MARITAL LITIGATION IN SOUTH CAROLINA

Substantive Law

Second Edition

By

Professor Roy T. Stuckey

and

F. Glenn Smith, Esquire

Published by the Continuing Legal Education Division of the South Carolina Bar

ISBN # 0-943856-76-0

PREFACE

This book discusses the substantive law of marital litigation in South Carolina. It does not include a volume of forms and it is not a how-to-do-it practice and procedure manual. It covers the substantive law. The first edition of this book was written by Professor Roy T. Stuckey and F. Glenn Smith, Esq. The book was updated in 1994 by Roy Stuckey and in 1995 by Glenn Smith. This second edition was prepared by Roy Stuckey.

The South Carolina Bar's library of CLE and other materials was an invaluable reference resource in the production of this book, and a paragraph, a page, or even more was occasionally adapted from those materials with permission of the Bar. The author appreciates the efforts of the many lawyers who have produced materials on marital litigation topics for the South Carolina Bar over the years. Especially helpful was *The Law of Domestic Relations in South Carolina* (S.C. Bar 1986) by Professor Randall Chastain, particularly with respect to chapters two, three and four.

A few unpublished opinions of South Carolina appellate courts are discussed in the book. Lawyers are reminded that these cases are not considered to have any precedential value and that it is improper to cite them to a court as authority for legal principles. They are included to assist practitioners in making predictions and in counseling clients about probable outcomes in cases involving similar factual circumstances.

The author and the board of editors tried to ensure that the revised edition is accurate and up-to-date through February, 1997. However, some mistakes and omissions inevitably slip by. Readers are encouraged to point out any errors you discover and to suggest ways in which the book could be clearer, more complete, or more helpful to the lawyers of South Carolina. Call Roy Stuckey at 803/777-2278 or send written comments to him at USC Law School, Columbia, SC 29208; fax 803/777-3401; e-mail Roy@law.law.sc.edu.

MARITAL LITIGATION IN SOUTH CAROLINA

Substantive Law

TABLE OF CONTENTS

MARITAL LITIGATION IN SOUTH CAROLINA
Substantive Law
DETAILED TABLE OF CONTENTS

CHAPTER FOUR
DIVORCE

CHAPTER SIX
ALIMONY

CHAPTER SEVEN
PROPERTY

CHAPTER EIGHT
PATERNITY

CHAPTER THIRTEEN
ATTORNEYS' FEES AND LITIGATION EXPENSES

CHAPTER FOURTEEN
AGREEMENTS

CHAPTER FIFTEEN
BANKRUPTCY

CHAPTER SIXTEEN
TAXATION

CHAPTER ONE
SUBJECT MATTER JURISDICTION

CHAPTER ONE
SUBJECT MATTER JURISDICTION

A. IN GENERAL

A failure to consider subject matter jurisdiction before initiating marital litigation may have disastrous (and embarrassing) consequences. The scope of family court jurisdiction can be confusing given the special nature of the family court and the relatively short time it has existed as an institution.

The family court is a court of limited jurisdiction. *Sims v. Sims*, 290 S.C. 190, 348 S.E.2d 835 (1986). As a statutory court, its jurisdiction is limited to that expressly or by necessary implication conferred by statute. *South Carolina Dept. of Mental Health v. State*, 301 S.C. 75, 390 S.E.2d 185 (1990).

The family court's jurisdiction is further limited by the pleadings. Ordinarily, a party may not receive relief not contemplated in the pleadings.

> While it is true that pleadings in the family court must be liberally construed, this rule cannot be stretched so as to permit the judge to award relief not contemplated by the pleadings. Due process requires that a litigant be placed on notice of the issues which the court is to consider. *Id.* [*Bass v. Bass*, 272 S.C. 177, 180, 249 S.E.2d 905, 906 (1978)]; *accord*, *Crocker v. Crocker*, 281 S.C. 154, 314 S.E.2d 343 (Ct. App. 1984), citing *Glass v. Glass*, 276 S.C. 625, 281 S.E.2d 221 (1981).

Loftis v. Loftis, 286 S.C. 12, 331 S.E.2d 372 (Ct. App. 1985) (finding the family court had no authority to order sale of house being used by wife if not requested in pleadings). *See also Dake v. Painter*, 288 S.C. 118, 341 S.E.2d 620 (1986) (finding the family court had no authority to reduce child support, if not requested in pleadings). *But see Pool v. Pool*, ___ S.C. ___, 467 S.E.2d 753 (Ct. App. 1996) (although attorneys' fees were not requested in the pleadings, the trial court was authorized to consider and properly awarded attorneys' fees to the husband upon a finding that the wife's claim of physical abuse was frivolous pursuant to the South Carolina Frivolous Civil Proceedings Act, S.C. Code Ann. § 15-36-10 through 15-36-50 (Law. Co-op. Supp.) which allows attorneys' fees to be awarded upon a finding that the procurement, initiation, continuation, or defense of any marital litigation is frivolous).

If the family court does not have subject matter jurisdiction over a particular matter, it cannot obtain it. Furthermore, the parties cannot waive this defect. *See Austelle v. Austelle*, 294 S.C. 19, 21, 362 S.E.2d 181, 183 (1987) (stating that "[o]f course, it is axiomatic that subject matter jurisdiction cannot be waived").

The parties cannot confer subject matter jurisdiction on the family court by stipulation or agreement. *State v. Richburg*, 304 S.C. 102, 105, 303 S.E.2d 315, 317 (1991); *Cox v. Lundsford*, 272 S.C. 527, 252 S.E.2d 918 (1979); *Harden v. South Carolina State Highway Dept.*, 266 S.C. 119, 124, 221 S.E.2d 851, 853 (1976). In *Leggett v. Leggett*, Op. No. 91-UP-056 (S.C. Ct. App. filed March 7, 1991), an unpublished opinion of the Court of Appeals, the parties had divided their marital property pursuant to an agreement providing that either party could seek enforcement in the family court. The former husband's father brought an action in family court attempting to clarify his interest in certain real estate which he had acquired from his son after the marital property had been divided pursuant to the agreement. The Court of Appeals held that the family court lacked subject matter jurisdiction to decide the issue, pointing out that, although *Moseley v. Mosier*, 279 S.C. 348, 306 S.E.2d 624 (1983), held that parties can agree to restrict the jurisdiction of the family court, there is no procedure through which parties can expand the court's jurisdiction, by agreement or otherwise. Just because something has once been marital property does not create perpetual jurisdiction in the family court. Once property has been divided between former spouses, the property is no longer marital property. Spouses become "legal strangers" after the divorce. The proper place to litigate issues involving former marital property is in the circuit court.

There is some precedent for the notion that the voluntary litigation of issues confers jurisdiction on the court to render a decision. *Cf. Moyle v. Moyle*, 262 S.C. 308, 204 S.E.2d 46 (1974). After noting that there had been no exception on appeal or other challenge to the trial court's authority to divide marital property without regard to which party's name it was titled in, the Supreme Court said, "We have heretofore recognized that voluntary litigation in a divorce case by the parties of their respective divorce rights confers jurisdiction on the court to consider questions raised thereby, regardless of whether the court otherwise would have jurisdiction." *Id.* at 312, 204 S.E.2d at 48 (citing *Piana v. Piana*, 239 S.C. 367, 123 S.E.2d 297 (1962).) *Piana* held that a family court could divide the parties' property, even though the action for divorce had been unsuccessful. It found such authority in the equity powers of the court, and it cited C.J.S. for the proposition that voluntary litigation by the parties confers jurisdiction on the court. The validity of this proposition should be viewed as suspect in light of the earlier discussion of subject matter jurisdiction, although the family court clearly has authority today to decide the issues which were presented in *Moyle* and *Piana*.

Defects in subject matter jurisdiction include failing to observe statutorily imposed time limits. In *Yarborough v. Yarborough*, 276 S.C. 416, 279 S.E.2d 130 (1981), the appellant-wife challenged the family court's jurisdiction to grant a divorce less than three months after the filing of the complaint seeking the divorce as this violated S.C. Code Ann. § 20-3-80 (Law. Co-op. 1976). The Supreme Court held that the trial court had no jurisdiction to grant the divorce before the expiration of the statutory time limit.

Whether the family court can enforce the terms of a *pendente lite* order after a case is administratively dismissed may be an unanswered question. The Administrative Order for the Family Courts dated June 5, 1992, *South Carolina Court Register*, FC ADMIN-5, clearly indicates that the family court does have jurisdiction to enforce such an order. "The striking of a case from the active docket is an administrative function only, and does not affect the merits of a case. Accordingly, all orders issued before such striking remain in full force and effect, unless limited by its terms." However, the Court of Appeals suggests in a footnote in *Cannon v. Cannon*, ___ S.C. ___, 467 S.E.2d 132 (Ct. App. 1996), that there may be a question about the validity of the Administrative Order. In an opinion requiring a former husband to pay alimony arrearages due under the terms of a *pendente lite* order in a case which was administratively dismissed, the court points out that the appellant did not argue that the order was not still in effect as a matter of law, and, therefore, the court did not address that issue. *Id.* at ___, 467 S.E.2d at 137, n.3.

The family court does not have jurisdiction to modify an order after the term of court in which the order is issued. In *Michel v. Michel*, 289 S.C. 187, 345 S.E.2d 730 (Ct. App. 1986), the Court of Appeals refused to allow the family court judge to vacate his own order when, two years after the order was entered, he discovered that it was not fair to one of the parties. The court held that the trial judge "loses jurisdiction to modify an order at the end of the term during which it is issued" and that only clerical errors that do not "involve the exercise of judgment or discretion on the merits" may be corrected. *Id.* at 190, 345 S.E.2d at 732 (citations omitted).

When a court lacks subject matter jurisdiction, it should dismiss the action under SCRCP Rule 12(h)(3), even if the parties have not requested dismissal. If the action is not dismissed, any action by a court which lacks subject matter jurisdiction is void. *Peake v. Peake*, 284 S.C. 591, 327 S.E.2d 375 (Ct. App. 1985); *State v. Funderburke*, 259 S.C. 256, 191 S.E.2d 520 (1972).

The issue of subject matter jurisdiction can be raised on appeal even if it is not presented to the trial court. *Cf. Knight Publishing Co. v. Univ. of South Carolina*, 295 S.C. 31, 33 n.3, 367 S.E.2d 20, 21 n.3 (1988); *Langford v. State Bd. of Fisheries*, 217 S.C. 118, 60 S.E.2d 59 (1950). Thus, a litigant can leave the family court feeling victorious only to have the case reversed on appeal due to a jurisdictional error that was not even mentioned during the trial of the case.

B. NECESSARY PARTIES

The family court has jurisdiction, in furtherance of the complete disposition of cases in the court's jurisdiction, to bring in and make parties to any proceeding pending before the court any person "whose presence to the proceedings may be found necessary to a complete determination of the issues therein or the relief to which the parties are entitled." S.C. Code Ann. § 20-7-420(19) (Law. Co-op. 1976). Under SCRCP Rule 19(a), which is applicable to the family courts (SCRFC Rule 2(a)), the court may order a person to be made a party where the person is subject to service of process and, in the person's absence, complete relief cannot be accorded among those already parties. The family court can add parties on its own motion, sua sponte, however, once parties are added they must be given an opportunity to present evidence on any issues involving them. *Frye v. Frye*, ___ S.C. ___, 448 S.E.2d 586

(Ct. App. 1994) (holding that the family court properly made a party's second wife a party to the action, sua sponte, but it erred in placing restrictions on the second wife without giving her an opportunity to respond to claims that the new wife had engaged in harassing behavior of a "bizarre" nature aimed at the previous wife); *Cleveland v. Cleveland*, No. 96-UP-433 (S.C. Ct. App. 1996) (affirming the family court's decision *sua sponte* to add the husband's criminal defense lawyer as a party to determine whether fees paid to the lawyer were marital property subject to equitable distribution).

C. EFFECT OF A PARTY'S DEATH

The death of either party to a divorce action terminates the action if it occurs before a divorce decree has been signed and delivered to the clerk. In *Bayne v. Bass*, 302 S.C. 208, 394 S.E.2d 726 (Ct. App. 1990), the wife committed suicide after the trial judge had orally granted her request for divorce but before he had signed a divorce decree. The judge signed the decree two days after she had died but vacated it on motion by the husband's counsel. The Court of Appeals held that the order granting the divorce was void and that the court had properly vacated its own order. The *Bayne* court cited *Case v. Case*, 243 S.C. 447, 134 S.E.2d 394 (1964), for the proposition that a divorce decree has no effect until it has been signed by the judge and delivered to the clerk of court because, until it has been delivered to the clerk, the judge can still modify, amend or rescind it.

The *Bayne* court also cited *Louthian and Merritt, P.A. v. Davis*, 272 S.C. 330, 251 S.E.2d 757 (1979), in support of its decision. In *Louthian*, the Supreme Court dealt with this issue in a somewhat different context. A law firm sought to collect attorneys' fees from the client's husband after her death. The wife initiated the divorce action and was awarded temporary alimony and attorneys' fees *pendente lite*. The action was subsequently heard before a standing master. Before he filed his report, the wife died. The attorneys sought to collect their fees. The Supreme Court, however, refused to allow the recovery saying "an action for divorce, being purely personal, terminates on the death of either spouse, and where the action for divorce is commenced, and one of the parties dies thereafter, but before the entry of the final decree, the action abates and the jurisdiction of the court to proceed with the action is terminated." *Id.* at 332, 251 S.E.2d at 758.

It does not appear, however, that the death of a party will have any effect on the jurisdiction of the family court to equitably apportion the marital party, if marital litigation has been initiated before the party dies. In *Hodge v. Hodge*, 305 S.C. 521, 409 S.E.2d 436 (Ct. App. 1991), the wife had brought an action for separate support and maintenance and property division. Both parties appealed, but the husband died during the appeal. The Court of Appeals held that, upon the filing of marital litigation, property acquired during a marriage becomes vested in an estate called marital property in which the spouses have a vested interest subject to equitable distribution. It further held that, with respect to marital property, marital litigation is not abated by the death of a spouse. The Court of Appeals went on to state that:

> [S]ince we hold that the wife's interest in the marital property was vested and therefore fixed by the institution of marital litigation, we hold that the only court which has jurisdiction to divide the marital estate is the Family Court, subject, of course, to appeal. Accordingly, we hold that upon the death of the husband, this action did not abate with respect to the issues relating to the equitable division of vested marital property.

Id. at 525, 409 S.E.2d at 439.

See also *Stone v. Guaranty Bank & Trust Co.*, 270 S.C. 331, 242 S.E.2d 404 (1978), in which the wife brought a suit for divorce and the husband counterclaimed for divorce. She was granted a divorce, but his counterclaim was still pending on appeal when he died. The Court determined that his death abated his counterclaim. The Supreme Court, however, said this did not abate the appeal dealing with the property rights of the parties. Since the wife had been awarded alimony, household furnishings, and attorneys' fees, the executor of the estate might still challenge these matters. The case was remanded to the lower court.

These cases leave open an important question about the effect of a party's death: do issues about the propriety of granting or denying a divorce survive the death of a party, if the death occurs after the decree becomes effective, but while an appeal is pending? The court in *Stone* said that the issue of the husband's counterclaim for divorce was abated on his death and the only issue it could deal with was the property rights of the parties. "Mr. Stone's death abates his counterclaim for a divorce and renders the contempt proceedings against him moot, but the appeal may continue in favor of his estate, to the extent of the lower court's order affects the property rights of the parties." *Id.* at 335-336, 242 S.E.2d at 406. However, it subsequently reversed the trial court's finding of a divorce for the wife on the basis that, if the deposition of a witness had been excluded as it should have been, there was no evidence of the husband's adultery, and it reversed and remanded the issue to the family court. In effect, while the court implied that the issue of divorce was not on appeal, it certainly dealt with that very issue in the appeal. Of course, on remand following a reversal of a divorce decree, it would seem that the family court would not have subject matter jurisdiction to grant a divorce for the wife under the holding in *Bayne*. For cases from other jurisdictions, *see* Annotation, *Effect of Death of a Party to Divorce Proceeding Pending Appeal or Time Allowed for Appeal*, 33 A.L.R.4th 47 (1984), which was cited in *Bayne*.

D. WHERE JURISDICTION EXISTS

The family court has exclusive jurisdiction to hear and determine actions involving all types of "marital litigation." S.C. Code Ann. § 20-7-420(2) (Law. Co-op. Supp.) gives the family court exclusive jurisdiction to hear and determine actions for "divorce *a vinculo matrimonii*, separate support and maintenance, legal separation[1] and in other marital litigation between the parties."

For many years, "marital litigation" was defined as litigation that sought to establish or modify the rights and obligations of married couples. If the action did not seek to affect the marital relationship, it was not marital litigation. Four types of actions have long been recognized as marital litigation in South Carolina: (1) actions to establish the validity of marriages; (2) annulments; (3) divorces *a vinculo matrimonii*; and (4) separate support and maintenance actions. The first two types of actions are specifically identified as marital litigation in the statute. Actions to determine the validity of marriages and annulments have been listed as other forms of marital litigation in case decisions. *See Brown v. Brown*, 295 S.C. 354, 358 n.3,

[1] Despite its inclusion in the statute, "legal separation" is not a recognized form of marital litigation in South Carolina. See discussion in the chapter on separate support and maintenance.

368 S.E.2d 475, 476 n.3 (1988), *cert. granted* 297 S.C. 73, 374 S.E.2d 897 (1989). The family court's authority to hear actions to determine the validity of marriages is found in S.C. Code Ann. § 20-7-420(5) (Law. Co-op. 1976), and its authority to hear actions for the annulment of marriages is found in S.C. Code Ann. § 20-7-420(6) (Law. Co-op. 1976).

The Supreme Court in *Brown* provided further clarification of the meaning of "marital litigation," pointing out the consequences of incorrectly concluding that an action in the family court was marital litigation.

> Marital litigation is litigation which seeks to alter or terminate the marital status of the parties. *See Sims v. Sims*, supra [290 S.C. 190, 348 S.E.2d 835 (1986)];and *Eichor v. Eichor*, 290 S.C. 484, 351 S.E.2d 353 (Ct. App. 1986). This is distinct from litigation between spouses or former spouses to determine their respective interests in property. *Id.* A family court lacks subject matter jurisdiction to settle a dispute between spouses involving their respective interests in property, unless the determination is incident to an action requesting alteration of their marital status. *Id.*

295 S.C. at 358, 368 S.E.2d at 477. In *Brown*, the wife sought an equitable interest in the marital home to prevent her husband from following through on his threats to evict her. Mrs. Brown argued that this was "other marital litigation between the parties" because the origin of the case was a marital dispute, that is, marital conflict was the reason she initiated the action. The court rejected her argument, holding that the family court lacks jurisdiction to settle a dispute between spouses involving their respective interests in property, unless the determination is incident to an action requesting an alteration of their marital status. She was not seeking to have the court alter or terminate her marital status. In fact, she expressed her desire to stay in the marital home with her husband.

Brown points out that it "is the nature of the cause of action, not the reason for bringing it, which controls" whether or not the family court has jurisdiction. *Id.* at 358, 368 S.E.2d at 476.

The Supreme Court may have broadened the definition of "marital litigation" in *Rivenbark v. Rivenbark*, 301 S.C. 175, 391 S.E.2d 232 (1990), but this is not clear. After listing the types of actions in which the family court is authorized to apportion marital property under S.C. Code Ann. § 20-7-472 (Law. Co-op. Supp.), the court stated: "'Other marital litigation' should include any type of action or proceeding involving a marital dispute." *Id.* at 179, 391 S.E.2d at 234. It is unclear whether the court really intended to modify the definition of marital litigation. There is no authority cited for the statement quoted above. It was not necessary for a decision in the case (the court could have apportioned the marital property without defining the action as marital litigation). The court did not discuss its previous cases defining marital litigation nor indicate any reason or intention to differ from them. Thus, *Rivenbark* does not appear to represent a considered, intentional decision to redefine "marital litigation." However, the Court of Appeals repeated the definition from *Rivenbark* in *Brown v. Brown*, No. 90-UP-164 (S.C. Ct. App. 1990) (finding in an unpublished opinion that attorneys' fees could be awarded in a child custody dispute because it is "marital litigation" as defined in *Rivenbark*). Again, however, the court made no mention of the earlier, more established definition of marital litigation, and the memorandum opinion has no precedential value. Therefore, one cannot be sure whether these cases truly represent any change.

If the definition of marital litigation which appears in the *Rivenbark* opinion ("any type of action or proceeding involving a marital dispute") really represents an intention to redefine the meaning of "marital litigation," there could be a significant potential impact on the family court's authority to decide property cases. If marital litigation involves all proceedings involving marital disputes, the fourth condition under which the family court is allowed to apportion marital property under the Equitable Apportionment of Marital Property Act ("other marital litigation between the parties") will be easier to satisfy.

The Supreme Court also used a broader term than "marital litigation" to describe the family court's jurisdiction in *Moseley v. Mosier*, 279 S.C. 348, 306 S.E.2d 624 (1983), in which it declared that thereafter "jurisdiction for all <u>domestic matters</u> whether by decree or by agreement, will vest in the family court." (emphasis added) *Id.* at 353, 306 S.E.2d at 627. Again, it is unlikely that the court intended to expand the family court's jurisdiction.

The opinion does not define "domestic matters," and its meaning was not important to the outcome of the case.

Irrespective of the meaning of "marital litigation," the family court has specific legislative authority to hear and determine additional types of disputes between spouses and former spouses, even if they are presented outside the context of marital litigation. These include disputes involving children (paternity, termination of parental rights, custody, visitation, and support — see the chapter on children); requests for spousal support (see the chapters on separate support and maintenance and on alimony); and certain disputes about the division of marital property (see the chapter on property). Specific jurisdictional issues related to these topics are discussed in the relevant chapters.

The family court's jurisdiction to consider, approve, or enforce separation or other agreements is limited to those situations in which it is authorized by statute to do so. The family court's jurisdiction over agreements that are executed during marital litigation proceedings is implicitly included in S.C. Code Ann. § 20-7-420(2) (Law. Co-op. 1976) (this statute gives the family court jurisdiction to hear and determine marital cases). *Funderburk v. Funderburk*, 286 S.C. 129, 332 S.E.2d 205 (1985), relied on § 20-7-420(2) to hold that the family court should exercise jurisdiction over a property division agreement that was submitted for its consideration at a divorce hearing, even if one party asks the court to approve the agreement and the other party claims it is unfair.

Some other agreements can be considered by the family court even if they are not incident to marital litigation. For example, the family court has jurisdiction over:

> [A]ll agreements which bear on the issue of alimony or separate maintenance and [spousal] support, whether brought before the court in actions for divorce from the bonds of matrimony, separate maintenance and [spousal support] actions, or in actions to approve agreement [sic] where the parties are living separate and apart. The failure to seek a divorce, separate maintenance, or a legal separation does not deprive the court of its authority and jurisdiction to approve and enforce the agreements.

S.C. Code Ann. § 20-3-130(G) (Law. Co-op. Supp.). (See further discussion about the family court's jurisdiction with respect to agreements in the chapter on agreements.)

E. WHERE JURISDICTION DOES NOT EXIST

The family court does not have subject matter jurisdiction to enforce agreements that are outside the scope of its statutory authorization. The following cases illustrate some of the specific instances in which the family court has been found to lack subject matter jurisdiction.

The family court has no authority to award money damages. In *Thompson v. Ballentine*, 298 S.C. 289, 379 S.E.2d 896 (1989), a settlement agreement approved by the family court gave the country club membership to the husband. Subsequently, the former wife obtained control of the membership, and the family court awarded $10,000 to the husband in damages. The Supreme Court held that S.C. Code Ann. § 20-7-420(2) (Law. Co-op. 1976) did not give the family court authority to make such an award. In *Peake v. Peake*, 284 S.C. 591, 327 S.E.2d 375 (Ct. App. 1985), the wife sought reimbursement for wages she lost while caring for her husband during his recuperation from injuries he had sustained in an accident. The court concluded that this factual stipulation by the parties required a finding that her claim was one for money damages, not for equitable distribution. Therefore, the family court lacked subject matter jurisdiction to make the award, and its action was void.

The family court lacks subject matter jurisdiction to permit a parent to litigate a claim for waste of marital property against a child, even in the context of marital litigation. *Gambrell v. Gambrell*, 295 S.C. 457, 369 S.E.2d 662 (Ct. App. 1988).

The family court lacks jurisdiction to hear actions for the collection of debts (although it can apportion marital debts). An unusual case which illustrates this point is *Lighty v. D.S.S.*, 285 S.C. 508, 330 S.E.2d 259 (1985). D.S.S. sought reimbursement in the family court from a mother for child support it had paid to a child's great aunt under the Aid to Families with Dependent Children program. The Supreme Court held that this was an action for debt, not for child support, and that the family court lacked subject matter jurisdiction. In his dissenting opinion, Justice

Ness argues persuasively that the family court has at least concurrent jurisdiction with the circuit court in such cases. S.C. Code Ann. §§ 20-7-420(11) & (14) (Law. Co-op. 1976 & Supp.) do appear to give the family court jurisdiction to hear all cases "to compel the support of a child" as Justice Ness argued. However, Justice Ness' dissenting opinion is not the law of the case. Perhaps this case is best understood in light of its very unusual facts, which seemed to influence the Court. There had been no court order awarding custody of the child to the great aunt. The mother had never been ordered to pay child support. D.S.S. only sought reimbursement for past payments, not for present or future child support. Perhaps if any of these facts had been different, the result would have been different, too. It is unclear why DSS did not petition the family court to order the mother to pay retroactive and prospective child support, which would have avoided the technical problem on which the opinion turns.

The family court does not have subject matter jurisdiction over an action brought by a third party seeking to compel one spouse to assume responsibility for the care of the other spouse. *Amisub of S.C., etc. v. Passmore, et al.*, 316 S.C. 112, 447 S.E.2d 207 (1994). In *Amisub*, a woman was no longer in need of hospitalization, but was unable to care for herself. Her husband refused to take responsibility for her care. The hospital filed an action in family court asking the court to order the husband to accept responsibility for his wife's care. The hospital relied on S.C. Code Ann. § 20-7-840 (Law. Co-op. 1976), which provides that "[a]ny interested persons may file a petition to the [family] court requesting the court to order persons legally chargeable to provide support as required by law;" and S.C. Code Ann. § 20-7-420(14) (Law. Co-op. 1976) which gives family courts the power to "[o]rder support of a spouse or child, or both, irrespective of whether they are likely to become a public charge." The Supreme Court held that the family court's jurisdiction under these statutes is limited to alimony and child support, not third party actions. The circuit court, not the family court, has jurisdiction over third party actions relying on the necessaries doctrine. (The court also ruled that the family court could not order DSS to assume financial obligations for an ill, adult person's care as "protective services" pursuant to S.C. Code Ann. § 43-29-10(7) (Law. Co-op. 1976).)

CHAPTER TWO
ESTABLISHING THE VALIDITY OF MARRIAGES

CHAPTER TWO
ESTABLISHING THE VALIDITY OF MARRIAGES

A. IN GENERAL

Questions about the validity of marriages may be presented in the context of actions seeking to establish their validity or to establish their invalidity (annulments). The same issues may also arise in the context of defenses either to actions for divorce or for separate support and maintenance if defendants claim that the alleged marriages were never valid in the first place.

In South Carolina, a valid marriage may be created by meeting the requirements of relevant statutory law or by satisfying the criteria of the common law.

The question of the age of consent to marriage in South Carolina presents interesting issues. One can enter into a valid common law marriage at a younger age than one can acquire a license for a statutory marriage. Even if a person is not old enough to obtain a marriage license, he or she can create a valid marriage by complying with the rules for establishing a valid common law marriage, in which case males need only be fourteen years old and females twelve years old. *State v. Ward*, 204 S.C. 210, 214, 28 S.E.2d 785, 786 (1944) (citing *Ex parte Blizzard*, 185 S.C. 131, 133, 193 S.E. 633, 634 (1937)). (There is a more detailed discussion about age requirements later in this chapter.)

B. JURISDICTION

The family court is authorized to hear and determine actions to determine the validity of marriages. S.C. Code Ann. § 20-7-420(5) (Law. Co-op. 1976). Also, S.C. Code Ann. § 20-1-520 (Law. Co-op. 1976) provides that "[w]hen the validity of a marriage shall be denied or doubted by either of the parties, the other may institute a suit for affirming the marriage and, upon due proof of the validity thereof, it shall be conclusive upon all persons concerned."

Other courts may have the authority to determine the validity of marriages if it is necessary to do so in order to decide the merits of the cases before them. "The Court of Probate possesses jurisdiction to determine the status of a common-law marriage when such question is relevant to determination of the proper heirs of an estate before the Probate Court." 1979 S.C. Att'y Gen. Ann. Rep. 212. *See also Campbell v. Christian*, 235 S.C. 102, 110 S.E.2d 1 (1959).

C. VENUE

It is not altogether clear what the proper venue is for actions to establish the validity of marriages. Unlike divorce and separate support and maintenance actions, there is no specific venue statute for actions to establish the validity of marriages. Therefore, venue is determined by reference to the general statutes governing civil actions. These are found at S.C. Code Ann. § 15-7-10 *et seq*. (Law. Co-op. 1976). Unfortunately, there have been no cases directly on point which provide guidance.

The proper location appears to be the county in which the defendant resides at the time of the commencement of the action. S.C. Code Ann. § 15-7-30 (Law. Co-op. 1976). This result may cause some inequity. In a particular case, the best place to bring the case might be where the marriage allegedly occurred, where the parties allegedly resided as husband or wife, or where the alleged breach of the marital contract occurred. Any of these locations may, in fact, be preferable to the defendant's present home due to the location of witnesses or property involved in the dispute. Perhaps the legislature will modify S.C. Code Ann. § 20-3-60 (Law. Co-op. Supp.) in the future to include all marital litigation.

Choosing an improper venue to initiate litigation is not necessarily detrimental to the merits of the plaintiff's case. If the venue is wrong, the proper remedy is to transfer the case, not to dismiss it. SCRCP Rule 82(b). *See also* Rule 12(b)(3), SCRCP.

D. STATUTORY LAW MARRIAGES

1. LICENSE REQUIREMENTS

It is "unlawful for any person to contract matrimony within this State without first procuring a license. . . ." S.C. Code Ann. § 20-1-210 (Law. Co-op. 1976). However, although this language would seem to eliminate common law marriages, South Carolina continues to recognize them (there is a discussion of common law marriages later in this chapter). Also, even marriages which have been contracted with invalid licenses or without a license are valid. *See* S.C. Code Ann. § 20-1-360 (Law. Co-op. 1976); *Johnson v. Johnson*, 235 S.C. 542, 112 S.E.2d 647 (1960).

The South Carolina Code provides that upon the filing of the application, the lapse of twenty-four hours, the payment of a fee, and the filing of a sworn statement that the parties are legally entitled to marry (along with their full names, ages and places of residence), the probate judge or clerk of court with whom the application was filed shall issue a [marriage] license." S.C. Code Ann. § 20-1-230 (Law. Co-op. 1976).

Licensing is supported by a number of public policies: vital statistics, health, and avoiding hasty marriages. These licensing statutes also help in determining those persons who are not qualified to marry because of age or because of prior marriages. In some states these statutes also serve as public health measures, but South Carolina is one of few states which does not require a physical examination or blood test. 1952-53 S.C. Att'y Gen. Ann. Rep. 153.

a. Waiting Period

South Carolina requires a twenty-four hour waiting period between the application for a license and its issuance. S.C. Code Ann. § 20-1-220 (Law. Co-op. 1976).

b. Nonresidents

Those persons who marry within the jurisdiction of this state must meet the requirements of law with respect to marriage irrespective of their status as citizens or aliens and, likewise, irrespective of the person who performs the ceremony. The laws of the country of celebrants' domicile shall have no application if the marriage takes place within the borders of this state. 1950-51 S.C. Att'y Gen. Ann. Rep. 210. Generally, the law of the place of celebration governs the formalities of marriage and determines its validity, and the marriage will generally be recognized in other states unless that would contradict strong public policy. *Zwerling v. Zwerling*, 270 S.C. 685, 686, 244 S.E.2d 311, 312 (1978) (citing 52 Am. Jur. 2d *Marriage* §§ 80, 82 (1970)).

c. Who May Perform a Marriage Ceremony

Only ministers of the Gospel, Jewish rabbis and officers authorized to administer oaths in this state (including notaries public) are authorized to administer a marriage ceremony. S.C. Code Ann. § 20-1-20 (Law. Co-op. 1976).

2. WHO MAY ENTER A LAWFUL MARRIAGE CONTRACT

"All persons, except mentally incompetent persons and persons prohibited" from marriage, may lawfully contract matrimony. S.C. Code Ann. § 20-1-10 (Law. Co-op. 1976). The statutory prohibitions are discussed below.

a. Affinity and Consanguinity

S.C. Code Ann. § 20-1-10 (Law. Co-op. Supp.) prohibits a man from marrying his "mother, grandmother, daughter, granddaughter, stepmother, sister, grandfather's wife, son's wife, grandson's wife, wife's mother, wife's grandmother, wife's daughter, wife's granddaughter, brother's daughter, sister's daughter, father's sister or mother's sister or another man." The same section prohibits a woman from contracting matrimony with males of the same degree of kinship as those listed for a man and from marrying another woman.

The statute includes relations of the half blood, such as stepsisters. *State v. Smith*, 101 S.C. 293, 85 S.E. 958 (1915) (holding that the statute includes relations of the half blood but affirming Mr. Smith's conviction for bigamy because his first marriage to his half-sister's daughter was voidable, not void).

A marriage contracted in violation of the consanguinity and affinity statute is voidable, not void, except that marriages between a man and another man or a woman and another woman are "void *ab initio* and against the public policy of this State." S.C. Code Ann. § 20-1-15 (Law. Co-op. Supp.). In *South Carolina v. Smith*, 101 S.C. 293, 85 S.E. 958 (1915), the Court held that the canonical impediments of consanguinity and affinity at the common law rendered a marriage voidable only and that this remains the law in South Carolina unless a statute specifically renders them void. The same conclusion was reached in *Bennett v. Bennett*, 195 S.C. 1, 10 S.E.2d 23 (1940). The daughter of Franklin Bennett sought to have his will declared invalid on the ground that his marriage to Louetta Chassereay was invalid because Louetta was Franklin's niece. Declaring that Franklin Bennett's marriage to his niece was merely voidable and not void, the Supreme Court affirmed the trial court's determination that "[A] consanguineous marriage . . . is not absolutely void, but rather is voidable only during the lives of the parties; and that if not so avoided during their lives it must be deemed valid to all intents and for all civil purposes." *Id.* at 3, 10 S.E.2d at 24 (quoting 18 R.C.L. 444).

Although one marrying one's mother or father, sister or brother in South Carolina need not be concerned with the validity of such marriage until it is contested in a court of competent jurisdiction, there is another problem with which a consanguineous marriage must contend — the state's incest law. S. C. Code Ann. § 16-15-20 (Law. Co-op. 1976) makes it a criminal act to engage in sexual intercourse with the persons named in the statute. The relationships listed in S.C. Code Ann. § 16-15-20 (Law. Co-op. 1976) and S.C. Code Ann. § 20-1-10 (Law. Co-op. 1976) are identical. The penalty for violation of the incest law is not less than a $500 fine or one year in jail or both.

b. Mental Competency

Mentally incompetent persons may not lawfully contract marriage. S.C. Code Ann. § 20-1-10 (Law. Co-op. 1976). However, a mental patient who has not been adjudicated to be an incompetent person may not be denied the right to marry. S.C. Code Ann. § 44-22-80 (Law. Co-op. Supp.). This right to marry would logically extend to people who are not mental patients.

The latter statute became effective on June 5, 1991, and it may have changed South Carolina case law. *See*, *e.g.*, *Clement v. Mattison*, 37 S.C.L. (3 Rich.) 93 (1846), which held in part that a marriage can be declared invalid on the basis of mental incompetency even though such incompetency has not been decreed by the state's judicial system.

For the time being, one should probably assume that no change in prior law was intended by the enactment of section 44-22-80, and that a marriage may still be declared invalid on the basis of mental incompetency, if it is proved later that the requisite degree of mental incompetency existed at the time of the marriage. However, this result is somewhat illogical in the face of a statute which specifically authorizes the marriage.

In any event, the following discussion of South Carolina case law should be read with the potential impact of section 44-22-80 in mind. South Carolina has long recognized that one may need less mental competency to contract matrimony than to make contracts binding an estate. In *Ex parte Glen*, 4 S.C. Eq. (4 Des.) 546 (1816), the petitioner sought to have one Maria Robinson declared a lunatic. Maria Robinson's father had bequeathed property to her, leaving a contingent remainder to her sister, who was married to the petitioner. Although the exact consequences are not clear from the case, the petitioner stood to gain the property bequeathed to Maria if her marriage was found void for lack of mental capacity. In declaring that Maria needed less mental capacity to contract marriage than to make contracts binding her property, the Court stated, "There may possibly be so much imbecility, as to render her incapable of making contracts which would bind her estate, but this imbecility does not appear to exist in so great a degree as to incapacitate her from contracting a marriage." *Id.* at 549.

The mental incompetency must exist at the time of marriage to invalidate the marriage. *Clement v. Mattison*, 37 S.C.L. (3 Rich.) 93 (1846). In *Clement*, a husband sought to dismiss a suit by his wife's father. The father wanted compensation for meals and lodging he provided to the wife after her husband had removed her from the marital home. The husband sought dismissal of the father's claim by having the marriage declared void because he was insane at the time of the marriage, suffering from delirium tremens. The Supreme Court ruled that insanity from delirium tremens will void a contract of marriage and returned the case to the lower court for determination of the fact.

An adjudication of mental incompetency may not be sufficient evidence standing alone to invalidate a marriage. In *Church v. Trotter*, 278 S.C. 504, 299 S.E.2d 332 (1983), a husband sought to have his former marriage declared a nullity on the basis of a 1969 adjudication that he was incompetent. He wished to recover alimony he had paid over a seven-year period. The Court indicated that "an adjudication of incompetency is but prima facie evidence of that fact." *Id.* at 506, 229 S.E.2d at 333. The Court also ruled that "it was the duty of the trial judge to make specific findings of fact with regard to respondent's competency at the time of the 1971 marriage and indeed during the pendency of the divorce action" and remanded for determination of competency at the relevant times. *Id.*

Because South Carolina does not explicitly declare marriages void which have been entered into by incompetent persons, *Church v. Trotter* indicates that marriages by mental incompetents in South Carolina are voidable rather than void.

Persons who suffer from lunacy at the time of marriage may consummate or validate their marriages during a lucid period. *Davis v. Whitlock*, 90 S.C. 233, 73 S.E. 171 (1911). The Court in *Davis* gave the following illustration:

> [A] ceremony having the form of a marriage when one of the parties is a lunatic or under compulsion would not be binding, but the lunatic, when reason is restored and the person under compulsion when force is removed, may consummate — that is complete — the marriage by cohabitation under the attempted contract.

Id. at 245, 73 S.E. at 174.

For an extreme example of the "lucid interval" rule, *see Fischer v. Adams*, 38 N.W.2d 337, 340 (1949).

> Mere weakness or imbecility of mind is not sufficient, nor eccentricity or partial dementia, but it must be such a derangement as prevents the party from comprehending the nature of the contract and from giving to it his free and intelligent consent in order to warrant a decree nullifying the purported marriage.

c. Bigamy

South Carolina statutory law concerning the validity of a bigamous marriage is found in S.C. Code Ann. § 20-1-80 (Law. Co-op. Supp.) which states in part: "All marriages contracted while either of the parties has a former wife or husband living shall be void." This statute codifies a basic religious and moral tenet of our society — one spouse per person at a time. However, in keeping with its policy to find, promote and maintain the institution of marriage, South Carolina courts will assume a second marriage is valid until the existence of a former spouse is proved:

> He or she may marry again, and, while the wife or husband remains absent, the parties under the second marriage are entitled to full legal recognition as man and wife with regard to the enforcement of rights and the assumption of obligations as such; but all this must be at the risk that if it turns out that the first spouse was alive at the time the second marriage was undertaken, then the second marriage will be void, and all supposed rights acquired under it will fall to the ground.

Davis v. Whitlock, 90 S.C. 233, 246, 73 S.E. 171, 175 (1911).

If a man and woman enter into a contract of marriage believing in good faith that they are capable of entering into the relation notwithstanding a former marriage, when in fact the former marriage is still of force, they become man and wife when the obstacle of the former marriage is removed if they continue the relation and hold themselves out as man and wife. *Id.* at 246, 73 S.E. at 175. Conversely, a failure to remove an impediment will render a putative second marriage invalid. *Day v. Day*, 216 S.C. 324, 58 S.E.2d 83 (1950).

An exception to the general rule prohibiting bigamy is contained in the second part of S.C. Code Ann. § 20-1-80 (Law. Co-op. Supp.):

> But this section shall not extend to a person whose husband or wife shall be absent for the space of five years, the one not knowing the other to be living during that time, not [sic] to any person who shall be divorced or whose marriage is declared void by sentence of a competent court.

[The number of years was reduced from seven to five when the statute was amended in 1990.]

This statute creates a presumption of death which operates as *prima facie* evidence of the death of the first spouse which will prevail over any presumption of continuance of life, in the absence of evidence to rebut the presumption. Statutes of this sort are known generically as "Enoch Arden" statutes after the famous Tennyson poem, being designed to avoid the dilemma faced by Enoch when he returned from shipwreck and found his wife remarried:

> Then Enoch Arden returned:
> Up the wall beyond the yew tree,
> Through the square of light
> Enoch saw his wife, his children grown,
> Beside the burnished board of the household
> To which he must be "the living dead";
> For he must have strength
> Not to tell her, never to let her know.
> He therefore, turning softly like
> A thief, lest he should swoon and tumble and be found,
> Left the window, crept to the gate and opened it and
> Closed it; and went his desolate way.
> [adapted from Tennyson, "Enoch Arden"]

A spouse wishing to rely on the "Enoch Arden" Rule must meet two requirements. First, he or she cannot abandon a spouse, leave the jurisdiction and remarry and use the section as a shield to protect the second marriage. A continuous unexplained five-year absence creates a presumption of death, but such a presumption "will not be indulged for the benefit of one who deserts his former spouse." *In re Duncan's Estate*, 190 S.C. 211, 217, 2 S.E.2d 388, 390 (1939).

Second, the abandoned or deserted spouse must also make a good faith effort to ascertain the whereabouts of the abandoning or deserting spouse. *Woodmen of the World Life Ins. Co. v. Irick*, 58 F. Supp. 202 (E.D.S.C. 1944), *aff'd* 150 F.2d 514 (4th Cir. 1945); *Day v. Day*, 216 S.C. 334, 339, 58 S.E.2d 83, 85 (1950). Both *Woodmen* and *Day* arose from circumstances wherein a wife remarried while a former spouse was living. The second husband died leaving certain death benefits. In *Woodmen* and *Day* the benefits were life insurance and workers' compensation death payments, respectively. In *Woodmen* the wife had not seen her former husband for eight years before her remarriage. The former husband left her and also survived the second husband. The Supreme Court declared the second marriage void because the wife had made no effort to ascertain the whereabouts of her former husband. The husband had returned to his hometown. The second marriage being declared void, the wife was no longer eligible for the insurance money. In *Day*, the wife left her former husband and married again. The second marriage took place seven years later. Again the wife failed to investigate the whereabouts of the former husband and, because she could have easily located the former husband, the court declared the second marriage void.

This harsh consequence can be avoided by obtaining a judicial declaration of presumed death pursuant to S.C. Code Ann. § 20-1-540 (Law. Co-op. 1976). The pertinent part of the statute reads:

> And when it shall be satisfactorily established to the presiding judge of such court or to a jury on an issue sent to the jury by the judge that such absent spouse has not been heard from for seven years the complaining spouse shall have an adjudication of the issue and such absent spouse shall be conclusively presumed dead in so far as any children or kindred resulting in any marriage of the abandoned spouse during such absence may be concerned, notwithstanding the fact that such absent spouse may later appear alive. The reappearance or return of the absent spouse shall not alter such adjudication or invalidate or upset any subsequent marriage entered into by the abandoned spouse.

[It is important to notice that, unlike S.C. Code Ann. § 20-1-80 (Law. Co-op. Supp.), this statute has not been amended to reduce the number of years from seven to five.]

Thus, a spouse abandoned for seven years who remarries, having made a reasonable effort to locate the abandoning spouse, should obtain a court order pronouncing the abandoning spouse presumed dead in order to be sure the second marriage survives should the abandoning spouse show up later. If a person believing a spouse to be dead obtains no court declaration of presumed death that person remarrying, even following a diligent search, takes the chance that the second marriage will be void upon the return of the former husband or upon proof that he is alive. *Ex parte Blizzard*, 185 S.C. 131, 193 S.E. 633 (1937).

Proving bigamy is a relatively easy matter, provided the undissolved marriage is of record. The real problem of proof of a prior undissolved marriage occurs when the prior marriage is one at common law. Consider this situation: *A* and *B* are married in Richland County. The marriage is "of record." Three years pass. *A*, while thumbing through old letters of *B*, determines that for ten years before her marriage to *B*, *B* lived with *C*. May *A* annul her marriage to *B* based on bigamy because *B's* common law marriage to *C* was not dissolved? The answer of course hinges on what constitutes a common law marriage, assuming *B* never got a divorce. The section on common law marriages in this chapter provides a detailed discussion of the requisites for establishing a common law marriage, but the short answer is that *A* must prove *B* and *C* held themselves out to the world as husband and wife through their actions and agreement to establish a prior marriage which makes the present marriage bigamous.

Another pitfall of the bigamous marriage is the criminal sanction against it. S.C. Code Ann. § 16-15-10. (Law. Co-op. 1976) provides a penalty of from six months to five years in the penitentiary or six months in jail and a fine of not less than $500 upon conviction of bigamy.

d. Age

South Carolina attempts to control the minimum ages at which persons may contract matrimony by prohibiting the issuance of a license to those who are not above the specified minimum age. *See* S.C. Code Ann. § 20-1-250 (Law. Co-op. 1976). The statute states:

> No such license shall be issued when the woman or child woman is under the age of fourteen or when the male is under the age of sixteen, provided that when the female applicant is between the ages of fourteen to eighteen and when the male is between the ages of sixteen to eighteen and when the applicant resides with father or mother, or other relative or guardian, the probate judge or other officer authorized to issue marriage licenses shall not issue a license for the marriage until furnished with a sworn affidavit by such father, mother, other relative or guardian giving his or her consent to the marriage.

Thus, the statute establishes the ages for obtaining a marriage license at fourteen for females and sixteen for males. However, if either applicant resides with a parent or guardian, parental consent by sworn affidavit is required before a license can be issued to applicants younger than eighteen.

The age of either party becomes irrelevant to the issuance of a marriage license when a female applicant is pregnant or has given birth to a child (and this fact is documented by a physician), if the proposed marriage is to the putative father and someone consents to the female's marriage who is authorized by statute to give such consent (this including the superintendent of the county department of social services). S.C. Code Ann. § 20-1-300 (Law. Co-op. 1976). No consent to the marriage of the putative father is required.

This attempt at controlling the minimum ages to contract matrimony is feeble. In fact, S.C. Code Ann. § 20-1-360 (Law. Co-op. 1976) declares that a failure to meet all the requirements to obtain a marriage license will not render illegal any marriage contracted anyway. Additionally, it is unlikely this section would survive if challenged today due to the differential treatment based on gender. In any event, the statute is completely defeated by the fact that one does not need a marriage license to create a valid common law marriage. Thus, even if a person is not old enough to obtain a marriage license, a valid marriage can be created by complying with the rules for establishing a valid common law marriage, in which case males only have to be fourteen years old and females only twelve. *State v. Ward*, 204 S.C. 210, 214, 28 S.E.2d 785, 786 (1944) (citing *Ex parte Blizzard*, 185 S.C. 131, 133, 193 S.E. 633, 634 (1937)).

Case law supports the view that entry into marriage by one or both parties under the age of competency does not render the marriage void. In *State v. Ward*, 204 S.C. 210, 28 S.E.2d 785 (1944), a twenty-six-year-old man introduced his thirteen-year-old girlfriend to his family, neighbors and friends as his wife. The two had had sexual relations. The father of the thirteen-year-old insisted on a marriage ceremony, as none had been performed. The twenty-six-year-old went to procure a marriage license but before the ceremony could be performed, the father had a warrant issued that led to the defendant's arrest and conviction for statutory rape. The Supreme Court reversed the conviction because it found a valid common law marriage between the parties and reasoned that a man cannot be guilty of raping his wife. Calling statutes such as S.C. Code Ann. § 20-1-250 (Law. Co-op. 1976) merely directory, the Court said:

> It is now generally held by the great weight of authority, that statutes prescribing the procurement of a license and other formalities to be observed in the solemnization of marriage, do not render invalid a marriage entered into according to the common law, but not in conformity with the statutory formalities, unless the statutes themselves expressly declare such marriage invalid; and this although the statutes prescribe penalties for ignoring their provisions.

Id. at 214, 28 S.E.2d at 786.

Although marital rape is now a criminal offense in South Carolina, it is unlikely that the existence of a marital rape statute would have affected the outcome in *Ward* because S.C. Code Ann. § 16-3-615 (Law. Co-op. Supp.) requires "the use of physical force or physical violence of a high and aggravated nature which results in some physical manifestation of that force or violence to overcome the victim, by one spouse against the other spouse if they are living together. . . ." Presumably, sexual intercourse incident to a common law marriage is consensual, not forced.

At common law the minimum age for consent to marriage was twelve years for females and fourteen for males. *State v. Ward*, 204 S.C. 210, 214, 28 S.E.2d 785, 786 (1944). Yet at common law a marriage by persons below the age of consent was not void unless one of the parties to the marriage was under seven years of age: "At common law a marriage of persons under the age of seven years was a nullity, but over that age, and under the age of consent, the marriage was not absolutely void, but only voidable." *State v. Sellers*, 140 S.C. 66, 73, 134 S.E. 873, 875 (1926) (quoting 18 R.C.L. 441 ¶ 70).

The *Sellers* case was one of criminal prosecution for bigamy. The defendant, who was in his second marriage, defended by claiming his first marriage was void, as his first wife had been married to someone else when he married her. Defendant's first wife was eleven years old when she contracted her first marriage which, of course, was not to the defendant. Her age was a central issue in determining the validity of her marriage, for if it were voidable the defendant would go free and if void he would be guilty of bigamy, having married a second time with a living spouse. After citing the rule above, the Court held that the defendant's first bride was a party to a voidable marriage and that it had not been annulled. This meant that the defendant's first marriage was void, and the defendant was thus not guilty of bigamy, being validly married this "second" (but really first) time. The Court also held that court action is necessary to annul marriages voidable for want of age, and indicated a need for nonconsummation:

> [W]e do conclude that the common-law right of a person to a marriage contract, voidable because of want of age of one of the contracting parties, to annul the same by his or her own act, without a decree of the court of common pleas, has been abrogated, and such marriages may only be declared void by that court when there has been no cohabitation between the contracting parties.

Id. at 93, 134 S.E. at 877.

Although it would not affect the validity of a marriage, another complicating factor is created by S.C. Code Ann. §§ 16-15-30 and -40 (Law. Co-op. 1976) which make it a criminal offense to deflower an unmarried female under the age of sixteen or to contract matrimony with a female under sixteen years of age without her father's permission or knowledge (or her mother's if her father is dead). Although there is no reported case of these statutes being applied to common law marriages or to other marriages involving females under sixteen years of age, their potential impact on the ability of the newlyweds to continue cohabiting should be considered before the marriage is created. The prohibition against deflowering is probably not applicable to females who have entered common law marriages in light of *State v. Ward*, 204 S.C. 210, 28 S.E.2d 785 (1944), which held that a similar statute prohibiting carnal knowledge of an unmarried woman under a certain age did not apply to women who had entered common law marriages. However, *Ward* does not speak to the effect of failing to have parental consent or knowledge.

e. Same Sex Marriages Prohibited

During its 1996 session, the South Carolina legislature enacted legislation stating that "[a] marriage between persons of the same sex is void *ab initio* and against the public policy of this State." S.C. Code Ann. § 20-1-15 (Law. Co-op. Supp.). This legislation is consistent with unpublished opinions of the Attorney General of South Carolina in 1976 and 1983 which conclude that a marriage license should not be issued to members of the same sex. In the 1983 Opinion, the Attorney General states that an exception to this is when one of the parties is undergoing sex-change surgery, as was contemplated in the case addressed in the Opinion. The Opinion says it is proper to issue a marriage license if medical authorities certify that the people seeking the marriage license are of opposite sexes. S.C. Att'y Gen'l Op. of Oct. 17, 1983, slip op. at 1.

The federal government passed legislation to allow states to refuse to recognize marriages consummated in other states between persons of the same sex. On September 21, 1996, President Clinton signed H.R. 3396, an Act "to define and protect the institution of marriage." It will be added to the U.S. Code in chapter 115, title 28, section 1738C. The main part of the text is:

> No State, territory, or possession of the United States, or Indian tribe, shall be required to give effect to any public act, record, or judicial proceeding of any other State, territory, possession, or tribe respecting a relationship between persons of the same sex that is treated as a marriage

> under the laws of such other State, territory, possession, or tribe, or a right or claim arising from such relationship.

The legislation also defines marriage to mean "only a legal union between one man and one woman as husband and wife, and the word 'spouse' refers only to a person of the opposite sex who is a husband or a wife."

Court challenges are expected to be made to the constitutionality of state laws barring same sex marriages and to the federal legislation allowing states to deny them full faith and credit.

3. CONSUMMATION BY COHABITATION REQUIRED

A marriage contract in South Carolina is not final until it has been consummated by cohabitation, which is considered to be evidence of the mutual consent required to create any valid contract. If the parties have not cohabited, the lack of consent of either party will be inferred, and the marriage is voidable pursuant to S.C. Code Ann. § 20-1-530 (Law. Co-op. 1976) which states:

> If any such contract has not been consummated by the cohabitation of the parties thereto the court may declare such contract void for want of consent of either party of the contracting parties or for any other cause going to show that, at the time the supposed contract was made, it was not a contract.

Cohabitation is a prerequisite for establishing a valid common law marriage; thus, lack of cohabitation will invalidate a common law marriage irrespective of this statute.

There remains some uncertainty about the meaning of "cohabitation" in South Carolina, with the particular question being whether or not any sexual activity is required before the parties will be deemed to have cohabited. One of the first cases to present an opportunity to define cohabitation was *Jakar v. Jakar*, 113 S.C. 295, 102 S.E. 337 (1920). The Court considered two issues: the first was whether the parties had cohabited sufficiently to validate a marriage; the second was whether the marriage was otherwise invalid due to fraud on the part of the defendant (the question of fraud is discussed in the chapter on annulment). In an era in which there was great reluctance to annul any marriage, the court was divided three to two in favor of upholding the trial court, which had decided that a common law marriage had been established by evidence that the plaintiff and defendant had "occupied the same room for several days after the marriage." *Id.* at 298, 102 S.E. at 338. Justice Fraser, a member of the majority, wrote: "' cohabit' means living together as man and wife. . . . A single act is enough to shut the door on annulment." *Id.* at 102 S.E. at 340. The minority strongly disagreed, stating that the trial court's finding of cohabitation (which was contrary to the ruling of a master) was wholly without evidence to support it and failed to take into account the following facts: the defendant was in default, and the plaintiff testified without contradiction that there was no cohabitation, that she had been confined in the room with the flu, that the defendant had been at Camp Jackson, and that the defendant had been enraged at her for having the flu. Neither Justice Fraser nor anyone else discussed whether "as man and wife" requires sexual activity.

The Supreme Court has recently provided dicta that sexual intercourse is not required to establish cohabitation under South Carolina law, but it is still not clear whether some sexual activity is required to consummate a marriage. In *E.D.M. v. T.A.M.*, 307 S.C. 471, 415 S.E.2d 812 (1992), the Court noted that "'[c]ohabitation' has been defined as 'living together in the same house,'"and went on to hold that the court "has never viewed actual sexual intercourse as distinguishable from other sexual activity in determining marital matters." *Id.* at 815, 415 S.E.2d at 815 (citing *R.G.M. v. D.E.M.*, 306 S.C. 145, 410 S.E.2d 564 (1991)). In *R.G.M.*, the Court held that homosexual activity does constitute adultery. The *E.D.M.* Court concluded that the evidence (a long relationship, sharing a bed, and some minimal sexual activity (oral sex performed on the wife by the husband)) supported a finding of cohabitation, even though there had been no penile-vaginal intercourse.

Guidance from other states is mixed. In New Jersey, a marriage was annulled although the parties had lived together for some period after the marriage (the marriage occurred on Nov. 27, 1920 and the petition for annulment was not filed until April 14, 1921). *Bissell v. Bissell*, 117 A. 252, 253 (N.J. Ch. 1922). The facts were that the husband had been physically and incurably impotent at the time of the marriage; the wife had not known of this, and she was still a virgin at the time of the hearing. The court found that the marriage had not been "ratified," and it granted the annulment.

In *Hunt v. Hunt*, 161 So. 119, 121 (Miss. 1935), the Mississippi Supreme Court held:

> The word "cohabitation" as used in the marriage laws means the public assumption by a man and a woman of the marital relation, and dwelling together as such, thereby holding themselves out to the public as being man and wife. . . . That cohabitation may be without coition is not expressly held . . . but is implicit therein. . . .

One could surmise that South Carolina will agree with Mississippi in light of the dicta in *E.D.M. v. T.A.M.*, but the issue has not yet been squarely addressed.

Lack of cohabitation can only be asserted as a ground for annulment when one spouse refuses to cohabit with the other spouse after marriage, and the other spouse knew nothing of the first one's plans beforehand. In other words, two people cannot be granted an annulment on the ground of noncohabitation when the parties agree before the marriage not to cohabit. In *Campbell v. Moore*, 189 S.C. 497, 1 S.E.2d 784 (1937), the parties agreed to marry to legitimize an unborn child. The parties contracted, among other things, not to live together after the marriage. The husband sought to have the marriage annulled based on the contract. The Court refused to annul the marriage, declaring the contract to be against public policy and therefore void. The Court stated that collateral or antecedent agreements will not affect marriages to which there was consent.

E. COMMON LAW MARRIAGES

1. IN GENERAL

South Carolina is one of the few states which still recognize common law marriages. *Rodgers v. Herron*, 226 S.C. 317, 85 S.E.2d 104 (1954). A common law marriage carries the same rights and obligations as a statutory law marriage. The laws of inheritance, descent and distribution, and other property rights apply to common law marriage. Even though S.C. Code Ann. § 20-1-250 (Law. Co-op. 1976) says a marriage without a license is illegal, S.C. Code Ann. § 20-1-360 (Law. Co-op. 1976) states that a failure to meet all requirements to obtain a marriage license will not render illegal any marriage contracted. As mentioned earlier, the Supreme Court has ruled that statutes such as S.C. Code Ann. § 20-1-250 (Law. Co-op. 1976) are merely directory and do not make marriages without licenses invalid. In *State v. Ward*, 204 S.C. 210, 28 S.E.2d 785 (1944), the Court stated: "[s]tatutes prescribing the procurement of a license and other formalities to be observed in the solemnization of marriage, do not render invalid a marriage entered into according to the common law, but not in conformity with the statutory formalities, unless the statutes themselves expressly declare the marriage invalid . . . ." *Id.* at 214, 28 S.E. at 786.

A valid common law marriage requires an informal (but mutually understood) agreement of a man and woman to be married, both having the capacity to marry, without obtaining a statutory marriage license, accompanied or followed by cohabitation, the couple publicly representing themselves to be married. No fixed minimum time period of cohabitation is required to establish a common law marriage. *Rodgers v. Herron*, 226 S.C. 317, 85 S.E.2d 104 (1954). Once a valid common law marriage has been established nothing less than death or a judgment of divorce can dissolve the relation.

2. REQUISITES: AGREEMENT, COHABITATION AND HOLDING OUT

A common law marriage does not require any ceremony or documentation to be a valid marriage. What must exist is an intention evidencing an actual and mutual agreement to live publicly together as husband and wife and not in concubinage. *Rodgers v. Herron*, 226 S.C. 317, 334, 85 S.E.2d 104, 113 (1954) (citing *Tedder v. Tedder*, 108 S.C. 271, 276, 94 S.E. 19, 20 (1917)). The parties must also consummate the marriage by cohabiting together. In *E.D.M. v. T.A.M.*, 307 S.C. 471, 415 S.E. 2d 812 (1992), the Supreme Court considered the impact of S.C. Code Ann. § 20-1-530 (Law. Co-op. 1976) which provides:

> If any such [marriage] contract has not been consummated by the cohabitation of the parties thereto the court may declare such contract void for want of consent of either of the contracting parties or for any other cause going to show that, at the time the supposed contract was made, it was not a contract.

The Court concluded that this statute "abrogated the common law right to annul a marriage for want of legal consent by adding the 'no cohabitation' requirement." *Id.* at 815, 415 S.E.2d at 814. Thus, it requires mutual consent and cohabitation to create a common law marriage.

In addition to consummating the marriage by cohabiting, the parties must hold themselves out to the public as husband and wife. This requirement has been satisfied by evidence such as the filing of joint tax returns, the wife's renunciation of dower rights in real estate transactions, and the parties' listing themselves as husband and wife on their children's birth certificates. *Kirby v. Kirby*, 270 S.C. 137, 241 S.E.2d 415 (1978).

Ordinarily, mere cohabitation is not enough to constitute a valid marriage in the absence of a mutual agreement to be married. *Johnson v. Johnson*, 235 S.C. 542, 550, 112 S.E.2d 647, 651 (1960). In *Tedder v. Tedder*, 108 S.C. 271, 276, 94 S.E. 19, 20 (1917), the Court stated:

> [T]he difference between marriage and concubinage rests in the intent of the cohabiting parties. . . . The intent in marriage consists of living together by agreement of a man and woman as husband and wife . . . according to what we believe to be the law of God. The intent in concubinage consists in a man and woman living together in the contrary fashion.

Id. at 276, 94 S.E. at 20. It should be noted that the court relied heavily on a presumption against interracial marriages in making this determination. *Id.* at 276-277, 94 S.E. at 20-21. It appears likely from the facts that a common law marriage would have been established but for this presumption.

However, the existence of a valid common law marriage may be inferred from evidence of well-established and long-continued cohabitation, even in the face of testimony that no express agreement to be married was ever made. *Campbell v. Christian*, 235 S.C. 102, 108, 110 S.E.2d 1, 4 (1959). *Campbell* involves an action by the alleged widow of the deceased contesting admission of his will to probate. The judge admitted it to probate and held that her marriage to the deceased was invalid because the deceased had a common law wife, Beulah. The deceased and Beulah had lived together openly and notoriously for twenty-four years, during which time five children were born to them. Two of the birth certificates stated that the deceased and Beulah were not married, and the other three stated that they were married. Even though there was no explicit mutual agreement as to their marriage, they held themselves out to the community as husband and wife. Because Beulah was "illiterate, uneducated and of childlike simplicity," the Court found that her testimony that she was not married was probably related to the notion that a marriage is not legal unless solemnized by a religious, or at least an official, ceremony. *Id.* at 108, 110 S.E.2d at 4. The Court, in finding a common law marriage to exist, wrote:

> [T]hey resided together, openly and continuously, over a period of at least twenty-four years, during which they were known and recognized in the community as husband and wife; and that the children born to them during this cohabitation were declared to the public authorities charged with the duty of registering their births, as having been born in wedlock. . . .

Id. A more recent case reaffirms the ideas expressed in *Campbell*. In *Owens v. Owens*, ___ S.C. ___, 466 S.E.2d 373 (Ct. App. 1996), the Court of Appeals reversed the trial court's finding that no common law marriage was established. The parties had lived together since 1984, as husband and wife since 1988 according to the wife. The Court of Appeals held that the wife's statements which the trial court found to be an admission of nonmarriage may well have been made with reference to a ceremonial marriage and it remanded the matter to the family court for disposition of the wife's divorce action.

> Assertions of both parties that their relationship was one of open concubinage, or admission of nonmarriage by one party, fortified by strong circumstances, <u>may</u> suffice to overcome the

> presumption of their marriage from cohabitation and reputation. Such an admission by the parties does not suffice to overcome the presumption, however, where it is shown that the admission may well have been made with reference to a ceremonial marriage, and not uttered with the idea of negativing broadly the existence of the marital status. *Campbell v. Christian*, 235 S.C. 102, 110 S.E.2d 1 (1959). There is a strong presumption in favor of marriage by cohabitation, apparently matrimonial, coupled with social acceptance over a long period of time. *Jeanes v. Jeanes*, 255 S.C. 161, 177 S.E.2d 537 (1970). A man and woman living together as husband and wife are generally presumed to be married, provided they have acquired a reputation as a married couple. While the presumption of marriage from cohabitation and reputation is ordinarily a rebuttable presumption, the degree of proof to overcome it is generally very high, especially where the parties have cohabited as husband and wife for a long time. *Id.* The presumption of marriage can be dispelled only by evidence which is "clear, distinct and satisfactory." *Id.*

Id. at ___, 466 S.E.2d at 375. Thus, the necessary agreement may be inferred under some circumstances from the nature and duration of open cohabitation coupled with actual intercourse. Therefore, couples genuinely wishing to avoid marriage while cohabiting should be explicit about their marital (or non-marital) status and document it.

On the other hand, living together for a short duration of time is not likely to create a common law marriage, absent clear evidence of an intention to be married and some representation to the public that two people intend to be married. The court determined that there had been no intention to create a common law marriage in *Cathcart v. Cathcart*, 307 S.C. 322, 414 S.E.2d 811 (Ct. App. 1992). In *Cathcart*, the former husband was attempting to prove that his former wife and her paramour had entered into a common law marriage so he could end his alimony obligation. The court made the following comments about the evidence in reaching its decision that no common law marriage had been created:

> [They] did not refer to each other as husband and wife. Both testified they had no intent to be married to each other. Indeed, the

> man testified he dated other women. Additionally, they did not file joint tax returns, did not have a joint bank account, and did not receive mail at the same address.

Id. at 812, 414 S.E.2d at 812.

In *Jennings v. Hurt*, 554 N.Y.S.2d 220 (1990), a New York court determined that the parties had not established a common law marriage while living in South Carolina. The plaintiff attempted to prove that five weeks of cohabitation in South Carolina, along with Hurt's purported statements to Jennings that they had a "spiritual marriage" and that they were "married in the eyes of God," had formed a common law marriage. The court relied on South Carolina case law (especially *Ex parte Blizzard*, 185 S.C. 131, 193 S.E. 633 (1937)) in determining that no such marriage existed. Because the court determined that Hurt's alleged statements, if true, did not indicate an intent to marry, it considered ancillary evidence relating to public perceptions of the couple's relationship to determine if a common law marriage existed. This included testimony and affidavits which showed that friends and neighbors believed them to be unmarried, and documents which listed the defendant as "single."

3. EFFECT OF IMPEDIMENTS

If any of the essentials which constitute a valid common law marriage are missing or if the relationship is illicit (e.g., one of the parties may be bound by an existing undissolved marriage), the relationship cannot ripen into a valid common law marriage no matter how long two people live together. Any marriage attempted between two parties while either of them has a subsisting marriage is void as a matter of public policy. In *Johns v. Johns*, 309 S.C. 199, 420 S.E.2d 856 (Ct. App. 1992), the court cited S.C. Code Ann. § 20-1-80 (Law. Co-op. Supp.) in support of this proposition and went on to hold that "[the marriage] was void from its inception, not merely voidable, and, therefore, cannot be ratified or confirmed and thereby made valid." *Id.* at ___, 420 S.E.2d at 858 (Ct. App. 1992).

Once an impediment has been removed and there is no longer a barrier to marriage, there must be a new mutual agreement to enter into a common law marriage. *Prevatte v. Prevatte*, 297 S.C. 345, 349, 377 S.E.2d 114, 117 (Ct. App. 1989); *Kirby v. Kirby*, 270 S.C. 137, 241 S.E.2d 415 (1978). This new agreement must be shown to exist by the preponderance of the evidence. A formal declaration of intent to enter a common law marriage is not required, but evidence of such agreement can be gathered from the conduct of the parties. *Kirby* at 140, 241 S.E.2d at 416 (citing *Ex parte Blizzard*, 185 S.C. 131, 133, 193 S.E. 633, 634 (1937)). *See also Cathcart v. Cathcart*, 307 S.C. 322, 324, 414 S.E.2d 811, 812 (Ct. App. 1992) (stating that a valid common law marriage requires evidence of an intention on the part of both parties to enter into a marriage contract, usually by an unequivocal public declaration of marriage).

Another case supporting this principal is *Day v. Sec. of Health and Human Servs.*, 519 F. Supp. 872 (D.S.C. 1981). An administrative law judge had ordered Myrtis Day to repay spousal insurance benefits following her third husband's retirement, for the reason that because her second marriage had not been dissolved, her third marriage was void. On appeal, the district court determined that her third marriage was not necessarily void. It relied on S.C. case law and S.C. Code Ann. § 20-1-80 (Law. Co-op. 1976) which states that any marriage formed while either party has a living former spouse is void. *Id.* However, the statute's first listed exception provides that the statute does not apply when one spouse has been absent seven years. *Id.* (The length of absence required has since been reduced to five years. S.C. Code Ann. § 20-1-80 (Law. Co-op. Supp.).) The court held that since more than seven years had passed between Day's last contact with her second husband and her application for benefits, she would have been eligible to remarry over a year before her application was filed. *Day*, 519 F. Supp. at 877.

Although she and Mr. Day had been formally married prior to her time of eligibility, the court found that a valid common law marriage may have been formed. Because the Days held themselves out to the public as husband and wife after the date of eligibility to remarry, the U.S. District Court determined that a South Carolina court would have held the common law marriage valid. *Id.* (citing *Ex parte Blizzard*, 185 S.C. 131, 133, 193 S.E. 633, 634 (1937)). Moreover, the South Carolina presumption that a conflicting second marriage is valid would also have led a court to find that the Days were married. *Day*, 519 F. Supp. at 877-878 (citing *Hallums v. Hallums*, 74 S.C. 407, 411, 54 S.E. 613, 614 (1905)).

South Carolina courts have not yet decided whether a valid common law marriage can be created if the parties do not have knowledge that an impediment has been removed. However, in *Prevatte v. Prevatte*, 297 S.C. 345, 349, 377 S.E.2d 114, 117 (Ct. App. 1989), the court came as close as it could without actually declaring that direct knowledge is not required. There the impediment had been a prior marriage of the wife. Her first husband had obtained a divorce from her in 1977 in which she was served by publication. Neither Prevatte became aware of the divorce decree until 1985, the year after they separated. Despite this, the court determined that, "at least by 1984, they must have come to the conclusion that they were married at that time." *Id.* at 350, 377 S.E.2d at 117. The opinion includes the following language:

> There appears to be a split of authority among the states requiring an agreement after removal of the impediment as to whether the parties must have knowledge that the impediment has been removed. Some of the earlier cases required knowledge of the removal of the impediment. The courts, in many of these cases, reasoned that unless the parties had such knowledge, there could be no agreement following the removal of the impediment. *E.g.* *Cartwright v. McGown*, 121 Ill. 388, 12 N.E. 737 (1887); *Rice v. Randlett*, 141 Mass. 385, 6 N.E. 365 (1908). Other courts have expressly rejected knowledge that the impediment has been removed as a criterion in deciding such cases. *E.g.* *Hess v. Pettigrew*, 261 Mich. 618, 247 N.W. 90 (1933); *In re Wells*, 123 App. Div. 79, 108 N.Y.S. 164 (1908), *aff'd*, 194 N.Y. 548, 87 N.E. 1129 (1909). We need not decide here which of these views to adopt.
>
> Mr. and Mrs. Prevatte knew of the impediment to their marriage at the time they first began living together as husband and wife. Thus, they recognized from the outset the illicit nature of their relationship. It is clear, however, that at least by 1984, they had come to the conclusion that they were married. After all, they both represented to the Court that they were married at that time. Mr. Prevatte made this representation when it was contrary to his best interest. It follows, therefore, that at least by 1984, they had somehow come to the conclusion that the impediment to their marriage had been removed. Finally, it is clear from their conduct that they

> thereafter gave every indication of their agreement to be married. The fact that they did not know exactly when the impediment to their marriage had been removed or even how it had been removed is of no consequence, under the circumstances.

Id. at 349-350, 377 S.E.2d at 117.

Although the court narrowly avoided answering the question of law directly, it appears that South Carolina courts will try to uphold the validity of marriages which can be ratified following the removal of impediments, even if the parties do not have direct knowledge of the removal of the impediment.

F. CONSEQUENCES OF MARRIAGE

1. IN GENERAL

The legal consequences of entering into a common law marriage are no different from the legal consequences of entering into a statutory law marriage. Marriage is marriage, and the same rights and obligations attach to either form.

Under the common law, the husband and wife became one person; the legal existence of the wife was considered "merged into that of the husband, under whose wing or cover she is," thus the term coverture. Irving Browne, *Elements of the Law of Domestic Relations and of Employer and Employed* 14 (Fred B. Rothman & Co. 1981). Therefore, the husband became entitled to all of the wife's property and responsible for all of her debts, whether she acquired such before or during the marriage. *Id.* The wife is "subordinate to the will and dominion of her baron or lord." *Id.*

> It is the wife's duty to love, honor, and obey the husband, and it is the husband's duty to love, protect, and maintain the wife. He is bound to furnish and guard the house; to provide according to his means and condition for her maintenance; to defend her from personal insult and

> wrong; to be kind to her; to see that the offspring are reared with care and tenderness.

Id. at 15.

A husband and wife are no longer considered one legal entity under South Carolina law. *McCall v. Bangs,* 262 S.C. 657, 207 S.E.2d 91 (1974) (holding that statutes of limitation are applicable to husbands and wives during marriage because the common law disability of coverture has been completely abolished in South Carolina). Today, most domestic laws which discriminate on the basis of gender have been held to be violations of the U.S. Constitution's guarantee of equal protection under the law, and the domestic law of South Carolina has moved toward gender-neutral treatment of husbands and wives. However, a few vestiges of the common law bias in favor of husbands remain, particularly in court decisions which have not yet been challenged.

2. PERMANENCY

A major consequence of marriage is that the parties to the marriage agreement cannot rescind or revoke it by mutual consent. Rather, the marriage continues until either a court issues an order of annulment or divorce, or one of the parties dies or is declared to be dead by a court. This is true for common law marriages as well as for statutory marriages.

S.C. Code Ann. § 20-1-80 (Law. Co-op. Supp.) permits a person to remarry without creating a bigamous marriage when a spouse has been absent and his or her whereabouts have been unknown for five years, but this does not invalidate the first marriage. The first marriage will be revived and the second marriage will become void if the existence of the former spouse is established. *Davis v. Whitlock*, 90 S.C. 233, 73 S.E. 171 (1911) (holding that the validity of the marriage depends on whether the former husband was alive at the time of the contract, but that the second marriage in this case became valid when the parties continued living together as husband and wife after the first husband's death). Where a wife marries within the seven years, the presumption of her innocence, with all the circumstances, may outweigh the presumption of the husband's being alive. *Chapman v. Cooper*, 39

S.C.L. (5 Rich.) 452 (1852) (holding that a wife of fifty years could claim dower in her second husband's estate although she had become married to him in less than seven years after her first husband had left and there were rumors at the time that he was still alive).

On the other hand, a judicial declaration of death pursuant to S.C. Code Ann. § 20-1-540 (Law. Co-op. 1976) can end the first marriage and allow remarriage without risk of bigamy or other nullification of the second marriage. This statute allows an abandoned spouse to have the absent spouse declared dead if the spouse has been missing and not heard from for seven years. If the absent spouse happens to return, any subsequent marriage entered into by the abandoned spouse will not be invalidated by such reappearance. The statute requires the action to be brought "in the court of common pleas or other court of competent jurisdiction." It is not clear whether the family court would be a court of competent jurisdiction, but it is doubtful, absent specific legislative authority.

3. INTERPERSONAL RIGHTS AND OBLIGATIONS

a. Cohabitation

There are probably no valid laws which distinguish between the mutual rights and obligations of people in the basis of whether or not they are married. Under the common law, women often lost some rights by becoming married. The husband's common law "right moderately to chastise his wife" once included the right to strike her with a stick no bigger around than his thumb, but modern common law prohibits the man from striking his wife "even if she is drunk or insolent." Irving Browne, *Elements of the Law of Domestic Relations and of Employer and Employed* 17 (Fred B. Rothman & Co. 1981) (1883). *See also State v. Bowen*, 209 S.C. 311, 40 S.E.2d 39 (1946), in which the Court found error in the trial judge's failure to direct a verdict of not guilty for a wife accused of killing her husband. The following language appears in the opinion: "[A]ppellant was far from a model wife and deserved punishment on the occasion above referred to, if ever an exasperated husband has the right to administer corporal punishment on his wife (which right under the law of course the husband does not have)." *Id.* at 314, 40 S.E.2d at 40.

One common law right of the husband which has not yet been successfully challenged is the common law rule which says that the husband has the right to choose where the family will live, and that the wife has the duty to follow him to that domicile or the husband is relieved of his obligation to support her and he is entitled to obtain a divorce on the ground of desertion. *Wolfe v. Wolfe*, 220 S.C. 437, 440, 68 S.E.2d 348, 349 (1951) (holding that, under the settled law of South Carolina, the husband has the right to choose where the family resides, and when the wife refuses to go with him she is guilty of desertion).

Wolfe and other cases supporting this common law rule have never been specifically overruled, and it is unlikely that the appellate courts will be presented with an opportunity to do so in light of the availability of divorce on the basis of one year separation. It is also unlikely that a family court judge will actually rule in these times that a wife deserts her husband by refusing to follow him to his unilateral choice of domicile. Other states have taken the position that the common law rule is "outmoded" and no longer applicable. *See Kerr v. Kerr*, 6 Va. App. 620, 371 S.E.2d 30 (Ct. App. 1988), in which the court affirmed the refusal of trial court to grant the husband a divorce on the ground of desertion for refusing to follow him to a new domicile when his job changed. The court avoided ruling on the wife's challenge that the common law rule violates the U.S. Constitution, because it found that the wife's refusal was justified because their marital relationship had deteriorated. However, the opinion contains the following statement: "[I]n response, the wife contends that this principle is unconstitutional. A law which explicitly discriminates based on gender is unconstitutional absent a showing that it substantially furthers an important government interest. *Kirchberg v. Feenstra*, 450 U.S. 455, 459-60, 101 S. Ct. 1195, 1198, 67 L. Ed. 2d 428, 434 (1981); U.S. Const. amend. XIV; . . . ." *Id.* at 623, 371 S.E.2d at 32.

One would anticipate that a South Carolina appellate court would hold that the common law rule is unconstitutional, but one cannot be certain.

b. Sexual Intercourse

Although it is no longer viewed by many people as a serious threat to their liberty, it remains the law in South Carolina that people who live together and engage in carnal intercourse without being married are committing the crime of fornication.

S.C. Code Ann. § 16-15-80 (Law. Co-op. 1976). *See* 3 *S.C. Juris.*, Adultery and Fornication (S.C. Bar - C.L.E. Division 1991).

Marriage creates a legal right and a social expectation that couples will engage in sexual intercourse, but the law does not impose an obligation on either spouse to do so. Under the common law, there was a duty to refrain from intercourse if the other spouse reasonably requested forbearance. 41 Am. Jur. 2d *Husband and Wife* § 7 (1968). It does not appear, however, that a husband faced any significant consequences if he ignored a request for forbearance and forced his wife to have sex. Times have changed.

The right of a spouse to say no is codified in South Carolina at S.C. Code § 16-3-615 (Law. Co-op. Supp.), Spousal Sexual Battery:

> (A) Sexual battery, as defined in Section 16-3-651(h), when accomplished through use of aggravated force, defined as the use of physical force or physical violence of a high and aggravated nature which results in some physical manifestation of that force or violence to overcome the victim, by one spouse against the other spouse if they are living together, constitutes the crime of spousal sexual battery and, upon conviction, is punishable according to the discretion of the court. (B) The offending spouse's conduct must be reported to appropriate law enforcement authorities within thirty days in order for that spouse to be prosecuted for this offense. (C) The provisions of Section 16-3-659.1 do not apply to any trial brought under this section.

c. Mutual Support

Any able-bodied person capable of earning a livelihood is, regardless of gender, responsible for the "reasonable support" of his or her spouse and minor children. S.C. Code Ann. §§ 20-7-40, -90 (Law. Co-op. 1976). Failure to provide such support constitutes a misdemeanor punishable by fine, imprisonment, or both. S.C. Code Ann. § 20-7-90 (Law. Co-op. 1976).

d. Confidentiality

South Carolina preserves the common law privilege against the disclosure of confidential communications made by one spouse to the other during the marriage. This has been codified with an exception for child abuse cases at S.C. Code Ann. § 19-11-30 (Law. Co-op. 1976 & Supp.).

> However, no husband or wife may be required to disclose any confidential or, in a criminal proceeding, any communication made by one to the other during their marriage.
>
> Notwithstanding the above provisions, a husband or wife is required to disclose any communication, confidential or otherwise, made by one to the other during their marriage where the suit, action, or proceeding concerns or is based on criminal sexual conduct involving a minor or the commission or attempting to commit a lewd act upon a minor.

Commentators have described the unusual nature of the South Carolina privilege as follows:

> The statute makes privileged in criminal cases "*any* communication" [made by one to the other. This distinction between disclosures in criminal cases] and those in civil cases would seem to add little to the common law rule however, because all communications made in private between husband and wife are presumed to be confidential unless the subject matter or the circumstances show to the contrary. (McCormick, § 72) However, in South Carolina it is the testifying spouse who owns the privilege, not necessarily the spouse who initially made the communication. *State v. Motes*, 264 S.C. 317, 215 S.E.2d 190 (1975). The South Carolina position is at odds with both Wigmore and McCormick who indicate that the owner of the privilege should be the communicator.

J. Thames and W.M. Vonzharen, *A Guide to Evidence Law in South Carolina* at 44 (S.C. Bar, 1987). (The bracketed language was inadvertently omitted from the 1987 revision.)

e. Common Surname

There is authority cited in C.J.S. in support of the following propositions: 1) a wife's maiden name is absolutely lost upon marriage and her husband's name becomes her legal name; 2) a woman may retain her surname after marriage by entering into an antenuptial contract and by exclusively continuing to use her maiden name; 3) a woman may retain her surname by evidencing a clear intent to consistently and nonfraudulently use her maiden name after marriage; and 4) a woman is not required by common law, statute or rule to assume the name of her husband upon marriage. 65 C.J.S., Names § 3 (1966 & Supp.) (the first rule is contained in the main volume, the others come from more recent cases cited in the supplement).

There is no requirement in South Carolina that married people have the same surname. It appears to be the law that any two people may choose to have a common name irrespective of whether or not they are married. If people choose to share a surname, it does not have to be either of their previous surnames. They can pick any name they desire, and they can change it whenever they want. This freedom does not appear to be available to minors, except those who get married before they are eighteen.

The statutes providing for court ordered name changes fix the time of a name change with some certainty, but they do not affect the common law right of a person to change his or her name. *Brayton v. Beall*, 73 S.C. 308, 53 S.E. 641 (1906).

> At common law, a man may lawfully change his name, or by general usage or habit acquire another name than that originally borne by him, without the intervention of Court or Legislature. *City Council v. King*, 4 McCord, 487; *Miller v. George*, 30 S.C., 528, 9 S.E., 659; 21 Ency. Law, 311.

Id. at 311, 53 S.E. at 642 (holding that statutes which provide a mode of changing a name "do not abrogate but are in affirmance and aid of the common law rule").

4. ASSETS AND LIABILITIES

a. In General

Under the common law, the husband was entitled to all of the wife's property and he was responsible for all of her debts, whether she acquired them before or during the marriage. Irving Browne, *Elements of the Law of Domestic Relations and of Employer and Employed* 14 (Fred B. Rothman & Co. 1981). Today, except for the doctrine of necessaries discussed below, assets and debts acquired prior to the marriage remain separate unless some conduct or expression of intent by the parties creates a joint interest. (See additional discussion in the chapter on property.)

Assets and debts acquired during the marriage may be distributed when the marriage ends either by agreement of the parties, or by equitable apportionment by the family court with reference to the factors set out in S.C. Code Ann. § 20-7-472 (Law. Co-op. Supp.). In *Hardy v. Hardy*, 311 S.C. 433, 429 S.E.2d 811 (Ct. App. 1992), the Court of Appeals held that the law relating to marital debts was "materially impacted" by S.C. Code § 20-7-472" and that "§ 20-7-472 creates a presumption that a debt either spouse incurred prior to marital litigation is a marital debt and must be factored into the totality of equitable apportionment. The presumption is rebuttable." *Id.* Although the Court's language was not specific, one assumes from the clear language of the statute that this applies only to debts acquired during the marriage, not before the marriage.

Marital debts subject to equitable apportionment may include debts incurred between the separation and the divorce, if they were incurred for the benefit of both parties. See *Peirson v. Calhoun*, 308 S.C. 246, 417 S.E.2d 604 (Ct. App. 1992) (affirming trial court's ruling that debts incurred by the husband following the separation were part of the marital estate subject to equitable apportionment).

b. Doctrine of Necessaries

As mentioned above, spouses are generally not responsible for each other's debts acquired before their marriage or after marital litigation commences. S.C. Code Ann. §§ 20-5-30, -70 (Law. Co-op. 1976). However, one spouse may be liable for the other spouse's debts contracted prior to or during the marriage if the goods or services provided to the spouse were "necessary." This is the "doctrine of necessaries."

S.C. Code Ann. § 20-5-60 (Law. Co-op. 1976) provides that "A husband shall not be liable for the debts of his wife contracted prior to or after their marriage, except for her necessary support and that of their minor children residing with her." Although the language of the statute would violate equal protection rights if it was applied literally, because it would impose liability on the husband but not the wife, the Supreme Court has held that the doctrine of necessaries remains a viable common law doctrine. *Richland Mem'l. Hosp. v. Burton*, 282 S.C. 159, 160-161, 318 S.E.2d 12, 13 (1984). The Court of Appeals more recently upheld the validity of the necessaries doctrine and refused to follow the example of other states which have abolished the necessaries doctrine in *Trident Regional Medical Center v. Evans*, 317 S.C.346, 454 S.E.2d 343 (Ct. App. 1995) (pointing out that marriage involves shared wealth, rights, and duties).

A third party providing necessary goods or services to either spouse may bring an action for recovery against the other spouse. *Burton, supra. See also Richland Mem'l. Hospital v. English*, 295 S.C. 511, 369 S.E.2d 395 (1988) (holding that the doctrine of necessaries includes actions to recover final illness expenses from the common law wife of a deceased patient).

However, a creditor may not rely on the doctrine of necessaries to recover from the spouse who is the secondary obligor unless it first seeks to recover from the assets of the spouse who is the primary obligor. *Anderson Mem'l. Hospital v. Hagen*, 313 S.C. 497, 443 S.E.2d 399 (Ct. App. 1994) (holding that the hospital could not recover from the husband under the doctrine of necessaries $62,089 worth of hospital services provided to the husband's deceased wife because it did not first seek to recover from the assets of the wife.)

A creditor is not required to sue and exhaust the assets of the debtor spouse before seeking reimbursement from the other spouse, but may bring a single action against both spouses after making demand for repayment upon the debtor spouse. *Trident Regional Medical Center v. Evans*, 317 S.C. 346, 454 S.E.2d 343 (Ct. App. 1995) (holding that a creditor seeking reimbursement from the nondebtor spouse must show: 1) necessaries were provided to the debtor spouse, 2) the parties were married at the time, and 3) despite demand therefor, payment for the necessaries has not been made by the person to whom the necessaries were provided).

A third party seeking to apply the necessaries doctrine must bring the action in the circuit court, not the family court. *Amisub of S.C., etc. v. Passmore, et al.*, 316 S.C. 112, 447 S.E.2d 207 (1994) (holding that the family court does not have subject matter jurisdiction over an action brought by a hospital seeking to have the court order a husband to accept responsibility for his ill wife's care).

5. INHERITANCE RIGHTS

a. Dower and Curtesy

South Carolina once recognized the common law rights of a wife to dower (a legal right or interest that a wife acquired in her husband's estate through marriage) and curtesy (a husband's right to his wife's property). Curtesy was abolished in South Carolina before 1900. *See* S.C. Const. art. 17, § 9 (1895). Dower was not abolished in South Carolina until 1984 in *Boan v. Watson*, 281 S.C. 516, 316 S.E.2d 401 (1984). That case abolished dower because it discriminated on the basis of gender. Because the Court abolished dower prospectively only, dower still applies to wives whose husbands died on or before May 22, 1984.

b. Intestacy

The surviving spouse of a person who dies intestate is entitled to a share of the decedent's estate. If there is no surviving issue of the decedent, the spouse is entitled to the entire intestate estate. If there are surviving issue of the decedent, the spouse receives one-half of the intestate estate. S.C. Code Ann. § 62-2-102 (Law. Co-op. 1976). A spouse who fails to survive the decedent by 120 hours is considered to have predeceased the decedent and is therefore not considered a surviving spouse for purposes of determining intestate share. S.C. Code Ann. § 62-2-104 (Law. Co-op. 1976).

If a child dies intestate and is not survived by a spouse or children, the parents of the child share equally in the child's estate. S.C. Code Ann. § 62-2-103(2) (Law.

Co-op. 1976). However, a parent who does not provide support for a child may be denied a share of an intestate child's estate. S.C. Code Ann. § 62-2-114 (Law. Co-op. Supp.) allows the probate court to deny or limit either or both parent's entitlement to a share of the proceeds of an intestate child's estate "if the court determines, by a preponderance of the evidence, that the parent or parents failed to reasonably provide support for the decedent as defined in Section 20-7-40 and did not otherwise provide for the needs of the decedent during his or her minority."

A parent who does not provide support for a child may be denied a share of damages awarded by a jury in a wrongful death action arising from the death of a child. S.C. Code Ann. § 15-51-40 (Law. Co-op. Supp.) allows the probate court to deny or limit either or both parents' entitlement for a share of the damages awarded by a jury in a wrongful death action "if the court determines, by a preponderance of the evidence, that the parent or parents failed to reasonably provide support for the decedent as defined in Section 20-7-40 and did not otherwise provide for the needs of the decedent during his or her minority."

c. Elective Share

The surviving spouse of a decedent domiciled at the time of his or her death in South Carolina has a right to take an elective share of one-third of the decedent's estate under S.C. Code Ann. § 62-2-201 (Law. Co-op. Supp.), minus funeral and administration expenses and enforceable claims. S.C. Code Ann. § 62-2-202 (Law. Co-op. 1976).

The surviving spouse must elect to take during his or her lifetime, personally or by his or her attorney in fact. S.C. Code Ann. § 62-2-203 (Law. Co-op. 1976). The election must occur within eight months after the decedent's death or six months after the probate of the decedent's will. S.C. Code Ann. § 62-2-205 (Law. Co-op. Supp.). Benefits the surviving spouse receives under the will or passing by intestacy, along with benefits in the form of exempt property, are chargeable against the elective share. S.C. Code Ann. § 62-2-206 (Law. Co-op. Supp.).

The right to an elective share may be waived by a written contract signed by the party waiving after fair disclosure. S.C. Code Ann. § 62-2-204 (Law. Co-op.

1976). Fair disclosure requires providing information about the assets of the party seeking the waiver.

> Considering the confidential relationship between parties to an antenuptial agreement, the affirmative duty imposed upon each party to disclose his or her financial status transcends what is normally required for a commercial transaction. [citation omitted]
>
> . . . .
>
> > Fair disclosure means that before signing an antenuptial agreement, each party must disclose to the other the facts that exist at the time of the agreement and which, in the absence of the antenuptial agreement, affect or determine the prospective intestate share of a surviving spouse in the disclosing party's estate or which otherwise affect or determine distribution of property at the disclosing party's death.
>
> *In re Estate of Stephenson*, 503 N.W.2d 540 (Neb. 1993).

Geddings v. Geddings, 319 S.C. 213, ___, 460 S.E.2d 376, 378 (1994) (upholding the circuit court's affirmance of the probate court's conclusion that a wife's waiver of her elective share in her husband's estate was void because there had not been fair disclosure. The evidence showed that the wife had no real or general knowledge of the total extent of her husband's assets. The attorney preparing the waiver document testified he did not discuss assets with the wife when it was executed. There was evidence that the husband was secretive about his financial affairs.)

d. Omitted Spouse

If a testator fails to provide in his or her will for a spouse married after the execution of that will, the omitted spouse shall receive the same share he or she would have received had the decedent died intestate, unless the will shows the omission to be intentional, or unless the testator provided for the spouse outside the will with the intention that the nontestamentary provisions be in lieu of any gifts under the will. S.C. Code Ann. § 62-2-301 (Law. Co-op. Supp.). Absent specific language in a will, or sufficient extrinsic evidence that a bequest was made "in contemplation of marriage" a spouse has not been "provided for" under the omitted spouse's statute. *Miles v. Miles*, 312 S.C. 408, 440 S.E.2d 882 (1994) (holding that a wife was not provided for in her capacity as a spouse where the will was executed a year before she agreed to marry the deceased and there was no evidence the will was written in contemplation of marriage).

e. Exempt Property

A surviving spouse is entitled to furniture, automobiles, furnishings, appliances, and personal effects to a value not exceeding $5000. S.C. Code Ann. § 62-2-401 (Law. Co-op. 1976). These rights are in addition to the homestead right, but are chargeable against the elective share or that spouse's share under the will or passing by intestacy. *Id.*

6. CHILDREN

a. Legitimacy

The status of legitimacy or illegitimacy is determined by whether the parents of a child were married at the time the child was conceived or born. The practical consequences of being born out of wedlock are virtually nonexistent in modern society. Parents of illegitimate children are required to support them the same as a child born during wedlock. Any social stigma is negligible given the large numbers of illegitimate children, the growing number of one-parent families and the high rate of divorce.

The distinction between legitimacy and illegitimacy was made largely for determining the heirs of an intestate parent. Until 1977, it was the law by statute in South Carolina that illegitimate children could not inherit from their fathers (former S.C. Code Ann. § 21-3-30 (Law. Co-op. 1976)). However, in *Trimble v. Gordon*, 430 U.S. 762, 97 S.Ct. 1459, 52 L.Ed. 31 (1977), the United States Supreme Court held an Illinois statute unconstitutional because it denied an illegitimate child any inheritance from its father. The South Carolina Supreme Court held that *Trimble* should be applied prospectively only in *Wilson v. Jones,* 281 S.C. 231, 314 S.E.2d 341 (1984). *See also Mitchell v. Hardwick*, 297 S.C. 48, 374 S.E.2d 681 (1988) (modifying *Wilson* under certain conditions). Today, S.C. Code Ann. § 62-2-109(2) (Law. Co-op. 1976 & Supp.) provides that a child born out of wedlock is entitled to inherit as a child of the deceased father if:

> (i) the natural parents participated in a marriage ceremony before or after the birth of the child, even though the attempted marriage is void; or
>
> (ii) the paternity is established by an adjudication commenced before the death of the father or within the later of eight months after the death of the father or six months after the probate of his estate and, if after his death, by clear and convincing proof, except that the paternity established under this subparagraph (ii) is ineffective to qualify the father or his kindred to inherit from or through the child unless the father has openly treated the child as his and has not refused to support the child.

Thus, a child born out of wedlock is entitled to share in his or her father's estate, even if no attempt to prove paternity is made until just after the father's death; but a father cannot try to get a share of his child's estate under similar circumstances unless he acted as a father toward the child during its lifetime.

Today, if the parents of a child born out of wedlock marry, that child is legitimized "as if born in lawful wedlock." S.C. Code Ann. § 20-1-60 (Law. Co-op. 1976). An illegitimate child will not, however, be legitimized merely because the child's natural mother marries someone. It must be the child's biological father. *Walton v. Walton*, 282 S.C. 165, 168, 318 S.E.2d 14, 16 (1984).

Even if the marriage proves to be bigamous, the children are still legitimate. S.C. Code Ann. § 20-1-60 (Law. Co-op. 1976). If a person remarries after the spouse has been absent for a period of seven years, such husband or wife not being heard from or known to be living during that period of time, the children of the subsequent marriage are legitimate. S.C. Code Ann. § 20-1-50 (Law. Co-op. 1976).

b. Care, Education and Welfare

Irrespective of whether they are married, parents are equally charged with the welfare and education of their minor children, along with the care and management of the children's estates. S.C. Code Ann. § 20-7-100 (Law. Co-op. Supp.). This statute also provides for parity of the husband and wife with respect to the right to custody of their children. It also grants to each parent, whether custodial or not, equal access to all educational and medical records of the children.

c. Children's Names

South Carolina case decisions have not considered this in modern times, but the law appears to be that parents have a right jointly to adopt any surname for their child they wish to adopt, just as they determine what shall be a child's given name. *See Lassiter-Geers v. Reichenbach*, 492 A.2d 303, 303 Md. 88 (1985) *cert. den.* 474 U.S. 1019, 106 S.Ct. 568, 88 L.Ed.2d 553 (affirming the trial court's decision denying the mother's request for the daughter to have her maiden name where the mother had remarried).

It is unclear in South Carolina which parent's surname a child should have if the parents cannot agree or if they are not married. An old opinion of the Attorney General of South Carolina concluded that, if the mother is unmarried, a child would take her name, but if the parents are married, it would take the name of the father, even if the father had deserted the family. 1938-39 Op. Atty. Gen. 164. This opinion may be ripe for challenge because it does not state a gender-neutral rule. A similar challenge may also be available to the validity of S.C. Code Ann. § 20-1-70 (Law. Co-op. 1976) which provides that a child who has been legitimized by the marriage of its parents following its illegitimate birth "shall take the name of his father" unless the child had been adopted and its name had already been changed by court decree.

Jurisdictions seeking a gender-neutral answer to the question have taken two approaches: a case by case analysis of the best interests of the child or a presumption in favor of the surname chosen by the custodial parent.

Courts applying the best-interests-of-the-child standard consider a number of criteria in determining the advantages and

> detriments to a child of assuming either the maternal or paternal surname. Those factors include the length of time that the child has used one surname, the identification of the child as a member or part of a family unit, the potential anxiety, embarrassment, or discomfort the child might experience if the child bears a surname different from the custodial parent, and any preferences the child might express, assuming the child possesses sufficient maturity to express a relevant preference. [citations omitted] Courts have experienced difficulty, however, in applying the factors underlying the best-interests-of-the-child standard, possibly because of the speculative quality of the inquiry into the effect that the chosen surname would have on the future welfare and happiness of the child.
>
> . . . .
>
> To enhance the predictability of the best interest standard, some commentators have suggested, and a few courts have adopted a presumption in favor of the surname chosen by the custodial parent.

Gubernat v. Deremer, 140 N.J. 120, 141, 657 A.2d 856, 867 (1995) (holding that in contested cases the surname selected by the custodial parent shall be presumed to be consistent with the child's best interests, a presumption rebuttable by evidence that a different surname would better serve those interests. The child was born to unmarried parents and was given the mother's surname at birth, the father having refused to acknowledge paternity. When his paternity was established seven months later, the father sought a change in the child's surname.)

G. MISCELLANEOUS

1. PALIMONY

"Palimony" is the term used to denote a monetary award or property settlement between unmarried partners. Litigation involving "palimony" would occur in circuit court, not in family court, because there is no specific statutory authority for the family court to hear and decide such cases.

It does not appear that South Carolina would be a friendly forum in which to bring palimony actions, but the case law is fairly old. In *Grant v. Butt*, 198 S.C. 298, 17 S.E.2d 689 (1941), a contract provided that a woman would live with a man in a state of concubinage and would refrain from marrying anyone else. As consideration the man was required to take out a life insurance policy naming the woman as the beneficiary, and he was to make a will giving her one-half of his estate if she survived him. Apparently she performed; he did not. When the man died intestate, the woman brought an action for breach of contract. The court cited *American Jurisprudence*:

> An agreement or understanding founded upon a consideration in whole or in part for the commencement or continuance of meretricious sexual intercourse is directly contrary to law or public policy and the best interests of society. Thus, a loan by a man to a woman on consideration that she serve as his mistress cannot be recovered.

Id. 198 S.C. at 306, 17 S.E.2d at 694 (citing 12 Am. Jur. *Contracts* § 176 (1936)).

Other jurisdictions have modified this approach, limiting contractual invalidity to consideration directly related to meretricious activity. See *Marvin v. Marvin*, 557 P.2d 106 (Cal. 1976). South Carolina's approach has not been altered in decisional law or by statute since *Grant v. Butt*. Thus, an action for "palimony" does not, at present, seem to be viable in South Carolina.

2. PROXY MARRIAGES

A proxy marriage occurs when one or both of the parties are represented at the ceremony by an authorized agent. South Carolina has no statute directly authorizing marriage except where both parties are present. 1959-60 S.C. Att'y Gen. Ann. Rep. 285.

A proxy marriage may be sustained either by meeting the statutory requirements for a ceremonial marriage or by creating a valid common law marriage. Given South Carolina's view of the formalities requirement as being merely directory, its strong policy favoring marriage, and its lack of a blood test requirement, no major public policy would seem to be violated by a recognition of proxy marriage. *But see* 8 U.S.C. § 1101(a)(35) (1987) (providing that for immigration purposes unconsummated proxy marriages shall not be recognized).

In *Brewington v. Brewington*, 280 S.C. 502, 313 S.E.2d 53 (Ct. App. 1984), the Court of Appeals held that an action for legal separation and related equitable relief could be brought by an attorney in fact in the name of the principal. It noted that divorce actions were purely personal and could not be so brought. Of course, entering into marriage is not the same as filing a lawsuit. Nonetheless, the relation sought is certainly a personal one.

CHAPTER THREE
ANNULMENT

CHAPTER THREE
ANNULMENT

A. IN GENERAL

Chapter Two concerns actions to establish the validity of marriages. Annulments on the other hand are actions to establish the invalidity of marriages. Of course, the question of whether a marriage is valid or invalid requires an examination of virtually identical factors; thus, readers should refer to Chapter Two for the bulk of the discussion on this topic.

An annulment declares that a marriage never occurred because of some defect. Defective marriages may be either void or voidable. In a void marriage, the circumstances are such that the marriage could never have come into being. A voidable marriage is recognized under the law as a valid marriage until an action is brought to prove it invalid.

A void marriage technically needs no judicial action to declare that it is void. The following examples illustrate the essential differences: suppose A and B are parties to a voidable marriage and one of them dies. The remaining spouse is legally entitled to all legal rights and obligations stemming from the marriage relationship, if there was no adjudication of voidness during the joint lifetimes of the parties. A void marriage, by contrast, creates none of the rights and obligations which stem from the marriage relationship and no adjudication is required before the void marriage has this effect. A void marriage may be declared void by judicial action at the request of any interested individual at any time.

B. JURISDICTION

Annulment of marriages, like divorce, has not always been possible in South Carolina. The mid-nineteenth century South Carolina cases held that jurisdiction to annul marriages lay only with the ecclesiastical courts of England and, because there was no constitutional or statutory grant of jurisdiction to annul marriages, South

Carolina courts were without jurisdiction to do so. The constitutional limitation was removed in 1868 when Article IV, § 15 of the South Carolina Constitution of 1868 was amended to provide that the court of common pleas should have jurisdiction in all civil cases. The statutory limitation was removed in 1873 by the Revised Statutes of that year which declared certain marriages to be void.

South Carolina's latest Constitution, that of 1895, retains the wording of Article IV, § 15 of the 1868 Constitution in Article V, § 7. In 1902, several statutes were enacted concerning the validity of marriages (S.C. Civil Code of 1902, §§ 2658, 2661 and 2664). In 1911, the Supreme Court put to rest any doubts regarding the authority of the court of common pleas to assume jurisdiction over the annulment of marriages. In *Davis v. Whitlock*, 90 S.C. 233, 73 S.E. 171 (1911), the Court unequivocally stated that the court of common pleas had jurisdiction over suits to annul marriages. Noting that the legislature had passed laws declaring all bigamous marriages void (as well as marriages between a white person and an Indian or black person), the Court stated:

> There ought to be no doubt of the proposition that, when the legislative department of the government enacts a law, it is not necessary to provide that the courts shall have jurisdiction to determine any substantial controversy between the individuals that may arise under the law. Such jurisdiction is necessarily implied.

Id. at 238-239, 73 S.E. at 173.

South Carolina's family courts now have exclusive jurisdiction over actions for annulment of marriages by virtue of S.C. Code Ann. § 20-7-420(6) (Law. Co-op. 1976).

Once the court has jurisdiction of the annulment suit it also has jurisdiction to resolve all other issues presented. *Splawn v. Splawn*, 311 S.C. 423, 429 S.E.2d 805 (1993) (affirming the trial judge's decision to equitably apportion marital property after declaring the marriage void because the husband had entered into the marriage with the mistaken belief that he was divorced from his first wife). This has been the rule in South Carolina for a long time. *See White v. White*, 283 S.C. 348, 323 S.E.2d 521 (1984), *Campbell v. Moore*, 189 S.C. 497, 1 S.E.2d 784 (1937) (child custody, maintenance, and attorney's fees); *Young v. Naylor*, 10 S.C.Eq. (1 Hill Eq.) 383 (1833) (division of property).

C. VENUE

It is not altogether clear what constitutes the proper venue for annulment actions. Unlike actions for divorce and separate support and maintenance, there is no specific statute establishing venue for annulment actions. Therefore, venue is determined by reference to the general statutes governing civil actions. These are found in S.C. Code Ann. § 15-7-10 *et seq*. (Law. Co-op. 1976). There have been no cases directly on point to provide guidance.

The proper location to initiate an annulment action appears to be the county in which the defendant resides at the time of the commencement of the action. S.C. Code Ann. § 15-7-30 (Law. Co-op. 1976). This may cause some inequity, for the best place to bring the case might be either at the place where the parties tried to become married or where they last resided together. Both of these locations may, in fact, be preferable to the defendant's present home due to the existence of witnesses or property involved in the dispute. Perhaps, the legislature will modify S.C. Code Ann. § 20-3-60 (Law. Co-op. 1992 Supp.) in the future to include all marital litigation.

Choosing an improper venue to initiate litigation is not necessarily detrimental to the merits of the plaintiff's case. If the venue is wrong, the proper remedy is to transfer the case, not to dismiss it. SCRCP Rule 82(b). SCRCP Rule 12(b) provides that the defense of "(3) improper venue" may be raised either in responsive pleadings or by motion. If it is raised by motion, it "shall be made before pleading, if a further pleading is permitted."

At least one of the parties to an annulment action must be a domiciliary of this state before personal jurisdiction attaches. In *Foster v. Nordman*, 244 S.C. 485, 137 S.E.2d 600 (1964), the parties were married in South Carolina but were North Carolina domiciliaries when the annulment suit was brought. The Court refused to grant the annulment even though the marriage was performed in South Carolina, stating:

> There is no jurisdiction of an annulment suit merely because the marriage was performed within the state. Jurisdiction lies in the courts of the state where the parties are residing, or where one of them resides at the time of suit, irrespective of the place where the marriage may have been contracted or solemnized.

However, South Carolina accepts the common law principles that the courts of the domicile of the parties have the right to determine the marital status of its citizens under its laws, and they have jurisdiction to annul a marriage celebrated elsewhere. *See Foster*; and *Everly v. Baumil*, 209 S.C. 287, 290, 39 S.E.2d 905, 906 (1946).

D. GROUNDS AND DEFENSES

1. IN GENERAL

The first question to consider is whether the requirements for establishing either a statutory law marriage or a common law marriage have been met. If not, the marriage will be annulled. The requirements for establishing valid marriages are discussed in the chapter on establishing the validity of marriages.

A basic requirement for seeking an annulment is lack of cohabitation. S.C. Code Ann. § 20-1-530 (Law. Co-op. 1976) provides:

> If any such [marriage] contract has not been consummated by the cohabitation of the parties thereto the court may declare such contract void for want of consent of either of the contracting parties or for any other cause going to show that, at the time the supposed contract was made, it was not a contract.

The Supreme Court has interpreted § 20-1-530 as barring an annulment on the basis of fraud if the parties have cohabited as husband and wife. *See E.D.M. v. T.A.M.*, 307 S.C. 471, 415 S.E.2d 812 (1992), discussed below in the section on fraud.

E.D.M. also says § 20-1-530 does not apply and cohabitation does not validate marriage by a person legally incompetent to contract marriage, i.e., a bigamous or incestuous spouse, citing *Hughey v. Ray*, 207 S.C. 374, 36 S.E.2d 33 (1945); *Davis v. Whitlock*, 90 S.C. 233, 73 S.E. 171 (1911). *E.D.M.* at 474, n.1, 415 S.E.2d at 814, n.1.

2. ADDITIONAL GROUNDS FOR ANNULMENTS

The common law contract defenses of fraud and duress have been recognized in South Carolina as appropriate considerations in determining the validity or invalidity of marriage contracts.

a. Duress

Duress is a well-recognized defense to formation of a contract. A marriage will be annulled if one of the parties enters into it under duress. *Campbell v. Moore*, 189 S.C. 497, 1 S.E.2d 784 (1937). The threats or violence constituting duress must be "of such nature as to inspire a great fear of bodily harm" in a person of ordinary firmness and it must "dominate throughout the transaction to such an extent that [the injured party] could not and did not act as a free agent." *Phipps v. Phipps*, 216 S.C. 248, 254, 57 S.E.2d 417, 420 (1950).

In *Phipps*, the petitioner agreed to marry the young woman when she became pregnant. Later, the petitioner informed her he was not going to marry her. A little more than one month before the child was born the young woman's father and two of her brothers rode over to the petitioner's house. He was restrained by the father, placed into his car and driven to the county probate court, where the father found that no marriage license had been issued to the couple. The following conversation took place outside the probate court:

Young woman's brother:	"You know what we should do with him?"
Petitioner:	"What, shoot me?"
Brother:	"That's exactly right."

Father: "This is too good for him. We should take him to the river and tie a rock around his neck and toss him in."

*Id.*at 251, 57 S.E.2d at 418. The petitioner should not have answered the way he did. The Court reasoned that he was not actually in fear of being injured or he never would have suggested that he be shot. The Court also noted that appellant had at least two chances to escape prior to the marriage but refused to attempt an escape. Apparently, the victim (usually the groom) of a "shotgun wedding" must attempt to escape from those attempting to force him to marry. Of course, the threat of harm also must be real or apparently so.

The court's reasoning in *Phipps* does not consider the impracticalities of escaping a shotgun wedding. Those with the shotguns will likely continue to threaten the reluctant party. A better solution would be to allow the defense of duress given the requisite amount of violence or threats, even if the reluctant spouse did have an avenue of temporary escape.

b. Fraud

A marriage procured by fraudulent means may be annulled in South Carolina, unless the marriage has been consummated by cohabitation. The leading case in this area of annulment law is *Jakar v. Jakar*, 113 S.C. 295, 102 S.E. 337 (1919). The Court considered two issues: the first was whether the parties had cohabited sufficiently to validate a marriage (the question of cohabitation is discussed in the chapter on establishing the validity of marriages); the second was whether the marriage was otherwise invalid due to fraud on the part of the defendant. The circuit court's order, as affirmed by the Supreme Court, defined the fraud necessary to annul a marriage as follows:

> The [marriage] contract, from its peculiar nature and on general grounds of public policy, the law regards as especially sacred and inviolable. It cannot be voided or set aside on the ground of fraud, except on the most plenary and satisfactory proof of deceit and imposition, touching matters which constitute the essentials of the marriage relation. "False representation of a party as to his character,

> social standing or fortune do not constitute such fraud on the opposite party as to avoid a marriage induced thereby," even though he conceals the fact that he has served a term in the penitentiary. "The fraudulent representations for which a marriage may be annulled must be of something essential to the marriage relation - of something making impossible the performance of the duties and obligations of that relation or rendering its assumption and continuance dangerous to health or life."

Id. at 298-299, 102 S.E.2d at 339 (citations omitted).

In *Jakar* the defendant represented himself to the plaintiff as a medical doctor of Belgian birth who had been an instructor at a medical school in Brussels, Belgium. He also told the plaintiff that he was a physician with twenty other physicians employed under him at the hospital at the then Camp (now Fort) Jackson. The defendant took the plaintiff to the best hotels and restaurants in Columbia. The plaintiff, a native Belgian, had immigrated to the United States twelve years before. Within a short time, a week or two, the defendant proposed marriage to the plaintiff. To hasten her decision, he told her she must answer quickly in order for him to qualify for housing allowances given to married officers. The plaintiff fell for it.

After the marriage, the plaintiff discovered that all the representations made by the defendant prior to marriage were false. The plaintiff also produced evidence that the defendant had killed a former wife, had assaulted the plaintiff's father and, in general, had behaved like a maniac. Still, these false representations did not constitute "deceit touching matters constituting the essentials of the marriage relation" in the eyes of the Court.

Specifically, what type of fraud will be found to render impossible the performance and duties and obligations of a marriage? As in *Jakar*, some other jurisdictions have required a greater degree of fraud to invalidate a marriage than will suffice to invalidate an ordinary contract in South Carolina, although the degree may depend on whether or not the marriage has been consummated. 55 C.J.S. *Marriage* § 34 (1948). In general, the fraud must go to the very fundamentals or essentials of the marital relations. *Id.* Thus, sufficient fraud has been found in the following situations: fraudulent representations about sanity or concealment of insanity (but not about being treated for mental illness); known impotency; known sterility; and an inclination to have children contrary to an antenuptial agreement. *Id.*

The Supreme Court was asked to annul a marriage on the basis of fraudulent concealment of a wife's sexual incapacity in *E.D.M. v. T.A.M.*, 307 S.C. 471, 415 S.E.2d 812 (1992); however, it specifically avoided deciding "whether concealment of a known sexual disfunction, is fraud sufficient to justify an annulment." 307 S.C. at 474, 415 S.E.2d at 815. The husband had sought an annulment based on the ground of fraud and lack of cohabitation. He claimed that the wife had concealed her psychological problems and resulting sexual incapacity. It was undisputed that they never engaged in penile-vaginal intercourse. However, they did have infrequent oral sex performed by the husband upon the wife. The trial court denied the husband's request for an annulment. The Supreme Court affirmed on two grounds: (1) the evidence did not support a conclusion that the wife had knowingly concealed her incapacity for sexual relations (the husband had not introduced any evidence that the wife knew the extent of her sexual problems before the marriage); and (2) an annulment on the ground of fraud was barred because the parties had consummated the marriage by cohabitation (the Court held that the parties having lived together, shared the same bed, and engaged in minimal sexual activity was evidence of an intimate relationship which supported a finding of cohabitation). One should note that the Supreme Court appears to have been influenced in its decision by the length of the parties' relationship which included a five year courtship and more than two years together after their wedding.

New York appears to have adopted a materiality rule by case decision. Basically, if the fraud is of such a material nature that the plaintiff would not have entered the marriage but for the fraud, the marriage may be annulled. *Kober v. Kober*, 211 N.E.2d 817 (N.Y. 1965) (granting an annulment because the husband had concealed from the Jewish wife that he had been a Nazi officer and was fanatically anti-Semitic). South Carolina courts would in all likelihood be bound, absent a statute designed to reach a result like that in New York, to limit their attention to matters having to do with sex and child bearing, given *Jakar*, although it is an old case which was decided when opinions about the inviolability of marriage were more entrenched than today. However, a representation by the wife that she could and would have children when she had had a hysterectomy before marriage and had concealed that fact would probably constitute a ground for annulment of marriage in

South Carolina. The same is probably true if a man made a similar representation to a woman knowing himself to be permanently impotent and not revealing the fact to her.

E. CONSEQUENCES OF ANNULMENT

This section should be read in conjunction with the consequences of marriage section in the chapter on marriage.

1. IN GENERAL

An annulment declares that a marriage never occurred due to some defect. Logically, if a marriage never occurred, then no legal rights or obligations could have been created by marriage. However, the relationship and conduct of the parties prior to an annulment may create legal issues which require court intervention, and public policy may dictate some illogical results to prevent inequities.

2. INTERPERSONAL RIGHTS AND OBLIGATIONS

a. Cohabitation

There are probably no longer any valid laws which create a distinction between couples who live together on the basis of whether or not they were married. If an annulled couple wishes to live together, there is nothing to stop them from doing so.

b. Sexual Intercourse

Annulment removes the legal right and social expectation that married couples will engage in sexual intercourse. In fact, annulment may serve as a declaration that any sexual intercourse between the parties was criminal fornication (*see* S.C. Code Ann. § 16-15-80 (Law. Co-op. 1976)). Although the threat of prosecution is quite remote, some individuals may be concerned about this technical violation. See 3 *S.C. Juris.*, Adultery and Fornication (S.C. Bar - C.L.E. Division 1991).

c. Mutual Support

An award of alimony is "a substitute for the support normally incident to the marital relationship." *McNaughton v. McNaughton,* 258 S.C. 554, 558, 189 S.E.2d 820, 822 (1972). Thus, if an person is judicially declared not to have been a spouse, there is no duty to support the other spouse and, logically following, no duty to pay alimony. The following statement appears at 27B C.J.S., *Divorce*, § 369 (1986):

> To warrant the allowance of alimony there must have been a valid marriage, since an award of alimony is incident to a valid binding marriage. Accordingly, no alimony may be awarded where the marriage was void by reason of the fact that at the time it was contracted one of the parties was married to a third person, or both parties had living undivorced spouses. It has been held, however, that permanent alimony may be granted, where the divorce is granted on the ground that the party against whom the divorce is granted had a spouse living at the time of the marriage.

Under this statement, therefore, alimony should not usually be awarded following an annulment. The issue of *pendente lite* support for a spouse while an annulment action is pending has not come before a South Carolina appellate court.

d. Confidentiality

There is no South Carolina case or statute regarding the survival of the privilege against disclosure of confidential communications made by one spouse to another during the marriage. Logically, since an annulment is a declaration that no marriage ever existed, there could have been no communication between spouses during the marriage which would be privileged. However, one should expect that the equities would be weighed and the result would be to favor recognizing the existence of the privilege.

e. Common Surname

Following an annulled marriage, a person can choose to continue using the surname used during the marriage or any other name he or she desires. South Carolina appears to continue to recognize the common law rule that "[a]t common law, a man may lawfully change his name, or by general usage or habit acquire another name than that originally borne by him, without the intervention of Court or Legislature. *City Council v. King*, 4 McCord, 487; *Miller v. George*, 30 S.C. 528, 9 S.E. 659; 21 Ency. Law, 311." *Brayton v. Beall*, 73 S.C. 308, 311, 53 S.E. 641, 642 (1906) (holding that statutes which provide a mode of changing a name "do not abrogate but are in affirmance and aid of the common law rule").

Those people who want court orders to prove that their names have been legally changed may apply to the family court. The family court is specifically authorized to, "upon the granting of final judgment [of divorce], allow a wife to resume her maiden name or the name of any former husband." S.C. Code Ann. § 20-3-180 (Law. Co-op. 1976). It does not appear that this statute permits similar treatment of a wife following an annulment. However, the family court is authorized to grant requests for name changes generally under S.C. Code Ann. § 20-7-420 (Law. Co-op. 1976). The statutes which govern the family court's consideration of requests for name changes are S.C. Code Ann. § 15-49-10 to -50 (Law. Co-op. 1976 & Supp.).

3. ASSETS AND LIABILITIES

a. In General

The family court has jurisdiction to equitably divide property following the annulment of a marriage. "S.C. Code Ann. § 20-7-420(6) (1985) vests Family Court with jurisdiction to consider and rule upon <u>all</u> matters in annulment actions." *Splawn v. Splawn*, 311 S.C. 423, 425, 429 S.E.2d 805, 806 (1993) (emphasis supplied by court). In *Splawn*, the Supreme Court affirmed the trial judge's decision to equitably apportion marital property after declaring the marriage void because the husband had entered into the marriage with the mistaken belief that he was divorced from his first wife.

The Court did not specifically discuss the possible implications of the language in the Equitable Apportionment of Marital Property Act (S.C. Code Ann. § 20-7-472 (Law. Co-op. Supp.)) which references actions for divorce and for separate support and maintenance, not annulment. However, even if the Court might consider this language to exclude division of property following an annulment, S.C. Code Ann. § 20-7-420(2) (Law. Co-op. Supp.) gives the family court jurisdiction to hear and determine actions for "other marital litigation," which includes annulments, and to settle "all legal and equitable rights of the parties in such actions in and to the real and personal property of the marriage and attorneys' fees, if requested by either party in the pleadings." Presumably, the family court would be guided by the factors and principles outlined in the Equitable Apportionment of Marital Property Act in discharging this responsibility.

Another case concerning property in an annulment action is the 1833 case of *Young v. Naylor*, 10 S.C.Eq. (1 Hill Eq.) 383 (1833), which involved the ownership of property acquired by the wife before marriage. Having discovered that her husband was married to another woman, she sought the return of property she owned prior to the marriage. The husband denied he was married when wed to her, a claim which if successful (prior to the enactment of the Equitable Apportionment of Marital Property Act) would have allowed him to keep her property. The Court decided in the wife's favor and awarded her the property.

b. Necessary Goods and Services

As with divorced people, the doctrine of necessaries would not apply to people whose marriages have been annulled. An interesting unanswered question is whether one party to an annulled marriage could sue the other party for reimbursement of "necessary" support provided during an annulled marriage.

4. INHERITANCE

Annulment revokes any disposition of property to a spouse under a will, any provision conferring on the spouse a power of appointment, and any nomination of the spouse as executor, trustee, conservator, or guardian, unless the will specifically states otherwise. S.C. Code Ann. § 62-2-507 (Law. Co-op. 1976). Subsequent remarriage of the parties reinstates such rights. *Id.* Property affected by revocation becomes part of the residue of the estate. S.C. Code Ann. § 62-2-604 (Law. Co-op. 1976).

5. CHILDREN

a. Legitimacy

There is no South Carolina case or statute on the effect of an annulment on the legitimacy of a child. Logically, the child would be deemed illegitimate since the annulment serves as a declaration that the marriage never existed. However, this would seem contrary to public policy which favors legitimacy of children. According to 14 C.J.S. *Children Out-of-Wedlock* § 3 (1991):

> In general, the issue of marriages void in law is illegitimate unless such issues are made legitimate by some statutory provision. The courts do not look with favor on the construction of a law as to the validity of a marriage, which results in the declaration that a child is illegitimate.
>
> The issue of marriages which are merely voidable is legitimate, notwithstanding the fact that the marriage is annulled after the birth of issue.

South Carolina handles the status of legitimacy or illegitimacy of children in relation to one type of void marriage in S.C. Code Ann. § 20-1-90 (Law. Co-op. 1976):

> When either of the contracting parties to a marriage that is void under the provisions of § 20-1-80 [bigamous marriage] entered into the marriage contract in good faith on or after April 13, 1951 and in ignorance of the incapacity of the other party, any children born of the marriage shall be deemed legitimate and have the same legal rights as a child born in lawful wedlock.

According to this statute, the state of mind of one of the child's parents controls its legitimacy or illegitimacy. There are no South Carolina cases or statutes concerning the legitimacy or illegitimacy of a child born to a merely voidable marriage.

See the chapter on establishing the validity of marriages for more information about how to determine whether a marriage is void or voidable.

b. Care, Education, and Welfare

The family court has jurisdiction to decide issues related to the care and custody of children of annulled marriages, even though no statute specifically governs these issues. There are no factual differences between children of annulled or divorced marriages. Both need shelter, food and clothing. S.C. Code Ann. § 20-3-160 (Law. Co-op. 1976) permits the family court to "make such orders touching the care, custody and maintenance of the children of the marriage" as are desirable in divorce cases. The statute further provides that such orders will be based upon "the best spiritual as well as other interests of the children." This language has been interpreted as meaning "the welfare of the child and what is for the child's best interest." *Sanders v. Sanders*, 232 S.C. 625, 103 S.E.2d 281 (1958). This approach was explicitly endorsed in *White v. White*, 283 S.C. 348, 323 S.E.2d 521 (1984), an action for annulment.

c. Children's Names

There is no South Carolina statute or case which considers the effect of an annulment on the names of parties' children. However, an annulment probably has no effect on a child's name unless a guardian *ad litem* asks the court for a name change on behalf of the child. The standard to be applied by the court would almost certainly be to examine the best interest of the child. This is the rule to be applied in disputes about the surnames of children following a divorce. The Supreme Court first announced this rule with respect to children of divorced parents in *Ex parte Shull*, 276 S.C. 512, 280 S.E.2d 209 (1981) (remanding the case because it was brought in the mother's name, not by a guardian), then confirmed it in *Stone v. Stone*, 285 S.C. 108, 328 S.E.2d 346 (1985) (remanding for a trial *de novo*, apparently because the father was not given a proper opportunity to participate and present evidence in the initial proceeding). See further discussion of this topic in the section on consequences of divorce in the chapter on divorce.

CHAPTER FOUR
DIVORCE

CHAPTER FOUR
DIVORCE

A. IN GENERAL

This chapter covers the substantive law of divorce. The only form of divorce recognized in South Carolina is divorce *a vinculo matrimonii* (divorce from the bonds of marriage).

The history of divorce is unusually important in South Carolina. The Supreme Court has consistently referred to that history in construing the divorce laws and has occasionally used it as part of its rationale in arriving at relatively narrow interpretations of the State's statutes. Thus, practitioners should be aware of the historical development of divorce law in South Carolina, not only out of a general desire to understand the context in which the courts operate, but also because that history may well have an independent present effect upon litigation of marital causes.

The overall trend of legislation and judicial decision-making in the Anglo-American jurisprudence of divorce has been one toward increasing the legal ability of spouses to separate. Our idea of marriage has developed largely from the teachings of the Christian religion, those being principally derived from interpretations of passages in the New Testament books of Matthew 19 and Mark 10, with Old Testament roots. In many Western societies the Roman Catholic tradition that marital matters are almost exclusively reserved for the church remains strong, and civil interference in home life is rare. Of course, Roman Catholic doctrine still teaches the indissolubility of marriage, this status stemming from the fact that marriage is regarded as a sacrament, administered by the parties to each other at the time the marriage contract is sealed or otherwise solemnized.

The Christian idea that marriage should be dissolvable was not well accepted in Rome and developed slowly even in medieval Europe. Ever since that time, there has been struggle between conflicting societal urges toward family stability and toward individual freedom of choice. Given the religious position noted above, the struggle has often taken the form of a conflict between Church and State (at least on the surface), as is perhaps most notably exemplified by the English Reformation and the establishment of the Church of England with the King as its head during the reign of Henry VIII, an act based at least in part upon the refusal of the Pope to authorize an annulment of Henry's marriage to Catherine of Aragon.

While it might have been thought that Henry's position would have been to liberalize legal/ecclesiastical approaches to marital separations (and there did, apparently, ensue in the sixteenth century in England some confusion about the extent to which remarriage after separation might be permissible), it became clear by the beginning of the seventeenth century that no judicial divorce would be permitted in England, a position which was adhered to until 1857. However, a device known as divorce by Act of Parliament did come into being by the end of that century. While it was difficult to obtain due to the time and expense involved (and was, in keeping with the nature of the society, almost always given to men rather than to women), its existence did serve to solidify the idea that the State — the political authorities as opposed to the religious authorities — had authority in marital matters. Further, the example set by the English Parliament was followed by a number of American colonial legislatures, with the practice of granting divorce by legislative act persisting in this country in some places into the middle of the nineteenth century.

Nonetheless, the fact remained that the ecclesiastical courts — an institution which was not imported into the colonies — exercised general jurisdiction over marital matters, including the judicial separation (divorce *a mensa et thoro*, or from bed and board) and its consequences. As a result, it has been generally held in this country that divorce jurisdiction is purely statutory, the courts not inheriting any rights from the English common law since the common law did not concern itself with marital matters (although the court of chancery did deal with alimony during the Protectorate). *See Nocher v. Nocher,* 268 S.C. 503, 234 S.E.2d 884 (1977) (holding that divorce *a mensa et thoro* does not exist in South Carolina). This view was taken in the courts of South Carolina early on and has colored the approach of our legal system to questions of divorce.

Courts in the Southern colonies in general were reluctant to address matrimonial matters, as were Southern legislatures. The South Carolina Court of Errors took perhaps the most extreme position in the colonies in this regard, explicitly refusing in 1848 any jurisdiction either to annul a marriage or to grant any form of divorce. In *Mattison v. Mattison,* 32 S.C. Eq. (1 Strob. Eq.) 387 (1846), Chancellor Dunkin confirmed that the Court had meant what it had indicated in dictum in the earlier case of *Rhame v. Rhame*, 12 S.C. Eq. (1 McCord Eq.) 197 (1826). It somewhat contradictorily admitted that South Carolina had equity jurisdiction to award alimony when marital partners had separated, such jurisdiction being based on the hard reality that there was no other court to exercise it since there were no ecclesiastical courts in the state; but the court lacked authority to "grant divorce." *Id.* at 205. This was odd because the courts would have to look to the grounds upon which divorces might be granted in England in order to determine whether to award alimony in South Carolina. In *Mattison* the Court acknowledged that a chancellor or a law court might have had the power to rule on the validity of a marriage if it were to arise collaterally to another matter properly before the court. However, insofar as a direct attack upon the marriage contract itself was concerned, based either upon alleged defects at its inception or upon conduct of the parties while married, the Court opined that the legislature had twenty years since the *Rhame* case in which to bestow upon the Chancellor (or someone) divorce jurisdiction, had not done so, and hence had foreclosed any exercise of that jurisdiction. Its language is instructive:

> The silence of the Legislature is conclusive — regarding the sacred nature of the marriage contract as a matter of public interest, they will neither interfere with it themselves, nor delegate to others the power to dissolve it. The distinction between the authority to declare a marriage null and void, or to grant a divorce, has no sanction either in reason or authority.
>
> Whether wisely or unwisely, the Legislature has thought proper to withhold these powers. They have delegated to no Court the authority to declare a marriage null and void, and they have never themselves exercised the authority. Cases of individual hardship have occurred, and will occur; but the observation of a different policy in other States, as well as the experience of our own, has served only to confirm the conviction that it is better to tolerate occasional sufferingthan to jeopardize the peace of society, and open a wide door to fraud, imposition and other immorality.

Mattison, at 392-393.

Drafted in the years following the Civil War, the South Carolina Constitution of 1868 provided, in Art. IV § 15, that the courts of common pleas should have exclusive jurisdiction in all cases of divorce, and in Article XIV § 5, required that no divorce should be granted but through the judicial process. In the legislative session of 1872, a divorce act, 15 Stat. 30, passed and for the next six years, until 1878, it was possible in theory to obtain a divorce in South Carolina on the grounds of adultery and willful desertion.

In 1878 the statute was repealed *in toto* by the Legislature (916 Stat. 719). The repeal served to terminate the only known divorce action which had apparently been brought under the Act, the Court ruling in *Grant v. Grant*, 12 S.C. 29 (1879), that the repeal did not violate the Contract Clause of the Federal Constitution and did render the suit unauthorized inasmuch as, although the action had been commenced eight days before the repeal, there was no law authorizing divorce by the time the cause came on for trial.

The Constitution of 1895 specifically prohibited divorces. Article XVII § 3 stated simply and directly: "[d]ivorces from the bonds of matrimony shall not be allowed in this State." This provision remained intact until 1949, at which time the Constitution was amended to authorize divorces from the bonds of matrimony (*a vinculo matrimonii*) on the grounds of adultery, desertion, physical cruelty, or habitual drunkenness. Article XVII § 3 of the South Carolina Constitution was amended further in 1969 to permit divorce to be granted on the ground of continuous separation for a period of at least three years and was further amended in 1979 to reduce the separation period to one year. This is the posture in which the Constitution currently stands. The statute (S.C. Code Ann. § 20-3-10 (Law. Co-op. 1946) was likewise amended with the addition of a section providing that habitual drunkenness was to be construed as including causation of drunkenness by use of any narcotic drug. This amendment came on April 4, 1952.

In the first case to come to it after the 1949 Constitutional amendments, the Court traced the history of divorce in South Carolina and then proclaimed the public policy of the state:

> It is generally recognized that the public policy relating to marriage is to foster and protect it, to make it a permanent and public

> institution, to encourage the parties to live together, and to prevent separation. This policy finds expression in probably every state in this country in legislative enactments designed to prevent the sundering of the marriage ties for slight and trivial causes, or in any case except on a full and satisfactory proof of such facts as the legislature has declared to be cause for divorce. Such provisions find their justification only in this well-recognized interest of the state in the permanency of the marriage relation.

Brown v. Brown, 215 S.C. 502, 508, 56 S.E.2d 330, 333 (1949).

In *Brown* the Court affirmed the trial court after it examined, and found wanting in sufficiency, evidence advanced to show that a husband was guilty of adultery and physical cruelty to his divorce-seeking spouse. In so doing, the Court signaled clearly that it intended to adhere closely to the tradition of encouraging the maintenance of the marital relationship which it perceived as permeating the state's legal history. While there has been some degree of relaxation of this strict attitude on the part of the Supreme Court in later years, it unquestionably behooves any attorney attempting to secure a ruling on an undetermined question to pay particular attention to the Court's consciousness of the history of divorce in South Carolina.

B. JURISDICTION

1. IN GENERAL

The exclusive jurisdiction of the family court over divorces is established in S.C. Code § 20-7-420 (Law. Co-op. 1976 & Supp.): "[t]he family court shall have exclusive jurisdiction: . . . (2) To hear and determine actions: For divorce *a vinculo matrimonii* . . . ."

As discussed in the chapter on subject matter jurisdiction, if the family court lacks subject matter jurisdiction, it cannot obtain it. A challenge to subject matter jurisdiction can be raised at any time during the proceeding, even at the appellate level. This includes an objection that statutorily imposed time limits have not been observed. In *Yarborough v. Yarborough*, 276 S.C. 416, 279 S.E.2d 130 (1981), the wife challenged the family court's jurisdiction to grant a divorce less than three months after the filing of the complaint seeking the divorce as this violated S.C. Code Ann. § 20-3-80 (Law. Co-op. 1976). The Supreme Court held that the trial court had no jurisdiction to grant the divorce before the expiration of the statutory time limit.

Issues which have been litigated and decided in a separate maintenance and support action cannot be relitigated in a subsequent divorce proceeding. Decisions in such actions could foreclose fault grounds for divorce, property division, alimony, or any other issue which was reached on the merits by the previous court. (See the discussion of this in the chapter on separate support and maintenance.)

2. RESIDENCY

A person seeking a divorce in South Carolina must satisfy one of three requirements for residence: (1) the plaintiff must have resided at least one year in the state prior to the commencement of the action, or (2) if the plaintiff is a non-resident, the defendant must have resided in the state for one year prior to the commencement of an action, or (3) if both parties are residents of the state, the plaintiff must have resided in South Carolina only three months prior to the commencement of an action. S.C. Code Ann. § 20-3-30 (Law. Co-op. 1976).

South Carolina is not unique in establishing a residence requirement for jurisdiction in a divorce proceeding. Yet residency in South Carolina, while considered sufficient as a basis for divorce, has not been enough to warrant full faith and credit recognition by other jurisdictions. *See* 24 Am. Jr. 2d *Divorce and Separation* § 246 (1966). This idea was debated at length in the two cases now known as *Williams I* and *Williams II*. *Williams v. N.C.*, 317 U.S. 287, 63 S. Ct. 207 (1942); *Williams v. N.C.*, 325 U.S. 226, 65 S. Ct. 1092, (1945). These decisions indicated that, if a state hopes for recognition of its decree for a divorce, it must establish that at least one of the parties was a domiciliary of the state. That is to say, one person must show that his or her connections go beyond mere presence there. *See Koebberling v. Koebberling*, 278 S.C. 204, 293 S.E.2d 857 (1982) (which held that the Texas divorce decree given full faith and credit where Texas residency was based upon the facts that the Respondent: 1) claimed Texas residency in order to pay in-state tuition for a child attending the University of Texas; 2) was registered to vote in Texas and had voted in the Texas general election the previous year; 3) maintained a bank account in Texas; and 4) had a Texas drivers license).

While the *Williams* cases have met considerable opposition in some of their findings, their "domiciliary" standard has generally been taken to heart. In 1965, in *Gasque v. Gasque*, 246 S.C. 423, 426, 143 S.E.2d 811, 812 (1965), the Supreme Court equated the "residency" required in the divorce statute (S.C. Code Ann. § 20-103 (1962) (now codified as S.C. Code Ann. § 20-3-30 (1976)) with domicile. The Court defined domicile as "the place where a person has his true, fixed and permanent home and principal establishment, to which he has, whenever he is absent, an intention of returning." *Id.* Thus, the primary issue in determining domicile is intent. Intent, in the Court's examination, is determined by "facts and circumstances of each case." *Id.* at 427, 143 S.E.2d at 812. In *Gasque*, the appellant husband sought a divorce from his wife in the South Carolina courts. The husband was a native of South Carolina, but was employed by the government and had worked and lived in the Washington, D.C., area for fourteen years prior to this action. The appellant testified that his employment was the only reason he was not living in South Carolina. Documentary evidence indicated that he had continuously declared South Carolina as his home and there was no evidence to the contrary. The Court determined that, absent proof to the contrary, the appellant's domicile was South Carolina and South Carolina courts had jurisdiction over him based on the statute.

Gasque shows that jurisdiction is based, not on the mere presence of the parties, but instead upon a more lasting contact with the forum by at least one party. The fact that divorce jurisdiction may be obtained after three months' residence by the plaintiff, if both parties are domiciliaries, does ameliorate the harshness of the one year provision to some extent and possibly is useful to the military personnel in the state. It may help avoid a challenge based on the constitutional problem (lack of domicile requirement) which exists in those states which have enacted some version of non-domicile residence test along the lines of Section 302 of the Uniform Marriage and Divorce Act (UMDA).

3. OUT-OF-STATE DIVORCES

South Carolina does not recognize the validity of divorces obtained by South Carolina domiciliaries in other jurisdictions. S.C. Code Ann. § 20-3-420 (Law. Co-op. 1976) precludes recognition of a divorce for this state's citizens in another state while they are both residents of South Carolina: "A divorce from the bonds of matrimony obtained in another jurisdiction shall be of no force or effect in this State if both parties to the marriage were domiciled in this State at the time the proceeding for divorce was commenced."

The effect of this statute is that residents of South Carolina must qualify for a divorce under the laws of South Carolina or remain married. This statute has been given modern application by the Supreme Court in *Powers v. Powers*, 273 S.C. 51, 254 S.E.2d 289 (1979), in which a Nevada divorce decree was nullified because the procurer thereof failed to overcome the presumption created by S.C. Code Ann. § 20-3-420 (Law. Co-op. 1976).

South Carolina has extended this principle to situations involving only one party obtaining a divorce out of the jurisdiction. S.C. Code Ann. § 20-3-430 (Law. Co-op. 1976) indicates that a person who leaves South Carolina to obtain a divorce but either returns within eighteen months or maintains a residence in South Carolina will be regarded *prima facie* as a domiciliary of South Carolina who simply has sought a different and improper forum in which to get a divorce. Obviously this puts the burden of proof on that party to show that the reason for his absence was proper within ordinary principles of domicile. That in turn gives a certain amount of discretion to the judge.

The *Powers* case illustrates this principle. The husband and wife were citizens and residents of Beaufort County, South Carolina. In late August the husband went to Nevada and in early October initiated an action for divorce there. Within a few days of filing he returned to South Carolina for approximately a month. On his return to Nevada in November, he was granted a divorce and he returned to South Carolina the next day. At the end of the month he remarried. The Court determined that his visits between the states did not indicate any intent to stay in Nevada, even though the appellant said that was his intention. This appears to be an obvious case, but others will presumably be solved by reference to the theory of conflicts of laws.

A person who obtains a foreign divorce decree and uses it to his or her benefit will be estopped from denying its validity if it would be detrimental to the other spouse. In *Smoak v. Smoak*, 269 S.C. 313, 237 S.E.2d 372 (1977), the husband, a prosperous lawyer, began an adulterous relationship which was little, if at all, concealed from anyone, including his wife of seventeen years. This resulted in his abandonment of his wife and three children on October 6, 1971. On February 18, 1972, the husband procured a divorce in Haiti, returned home and presented his wife with an authenticated copy of the decree. She believed the decree to be valid, although it was not. He thereafter posed as an unmarried man, executing deeds and mortgages without mentioning dower renunciation. The court cited this as part of the evidence that he relied on the Haitian divorce to his benefit and to his wife's detriment. He then proceeded for the next three years to hold out his paramour as his new wife.

In 1975, he filed for divorce on the ground of three years continuous separation. When his wife filed a claim for alimony, he responded that she had committed adultery with at least three men since he had presented her with the Haitian divorce decree, and, since the Haitian decree was invalid, she was barred from seeking alimony. The trial court agreed with him. The Supreme Court did not. In reversing the trial judge, the Court stated:

> We need not delicately weigh the circumstantial evidence to determine if adultery on the part of the wife had been proved. Nor need we decide whether pleading the Fifth Amendment has had any effect on her claim.
>
> The evidence recited hereinabove conclusively proves that the husband accepted the privileges, benefits and fruits of the Haitian judgment of divorce. He has in effect said to this court: "Even after the Haitian decree and my subsequent conduct, I was still entitled to the loyalty of my wife." However, it is the position of the wife that a party who has obtained a fraudulent judgment of divorce should not be permitted to enjoy its benefits, or be allowed to assert its invalidity for his own advantage. We agree. The position of the husband is untenable, and we hold that he is estopped to assert the invalidity of

> the Haitian judgment of divorce. The wife could attack it, but he, having accepted its benefits, may not.

Id. at 319, 237 S.E.2d at 374.

The Uniform Divorce Recognition Act (S.C. Code Ann. § 20-3-410 (1976)) has only been adopted in a handful of states besides South Carolina. The Act appears questionable in terms of full faith and credit. *See Comment*, 24 Wash. L. Rev. 259 (1949). That challenge, however, has not been made in South Carolina courts. Additionally, the issue of its international applicability has not arisen here.

While South Carolina goes far to guard its autonomy over its citizens and their marriage relations, it has evidenced its reluctance to interfere with those decisions properly made in other states. In *Zwerling v. Zwerling*, 270 S.C. 685, 244 S.E.2d 311 (1978), the appellant wife sought a divorce from her husband. The couple was married in New York after she had received a Mexican divorce from her former husband. She and her husband, the respondent here, then moved to South Carolina where she sought a divorce. The respondent defended by saying that their marriage was not lawful because the Mexican divorce was not recognized in South Carolina pursuant to the Uniform Divorce Recognition Act discussed earlier.

The Court determined that "'the validity of a marriage is determined by the law of the place where it is contracted' and will be recognized unless 'such recognition would be contrary to a strong public policy of that State.'" *Id.* at 686, 244 S.E.2d at 312 (citing 52 Am. Jur. 2d *Marriage* §§ 80, 82 (1970)). In light of the New York case of *Rosenstiel v. Rosenstiel*, 16 N.Y.S.2d 64, 262 N.Y.S.2d 86, 209 N.E.2d 709 (1965) (which recognized the validity in New York of a Mexican divorce and subsequent marriage) and, absent any public policy contrary to the finding, the Court recognized the divorce since it would have likewise been recognized in New York.

A limitation upon this is found in *Payton v. Payton*, 270 S.C. 275, 241 S.E.2d 901 (1978), *cert. den.*, 439 U.S. 847, 99 S. Ct. 145 (1978). Elizabeth Payton and the deceased husband had been married in Alabama in 1951. She had received a divorce from her husband in 1963 in Florida, but she now claimed that the Florida decree was void because the husband did not have notice of the action. The husband had married

Evelyn Payton in 1958. In 1972, he had received an annulment from Evelyn Payton on the basis that he was still married to Elizabeth Payton. That same year, he was granted a divorce from Elizabeth Payton, although there was no evidence that she was served with process or had knowledge of the proceeding. In 1973, he had again married Evelyn Payton. The husband died in 1975, and both women claimed rights as the lawful wife.

The Supreme Court agreed with Elizabeth Payton's claim that, because the husband had no notice of the divorce proceeding in Florida, the Florida court had lacked jurisdiction to grant a divorce and, thus, the divorce would not be recognized in South Carolina. The proof of this lack of notice was the testimony of Elizabeth Payton and the husband's action in seeking an annulment from Evelyn Payton on the basis of his marriage to Elizabeth Payton. *Id.* at 279, 241 S.E.2d at 903. As further support for the need and relevancy of actual notice, *see Koebberling v. Koebberling*, 278 S.C. 204, 293 S.E.2d 857 (1982), which held that a Texas divorce decree was entitled to full faith and credit where the husband knew of and participated in the initial divorce proceedings but made no later inquiry as to their progress, and merely asserted that he could not recall if he had received notification of the hearings.

There is a conceptual way to reconcile the decisions in *Zwerling* and *Payton*. In *Zwerling*, the Court did not actually make a decision concerning the Mexican divorce but, instead, recognized New York's recognition of that divorce and the subsequent marriage. In *Payton*, on the other hand, the Court was not asked to recognize a sister state's recognition of a marriage after a "questionable divorce," as in *Zwerling*, but to recognize the divorce itself. More interesting is the Court's permitting Elizabeth to raise the notice issue.

4. EFFECT OF COHABITATION AT TIME OF FILING FOR DIVORCE

The family court may hear divorce cases based on adultery, habitual drunkenness, or physical cruelty even if the parties are still living in the same house. *Watson v. Watson*, 319 S.C. 92, 460 S.E.2d 394 (1995). In *Watson*, the husband brought a divorce action on the ground of adultery. The family court granted the wife's motion to dismiss on the basis that it had no subject matter jurisdiction because the parties continued to reside in the marital home at the time the action was commenced. The Supreme Court reversed.

> If we were to require physical separation of the parties in order to bring a divorce action, divorcing parents who seek custody of their children would have these choices: either vacate the home, taking the children with them and thereby cause additional disruption in the children's lives; vacate the home and abandon the children to their spouse; or continue in the marriage. We hold that public policy permits a party to remain in the home and institute divorce litigation premised on fault grounds other than desertion. In such cases, the living arrangements of the parties and the children during the pendency of the litigation should be decided at the temporary hearing.

Id. at 94, 460 S.E.2d at 395.

5. EFFECT OF A PARTY'S DEATH

The death of either party to a divorce action terminates the action if it occurs before a divorce decree has been signed and delivered to the clerk. In *Bayne v. Bass*, 302 S.C. 208, 394 S.E.2d 726 (Ct. App. 1990), the wife committed suicide after the trial judge had orally granted her request for divorce but before he had signed a divorce decree. The judge signed the decree two days after she had died but vacated it on motion by the husband's counsel. The Court of Appeals held that the order granting the divorce was void and that the court had properly vacated its own order. The *Bayne* court cited *Case v. Case*, 243 S.C. 447, 134 S.E.2d 394 (1964), for the proposition that a divorce decree has no effect until it has been signed by the judge and delivered to the clerk of court because, until it has been delivered to the clerk, the judge can still modify, amend or rescind it.

The *Bayne* court also cited *Louthian and Merritt, P.A. v. Davis*, 272 S.C. 330, 251 S.E.2d 757 (1979) in support of its decision. In *Louthian*, the Supreme Court had dealt with this issue in a somewhat different context. A law firm sought to collect attorneys' fees from the client's husband after her death. The wife initiated the divorce action and had been awarded temporary alimony and attorneys' fees *pendente lite*.

The action was subsequently heard before a standing master. Before he filed his report, the wife died. The attorneys sought to collect their fees. The Court, however, refused to allow the recovery saying "an action for divorce, being purely personal, terminates on the death of either spouse, and where the action for divorce is commenced, and one of the parties dies thereafter, but before the entry of the final decree, the action abates and the jurisdiction of the court to proceed with the action is terminated." *Id.* at 332, 251 S.E.2d at 758.

It does not appear, however, that the death of a party will have any effect on the jurisdiction of the family court to equitably apportion the marital party, if marital litigation has been initiated before the party dies. In *Hodge v. Hodge*, 305 S.C. 521, 409 S.E.2d 436 (Ct. App. 1991), the wife had brought an action for separate support and maintenance and property division. Both parties had appealed, but the husband died during the appeal. The Court of Appeals held that, upon the filing of marital litigation, property acquired during a marriage becomes vested in an estate called marital property in which the spouses have a vested interest subject to equitable distribution. It further held that, with respect to marital property, marital litigation is not abated by the death of a spouse. The Court of Appeals went on to state that:

> [S]ince we hold that the wife's interest in the marital property was vested and therefore fixed by the institution of marital litigation, we hold that the only court which has jurisdiction to divide the marital estate is the Family Court, subject, of course, to appeal. Accordingly, we hold that upon the death of the husband, this action did not abate with respect to the issues relating to the equitable division of vested marital property.

Id. at 525, 409 S.E.2d at 439.

See also Stone v. Guaranty Bank & Trust Co., 270 S.C. 331, 242 S.E.2d 404 (1978), in which the wife brought a suit for divorce and the husband counterclaimed for divorce. She was granted a divorce, but his counterclaim was still pending on appeal when he died. The Court determined that his death abated his counterclaim. The Court, however, said this did not abate the appeal dealing with the property rights of the parties. Since the wife had been awarded alimony, household furnishings, and attorneys' fees, the executor of the estate might still challenge these matters. The Court remanded the case to the lower court.

These cases leave one important question about the effect of a party's death: do issues about the propriety of granting or denying a divorce survive the death of a party, if the death occurs after the decree becomes effective, but while an appeal is pending? The Court in *Stone* said that the issue of the husband's counterclaim for divorce was abated on his death and the only issue it could deal with was the property rights of the parties. "Mr. Stone's death abates his counterclaim for a divorce and renders the contempt proceedings against him moot, but the appeal may continue in favor of his estate, to the extent of the lower court's order affects the property rights of the parties." *Id.* at 335-336, 242 S.E.2d at 406. However, it subsequently reversed the trial court's finding of a divorce for the wife on the basis that, if the deposition of a witness had been excluded as it should have been, there was no evidence of the husband's adultery, and it reversed and remanded the issue to the family court. In effect, while the Court implied that the issue of divorce was not on appeal, it certainly dealt with that very issue in the appeal. Of course, on remand following a reversal of a divorce decree, it would seem that the family court would not have subject matter jurisdiction to grant a divorce for the wife under the holding in *Bayne*. For cases from other jurisdictions, *see* Annotation, *Effect of Death of a Party to Divorce Proceeding Pending Appeal or Time Allowed for Appeal*, 33 A.L.R.4th 47 (1984), which was cited in *Bayne*.

C. VENUE

Litigants seeking a divorce may have a choice of locations in which they can properly file their pleadings.

> Actions for divorce from the bonds of matrimony . . . must be tried in the county (a) in which the defendant resides at the time of the commencement of the action, (b) in which the plaintiff resides if the defendant is a nonresident or after due diligence cannot be found, or (c) in which the parties last resided together as husband and wife

> unless the plaintiff is a nonresident, in which case it must be brought in the county in which the defendant resides.

S.C. Code Ann. § 20-3-60 (Law. Co-op. Supp.).

Any question about whether the statute intended these options to be in any particular order of priority was put to rest in *Voravudhi v. Voravudhi*, 273 S.C. 407, 257 S.E.2d 156 (1979), where the Court held that a divorce could be tried in any of the three places indicated.

The Court has also interpreted the "due diligence" language of the venue statute. In *Collins v. Collins*, 237 S.C. 230, 116 S.E.2d 839 (1960), the wife sought a divorce from her husband. The couple lived in Athens, Georgia, where he was a student. (The opinion does not indicate that the residency of the parties was an issue in terms of the residency requirement.) She returned to South Carolina and filed for divorce in Kershaw County where she was living with her family. Appellant husband sought a change of venue, and she was given a nonsuit in that proceeding so she might file in Horry County, the place of her husband's residence. Service of the summons and complaint was attempted on the husband by a deputy sheriff who indicated that he "was unable to locate him [the husband] within the bounds of Horry County despite due diligence on my part." *Id.* at 234, 116 S.E.2d at 841. At the hearing the husband appeared and sought to set aside the service deeming it "ineffectual." *Id.* The wife again sought an order of dismissal, which was granted. She again filed for divorce in Kershaw County, and the husband again made a motion for change of venue. The Supreme Court determined that the deputy sheriff's attempts to serve the appellant were sufficient to constitute "due diligence" as required by statute and the respondent was entitled to bring the action in Kershaw County, the county of her residence.

The Court determined that due diligence means "some attempt to find the party, in the county of his alleged residence, which the court or judge shall be satisfied is reasonable under the circumstances." *Id.* at 236, 116 S.E.2d at 842. Citing a Wisconsin case and a South Dakota case, *Winner v. Hoyt*, 68 Wis. 278, 32 N.W. 128 (1887) and *Cone v. Ballard*, 68 S.D. 593, 5 N.W.2d 46 (1942), the Court indicated that the attempt did not require the "utmost diligence" nor all "possible means . . . be used," but only "reasonable means." *Id.*

The Supreme Court has decided that if a request for a change in venue is proper within the statute, the judge must grant the change, as that is a question of law not within the judge's discretion. *Brockman v. Brockman*, 253 S.C. 528, 171 S.E.2d 862 (1970). At the same time, however, a change in venue must "serve the ends of justice" and the discretion of the judge will not be disturbed unless there has been an abuse of discretion. *Graham v. Beverly*, 235 S.C. 222, 110 S.E.2d 923 (1959).

The issue of the refusal of a trial judge to change venue from Charleston County to Berkeley County was raised in *Christy v. Christy*, 317 S.C. 145, 452 S.E.2d 1 (Ct. App. 1994). The husband resided in Charleston County at the commencement of the divorce action and later moved to Berkeley County. Subsequently, a contempt proceeding was initiated against husband by his former wife to enforce the judgment entered in the divorce action. He asked for a change of venue from Charleston County to Berkeley County and the trial judge refused his motion. The family court judge was upheld because the contempt action was a direct outgrowth of the divorce action which was brought in Charleston County.

D. STANDING AND CAPACITY TO SUE

The capacity of a party to sue or be sued shall be determined by the law of South Carolina. SCRCP Rule 17(b). A mental health patient who has not been adjudicated incompetent is entitled to contract marriage or to seek a divorce. S.C. Code Ann. § 44-22-80 (Law. Co-op. Supp.) provides that "[u]nless a patient has been adjudicated incompetent, no patient may be denied the right to: . . . (6) marry or divorce."

Simply because a person has been told by doctors that he or she needs a fiduciary to handle financial matters this does not necessarily mean that the person is incompetent to maintain a divorce action without appointment of a guardian *ad litem*. *In Zaragoza v. Zaragoza*, 309 S.C. 149, 420 S.E.2d 516 (Ct. App. 1992), a husband filed an action seeking a divorce on the ground of one year continuous separation. His wife defended *pro se*. The Court of Appeals affirmed the trial court's decision to grant the divorce and the wife appealed, claiming that a guardian *ad litem* should have been appointed because her husband was incompetent. The Court of Appeals pointed out that no application had been made for appointment of a guardian *ad litem*. It further found that the trial judge had considered the husband's mental capacity, and it had found that he was sufficiently competent to proceed without the benefit of a guardian *ad litem*. Although the husband was told by doctors that he needed a fiduciary to handle his financial affairs and his driver's license was suspended, other evidence showed that he lived by himself, traveled on his own, and made his own plans after talking with his mother.

In *Murray v. Murray*, 310 S.C. 336, 426 S.E.2d 781 (Ct. App. 1993), the Court of Appeals remanded a similar case to the family court to make specific findings of fact with regard to the husband's competency to initiate an action for divorce. The court specifically declined to adopt an absolute rule denying the right to seek a divorce if the spouse, although mentally incompetent with respect to the management of his estate, is capable of exercising reasonable judgment as to his personal decisions, is able to understand the nature of the action and is able to express unequivocally a desire to dissolve the marriage. The facts in *Murray* are that an action for divorce was brought on behalf of an 87 year old man against his 80 year old second wife by his son from his first marriage in his capacity as attorney-in-fact. A guardian *ad litem* was then appointed to represent the interests of the husband. It did not appear from the record that the husband had ever been adjudicated incompetent, simply that he was totally disabled and incapacitated and confined to a nursing home. However, his son represented that it was the husband's desire to obtain a divorce. The court ruled that, if the husband is able to express a desire to obtain a divorce, he could maintain it through his guardian *ad litem* (although the court also stated that the son had a clear conflict of interest and, therefore, should not serve as his father's guardian in this matter).

However, *Murray* is more noteworthy for other statements of law in the opinion, especially its decision to adopt the majority rule that, if a spouse is mentally incompetent as to his property and his person, he may not bring an action for divorce either on his own behalf or through a guardian, notwithstanding SCRCP Rule 17(c) which provides: "[W]henever a[n] . . . incompetent person has a representative, such as a general guardian, committee, conservator, or other like fiduciary, the representative may sue or defend on behalf of the . . . incompetent person." Somehow, the court did not feel that this language answered the question of whether a guardian may sue for *divorce* on behalf of an incompetent person, and it declared that a guardian could not (the court noted that many other jurisdictions had held that statutes which give guardians the general authority to maintain actions on behalf of incompetents had ruled that these statutes do not apply to divorce actions unless the statute expressly so states). As this holding was not necessary for the result reached in the case, it is *dicta*, but the Court of Appeals has clearly indicated its position on the issue.

The Court of Appeals also ruled in *Murray* that a conservator may not bring suit on behalf of an incompetent person, but it avoided ruling on whether a person acting pursuant to a power of attorney could do so by ruling that, pursuant to S.C. Code Ann. § 62-5-501 (Law. Co-op. Supp.), the son's power of attorney had been terminated by the appointment of a guardian *ad litem* because there was no evidence that it specifically provided that it would not terminate upon such appointment (the power of attorney had not been included in the record on appeal).

However, the Court of Appeals implied in *Murray* that an attorney-in-fact could maintain a divorce action for an incompetent person. This is at odds with the implication in *Brewington v. Brewington*, 280 S.C. 502, 313 S.E.2d 53 (Ct. App. 1984), that an attorney-in-fact could not maintain a divorce action on behalf of an incompetent person, although the court held that one could bring an action for separate support and maintenance. In *Brewington*, a wife instituted an action for legal separation, separate support and maintenance, property division and attorneys' fees by her attorney-in-fact shortly before she was confined in Crafts-Farrow mental hospital. The trial court granted her a legal separation, divided the marital home fifty-fifty, and ordered the husband to pay $500 in attorneys' fees. The Court of Appeals first considered the husband's claim that the attorney-in-fact lacked the capacity to bring the action, and it held that the right to object to this had been waived by failing to demur or to file an answer raising this challenge. It then considered the possibility that the claim was one that the attorney-in-fact lacked standing, which would have raised an issue of subject matter jurisdiction which cannot be waived. The court decided that it did not matter. "We hold that an agent possessed of a valid and durable power of attorney may institute in the name of a principal an action for legal separation[2] and related equitable relief." *Id.* at 506, 313 S.E.2d at 55. The Court

[2] Although it has since been made clear that there is no cause of action in South Carolina for a legal separation (see the discussion of this issue in the chapter on separate support and maintenance), *Brewington* also involved a claim for separate support and maintenance.

dismissed authority cited from C.J.S. in support of his claim that the action was too personal in nature to allow an agent to bring it on behalf of the principal, saying that an action for legal separation was different from a divorce action because it does not seek to terminate the marriage. Thus, there is *dicta* in two cases which seems to point toward different conclusions.

E. GROUNDS (AND PROOF)

1. IN GENERAL

There are only five grounds for divorce in South Carolina: (1) adultery; (2) desertion for a period of one year; (3) physical cruelty; (4) habitual drunkenness, provided, that this ground shall be construed to include habitual drunkenness caused by the use of any narcotic drug; and (5) living separate and apart without cohabitation for a period of one year. S.C. Code Ann. § 20-3-10 (Law. Co-op. 1976).

If a divorce is granted on any ground, it moots the question of whether a divorce should have been granted on any other ground. *Karle v. Karle*, No. 92-UP-135 (S.C. Ct. App. 1992) (holding that it was a moot question on appeal as to whether the family court had incorrectly refused to give the wife a divorce on the ground of habitual drunkenness, because a divorce had been given to her on the basis of one year continuous separation during the time between the trial and the appeal); *Smith v. Smith*, 294 S.C. 194, 363 S.E.2d 404 (Ct. App. 1987) (holding that the trial court had acted properly in refusing to consider the husband's counterclaim for divorce on the ground of adultery where the court had divorced the parties on the basis of the wife's request for a divorce on the ground of one year separation).

What difference does it make today whether the divorce is sought on the basis of the no fault one year separation ground or on the basis of one of the fault grounds? A major practical consideration is speed. A divorce action can be filed as soon as the ground arises on the basis of adultery, physical cruelty or habitual drunkenness and a divorce can be granted three months after such filing. S.C. Code Ann. § 20-3-80 (Law. Co-op 1976).

As a technical matter, it makes increasingly less difference whether one uses a fault ground or a no fault ground as the basis for the divorce. To the extent that fault is relevant, evidence of the relative misconduct of the parties can be presented to and considered by the court even where the ground being used for the divorce is one year separation. Still, from the perspective of litigation strategy, some litigants may desire to use a fault ground for emotional satisfaction, for negotiation leverage, or due to a sense that it will have some beneficial impact on the trial judge. Some attorneys believe that stating fault grounds in the pleadings has an important psychological effect on trial judges.

In *Gainey v. Gainey*, 277 S.C. 519, 290 S.E.2d 242 (1982), the court was faced with an effort on the part of the petitioning spouse to prove both one year's separation and adultery; his motive for proving adultery, of course, was to bar his wife from alimony. The Supreme Court held, *inter alia*, that adultery had been proved along with the one year's separation and that the adulterous wife should therefore have been permanently barred from alimony in accordance with S.C. Code Ann. § 20-3-120 (Law. Co-op. 1976). The evidence of adultery was circumstantial, but the Court held that a clear preponderance of the evidence had established it.

Today, alimony can be barred on the basis of adultery, irrespective of the ground used as the basis for divorce, but only if the adultery was committed before either (1) the formal signing of a written property or marital settlement agreement or (2) entry of a permanent order of separate maintenance and support or of a permanent order approving a property or marital agreement of the parties. S.C. Code Ann. § 20-3-80 (Law. Co-op. Supp.).

a. The Significance of Fault

The relative fault of the parties is one factor to be considered by the court in making an equitable division of property award. In *Rampey v. Rampey*, 286 S.C. 153, 332 S.E.2d 213 (Ct. App. 1985), the trial court had considered in dividing the marital property the fact that the wife's desertion without cause was directly responsible for the breakup of the marriage. "Although fault does not justify a severe penalty in making a division of the marital property, it is a factor the Court may consider in determining the equities between spouses." *Id.* at 156, 332 S.E.2d at 214. However, fault does not justify a severe penalty. *Noll v. Noll*, 297 SC 190, 375 S.E.2d 338 (Ct.

App. 1988). *See also Peirson v. Calhoun*, 308 S.C. 246, 417 S.E.2d 604 (Ct. App. 1992) (remanding the issue of the husband's fault in dividing marital property to the trial court for proper consideration).

The effect of a counterclaim for a divorce based on a fault ground when the plaintiff has asked for a divorce on the no-fault ground was addressed in *Dunson v. Dunson*, 278 S.C. 210, 294 S.E.2d 39 (1982). The husband had asked for divorce on the ground of one year's separation, and the wife had counterclaimed for divorce on the basis of desertion. The Supreme Court wrote in relevant part:

> Both parties seek a divorce; one asserted separation for one (1) year as a ground, the other desertion. *The failure to sustain the wife's allegation of desertion has not prejudiced any of her rights.* The award of the divorce on the ground of separation for one (1) year has not denied to her any personal or property right nor has it imposed on her any burden or obligation. *She has been properly declared entitled to alimony from which there is no appeal.* She is simply not an aggrieved party insofar as this issue was concerned.

Id. at 212, 294 S.E.2d at 40 (emphasis supplied).

An example of the ability to prove fault, even when it is not relevant to the grounds for divorce can be found in *Peirson v. Calhoun*, 308 S.C. 246, 417 S.E.2d 604 (Ct. App. 1992). The parties had been divorced in North Carolina on no fault grounds and were in the family court in South Carolina seeking a division of marital property. At issue on appeal was the trial court's finding that there had been no misconduct of the husband that had adversely affected the economic circumstances of the parties or contributed to the breakup of the marriage. The wife had left the husband, and she claimed that his heavy drinking was the reason. The husband denied this and said he had stopped drinking 6-8 months before the divorce. The Court of Appeals determined that the trial court had ignored the question of his fault, and it sent the case back to the family court to consider what impact, if any, the husband's fault had on the breakup of the marriage and the economic circumstances of the parties.

The foregoing discussion reflects a clear separation in the Court's view between the existence of fault as a ground for divorce on the one hand and the effect of evidence of such fault upon other matters involved in marital litigation on the other hand. Thus, the Court carefully pointed out that the wife in *Dunson* had properly been declared entitled to alimony. The rather clear implication is that it would be inappropriate for a trial court to rule that a litigant's reliance on the no fault ground for getting a divorce precludes evidence of marital fault, if such fault is relevant to other issues in the litigation. This, of course, is bolstered by the holding in *Gainey* (discussed earlier).

In the final analysis, the decision to use a fault ground (other than adultery) when the parties have been separated for more than one year may be determined more by the client's interest in making a record of the fact that the divorce was caused by the spouse rather than by consideration of any legal consequences.

b. Corroboration

Corroboration of testimony used to sustain a ground for divorce is normally required, although this requirement can be waived where the possibility of collusion is not a consideration. The law with respect to corroboration is stated in *McLaughlin v. McLaughlin*, 244 S.C. 265, 136 S.E.2d 537 (1964):

> [A] divorce will not be granted on the uncorroborated testimony of a party or the parties to the suit; however, as the main reason for the rule is to prevent collusion, it is not generally deemed inflexible and may be relaxed where it is evident that collusion does not exist. When the rule is deemed applicable, corroboration is required of all material allegations of the complaint necessary to sustain a decree of divorce; but such corroboration need not in itself be sufficient to warrant such relief. Corroboration may be by either direct or circumstantial evidence. All testimony is not required to be corroborated in every particular. It may be corroborated by testimony of third persons as to some of the causes alleged or by testimony to acts other than those specifically alleged which tend to prove those that are.

> The testimony of plaintiff's witnesses does not corroborate her charges of physical cruelty. She, however, contends that corroboration is not required where the divorce is contested and there is no question of collusion between the parties; and, further, that if in this case the Court requires corroboration, the testimony of the defendant sufficiently corroborates plaintiff's allegations of cruelty.
>
> In South Carolina the rule requiring corroboration is not mandatory and the necessity of such to a large extent depends upon the facts and circumstances of each case. Some states have adopted a rule that, where a divorce case is contested, the Court may grant a divorce on plaintiff's uncorroborated testimony. This does not appear to us to be the proper basis upon which to require the rule. The degree of corroboration required may be greater when the divorce is uncontested and only slight corroboration may be sufficient in certain contested divorces; however, if no corroboration is shown, then the burden is upon the plaintiff to show why.
>
> . . .
>
> In the absence of collusion or connivance testimony of the adverse party may furnish necessary corroboration in certain instances; however, such corroboration is looked upon with suspicion if there is an absence of other corroborating testimony or circumstances.

Id. at 270-271, 136 S.E.2d at 539-540.

In *McLaughlin* the Court of Appeals ruled that the testimony of the wife with respect to physical cruelty was only partly corroborated by her husband's testimony, and that, even if his testimony was allowed to corroborate hers, the single act of physical cruelty which was corroborated was insufficient to justify a divorce on the ground of physical cruelty.

The Court of Appeals has held that the uncorroborated testimony of a wife that her husband had admitted to her that he had committed adultery was sufficient to grant a divorce. In *Harvley v. Harvley*, 279 S.C. 572, 310 S.E.2d 161 (Ct. App. 1983), the Court of Appeals stated that

> The main reason for the rule requiring corroboration is to prevent collusion. Where it is evident that collusion does not exist, the rule may be relaxed. Upon a review of the entire record, there is no evidence that parties [sic] colluded to obtain the divorce. The husband admitted his adulterous behavior on several occasions. There is no need to corroborate the uncontradicted admission of appellant against his own interests. The ground for divorce is sustained.

Id. at 574, 310 S.E.2nd (citations omitted).

Another case in which the Court of Appeals sustained a finding of adultery based solely on the husband's admission of adultery is *McLaurin v. McLaurin*, 294 S.C. 132, 363 S.E.2d 110 (Ct. App. 1987). The court ruled that corroboration was not needed because the husband had vigorously contested the allegation of adultery and the suit was not collusive. However, the court also determined that sufficient corroboration was provided by the testimony of a process server who served the husband at the alleged paramour's home and observed that she had come to the door dressed in a flimsy gown, although the husband had been fully dressed.

Also in *McLaurin*, the court declined to comment on the husband's claim that the trial court had erred by inferring guilt from his invoking the Fifth Amendment's protection against self incrimination. The court said that, because corroboration was not needed and sufficient corroboration existed, it was not necessary to decide what, if any, inference may be drawn from a witness' invocation of the privilege against self incrimination in a civil case.

Other cases which found insufficient corroboration include: *Frazier v. Frazier*, 228 S.C. 149, 89 S.E.2d 225 (1955) (holding that the wife had insufficient corroboration of her testimony that she had cohabited with her husband during the preceding year to defeat the husband's request for a divorce on the ground of desertion); *Brown v. Brown*, 215 S.C. 502, 56 S.E.2d 330 (1949) (sustaining the trial court's denial of a divorce and stating that "[w]e have the bare statement that at some time, shortly before they parted, appellant found her husband in bed with her sister-in-law. None of the circumstances are given." *Id.* at 511, 56 S.E.2d at 335.)

2. THE NO FAULT GROUND: LIVING SEPARATE APART AND WITHOUT COHABITATION FOR ONE YEAR

a. In General

This ground, contained now in S.C. Code Ann. § 20-3-10(5) (Law. Co-op. 1976), was originally added to the allowable grounds for divorce in South Carolina with the 1969 amendment to the State Constitution. At that time, the required duration of the separation period was three years, but it was amended in 1979 to reduce the period to the present one year. Although the three year separation ground was not a terribly significant ground for divorce, the one year separation ground is now the most common ground upon which divorces are sought in South Carolina.

One may obtain a divorce on this ground (or desertion) immediately after the filing of the action if responsive pleadings are filed or thirty days after the defendant is served, if the defendant does not respond. The ordinary three-month delay between filing and the effective date of any decree is abrogated for purposes of these two grounds. S.C. Code Ann. § 20-3-80 (Law. Co-op. 1976).

Neither spouse is more or less entitled to a no fault divorce than the other. At either party's request, the court may grant a divorce to either or both parties on the ground of one year separation. *Miles v. Miles*, 303 S.C. 33, 397 S.E.2d 790 (Ct. App. 1990).

b. Voluntariness

Both parties must be conscious of the fact of the separation before a divorce on the basis of one year separation can be granted, even though it is possible for a separation to take place at the unilateral insistence of one party.

The initial case to construe the no fault ground in South Carolina was *Shaw v. Shaw*, 256 S.C. 453, 182 S.E.2d 865 (1971). In that case, the Supreme Court determined that the living separate and apart ground would not apply where the defendant was living separate and apart in a physical sense merely due to her commitment to the South Carolina State Hospital as a mental patient. The Supreme Court relied upon and cited extensively from the Virginia case of *Crittenden v. Crittenden*, 210 Va. 76, 168 S.E.2d 115 (1969). Our Court was concerned that the living separate and apart ground should not be treated as tantamount to a divorce ground of insanity.

Similarly, separations caused by military service cannot be used as a basis for divorce. However, if the parties separate before one of them is ordered to move by the military or if the reasons for separating are independent of the military service, the time for establishing the year's separation can continue to run while a spouse is away in military service. The Court of Appeals addressed this issue in *Niemann v. Niemann*, 282 S.C. 127, 317 S.E.2d 472 (Ct. App. 1984). The husband had appealed a divorce granted to the wife on the ground of continuous separation for a year. He was a naval officer on involuntary sea duty during seven months of the one year period. He contended that including his time of sea duty in the one year period violated the equal protection clause of the Fourteenth Amendment to the U.S. Constitution and was contrary to public policy.

The court disagreed and adopted the general rule, holding that "when one's spouse serves in the military and the parties were separated before the military service began or when the separation is independent of military service, though during service, a divorce on the grounds of separation is proper." *Id.* at 128, 317 S.E.2d at 473. The Court held that the Niemanns' separation was of the latter type: independent of the military service. The wife had indicated her clear intent to separate before the husband left for duty. The parties had also lived separate and apart for two months prior to the sea duty. The Court concluded the discrimination issue was avoided by its holding that the separation must be independent of involuntary sea duty.

It remains for future case decisions to determine which other kinds of "involuntary" separations would nonetheless be satisfactory separations for purposes of this divorce ground. Conceivably, transfers in a civilian work situation could arise just as they do in the military. There is an extensive annotation which deals with the general question of voluntariness in living separate and apart statutes, and which lists

Shaw v. Shaw, 256 S.C. 453, 182 S.E.2d 865 (1971), as one of those cases which espouse voluntariness as being an element of living separate and apart which must be met before the ground will be established. Presumably, this interpretation means that one party must be voluntarily living separate and apart, and that both parties must be conscious of it.

c. "Separate and Apart"

Spouses are not living "separate and apart" for purposes of the divorce statute if they continue to maintain a single household under one roof. In *Barnes v. Barnes*, 276 S.C. 519, 280 S.E.2d 538 (1981), the parties both testified that they lived in separate rooms of the marital home and had no sexual relations for more than a year. The Supreme Court wrote, "while a husband and a wife lived together in the marital home the only evidence of separation would exist behind the closed doors of the matrimonial domicile. This situation encourages collusion between the dissatisfied partners of the marriage. . . . We therefore hold that the 'living separate and apart' language of § 20-3-10(5) requires that the parties live in separate domiciles for a period of a year." 276 S.C. at 520, 280 S.E.2d at 539. *See also Ariail v. Ariail*, 295 S.C. 486, 369 S.E.2d 146 (Ct. App. 1988) (living in the same house is not living separate and apart for the purpose of obtaining a divorce).

d. "Without Cohabitation for One Year"

The statute requires spouses to live separate and apart "without cohabitation for one year" to obtain a divorce on this ground. S.C. Code Ann. § 20-3-10(5) (Law. Co-op. 1976). No explanation of the meaning of "cohabitation" is supplied in the statute. Cohabitation has been defined as "living together as man and wife," (Jakar v. Jakar, 113 S.C. 295, 302-303, 105 S.E. 337, 338 (1920)), and as "living together in the same house" (*E.D.M. v. T.A.M.* 307 S.C. 471, 475, 415 S.E.2d 812, 815 (1992) (citing *Barksdale v. United States*, 4 F. Supp. 207 (D.S.C. 1931)). (For additional discussion about the meaning of "cohabitation," see the chapter on establishing the validity of marriages.)

There are other questions presented by the "without cohabitation" requirement which have not squarely answered by case decisions, including whether

(1) having sexual relations, or (2) attempting a reconciliation, requires the one year clock to start over.

(1) Effect of Sexual Relations

There is no South Carolina case directly on point nor should one be expected, unless it is presented as a secondary issue in an appeal. If a divorce is denied on the basis that one year has not passed since the parties have had sexual relations, not many clients will be willing to spend the money and effort to appeal that ruling. A new one year period will very likely be established before an appellate decision is rendered.

However, there is no apparent reason why spouses should not be able to obtain no fault divorce just because sexual relations have happened during the year. This determination should be based on an examination of the intentions of the parties and the facts surrounding the sexual intercourse. In discussing reconciliation (which means a resumption of marital cohabitation in its fullest sense) the following language appears in C.J.S.:

> If the parties casually cohabit, or if the cohabitation is sporadic, conditional, or provisional, there is no reconciliation because of the absence of the required intent to settle their differences on a permanent basis. Thus, isolated acts of sexual intercourse between judicially separated spouses are not conclusive of an intent to reconcile, but are merely one of the factors to be considered in determining mutual consent and agreement to reconcile.

27A C.J.S. *Divorce* § 85 (1986). Thus, if isolated acts of sexual intercourse are not enough to establish the defense of reconciliation because true marital cohabitation has not occurred, then it would be inconsistent to permit the same acts to bar a no fault divorce. One should also take into account that sexual intercourse is not enough, in and of itself, to establish a common law marriage (see the chapter on establishing the validity of marriages). Logically then, sexual intercourse alone should not be enough to revive a broken marriage.

The more important issue in determining whether cohabitation has resumed is whether the parties mutually intended to resume cohabitation as man and wife. Evidence of their intention, or lack thereof, can be gleaned from the facts surrounding the sexual intercourse. Did the parties resume living under the same roof and stop maintaining separate households? Did they tell anyone they had resumed their marriage? How frequently and over what period of time did they engage in sexual relations? What other things did they do or fail to do that would indicate they were trying to save their marriage? How long did they live together? If there was really no mutual intention to resume cohabitation as a family, there is no apparent public policy served by requiring the parties to wait another full year for a divorce.

(2) Effect of Attempted Reconciliation

At first glance, one might conclude that an attempted reconciliation requires restarting the one year period needed for a divorce. Perhaps it does, but there is not yet a South Carolina case on point, and such a result would be contrary to the long standing public policy in South Carolina of encouraging reconciliation. In appropriate cases, litigants may want to consider asking the family court to ignore a period of attempted reconciliation (especially if very brief) in its calculations — that is, not to include it as part of the twelve month period required to qualify for a no fault divorce. (A more extensive discussion of this point is in the section on reconciliation in the divorce defenses portion of this chapter.)

3. ADULTERY

a. In General

Historically, adultery has been one of the most common grounds for divorce. Often it was the only ground for divorce. Currently, South Carolina adheres to the common law definition espoused in *Hull v. Hull*, 21 S.C. Eq. (1 Strob. Eq.) 174 (1848), which states, "[a]dultery is the illicit intercourse between two persons, one of whom, at least, is married." This definition was used in *R.G.M. v. D.E.M.*, 306 S.C. 145, 410 S.E.2d 564 (Ct. App. 1991); and *Panhorst v. Panhorst*, 301 S.C. 100, 390 S.E.2d 376 (Ct. App. 1990).

"Illicit intercourse" does not require the normal act of consummation between a man and a woman. In *Panhorst*, the court was asked to decide exactly what sex acts do and do not constitute adultery. The wife, who was accused of adultery, took the position that illicit sexual intercourse consists solely of the normal act of consummation between a man and a woman. Her complaint on appeal was that the trial court had refused to allow her to testify that her alleged paramour was impotent and thus was incapable of having normal sexual intercourse with her. The court declined to define the sex acts that constitute adultery, finding that enough evidence was produced in this case to support the trial judge's ruling that the wife had committed adultery. The court wrote:

> This evidence showed both an inclination and the opportunity to commit adultery. Proof of inclination and opportunity is sufficient to establish a *prima facie* case. See *Hartley v. Hartley*, 292 S.C. 245, 355 S.E. (2d) 869 (Ct. App. 1987) (adultery may be proven by circumstantial evidence showing inclination and opportunity to commit adultery).
>
> . . .
>
> At common law, marriage is both a contract and a status. As a status, it gives rise to rights and duties imposed by law on the marriage partners. Among these are material support and consortium, i.e., the conjugal society, comfort, companionship, and affection of each other. Sexual fidelity is a fundamental duty of the marital relationship. As far as the law is concerned, the contract of marriage is, in its essence, a consent on the part of a man and a woman to cohabit with each other and with each other only. This means a husband and wife must confine their sexual activity exclusively to one another. Sexual relations with a person other than the marriage partner are illicit because they violate this marital duty of exclusiveness.
>
> . . .

> Suffice it to say that where, as here, a married woman with a history of having committed adultery, spends the night, undressed, in the same bed with a man, with whom it appears she is romantically involved and to whom she is not married, her actions warrant the finding that she has committed adultery. (citations omitted).

Id. at 103-104, 390 S.E.2d at 378.

Prove of "sexual intimacy" is enough to support a finding of adultery. The Court of Appeals reversed a family court's ruling that a woman did not commit adultery based upon its finding "that the relationship between the Wife and Gooding was sexually intimate, thus compelling a finding that the Wife committed adultery." *Nemeth v. Nemeth*, Op. No. 2616 (S.C. Ct. App. filed Jan. 13, 1997)(Davis Adv. Sh. No. 1 at 47). The facts are that Mrs. Nemeth shared a cabin with Mr. Gooding, who was not her husband, during a cruise to Alaska so that two other people who became engaged shortly before the cruise could share a cabin (there were no other cabins available). At the end of the cruise they shared a room in a hotel. There was some evidence that the wife was favorably inclined to have a sexual relationship with Mr. Gooding, and the husband testified that the wife confessed that she had an affair with Mr. Gooding. The wife denied committing adultery and presented evidence that she had a disease which caused chronic pain in the vaginal area which made intercourse painful for her. The Court of Appeals determined that inclination and opportunity existed for her to commit adultery. It concluded that the wife's medical evidence did not establish that she was totally incapacitated during the Alaska trip; but, even if it had, it would not matter because actual sexual intercourse is not required to establish adultery. Sexual intimacy is enough.

Adultery must be plead as a defense. If it is not raised in the pleadings, it cannot be proved at trial. *Doe v. Doe*, ___ S.C. ___, 478 S.E.2d 854 (Ct. App. 1996) (affirming the trial court's decision to bar the husband's attorney from cross-examining the wife about extramarital relationships). "Husband did not plead Wife's adultery and thus was not entitled to question her on the issue at trial. ... adultery is an avoidance to an action for alimony which must be pled under Rule 8(c), SCRCP." *Id.* at ___, 478 S.E.2d at 858.

Proof of adultery must be "clear and positive, and the infidelity must be established by a clear preponderance of the evidence." *McLaurin v. McLaurin*, 294 S.C. 132, 133, 263 S.E.2d 110, 111 (Ct. App. 1987). Preponderance of the evidence has been defined by the Supreme Court as "that evidence which convinces as to its truth. A preponderance of the evidence is not made out by the greater number of witnesses." *Lee v. Lee*, 237 S.C. 532, 118 S.E.2d 171 (1961) (affirming a divorce given to the husband based solely on the testimony of a game warden who said he saw the wife and her alleged paramour engaging in sexual intercourse in the woods, despite her and the alleged paramour's testimony that they had not committed adultery).

Proof of adultery may be by circumstantial evidence, and proof of opportunity and inclination to commit adultery is sufficient to sustain a finding of adultery.

> Because "adultery, by its very nature, is an activity which takes place in private, it may be proved by circumstantial evidence." *McLaurin v. McLaurin*, 294 S.C. 132, 133, 363 S.E.2d 110, 111 (Ct. App. 1987). Indeed, if it were not for circumstantial evidence, the practice of adultery would scarcely be known to exist. A finding of adultery is allowed where there is evidence of both the opportunity to commit adultery and the disposition to commit adultery. *Hartley v. Hartley*, 292 S.C. 245, 355 S.E.2d 869 (Ct. App. 1987). State of mind can be inferred from circumstances. For example, it can be inferred that a piano player in a bawdy house knows what is going on upstairs. The same evidence which proves the opportunity can also prove the disposition. For example, where a married man is observed going upstairs in a bawdyhouse, unless something to the contrary appears, no other evidence is required to warrant a finding of adultery.
>
> The opportunities available to Mr. Prevatte are quite apparent. His disposition can be inferred from the circumstances in which he was observed, coupled with his response when questioned regarding his whereabouts. When two people, a man and a woman, park by themselves at night in lonely places and purposely sit very close together, unless some other reason appears for their behavior, even

> the most dispassionate observer may very well infer that they are romantically disposed toward each other. Such is life.
>
> Moreover, insufficiency of proof "should not be allowed to defeat a divorce where the court is fully convinced adultery has been committed and a party has had full opportunity to defend or refute the charge." *McLaurin*, 294 S.C. at 134, 363 S.E.2d at 111.

Prevatte v. Prevatte, 297 S.C. 345, 351, 377 S.E.2d 114, 118 (Ct. App. 1989).

In *McLaurin* the only evidence of adultery was the wife's testimony that he had admitted committing adultery to her and a process server's testimony that the divorce pleadings had been served on the husband at the alleged paramour's house, where she had answered the door wearing a flimsy gown but he had come to the door fully dressed. The Supreme Court affirmed the trial court's decision to grant the wife a divorce on the ground of adultery. *See also Harvley v. Harvley*, 279 S.C. 572, 310 S.E.2d 161 (Ct. App. 1983) (affirming a finding of adultery solely on the basis of uncontradicted testimony that the husband had admitted committing adultery).

There is some question about the degree of specificity which is required to sustain a finding of adultery. In *Odom v. Odom*, 248 S.C. 144, 149 S.E.2d 353 (1966), the Supreme Court said "[t]he proof must be sufficiently definite to identify the time and place of the offense, and the circumstances under which it was committed." *Id.* at 146, 149 S.E.2d at 354 (reversing a divorce granted on the basis of adultery for lack of evidentiary support). However, in *Dubose v. Dubose*, 259 S.C. 418, 192 S.E.2d 329 (1972), the Supreme Court held that "approximate times, places and circumstances" are sufficient to prove adultery. *Id.* at 424, 192 S.E.2d at 331 (affirming divorce, over Justice Littlejohn's dissent that the evidence did not meet the *Odom* standard of specificity). It appears under *McLaurin* and *Prevatte* that the appellate courts will allow a divorce to be granted with less specific evidence of the time, place and circumstances of the adultery "where the court is fully convinced adultery has been committed and a party has had full opportunity to defend or refute the charge." *McLaurin*, 294 S.C. at 134, 363 S.E.2d at 111; *Prevatte*, 297 S.C. at 351, 377 S.E.2d at 118.

Simply placing a spouse and an alleged paramour together, without more, will not support a finding of adultery. In *Fox v. Fox*, 277 S.C. 400, 288 S.E.2d 390 (1982), the Supreme Court wrote: "Husband and Terry conceded to being close friends and to dating, but emphatically denied adulterous relationship. While the evidence undoubtedly places Husband and Terry together on several occasions, that fact alone, without more, does not warrant the conclusion that adultery was committed." *Id.* at 402, 288 S.E.2d at 391 (reversing the trial court's granting of a divorce on the ground of adultery, but finding that a divorce should have been granted on the basis of one year separation). The Court of Appeals in *Fulton v. Fulton*, 293 S.C. 146, 359 S.E.2d 88 (Ct. App. 1987) affirmed the trial court's refusal to grant a divorce on the ground of adultery where the husband's only evidence that his wife had committed adultery was that she and another woman had spent three nights in a house occupied by two men, one of whom was her sponsor at Alcoholics Anonymous.

A husband's testimony that he found his wife "living in adultery in his said home with another man" and evidence that the wife had been seen in the company of the alleged paramour and four other men was not enough to support a finding of adultery in *McAteer v. McAteer*, 262 S.C. 475, 205 S.E.2d 377 (1974). The testimony about the other "sightings" was held to be inappropriate since Mrs. McAteer had no notice of this claim. The husband's accusation of a single incident at the residence was insufficient to support the allegations of adultery. The Court held that consideration of a divorce on the grounds of adultery will ordinarily be confined to the specific acts alleged in the pleadings.

The circumstantial evidence described in *Husband v. Wife*, 301 S.C. 531, 392 S.E.2d 811 (Ct. App. 1990), was held to be sufficient to sustain a finding of adultery.

> She worked until the wee hours of the morning. She would come home, get dressed, and leave again, not returning until just before the children left for school. At least twice, she rented a motel room for the night. Once, two days before Christmas, she checked into a motel, checked out the same day, checked back in later that day, and stayed until Christmas Eve. She explained that she did this because she wanted to be alone. But the husband testified he and the children were out of town at the time. Then there was the matter of the duffle bags

> in her car. The husband noticed one of the bags contained a number of personal items, including nightgowns, pajamas and underpants. He noticed the other bag contained condoms, things people do not usually carry with them when they want to be alone. The husband testified she admitted sleeping with a man in the motel but denied anything "took place between her and him." He did not believe her denial. Nor did the trial judge. Nor do we.

Id. at 533, 392 S.E.2d at 812.

b. Homosexual Acts

A divorce can be granted in South Carolina on the ground of adultery where one spouse is involved in a homosexual relationship. In *R.G.M. v. D.E.M.*, 306 S.C. 145, 410 S.E.2d 564 (1991), the Supreme Court held, "explicit extramarital sexual activity constitutes adultery regardless of whether it is of a homosexual or heterosexual character. Accordingly, we conclude that homosexual activity between persons, at least one of whom is married to someone other than the sexual partner, constitutes adultery." *Id.* at 567.

c. Artificial Insemination

No case in South Carolina has dealt directly with the issue of artificial insemination and adultery. However, in *Panhorst v. Panhorst*, 301 S.C. 100, 390 S.E.2d 376 (Ct. App. 1990), Justice Bell discussed *Orford v. Orford*, 49 Ont. L. 15, 58 Dom. L. Rep. 251 (1951) and artificial insemination in a footnote but declined to "decide exactly what sex acts do and do not constitute adultery." *Orford* held that a wife who underwent artificial insemination without the express consent of the husband would be guilty of adultery. *Orford* relied on the now discredited reasoning of *Matchin v. Matchin*, 6 Penn. (6 Barr.) 332 (1847), that the question of how the wife was impregnated was irrelevant to the real purpose of the adultery ground, which was to insure against the introduction of spurious offspring into the family. *See also Doornbos v. Doornbos*, No. 54 S. 1498 (Superior Court, Cook Co., December 13, 1954) (holding that, where the precise issue of legitimacy has been squarely presented for determination, it has been held that heterologous artificial insemination by a third-party donor with or without the consent of the husband, constitutes adultery on the part of the mother and that a child so conceived is not a child born in wedlock and is therefore illegitimate.). *But see People v. Sorenson*, 437 P.2d 495 (Cal. 1968) (holding that artificial insemination is not considered adultery).

It is unclear where the courts of this state would stand if ever faced with the issue of whether artificial insemination constitutes adultery. It is a topic which the common law has dealt with poorly on a case-by-case basis. Perhaps, therefore, it should be the subject of statutory regulation. *See Artificial Insemination — A Model Statute*, 24 Cleveland State L. Rev. 341, Spring, 1975; Annotation, *Legal Consequences of Human Artificial Insemination*, 25 A.L.R.3d 1103, 1107 (1969). The better reasoned cases reject the notion that artificial insemination may be regarded as adultery, but clearly the danger lurks in the background, ready to spring at the unwary wife whose husband later regrets (or did not consent to) the action.

d. Voluntary, Knowing, and Intentional

Since the sexual intercourse involved must be "voluntary," it has generally been held that an element of adultery is a guilty intent. In other words, the person engaging in adultery must know that he or she is doing so. *See* Annotation, *Cohabitation Under Marriage Contracted After Decrease as Adultery Where Decree is Later Reversed or Set Aside*, 63 A.L.R.2d 816 (1956). It follows that a substantial mistake of fact, or an incapacity on the part of the accused, will serve to prevent a finding of adultery. Thus, it has been said it is not adultery "where the wife has intercourse with a man not her husband through mistake, she believing him to be her husband . . . ." *See Gordon v. Gordon*, 141 Ill. 160, 30 N.E. 446, 448 (1892). Similarly, if the person is insane, it is generally held that there exists in him or her no capacity to commit adultery. *See* Annotation, *Insanity as Affecting Right to Divorce or Separation on Other Grounds*, 19 A.L.R.2d 174 (1951).

South Carolina's highest court addressed the issue of mental illness and adultery in *Rutherford v. Rutherford*, 307 S.C. 199, 414 S.E.2d 157 (1992). *Rutherford* involved a wife who suffered from multiple personality disorder and who had admittedly committed the physical act of adultery. However, she urged the court to excuse her from legal responsibility due to her mental illness. The Court found that lower standard of mental impairment establishing in divorce actions would be inappropriate and further stated, "in order to avoid the husband's action for divorce on the ground of adultery and the bar of alimony, the wife bore the burden of proving by the preponderance of the evidence that at the time she committed adultery, she was unable to appreciate the wrongfulness of her conduct." *Id.* at 206, 414 S.E.2d at 161. Therefore, while South Carolina still allows the defense of mental illness to legally excuse one from divorce on the ground of adultery, the standard of proof necessary to establish this defense has not been lowered.

There exists considerable confusion in one sub-area of analysis: if a person engages in intercourse with another, honestly believing himself or herself to be free from matrimonial obligations either through divorce or believed death of a (presumptively) former marital partner, and it is later discovered that for some reason the individual in question is in fact still married to the former partner, can the former partner (actual partner, in fact) obtain a divorce on the grounds of the individual's adultery? It would seem that to the extent a guilty (knowing) intent is required before adultery can be proved there should be no adultery under the facts outlined, and most of the cases so hold. A leading case in this area is *Harmon v. Harmon*, 245 N.C. 83, 95 S.E.2d 355 (1956), which holds that only a lack of good faith on the part of the defendant when the second marriage was entered into (i.e., knowledge that a supposed divorce was invalid) would serve to render the cohabitation under the putative second marriage adulterous. However, *see Gordon v. Gordon*, 141 Ill. 160, 30 N.E. 446 (1892), which holds that a wife's cohabitation under a second marriage is adulterous when there has in fact been no initial divorce, although she in good faith thought there had been an initial divorce since she had been misled by her attorney.

Although there is no South Carolina case on point, it is likely that South Carolina courts would rule that intercourse brought on by intoxication will not be shielded from designation as adulterous, since an intoxicated person is held to have entered that state voluntarily. This would be consistent with its rulings that intoxication is not a defense to a criminal charge because the act of becoming intoxicated is voluntary. *See State v. Hatfield*, 300 S.C. 469, 388 S.E.2d 802 (1990); *State v. Vaughn*, 268 S.C. 119, 125, 232 S.E.2d 328, 330 (1977).

e. Criminal Adultery

The criminal offense of adultery is not precisely the same thing as the marital offense. S.C. Code Ann. § 16-15-60 (Law. Co-op. 1976), a statute close to 100 years old, makes adultery or fornication punishable by a fine of from $100.00 to $500.00, or imprisonment for from six months to one year, or both. S.C. Code Ann. § 16-15-70 (Law. Co-op. 1976) defines adultery as "the living together and carnal intercourse with each other or habitual carnal intercourse with each other without living together of a man and woman when either is lawfully married to some other person." (Fornication is similarly defined in the next section of the Code, substituting the words "both being unmarried" for the words "when either is lawfully married to some other person" in the adultery definition section.)

Thus, where a single act of illicit intercourse will apparently suffice for proof of marital offense, repetition is the key for the criminal offense. How much repetition? The best our courts have been able to do may be found in *State v. Carroll*, 30 S.C. 85, 8 S.E. 433 (1889), where the Supreme Court approved a jury charge which basically held that the acts of intercourse involved must be "frequent, not occasional," and otherwise left things up to the jury.

Prosecutions are not undertaken frequently under these statutes, but they do take place. It is perhaps worth pointing out that a mistaken belief on the part of one partner that he or she is not married has been held to be no bar to a prosecution and conviction under these sections. *State v. Westmoreland*, 76 S.C. 145, 56 S.E. 673 (1907). Under the same principle, of course, simple ignorance of the existence of the prohibition would not be a defense. *Quaere*, the appropriateness of the continuance of these sections on our statute books in view of the more relaxed state of social relations which exists in South Carolina today, when compared to the time in which the statutes were originally enacted, particularly since it has been held that adultery was not an indictable offense at common law in *State v. Brunson*, 18 S.C.L. (2 Bail.) 149 (1831).

4. DESERTION

a. In General

For all practical purposes, there is no reason for desertion to remain as a ground for divorce in South Carolina. A no fault divorce can be proved more easily than desertion, and the courts will consider the same factors in deciding any disputed issues, irrespective of the basis on which the divorce is being sought. If one party deserves better treatment from the court because the other spouse is a deserter, such misconduct and any advantage to be derived from it can be presented to and considered by the court in a no fault divorce, if it is relevant to issues before the court. Thus, the information presented in this section is largely of academic, not practical, interest to modern litigators. However, it may be of some use in those cases in which there is an advantage to be gained in negotiation or client satisfaction by labeling someone as a deserter, or when one believes that alleging desertion will have a positive psychological effect on the trial judge.

The statutory authorization for desertion as a ground for divorce is found in S.C. Code Ann. § 20-3-10 (Law. Co-op. 1976) which provides that "[n]o divorce from the bonds of matrimony shall be granted except upon one or more of the following grounds, to wit:

. . .

(2) Desertion for a period of one year."

Desertion was once the most common ground upon which divorces were granted in South Carolina. It is now rarely used due to the advent of the one year separation ground. "Prior to the addition in 1969 of three years' continuous separation as grounds for divorce, dissolution on the grounds of desertion accounted for approximately one-half of all divorces awarded, whereas they now constitute less than one-half of one percent." 13 S.C. Juris. *Divorce* § 15(a), (S.C. Bar-C.L.E. Division, 1992).

The South Carolina constitutional authorization for divorce based on desertion makes no mention of a time period; however, the one year provision was sustained against a constitutional challenge in *Nolletti v. Nolletti*, 243 S.C. 20, 132 S.E.2d 11 (1963). The Court pointed out that the one year provision should serve "to insure that the separation is not for a light or trivial reason," and that it thus should "safeguard the institution of marriage in furtherance of the well established public policy of the State." *Id.* at 25-26, 132 S.E.2d at 14.

The overall approach taken by the South Carolina cases to desertion squares in essence with the general case law through the nation. Numerous South Carolina cases have held that the essentials of desertion are:

(1) cessation from cohabitation for one year,
(2) intent of the absenting party not to resume cohabitation,
(3) absence of consent, and
(4) absence of justification for the cessation.

See Fort v. Fort, 270 S.C. 255, 241 S.E.2d 891 (1978); *Bennefield v. Bennefield*, 263 S.C. 233, 209 S.E.2d 563 (1974); *Machado v. Machado*, 220 S.C. 90, 66 S.E.2d 629 (1951).

There is a fair amount of case law about issues related to desertion, most of which predate the approval of a no fault divorce ground.

b. Cessation of Cohabitation for One Year

(1) Measurement of One Year

The cessation from cohabitation must persist for a full year. The time period is measured from the date of initial desertion to the time of filing. Subsequent litigation time does not count toward the expiration of the year. *See Cleveland v. Cleveland*, 238 S.C. 547, 121 S.E.2d 98 (1961); *Simonds v. Simonds*, 229 S.C. 376, 93 S.E.2d 107 (1956). In *Simonds*, the Court was explicit in denying a divorce on desertion grounds (constructive desertion, to be precise) "because a year had not elapsed from the date of the desertion to the commencement of this action." *Id.* at 386, 93 S.E.2d at 111 (citing *Mincey v. Mincey*, 224 S.C. 520, 80 S.E.2d 123 (1954)).

It is less clear when the clock begins to run. Some jurisdictions have taken the approach that the durational period will begin to run from the time the intent to desert was first formed, even though physical absence did not occur until later. South Carolina apparently takes the opposite approach, focusing upon the physical absence and permitting the intent to be formed later. *See Frazier v. Frazier*, 228 S.C. 149, 89 S.E.2d 225 (1955). How long after the departure the intent may be formed is unclear. Often, of course, formulation of intent and initiation of one act will be simultaneous, or the intent will have been formed prior to the departure, so the issue will not arise. Nonetheless, it should be pointed out that a position that an after-formed intent may relate back to an earlier departure is logically inconsistent with the need to have all four elements of the marital offense present throughout the year period. Thus, the safest course would be not to file for a divorce on desertion grounds until a year has passed from the time of the first objective manifestation of intent to desert, if the physical departure itself could not be said to be such (e.g., was brought about by an armed forces transfer or the like).

In an action for desertion based upon a failure to renew cohabitation after a good-faith offer to do so has been made on the part of the spouse who originally departed (i.e., when the initially deserting spouse has a change of heart and offers to return and is rejected, always assuming the existence of the four elements of the marital offense), "[t]he statutory period commences to run from the date of the refusal to resume marital relations." *Cleveland* at 553, 121 S.E.2d at 101.

(2) Examples of Cessation From Cohabitation

A refusal to engage in sexual relations for a year, without a physical departure, does not constitute desertion inasmuch as "cohabitation" connotes more than physical intimacy. The Court wrote in *Bennefield v. Bennefield*, 263 S.C. 233, 237, 209 S.E.2d 563, 565 (1974):

> The sole contention of the husband is that the refusal of the wife to engage in sexual relations with him for over a year prior to the institution of this action constituted cessation from cohabitation within the meaning of the divorce law. There is no merit in the contention. We have held that mere refusal of the wife to engage in sexual relations with the husband does not constitute cessation from cohabitation so as to constitute desertion as a ground for divorce.

See also Vickers v. Vickers, 255 S.C. 25, 176 S.E.2d 561 (1970) (treating husband with coldness and contempt and refusing to have sex is not desertion).

Locking a spouse out of the marital home may constitute cessation from cohabitation. In *Fort v. Fort*, 270 S.C. 255, 241 S.E.2d 891 (1978), the husband and wife were married in 1944. He was a medical doctor and together they acquired substantial assets. Beginning with the 1970's the marriage began to decline. The Court explained:

> In June of 1975, the wife, while continuing to live under the same roof with the husband, commenced this action for divorce. In early July, the husband went to North Carolina to attend a checker tournament and, upon his return, found that the wife had changed the locks on the doors of their home such that he could not gain entrance. In addition, she had packed all of his clothing and personal effects into plastic garbage bags and taken them to a motel.

Id. at 259, 241 S.E.2d at 893. The Court looks to the *Bennefield* case to illustrate the essentials of desertion and concludes:

> By moving the husband's clothes out and changing the locks on the doors so as to prevent his return home, the wife has intentionally absented herself from him just as effectively as if she had departed the premises herself. Such was clearly without the husband's consent, and justification for her action does not appear in the record. She has not shown a bona fide intent to resume the marital relation. Her testimony that she gave a set of keys to her preacher and set forth in a letter the conditions under which she would allow [the husband] to return, is neither appealing nor convincing. He has proved the four elements of actual desertion by the preponderance of the evidence.

Id. at 260, 241 S.E.2d at 893-94.

There are no South Carolina decisions further elaborating the element of cessation of cohabitation, either accepting or rejecting contentions that a course of conduct short of a physical departure by the alleged deserter from the marital residence but involving a greater estrangement than simple denial of sexual relations should amount to a desertion.

(3) Intent Not to Resume Cohabitation

Intent is a question of fact. The Supreme Court has twice referred to the following statement from American Jurisprudence, now found at 24 Am. Jur. 2d *Divorce and Separation* § 371 (1983):

> In proceedings for divorce on the ground of desertion, no general rule can be formulated as to what evidence is or is not admissible, each case depending upon its own particular circumstances. Since the intent to abandon is largely a matter of inference and presumption, the subsequent conduct of the parties frequently makes plain the intent with which a previous act was performed, and evidence of such conduct is admissible to ascertain the intent. The failure of the defendant to appear in a proceeding for divorce on the ground of desertion, although he is within easy access of the court, should be considered, in connection with other proof, upon the question of the mental attitude of the defendant. (footnotes omitted)

In *Frazier v. Frazier*, 228 S.C. 149, 89 S.E.2d 225 (1955), the Court found sufficient circumstantial evidence to uphold the trial court's decision that the wife had intended to desert her husband and remain apart when she left him at his military post in North Carolina and returned to her mother's house. In *Oswald v. Oswald*, 230 S.C. 299, 95 S.E.2d 493 (1956), the Court upheld a finding of desertion where the wife remained with her parents and did not follow her husband to Connecticut where he had been assigned by the Navy.

Physical separation alone does not establish intent to desert. The Supreme Court made the following statement in *Boozer v. Boozer*, 242 S.C. 292, 130 S.E.2d 903 (1963):

> Although it is clear in this case that friction between the parties caused the establishment and occupation of two domiciles during the period of time involved, there is nothing unusual under present day conditions about more than one domicile being maintained by husband and/or wife. Such is frequently the result of

> the occupational or economic status of the parties, even when husband and wife are living in perfect harmony.

Id. at 296, 130 S.E.2d at 905.

In *Bond v. Bond*, 252 S.C. 363, 166 S.E.2d 302 (1969), the Court declined to uphold a divorce granted on desertion grounds where the wife had returned to Columbia from Birmingham, Alabama, where she and her husband had been visiting his mother when he had decided to seek new employment. His search had proved unsuccessful and his mother had informed the couple that she could not support them for any substantial period of time, whereupon the wife, apparently with the consent of the husband, returned with the children to Columbia where her parents resided. In the ensuing year and a half the husband paid five or six visits to Columbia, and the wife eventually instituted divorce proceedings with desertion as the claimed ground. Neither party had offered to resume physical cohabitation in the interval in question. The Court wrote:

> We think that the evidence is insufficient to sustain the finding of the lower court that the husband was guilty of desertion within the meaning of the divorce statute. This record shows that the return of the wife to her parents was apparently the result of a mutual understanding that economic necessities required it and neither contemplated at the time that it would be permanent.
>
> A separation by mutual consent does not constitute desertion. *Cleveland v. Cleveland*, 238 S.C. 547, 121 S.E.2d 98.
>
> The record fails to show an intent to end the marriage at the time of the separation and there is no showing from which a reasonable conclusion can be drawn as to when any intent was formed to permanently cease the marital relationship, other than the certificate of the trial judge as to an unsuccessful attempt to effect a reconciliation. The wife was required to show that the husband deserted her and that such desertion continued for a period of at

> least one year prior to the institution of this action. This she has failed to do.

Id. at 367-68, 166 S.E.2d at 304.

The Court in *Bond* indicated that a manifestation of intent to desert did take place when the trial judge was unable to effect a reconciliation. Other circumstances, such as infrequent visits to Columbia by the husband and sporadic support payments by him, were apparently viewed as being consistent with conditions which had brought about the voluntary separation to begin with, and hence insufficient to indicate formation of an intent to desert.

(4) Absence of Consent

Since the party seeking the divorce on the ground of desertion must, by definition, not have consented to the conduct of the other party, a separation by mutual consent cannot, without more, lead to a divorce for desertion. *See Bond v. Bond*, 252 S.C. 363, 166 S.E.2d 302 (1969); *Cleveland v. Cleveland*, 238 S.C. 547, 121 S.E. 2d 98 (1961) and 243 S.C. 586, 135 S.E. 2d 84 (1964); *Machado v. Machado*, 220 S.C. 90, 66 S.E.2d 629 (1951).

A refusal by the deserted spouse to accept a bona fide reconciliation offer could create a desertion ground in favor of original deserter. If a party to a mutual agreement to separate has a change of heart and desires to effect a reconciliation, and the other party refuses, the refusing party becomes a deserter a year from the date of the refusal. *Cleveland v. Cleveland*, 238 S.C. 547, 121 S.E.2d 98 (1961).

A refusal to accept a reconciliation offer will not make one a deserter, if the offer is insufficient. Such an offer must be made in good faith and must ordinarily be made before the cause of action accrues, i.e., before the end of the one year period following the cessation of cohabitation. "Good faith" is a matter of fact and its existence is to be determined from an examination of all surrounding circumstances. The South Carolina cases speak in terms of a bona fide offer of reconciliation. *See Inabinet v. Inabinet*, 249 S.C. 65, 152 S.E.2d 553 (1967), where the husband's offer to accept his wife back into the home was rejected by the Court with the following language:

> Under the circumstances, the offer which the husband allegedly made amounted to nothing more than mere permission to the wife to return to an unhappy home, which the husband neither owned nor controlled, and from which only one of the causes of friction and unhappiness had been removed by death. His alleged offer contained no apology or excuse for the prior shortcomings of the husband, which caused the separation of the parties, and nothing to indicate that the husband sincerely desired that his offer be accepted or that the wife's lot in life would be a happy one if she did return. Instead of evincing any willingness to atone for his shortcomings, he was still engaged in attempting to charge her with desertion in [a] former action.
>
> We conclude that, even accepting the husband's testimony as literally true, he has failed to prove a bona fide offer of reconciliation, the refusal of which would constitute the wife a deserter and entitle the husband to a divorce on that ground.

Id. at 70-71, 152 S.E.2d at 555.

See also Miller v. Miller, 225 S.C. 274, 282, 82 S.E.2d 119, 122-23 (1954) (noting that the issue of reconciliation was not preserved for appeal, but that in any event the husband's request of the wife while she was hospitalized for gall bladder surgery to "come back out there" was a "gesture of peace . . . hardly consistent" with the husband's later actions); *Mincey v. Mincey*, 224 S.C. 520, 532-533, 80 S.E.2d 123, 130 (1954) (holding that the husband's offer of reconciliation was "questionable in view of [his] past marital record" and that the wife was "not required to blindly accept the same, but may judge the offer by its background"); *Wolfe v. Wolfe*, 220 S.C. 437, 68 S.E.2d 348 (1951) (finding the husband's offer to build a separate home to be a good faith offer to reconcile where the parties and their children had previously been living with the husband's parents and two of the husband's brothers, one of whom was also married); *Briggs v. Briggs*, 24 S.C. 377 (1886) (relied upon by the *Inabinet* Court to illustrate the degree of sincerity and the nature of the circumstances which should be shown to prove that an offer of reconciliation is sincere).

The desertion ground is lost if the abandoned spouse agrees to the separation during the year. A desertion can be turned into a separation by mutual consent if the initially innocent spouse at some point during the statutory period manifests an unwillingness to have the departed spouse return. *See Reaves v. Reaves*, 262 S.C. 499, 206 S.E.2d 405 (1974), where the conduct evidencing an unwillingness to accept the return was a changing of the locks on the marital home.

However, the mere silence of an abandoned spouse is probably not consent. While the question has not directly arisen in South Carolina, it seems safe to assume from the cases that mere silence on the part of complaining party during the absence of the other will not ripen into a consent. This is the nearly universal rule. *See Woodson v. Woodson*, 256 A.2d 410 (D.C. 1969). Nonetheless, a genuine offer to resume cohabitation on the part of the abandoned party would obviously be excellent proof that no consent to the departure existed.

(5) Absence of Justification

Not all departures from the marital abode will be sufficient to give rise to a cause of action for divorce, even though they are intentional and the remaining spouse does not consent to the departure. Conduct on the part of the remaining party can be such as to justify the departing spouse's action. If this conduct rises to the level, itself, of a ground for divorce the absenting spouse may avail herself or himself of the South Carolina version of the doctrine of "constructive desertion." If there is justification for the departure, but there is not an independent ground for divorce establishable, neither party may use desertion as the basis for a divorce.

(a) Constructive Desertion

Constructive desertion was nominally approved by the Supreme Court in *Machado v. Machado*, 220 S.C. 90, 66 S.E. 2d 629 (1951). The Court did not there determine what conduct would be necessary on the part of the offending spouse to permit the other to claim constructive desertion. However, it did determine that there was no constructive desertion by Mr. Machado due to a number of circumstances. Chief among these were that the parties had signed a separation agreement (which was proof that the separation had become mutually agreeable) and they had cohabited at his brother's house after the date on which Mrs. Machado said the desertion had occurred. In *Mincey v. Mincey*, 224 S.C. 520, 80 S.E.2d 123 (1954), the Court resolved the issue, holding that only conduct which would otherwise amount to a ground for divorce would be sufficient to allow a spouse who chose to cease cohabitation to make a technical deserter out of the other. The Court wrote:

> In order to constitute constructive desertion, the abandoning party seeking to make a technical deserter out of the one abandoned, must establish misconduct on the part of the other in itself, and independently, amounting to one or more of the recognized permitted grounds for divorce. The conduct complained of must in itself be a sufficient cause for divorce, one or more of the four grounds permitted by the constitutional amendment.

Id. at 531, 80 S.E.2d at 129.

The Court was careful in both *Machado* and *Mincey* to point out that the conduct of the husbands, while falling short of that which would permit their wives to obtain divorces, was such as to justify the wives' departure, from the marital abode and hence sufficient to permit awards of separate maintenance. By implication neither husband would, therefore, have been entitled to a divorce from his wife on the ground of her desertion because she was justified in leaving the home.

(b) Other Justifications

A spouse's failure to work and provide the necessities of life for the other spouse may justify a departure from the marital home. In *In re Duncan's Estate*, 190 S.C. 211, 2 S.E.2d 388 (1939), the Court indicated that the wife was justified in leaving the marital home where her husband had refused to work and provide the necessities of life. The other factor cited as justification was the husband's ill treatment of the wife, but the nature of this mistreatment is not specified in the opinion.

A failure to provide reasonable living conditions could be sufficient justification to leave a spouse. Choice of the marital abode in South Carolina is for the husband to decide (at least until challenged on equal protection grounds), and a wife will ordinarily be a deserter if she fails to follow her spouse wherever he might determine it appropriate to live. The other side of this coin is that a husband is required to provide a reasonable living situation for the wife, and his failure to do so will justify her in leaving his bed and board even though it is not ordinarily sufficient to constitute him a constructive deserter. These rules are rather completely spelled out and have essentially been in force in South Carolina since colonial times. Since the decision of the United States Supreme Court in *Orr v. Orr*, 440 U.S. 268, 99 S.Ct. 1102, 59 L.Ed.2d 306 (1979), however, this doctrine may be viewed with legitimate suspicion. *Cf. Crosby v. Crosby*, 434 So.2d 162 (La. 1983) (holding unconstitutional in light of *Orr* a Louisiana statute that set forth the mutual obligations of husbands and wives, including the obligation of the wife to follow the husband wherever he chose to reside).

Making life intolerable for a spouse might justify the departure of that spouse. *See Smith v. Smith*, 260 S.C. 65, 194 S.E. 2d 199 (1973) (the husband committed unspecified abusive treatment and made threats against his wife's life).

South Carolina cases make an interesting distinction between conduct engaged in by one of the spouses (ordinarily the husband) and conduct engaged in by the spouse's live-in relatives. According to what might be called "the Rule of the Cantankerous Mother-in-Law," one is required to accept more onerous conduct on the part of a spouse than on the part of his or her relatives. *See State v. Bagwell*, 125 S.C. 401, 118 S.E. 767 (1923), in which a husband was successfully prosecuted for nonsupport despite evidence that the wife had left the marital home. It was pointed out that she had done so only after the husband's mother (whose home it was) had called her a "red-headed whore" and a "red-headed bitch," among numerous other things. Justice Marin pointed out that a wife could not find justification for leaving the marital abode simply because a husband used abusive and insulting language, but that the same did not hold for the mother-in-law: "the wife's marital duty to put up with coarse and abusive language from a husband, whom she has taken for better or for worse, may not be extended to cover the tongue of a cantankerous mother-in-law." *Id.* at 405, 118 S.E. at 768.

The most recent substantial statement of the mutual obligations of husband and wife in South Carolina is found in the first of two Inabinet cases, *Inabinet v. Inabinet*, 236 S.C. 52, 113 S.E.2d 66 (1960):

> It is the duty of a husband to provide for his wife, in accordance with his means, a home wherein she may live as the object of his care and affection without interference from members of the household; and if he fails or refuses to provide such a home she will be justified in leaving and will not be guilty of desertion if she does so. She marries him, not his family .... Her obligation to be tolerant, within reason, of his shortcomings is one thing; her right to freedom from ill-treatment, nagging, and unwarranted interference on the part of his parents, is another.
>
> . . .
>
> Each case of this kind must be decided on its own circumstances, which should be considered as a whole.

Id. at 56, 113 S.E.2d at 68 (citations omitted).

Although disruptive relatives may justify one spouse's leaving the marital home, their presence does not justify one spouse ordering the other to leave. In *Thomas v. Thomas*, 182 S.C. 16, 188 S.E. 367 (1936), the Court held that the wife did not desert the husband when she left the marital home at his insistence because he was unhappy about the presence of unwanted relatives of the wife in the home. The Court noted that he had the power to order the relatives to leave, but he should not have ordered the wife to leave and refused to support her.

5. PHYSICAL CRUELTY

a. In General

Some sort of physical violence is required to give rise to a cause of action for a divorce upon the ground of physical cruelty. The nature of conduct that will give rise to a cause of action as physical cruelty was defined in *Brown v. Brown*, 215 S.C. 502, 56 S.E.2d 330 (1949) (*Brown I*), as "actual personal violence, or such a course of physical treatment as endangers life, limb, or health, and renders cohabitation unsafe." This definition is followed by *Gambrell v. Gambrell*, 295 S.C. 457, 460,

369 S.E.2d 662, 663 (Ct. App. 1988); *Canady v. Canady*, 289 S.C. 512, 514, 347 S.E.2d 115, 117 (Ct. App. 1986); *Gibson v. Gibson*, 283 S.C. 318, 322, 322 S.E.2d 680, 682 (Ct. App. 1984). It must be noted, however, that the case decisions have emphasized that the determination of whether conduct constitutes physical cruelty is "governed by the particular circumstances of each case." *Crowden v. Crowden*, 246 S.C. 299, 143 S.E.2d 580 (1965). Furthermore, numerous interpretations of the *Brown I* definition of physical cruelty alter its scope under certain factual situations.

South Carolina courts make frequent reference to *Brown I* in physical cruelty cases. There, in addition to claiming adultery, the wife claimed physical cruelty against the husband, with no greater success than she had in establishing the former. The wife's testimony was that she was slapped twice during the marriage and was once caused pain when her husband pinched her. In denying the divorce, the Court wrote in language which has often been quoted since:

> Physical cruelty, as used in divorce law, has generally been defined by our courts as actual personal violence, or such a course of physical treatment as endangers life, limb or health, and renders cohabitation unsafe. With this definition, we are in accord. In determining what acts constitute cruelty under our statute authorizing a divorce, regard must be had, not only to the provisions of the statute, but also to the circumstances of each particular case.
>
> Continued acts of personal violence producing physical pain or bodily injury and a fear of future danger are recognized as sufficient cause for a divorce for cruelty in nearly all jurisdictions, especially where accompanied by other acts of ill treatment. 27 C.J.S., *Divorce*, § 26, page 549. It is not every slight violence, however, committed by the husband or wife against the other, even in anger, which will authorize the divorce.
>
> It is generally held that a single act of physical cruelty does not ordinarily constitute ground for divorce, unless it is so severe and atrocious as to endanger life, or unless the act indicates an intention to do serious bodily harm or causes reasonable apprehension of serious danger in the future. A single act of aggravated cruelty may,

> however, warrant a divorce if accompanied with such precedent or attendant circumstances as to satisfy the court that such acts are likely to be repeated. 27 C.J.S., *Divorce*, § 258, page 548; *Phinizy v. Phinizy*, 154 Ga. 199, 114 S.E. 185; *Smith v. Smith*, 125 W. Va. 489, 24 S.E. 2d 902; *Nye's Appeal*, 126 Pa. 341, 17 A. 618, 12 Am. St. Rep. 873; Annotation, 65 Am. St. Rep. 69.
>
> However, as courts are loath to grant a divorce for a single act of physical violence by one of the married parties to the other as constituting such cruelty as will justify a decree for divorce, the facts and circumstances accompanying its infliction should be fully laid before the court; a full history of the assault should be given.
>
> The burden was upon the plaintiff to make good of physical cruelty by the preponderance of the evidence, by detailing what went before and what followed the physical violence of which she complained.

215 S.C. at 508, 56 S.E.2d at 333.

b. Conduct Constituting Cruelty

Although "slight violence" ordinarily does not constitute physical cruelty, the appellate courts have held in some instances that a single episode of violence may warrant a divorce. In *McDowell v. McDowell*, 300 S.C. 96, 386 S.E.2d 468 (Ct. App. 1989), the Court of Appeals stated, "[a] single assault by one spouse upon the other spouse can constitute physical cruelty. The assault must, however, be life threatening or must be either indicative of an intention to do serious bodily harm or of such a degree as to raise a reasonable apprehension of great bodily harm in the future." *McDowell* involved a husband who obtained a divorce on the grounds of physical cruelty because his wife had shot him once in the chest at pointblank range. Another example of physical cruelty based on a single assault and/or battery is found in *McKenzie v. McKenzie*, 254 S.C. 372, 175 S.E.2d 628 (1970), where the wife shot her husband in the chest as he was leaving a social club.

It should be noted that *McKenzie* and *McDowell* are rare instances where the courts have granted a divorce on a single assault/battery. *Brown I* emphasizes their reluctance to do so stating that "courts are loath to grant a divorce for a single act of physical violence by one of the married parties to the other as constituting such cruelty as will justify a decree for divorce, the facts and circumstances accompanying its infliction should be fully laid before the court; a full history of the assault should be given." *Brown*, 215 S.C. at 509, 56 S.E.2d at 334.

It was not until 1984 that South Carolina courts recognized that a single assault by one spouse upon the other spouse (not accompanied by a battery or actual bodily injury) might constitute a basis for a divorce on the ground of physical cruelty. However, the violence directed at the plaintiff must be sufficient to put him or her reasonably in fear of his or her bodily integrity. In *Gibson v. Gibson*, 283 S.C. 318, 322 S.E.2d 680 (Ct. App. 1984), a wife, after arguing with her husband, went to her bedroom and fired 16 shots through her closed door with a .22 caliber rifle. None of the bullets struck the husband, but he did claim that a "small splinter" hit him after she fired the first shot. The husband went to work following the incident and the wife subsequently set fire to the home, severely damaging it. The Court wrote, "[w]e therefore hold that if the wrongful act involves actual violence directed by one spouse at the other, 'bodily injury' is not required in order to find 'physical cruelty.'" *Id.* at 323, 322 S.E.2d at 683. However, the Court of Appeals did not decide whether Mr. Gibson was entitled to a divorce. It remanded the case for further proceedings in light of the opinion, saying: "Here, there is evidence that the wife committed an act of actual violence. She discharged a firearm. What is not clear, however, is whether she committed an act of actual personal violence, i.e., whether the wife directed actual violence at her husband." *Id.* at 323-24, 322 S.E.2d at 683.

Thus, if a single assault by one spouse upon the other spouse is relied on as the basis for a divorce, the assault must be life threatening or it must either indicate an intention to do serious bodily harm or raise a reasonable apprehension of great bodily harm in the future.

c. Conduct Not Constituting Cruelty

"Slight violence" will not suffice to obtain a divorce for physical cruelty. In *Anders v. Anders*, 285 S.C. 512, 331 S.E.2d 340 (1985), the Court stated held that one instance where the husband pushed his wife after an argument was not enough to warrant a finding of physical cruelty. Other cases where the courts have denied a divorce where only "slight violence" occurred are *Wood v. Wood*, 269 S.C. 600, 239 S.E.2d 315 (1977) (husband "manhandled" wife, occasionally forcing her to sit in a chair and backing her into corners "to make her listen to him"); *Gill v. Gill*, 269 S.C. 337, 237 S.E.2d 382 (1977) (wife possibly attacked husband at a hotel room on one occasion, rammed her car into his truck on another, and another time threatened him with a BB pistol (he admitted he was not afraid)); *Barstow v. Barstow*, 223 S.C. 136, 74 S.E.2d 541 (1953) (wife nagged and abused the husband and struck him with the spike of a high-heel shoe); and *Jones v. Jones*, 270 S.C. 143, 241 S.E.2d 417 (1978) (wife claimed husband inflicted bruises and threatened her with a pistol).

In *Godwin v. Godwin*, 245 S.C. 370, 140 S.E.2d 593 (1965), the Court found that the husband was provoked into using physical violence by the wife. The provocation was the unjustified refusal by the wife to follow the husband to a new place of employment. The physical conduct complained of occurred when the husband came to the wife's aunt and uncle's house to discuss reconciliation (according to him). After he picked her up and carried her outside against her struggles, he grabbed her arm when she tried to turn away from him and he slapped her hard enough to leave a hand print (after she slapped him) in an attempt to "quiet her down." The Court denied her request for a divorce, relying on *Brown I* to hold that the evidence presented was not "sufficient to warrant any reasonable conclusion that such acts constituted physical cruelty." *Id.* at 377, 140 S.E.2d at 597.

> The alleged acts of physical cruelty upon which the appellant here relies were not of a violent or a serious nature, nor is it shown by the evidence that the acts of the respondent indicated an intention to do serious bodily harm to the appellant or to cause her reasonable apprehension of serious danger in the future. We cannot adopt a policy of awarding a divorce for slight or trivial causes. The testimony of the appellant does not show physical cruelty within the contemplation of our divorce statute.

Id.

A difference in size or physical strength may be considered in determining that physical violence is insufficient to warrant a divorce on the ground of physical cruelty. In a different *Brown v. Brown* case, 250 S.C. 114, 156 S.E. 2d 641 (1967) (*Brown II*), the husband claimed physical cruelty because his wife restricted his physical freedom of movement when he was attempting to make a telephone call and she scratched him across the face. She admitted that she scratched him after pushing him aside when he blocked her access to the bedroom, but she claimed he provoked her by twisting her arm. A policeman called to the scene by the wife agreed that there were some scratches on the husband's face, but he testified that they were not serious. Another incident was not corroborated and the testimony of the parties regarding it was characterized by the Court as being "hopelessly in conflict."

After again quoting from *Brown I*, the Court pointed out that the husband was five feet, eleven inches tall and weighed two hundred twenty pounds. The Court stated that "[t]he courts seem to be particularly skeptical of the existence of fear or danger where a husky husband, in good health, is complaining of physical cruelty on the part of his frail consort." *Brown*, 250 S.C. at 121, 156 S.E.2d at 645. It continued by pointing out that there were no observable facts from which fear on the part of the husband could reasonably be inferred (i.e., he did not call the police, he lodged no complaint, and he admitted that he could have walked away from any of the incidents with his wife), thus implying that, had the husband in fact felt fear, it would at least have been a relevant consideration. At the same time, though, the tenor of the discussion was that the husband could hardly have been reasonable in feeling fearful under the circumstances. The Court concluded its discussion of this aspect of the case by observing that each party had provoked cruel conduct on the part of the other, after noting that "[t]he general unpleasantness of the wife is a risk assumed by the husband with marriage; however, it is not a statutory ground for divorce." *Id.*

A conspiracy to murder a spouse is not physical cruelty if no attempt is made to carry out the plan. In *Sharpe v. Sharpe*, 307 S.C. 540, 416 S.E.2d 215 (Ct. App. 1992), the Court of Appeals denied a husband a divorce on the ground of physical cruelty where the wife formulated a conspiracy to murder him. The attempt failed when the husband learned of the plan. Had the wife actually reach the level of attacking her husband with a lethal weapon (similar to *Gibson*) the appellate court may have ruled differently.

A denial of sex does not constitute physical cruelty. In *Vickers v. Vickers*, 255 S.C. 25, 176 S.E.2d 561 (1970), the Court held that a denial of sex does not constitute physical cruelty, even where it is alleged that the denial threatens the mental health of the plaintiff. The Court emphasized the *Brown I* definitional elements of personal violence and causes of physical mistreatment, stating that treating the husband with coldness and contempt and refusing to have sexual relations with him did not fit that definition.

A nagging wife is not physical cruelty, even if it prevents sleep. *Lindsey v. Lindsey*, 246 S.C. 282, 143 S.E.2d 524 (1965), involved a husband who maintained that he was unable to sleep due to continual nagging on the part of the wife. The Supreme Court decided that this constituted no more than incompatibility between the parties. The Court was clearly unwilling to let a form of mental cruelty creep into our divorce statute by the device — adopted in some other states — of looking to the effect upon the plaintiff of non-physical conduct on the part of the defendant.

6. HABITUAL DRUNKENNESS AND DRUG ABUSE

a. In General

S.C. Code Ann. § 20-3-10 (Law. Co-op. 1976) provides that "[n]o divorce from the bonds of matrimony shall be granted except upon one or more of the following grounds, to wit: . . . (4) Habitual drunkenness: provided, that this ground shall be construed and include habitual drunkenness caused by the use of narcotic drug."

"In order to prove habitual drunkenness, there must be a showing that the abuse of alcohol caused the breakdown of the marriage and that such abuse existed at or near the time of filing for divorce. *Fisher v. Fisher*, 276 S.C. 375, 278 S.E.2d 780 (1981)." *Epperly v. Epperly*, 312 S.C. 411, 414, 440 S.E.2d 884, 885 (1994) (affirming the trial court's ruling that there was insufficient evidence of habitual drunkenness to grant a divorce).

b. Meaning of "Habitual Drunkenness"

There is no clear definition of "habitual drunkenness." The Supreme Court used one from Black's law dictionary in *Rooney v. Rooney*, 242 S.C. 503, 131 S.E. 2d 618 (1963), where it stated that habitual drunkenness is "the fixed habit of frequently getting drunk; but it does not necessarily imply continual drunkenness." *Id.* at 505, 131 S.E.2d at 619. It determined that the trial judge had ruled correctly in granting Mr. Rooney a divorce on the ground of Mrs. Rooney's habitual drunkenness. The facts were that she had had a serious drinking problem for several years leading up to the divorce action, quite frequently drinking a pint to a fifth of liquor a day. She had been hospitalized twice and diagnosed as an alcoholic, and witnesses referred to her as a drunk.

The Court of Appeals cited *Rooney* and used the same definition in *Karle v. Karle*, No. 92-UP-135 (S.C. Ct. App. 1992), in which it affirmed the family court's ruling that the wife had not proven habitual drunkenness, saying "[t]here was no testimony that the husband actually drank beer on a daily basis. Nothing in the record indicates the husband's beer drinking caused the break-up of the marriage or that his drinking affected his work." *Id.* at 2.

Thus, on the one had, it appears clear that a divorce can be obtained on this ground from a person who consumes a large amount of alcohol or other drugs and stays regularly intoxicated, such as the wife in *Rooney*; however, it is not clear what other circumstances would sustain a divorce for habitual drunkenness. The *Karle* opinion suggests that one must show drinking, if not drunkenness, on a daily basis.

Practitioners dealing with an allegation of habitual drunkenness would appear to be well-advised to seek testimony regarding the client's demeanor in different settings where alcoholic beverages were generally available in order to determine the extent of the defendant's aberrant behavior and his or her ability to refrain from such behavior in varying social conditions.

c. Extent of Habit

It should initially be noted that the statute speaks in terms of "habitual drunkenness" (including that brought on by the use of any narcotic drug) rather than alcoholism *per se*. In *Lee v. Lee*, 282 S.C. 76, 316 S.E.2d 435 (Ct. App. 1984), the Court of Appeals looked to the statute and the definition in *Rooney* and indicated ". . . one need not be an alcoholic to be guilty of habitual drunkenness. It is sufficient if the use or abuse of alcohol causes the breakdown of normal marital relations." *Id.* at 79, 316 S.E.2d at 437. It seems likely that one who is an admitted alcoholic would be subject to divorce under this statute, but no further effort should be made to equate the statutory term with the medical one.

As noted above, in *Rooney* the Court accepted evidence that the wife for several years prior to the commencement of the action had "a serious drinking problem" which increased to the point where she quite frequently was drinking a pint to a fifth of liquor a day. There was medical evidence that she had been diagnosed as being alcoholic, but the Court appeared to give as much weight to lay testimony that the wife had generally been "just a plain drunk." *Rooney*, 242 S.C. 503, 505, 131 S.E.2d 618, 619.

In *Lee v. Lee*, the Court of Appeals looked to the frequency of the habit when it indicated that "[t]he record provides more than one instance in which Mr. Lee was required to provide assistance to Mrs. Lee when she was publicly intoxicated and unable to return home. These situations would occur during the day and were a source of considerable embarrassment to Mr. Lee. Mr. Lee's testimony as to Mrs. Lee's habitual drunkenness was corroborated by the parties' neighbors." *Lee*, 282 S.C. at 79, 316 S.E.2d at 437. The Court held the divorce was properly granted to Mr. Lee based upon the preponderance of the evidence. *See also Bailey v. Bailey*, 283 S.C. 482, 323 S.E.2d 63 (Ct. App. 1984), where the wife was granted a divorce based on the husband's habitual drunkenness. The husband drank a pint of liquor daily.

In *Fisher v. Fisher*, 276 S.C. 375, 278 S.E.2d 780 (1981), the wife petitioned for divorce on ground of habitual drunkenness or, in the alternative, for separate support and maintenance. The Supreme Court held the following testimony established a *prima facie* case of habitual drunkenness according to the *Rooney* case.

> (1) Appellant testified respondent drinks every weekend and frequently during the week, that he goes on drinking binges and that he drinks approximately one-half gallon of liquor during such periods;

(2) Respondent admitted to drinking moderately and as much as one-half gallon of liquor over a weekend. He concedes he has on occasion gone on drinking binges;

(3) A private investigator testified that when he served "the petition of divorce, respondent both sounded and acted as if he were under the influence of alcohol as early as 11 am.";

(4) Appellant testified that while drinking, respondent has: cursed her in the presence of their three-year old son; physically struck her; and has ordered her and the minor child to leave the marital home on several occasions.

Id. at 377, 278 S.E.2d at 781. From this case it appears that the courts are to look into the amount of drinking and its effect, as well as the frequency of imbibing.

In *Herbert v. Herbert*, 260 S.C. 86, 194 S.E.2d 238 (1973), the Supreme Court noted the ambivalence with which society views alcoholism, pointing out its invidiousness but noting as well the harm it can cause to innocent spouses and families. It affirmed as within the discretion of the trial judge an award of alimony based on a finding that the wife's drunkenness should not be "used as the basis for determining real moral wrongdoing on her part." *Id.* at 91, 194 S.E.2d at 240.

In *Grubbs v. Grubbs*, 272 S.C. 138, 249 S.E.2d 747 (1978), the wife sought a divorce on the grounds of physical cruelty and/or adultery. The husband counterclaimed on the grounds of habitual drunkenness or habitual use of drugs and/or adultery. The family court denied both parties a divorce and made certain awards of relief for the wife. The Supreme Court agreed with the family court in denying the husband a divorce on the ground of habitual drug use. The Court opined, "[w]hile the husband produced evidence of his wife's use of die't pills, we do not believe he established she was sufficiently dependent on drugs to classify her as a habitual user or that her use continued up to the time of trial. Accordingly, this contention is without merit." *Id.* at 141, 249 S.E.2d at 749. The opinion cited to the *Simonds* case (discussed below) and would seem to indicate that the Court will hold the habitual drug user to a similar standard.

d. Duration of Habit

The condition must exist at or near the time of filing for divorce. This issue was the principal one with which *Simonds v. Simonds*, 229 S.C. 376, 93 S.E.2d 107 (1956) was concerned. The husband who was charged with habitual drunkenness had admittedly been "totally abstemious" for approximately one year prior to the commencement of the action. In keeping with the approach of most jurisdictions, the Supreme Court held that habitual drunkenness, to be a ground for divorce, must "exist at or near the time of the filing of the action for a divorce." *Id.* at 381, 93 S.E.2d at 110. Thus, the wife was not entitled to a divorce upon the ground of habitual drunkenness. *See also Gambrell v. Gambrell*, 295 S.C. 457, 369 S.E.2d 662 (Ct. App. 1988) (denying a divorce where the wife failed to establish that the husband had a drinking problem at or near the time the action was filed); *Lee v. Lee*, 282 S.C. 76, 316 S.E.2d 435 (Ct. App. 1984) (sustaining a divorce where the wife's bouts of drunkenness occurred for several years, continuing at least until the separation hearing).

How long a habit of becoming drunk must continue before it becomes "habitual" has not been much addressed by the courts or commentators. It is typically not separated out from the general definitional issue, although several states' statutes do specify a time period (generally one year). No South Carolina case has dealt with the question, so practitioners must depend upon general sources such as the definition quoted from Black's Dictionary earlier indicating the need for a "fixed habit." Such cases as have dealt with the issue elsewhere have indicated simply that a few instances of becoming intoxicated will not suffice. Such holdings seem superfluous in view of the statutory mandate of habitualness. *See* E.W.H., Annotation, *What Amounts to Habitual Intemperance, Drunkenness, etc., Within Statute Relating to Substantive Grounds for Divorce*, 120 A.L.R. 1176 (1939); C.C. Marvel, Annotation, *What Amounts to Habitual Intemperance, Drunkenness and the Like Within Statute Relating Substantive Grounds for Divorce*, 29 A.L.R.2d 925 (1953).

Finally, it should be noted that the South Carolina courts' conclusion that the marital offense must continue until substantially the time of the filing for the divorce would seem to point to this jurisdiction's having accepted the idea that habitual drunkenness is a continuing offense (as opposed to a single occurrence offense, like adultery). This has consequences when one is considering possible defenses.

F. DEFENSES NOT RELATED TO PROOF OF THE GROUNDS FOR DIVORCE: COLLUSION, CONNIVANCE, RECRIMINATION, CONDONATION, RECONCILIATION, PROVOCATION AND INSANITY

1. COLLUSION

"If it shall appear to the satisfaction of the court that the parties to any divorce proceeding colluded or that the act complained of was done with the knowledge or assent of the plaintiff for the purpose of obtaining a divorce the court shall not grant such divorce." S.C. Code Ann. § 20-3-20 (Law. Co-op. 1976).

Problems regarding collusion are, as a practical matter, not very likely to arise today. However, collusion was a significant issue during the period when desertion was a frequent ground for divorce and no fault divorces were not yet allowed. Desertion was viewed by many spouses in unhappy marriages as the least messy way out of the situation. It was almost impossible for the courts to identify abuses when the parties would testify that one spouse left against the will of the other and that the abandoned spouse continued to want the other to return. In fact, the extent of collusion in establishing desertion grounds was a significant motivation for the adoption of no fault divorce in South Carolina. Nonetheless, there is still a statutory ban on collusive divorces so we must pay some attention to it.

South Carolina has not undertaken to define collusion in the context of marital litigation. However, it has been defined in a case involving insurance fraud as "fraud which, in judicial proceedings, is a secret agreement between two persons that one should institute suit against the other in order to obtain the decision of a judicial tribunal for some sinister purpose, or on perjured testimony." 13 S.C. Juris. *Divorce* § 17 (S.C. Bar — C.L.E. Division 1992) (citing *Walker v. New Amsterdam Cas. Co.*, 157 S.C. 381, 154 S.E. 221 (1930)). In West's Ann. Civ. Code (Cal.) § 114, one finds: "Collusion is an agreement between a husband and wife that one of them shall commit, or appear to have committed, or to be represented in court as having committed, acts constituting a cause of divorce, for the purpose of enabling the other to obtain a divorce."

Note that there are two principal facets to the above: first, that there must be an *agreement* between the spouses; second, that the agreement must have to do with the substance of the act or acts alleged to be the ground for divorce. Thus, a defaulting defendant does not interpose a barrier to the divorce on the grounds of collusion, nor does one ordinarily participate in collusion by procedural acts undertaken to facilitate the speedy granting of a divorce, once the underlying substantive marital fault has already taken place. *See Mitchell v. Mitchell*, 312 Ky. 810, 229 S.W.2d 967 (1950) (holding that the husband's decision to forego defense of the divorce action and to seek prompt resolution of the case did not amount to collusion).

Nationally there have been many problems with the collusion defense to divorce. One can anticipate, however, that issues related to collusion will become increasingly rare in light of widespread "no fault" or voluntary separation-based decrees. The reason for this is that the statutory changes represent an alteration in public policy. It has always been assumed that the state is vitally interested in the maintenance of the marriage relation. While "no fault" divorce does not alter this, it does represent a recognition that the state might in some circumstances better serve the goal of promoting human welfare by permitting the parties to say that their relationship is over and done rather than by condemning them willy-nilly to continue to live in a dead relationship. If this is the case, collusion is no longer of very great significance since its primary function was to vindicate the integrity of the judicial system by preventing the parties from improperly invoking the court's jurisdiction absent a true adversary contest which could be relied upon to provide access to the facts.

At the same time, the public policy in South Carolina is that spouses who mutually want a divorce should not be allowed to have one without proving marital fault until they have been living separate and apart for one year. Therefore, collusion in an effort to obtain an earlier divorce would presumably still run afoul of both the statute and underlying public policy.

2. CONNIVANCE

The defense of connivance probably exists in South Carolina. S.C. Code Ann. § 20-3-20 (Law. Co-op. 1976) says: "If it shall appear to the satisfaction of the court that the parties to any divorce proceeding colluded *or that the act complained of was done with the knowledge or assent of the plaintiff for the purpose of obtaining a divorce* the court shall not grant such divorce." (emphasis added)

This, coupled with an understanding of the general definition of the term, indicates that connivance is a recognized defense to a divorce action in South Carolina. In addition, South Carolina having adopted the English common law and connivance being a nonstatutory defense in ecclesiastical practice, it has been adopted to the extent that other domestic equity practice short of divorce has been received into the common law of South Carolina. *See generally* 6 S.C. Juris, *Common Law* (S.C. Bar - C.L.E. Division 1991).

> Connivance in the law of divorce is the complainant's consent, express or implied, to the misconduct alleged as a ground for divorce. A corrupt intent on the part of the complainant that the party at fault should engage in misconduct is generally considered to be an essential element of connivance. If the consent was actively given, the intent is impliedly corrupt and the defense is complete.

C.J.S. *Divorce* § 86 (1986).

Although it is true that the defense of connivance is most often associated with the charge of adultery, it can be raised in other contexts. *See Greene v. Greene*, 15 N.C. 314, 190 S.E.2d 258 (1972), where the connivance consisted of a husband employing prostitutes to induce his wife to perform abnormal sex acts; and *Muir v. Muir*, 46 Del. 578, 86 A.2d 857 (1952), which held that the connivance defense to habitual drunkenness was not established by evidence that the husband knew of his wife's weakness for alcohol and made it available to her.

The defense obviously has certain similarities to that of collusion. The most obvious distinction lies in the fact that only one spouse needs to be planning for or agreeing to the commission of the marital offense to establish connivance, while collusion requires that both be participants with ill motives. Additionally, the presentation of a collusive divorce may involve fabrication of the entire marital offense. The presentation of a divorce wherein connivance is a reasonable defense will necessarily involve the actual commission of a marital wrong. To an extent, both defenses come about as a result of the state's obligation to keep its court system free from mistaken decisions and to prevent the misleading of judicial officers.

From the perspective of the effect of the defense on marital litigants, it is less easy to see the justification. Presumably if one spouse is willing to commit a marital offense and the other is willing to consent to it or arrange for it, there is not much left in the marriage to preserve. However, it is possible that a scheming spouse could arrange a situation in which the other spouse would succumb to temptation even though that spouse was genuinely desirous of maintaining the marriage relation. To the extent that the law of divorce is supposed to continue to contain an element of punishment for spouses who are "guilty," it thus makes sense to maintain the defense of connivance.

As both the South Carolina statute and the general definition reflect, the essential element of connivance is the finding of the corrupt consent of one spouse to the commission of a marital wrong by the other spouse. Ordinarily, this "wrong" must, of course, be one which would be a ground for divorce (otherwise, to what is the defense a defense?). The consent may be active or passive in manifestation but cannot rise from mere negligence. *See McMillan v. McMillan*, 120 Fla. 209, 162 So. 524 (1934). As might be expected, the cases are not entirely uniform on this, and there are some to be found which claim that active participation by the spouse against whom the defense is raised in the commission of the marital wrong will be necessary. *See Hayden v. Hayden*, 326 Mass. 587, 96 N.E.2d 136 (1950). Since the principal function of the defense these days is really to serve as a form of "club," in which the spouse raising the defense, or potentially able to raise it, is able to extract more favorable terms from the other spouse because of its existence, it seems desirable to give it a relatively narrow interpretation so that it will not be utilized except in those cases where it would be manifestly unjust to penalize a basically innocent but deceived spouse. Another situation in which the defense has proved useful to a few courts is that in which the spouses have participated in obtaining a void divorce, one of them remarries, and the other brings a suit for divorce in a proper forum based upon the adultery of the remarried spouse. *See Shannon v. Shannon*, 286 N.Y.S. 27

(N.Y App. Div. 1936). Perhaps it would be more logical to apply a straightforward estoppel doctrine in these situations than to call the problem one of connivance.

3. RECRIMINATION

The statute providing for a no fault divorce (S.C. Code Ann. § 20-3-10(5) (Law. Co-op. 1976)) specifies that recrimination is not a defense to the maintenance of an action for divorce based upon one year's separation. It is commonly assumed throughout the Bar that the defense of recrimination is otherwise effective in South Carolina.

The Court of Appeals, citing 24 Am. Jur. 2d *Divorce and Separation* § 226 (1966), defined recrimination stating, "[a]s a general rule, to constitute the defense of recrimination, the misconduct of which the plaintiff is guilty must be such as to provide the defendant with grounds for divorce." *Allen v. Allen*, 287 S.C. 501, 339 S.E.2d 872 (Ct. App. 1986). *Allen* involved a husband who sought a divorce on the basis of adultery and physical cruelty. In her answer, the wife raised the defense of recrimination, alleging desertion on part of the husband. The court found this defense ineffective because the husband had not deserted the home for one year as required by S.C. Code Ann. § 20-3-10(2) (Law. Co-op. 1976).

Although recrimination is recognized as a valid defense in South Carolina, the doctrine, even if established in a divorce proceeding, can easily be circumvented if a no fault divorce is proven. S.C. Code Ann. § 20-3-10(5) (Law. Co-op. 1976) provides that "[a] plea of . . . recrimination with respect to any other provision of this section shall not be a bar to either party obtaining a divorce on this ground [one-year separation]." The principal case applying this rule is *Spires v. Spires*, 296 S.C. 422, 373 S.E.2d 698 (Ct. App. 1988), where the wife pled recrimination as a defense to her husband's request for divorce. The court found that both parties had committed adultery and then overcame the normal effect of a recrimination defense by granting a divorce on the ground of one year separation.

Spires also held that "recrimination is not a proper defense to the statutory bar to alimony" and terminated the alimony awarded by the trial judge. *Id.* at 423, 373 S.E.2d at 699. The wife had pled recrimination as a defense to her husband's cause of action which asked that alimony be barred under S.C. Code Ann. § 20-3-130 (Law. Co-op. 1976) ("no alimony shall be granted an adulterous spouse"). The Court of Appeals did not comply with the wife's request stating, "[r]ecrimination does not constitute an exception to this statute. We hold the violation of the law by one's spouse does not justify nor give license to the other to violate the same law without penalty." *Id.* Followed by *R.G.M. v. D.E.M.*, 306 S.C. 145, 410 S.E.2d 564 (Ct. App. 1991).

For those inclined to an interest in history that has given rise to the existence of the doctrine, a good account will be found in Beamer, *Recrimination in Divorce Proceedings*, 10 Kan. City L. Rev. 213 (1942). There is extensive additional literature on the subject, almost all of it highly critical. This is presumably for the reason that it is difficult to envision the social improvement likely to result from forcing two persons to remain in a marriage which is so dead that both of them have committed acts which are grounds for divorce. The vindictive notion that they should be left in the beds that they have made and not unleash them upon the rest of the world has a certain gruff appeal but no longer seems compatible with our understanding of how human interaction works. *See* Note, *Recrimination and Alimony — Are They Compatible*, 13 Syra. L. Rev. 562 (1962); Annotation, *Fault of Spouse as Affecting Right to Divorce Under Statute Making Separation a Substantive Ground of Divorce*, 14 A.L.R.3d 502 (1967).

In any event, it is ordinarily the case that recrimination may arise from any conduct which has not been condoned and which would independently be sufficient as a ground of divorce itself. *See Jeffords v. Jeffords*, 216 S.C. 451, 58 S.E.2d 731 (1950). For additional cases, *see* Annotation, *Recrimination as an Absolute or Unqualified Defense in Divorce Cases*, 170 A.L.R. 1076 (1946). The time at which the recriminatory offense occurs is not limited to that time prior to the filing of the action for divorce; it can accrue up to the time of the granting of the decree. *See* Annotation, *Subsequent Adultery as Recrimination Defense to Desertion or Cruelty*, 101 A.L.R. 646 (1936). *See also Roddis v. Roddis*, 18 Wis.2d 118, 118 N.W.2d 109 (1962), where an interlocutory divorce decree had prohibited remarriage within one year. The wife remarried after eleven months, proving her adultery. The husband obtained a vacation of the interlocutory decree which had been granted on the basis of his cruel and inhumane treatment.

As the case of *Pride v. Pride*, 269 S.C. 70, 236 S.E.2d 404 (1977), points out, condonation of a marital offense will ordinarily deprive the condoner of the use of that offense as a basis for raising the defense of recrimination as well as the ability to raise it as an affirmative ground upon which to base an action for divorce. In *Pride*, the wife had committed adultery and the husband had committed physical cruelty. However, the Court found that the husband's acts of cruelty were condoned and the wife failed to prove any other ground for divorce. The Court, therefore, refused to consider whether a defense of recrimination could exist to bar the divorce. The husband did not condone the wife's adultery; therefore, he was awarded the divorce and she was barred from alimony. Thus, condonation can be effectively employed either as a defense to a divorce or as a reply to the defense of recrimination.

For a more detailed discussion of the recrimination defense *see* "An Examination of the Recrimination Doctrine," 20 S.C.L.Rev. 685 (1968). The author of that article concludes that the doctrine of recrimination will eventually go the way of the dinosaur because the questionable merits of the rule are outweighed by its objectional features (encouraging illicit alliances and pre-divorce blackmail and perpetuating the unhappiness of mismated couples).

4. CONDONATION

Condonation is one of the most important defenses in South Carolina marital litigation. Proof of condonation will not only defeat a divorce action brought on a fault ground, it will also (as was pointed out in the section on recrimination) suffice to destroy the recriminatory defense if the conduct condoned is the same conduct alleged to constitute the recriminatory act.

a. Elements

The basic elements needed to establish the defense of condonation are forgiveness, a mutual intention to renew the full marital relationship, usually cohabitation, and full knowledge of the marital offense. 27A C.J.S. *Divorce* § 81 (1986).

In the leading South Carolina case on condonation, *McLaughlin v. McLaughlin*, 244 S.C. 265, 136 S.E.2d 537 (1964), the Court approvingly quoted from 27A C.J.S. *Divorce* § 59 (1986) stating, "[c]ondonation in the law of divorce means forgiveness, express or implied, by one spouse for a breach of marital duty by the other. More specifically, it is the forgiveness of an antecedent matrimonial offense on condition that it shall not be repeated, and that the offender shall thereafter treat the forgiving party with conjugal kindness." *Id.* at 272, 136 S.E.2d at 540.

The defense is as old as our jurisprudence. *See Hair v. Hair*, 31 S.C. Eq. (10 Rich. Eq.) 163 (1858), where the Court held that the wife deserted her husband by not following him to Louisiana (even though he left at midnight, taking their slaves and money with him) but that the husband had condoned her desertion when he attempted to reconcile with her, promising conjugal affection if she returned to Louisiana with him. Her refusal to do so voided the condonation and alimony was disallowed. In *Thompson v. Thompson*, 32 S.C. Eq. (10 Rich. Eq.) 416 (1859), after a long separation, the husband moved back into the house with his wife for one week. This was held to have condoned his misconduct which occurred prior to the brief reconciliation. The continuing vitality of the defense was reaffirmed in *Rabon v. Rabon*, 289 S.C. 49, 344 S.E.2d 615 (Ct. App. 1986), which held that the husband's threats to kill the wife and his choking of her had been condoned. However, these were revived as grounds when he committed additional, albeit less serious, acts of violence against her.

On the question of whether sexual intercourse alone can be sufficient evidence of condonation, South Carolina's position is not without some degree of ambiguity. However, it appears clear that more than sexual intercourse (i.e., attendant forgiveness, proved somehow) is needed to establish the defense in South Carolina. In *Wilson v. Wilson*, 274 S.C. 236, 262 S.E.2d 732 (1980), the Supreme Court has written, "[condonation] is primarily a state of mind, the existence of which may appear either from the language used, from conduct, or both. The presence or lack of sexual access is a pertinent factor in determining that requisite state of mind necessary for the existence of condonation." *Id.* at 238, 262 S.E.2d at 733 (the family court erroneously refused to allow evidence concerning lack of sexual access before ruling that condonation occurred by the parties continuing to share the same house for three months after the most recent episode of physical cruelty). *See also Horton v. Horton*, 282 S.C. 317, 317 S.E.2d 778 (Ct. App. 1984), which held that the wife's state of mind was such that condonation was not present. Even if she had condoned the husband's earlier acts of adultery, his later acts revived the first.

Thus, it would seem that in South Carolina it is necessary to prove principally the fact or act of forgiveness on the part of the injured spouse. It would further seem relevant to prove sexual intercourse when proving forgiveness and that there could be cases in which the circumstances surrounding the sexual intercourse proved would suffice to support proof of condonation. However, it would finally seem from the reference to "state of mind" that proof of an act of intercourse without more would not suffice, and that condonation could be proved without proving sexual intercourse. Nevertheless, it would seem that in most instances it would be unwise to attempt such a proof. If the purpose of the doctrine of condonation is, as most writers seem to believe, to give legal sanction to the view of the parties that they find themselves on the same footing in the marriage relationship as they were prior to the commission of the marital offense which has been condoned, the law ought to expect objective proof of the existence of the forgiving state. Under most circumstances, the best such objective proof will be the resumption of a normal pattern of marital life, which is ordinarily thought to include regular sexual intercourse.

Condonation can be implied by continuing to cohabit with a misbehaving spouse after learning of the misconduct. *See Grubbs v. Grubbs*, 272 S.C. 138, 140, 249 S.E.2d 747, 749 (1978) (ten years); *McLaughlin v. McLaughlin*, 244 S.C. 265, 136 S.E.2d 537 (1964) (approximately five years, during which the relationship was strained); *Doe v. Doe*, 286 S.C. 507, 334 S.E.2d 829 (Ct.App. 1985) (no length of time given in the opinion).

Condonation is not a valid defense unless the supposed condoner has full knowledge of the marital offense he or she is allegedly condoning, and not merely a suspicion that the marital offense has occurred. A presumption that a spouse has knowledge of the marital misconduct of the other spouse can be created by the passage of time, that is, the courts will assume knowledge of marital misconduct which occurred a long time ago. In *Grubbs*, the husband denied learning of the wife's adultery until shortly before the divorce proceedings; but the Court felt that he must have learned of it earlier and it held that the passage of ten years created a "presumption of condonation," thus shifting the burden of proof to the husband.

Actual knowledge of a marital offense, not a mere suspicion of it, is required before condonation will be found. In *Pride v. Pride*, 269 S.C. 70, 236 S.E.2d 404 (1977), the Supreme Court refused to find that the husband had condoned the adulterous activities of his wife by remaining in the marital home with her, although without having sexual relations, for a period of some two weeks after he gained final proof of her adulterous activities. The record also reflects that the husband had good cause to be suspicious of the wife's activities for a substantial period of time prior to his leaving. Thus, the case seems to stand for the sensible proposition that the putative condoner has to have actual knowledge of the existence of the marital offense he or she is allegedly condoning, not merely to have suspicions. This approach is sensible inasmuch as it is consistent with the obligation of the courts to encourage the marital state and thus to encourage continuance of the marriage by making it legally undesirable for parties to a marriage to separate as soon as either of them has suspicions of the other. *See also Thompson v. Thompson*, 31 S.C. Eq. (10 Rich. Eq.) 416 (1859), where after a long separation, the husband moved back into the house with his wife for one week. This was held to have condoned his misconduct which occurred prior to the brief reconciliation; *McLaughlin*, which held that the husband's losing his temper and leaving the room were not enough to let the wife revoke her condonation of his earlier physical cruelty.

b. Revival of Condoned Grounds by Subsequent Marital Misconduct

Condonation is a conditional forgiveness, the implied condition being that the guilty party shall in the future refrain from committing any matrimonial offense. Subsequent marital misconduct may revive the condoned conduct as a viable ground for divorce.

As noted in *Wilson v. Wilson*, 274 S.C. 236, 262 S.E.2d 732 (1980), an offender whose marital misconduct has been condoned is required to treat the forgiving party "with conjugal kindness." *Id.* at 238, 262 S.E.2d at 733. (The rule was restated in *Horton v. Horton*, 282 S.C. 317, 317 S.E.2d 778 (Ct. App. 1984).) The Supreme Court made it clear in *McLaughlin* that it is among those states which view condonation as a conditional forgiveness: "The authorities appear to be in agreement that condonation is a conditional forgiveness or remission of the previous offense or misconduct of the offending spouse, the implied condition being that the guilty party shall in the future refrain from committing any matrimonial offense." 244 S.C. at 275, 136 S.E.2d at 542.

McLaughlin raised the issue of whether the husband's acts of losing his temper and leaving the room constituted a sufficient failure to treat his plaintiff wife with conjugal kindness as required by *Wilson.* The Supreme Court held that these acts were not sufficient to negate the husband's defense of condonation to his alleged physical cruelty toward his plaintiff wife. The Court established that it would be possible to revive previously condoned offenses, and that the kind of conduct necessary to perform the revival need not in and of itself amount to a marital offense directly. Quoting from *Currence v. Currence*, 123 W. Va. 599, 18 S.E.2d 656 (1941), the Court stated:

> In order to revoke or nullify the condonation and revise [revive] the original offense as a cause for divorce, the subsequent conduct must be of such nature as to lead other party [sic] to reasonably believe that the original offense will be repeated or that some other act constituting a ground of divorce will be committed. 'No definition of such subsequent conduct is possible, but common sense and authority seem to require that it shall sink to the grade approaching a marital offense and partaking in at least a substantial degree of such an offense.'

McLaughlin, 244 S.C. at 275, 136 S.E.2d at 542. The Court relied upon the case of *Threewits v. Threewits*, 4 S.C. Eq. (4 DeSaus. Eq.) 558 (1815), wherein the Court wrote:

> To be sure, if a woman forgives ill usage and returns to her husband, on promises of good usage, she shall not afterwards obtain the protection and assistance of this Court, if those promises had [sic] been faithfully kept, and she again leaves her husband from caprice; but if there are clear indications of a breach of those promises, and some actual ill usage, she is not bound to wait for extremities as in the first instance, but may depart as soon as she finds the promises violated, and her husband returning to his old bad habits. She has a

> right to judge of the future by the past; and the Court will connect the whole of his conduct, in order to form a correct judgment.

Id. at 574.

The net effect of the these two cases seems to be that a forgiven spouse lies under a cloud to some extent, and that the necessity he or she faces to treat the other spouse with "conjugal kindness" imposes a requirement of somewhat more pleasant treatment than that which is ordinarily demanded of husband and wife (see the section on physical cruelty). This notion is reinforced in *Horton v. Horton*, 282 S.C. 317, 317 S.E.2d 778, 780 (Ct. App. 1984), in which the court noted that even if the wife is viewed as having condoned her husband's conduct originally, the condonation was nullified by his subsequent acts of adultery. *See also R.G.M. v. D.E.M.*, 306 S.C. 144, 410 S.E.2d 564 (Ct. App. 1991) (holding that appellant's continued lesbian activity revived the ground of adultery); *Rabon v. Rabon*, 289 S.C. 49, 344 S.E.2d 615 (Ct. App. 1986) (holding that the husband's first acts of physical cruelty were condoned by the wife, but the husband's subsequent cruel conduct revived the former act and they, together with the more recent incident of actual personal violence, provided a basis for divorce on the ground of physical cruelty).

In some jurisdictions there has been a debate over whether condonation should be allowed as a defense when the marital offense charged is physical cruelty. *See* Annotation, *Condonation of Cruel Treatment as Defense to Action for Divorce or Separation*, 32 A.L.R. 2d 107 (1953). In South Carolina, the case of *Rabon v. Rabon* (discussed above) makes it clear that physical cruelty can be condoned.

Some case decisions in other jurisdictions have suggested that condonation becomes irrefutable following the passage of a reasonable period of time. *See Niresi v. Niresi*, 229 Ark. 1059, 320 S.W.2d 757 (1959) (holding that condonation occurred when the separated husband and wife decided to cohabit for two more years before their separation).

5. RECONCILIATION

Reconciliation is similar to condonation. The major difference is that it does not necessarily involve the forgiveness of marital misconduct, e.g., reconciliation may occur following a period of separation which was prompted by a mutual feeling by spouses that they no longer loved each other. Another difference is that reconciliation is associated with ending a period of physical separation while condonation may occur while spouses are continuing to live together: "Reconciliation . . . means a resumption of marital cohabitation in its fullest sense, with the husband and wife resuming their status, positions, services, privileges and duties as marital partners in all material respects. Reconciliation is a matter of mutual intent to resume married life entirely . . . ." 27A C.J.S. *Divorce* § 85 (1986).

For practitioners, the most significant difference between reconciliation and condonation is that condonation is always conditional (the antecedent matrimonial offense is forgiven on condition that it shall not be repeated) whereas a true reconciliation is unconditional. As stated in C.J.S.:

> If the parties casually cohabit, or if the cohabitation is sporadic, conditional, or provisional, there is no reconciliation because of the absence of the required intent to settle their differences on a permanent basis. Thus, isolated acts of sexual intercourse between judicially separated spouses are not conclusive of an intent to reconcile, but are merely one of the factors to be considered in determining mutual consent and agreement to reconcile.

27A C.J.S. *Divorce* § 85 (1986).

The potential significance of this language has not yet been fully explored in South Carolina case decisions. The greatest impact of distinguishing between conditional, or trial, reconciliations and unconditional reconciliations might be with respect to no fault divorces. The particular issue is whether parties to an attempted reconciliation which fails should be required to wait another full twelve months before they can be divorced or whether they could add together the time before and after the failed reconciliation to meet the statutory twelve month requirement.

This question has not yet been addressed in South Carolina. In *Machado v. Machado*, 220 S.C. 90, 66 S.E.2d 629 (1951), the Supreme Court considered the impact of reconciliation on desertion grounds and said, "[a] complete and unconditional resumption of cohabitation puts an end to desertion or abandonment." *Id.* at 102, 66 S.E.2d at 634. The Court did not address the issue of whether a trial or conditional reconciliation would have the same impact.

If adopted in South Carolina, the language quoted above from C.J.S. would support a conclusion that an attempted reconciliation should not necessarily require the clock to start over, so long as the parties never had the required intent to settle their differences on a permanent basis.

The Supreme Court of Alabama ruled in *Euler v. Euler*, 515 So.2d 710 (Ala. 1987) that no reconciliation occurred although a husband and wife resumed living together for one month while her suit for divorce was pending. It held that whether there has been a reconciliation is a question of fact which the trial court must determine from all the evidence before it and that reconciliation is largely a state of the minds of both of the parties. The opinion states:

> For a reconciliation to take place, "'[t]he intention of the parties must be to resume married life entirely, and not merely to enjoy each other's society temporarily, for limited purposes, or as a trial of whether they want to be reconciled.'" *Rikard [v. Rikard]*, 387 So.2d [842] at 844 [(Ala. Civ. App. 1980)] (quoting Homer F. Clark, Jr., The Law of Domestic Relations in the United States, p. 541).

Id. at 711. The testimony of neither party showed an intention to resume true marital cohabitation on a permanent basis (the wife said she returned to the marital home to try to enter into a settlement with the husband), thus the court held that no reconciliation took place.

North Carolina has a statute which sets out the test by which conduct between separated parties is measured in order to determine if reconciliation has been affected. N.C. Gen. Stat. 52-10-2. It defines "resumption of marital relations" as voluntary renewal of the husband and wife relationship, as shown by the totality of the circumstances. Isolated incidents of sexual intercourse between the parties shall not constitute resumption of marital relations." The North Carolina Court of Appeals applied this statute in holding that a couple's isolated acts of sexual intercourse during a six day period was not a reconciliation warranting recision of their separation agreement. *Fletcher v. Fletcher*, 123 N.C. 744, 474 S.E.2d 802 (Ct. App. 1996). The court noted that the wife did not move back into the marital home, the time period was less than a week, they did not resume the sharing of chores or household duties, they did not hold themselves out as husband and wife, and they did not indicate to friends or family that they had worked out their problems.

The statute which establishes the no fault ground for divorce, S.C. Code Ann. § 20-3-10(5) (Law. Co-op. 1976), does not specifically state whether the required one year period of separation has to be continuous. Thus, it is open to interpretation that a divorce can be obtained under the statute, even if the twelve months are interrupted by a trial or conditional reconciliation which fails. Before reaching such a conclusion, however, the courts will examine the public policies related to the issue.

A decision requiring a continuous twelve month period would appear to work against the public policy in favor of reconciliation, and, perhaps, against the public policy supporting the permanence of marriage. Parties who have been separated for almost twelve months might hesitate to attempt a reconciliation out of fear of losing their ground for divorce, even if they think one might be possible. It would be less risky for most couples in this situation to wait until they have become divorced, then give their relationship another shot without getting married again. Thus, a rigid rule that attempted reconciliations require the clock to start over for no fault divorces would not only discourage attempted reconciliations, it would encourage people considering reconciliations to live together out of wedlock.

If a reconciliation occurs, the parties cannot restrict their fundamental marital rights and responsibilities. In *Towles v. Towles*, 256 S.C. 307, 182 S.E.2d 53 (1971), the Supreme Court refused to enforce a reconciliation agreement in which the wife agreed never to sue her husband again for the reason that the agreement could have the effect of relieving the husband of his fundamental duty to support his wife.

> Our decision herein is not inconsistent with the established public policy to encourage and promote reconciliation between estranged spouses. That policy contemplates preservation of marriage

> under conditions which recognize the mutual obligations and liabilities of the parties. The present resumption of the marital relationship was not on that basis.

Id. at 312, 182 S.E.2d at 55.

6. PROVOCATION

The provocation defense is essentially "yes, I did it, but I would not have done it but for his (or her) provocation." When raised, it is usually in the context of physical cruelty allegations. However, the defense is not often pleaded, in large part because South Carolina courts have not accepted the defense if the retaliatory conduct is disproportionate to the conduct alleged to have provoked it.

Physical cruelty out of proportion to the provoking conduct would still entitle a spouse to a decree. In *Godwin v. Godwin*, 245 S.C. 370, 140 S.E.2d 593 (1965), the Supreme Court wrote:

> The general rule is that a divorce will not be granted on the ground of physical cruelty when the acts of cruelty complained of were provoked by the misconduct of the complaining spouse. However, that there was some provocation will not disentitle a spouse to relief if the retaliatory conduct complained of was out of proportion to the provoking conduct.

Id. at 376, 140 S.E.2d 596 (citations omitted). Thus, unless both parties have engaged in misconduct which give each other grounds for divorce (the first misconduct provoking the second), the defense of provocation does not appear to be viable. In such cases, of course, recrimination would be an equally valid defense.

The proposition that provocation will not prevent a divorce if the retaliation is out of proportion to the provoking conduct is illustrated in *Miller v. Miller*, 225 S.C. 274, 82 S.E.2d 119 (1954). *Miller* involved a battling couple, she in her forties, he in his sixties, the more violent of whom appeared to be the husband. The wife was seeking a divorce based on cruelty, and the husband claimed that his conduct had been provoked by the wife's actions. With regard to the most serious incident, the evidence indicated that the husband had been the aggressor and that the wife had acted in self-defense. The Court wrote approvingly of the following statement from 3 Nelson, *Divorce & Annulment*, 6th Ed., § 32.21 stating:

> While a wife need not be wholly blameless in order to recover, if she is chargeable with substantial fault or misconduct, either by way of act or omission, which materially contributed to the disruption of the marital relation or induced the action by the husband upon which she relies to justify their separation, she is precluded from maintaining a proceeding for separate maintenance.

Id. at 280, 82 S.E.2d at 122. *See also McDowell v. McDowell*, 300 S.C. 96, 386 S.E.2d 468 (Ct. App. 1989) (holding that a divorce on the ground of physical cruelty will not be granted when the physical cruelty is provoked by the complaining spouse and the physical cruelty is not out of proportion to the provocation); *Rabon v. Rabon* 289 S.C. 49, 344 S.E.2d 615 (Ct. App. 1986) (holding that the wife's ridicule of the husband about his lack of education and her refusal to discuss the possibility of him returning home did not constitute the provocation necessary to justify the husband's subsequent acts of physical cruelty).

If the provoking act and the retaliatory act are similarly violent and amount to mutual combat, it appears that the defense of provocation will be allowed and no divorce will be granted in South Carolina, even if it means that two people who are capable of killing each other are forced to remain married. In *Brown v. Brown*, 250 S. C. 114, 156 S. E. 2d 641 (1967), the trial court awarded the husband a divorce on the ground of physical cruelty. The Supreme Court reversed. In addition to pointing out that there was insufficient corroboration, the Court recounted two instances wherein the parties struggled, one a minor skirmish and the other admittedly involving knives and substantial violent conduct on the part of both parties. The Court wrote in relevant part:

> The record reasonably suggests that each party shared in the responsibility for provoking the difficulties, that neither was unwilling to turn the other cheek. Perhaps we could call it a case of mutual stubbornness. Harmony between the parties is not automatic

> in marriage. The general unpleasantness of the wife is a risk assumed by the husband with marriage; however, it is not a statutory ground for divorce.
>
> A careful review of the evidence in this case convinces us that the mutual provocations of the parties met retaliatory cruelty in kind.

Id. at 121-22, 156 S.E.2d at 645. The Court reversed the granting of a divorce to the husband, and reversed as well the property settlement. This presumably left the parties where they had been prior to the filing of the divorce action.

The *Brown* case does suggest a social problem with too vigorous use of the provocation defense. While that defense can be beneficial where it is genuinely desired by the party raising it that the marriage continue, or where the nature of the provocation is such that it would be unjust to grant a divorce against the provoked party, its overall social utility is difficult to see in a context such as that in *Brown.* Used in this fashion, provocation becomes very closely akin to recrimination, and the same policy considerations described in the section on that defense could reasonably come into play with regard to provocation.

The Supreme Court, in *Quarles v. Quarles*, 278 S.C. 251, 294 S.E.2d 341 (1982), held that provocation can operate as a partial offset of marital fault for alimony purposes. In that case the Court reversed a decision barring an alcoholic wife of all right to support. Her drinking (which had stopped prior to the action) was at least possibly brought on by adulterous behavior on the part of the husband, therefore, the Court felt that she should not have had all the responsibility for the end of the marriage allocated to her.

Although its utility will remain limited to a very restricted range of circumstances, provocation is an active, viable defense in South Carolina. This is as it should be in a fault—based divorce system, even with the problems noted. It takes heed of human frailty.

7. INSANITY

Unlike some jurisdictions, South Carolina has no specific statutory provision dealing with insanity as a defense to a matrimonial action or as a ground for divorce. As was pointed out at the beginning of this chapter, the Supreme Court, in *Shaw v. Shaw*, 256 S.C. 453, 182 S.E.2d 865 (1971), held specifically that the continuous separation ground for divorce did not contemplate, and hence did not include, a separation brought about by the confinement of one party to the South Carolina State Hospital on account of insanity.

In *Shaw* the Court quoted at length with approval from a Virginia decision, *Crittenden v. Crittenden*, 210 Va. 76, 168 S. E.2d 115 (1969), and specifically indicated its endorsement of the logic of that opinion. The Virginia court placed particular emphasis upon a need for both parties to be . . . sufficiently competent to be conscious of the fact that the act of separation has occurred." *Shaw* at 456, 182 S. E. 2d at 866. This was coupled, as was indicated earlier, with the general history of divorce in South Carolina, the Supreme Court pointing out that the legislature would well have been able to state its desire for a mental incompetence or insanity ground for divorce had it wished to do so, there being no justification in history for a liberal interpretation of the grounds of divorce here.

Although *Shaw* was decided when the period of separation required was three years, the Court of Appeals provided *dicta* in a more recent case which make it pretty clear that the same rule applies under the one year separation statute. In *Rish v. Rish*, 296 S.C. 14, 370 S.E.2d 102 (Ct. App. 1988), the court was asked to decide whether the wife was entitled to attorneys' fees. The husband had brought, then withdrawn, a divorce action based on one year separation against his wife who was in the mental hospital. Before deciding that the wife was entitled to attorneys' fees, the court said that *Shaw* "clearly stands for the proposition that the husband in this case is not entitled to a divorce on the ground of one year separation as alleged in the Complaint." *Id.* at 16, 370 S.E.2d at 103.

The Supreme Court addressed the defense of mental illness in the case of *Rutherford v. Rutherford*, 307 S.C. 199, 414 S.E.2d 157 (1992). In *Rutherford*, the wife suffered from multiple personality syndrome and attempted to use her mental illness as a defense to her physical act of adultery which she admittedly committed.

She claimed that "she was unable to control the acts of her alter personalities, therefore, she argued she should not be held responsible for those acts." *Id.* at 205, 414 S.E.2d at 161. While the court did not recognize mental illness as a ground for divorce, it appears to have recognized such illness as a form of lack of capacity which can be used as a defense for the ground of adultery and the statutory bar of alimony. This assessment of the wife's mental illness defense was remanded "to determine whether or not the wife at the time of her adulterous affair had the ability to realize it was adultery and, therefore, wrong." *Id.*

As was pointed out in the discussion of the substantive grounds themselves, there are probably mental elements which technically must be proved with regard both to adultery and desertion. *See Pollard v. Pollard*, 204 Va. 316, 130 S.E.2d 425 (1963) (holding that a defendant must have had the mental competence necessary to maintain an intent to desert throughout the entire desertion period). However, this decision was later overturned by statute, as was *Crittenden. See* Va. Code Ann. § 20-93 (Michie 1960).

The problems with physical cruelty and insanity are related. Essentially, what must be shown theoretically in order to justify a divorce based upon physical cruelty is so substantial that keeping a couple together, where the conduct of the charged party genuinely amounts to physical cruelty, simply because that party has a mental defect which arguably created the physical conduct, would place the innocent party at a very great risk for very little discernible value to society. Of course, it is arguable that a defendant spouse who has been committed, and who could show that the cause of the commitment was also the cause of the physical conduct being complained of, should be able to argue insanity as a defense. His or her confinement makes the element of repetition and reasonable fear for one's life or physical well-being difficult to prove. The social utility of such an approach would presumably be similar to that of the *Shaw* decision.

G. CONSEQUENCES OF DIVORCE

This section should be read in conjunction with the consequences of marriage section in the chapter on marriage.

1. IN GENERAL

Divorce ends the marriage, but it does not necessarily affect each of the legal rights and obligations created by the marriage.

2. INTERPERSONAL RIGHTS AND OBLIGATIONS

a. Cohabitation

There are probably no longer any valid laws which create a distinction between couples who live together on the basis of whether or not they are married. If a divorced couple wishes to continue living together, there is nothing to stop them from doing so.

b. Sexual Intercourse

Divorce removes the legal right and social expectation that married couples will engage in sexual intercourse.

Although it is no longer viewed by many people as a serious threat to their liberty, it remains the law in South Carolina that people who live together and engage in carnal intercourse without being married are committing the crime of fornication. S.C. Code Ann. § 16-15-80 (Law. Co-op. 1976). *See* 3 S.C. Juris. *Adultery and Fornication* (S.C. Bar - C.L.E. Division 1991).

c. Mutual Support

Divorce ends the statutorily imposed obligation of spouses to provide support for each other. The only support obligations between former spouses are those which are imposed by the family court in its divorce decree.

d. Confidentiality

There is no privilege against the disclosure of confidential communications made between former spouses, except as to communications during the marriage.

e. Common Surname

A divorced person can choose to continue using the surname used during the marriage or any other name he or she desires. South Carolina appears to continue to recognize the common law rule that "[a]t common law, a man may lawfully change his name, or by general usage or habit acquire another name than that originally borne by him, without the intervention of Court or Legislature. *City Council v. King*, 4 McCord, 487; *Miller v. George*, 30 S.C. 528, 9 S.E. 659; 21 Ency. Law, 311." *Brayton v. Beall*, 73 S.C. 308, 311, 53 S.E. 641, 642 (1906) (holding that statutes which provide a mode of changing a name "do not abrogate but are in affirmance and aid of the common law rule").

Those people who want some proof that they have legally changed their names can ask the family court to issue an order allowing them to change their names. The family court is specifically authorized to, "upon the granting of final judgment [of divorce], allow a wife to resume her maiden name or the name of any former husband." S.C. Code Ann. § 20-3-180 (Law. Co-op. 1976). If a divorced person wants to use a different name than specifically designated in this statute, or if a married or divorced person wishes to request a name change independent of the divorce action (perhaps, even before filing for divorce), the family court has jurisdiction to grant such relief under S.C. Code Ann. § 20-7-420 (Law. Co-op. 1976). The statutes which govern the family court's consideration of requests for name changes are S.C. Code Ann. § 15-49-10 to 15-49-50 (Law. Co-op. 1976 & Supp.).

3. ASSETS AND LIABILITIES

a. In General

Divorce has no effect on the property rights of either party, unless one or both spouses seek intervention by the family court. However, neither party continues to acquire any interest in the assets of the other.

b. Necessary Goods and Services

The "doctrine of necessaries" does not apply to divorced people. However, the duty to provide "necessaries" to a spouse continues during the pendency of a suit for divorce, even if the spouse does not request temporary alimony. 41 C.J.S. *Husband and Wife* § 49 (1991).

4. INHERITANCE

Perhaps the most significant consequence of divorce is that divorced persons lose their right to share in the distribution of each other's intestate estates. Divorce revokes any disposition of property to a spouse under a will, any provision conferring on the spouse a power of appointment, and any nomination of the spouse as executor, trustee, conservator, or guardian, unless the will specifically states otherwise. S.C. Code Ann. § 62-2-507 (Law. Co-op. 1976). Subsequent remarriage of the parties reinstates such rights. *Id.*

Property affected by revocation becomes part of the residue. S.C. Code Ann. § 62-2-604 (Law. Co-op. 1976).

5. CHILDREN

a. Legitimacy

Divorce does not affect the legitimacy of children.

b. Obligations

Divorce has no legal effect on the obligations of parents for the welfare, education and care of their children. If the parents can agree between themselves how to raise and care for the children, there is no obligation for the parents to seek judicial approval or intervention. However, the family court may be asked to approve all or some of any agreements between the parents (*see* the chapter on agreements). Also, the family court may be asked to resolve any disputes about the children (see the chapter on children).

c. Children's Names

The family court is authorized to change the names of children following divorces, if it determines that it would be in their best interest. The Supreme Court first announced this rule in *Ex parte Shull*, 276 S.C. 512, 280 S.E.2d 209 (1981) (remanding the case because it was brought in the mother's name, not by a guardian), then confirmed it in *Stone v. Stone*, 285 S.C. 108, 328 S.E.2d 346 (1985) (remanding for a trial *de novo*, apparently because the father was not given a proper opportunity to participate and present evidence in the initial proceeding). These cases are rather remarkable because they make no mention of the common law rule which they abolished (the father had a right to have his child bear his surname) and because they do not provide any guidance for determining what is in a child's best interest.

The result is in accord with decisions in other states. *See Lassiter-Geer v. Reichenbach*, 492 A.2d 303, 303 Md. 88 (1985), *cert. denied* 106 S.Ct. 568, 88 L.Ed.2d 553 (affirming the denial of a mother's request to change the surname of her child to her maiden name where the mother had remarried since the divorce); *In re Marriage of Schiffman*, 169 Cal. Rptr. 918, 620 P.2d 579, 28 Cal.3d 640 (1980) (abolishing the rule that a father had a primary right to have the child bear his surname and deciding that the sole consideration should be the child's best interest). *Schiffman* is noteworthy in several respects. It includes a fascinating discussion of the evolution of the common law rule and the reasons why it should not survive. A concurring opinion argues for a rule which would recognize a rebuttable presumption that the parent with custody has acted in the child's best interest in selecting a name. A lone dissenter argues in favor of leaving the rule alone in the absence of evidence that it has resulted in any evil. The *Schiffman* majority also explains how the trial courts should determine what is in the best interest of the child:

> Under the test thus revised the length of time that the child has used a surname is to be considered. If, as here, the time is negligible because the child is very young, other facts may be controlling. For instance, the effect of a name change on preservation of the father-child relationship, the strength of the mother-child relationship, and

> the identification of the child as part of a family unit are all pertinent. The symbolic role that a surname other than the natural father's may play in easing relations with a new family should be balanced against the importance of maintaining the biological father-child relationship. "[T]he embarrassment or discomfort that a child may experience when he bears a surname different from the rest of his family" should be evaluated.

620 P.2d at 583 (citations omitted).

CHAPTER FIVE
SEPARATE SUPPORT AND MAINTENANCE

CHAPTER FIVE
SEPARATE SUPPORT AND MAINTENANCE

A. IN GENERAL

This chapter considers issues related to actions for separate support and maintenance.[3] It should be read in conjunction with Chapter Six, for some of the issues which are common to both alimony and separate support and maintenance are discussed in that chapter but not here. For example, the factors to be considered in awarding spousal support and the forms and methods of payment allowed are discussed in the alimony chapter.

An action for separate support and maintenance is essentially an action for alimony, but it is not a divorce. It is probably technically incorrect to file an action for separate support and maintenance which does not include a request for spousal support, but it has become a vehicle for resolving a wide variety of disputes between married people who no longer want to live together. The absence of a request for spousal support really makes little practical difference today because the family court has subject matter jurisdiction to hear and decide marital disputes about property, children and domestic violence as independent causes of action, as well as parts of actions for separate support and maintenance or divorce. There is no difference in the meanings of "spousal support," "separate support and maintenance" and "alimony." They all refer to money which one spouse is ordered to pay the other spouse while they are separated or divorced.

The family court is authorized to treat a divorce action as an action for separate support and maintenance if a divorce is not granted to either party. *See Machado v. Machado*, 220 S.C. 90, 66 S.E.2d 629 (1951); *Piana v. Piana*, 239 S.C. 367, 123 S.E.2d 297 (1962); *Gill v. Gill*, 269 S.C. 337, 237 S.E.2d 382 (1977).

---

[3] For unknown reasons, such actions are referred to in the S.C. Code of Laws both as actions for separate support and maintenance (see S.C. Code Ann. § 20-7-420(2) (Law. Co-op. 1976 & Supp.)) and as actions for separate maintenance and support (see S.C. Code Ann. § 20-3-130(A) (Law. Co-op. Supp.)).

The enactment in 1990 of S.C. Code § 20-3-130 (Law. Co-op. Supp.) has resolved many of the issues related to actions for separate support and maintenance, but some myths persist and traps remain for the unwary practitioner.

1. ISSUES LITIGATED AND DECIDED CANNOT BE RELITIGATED

Issues which have been litigated and decided in a separate maintenance and support action cannot be relitigated in a subsequent divorce proceeding. In *Powell v. Powell*, 249 S.C. 663, 156 S.E.2d 305 (1967), the wife had brought an earlier action for separate maintenance and support, claiming successfully that her departure from the marital home was justified and she was entitled to support. The husband later brought an action for divorce on the ground of desertion. The Court held that his action was barred by the wife's action for separate support and maintenance:

> It is hornbook law that a prior judgment of a court having jurisdiction of the parties and the subject matter is conclusive in any subsequent action between the parties, or their privies, of all questions which were actually litigated in the prior action and determined by the judgment, regardless of whether the subsequent action involves the same or a different cause of action.

Id. at 665, 156 S.E.2d at 306. A similar situation and the same result are found in *Blackmon v. Blackmon*, 294 S.C. 187, 363 S.E.2d 400 (Ct. App. 1987) (holding that evidence of changed circumstances were not allowed where the wife pleaded the prior ruling in a separate support action and that no changed circumstances existed and the husband merely alleged she was not entitled to alimony).

This issue is confused somewhat by *Page v. Page*, 260 S.C. 298, 195 S.E.2d 613 (1973). The wife had brought an action in the circuit court, alleging physical cruelty and seeking separate support, but she was unsuccessful. Later, the husband obtained a divorce on the ground of desertion. The trial court found that the wife's request in the same action for a divorce on the ground of physical cruelty was not supported by the evidence, and the Supreme Court upheld this ruling and refused to review the evidence, stating that "[t]he prior judgment precludes the wife from relitigating that issue although the cause of action is not the same as in the first action." *Id.* at 301, 195 S.E.2d at 614. Somewhat incongruously, however, the Supreme Court held that it was an error for the trial judge to refuse to consider the wife's claim to alimony. The trial judge had ruled that the claim was barred by the prior adjudication in the circuit court. The Supreme Court said this was an error and remanded the case for consideration of her alimony claim, stating:

> Regarding the former adjudication that the wife left the marital abode without just cause or excuse as conclusive against her claim to alimony in the divorce action, the court refused to hear her evidence relating to this claim. This was error. Only an adulterous wife is automatically barred from alimony by the terms of the statute. Sec. 20-113, Code of 1962. In all other cases, "the circumstances and conduct of an offending spouse might be such as to bar her from alimony but this is a matter solely for the trial judge, governed by equity and justice and the condition of both parties. The exercise of such a discretion will not be disturbed on appeal unless an abuse thereof is shown." *Herbert v. Herbert*, S.C., 194 S.E.2d 238, 239 (1973); *McKenzie v. McKenzie*, 254 S.C. 372, 175 S.E.2d 628 (1970).

*Id.*at 301, 195 S.E.2d at 614. It is difficult to understand why the prior determination that the wife was not entitled to separate support and maintenance would not have bound the subsequent court on the issue of alimony, absent proof of changed circumstances, in light of the fact that the factors for determining whether or not spousal support should be awarded are the same irrespective of whether one is seeking it in an action for separate support and maintenance or in a divorce proceeding. Perhaps the Supreme Court felt that separate support should have been awarded in the initial circuit court action, even though it agreed with the trial court that the husband's misconduct was not sufficient to grant a divorce. However, it did not say this, so the results in the case are difficult to explain.

If spousal support is requested in the pleadings in a separate support and maintenance action, an agreement to forego it could bar a subsequent request for alimony in a divorce action. In *Lawter v. Lawter*, 287 S.C. 298, 345 S.E.2d 479 (1986), the Supreme Court held that the family court had no authority to award alimony in a divorce action where the parties had stipulated, and the family court had noted as a finding of fact, that the wife waived her right to spousal support at the separate maintenance hearing.

Settlement agreements in separate support and maintenance actions do not preclude subsequent litigation if the parties fail to obtain a clear ruling from the trial court based on some proof other than the submission of the agreement. Care must be taken to get a ruling by the trial judge on the merits of the issues, if one wants to rely on a separate maintenance and support action as a final disposition of disputed issues. In *Clayton v. Clayton*, 287 S.C. 308, 338 S.E.2d 326 (1985), an action for separate maintenance and support was ended by agreement of the parties, the terms of which were included in the court's order. However, the Supreme Court held that the issues covered in the agreement could be reconsidered by the family court in a subsequent divorce proceeding because the entitlement to support had not been "litigated or decided." Rather, the order had simply recited the agreement and made no ruling as to fairness. The holding in *Clayton* was distinguished in *Murphy v. Murphy*, 293 S.C. 151, 359 S.E.2d 91 (Ct. App. 1987), where the agreement in question had been approved and incorporated into the order of the court, not just merely recited. Moreover, in the action brought to attack the prior order in *Murphy*, the trial judge had determined the award of support to be reasonable.

In *Witt v. Witt*, 271 S.C. 541, 248 S.E.2d 494 (1978), the Supreme Court held that it is not necessary to show changed circumstances when a former husband requests reconsideration of the appropriate amount of spousal support where there was no evidence introduced at the original trial about the husband's ability to pay support. There was no original condition established; therefore, it would have been impossible for him ever to establish changed conditions. The Court emphasized that no decree should ever be issued without further proof than the terms of the parties' agreement.

2. REPAYMENT OF SPOUSAL SUPPORT MAY BE REQUIRED

When a person is seeking *pendente lite* spousal support, the other spouse should be given an opportunity to present evidence of adultery or other reasons why the request should be denied. In *Watson v. Watson*, 291 S.C. 13, 351 S.E.2d 883 (Ct. App. 1986), the wife was awarded *pendente lite* alimony. The court refused to consider the husband's evidence of adultery. At the final hearing on the merits, the husband was given a divorce on the ground of adultery. The court wrote: "We hold it was error under the circumstances of this case for the trial judge to preclude the husband from attempting to prove that the wife was an adulterous spouse, as contemplated by the statute, and was not entitled to temporary alimony." *Id.* at 23, 351 S.E.2d at 889. This was further explained in a footnote:

> We recognize that time constraints may preclude the taking of testimony in every case where adultery is denied by the offending spouse. However, where there has been a *prima facie* showing of adultery through testimony or affidavits, it is incumbent upon the spouse charged with adultery to present a *prima facie* showing that he or she did not commit the alleged adulterous acts. At a minimum, a trial judge must in such situations provide for reimbursement to the payor spouse if adultery is proven at the merits hearing.

Id. at 23, 351 S.E.2d at 889-890, n.4. *Watson* was remanded with instructions to reduce the wife's equitable distribution by the amount of alimony paid by the husband.

This has potentially significant consequences for a spouse who is awarded *pendente lite* or permanent separate support and maintenance, but who might not be entitled to it. Such a spouse may be required to repay the entire amount of support which has been paid between the time of a temporary hearing on a separate support and maintenance action and the final decision on a divorce petition. One way of protecting a client against this risk is to be sure that a finding on the merits of the spouse's entitlement is made by the trial judge at the merits hearing on the request for separate support and maintenance. If no finding on the merits is made, e.g., if the parties simply ask that their agreement be approved, the spouse receiving support could be at risk. *See Witt v. Witt*, 271 S.C. 541, 248 S.E.2d 494 (1978) (discussed above).

B. JURISDICTION

1. IN GENERAL

The family court is given exclusive jurisdiction over actions for separate support and maintenance in S.C. Code Ann. § 20-7-420(2) (Law. Co-op. 1976), which provides that the family court has exclusive jurisdiction:

> To hear and determine actions: For . . . separate support and maintenance. . . (14) To order support of a spouse or child, or both, irrespective of whether they are likely to become a public charge.

Authority and guidance for determining whether to award separate support and maintenance are provided in S.C. Code Ann. § 20-3-130 (Law. Co-op. Supp.):

> (A) In proceedings for . . . actions for separate maintenance and support, the court may grant . . . separate maintenance and support in such amounts and for such term as the court considers appropriate as from the circumstances of the parties and the nature of the case be just, *pendente lite* and permanently.
>
> . . .
>
> (B) . . . separate maintenance and support awards may be granted *pendente lite* and permanently in such amounts and for such periods of time subject to conditions as the court considers just including, but not limited to:
>
> . . .
>
> (5) Separate maintenance and support to be paid periodically, but terminating upon the divorce of the parties, or upon the death of either spouse (except as secured in subsection (D)) and terminable and modifiable based upon changed circumstances in the future. The purpose of this form of support may include, but not be limited to, circumstances where a divorce is not sought, but it is necessary to

provide for support of the supported spouse by way of separate maintenance and support when the parties are living separate and apart.

2. ACTIONS FOR LEGAL SEPARATION DO NOT EXIST IN S.C.

There is no cause of action in South Carolina for a "legal separation," although there remains more than a little confusion about this. The Supreme Court ended some of the confusion when it explicitly held, in *Nocher v. Nocher*, 268 S.C. 503, 234 S.E.2d 884 (1977), that the common law action for a divorce *a mensa et thoro* does not exist in South Carolina. Other phrases that are equivalent to "divorce *a mensa et thoro*" are "divorce from bed and board," "legal separation," and "limited divorce." *See Ariail v. Ariail*, 295 S.C. 486, 487, 369 S.E.2d 146, 147 (Ct. App. 1988). However, some case decisions and statutory language have muddied the waters about the status of a cause of action for "legal separation" by continued use of the term. For example, S.C. Code Ann. § 20-7-420 (Law. Co-op. Supp.) contains the following language in describing the family court's jurisdiction: "The family court shall have exclusive jurisdiction: (2) To hear and determine actions: For divorce *a vinculo matrimonii*, separate support and maintenance, *legal separation*, and in other marital litigation between the parties" . . . . (emphasis added).

In a number of cases, the appellate courts have affirmed the granting of a legal separation without commenting on whether or not it was a valid cause of action. *See Murray v. Murray*, 271 S.C. 62, 244 S.E.2d 538 (1978); *Miller v. Miller*, 225 S.C. 274, 82 S.E.2d 119 (1954); *Brewington v. Brewington*, 280 S.C. 502, 313 S.E.2d 53 (Ct. App. 1984). In *Brewer v. Brewer*, 242 S.C. 9, 129 S.E.2d 736 (1963), the Supreme Court discussed the nature of divorces *a mensa et thoro* at great length, although Justice Bussey wrote a long opinion concurring in the result in which he pointed out that the cause of action did not exist in South Carolina.

The Court of Appeals has made it clear that neither the statutory language quoted above nor any inadvertent language in case opinions has created a cause of action for "legal separation." In *Ariail v. Ariail*, 295 S.C. 486, 369 S.E.2d 146 (Ct. App. 1988), the wife had sought a legal separation although she and her husband continued to live in the same house. The Court saw the issue as whether a family court has a right to issue a limited decree of divorce. The wife's argument was that *Brewington v. Brewington*, 280 S.C. 502, 313 S.E.2d 53 (Ct. App. 1984), had held that there was an action for legal separation. The Court rejected this argument, stating "[w]e did not hold in *Brewington* . . . that a family court has the power to award a legal separation or limited divorce in the absence of a statute or constitutional provision." *Ariail* at 493, 369 S.E.2d at 149 (order on petition for rehearing). *See also Rivenbark v. Rivenbark*, 301 S.C. 175, 391 S.E.2d 232 (1990) (affirming *Ariail*'s holding that there is no cause of action for a "legal separation" in South Carolina).

The *Ariail* court went on to cite with favor the portion of Justice Bussey's concurring opinion in *Brewer v. Brewer*, 242 S.C. 9, 129 S.E.2d 736 (1963), in which he distinguishes separate maintenance and support actions from divorce *a mensa et thoro*. In *Brewer*, Justice Bussey wrote:

> To return to the primary contention of the appellant [that a cause of action for legal separation exists], it is, in my opinion, totally unsound and is based upon what seems to me to be a rather wide-spread erroneous impression to the effect that 'divorces *a mensa et thoro*' were in fact traditionally recognized by our courts independently of any statutory or constitutional provision. This erroneous impression has risen, I think, probably from a somewhat indiscriminate and interchangeable use of the terms 'divorce *a mensa et thoro*,' 'separate support and maintenance,' and 'legal separation,' without due regard for the real meaning of such terms. On more than one occasion, this erroneous impression has been contributed to by *dicta* in the opinions of this court.
>
> . . .
>
> From early days, courts of equity in this state have, in proper cases, ordered separate support and maintenance but, whenever the issue has been squarely raised, have declared that no court in this state had the power to grant a divorce *a mensa et thoro* . . . .

Id. at 20-21, 129 S.E.2d at 741-42 (Bussey concurring in result).

Surprisingly, some practitioners continue to seek legal separations and some family court judges continue to grant them. *See Rivenbark v. Rivenbark*, 301 S.C. 175, 391 S.E.2d 232 (1990), in which a wife had petitioned for and had been granted a legal separation. The Supreme Court noted:

> An action for legal separation cannot be maintained in South Carolina in the absence of constitutional or statutory authority. *Ariail v. Ariail*, 295 S.C. 486, 369 S.E.(2d) 146 (Ct. App. 1988). Although this action was brought in a peculiar form, we construe this action to be one for separate support and maintenance.

Id. at 176, 391 S.E.2d at 233, n.1.

There is some importance in the fact that there is no divorce *a mensa et thoro* in South Carolina. If it existed, such a decree would authorize the parties to live apart, whereas an action for separate support and maintenance does not. As Justice Bussey explained in his concurring opinion in *Brewer*:

> A divorce *a mensa et thoro* may be defined as a judicial decree which terminates the obligation and right of cohabitation but does not affect the status of the parties as married persons or dissolve the marriage. When a divorce *a mensa et thoro* is decreed there is no severance of the marriage bond. The marital status is not affected thereby; and the parties remain husband and wife, although authorized to live in separation.

Brewer v. Brewer, 242 S.C. 9, 13, 129 S.E.2d 736, 737.

However, there is very little practical impact of being separated without a court's permission in today's society, especially after the enactment of S.C. Code Ann. § 20-3-130 (Law. Co-op. Supp.), which makes marital misconduct irrelevant to an award of separate support and maintenance after the earliest of (a) the formal signing of a written property or marital settlement agreement or (b) entry of a permanent order of separate maintenance and support or of a permanent order approving a property or marital settlement agreement. S.C. Code Ann. § 20-3-

130(C)(10) (Law. Co-op. Supp.). Even though there is no such thing as a "legal separation" in South Carolina, neither is there an "illegal separation."

3. MARITAL PROPERTY CAN BE DIVIDED

It would be logical for courts to refuse to make a final division of marital property in actions for separate support and maintenance. Public policy in South Carolina encourages reconciliation, and the division of marital property would seem to remove one incentive for parties to attempt a reconciliation and resume marital cohabitation. However, the legislature erased any doubts about the family court's authority to do this in 1986 when it adopted S.C. Code Ann. § 20-7-472 (Law Co-op. Supp.): "In a proceeding for . . . separate support and maintenance . . . the court shall make a final equitable apportionment between the parties of the parties' marital property upon request by either party in the pleadings."

Before this statute was enacted, there was some confusion about whether division of marital property was appropriate in separate support and maintenance actions. The Supreme Court had indicated that the family court was authorized to divide marital property in a support action in its discretion, even though it suggested that exercising such discretion would not usually be appropriate:

> In this State the courts in such a proceeding may exercise full equity powers and the right to exercise those powers is not dependent on the success or failure of the divorce action.
>
> . . .
>
> Assuming that in such a proceeding, particularly when the divorce is denied, the Court should refrain from undertaking any adjudication of property rights, the question is not one of jurisdiction but the proper exercise of jurisdiction. The remedy for any mistake is by direct appeal and not by collateral attack.

Piana v. Piana, 239 S.C. 367, 373 & 375, 123 S.E.2d 297, 300 & 301 (1962). The court apparently felt that it was appropriate for the family court to divide the marital property in *Piana* because the husband had obtained a divorce in the meantime, thus removing any issue about the public policy favoring reconciliation, and because the parties had voluntarily submitted the issue to the trial court for a decision. However, the Court's statement that voluntary litigation of the property issues conferred subject matter jurisdiction on the family court appears to be incorrect. See the chapter on subject matter jurisdiction.

As mentioned earlier, however, the 1986 legislation removed any doubt about the ability of the family court to make a final distribution of marital property in actions for separate support and maintenance. In fact, if one spouse requests it, the court is required to divide the marital property. Once marital property has been divided, it becomes nonmarital property. Thus, if the parties reconcile, the divided property remains nonmarital in nature unless it is transmuted, although any increase in its value due to the joint efforts of the spouses following the reconciliation is subject to equitable apportionment. *Crawford v. Crawford*, 301 S.C. 476, 392 S.E.2d 675 (Ct. App. 1990) (affirming trial court's decision to equitably apportion property acquired after reconciliation as well as the increased value of property which had been divided during a previous period of separation).

4. MAYBE SPOUSES CAN BE FORCED TO SEPARATE

One of the important unanswered questions in South Carolina marital litigation is how to determine who moves out of the marital home absent an agreement between the parties. As mentioned earlier and discussed later in the section on entitlement, if either spouse moves out of the marital home without adequate justification, there is a risk that he or she will be considered a deserter and, perhaps, forfeit spousal support. It appears equally clear that a spouse who forcefully evicts the other spouse, by changing the locks or otherwise, could be held to be a constructive deserter or, at least, be seen as coming to the court with unclean hands (see the discussion of constructive desertion in the chapter on divorce).

It seems more likely than not that an action for separate support and maintenance can be filed even if the parties are living together. In 1995, the Supreme Court held that the family court may hear divorce cases based on adultery, habitual drunkenness, or physical cruelty even if the parties are still living in the same house.

Watson v. Watson, 319 S.C. 92, 460 S.E.2d 394 (July 24, 1995). In *Watson*, the husband brought a divorce action on the ground of adultery. The family court granted the wife's motion to dismiss on the basis that it had no subject matter jurisdiction because the parties continued to reside in the marital home at the time the action was commenced. The Supreme Court reversed.

> If we were to require physical separation of the parties in order to bring a divorce action, divorcing parents who seek custody of their children would have these choices: either vacate the home, taking the children with them and thereby cause additional disruption in the children's lives; vacate the home and abandon the children to their spouse; or continue in the marriage. We hold that public policy permits a party to remain in the home and institute divorce litigation premised on fault grounds other than desertion. In such cases, the living arrangements of the parties and the children during the pendency of the litigation should be decided at the temporary hearing.

Id. at 94, 460 S.E.2d at 395. The same poor choices confront married couples who want to separate but cannot agree on which party will remain in the marital home. One might predict that the Supreme Court or the Court of Appeals will adopt the same policy with respect to actions for separate support and maintenance when it has an opportunity to do so.

Although there appear to be some judges and members of the bar who believe there is no judicial remedy available in these unfortunate situations except in cases of domestic abuse (*see* S.C. Code Ann. § 20-4-60 (Law. Co-op. 1976)), S.C. Code Ann. § 20-7-420(30) (Law. Co-op. 1976) appears to provide authority for the family court to act. It indicates that the family court has exclusive jurisdiction "to make any order necessary to carry out and enforce the provisions of this chapter, and to hear and determine any questions of support, custody, separation or any other matter over which the court has jurisdiction without the intervention of a jury."

In any event, there is no statute or case which prohibits the family court from hearing an action for separate support and maintenance while the parties are still living together, especially if the action includes a request to order one of the parties out of the marital home. The Supreme Court determined in *Barnes v. Barnes*, 276

S.C. 519, 280 S.E.2d 538 (1981), that a divorce on the ground of living separate and apart for one year could not be granted to two people who were still living under the same roof, even if they had lived in separate rooms for more than a year. The Court held that separate domiciles are required. However, it justified this holding on the basis that any other result would encourage collusion. Collusion is not a concern in considering requests for separate support and maintenance.

The Court of Appeals came close to deciding this issue squarely in *Ariail v. Ariail*, 295 S.C. 486, 369 S.E.2d 146 (Ct. App. 1988). As mentioned earlier, the primary contribution of *Ariail* to our understanding of the law is its unequivocal statement that there is no cause of action for a "legal separation" (a.k.a. divorce *a mensa et thoro*) in South Carolina. However, there are other interesting aspects to this case. The parties were living in the same house when the wife brought an action for legal separation, alimony, and child custody and support. The family court apparently awarded her alimony. However, the Court of Appeals vacated that portion of the order because the wife had withdrawn her request for alimony by the time of the hearing; the family court, therefore, lacked subject matter jurisdiction to award it. The Court of Appeals did not provide any *dicta* with respect to whether spousal support could have been awarded if she had not withdrawn the request. (Even though the action had been brought improperly as an action for legal separation, the court could have construed it as an action for separate support and maintenance. *See Rivenbark v. Rivenbark*, 301 S.C. 175, 391 S.E.2d 232 (1990).)

However, in also denying the wife's request for child support, the *Ariail* court based its decision partly on its finding that there was nothing in the record to suggest that the husband was not providing support to the children who were living in the house with them. This implies that a child support action can be maintained against a spouse who is not providing his or her fair share of child support, even while living in the same home. If this is so, the same logic would extend to actions for separate support and maintenance in which one spouse claims that the other is not providing sufficient spousal support. Thus, while it is not entirely clear that actions for separate support and maintenance can be brought while spouses are still living together, neither is it clear that they cannot.

Although there appears to be no bar to such actions, the courts might be understandably reluctant to begin entertaining cases in which they are asked to decide how much money a husband should give his wife or his children while they are still living in the same house. However, this reluctance should not exist if a request for separate support and maintenance includes a request for the court to order one party to move out of the marital home.

As discussed earlier, the family court has the authority to divide marital property in actions for separate support and maintenance. The authority to divide marital property has traditionally included the power to determine whether either party should have the exclusive use and possession of the marital home, at least *pendente lite*. That is, a family court judge should be able to order one spouse to move out. There does not appear to be any public policy which would be detrimentally affected by the exercise of such authority. On the other hand, there is a clear need for married couples to be able to obtain a judicial determination of spousal support and possession of the marital property without one spouse having to move out first at the risk of jeopardizing his or her property and support rights.

If the family court does not have authority to hear actions for separate support and maintenance while spouses are living under the same roof and to order one of the parties to move out of the marital home, the options are limited for people who want to avoid an accusation of desertion or other detrimental effects of moving out. One option is for both parties to obtain counsel and negotiate a settlement agreement before the separation occurs. If a full settlement is not possible, an agreement at least that the separation is mutually voluntary and that neither party will try to take advantage of the fact that the other moves out of the marital home will provide some protection.

In sum, the family courts are neither clearly prohibited nor required to hear actions for separate support and maintenance while the parties are living in the same residence. There is a clear need for them to exercise jurisdiction in such cases, especially where the pleadings include a request that one spouse be ordered to move out of the marital home. Otherwise, people in need of judicial assistance may be left with none. There appears to be no public policy which would be violated by the family court assuming and exercising such authority, other than to encourage spouses to stay together. While keeping spouses together is an important objective, it must be weighed against the inequities created when an innocent spouse in an unhappy marriage is forced to remain in the marital home simply because of a lack of independent resources. On balance, the equities would seem to favor the family court assuming jurisdiction to hear and decide separate support and maintenance actions even if the parties are still living together. Whether or not support should be awarded is a separate issue which would be determined by reference to the factors set forth in S.C. Code Ann. § 20-3-130 (Law. Co-op. Supp.).

C. VENUE

Litigants preparing to bring an action for separate support and maintenance can choose from among as many as three different locations for filing their pleadings.

> Actions . . . for separate support and maintenance must be tried in the county (a) in which the defendant resides at the time of the commencement of the action, (b) in which the plaintiff resides if the defendant is a nonresident or after due diligence cannot be found, or (c) in which the parties last resided together as husband and wife unless the plaintiff is a nonresident, in which case it must be brought in the county in which the defendant resides.

S.C. Code Ann. § 20-3-60 (Law. Co-op. Supp.).

Any question about whether the statute intended these options to be in any particular order of priority was put to rest in *Voravudhi v. Voravudhi*, 273 S.C. 407, 257 S.E.2d 156 (1979), in which the court held that a divorce could be tried in any of the three places indicated. Although *Voravudhi* was decided before separate support and maintenance actions were added to the statute, the reasoning of the court would seem to extend to them as well.

D. ENTITLEMENT: THE ROLE OF MARITAL FAULT

1. IN GENERAL: FAULT IS ONE OF MANY FACTORS TO CONSIDER

The factors to be considered in awarding separate support and maintenance are exactly the same as those to be considered in awarding alimony. S.C. Code Ann. § 20-3-130(C) (Law. Co-op. Supp.). These factors are discussed in the chapter on alimony, but the role of marital fault is also discussed here because of the historical confusion about its role in actions for separate support and maintenance. The confusion has involved two separate, but related issues: 1) the circumstances in which a spouse is barred from seeking support that is, when a judge should not accept evidence about the factors set forth in section 20-3-130(C); and 2) the kinds of misconduct which will result in support being denied by the court after considering those factors.

As with alimony awards, the appellate courts have not yet developed a clear judicial philosophy based on public policy considerations to guide the family courts in awarding separate support and maintenance. Some family court judges have been slower than others in shifting from a fault-based approach in which assigning blame was the primary judicial function to an equity-balancing approach in which all relevant factors are to be considered in determining whether one spouse should provide support to another spouse while they are living apart. Practitioners report that family court judges will sometimes not award any support to a spouse who leaves the marital home without "good reason," while at other times they appear to unduly penalize an abandoned spouse upon allegations of marital misconduct that are neither substantial nor material.

Although the transition from a fault-based to an equity-balancing approach has been slow, case law and legislation clearly reflect that trend. However, a judicial philosophy based on public policy considerations is needed to enhance uniformity and equitable results in separate support and maintenance decisions. The section on the purposes of alimony in the alimony chapter suggests some guidelines for developing a policy-based approach.

The basic rule is that a *prima facie* case for support is established by showing that one spouse is in need of support and the other spouse is able to pay it. Once this has been established, the court looks to other relevant factors to decide whether to award support.

> Only an adulterous wife is statutorily denied alimony. Conversely, it is an irrefutable judicial principal that any alimony award rests in the sound discretion of the trial judge.
>
> "Alimony is founded upon the legal duty of the husband to support his wife. It is not intended as a penalty against him nor as a reward to the wife. While the financial condition of the husband, and the needs of the wife are important, they are not the only essentials to consider in determining the amount. There must also be considered all other circumstances of the particular case such as the age and health of the parties, their respective earning capacity, their individual wealth, the amount she contributed to the accumulation thereof and the conduct of the parties. *Graham v. Graham*, 253 S.C. 486, 171 S.E.(2d) 704 (1970)." *Beasely v. Beasely*, 264 S.C. 611, 612-613, 216 S.E.(2d) 535, 535-536 (1975).

Nienow v. Nienow, 268 S.C. 161, 170, 232 S.E.2d 504, 509 (1977) (holding that a wife was entitled to bring an action for alimony in South Carolina after her husband had obtained a divorce from her in Florida). *See also Machado v. Machado*, 220 S.C. 90, 108, 66 S.E.2d 629, 637 (1951) (discussed below).

Marital fault has been one of the most important factors in determining whether a spouse is entitled to support, and it will continue to be a significant consideration. Under the 1990 alimony statute, however, fault is not to be considered in deciding whether to award support if the misconduct has neither affected the economic circumstances of the parties nor contributed to the breakup of the marriage. *See* S.C. Code Ann. § 20-3-130(C)(10) (Law. Co-op. Supp.); *McKnight v. McKnight*, 283 S.C. 540, 324 S.E.2d 91 (Ct. App. 1984); *Welch v. Welch*, 250 S.C. 264, 157 S.E.2d 249 (1967). This section of the Code and both cases are discussed below.

2. "GROUNDS" ARE NOT NEEDED TO SEEK SUPPORT

The family court is not required to find that "grounds" exist before it can award separate support and maintenance. That is, it is not necessary to show any misconduct on the part of the spouse being asked to pay support for the family court to consider awarding it. This issue warrants attention because some commentators have indicated that there is a need to have grounds before separate support and maintenance can be awarded. For example, *see* 13 S.C. Juris. *Divorce* § 41 (S.C. Bar C.L.E. - Division, 1992): "Not all spouses, however, are entitled to alimony or support. As a threshold issue the party must have either grounds for divorce or grounds for separate support and maintenance." As authority for this proposition, S.C. Jurisprudence cites *Machado v. Machado*, 220 S.C. 90, 66 S.E.2d 629 (1951), and *Simmons v. Simmons*, 229 S.C. 376, 93 S.E.2d 107 (1956). These cases are discussed later.

The source of the confusion began long before *Machado* and *Simmons* were decided. Three South Carolina cases reflect the common law rule that a finding of fault is required before spousal support can be awarded: *Levin v. Levin*, 68 S.C. 123, 46 S.E. 945 (1904); *Wise v. Wise*, 60 S.C. 426, 38 S.E. 794 (1901); *Hair v. Hair*, 31 S.C. Eq. (10 Rich. Eq.) 163 (1858). Each of these cases contains statements to the effect that spousal support can only be granted if the person being asked to pay support has engaged in at least one of the following kinds of misconduct: (a) *saevitia* (actual or threatened violence affecting health or life, or particularly strong words of reproach or accusation); (b) desertion; or (c) obscene and revolting indecent practices.

It is doubtful that these cases have any relevance to modern questions of law and equity. They were written in an age when marital relationships were viewed quite differently than today. The cases spend many words describing the duties of a wife to follow her husband to his choice of domicile and discussing the various forms and degrees of abuse which a wife was expected to suffer before she would be justified in leaving the marital home. The following statement from *Levin* illustrates turn-of-the-century views about marital relations: "The husband's right of domination and the wife's duty to live with him and obey him cease to exist when the husband ceases to support them by at least decent respect and consideration." *Levin v. Levin*, 68 S.C.

123, 125, 46 S.E. 945, 946 (1904). It was unthinkable in that day that a woman should live apart from her husband without good cause.

The belief that grounds were required for awarding spousal support has persisted, due in large part to the long lasting uncertainty as to whether South Carolina recognized a cause of action for divorce *a mensa et thoro*. If it existed in South Carolina, some finding of some fault by the supporting spouse would be required before the court could grant that form of divorce. Some cases have proceeded as if divorce *a mensa et thoro* was a valid cause of action. For example, in *Miller v. Miller*, 225 S.C. 274, 82 S.E.2d 119 (1954), the Supreme Court said there is a need to have grounds to seek spousal support in connection with a request for a divorce *a mensa et thoro*, and it found sufficient fault to grant the request in an unprovoked assault on the wife by the husband. This would have been a correct ruling, but for the fact that South Carolina does not recognize that cause of action. The nonexistence of divorce *a mensa et thoro* in South Carolina was not conclusively stated until 1988 (see previous discussion in the section on jurisdiction).

The greatest source of current confusion about this issue was produced by *Machado v. Machado*, 220 S.C. 90, 66 S.E.2d 629 (1951), which, as mentioned earlier, is cited in S.C. Jurisprudence as standing for the proposition that grounds are needed. (*Simonds v. Simonds*, 229 S.C. 376, 93 S.E.2d 107 (1956), is also cited, but *Simonds* did not reach the merits of the spousal support issue. The Supreme Court remanded the case, holding that the trial judge had erred in not ruling on the wife's request for separate support and maintenance after it had denied her a divorce on the basis of constructive desertion because a full year had not yet run.) The following statement was quoted from *Machado* in *Simonds* and in other cases:

> The *causes* for which separate maintenance and support may be granted are not confined to those which constitute grounds for divorce . . . . In actions for divorce, we are limited by the terms of the Constitution. There is no statute in this state undertaking to fix the *grounds* for separate maintenance and support. This is left to the broad discretion of a court of equity.

Id. at 103, 66 S.E.2d at 635 (citations omitted) (emphasis added).

Machado is an interesting case, even though it has led to some confusion on the issue of spousal support. The primary issue was whether or not an absolute divorce could be granted on the basis of constructive desertion. The trial court concluded that it could and granted the divorce. The Supreme Court agreed that constructive desertion could serve as a ground for divorce, but it reversed the decision of the trial judge, finding that all of the requisite elements had not been met because the separation had been by mutual agreement. "Her departure was, therefore, by mutual agreement and did not constitute desertion." *Id.* at 101, 66 S.E.2d at 634. It also supported its conclusion by finding that the husband and wife had cohabited together after the separation by sleeping together for several nights at the husband's brother's house. Apparently, the court was implying that the husband's misconduct had been condoned. The wife subsequently moved to New York and other places before bringing the divorce action. She never returned to the marital home.

After finding that the wife was not entitled to a divorce, the Supreme Court considered whether she was entitled to support. The original opinion of the Court leaves the impression that the wife needed to show fault by the husband before support could be awarded. It even cited *Levin v. Levin*, 68 S.C. 123, 46 S.E. 945 (1904) (see above), among other cases, to support its conclusion that she was entitled to support because the husband had accused her of adultery on numerous occasions while flaunting his love affair with his secretary. This finding may be reconcilable with the Court's earlier conclusion that the separation had been by mutual agreement and its implication that the husband's misconduct had been condoned, in that some of the husband's accusations occurred after the separation.

The language quoted earlier from *Machado* has been read to imply that there is a need to find some misconduct on the part of the spouse who is being asked to pay support. This is not an unreasonable reading of the original opinion, although it makes no affirmative statement to this effect. However, the Supreme Court indicated that this interpretation is probably incorrect when it later explained its justifications for allowing the wife's request for separate support to be heard without requiring her to file a separate action. The following language appears in the Court's *per curium* opinion denying both parties' petitions for rehearing:

> But it is contended that the counterclaim did not allege a cause of action for support and separate maintenance . . . . The counterclaim

> or cross-bill contains the usual allegations in an action of this kind. Among other facts, it was alleged that the appellant "is well able to and has sufficient means to provide for the support and maintenance of the defendant and for the support, maintenance and education of the infant children born of their marriage," and "that the defendant is without sufficient funds or property to wholly maintain the support of herself and the said infant children, either permanently or during the pendency of this action." We think the counterclaim includes appropriate allegations for separate maintenance and support.

Id. at 108, 66 S.E.2d at 637. The Court does not mention any need to allege fault by the husband in order to establish a *prima facie* case for support.

Thus, *Machado* is probably best interpreted as saying that a showing of a need for support by one spouse, coupled with the ability to pay support by the other, establishes a *prima facie* case for support; and the court should then consider all relevant factors in deciding whether to award it. No case since *Machado* has said anything to the contrary. In fact, references to the need to have "grounds" for spousal support disappeared for the most part after *Machado*. In its place came the oft-repeated statement: "Only an adulterous wife is statutorily denied alimony. Conversely, it is an irrefutable judicial principle that any alimony award rests in the sound discretion of the trial judge." *Nienow v. Nienow*, 268 S.C. 161, 170, 232 S.E.2d 504, 509 (1977) (citations omitted).

In sum, there is no need for the court to find "grounds" before it can award separate support and maintenance. The basic obligation to support a spouse exists whether a husband and wife are living together or apart, unless the spouse seeking support has committed adultery. Whether or not spousal support will be awarded will be determined by the trial judge after considering each of the factors set forth in S.C. Code § 20-3-130(C) (Law. Co-op. Supp.).

It should be noted before concluding that the Supreme Court decided in 1952 that spousal support can be awarded when spouses separate by mutual agreement. In *Owens v. Owens*, 221 S.C. 84, 69 S.E.2d 74 (1952), the Supreme Court held that spousal support could be awarded where the parties separated by mutual agreement on the theory that the supporting spouse had elected to support his wife and children separately, rather than to live with them as husband and father. The Court's ruling that an implicit agreement to pay support exists whenever spouses voluntarily separate is a fiction, of course, but it is consistent with the rule that husbands and wives have a mutual support obligation, absent adultery. However, this fiction is no longer needed as the justification for awarding spousal support following mutually agreeable separations in light of S.C. Code Ann. § 20-3-130 (Law. Co-op. Supp.). The absence of fault as well as the existence of fault would be taken into consideration by the court along with all other relevant factors.

3. MISCONDUCT MUST BE SUBSTANTIAL AND MATERIAL TO BAR SUPPORT

a. In General

Courts have come to recognize that when a marriage has failed, both spouses were usually somewhat at fault in causing the deterioration of the marital relationship. However, a spouse will be denied support if he or she engaged in substantial misconduct which materially contributed to the failure of the marriage, unless the other spouse was equally at fault.

In holding that a wife was not absolutely barred from seeking support just because she removed herself from the marital home, the Supreme Court made the following observations in *McKnight v. McKnight*, 283 S.C. 540, 324 S.E.2d 91 (Ct. App. 1984):

> Her entitlement to separate maintenance and support is not affected "unless she is guilty of disqualifying fault in bringing about or causing the disruption of the marital relation, which her physical departure from the home merely signifies." *Welch v. Welch*, 250 S.C. [264] at 268, 157 S.E.2d 249 [1967].
>
> > As to what constitutes fault which will bar a wife from separate maintenance and support, this Court in *Miller v. Miller*, 225 S.C. 274, 82 S.E.(2d) 119 [1954], recognized that most marital difficulties

> are to some extent the fault of both parties and approved the rule that the wife need not be blameless in order to recover. Relief should be denied to her on this ground only if she was guilty of substantial fault or misconduct "which materially contributed to the disruption of the marital relation or induced the action by the husband upon which she relies to justify their separation . . . ."
>
> *Welch*, 250 S.C. at 251, 157 S.E.(2d) 249 (citations omitted).
>
> The evidence in this case sheds little light on which of the parties, if either, engaged in substantial misconduct which materially contributed to the disruption of the marital relationship. What is clear is that Mrs. McKnight's departure was not the cause of but only signified that disruption.

Id. at 544, 324 S.E.2d at 93. *See also Brown v. Brown*, 239 S.C. 444, 123 S.E.2d 772 (1962), which held, after reciting similar language as set forth above, that the wife was not entitled to support because she was substantially at fault in the separation and materially provoked the difficulties of which she had complained in her unsuccessful attempt to divorce her husband on the ground of physical cruelty.

Where marital misconduct exists, but it is equally divided, support is not barred even if a divorce has been awarded to one spouse on the ground of misconduct by the other spouse. *Clardy v. Clardy*, 266 S.C. 270, 222 S.E.2d 771 (1976). *Clardy* determined that the trial court properly awarded support to a wife, although the husband had been granted a divorce on the basis of her desertion. "Although the divorce was granted to the husband, it is inferable that fault is about equally divided. The divorce law of this State does not deny to a wife alimony except in case of adultery." *Id.* at 273, 222 S.E.2d at 772.

b. Habitual Drunkenness Alone is Not a Bar To Support

Habitual drunkenness will not bar support, unless misconduct resulting from the condition materially contributed to the disruption of the marital relationship. The

Supreme Court held that the trial court properly awarded support in *Herbert v. Herbert*, 260 S.C. 86, 194 S.E.2d 238 (1973), after the husband had been granted a divorce on the ground of the wife's habitual drunkenness:

> Admittedly, the respondent is a chronic alcoholic and it was determined in this case that she was a habitual drunkard within the meaning of Section 20-101(4) of the Code.
>
> In the case of *DeSipio v. DeSipio*, D.C. Mun. App., 186 A.(2d) 624, the Court held that the wife's chronic alcoholism was not misconduct precluding separate support and maintenance and went on to say that "chronic alcoholism, although frequently a cause of much unhappiness in family relationships, is not to be equated with misconduct. It is a disease, difficult to control or permanently cure, and seriously affects the employability of the victim."
>
> . . .
>
> The record here shows that the trial judge took into consideration, in making an award of alimony to the wife, the fact that she was a habitual drunkard but that such addiction should not be "used as the basis for determining real moral wrongdoing on her part."

Id. at 91, 222 S.E.2d at 239.

c. Adultery is Sometimes an Absolute Bar to Support

Adultery will be an absolute bar to separate support and maintenance only if it is committed before the earliest of two events: (1) the formal signing of a written property or marital settlement agreement or (2) entry of a permanent order of separate maintenance and support or of a permanent order approving a property or marital settlement agreement between the parties. S.C. Code Ann. § 20-3-130(A) (Law. Co-op. Supp.). This was not always the case. Until the statute was enacted, a spouse risked having support barred if he or she committed adultery at any time before the final divorce decree. *See Morris v. Morris*, 295 S.C. 37, 41, 367 S.E.2d 24, 26

(1988): "We hold that she was no less a 'spouse' under the separate maintenance decree, her romantic interludes no less 'adulterous,' than as the parties had never separated."

The implications of the statutory language are potentially quite significant. A strict reading would appear to permit married couples to engage in adultery without fear of losing their rights to spousal support if they have signed a property agreement at any time during the marriage, perhaps including a premarital agreement. It is doubtful that our courts would interpret the statute so liberally. The unanswered questions about this language pose risks for litigants, particularly since the statute does not define the parameters of "written property or marital settlement agreement." Does the agreement have to be complete — that is, does it have to settle every detail of every issue between the parties? Or could an agreement suffice which settles some or a significant portion of property or other issues? What if the agreement is found to be invalid, either in part or in its entirety for any of the reasons discussed in the chapter on agreements? Could a spouse who commits adultery in good faith (if such term can be applied to an adulterer) reliance on the existence of the agreement be required to pay support due to some unknown and unintended defect in the agreement? For the answers to these questions, we will have to wait for legislative clarification, or more likely, for appellate case decisions.

d. Abandonment is Not Necessarily a Bar to Support

Under the common law, and for many years in South Carolina, abandonment of a spouse was an absolute bar to an award of spousal support, unless the abandonment was "justified." This is no longer the case.[4]

Although in several jurisdictions, desertion absolutely bars a spouse from alimony, that is not the case in South Carolina. In *Welch*

---

[4] The statute which makes child and spousal nonsupport a criminal offense, S.C. Code Ann. § 20-7-90 (Law. Co-op. 1976), provides in part: "A husband or wife abandoned by his or her spouse is not liable for the support of the abandoning spouse until such spouse offers to return unless the misconduct of the husband or wife justified the abandonment." While this language might help a nonsupporting spouse avoid going to jail, this statute has not been cited in a civil spousal support case and it appears to be irrelevant to marital litigation.

v. Welch, 250 S.C. 264, 157 S.E.(2d) 249 (1967), an action for separate support and maintenance, the Court stated that the fact that the wife removed herself from the marital home was entitled to little, if any, weight. Her entitlement to separate maintenance and support is not affected "unless she is guilty of disqualifying fault in bringing about or causing the disruption of the marital relation, which her physical departure from the home signifies." *Welch*, 250 S.C. at 268, 157 S.E.(2d) 249.

> As to what constitutes fault which will bar a wife from separate maintenance and support, this Court in *Miller v. Miller*, 225 S.C. 274, 82 S.E.(2d) 119 [1954], recognized that most marital difficulties are to some extent the fault of both parties and approved the rule that the wife need not be blameless in order to recover. Relief should be denied to her on this ground only if she was guilty of substantial fault or misconduct "'hich materially contributed to the disruption of the marital relation or induced the action by the husband upon which she relies to justify their separation . . . .'[citations omitted]."
>
> *Welch*, 250 S.C. at 251, 157 S.E.(2d) 249.

The evidence in this case sheds little light on which of the parties, if either, engaged in substantial misconduct which materially contributed to the disruption of the marital relationship. What is clear is that Mrs. McNight's departure was not the cause of but only signified that disruption.

McKnight v. McKnight, 283 S.C. 540, 544, 324 S.E.2d 91, 93 (Ct. App. 1984).

This statement essentially represents the current law codified in S.C. Code Ann. § 20-3-130(B)(10) (Law. Co-op. Supp.), which provides that, in making an award of alimony or separate maintenance and support, the court must consider and give weight to "marital misconduct or fault of either or both parties whether or not used as a basis a divorce or separate maintenance decree if the misconduct affects or has effected the economic circumstances of the parties, or contributed to the breakup of the marriage . . . ."

To understand how much the law has changed, a review of relevant South Carolina cases is instructive. At the beginning of the twentieth century, it was inconceivable that a wife should be allowed to leave (abandon) her husband absent very significant justification. The three cases mentioned earlier in connection with the common law rule that a husband could not be ordered to pay support if he was not at fault provide extreme examples of the old rules. The facts in all three cases are reasonably similar. The husbands had deserted their wives, at least temporarily. The question for the courts then became whether the wives were justified in not following their husbands to their new domiciles or whether they were justified in refusing to live with them when they returned. In *Levin v. Levin*, 68 S.C. 123, 46 S.E. 945 (1904), the wife was found to be justified in refusing to live with her husband because his invitation for her to return to the marital home was not bona fide and because he had accused her of unchastity. In *Wise v. Wise*, 60 S.C. 426, 38 S.E. 794 (1901), the Court found that the seventeen year old wife was justified in refusing to live with her fifty-eight year old husband on the basis of *saevitia* which included his refusal to provide assistance for her during and after the birth of her first child and his rude and insulting comments about her, including an accusation that she had engaged in sex with a Negro boy and others (however, there was a dissenting opinion which would have held her to be a deserter). In *Hair v. Hair*, 31 S.C. Eq. (10 Rich. Eq.) 163 (1858), the holding was that the wife was not justified in refusing to follow her husband to Louisiana once he had issued a bona fide invitation to her (his promise never to make her leave South Carolina which had induced her to marry him was held to create a moral, not a legal duty).

Many subsequent cases have struggled over the question of whether or not a spouse, usually the wife, is justified in leaving the marital home or is otherwise at fault in bringing about the marital problems. A brief survey follows: *Machado v. Machado*, 220 S.C. 90, 80 S.E.2d 123 (1951), held that the wife was justified in leaving the marital home because of the husband's false accusations of marital infidelity while he flaunted his own love affair. In *Mincey v. Mincey*, 224 S.C. 520, 80 S.E.2d 123 (1954), the wife was found to have had just cause to leave her husband based on his "reprehensible conduct" which was not sufficient to serve as a ground for divorce. *Inabinet v. Inabinet*, 236 S.C. 52, 113 S.E.2d 66 (1960), determined that the wife was not required to live with her husband in his parents' home because they were rude and interfered. In *Brown v. Brown*, 239 S.C. 444, 123 S.E.2d 772 (1962), the Supreme Court determined that the wife was not entitled to a divorce on the ground of physical cruelty and should not receive any support because she had invited arguments with her husband and pursued them rather diligently and vigorously at times, thus substantially provoking the difficulties about which she complained (that is, she asked for it).

The modern rule began to take shape in the late 1960's in *Welch v. Welch*, 250 S.C. 264, 157 S.E.2d 249 (1967) (quoted at the beginning of this section from *McKenzie v. McKenzie*, 254 S.C. 372, 175 S.E.2d 628 (1970)), and other cases in the early to mid 1970's. This, of course, was the same period in our country's history when increased attention was beginning to be paid to women's rights in general. Although the husband had been granted a divorce on the ground of desertion in *Page v. Page*, 260 S.C. 298, 195 S.E.2d 613 (1973), the Supreme Court held that the trial court had erred in ruling that the wife's request for alimony was barred by a prior adverse ruling in an action brought by the wife charging the husband with physical cruelty and seeking separate support. A divorce had been awarded to the husband on the ground of desertion, and the wife's request for a divorce on the ground of physical cruelty had been denied.

> Regarding the former adjudication that the wife left the marital abode without just cause or excuse as conclusive against her claim to alimony in the divorce action, the court refused to hear her evidence relating to this claim. This was error. Only an adulterous wife is automatically barred from alimony by the terms of the statute. Sec. 20-113, Code of 1962. In all other cases, "the circumstances and conduct of an offending spouse might be such as to bar her from alimony but this is a matter solely for the trial judge, governed by equity and justice and the condition of both parties. The exercise of such a discretion will not be disturbed on appeal unless an abuse thereof is shown." *Herbert v. Herbert*, S.C., 194 S.E.2d 238, 239 (1973); *McKenzie v. McKenzie*, 254 S.C. 372, 175 S.E.2d 628 (1970).

Id. at 301, 195 S.E.2d at 614. The case was remanded for consideration of the wife's alimony claim.

The Supreme Court ruled that a wife should have been awarded alimony in *Clardy v. Clardy*, 266 S.C. 270, 222 S.E.2d 771 (1976), although the husband had been granted a divorce on the basis of her desertion. "Although the divorce was granted the husband, it is inferable that fault is about equally divided. The divorce law of this State does not deny to a wife alimony except in case of adultery . . . ." *Id.* at 273, 222 S.E.2d at 772.

As explained at the beginning of this section, the fact that one spouse abandons another appears to no longer be significant in and of itself. The important issue is whether the act of abandonment caused the disruption of the marital relationship or only served as evidence that the marital relationship had already been disrupted. *McKnight v. McKnight*, 283 S.C. 540, 544, 324 S.E.2d 91, 93 (Ct. App. 1984). This essentially represents the law which is codified in S.C. Code Ann. § 20-3-130(C)(10) (Law. Co-op. Supp.).

E. TERMINATION AND MODIFICATION

Spousal support which has been awarded pursuant to an action for separate support and maintenance can be modified for the same reasons as alimony: a material change in circumstances. Unlike alimony, of course, it cannot terminate upon remarriage because the parties are not yet divorced and remarriage is impossible. However, separate support and maintenance does terminate if the parties become divorced unless the divorce decree provides for alimony.

> Alimony and separate maintenance and support awards may be granted *pendente lite* or permanently in such amounts and for periods of time subject to conditions as the court considers just, including, but not limited to:
>
> . . .

(5) Separate maintenance and support to be paid periodically, but terminating upon the divorce of the parties, or upon the death of either spouse (except as secured in subsection (D)) and terminable and modifiable based upon changed circumstances in the future.

S.C. Code Ann. § 20-3-130(B) (Law. Co-op. Supp.).

In seeking a modification of support on the basis of a material change in circumstances, the practitioner should keep in mind the holding in *Witt v. Witt*, 271 S.C. 541, 248 S.E.2d 494 (1978), that no showing of changed circumstances is necessary to request reconsideration of spousal support where there was no evidence introduced at the original trial about the husband's ability to pay support. If there has been no original condition established, it would be impossible for a person seeking a modification to establish changed conditions. The Court emphasized in *Witt* that no decree should ever be issued without further proof than the terms of the parties' agreement.

Reconciliation terminates any ongoing or prospective obligations created by a separate support and maintenance agreement or order, although it has no effect on those provisions which have been executed by the time of the reconciliation. That is, prospective support payments will end, but the supported spouse does not have to return any payments received before the reconciliation. Also, marital property which was equitably apportioned by the family court remains nonmarital property unless it is transmuted after the reconciliation. *Crawford v. Crawford*, 301 S.C. 476, 392 S.E.2d 675 (Ct. App. 1990). In *Crawford*, the parties had separated and the family court had approved their property settlement agreement and had equitably apportioned the marital property. The property was divided accordingly. The parties subsequently reconciled, then separated again. The family court ruled that the previously divided marital property had remained nonmarital property after the reconciliation, and it ordered equitable apportionment of property which had been acquired after the reconciliation, been transmuted, or increased in value due to joint efforts of both parties. The Court of Appeals affirmed, holding that reconciliation terminates any executory support provisions contained in separation agreements or orders but it has no effect on executed property provisions. See additional discussion about reconciliation agreements in the chapter on agreements.

CHAPTER SIX
ALIMONY

CHAPTER SIX
ALIMONY

A. IN GENERAL

Alimony is money which one spouse is ordered to pay for the support of the other spouse in an action for divorce, whether *pendente lite* or on the merits of the case. There is no difference between alimony and separate support and maintenance, except that separate support and maintenance is what spousal support is called in actions for separate support and maintenance, and alimony is what it is called in divorce actions. (There is a separate chapter on actions for separate support and maintenance.)

Comprehensive legislation about alimony was enacted in 1990, and it applies to all actions for divorce or for separate maintenance and support filed on or after November 29, 1990. S.C. Code Ann. § 20-3-130 (Law. Co-op. Supp.) now codifies much of the pre-existing case law about alimony, but it also contains some significant revisions to the law. The text of the statute is included in the section on jurisdiction.

The family court is required to allocate support between spousal support and child support. S.C. Code Ann. § 20-3-150 (Law. Co-op. 1976) provides:

> In the event the court shall award the custody of the children to the spouse receiving alimony the court shall, by its decree, unless good cause to the contrary be shown, allocate any award for permanent alimony and support between the supported spouse and the children and in the event of the remarriage of the supported spouse the amount fixed in such decree for his or her support shall forthwith cease and no further alimony payments shall be required from the supporting spouse.

See Aycock v. Aycock, 284 S.C. 193, 324 S.E.2d 650 (Ct. App. 1984); *Radtke v. Radtke*, 297 S.C. 260, 376 S.E.2d 275 (1989) (both holding that if an award of unallocated support and alimony payments is to be made, there must be a finding of fact in the decree that there is good cause to make this award rather than allocated awards). In *Delaney v. Delaney*, 278 S.C. 55, 293 S.E.2d 304 (1982), the Court found that good cause existed for making an unallocated award because the tax burden shifted to the supported spouse who had little or no income, thus making it possible for the supporting spouse to pay more support. *Delaney* should be read in conjunction with *Beinor v. Beinor*, 282 S.C. 181, 318 S.E.2d 269 (1984), where the Supreme Court held that the trial court's finding of good cause for allowing the support to be unallocated was not supported by the record. The husband was a medical doctor. The court found that he was capable of paying the necessary taxes and the amount of support needed to maintain the wife at the standard of living of the marriage. "An award of unallocated alimony and child support should not be made purely as an accommodation for the Husband." *Id.* at 183, 318 S.E.2d at 270. The opinion does not explain how the facts in *Beinor* are distinguishable from *Delaney*, but Justice Gregory's concurring opinion expresses his continuing adherence to *Delaney*.

1. PURPOSES OF ALIMONY

a. The Current State of the Law

Alimony, like divorce, was unknown at the common law. It exists because statutes authorize it and courts have seen fit to award it. Insight into the origin and purposes of alimony is provided in C.J.S., which explains:

> Alimony is founded on the natural and legal duty, the common-law and statutory obligation, of one spouse to support the other spouse, which continues as long as they remain husband and wife, and which is not removed by asking for or obtaining a divorce. Alimony for one spouse by another has been called a substitute for the statutory right to marital support during coverture, and it has also been termed an allowance in lieu of a spouse's legal obligation to support the other spouse.

27B C.J.S. *Divorce* § 307.

When alimony was first considered in South Carolina, the political, social, and economic realities were quite different than those of today. Divorce was rare. Those marriages that ended in divorce were often lengthy marriages in which the wife had no job skills and less education than the husband. In most cases she remained faithful to her husband while raising the children and taking care of the household. This paradigm divorce situation also involved fault by the husband.

It is significant, in understanding where alimony came from and where it is going, to recognize that for many years alimony could only be awarded when fault existed because no fault divorces were not allowed. Litigation involving the wife's fault was mostly related to her entitlement to alimony (adultery always barred it, and desertion usually did . . . wives were less capable of physical cruelty and less likely to become habitual drunkards). Litigation involving the husband's fault was almost always related to the amount of alimony to be awarded. The existence of fault on the part of the husband added additional justification for the development of permanent periodic alimony and the concept that the wife should be maintained at the lifestyle she had become accustomed to during the marriage.

It is also significant to remember that, until recently, wives had no legal entitlement to share in the marital property generated by the labors of their husbands, other than dower. The concept of equitable apportionment did not exist. Alimony was the only tool the courts had available to recognize the sacrifices and contributions of housewives. It was in this context that the preference for permanent periodic alimony was developed.

The paradigm divorce case around which the initial principles of alimony were developed is no longer the norm. Today, divorce, not death, has become a more frequent way for marriages to end, and long-term marriages are seen less frequently in the family court than marriages of less than five years. Another modern reality is that no fault divorces have brought many parties into the family court who are equally blameless for the breakup of the marriage. Equitable apportionment of marital property attempts to provide both spouses a fair share of the marital property. An increasing number of women have entered the work force and they are making progress in closing gender-based employment and income discrepancies, although significant disparities persist.

The courts have been slow to recognize the consequences of these changes with respect to alimony awards, and they have not yet articulated a judicial philosophy which adequately responds to the varied needs of modern society. The 1990 alimony statute provides a greater range of tools with which the courts can work to forge new judicial leadership; however, it does not provide assistance in determining the appropriate purposes of alimony because it does not supply any criteria by which the factors listed in the statute are to be applied.

The family law practitioner is faced with inconsistent and conflicting statements about the justifications and purposes of alimony. This allows particular cases to be decided on the basis of judicial whim, not judicial philosophy grounded in public policy. This situation neither assists litigants in predicting the outcome of litigation nor serves the purposes of the judiciary of South Carolina. The less clarity and predictability there is about alimony, the fewer settlements and more appeals one can expect. This also causes litigants to incur greater costs, economically and emotionally.

The case which most clearly illustrates the current state of the law with respect to alimony in South Carolina, as well as some of the concerns about it, is *Johnson v. Johnson*, 296 S.C. 289, 372 S.E.2d 107 (Ct. App. 1988). Dr. Johnson, a dentist, married his dental hygienist on May 11, 1985. They had signed an antenuptial agreement. The wife left after fourteen months on July 14, 1986, due to verbal and physical abuse. Dr. Johnson sought enforcement of the antenuptial agreement, and the wife counterclaimed for a divorce, alimony, and other relief. The trial court held that the agreement was invalid and granted rehabilitative alimony of $300 per month for twelve months. Mrs. Johnson appealed, arguing that the alimony was inadequate to maintain the standard of living which she enjoyed during the marriage and that there was no evidence to show she would be able to support herself at that level after a twelve month rehabilitative period. The following quote from the Court of Appeals' opinion provides an overview of the law of alimony in South Carolina:

> Alimony is a substitute for the support which is normally incident to the marital relationship. *Lide v. Lide*, 277 S.C. 155, 283 S.E.2d 832 (1981). Ordinarily, the purpose of alimony is to place the supported spouse, as nearly as is practical, in the position of support

she enjoyed during the marriage. *See Voelker v. Hillock*, 288 S.C. 622, 344 S.E.2d 177 (Ct. App. 1986).

Alimony may be awarded as periodic payments or in a lump sum. Section 20-3-130, Code of Laws of South Carolina, 1976; *McCune v. McCune*, 284 S.C. 452, 327 S.E.2d 340 (1985). It may also be awarded as permanent support or as temporary, rehabilitative support. *See* Section 20-3-130; *cf. Brewer v. Brewer*, 242 S.C. 9, 129 S.E.2d 736 (1963) (permanent alimony); *Herring v. Herring*, 286 S.C. 447, 335 S.E.2d 366 (1985) (temporary, rehabilitative support). If a claim for alimony is well founded, the law favors the award of permanent, periodic alimony. *See O'Neill v. O'Neill*, 293 S.C. 112, 359 S.E.2d 68 (Ct. App. 1987).

The power to award lump sum alimony should be exercised only where special circumstances require it. *Millis v. Millis*, 282 S.C. 610, 320 S.E.2d 66 (Ct. App. 1984). Lump sum awards are not favored and should be given only in exceptional cases or when consented to. *Matheson v. McCormac*, 186 S.C. 93, 195 S.E. 122 (1938). An award of lump sum alimony must be supported by some impelling reason for its necessity or desirability. *Millis v. Millis*, *supra*.

Similarly, rehabilitative alimony may be awarded only upon a showing of special circumstances justifying a departure from the normal preference for permanent, periodic support. The purpose of rehabilitative alimony is to encourage a dependent spouse to become self supporting after a divorce. *Toler v. Toler,* supra. [292 S.C. 374, 356 S.E.2d 429 (Ct. App. 1987)]. It permits former spouses to develop their own lives free from obligations to each other. *Id.* However, it should be approved only in exceptional circumstances, in part, because it seldom suffices to maintain the level of support the dependent spouse enjoyed as an incident to the marriage. *See Id.*; *Voelker v. Hillock, supra.*

The factors to be considered in awarding rehabilitative alimony include: (1) the duration of the marriage; (2) the age, health, and education of the supported spouse; (3) the financial resources of the parties; (4) the parties' accustomed standard of living; (5) the ability of the supporting spouse to meet his needs while meeting those of the supported spouse; (6) the time necessary for the supported spouse to acquire job training or skills; (7) the likelihood that the supported spouse will successfully complete retraining; and (8) the supported spouse's likelihood of success in the job market. There must be evidence demonstrating the self sufficiency of the supported spouse at the expiration of the ordered payments in order for rehabilitative alimony to be granted. *Toler v. Toler, supra.*

In this case, the court found as a fact that Mrs. Johnson's standard of living during the marriage was much higher than her premarital standard of living and more than her income after dissolution of the marriage could sustain. Without explaining why rehabilitative alimony was appropriate, the judge fixed alimony at an amount which, at best, would restore her to her standard of living *before* she married, not, as the law requires, the standard of living she enjoyed *during* the marriage. This was an error of law amounting to an abuse of discretion.

The record reveals a great disparity in the financial resources and earning capacities of the parties. Moreover, it shows that Dr. Johnson has the financial ability to meet his own needs while supporting Mrs. Johnson at the standard of living she enjoyed during the marriage. It is likewise apparent that Mrs. Johnson could not possibly sustain her marital standard of living on her own earnings at the end of the period of rehabilitation. To require Dr. Johnson to pay a paltry $3,600 in support of his former spouse is plainly insufficient. These circumstances mandate an award of permanent, periodic alimony.

Dr. Johnson argues, and the family court agreed, that the short duration of this marriage weighs in favor of rehabilitative alimony.

> He overlooks the fact that his own conduct was responsible for its quick demise. Mrs. Johnson was entirely blameless for the failure of the marriage. When she married, she was entitled to expect a lifelong partnership which would provide her with a high standard of living and great financial security. Without cause, Dr. Johnson brought those prospects to an end. In effect, he now asks us to treat the result of his own misconduct as an equity in his favor.
>
> Unlike most cases, fault is a substantial factor in awarding alimony in this case. Dr. Johnson, not Mrs. Johnson, is to blame for the shortness of the marriage. When the duration of the marriage is seen in its proper light, the equities favor Mrs. Johnson, not Dr. Johnson. An at fault spouse cannot destroy a marriage and then claim its short duration entitles him to more favorable consideration when the economic adjustments attendant to divorce are made.
>
> We reverse the award of rehabilitative alimony and remand for an award of permanent, periodic alimony. *See Voelker v. Hillock, supra.* The factors which should guide the judge's discretion in making the award are set forth in *Lide v. Lide, supra.* While based upon the reasonable needs of the wife to maintain her marital standard of living, the award should also take into account her own earning capacity. Alimony should not serve as a disincentive for her to improve her employment potential nor dissuade her from providing, to the extent feasible, for her own support. *Josey v. Josey*, 291 S.C. 26, 351 S.E.2d 891 (Ct. App. 1986).

Id. at 300-303, 372 S.E.2d at 113-115.

As in *Johnson*, South Carolina courts have stated time and again that there is a preference in South Carolina for awarding permanent periodic alimony which has as its purpose: to "place the supported spouse, as nearly as practical, in the position of support she enjoyed during the marriage." *Cf. Mallett v. Mallett*, ___ S.C. ___, ___, 473 S.E.2d 804, 809 (Ct. App. 1996) (increasing the amount of alimony to fully meet the wife's needs following a twenty-one year marriage). However, they have not explained the rationale or public policies behind either the preference or the stated purpose served by it.

One problem with setting the standard of living enjoyed during the marriage as the purpose of periodic alimony is that it sets an impossible goal in the vast majority of cases. While this objective may be laudable, the reality is that two households cost more to operate than one household. After a divorce, both spouses should expect their standards of living to diminish, for this is what usually occurs. The courts have recognized this in practice, but the phrase quoted above is still repeated in many case decisions. Another problem is that it is not a fair objective to apply to marriages of short duration. Perhaps the most troubling aspect of the standard of living measure is that it is given great weight in some cases, but ignored in others.

b. A Suggested Policy-Based Approach

A more helpful way to approach alimony decisions would be for the courts to more fully analyze the public policy considerations which justify making an award of alimony in each case. This would help ensure that each alimony award is appropriate in light of the circumstances of each case, and it would lead to more consistency and predictability.

Of the public policy justifications which have been advanced in support of alimony, three appear to be particularly useful:

1) to express moral judgments regarding the marital behavior of each spouse;

2) to compensate the supported spouse for "faithful service"; and

3) to prevent the spouse in need of financial support from becoming a charge on public resources.

R. Chastain, *The Law of Domestic Relations in South Carolina*, 55 (S.C. Bar, 1986).[5]

The implications of these proposed policy justifications for alimony are discussed below.

(1) To Express Moral Judgments Regarding the Marital Behavior of Each Spouse

The use of fault as a factor in awarding alimony serves the purpose of expressing moral judgments regarding the marital behavior of each spouse. This is a controversial purpose, but one which has long been a reality in divorce litigation. South Carolina courts have made it very clear that, at least at the appellate level, fault will often make a significant difference in the decision to award periodic alimony. The marital misconduct of the parties has long been one of the factors used in calculating the amount of an alimony award. *See Riggin v. Riggin*, 282 S.C. 171, 318 S.E.2d 117 (1984); *McKinney v. McKinney*, 282 S.C. 96, 316 S.E.2d 728 (Ct. App. 1984); *Kane v. Kane*, 280 S.C. 479, 313 S.E.2d 327 (Ct. App. 1984); *Deglman v. Deglman*, 276 S.C. 600, 281 S.E.2d 123 (1981). Under the 1990 alimony statute, fault will continue to be a factor, but it can only be considered by the courts if "it affects or has affected the economic circumstances of the parties, or contributed to the breakup of the marriage." S.C. Code Ann. § 20-3-130 (Law. Co-op. Supp.).

Fault has been cited as a basis for increasing the amount of alimony to be paid by a supporting spouse, for reducing the amount to be received by the supported spouse, or for denying alimony altogether. In *Murray v. Murray*, 271 S.C. 62, 244 S.E.2d 538 (1978), the Supreme Court pointed out in some detail that the wife's misconduct weighed in the balance, along with other factors, in convincing the Court that $400 per month limited to a six-month period was not an inadequate award of alimony. The next year, in *Powers v. Powers*, 273 S.C. 51, 254 S.E.2d 289 (1979), Mr. Powers appealed specifically upon the ground that the alimony awarded his wife was excessive. Mr. Powers had an annual income of roughly $16,000, and his wife

[5] Chastain also suggests two other policies alimony should foster: 1) to protect the children of the divorce (in addition to child support monies); and 2) to minimize the financial impact of divorce on the less affluent spouse, while recognizing that divorce inevitably must have a substantial impact on both parties.

was awarded $3,600 per year ($300/month). The court wrote: "The breakup of the marriage was caused by Mr. Powers' infatuation with another woman and his subsequent desertion of Mrs. Powers. There is no evidence of any misconduct by Mrs. Powers." *Id.* at 55, 254 S.E.2d at 291. At the same time, however, it must be noted that the alimony in question was only slightly more than twenty percent of the gross income of the husband. It is, thus, somewhat difficult to see the extent to which the husband was in fact penalized for his conduct, although the Court did speak in terms indicating that it was appropriate to so penalize him.

The case of *Thompson v. Thompson*, 31 S.C. (10 Rich. Eq.) 416 (1859), held that "the amount of alimony depends largely on the extravagance of the husband's misconduct." *Id.* at 424. The court discussed in detail the husband's adultery with another woman: "[E]very portion of the testimony on point, without a particle of contradiction, compels the conclusion that the defendant is living in degrading concubinage with his menial servant. We may properly consider his misconduct as entitling the wife and children, whom he has abandoned, to a large share of his income." *Id.* at 425-426. No cases subsequent to *Thompson* have been found which actually made it a point overtly to punish a guilty spouse by ordering that spouse to pay additional amounts of alimony.

In light of the history showing that fault has been a significant factor in many cases, it is curious that numerous cases have asserted that alimony is "not intended to penalize one spouse while rewarding the other." *Donahue v. Donahue*, 299 S.C. 353, 362, 384 S.E.2d 741, 746 (1989). *See also Beasely v. Beasely*, 264 S.C. 611, 612, 216 S.E.2d 535, 536 (1975), stating that "[a]limony is founded in the legal duty to support his wife. It is not intended as a penalty against him, nor as a reward to the wife." While this may be an accurate statement in some no fault divorces, it is simply misleading in cases in which one spouse is more at fault than the other spouse. Perhaps what the courts have intended to communicate is that the punishment should not be disproportionate to the level of marital misconduct.

Fault does make a difference and a spouse who has caused the breakup of a marriage can expect to be penalized. The notion that the amount of alimony should be determined by reference to the moral conduct of the parties should either be given full expression or dropped altogether. It would seem preferable to give it expression. The Court of Appeals has come fairly close to doing so. In *Dooley v. Dooley*, 280

S.C. 514, 313 S.E.2d 331 (Ct. App. 1984), the Court of Appeals stated, "We affirm the award of alimony. The Husband was flagrantly at fault and proven so. The amount awarded is reasonable in light of the relative incomes of the parties and the approaching majority of the seventeen year old minor child." *Id.* at 516, 313 S.E.2d at 332. Similarly, in *Johnson v. Johnson*, 296 S.C. 289, 372 S.E.2d 107 (Ct. App. 1988), the court wrote:

> Unlike most cases, fault is a substantial factor in awarding alimony in this case. Dr. Johnson, not Mrs. Johnson, is to blame for the shortness of this marriage. When the duration of the marriage is seen in its proper light, the equities favor Mrs. Johnson, not Dr. Johnson. An at fault spouse cannot destroy a marriage and then claim its short duration entitles him to more favorable consideration when the economic adjustments attendant to divorce are made.

Id. at 302-303, 372 S.E.2d at 115.

If one of the parties is primarily to blame for the dissolution of the marriage, it may be appropriate to punish that spouse by awarding alimony even in marriages of short duration, as in *Johnson*. However, it is not clear why the appellate courts have preferred to rely exclusively on periodic alimony to accomplish this purpose - it would be terminated if the supported spouse remarries - rather than, for example, ordering an appropriately sizeable payment of lump sum alimony. If punishment is the justification for awarding a different amount of alimony than other factors would appear to warrant, the courts should make it clear what they are doing. One case in which the Supreme Court may have used another form of spousal support to punish spousal misconduct is *C.A.H. v. L.H.*, 315 S.C. 389, 434 S.E.2d 268 (1993). The wife left the marital home after six years of marriage when her daughters from a previous marriage told her that her husband had sexually abused them. She obtained a divorce on the ground of adultery based on that abuse. The wife sought "relocation alimony," and the trial judge awarded the wife "$105.00 per month as rehabilitative alimony for a period of one year." The husband appealed, arguing that the alimony award did not fall under S.C. Code Ann. § 20-3-130 (Law. Co-op. Supp.). The Supreme Court agreed that rehabilitative alimony may not have been appropriate under the circumstances, but it found "ample support in the record" for alimony under § 20-3-130(B)(6) which authorizes the family court to award "such other form of spousal support, under terms and conditions as the court may consider just," and it affirmed the award. It is not entirely clear what support the court found in the record for the award of alimony other than the misconduct of the husband.

(2) To Compensate the Supported Spouse For "Faithful Service"

This policy supports awarding significant amounts of periodic alimony in situations resembling the paradigm divorce cases which involve long marriages, disparate earning capacities, and, often, fault. One might use a contract law term to describe the same concept, saying that the supported spouse is entitled to the "benefit of the bargain."[6]

Irrespective of the terminology used to express the policy, it is quite legitimate to declare as a matter of public policy that a spouse who gives up other marital prospects, who gives up or detrimentally alters career plans, who takes primary responsibility for raising the parties' children, who is faithful, and who does not cause the breakup of the marriage should not be left without support from the other spouse, even if the other spouse is also without fault. Again, a contract term seems fitting: "substantial performance."

A "faithful service" reward will support the continuation of awarding periodic alimony in situations similar to those which originally gave rise to the concept of divorce, and it will preserve much of the case law developed in South Carolina. For example, statements about periodic alimony such as the following from *Eagerton v. Eagerton*, 285 S.C. 279, 328 S.E.2d 912 (Ct. App. 1985), would remain valid: "We would recognize that where a spouse has been out of the job market performing spousal duties over the course of a lengthy marriage, rehabilitative alimony will

---

[6] One should be careful, however, about trying to analyze marriages from the perspective of contract law. "The marriage commitment is not a contract in the sense of bargained-for promises with defined performance. Rather, it is a commitment to the relationship: to live and work together to maintain the transactions that tie them together and to address the future as a unit, making choices that benefit them as a whole." Cornell, *When Two Become One, and Then Come Undone: An Organizational Approach to Marriage and Its Implications for Divorce Law*, 26 Fam. L. Q. 103, 116 (ABA Section of Family Law, 1992).

rarely be approved; in these cases permanent alimony generally is required." *Id.* at 284, 328 S.E.2d at 915.

Indeed, it is difficult to criticize results such as found in *Canady v. Canady*, 296 S.C. 521, 374 S.E.2d 502 (Ct. App. 1988), where periodic alimony was awarded after an eighteen-year marriage. Both parties had enjoyed a comfortable standard of living, had no health problems, and were both employed. However, the husband's income was twice as much as the wife's, and there was no indication that she could attain further job training or skills at her age and with her employment background. Similarly, the result in *Mallett v. Mallett*, ___ S.C. ___, 473 S.E.2d 804 (Ct. App. 1996), seems equitable. The wife remained out of the work force during the final seventeen years of a twenty-one year marriage and cared for the children while the husband successfully pursued an insurance career. The court concluded that, in light of the husband's ample assets, the wife was entitled to sufficient periodic alimony to sustain the life style to which she had become accustomed.

Rather than using the "marital standard of living" language, however, it would be more helpful for the courts in such cases to explain their objective as striving to structure an alimony award which will equalize the lifestyles of the parties following the divorce. This would be consistent with the purpose of periodic alimony described in C.J.S.:

> Permanent alimony is awarded on considerations of equity and public policy. The responsibility of the court is to provide a just and equitable adjustment of the economic resources of the parties so that they can reconstruct their lives, by attempting to insure that the parties separate on an equal a basis as possible.

27B C.J.S. *Divorce* § 369 (1986).

An "equalization of lifestyles" approach would also be consistent with the statutory definition of "reasonable support" found in the criminal nonsupport statute, S.C. Code Ann. § 20-7-90(A) (Law. Co-op. 1976), which provides in part:

> Any able-bodied person capable of earning a livelihood who shall, without just cause or excuse, abandon or fail to provide

> reasonable support to his or her spouse . . . shall be deemed guilty of a misdemeanor . . . .
>
> As used in this section 'reasonable support' means an amount of financial assistance which, when combined with the support the member is reasonably capable of providing for himself or herself, will provide a living standard for the member substantially equal to that of the person owing the duty to support. It includes both usual and unusual necessities.

It is surprising that the appropriateness of applying this statutory definition of "reasonable support" to alimony decisions does not appear to have been considered by the appellate courts.

Of course, if the parties are already equally capable of supporting themselves, there is no need for alimony. Continued reliance on the "marital standard of living" objective could confuse this fact and lead to inequitable results. This possibility has already been recognized in some cases. For example, in *Trammell v. Trammell*, 268 S.C. 144, 232 S.E.2d 339 (1977), the court pointed out that the alimony awarded created a disproportionate income situation (with the supporting spouse having available some $260 per month after paying alimony and the supported spouse having available some $650 per month after receiving alimony). The court remanded the case for reconsideration, apparently feeling that, where income and asset postures were relatively equal between the parties and fault played no major part, the parties should have been left where they were found. Also, in *Collins v. Collins*, 283 S.C. 526, 324 S.E.2d 82 (Ct. App. 1984), the court said:

> We find that the court's denial of alimony and attorney's fees to the wife . . . is supported by the evidence. The husband earns approximately $740 monthly and the wife, $659 to $750. At the time of the separation, the husband had no separate assets. Both parties are able to work. An award of alimony is in the sound discretion of the trial judge, *McNaughton v. McNaughton*, 258 S.C. 554, 189 S.E.2d 820 (1972), upon a consideration of, among other things, the needs of the petitioner and the ability of the respondent to pay.

Id. at 531, 324 S.E.2d at 85. There is no discussion in *Collins* as to whether the wife's lifestyle after the divorce was going to be the same as it had been during the marriage. Thus, the objective of periodic alimony to maintain the marital standard of living, as discussed in *Johnson* and many other cases, was apparently not considered an important goal in this case.

(3) To Prevent the Spouse in Need of Financial Support From Becoming a Charge on Public Resources

In long-term marriages, there is logical support for attempting to equalize the financial situations of divorced spouses. There is no logical reason for trying to do so in marriages of short duration in which neither spouse gave up educational or career opportunities, or in which such losses could be made up fairly quickly. Where a marriage ends quickly for any reason and both spouses can be restored to their pre-divorce situations, permanent periodic alimony does not appear to be justified. In cases involving short term marriages, a presumption against awarding alimony would make sense, so long as neither party is likely to become a public charge.

If alimony is considered, a reasonable objective for cases involving short-term marriages would be to try to ensure that both spouses are able to live at a standard of living as near as possible to their respective situations before the marriage. This goal has been specifically rejected so far in South Carolina. As noted earlier, *Johnson* makes it clear that the standard of living to be achieved with alimony is that which was enjoyed during the marriage, not before: "Without explaining why rehabilitative alimony was appropriate, the judge fixed alimony at an amount which, at best, would restore her to her standard of living *before* she married, not, as the law requires, the standard of living she enjoyed *during* the marriage." *Johnson v. Johnson*, 296 S.C. 289, 302, 372 S.E.2d 107, 114 (Ct. App. 1988) (emphasis supplied).

However, the rationale for this position of the appellate courts has never been articulated, and it is inconsistent with other cases. For example, in *Nienow v. Nienow*, 268 S.C. 161, 232 S.E.2d 504 (1977), the Supreme Court affirmed an award of lump sum, rather than periodic, alimony following a marriage of short duration, although it determined that the amount of the lump sum award was inadequate. The trial court had ordered a lump sum award of $15,000 to a wife of approximately twenty-one months. The parties separated after about fourteen months of marriage, and they had lived together for over two years prior to getting married. The husband had an admitted net worth in excess of $4 million to which the wife had made no contributions. The court recited a series of circumstances including the relative youth of the wife, her good health, and her admitted capability for self support, as well as the fact that the husband was old enough to have been retired for some nine years at the time of the court's decision and had recently undergone open-heart surgery. It also pointed out that there was "insufficient evidence of any substantial marital misconduct on the part of either party." *Id.* at 171, 232 S.E.2d at 509.

The court then went on to write: "Yet, we conclude a lump sum of $15,000 is unreasonable in light of the wife's accustomed standard of living, the disparity between the parties wealth, and their respective earning capacities." *Id.* at 172, 232 S.E.2d at 501.

A presumption against periodic alimony except in exceptional circumstances might make more sense in marriages of short duration. Such a presumption could be overcome in cases involving fault or where other special circumstances exist, such as a risk that the spouse might become a public charge, e.g., due to bad health. In the normal case involving a short marriage, however, lump sum or rehabilitative alimony would be a more rational method for returning the supported spouse to society.

An example of such a case is *Shambley v. Shambley*, 296 S.C. 408, 373 S.E.2d 689 (Ct. App. 1988). Although the Court of Appeals used the term "temporary alimony," the award was actually rehabilitative alimony. The wife appealed the refusal of the family court to award periodic alimony. She was awarded $600 per month for a period to last four months after the date by which the court believed she should be able to gain employment. The facts found by the trial judge were that the "parties had the capacity to earn approximately the same income, that their standard of living was commensurate with that of a young couple starting out in marriage, that they had not accumulated any joint wealth to speak of, that the marriage was relatively short in duration, and that neither party was primarily at fault in its dissolution." *Id.* at 408, 373 S.E.2d at 690. The other facts were that the wife was twenty-eight years old, in good health, had high credentials, and immediate employment prospects. However, the "standard of living" factor was still a consideration given weight by the court. It came to "the conclusion that the wife, within a few months, would be capable of supporting herself at the marital standard of living." *Id.*

However, the statement in *Johnson* and other cases remains the law of South Carolina and, until it is changed, the objective of alimony is to maintain the spouse in the style enjoyed during the marriage, not before.

c. The Role of Rehabilitative Alimony

The family courts have broader authority under the 1990 alimony statute to fashion alimony awards that best serve the needs of the parties. This includes the ability to award more than one kind of alimony in the same case. For example, the courts could fashion a support award which combines periodic alimony with rehabilitative alimony in situations in which some, but less than full, rehabilitation can be accomplished. In an appropriate case, this could ultimately reduce the amount of periodic alimony being paid by the supporting spouse, while providing adequate support during a period of rehabilitation.

The appellate courts have been reluctant to approve awards of rehabilitative alimony alone. This reluctance reflects the reality that full rehabilitation is impossible to achieve in many cases. A spouse who quits work or decides not to pursue advanced education or training in order to raise a family and run a household cannot regain all of the career opportunities which are lost. Even if the means are provided to enable the spouse to become qualified to enter the job market again at the same level as before, that spouse can never regain the same opportunity for full advancement in a career because the number of years before retirement will be limited. In many cases, the spouse will continue after a divorce to face the same child care and other responsibilities which served as the basis for the original decision to forego career opportunities. In a marriage of significant duration, it is unlikely that a spouse who has stayed home to raise the family can ever become fully rehabilitated. Some have proposed that a fairer approach would be to make an award at the time of divorce which would be based on a calculation of the actual loss of earning capacity which has been caused by the marriage, while other proposals have suggested granting what amounts to a contractual expectation remedy. *See When Two Become One, and Then Become Undone: An Organizational Approach to Marriage and Its Implications for Divorce Law,* 26 Fam. L. Q. 103, 130 (ABA Section of Family Law 1992).

Although rehabilitative alimony awards have often been disapproved by the appellate courts, there appears to be a growing expectation that both spouses will work after the divorce or, at least, that the earning capacity of the supported spouse should be taken into consideration in setting the amount of periodic alimony to be paid. One should expect this trend to continue. The appellate courts have made it very clear that children are now required to make every effort possible to help themselves obtain a college education before their parents will be forced to contribute. (See the section on child support in the chapter on children.) It would be logically inconsistent for the courts to fail to require a similar effort on the part of supported spouses.

Some cases have begun considering the effect of periodic alimony on the supported spouse's motivation to earn independent income that is, whether alimony, or a particular amount or form of it, serves as a disincentive for the supported spouse to work. The leading case on the disincentive topic is *Josey v. Josey*, 291 S.C. 26, 351 S.E. 2d 891 (Ct. App. 1986). The Court of Appeals reversed the trial court's award of $48,000 per year, agreeing with the husband that such an award could only serve to deter self-improvement by the wife and precluded any viable option of her remarriage: "The ultimate alimony award, based upon the reasonable needs of the wife, should not serve as a disincentive for her to make reasonable efforts to improve her employment potential or dissuade her, to the extent feasible, from becoming self-supporting." *Id.* at 33, 351 S.E.2d at 896.

Johnson v. Johnson, 296 S.C. 289, 372 S.E.2d 107 (Ct. App. 1988), also includes a statement that alimony should not serve as a disincentive for the supported spouse to improve her employment potential nor dissuade her from providing, to the extent feasible, for her own support. The Supreme Court noted in *Williamson v. Williamson*, 311 S.C. 47, 49, 426 S.E.2d 758, 760 (1993), that "an alimony award should not serve as a disincentive for a spouse to make reasonable efforts to improve her employment potential or become self-sufficient." *Williamson* affirmed the trial court's denial of alimony on the basis that the wife had not presented sufficient evidence to establish the effect of her epilepsy on her ability to work.

If *Josey* becomes accepted as the more appropriate way to view the purposes of rehabilitative alimony (to provide an incentive to supported spouses to become self-sufficient), one could expect an increase in the use of rehabilitative alimony to provide an incentive for former spouses to rehabilitate themselves, perhaps in combination with smaller awards of periodic alimony.

However, in another case, the Court of Appeals found that periodic alimony did not provide a disincentive for the supported spouse to work. In *Curry v. Curry*, 309 S.C. 539, 424 S.E.2d 552 (Ct. App. 1992), the wife had not worked during the marriage at the husband's request. The husband was in the Navy and the wife had sole responsibility for raising their two children. The marriage lasted twenty-four years before the parties separated. The divorce was granted on the basis of the husband's adultery. At the time of the hearing, the husband had retired from the Navy, and he had a new job at which he was earning $29,000 annually and drawing retirement of $803 per month. The wife was earning $120 per month cleaning houses. The trial court's award of $719.10 per month in periodic alimony and forty percent of the husband's retirement was upheld. The husband contended that the amount of alimony awarded served as a disincentive for the wife to work. "Under the circumstances, we find no disincentive for the wife to work and hold there was no abuse of discretion in the amount of alimony received." *Id.* at 541, 424 S.E.2d at 554.

The presence of a child in the supported spouse's home may be an important factor in deciding whether to provide an incentive for the supported spouse to seek employment. In *Mallett v. Mallett*, ___ S.C. ___, 473 S.E.2d 804 (Ct. App. 1996), the Court of Appeals noted that an award of alimony should not be set so high as to take away from the supported spouse, who has no good reason not to seek gainful employment, all incentive to find such employment. However, the Court increased the periodic alimony award to fully meet the wife's needs to sustain the affluent life style she enjoyed during the marriage. The Court reasons for this were the husband's more than adequate income, the unsettled nature of the wife's earning potential, and the fact that the parties' teenage son "could benefit from the wife being in the home full-time." *Id.* at ___, 473 S.E.2d at 809. Based on these reasons, the court concluded that the husband "should be required to fully meet her needs, at least for the time being." *Id.* Although it is not explicitly stated in the opinion, the implication is that the wife will be expected to seek employment to reduce the husband's alimony burden when the child is no longer in the home. She has a college degree, and the trial court found that she is an able-bodied adult who has had ample time to complete any further education or training which she felt would have been necessary for her to reenter the work force. When the child leaves home, it will be difficult for her to justify staying out of the work force.

Most appellate court decisions have insisted that rehabilitative alimony should not be awarded unless it can be demonstrated that the supported spouse will become self-sufficient at the end of the rehabilitation period. *See Therrell v. Therrell*, 299 S.C. 210, 383 S.E.2d 259 (Ct. App. 1989) (holding that there must be evidence demonstrating *the self-sufficiency* of the supported spouse at the expiration of the ordered payments); *Hickman v. Hickman*, 294 S.C. 486, 366 S.E.2d 21 (Ct. App. 1988) (holding that the record did not show that after a period of time, Ms. Hickman would become *more self-sufficient* than she was at the time of trial); *Crawford v. Crawford*, 301 S.C. 476, 392 S.E.2d 675 (Ct. App. 1990) (holding that no evidence existed to demonstrate that the wife would be *reasonably self-sufficient* at the termination of the alimony payments).

Although they have not been consistent, most of the cases have indicated that "self-sufficiency" means the ability to support oneself at the marital standard of living. *See Eagerton v. Eagerton*, 285 S.C. 279, 328 S.E.2d 912 (Ct. App. 1985). In *Voelker v. Hillock*, 288 S.C. 622, 344 S.E.2d 177 (Ct. App. 1986), the Court of Appeals held that it was an abuse of discretion to award the wife rehabilitative alimony instead of periodic alimony. The marriage lasted eleven years and produced two children. The husband earned $100,000 per year, and the wife anticipated earning up to $30,000 per year if she could successfully retrain in the field of secretarial science. *See also Toler v. Toler*, 292 S.C. 374, 356 S.E.2d 429 (Ct. App. 1987) (finding that the trial court's order contained no findings regarding the wife's ability to obtain self-sufficiency at the end of the ordered payments nor any explanation for the amount or duration of the award.); *Crim v. Crim*, 289 S.C. 360, 345 S.E.2d 515 (Ct. App. 1986) (finding that rehabilitative alimony was not appropriate following a lengthy marriage where the husband's income potential vastly exceeded that of the wife, even if she became as rehabilitated as possible).

However, in *Bryan v. Bryan*, 296 S.C. 305, 372 S.E.2d 116, (Ct. App. 1988), the Court of Appeals allowed an award of rehabilitative alimony to stand, without discussing whether it would allow the wife to maintain the standard of living of the marriage. She had been awarded $1,700 per month rehabilitative alimony through August, 1987. She was to complete her degree in May 1987. The award allowed reasonable time to find a job. The wife's contention that she needed $2,500 per month and one year to secure a job was found unreasonable.

The future of rehabilitative alimony in South Carolina is unclear. However, one should anticipate that rehabilitative alimony will play an increasingly frequent role in the alimony equation, especially in marriages of short duration where true rehabilitation is a viable possibility. The concept of partial rehabilitation will probably influence awards of periodic alimony as courts struggle to create alimony awards which do not take away all incentive for the supported spouse to seek gainful employment.

d. Conclusion

A clearer judicial philosophy based on public policy considerations is needed if there is to be more consistency in alimony awards. The courts should consider abandoning the marital standard of living as the stated purpose of alimony. The policy of compensating the supported spouse wife for "faithful service" supports a continuation of a presumption in long marriages in favor of periodic alimony, where it is needed to equalize the post-divorce lifestyles of the parties. The courts should consider adopting a presumption against alimony following brief marriages, unless justified by a public policy, such as to prevent the spouse in need of financial support from becoming a charge on public resources. If the courts continue to consider fault as a significant factor in awarding alimony, as expected, they could be more explicit about the use of alimony as a way of expressing judgments regarding the marital behavior of each spouse. Appropriate roles for rehabilitative and other forms of alimony should continue to be explored as ways of creating alimony awards which are as fair as possible to divorcing spouses, particularly in cases which cannot be resolved by reference to the policy statements discussed above.

2. FAILURE TO OBTAIN SUPPORT IN SEPARATE MAINTENANCE ACTION MAY BAR ALIMONY IN DIVORCE ACTION

If the issue of spousal support has been litigated and decided in a separate maintenance and support action, it cannot be relitigated in a subsequent divorce proceeding. In *Powell v. Powell*, 249 S.C. 663, 156 S.E.2d 305 (1967), the wife had brought an earlier action for separate maintenance and support, claiming successfully that her departure from the marital home was justified and she was entitled to support. The husband later brought an action for divorce on the ground of desertion. The Court held that his action was barred by the wife's action for separate maintenance and support:

> It is hornbook law that a prior judgment of a court having jurisdiction of the parties and the subject matter is conclusive in any subsequent action between the parties, or their privies, of all questions which were actually litigated in the prior action and determined by the judgment, regardless of whether the subsequent action involves the same or a different cause of action.

Id. at 665, 156 S.E.2d at 306. A similar situation and the same result are found in *Blackmon v. Blackmon*, 294 S.C. 187, 363 S.E.2d 400 (Ct. App. 1987) (refusing to allow evidence of changed circumstances where wife pleaded prior ruling in separate support action and no changed circumstances and husband merely alleged she was not entitled to alimony).

If spousal support is requested in the pleadings in an action for separate support and maintenance, an agreement to forego it could bar a subsequent request for alimony in a divorce action. In *Lawter v. Lawter*, 287 S.C. 298, 345 S.E.2d 479 (1986), the Supreme Court held that the family court had no authority to award alimony in a divorce action where the parties stipulated and the family court noted as a finding of fact that the wife waived her right to spousal support at the separate maintenance hearing.

Settlement agreements in separate support and maintenance actions do not preclude subsequent litigation if the parties fail to obtain a clear ruling from the trial court based on some proof other than the submission of the agreement. Care must be taken to get a ruling by the trial judge on the merits of the issues, if one wants to rely on a separate maintenance and support action as a final disposition of disputed issues. In *Clayton v. Clayton*, 287 S.C. 308, 338 S.E.2d 326 (1985), an action for separate maintenance and support was ended by agreement of the parties, the terms of which were included in the court's order. However, the Supreme Court held that the issues covered in the agreement could be reconsidered by the family court in a subsequent divorce proceeding because the entitlement to support had not been "litigated or decided." Rather, the order had simply recited the agreement and made no ruling as to fairness. The holding in *Clayton* was distinguished in *Murphy v. Murphy*, 293 S.C. 151, 359 S.E.2d 91 (Ct. App. 1987), where the agreement in question had been approved and incorporated in the judgment of the court, not just merely recited. Moreover, in the action brought to attack the prior order in *Murphy*, the trial judge had determined the award of support to be reasonable.

In *Witt v. Witt*, 271 S.C. 541, 248 S.E.2d 494 (1978), the Supreme Court held that no showing of changed circumstances is necessary for a former husband to request reconsideration of the appropriate amount of spousal support where there was no evidence introduced at the original trial about the husband's ability to pay support. There was no original condition established; therefore, it would have been impossible for him ever to establish changed conditions. The court emphasized that no decree should ever be issued without further proof than the terms of the parties' agreement.

B. JURISDICTION

1. IN GENERAL

The general jurisdictional authority of the family court to award spousal support is found in S.C. Code Ann. § 20-7-420 (Law. Co-op. Supp.) which provides that the family court shall have exclusive jurisdiction:

(2) To hear and determine actions:

For divorce *a vinculo matrimonii*, separate support and maintenance, legal separation, and in other marital litigation between the parties, and for settlement of all legal and equitable rights of the parties in such actions in and to the real and personal property of the marriage and attorneys' fees, if requested by either party in the pleadings.

. . .

(11) To hear and determine proceedings within the county to compel the support of a spouse.

. . .

(14) To order support of a spouse . . . irrespective of whether [he or she is] likely to become a public charge.

. . .

(17) To make all orders for support run until further order of the court.

In order to be granted alimony a party must pray for the allowance "in his or her complaint, answer, or by petition." S.C. Code Ann. § 20-3-120 (Law. Co-op. 1976). A failure to obtain alimony or reserve the future right to seek it before a divorce decree is issued precludes the court from considering a post-decree request for alimony, even if a change of circumstances would warrant such an award. The reservation must be express and clear in the decree. In *Taylor v. Taylor*, 241 S.C. 462, 128 S.E.2d 910 (1962), no alimony was awarded at the time of the divorce because the wife earned enough for her support. She later sought alimony due to changed circumstances, but the trial court had no authority to grant alimony.

If alimony is not specifically requested in the pleadings, it may not be awarded, absent a later waiver of objection. In *Hopkins v. Hopkins*, 266 S.C. 23, 221

S.E.2d 113 (1975), the wife sought a divorce. There was no mention of alimony in the pleadings. The husband was in default.

Although it has not come up since the 1990 amendments to the alimony statute, the case law is that a court can award any form of alimony it finds to be appropriate if the pleadings ask for alimony, but only periodic alimony can be awarded in a default divorce unless another form of alimony is specifically requested in the pleadings.

> [O]rdinarily a trial court would have authority to direct payment of alimony in installments or in a lump-sum under a general prayer for such relief. . . . None of these cases involved default judgments. We are thus called upon to address a novel question, and it is our view that a general prayer for alimony does not provide sufficient notice to a defendant to support a subsequent award of lump-sum alimony upon a default judgment.

Harris v. Harris, 279 S.C. 148, 152, 303 S.E.2d 97, 100 (1983) (citations omitted) (reversing an award of lump-sum money).

This case seems to be inconsistent with the spirit of the 1990 alimony statute which provides greater flexibility to the trial judge in fashioning equitable spousal support awards. However, until the appellate courts clarify this issue, litigants seeking alimony should pray for alternative forms of alimony.

In cases not involving default, however, the family court has the power to award lump sum alimony even if it is not requested in the pleadings. In *Richardson v. Richardson*, 309 S.C. 31, 419 S.E.2d 806 (Ct. App. 1992), an order for the husband to pay the wife lump sum alimony equal to the fair market value of the marital home was upheld although the wife had not requested lump sum alimony. The husband had agreed to transfer title to the house, but later claimed he could not do so because it was titled in his mother's name. Because the husband was unable to comply strictly with the terms of the agreement with respect to alimony, the appellate court reasoned that the family court had the authority to effect the intent of the agreement in the best way possible.

If one pleads for a specific form of alimony, it may tie the hands of the court to award any other form. It appears that one might have to plead specifically for reimbursement alimony in order for the trial court to be able to award it, although it is not clear why pleas for "alimony" would not permit the trial judge to award any form of alimony which was deemed fair and appropriate. In *Heath v. Heath*, 295 S.C. 312, 368 S.E.2d 222, 295 S.C. 312 (Ct. App. 1988), however, the wife failed to get any reimbursement alimony because she sought only equitable distribution and lump sum alimony. The parties were married in March 1983, while the husband was in medical school. They separated in January 1985, during the husband's last semester of medical school. The trial court awarded the wife $20,000 as equitable division of husband's medical practice. The Court of Appeals reversed this and remanded the case for reconsideration of the appropriateness of lump sum alimony.

2. RESERVATION OF ALIMONY

It is possible to reserve the question of alimony for a future determination by the family court. *Taylor v. Taylor*, 241 S.C. 462, 128 S.E.2d 910 (1962).

The circumstances under which alimony is properly reserved are narrow. There must be a "determination that there exists an identifiable set of circumstances that is likely to generate a need for alimony in the reasonably near future." *Donahue v. Donahue*, 299 S.C. 353, 363, 384 S.E.2d 741, 746-747 (1989) (quoting *Tarrisi v. Sanzaro*, 308 Md. 515, 531, 520 A.2d 1080, 1088 (Ct. App. 1987)). In *Donahue*, the trial court had reserved the question of alimony, although the wife was able to earn more than the husband, due to the probable success of the husband's business. The Supreme Court reversed, finding that the wife had no need for alimony at the time of trial, did not have any health problems or expectation of health problems in the future, or some other extenuating circumstance to warrant reserving her right to alimony. "Where . . . there is no need for alimony at the time of trial; and no indication of physical or mental illness, foreseeable change in need in the future, or such other extenuating circumstance, the question of alimony should not be reserved." *Id.* at 363, 384 S.E.2d at 747. (However, *Donahue* was remanded with permission for the wife to amend her complaint to seek reimbursement alimony. She had helped support her husband for five years while he attended dental school, following which he began having an affair.) The Court of Appeals held that it was improper to reserve alimony in *Hardy v. Hardy*, 311 S.C. 433, 429 S.E.2d 811 (Ct. App. 1992), because at the time of the trial there was no present or foreseeable circumstance which would warrant the reservation of alimony.

The Supreme Court preserved a husband's right to seek alimony in the future in view of his permanent disability and his wife's prospects for future employment in *Stevenson v. Stevenson*, 295 S.C. 412, 368 S.E.2d 901 (1988), where the wife had returned to college and was about to graduate with a degree in practical nursing. Although the Supreme Court affirmed the trial court's denial of alimony on the basis that the wife had not presented sufficient evidence to demonstrate the effect of her epileptic disability on her ability to work in *Williamson v. Williamson*, 311 S.C. 47, 426 S.E.2d 758 (1993), it held that the question of alimony should have been reserved given the possibility that her condition might deteriorate. Reservation of alimony was also required by the Court of Appeals in an unpublished opinion, *Bryant v. Bryant*, No. 92-UP-036 (S.C. Ct. App. 1992). The trial court's denial of alimony was reversed. Although the wife was employed and both were "able to support themselves reasonably well," the wife suffered from lupus and it was foreseeable that her condition might worsen and force her to quit working. The Court of Appeals felt that the family court should have reserved jurisdiction over alimony:

> Were this appellant in robust health, we might hold that the trial judge did not abuse his discretion in denying alimony. We would find no difficulty in holding that he abused his discretion if the wife were unemployable at this time. We find that the likelihood of her becoming unemployable and needing medical attention in the future is sufficiently strong and that the question of alimony should be left open for later determination.

If the question of alimony is reserved, the family court should be specific about the events which will allow it to be reconsidered in the future. The Court of Appeals explained this in another unpublished opinion, *Markus v. Markus*, No. 92-UP-106 (S.C. Ct. App. 1992). The trial court had found the wife was currently in good health and did not order alimony, but it reserved jurisdiction to award wife alimony in the future "in the event of an unfortunate medical setback" or "other adverse circumstance." The Court of Appeals held that the order had to be modified by striking the phrase "or other adverse circumstance" as the language was too broad and the need for alimony must grow out of health problems supported by evidence at trial. The court held that alimony may be reserved if "there is evidence of a significant risk for the need of alimony in the reasonably near future."

Thus, while reservation of alimony is possible, it will not be granted routinely.

3. ASSISTANCE FROM DSS CHILD SUPPORT ENFORCEMENT DIVISION

The Child Support Enforcement Division of the Department of Social Services (the Division) is required to help collect past due alimony payments if it is also assisting a parent with the enforcement of a child support order. 42 U.S.C. § 654(6). The Division will not help establish an alimony obligation, although it may be required to do so in interstate cases (see discussion of UIFSA below). It will only help enforce an alimony obligation which has already been set by a court order and only when it is also helping the parent enforce a child support obligation which arises from the same court order as the alimony obligation.

Any person can receive assistance from the Division. Individuals who are not receiving public assistance benefits can secure the Division's services by completing and submitting an application form and paying a $1.00 fee.

4. INTERSTATE ALIMONY MATTERS

a. Jurisdiction to Award Alimony

A court with personal jurisdiction over the parties in a divorce proceeding has jurisdiction over matters such as alimony. *See Williams v. North Carolina*, 317 U.S. 287, 63 S.Ct. 207 (1942) (*Williams I*); *Williams v. North Carolina*, 325 U.S. 226, 65 S.Ct. 1092 (1945) (*Williams II*); *Vanderbilt v. Vanderbilt*, 354 U.S. 416, 77 S.Ct. 1360 (1957); *Nienow v. Nienow*, 268 S.C. 161, 232 S.E.2d 504 (1977).

Minimal contacts with the state are necessary to obtain personal jurisdiction over a person who does not reside in South Carolina. In *Carnie v. Carnie*, 252 S.C. 471, 167 S.E.2d 297 (1969), the respondent wife was granted a divorce from her husband who was stationed in Iran, was a resident of Virginia and had never been a resident of South Carolina. Service of the summons and complaint was apparently made by mail. This was not sufficient at that time for purposes of personal jurisdiction. The husband subsequently challenged South Carolina's jurisdiction concerning the award of alimony and attorneys' fees. He chose not to challenge the divorce or the child support award. The court determined that this constructive service might establish jurisdiction for marriage, as that is "a judgment *in rem.*" However, the other elements were "judgment[s] *in personam*," and personal jurisdiction was required. *Id.* at 475, 167 S.E.2d at 299. Without personal jurisdiction, the court had no jurisdiction to deal with these matters. However, in *Crowe v. Crowe*, 289 S.C. 330, 345 S.E.2d 498 (1986), the court determined that South Carolina had jurisdiction over a husband who moved to Georgia from South Carolina twenty years earlier, leaving his family in South Carolina. The court distinguished the facts from those in *Carnie* by pointing out that "[i]n *Carnie*, the parties *last marital residence was in Virginia.* We held no personal jurisdiction existed in South Carolina over the husband who remained a Virginia resident." *Id.* at 332, 345 S.E.2d at 499 (emphasis in original).

The Supreme Court affirmed *Crowe* and established the minimal contact rule in *Keller v. Keller*, 296 S.C. 412, 373 S.E.2d 692 (1986). The parties were married in South Carolina while Mr. Keller was in the Navy. They immediately left the state, but they returned to South Carolina just before Mr. Keller was transferred to the Philippines. The family stayed in South Carolina. The Court recognized that *Kulco v. Superior Court of California*, 486 U.S. 84, 98 S.Ct. 1690, 56 L.Ed.2d 132 (1978), required South Carolina to determine whether Mr. Keller had minimum contacts with South Carolina such that the maintenance of the suit would not offend traditional notions of fair play and substantial justice. In *Kulco*, the United States Supreme Court had determined that California could not exercise *in personam* jurisdiction over a nonresident, nondomiciliary parent of minor children domiciled within the state. As provided in *Kulco*, the Supreme Court determined that an essential criterion was whether the quality and nature of the activity of the defendant make it reasonable and fair to require him to conduct his defense in this state. The Court held that sufficient contacts with South Carolina existed to exercise personal jurisdiction over

Mr. Keller. It distinguished the facts from *Kulco* where the husband had only been in California on three brief occasions and both he and his wife were domiciliaries of New York and had spent almost their entire married life there, although they had been married in California. The Kellers, on the other hand, were married in South Carolina, last resided together as man and wife here, and the wife and the children had continued to reside here since the separation. (Given the statement of facts in *Carnie*, it does not appear that the "minimal contacts" analysis employed in *Keller* would have led to a different result in *Carnie*. The facts appear to be very similar to those that were found not to pass constitutional muster in *Kulco*.)

The Uniform Interstate Family Support Act (UIFSA) extends the concept of long arm jurisdiction as broadly as possible. It lists the "minimal contacts" which allow South Carolina tribunals to exercise personal jurisdiction over defendants in proceedings to establish, enforce, or modify spousal or child support orders or to determine parentage, including when:

> (1) the individual is personally served in South Carolina;
>
> (2) the individual submits to the jurisdiction of this state by consent, by entering a general appearance, or by filing a responsive pleading having the effect of waiving any contest to personal jurisdiction;
>
> (3) the individual resided with the child in South Carolina;
>
> (4) the individual resided in South Carolina and provided prenatal expenses or support for the child;
>
> (5) the child resides in South Carolina as a result of the acts or directives of the individual;
>
> (6) the individual engaged in sexual intercourse in South Carolina and the child may have been conceived by that act of intercourse; or
>
> (7) there is any other basis consistent with the constitutions of South Carolina or the United States for the exercise of personal jurisdiction.

S.C. Code Ann. § 20-7-980 (Law. Co-op. Supp.).

South Carolina courts may be required to recognize a divorce granted by another state's court, yet be able to disregard the other court's rulings on alimony and other issues which require personal jurisdiction. In *Murdock v. Murdock*, 243 S.C. 218, 133 S.E.2d 323 (1963), a husband and wife were married in South Carolina and were divorced in Kentucky on his motion and constructive service. The divorce decree in Kentucky purported to bar alimony. The wife, still present in South Carolina, sought alimony in South Carolina. Since South Carolina had personal jurisdiction over the husband and the wife, the Supreme Court ruled that South Carolina had the power to adjudicate the alimony issue. Inasmuch as the Kentucky Court lacked personal jurisdiction over the parties, its pronouncement on the alimony issue was a nullity.

The doctrine set forth in *Murdock* is the "divisible divorce" doctrine recognized in *Vanderbilt v. Vanderbilt*, 354 U.S. 416, 77 S.Ct. 1360 (1957). In *Vanderbilt* the husband and wife were married in California. The couple subsequently separated, the wife establishing a domicile in New York. The husband, in the meantime, obtained a divorce in Nevada, absent the appearance of the wife. The wife then filed suit for separation and alimony. She was granted alimony in New York. The husband challenged the award, contending that full faith and credit barred New York from granting alimony after Nevada had granted a divorce absent that obligation. The United States Supreme Court determined that, without personal jurisdiction over the wife, the Nevada Court could not deal with the issue of alimony. While New York was bound to recognize the divorce decree, it was not bound to recognize the *ex parte* alimony award. *Id.* at 418-19; 77 S. Ct. at 1362-63.

The Supreme Court of South Carolina affirmed the *Murdock* decision and noted its acceptance of *Vanderbilt* and the divisible divorce doctrine in *Nienow v. Nienow*, 268 S.C. 161, 232 S.E.2d 504 (1977). The parties were married in Florida. On their separation the wife moved to South Carolina. The husband remained in Florida and filed for divorce. She subsequently filed in South Carolina for divorce, alimony, and attorneys' fees. While the wife's suit was pending in South Carolina, the Florida courts granted the husband a divorce. The Supreme Court determined that, while it could not grant the wife a divorce because she had not resided in the state for a year prior to the commencement of her suit, it could decide whether or not the wife was entitled to alimony. The trial court obtained personal jurisdiction over the husband by virtue of a voluntary general appearance.

b. UIFSA and Assistance from DSS Child Support Enforcement Division

The status of alimony under the Uniform Interstate Family Support Act (UIFSA) (S.C. Code Ann. §§ 20-7-960 through 20-7-1220 (Law. Co-op. Supp.)) is unclear. UIFSA reads as though it applies to interstate spousal support actions as well as to interstate actions involving child support and paternity. However, the Child Support Enforcement Division of the Department of Social Services (the Division) claims that it is not required to do any more than to help collect past due alimony payments if the alimony obligation is set in the same order as a child support obligation which the Division is helping enforce. While this seems to be the extent of its obligations with respect to cases in which both parties are residents of South Carolina (*see* 42 U.S.C. § 654(6), the language of UIFSA implies that its obligations with respect to interstate disputes may be much broader. However, the author has been unable to locate any case which says one way or another if UIFSA applies more broadly to spousal support disputes.

In a UIFSA proceeding, a tribunal may do one or more of the following, if it has jurisdiction under UIFSA and to the extent it is otherwise authorized by law:

(1) modify an order of child support or spousal support issued by a tribunal of this State;

(2) establish an original order for spousal or child support:

(3) enforce a support order and income withholding order of another state without registration;

(4) register a spousal support order or child support order of another state for enforcement;

(5) register a child support order of another state for modification; and

(6) determine parentage.

S.C. Code Ann. § 20-7-1025(B) (Law. Co-op. Supp.) (emphasis added).[7]

Thus, UIFSA appears to contemplate that it will be used as a vehicle for "establishing an original order for spousal support." Also, there is nothing in federal or state legislation which supports the Division's policy of refusing to assist with the interstate enforcement of an existing spousal support order if the order does not also create a child support obligation which the Division is helping enforce.

Furthermore, UIFSA appears to provide clearly that the Division is supposed to provide assistance in such actions. Section 20-7-1025(C) (part of the same section which says tribunals may establish original spousal support orders under UIFSA) says:

> An individual plaintiff or a support enforcement agency may bring a proceeding authorized under this subarticle by filing a complaint in an initiating tribunal for forwarding to a responding tribunal or by filing a complaint directly in an appropriate tribunal of another state which has or can obtain jurisdiction.

The duties of the Division are defined in S.C. Code Ann. § 20-7-1050 (Law. Co-op. Supp.):

> (A) A support enforcement agency of this State shall provide services upon request to a plaintiff in a proceeding under this article.

Thus, it appears that the drafters not only intended UIFSA to be a vehicle for establishing original orders of spousal support, but also intended for the Division to help establish them.

This possibility is not without some practical problems. While there does not appear to be a good reason for the Division to refuse to help enforce any existing spousal support award, there are some reasons why it may be inappropriate to expect

---

[7] The family court does not have jurisdiction to modify a spousal support order of another state, unless it has obtained continuing, exclusive jurisdiction. S.C. Code Ann. § 20-7-1005(C) (Law. Co-op. Supp.).

it to help establish original spousal support obligations. The child support guidelines make it a relatively simple matter to calculate the amount of child support which should be paid. There are no spousal support guidelines. Instead, the family court is required to evaluate fifteen separate factors in deciding whether to award alimony, what kind, and how much. Thus, administratively negotiated settlements are not likely.

If the Division is required to help establish original spousal support obligations, it will need a much larger staff to conduct discovery and try cases in the family court. It is uncertain how much of this expense could be offset by UIFSA's special provisions for attorneys' fees. Efforts by the Division to establish orders of spousal support may also have unintended effects on other issues involved in the separation or divorce, such as property division which the Division is clearly not authorized to help with. Since spousal support must be awarded before the final divorce decree or is lost forever (unless reserved by the court for good cause), an effort by the Division to help establish a original spousal support obligation would often coexist with the efforts of private counsel to resolve other issues. Neither UIFSA nor any other legislation provides guidelines for resolving dilemmas arising from these situations.

If the Division begins providing expanded assistance with spousal support, anyone will be eligible to use its services, not just those who are receiving public benefits. The procedures and rules would be the same as those in UIFSA proceedings to establish and collect child support. See the discussion of UIFSA in the child support chapter.

Unless the Division begins providing additional assistance with spousal support, those people who wish to establish spousal support obligations or to enforce alimony awards not connected with child support awards must proceed *pro se* or with private counsel.[8]

---

[8] If a person with an interstate spousal support problem proceeds with private counsel, as permitted by S.C. Code Ann. § 20-7-1065 (Law. Co-op. Supp.), special provisions for attorneys' fees under UIFSA may apply. UIFSA allows attorneys' fees to be awarded by the family court. If attorneys' fees are awarded, they may be ordered paid directly to the attorney and collected in the attorney's own name. S.C. Code Ann. § 20-7-1085(B) (Law. Co-op. Supp.). The court must award

5. THE 1990 ALIMONY STATUTE

Many of the rules and principles about alimony which were developed prior to 1990 in South Carolina case law must be reexamined in light of comprehensive alimony legislation which substantially amended S.C. Code Ann. § 20-3-130.[9]

The 1990 alimony statute began as House Bill 2654, which intended to eliminate the absolute bar of alimony awards to spouses who had committed adultery as provided in § 20-3-130, and to provide for a more consistent approach to the award of alimony.

House Bill 2654 was then referred to the General Laws Subcommittee of the House. The General Laws Subcommittee invited comments from the Family Law Section of the South Carolina Bar. A comprehensive Bill was then drafted to codify existing alimony law and to include provisions eliminating the absolute bar to alimony for adulterous spouses. Although the initial focus of the drafting efforts was to eliminate the perceived inequities of the absolute bar to alimony arising from adultery, particularly post separation, the authors' emphasis shifted to drafting comprehensive alimony legislation.

The Family Law Section polled its members and the family court judiciary and received substantial support for the Bill. The Bill was then endorsed by the South

---

costs and attorneys' fees if it determines that a hearing was requested primarily for delay. In cases arising from requests to register foreign support orders, courts are required to presume that a hearing is requested primarily for delay if a registered support order is confirmed or enforced without change. S.C. Code Ann. § 20-7-1085(C) (Law. Co-op. Supp.).

[9] Before it was amended, section 20-3-130 read as follows:

> In every judgment of divorce from the bonds of matrimony the court shall make such orders touching the maintenance, alimony and suit money of either party or any allowance to be made to him or her and, if any, the security to be given as from the circumstances of the parties and the nature of the case may be just. No alimony shall be granted an adulterous spouse. In any award of permanent alimony the court shall have jurisdiction to order periodic payments or payment in a lump sum.

Carolina Bar. The Bill began the legislative process by receiving overwhelming approval in the House Judiciary Committee. The full House modified the section of the Bill which removed the bar to alimony, but passed the balance of the Bill without amendment. The Bill then moved to the Senate side and was addressed by the Senate Judiciary Committee. The bar to alimony and security sections were further amended in the Senate Judiciary Committee. The statute was fine-tuned and was ultimately signed by the Governor on May 29, 1990, to be effective November 29, 1990. All in all, the legislative process took approximately three years to complete (a Bill removing the bar to alimony was first introduced during the 1988 Session).[10]

In large part the new alimony statute codifies existing law, with certain important differences. The text of the statute is set forth below. The implications of each section are discussed later in this chapter.

C. PENDENTE LITE ALIMONY

1. IN GENERAL

The authority of the family court to award temporary alimony is clear. S.C. Code Ann. § 20-3-130(A) (Law. Co-op. Supp.) states:

> In proceedings for divorce from the bonds of matrimony, and in actions for separate maintenance and support, the court may grant alimony or separate maintenance and support in such amounts and for such term as the court considers appropriate as from the circumstances of the parties and the nature of case may be just, *pendente lite*, and permanently.

---

[10] Credit for this legislative history goes to Peter L. Fuge, Esq., Joseph T. McElveen, Esq., and James T. McLaren, Esq., who included it in CLE materials for a S.C. Bar JCLE seminar on November 9, 1990, "Family Law Issues: the 1990 Alimony Statute and Other Alimony Issues."

Two other statutes also provide authority to grant alimony *pendente lite*. S.C. Code Ann. § 20-3-120 (Law. Co-op. 1976) speaks to temporary spousal support in divorce actions:

> In every divorce action from the bonds of matrimony either party may in his or her complaint or answer or by petition pray for the allowance to him or her alimony and suit money and for the allowance of such alimony and suit money *pendente lite*. If such claim shall appear well-founded the court shall allow a reasonable sum therefor.

S.C. Code Ann. § 20-3-140 (Law. Co-op. Supp.) accomplishes the same thing with respect to actions for separate support and maintenance and other marital litigation.

> In all actions for separate support and maintenance, legal separation, or other marital litigation between the parties, allowances of alimony and suit money and allowances of alimony and suit money pendente lite shall be made according to the principles controlling such allowance in actions for divorce a vinculo matrimonii.

The principal objective of temporary alimony is to give the spouse seeking support sufficient means for her support and to enable her to prosecute or defend her suit. *See Armstrong v. Armstrong*, 185 S.C. 518, 194 S.E. 640 (1938). To this end, it has traditionally been viewed as appropriate to award temporary alimony without making any investigation into the merits of the underlying cause if the wife is unable to maintain herself separately from her husband and he is able to maintain her. Thus, the principal inquiries at the temporary alimony hearing are related to the relative financial positions of the spouses. *See Smith v. Smith*, 51 S.C. 379, 29 S.E. 227 (1898). In *Armstrong*, the court wrote:

> As the purpose of temporary alimony is to provide maintenance for the wife during the pendency of the suit, the reason for making her a temporary allowance for such purpose does not exist when the income of her separate estate is sufficient; accordingly, a

> temporary award will not be made unless it is shown that she is without sufficient means.

Id. at 522, 194 S.E. at 641.

The spouse seeking temporary alimony must make out a *prima facie* case. *See Fisher v. Fisher*, 276 S.C. 375, 278 S.E.2d 780 (1981) (reversing the trial court's ruling that the wife had not made out a *prima facie* case of habitual drunkenness). In *Poliakoff v. Poliakoff*, 221 S.C. 391, 70 S.E.2d 625 (1952), the Court characterized this as a showing "that she has a probable cause for divorce, or, if she is defendant, that she has a valid defense to the action." *Id.* at 396, 70 S.E.2d at 627.

2. REPAYMENT OF TEMPORARY SUPPORT MAY BE REQUIRED

When a person is seeking *pendente lite* spousal support, the other spouse should be given an opportunity to present evidence of adultery or other reasons why the request should be denied. In *Watson v. Watson*, 291 S.C. 13, 351 S.E.2d 883 (Ct. App. 1986), the wife was awarded *pendente lite* alimony. The court refused to consider the husband's evidence of adultery. At the final hearing on the merits, the husband was given a divorce on the ground of adultery. The husband appealed the *pendente lite* order. Both parties appealed provisions of the decree. The court wrote: "We hold it was error under the circumstances of this case for the trial judge to preclude the husband from attempting to prove that the wife was an adulterous spouse, as contemplated by the statute, and was not entitled to temporary alimony." *Id.* at 23, 351 S.E.2d at 889. This was further explained in a footnote:

> We recognize that time constraints may preclude the taking of testimony in every case where adultery is denied by the offending spouse. However, where there has been a *prima facie* showing of adultery through testimony or affidavits, it is incumbent upon the spouse charged with adultery to present a *prima facie* showing that he or she did not commit the alleged adulterous acts. At a minimum, a trial judge must in such situations provide for reimbursement to the payor spouse if adultery is proven at the merits hearing.

Id. at 23, 351 S.E.2d at 889-890, n.4. *Watson* was remanded with instructions to reduce the wife's equitable distribution by the amount of alimony paid by the husband.

If an award of temporary alimony is made at the *pendente lite* hearing and the temporary order is not appealed, the supporting spouse may not be allowed to seek reimbursement of the alimony paid under the temporary order. See *E.D.M. v. T.A.M.*, 307 S.C. 471, 415 S.E.2d 812 (1992), in which the court reversed an award of periodic alimony, then denied the husband's contention that he was entitled to reimbursement for the temporary alimony payments because he did not appeal the temporary order.

The possibility of having to repay temporary alimony has potentially significant consequences for a spouse who is awarded *pendente lite* alimony or permanent separate support and maintenance, but who might not be entitled to it. Such a spouse may be required at the final hearing on divorce to repay the entire amount of support which has been received as far back as the date of a temporary hearing on a separate support and maintenance action.

One way to protect a client against this risk in an action for separate support and maintenance is to be sure that a finding on the merits of the spouse's entitlement is made by the trial judge at the final hearing. If no finding on the merits is made, e.g., if the parties simply ask for an agreement to be approved, the receiving spouse could be at risk of having to pay back everything, if it is determined in a subsequent divorce action that the spouse is not entitled to alimony. *See Clayton v. Clayton*, 287 S.C. 308, 338 S.E.2d 326 (1985), holding that issues covered in an agreement submitted to the trial judge could be reconsidered by the family court in a subsequent divorce proceeding because the entitlement to support had not been "litigated or decided." The result would be different if the agreement had been approved and incorporated into the order of the court. *See Murphy v. Murphy*, 293 S.C. 151, 359 S.E.2d 91 (Ct. App. 1987), in which the agreement in question had been approved and incorporated in the order of the court, not just merely recited, and the trial judge had determined the award of support to be reasonable.

D. SECURITY FOR PAYMENT OF ALIMONY

S.C. Code Ann. § 20-3-130(D) (Law. Co-op. Supp.) provides:

> In making an award of alimony or separate maintenance and support, the court may make provision for security for the payment of the support including, but not limited to, requiring the posting of money, property, and bonds and may require a spouse, with due consideration of the cost of premiums, insurance plans carried by the parties during marriage, insurability of the payor spouse, the probable economic condition of the supported spouse upon the death of the payor spouse, and any other factors the court may deem relevant, to carry and maintain life insurance so as to assure support of a spouse beyond the death of the payor spouse.

The statute significantly departs from pre-existing statutory and case law as to security for support. Under section 20-3-130 before it was amended in 1990, the family court had the jurisdiction to require security for support. However, the appellate courts have only allowed security for support to be required in exceptional circumstances, and they have very seldom, if at all, approved the use of life insurance. The rationale was that the obligation to support a spouse terminates upon death. *See Hardin v. Hardin*, 294 S.C. 402, 365 S.E.2d 34 (Ct. App. 1987); *Ferguson v. Ferguson*, 300 S.C. 1, 386 S.E.2d 267 (Ct.App. 1989). In *Hardin*, the court wrote:

> The prevailing view, which we adopt, is that absent special circumstances or specific statutory authority, both of which are lacking here, the Family Court does not have the inherent power to require a supporting spouse to obtain or maintain, solely as an incident of support, a life insurance policy naming the dependent spouse as a beneficiary, the rationale being that such a requirement is in the nature of alimony, for which liability ceases upon the death of the supporting spouse.

Hardin, 294 S.C. at 404, 365 S.E.2d at 36.

Under the 1990 alimony statute, security for support, including life insurance, is allowed "to assure support of the supported spouse beyond the death of the payor spouse," and it lists some factors to be considered before requiring it. However, the statute does not require the family court to provide for support beyond the death of the payor spouse. It does not even say that it should ever be required, and it does not set forth any criteria for determining the circumstances under which it might be appropriate. Thus, it remains to be seen whether the changes in the statute result in any changes in practice. Note that life insurance to ensure the satisfaction of a child support obligation can only be required for a "compelling reason, amounting to necessity." *See Shambley v. Shambley*, 296 S.C. 408, 373 S.E.2d 689 (Ct. App. 1988).

E. METHOD OF PAYMENT

1. IN GENERAL

S.C. Code Ann. § 20-7-420(21) (Law. Co-op. 1976) provides that "The family court shall have exclusive jurisdiction: To determine the manner in which sums ordered paid for support shall be paid and applied, either to a person through the court or through the clerk of court."

S.C. Code Ann. § 20-3-130(E) (Law. Co-op. Supp.) provides: "In making an award of alimony or separate maintenance and support, the court may order the direct payment to the supported spouse, or may require that the payments be made through the Family Court and allocate responsibility for the service fee in connection with the award. The court may require the payment of debts, obligations, and other matters on behalf of the supported spouse."

This language codifies existing law and makes it clear that the family court can allocate payment of the service fee. The family court also continues to have the jurisdiction to order the support of a spouse by directing that payments such as house payments, car payments, and the like be paid on behalf of the supported spouse.

The normal rule is that spousal support will be paid in cash and the court cannot order a supporting spouse to transfer property in lieu of money. The Supreme Court, in *Smith v. Smith*, 264 S.C. 624, 216 S.E.2d 541 (1975), stated:

> The general rule is that the word "alimony" is restricted to payments in money. We think that the only reasonable conclusion that can be reached is that our statute contemplates the payment of alimony in money. This being true, the court has no power to award any specific property of the husband as alimony. . . . It follows that the court is without authority to set apart to the wife as alimony any specific property of the husband.

Id. at 630-631, 216 S.E.2d at 544-545 (citations omitted).

An alimony award in the form of health insurance is allowed in appropriate situations. In *Sharpe v. Sharpe*, 307 S.C. 540, 416 S.E.2d 215 (Ct. App. 1992), an award of alimony was upheld which included requiring the husband to maintain health insurance for the wife through his business, because the wife was terminally ill (the fact that the husband had tried to kill her was also given some weight by the court).

2. TRANSFER OR USE OF MARITAL PROPERTY

The alimony statute does not address the ability of the family court to order the transfer of property to satisfy a support obligation. Presumably, requiring such a transfer continues to be prohibited under existing case law.

As mentioned above, the normal rule is that the court cannot order a supporting spouse to transfer property in lieu of money. *Smith v. Smith*, 264 S.C. 624, 216 S.E.2d 541 (1975). In *Hendricks v. Hendricks*, 285 S.C. 591, 330 S.E.2d 553 (Ct. App. 1985), the court said:

> The court properly disregarded Mrs. Hendricks' request for the home as alimony because it "is well settled a court may not order the

> transfer of property as alimony or in lieu thereof." *Poniatowski v. Poniatowski*, 275 S.C. 11 [,12], 266 S.E.2d 787, 788 (1988).

Id. at 593, 330 S.E.2d at 554. Mrs. Hendricks had received the house as part of equitable distribution in addition to lump sum alimony.

Although the court cannot order the transfer of property to satisfy alimony, it can offer such transfer to the paying spouse as an alternative way to satisfy the obligation. As the Supreme Court noted in *Wilson v. Wilson*, 270 S.C. 216, 241 S.E.2d 566 (1978):

> Mr. Wilson next appeals the lower court's order that he convey his own one half interest in the Anderson residence and the lake property to Mrs. Wilson as an equitable division of property in lieu of alimony. Although the lower court could have specified such property transfer as an alternate method of satisfying an alimony award, it could not order the property transferred in lieu of alimony.

Id. at 222, 241 S.E.2d at 569. *See also Jones v. Jones*, 270 S.C. 280, 241 S.E.2d 904 (1978) (Mr. Jones was offered the option of paying Mrs. Jones "$36,000 as lump sum alimony or in lieu thereof to pay $150.00 per month from January 1977 through October 1977 and then convey to Mrs. Jones all of the cleared land on his farm for a term of twelve years so she can rent the same for her support"); *Hussey v. Hussey*, 280 S.C. 418, 312 S.E.2d 267 (Ct. App. 1984) ("it is entirely proper for a family court to permit an award of lump sum alimony or a monetary property distribution to be satisfied by the transfer of specific property").

A broad exception to the rule against transferring property in lieu of alimony may have been created in *Poniatowski v. Poniatowski*, 275 S.C. 11, 266 S.E.2d 787 (1988). In *Poniatowski* the husband was ordered to transfer his interest in a bookstore to his wife as division of property and in lieu of alimony. The Supreme Court upheld the trial court's decision and explained that it was not changing the rule against transfers of property in lieu of alimony:

> Here, the court effected a division of the marital property while preserving respondent's future right to alimony.

> Upon holding respondent entitled to both alimony and an equitable share of appellant's business interest, the family court recognized the proposed property division would make payment of the alimony unnecessary and perhaps unduly difficult for appellant *at the present time*. It is clear from this finding the court did not intend the transfer of the bookstore to take the place of alimony. We construe the decree as awarding respondent appellant's interest in the bookstore only in lieu of *present* alimony.

Id. at 12-13, 266 S.E.2d at 788 (emphasis supplied). Thus, the appellant came to the appellate court arguing that it was unfair to take his bookstore as alimony, only to leave the court with the bookstore still owned by his wife and now facing the possibility of alimony being awarded against him in the future.

It is difficult to reconcile *Poniatowski* with the cases cited earlier. One way to distinguish it is to consider it simply as a case in which the marital property was divided, with the question of alimony being reserved for future consideration on the basis that the husband was unable to pay any alimony now, but his income was expected to go up. However, this is not what the trial court or the Supreme Court held. The Supreme Court's holding seems to be that a transfer of property can be ordered to partially, but not totally, satisfy an obligation to pay alimony. Most likely, *Poniatowski* should be read narrowly. The notion that property can be transferred in lieu of alimony, whether present or otherwise, is inconsistent with all other appellate decisions on this issue.

The family court is allowed to award the use of the marital home as spousal support, but only temporarily and only if special circumstances exist. A statement of the principles to be followed in deciding whether to award a spouse the exclusive possession of the marital home is found in *Johnson v. Johnson*, 285 S.C. 308, 329 S.E.2d 443 (Ct. App. 1985):

> First, the family court must begin with the premise that division and distribution of the marital home should be accomplished at the time of entry of the judgment of divorce. If possible, all issues between the parties should be resolved at that point so that disputes and irritants do not linger and present further incentives to litigation.

The family court's objective should be to dissolve the marriage, sever all entangling legal relations and place the parties in a position from which they can begin anew. In most cases, the parting of the ways should be accompanied by clearly stated obligations for the future, put in monetary terms as far as possible.

Second, the court must carefully consider the claim of a party that the interests of that party or the children are so predominant, when balanced against the interests of the other, that an award of the use of the marital home is compelled. In *Thompson v. Brunson, supra* [283 S.C. 221, 321 S.E.2d 622 (Ct. App. 1984)], and *Shafer v. Shafer, supra* [283 S.C. 205, 320 S.E.2d 730 (Ct. App. 1984)], we noted some of the interests which may be considered compelling: (1) adequate shelter for minors; (2) suitable housing for a handicapped or infirm spouse; and (3) the inability of the occupying spouse to otherwise obtain adequate housing.

In the same context, the court must consider the interests of the non-occupying spouse. An award of exclusive possession to one party requires that the other defer the realization of the value of his share of the marital home. Such a requirement is usually a burden. Therefore, before the family court imposes such a burden, it should consider the size and expansiveness of the home in relation to the expected use and the cost of maintaining the home in comparison to the benefits received. Further, the court must consider the potential duration of the exclusive possession. The family court may not award exclusive possession of the marital home for an unlimited period of time. In the exercise of sound discretion, the court must make the award for a reasonable time based on the circumstances warranting the award in the first place.

Finally, the family court must make such provision in its order for eventual distribution of the marital home and state the terms upon which such distribution will be made.

Id. at 311-312, 329 S.E.2d at 445-446 (citations omitted). In *Johnson*, the Court of Appeals reversed the award of exclusive use of the marital home to the wife and remanded the case because the trial judge did not identify any compelling reasons for making the award, establish the value of the husband's interest in the home, consider the reasonableness of the period of time he would be deprived of this interest, or provide for the eventual distribution of the home.

An award of exclusive possession of the marital home to the wife was also reversed, and the marital home was ordered to be sold in *Smith v. Smith*, 280 S.C. 257, 312 S.E.2d 560 (Ct. App. 1984), where the court stated:

> [T]he family court should not have granted the wife the exclusive use and possession of the marital home. A court should not give a spouse exclusive possession of a residence as an incident of support where the evidence reflects that a substantial portion of the other spouse's assets are invested in the home and there is no evidence either that the other spouse has custody of the parties' minor children, that the other spouse is severely handicapped, or that some other special circumstance exists which would warrant such an award.

Id. at 264-265, 312 S.E.2d at 565.

The only "special circumstance" which is evident from the opinion in *Hickman v. Hickman*, 294 S.C. 486, 366 S.E.2d 21 (Ct. App. 1988), is that the wife had custody of the children. In *Hickman*, the Court of Appeals upheld the trial court's award to the wife of the exclusive use of the marital home "at least until July, 1991 at which time [the older son's] four-year college term should have ended . . . ." *Id.* at 491, 366 S.E.2d at 25. This suggests that the award may have been one for child support, not spousal support, but the opinion is not clear about this.

The appellate cases frequently fail to indicate whether the use of the marital home has been awarded as spousal support or child support. For example, in *Stafford v. Stafford*, 296 S.C. 423, 373 S.E.2d 699 (Ct. App. 1988), the court noted that the wife was awarded use of the marital home as support and the husband made certain payments toward its operation. It appeared that the use of the home may have been awarded as spousal support. However, it was noted that one-half of the husband's payments were designated as child support and one-half as spousal support. The court held in *Stafford* that the disposition of the marital home was merely incidental to separation and not a true property settlement; therefore, the husband was not barred from seeking equitable distribution of his interest in the house.

The failure to explain whether the use of the marital home is being awarded as spousal support or as child support is potentially significant for tax reasons and also because one difference between spousal and child support is that a child support obligation usually ends as soon as the children are emancipated, while an obligation to provide spousal support may continue until one of the parties dies. When the supporting spouse's interest in obtaining his or her equity out of the marital home is balanced against the supported spouse's interest in continuing to live in the marital home, one would expect the court to order the marital home to be sold in virtually every case, as it did in *Smith*, absent a finding of special circumstances.

The practitioner should note that the sequestration statute, S.C. Code Ann. § 20-7-475 (Law. Co-op. Supp.), applies only to enforcement of equitable apportionment, not to alimony. The policy reasons for not allowing sequestration also to enforce alimony awards are not apparent.

F. TAX CONSEQUENCES

S.C. Code Ann. § 20-3-130(F) (Law. Co-op. Supp.) provides:

> The court may elect and determine the intended tax effect of the alimony and separate maintenance and support as provided by the Internal Revenue Code and any corresponding state tax provisions. The Family Court may allocate the right to claim dependency exemptions pursuant to the Internal Revenue Code and under corresponding state tax provisions and to require the execution and delivery of all necessary documents and tax filings in connection with the exemption.

This language grants power to the family court to elect and determine the intended tax effect of alimony and separate maintenance and support as provided by the Internal Revenue Code and any corresponding state tax provisions. This means, in effect, that the family court may deem alimony deductible to the payor spouse and taxable to the payee spouse, or direct that the payment be non-deductible to the payor spouse and nontaxable to the payee spouse. The family court also has jurisdiction to allocate the right to claim the dependency exemptions and to require the execution and delivery of all necessary documents and tax filings in connection with the exemption.

The language grants the family court considerable discretion to fashion its intended support remedy, and it is a significant departure from prior case law. If the court intends for the supported spouse to have a specific sum of money to meet his or her expenses on a monthly basis, the court can fashion that remedy by deeming the alimony award non-deductible and non-taxable. The supported spouse will then have the amount of support the family court intended for the payment of monthly and other expenses. *Wood v. Wood*, No. 96-UP-124 (S.C. Ct. App. 1996) (finding no abuse of discretion for the family court judge to order the wife's alimony taxable as income to her and deductible to the husband).

On the other hand, if there appears to be an advantage to structure the alimony award as taxable to the payor spouse and deductible to the payee spouse, the court may structure the alimony as deductible to the payor spouse and taxable to the supported spouse. The court should, however, make a determination of the spendable income of each of the parties after considering tax effects, as required by S.C. Code Ann. § 20-3-130(C)(11) (Law. Co-op. Supp.).

Under current tax law the custodial spouse is generally entitled to claim the dependency exemption for the child or children in his or her legal custody, subject to certain qualifications. The new statute, in conjunction with the applicable tax code provisions, allows the family court to allocate the right to claim the children as exemptions for tax purposes.

The practitioner should take care to ensure that the family court's order accomplishes the intended effect and that the language conforms to the technical requirements of the Internal Revenue Code.

G. ATTORNEYS' FEES AND LITIGATION EXPENSES

S.C. Code Ann. § 20-3-130(H) (Law. Co-op. Supp.) provides:

> The court, from time to time after considering the financial resources and marital fault of both parties, may order one party to pay a reasonable amount to the other for attorney fees, expert fees, investigation fees, costs, and suit money incurred in maintaining an action for divorce from the bonds of matrimony, as well as in actions for separate maintenance and support, including sums for services rendered and costs incurred before the commencement of the proceeding and after entry of judgment, pendente lite and permanently.

This clarifies the power of the family court (which probably existed before the enactment of the 1990 amendments) to order the payment of attorneys' fees, expert fees, investigation fees, costs and suit money. It also makes it clear that the court can award fees and costs incurred before the commencement of the proceeding and after entry of the judgment, both *pendente lite* and permanently. The statute does require, however, specific consideration of "the financial resources and marital fault of both parties."

There is a special provision for attorneys' fees in interstate actions to establish or enforce spousal support actions under the Uniform Interstate Family Support Act (UIFSA). Private counsel may be used in UIFSA proceedings, and attorneys' fees may be awarded by the family court. S.C. Code Ann. § 20-7-1065 (Law. Co-op. Supp.) If attorneys' fees are awarded, they may be ordered paid directly to the attorney and collected in the attorney's own name. S.C. Code Ann. § 20-7-1085(B) (Law. Co-op. Supp.). The court must award costs and attorneys' fees if it determines that a hearing was requested primarily for delay. In cases arising from requests to register foreign support orders, courts are required to presume that a hearing is requested primarily for delay if a registered support order is confirmed or enforced without change. S.C. Code Ann. § 20-7-1085(C) (Law. Co-op. Supp.).

Attorneys' fees and litigation expenses are discussed more fully in a separate chapter.

H. TYPES OF ALIMONY (AND TERMINATION AND MODIFICATION)

1. IN GENERAL

S.C. Code Ann. § 20-3-130 (Law. Co-op. Supp.) defines six different types of spousal support that may be awarded by the family court: 1) periodic alimony; 2) lump sum alimony; 3) rehabilitative alimony; 4) reimbursement alimony; 5) separate maintenance and support; and 6) such other form of spousal support, under terms and conditions as the Court may consider just, as appropriate under the circumstances without limitation to grant more than one form of support.

Each of these may be awarded *pendente lite* and permanently "in such amounts and for periods of time subject to conditions as the court considers just." The statute defines the general circumstances under which each type of spousal support may be appropriate, and grants the family court more discretion in fashioning a support award.

Permanent periodic alimony is the form of alimony favored in South Carolina. *See Johnson v. Johnson*, 296 S.C. 289, 372 S.E.2d 107 (Ct. App. 1988); *Gill v. Gill*, 269 S.C. 337, 237 S.E.2d 382 (1977). However, in light of the 1990 alimony statute, one might anticipate that family courts will begin awarding a broader range of forms of alimony in appropriate cases, especially rehabilitative alimony.

Special circumstances must exist to award any form of alimony other than periodic alimony, and the family court must make it clear which form of alimony is being awarded. In *Carroll v. Carroll*, 309 S.C. 22, 419 S.E.2d 801 (Ct. App. 1992), the trial court's award of alimony was reversed for failing to designate which form of alimony had been awarded (it was either lump sum or rehabilitative) and for failing to make any finding of special circumstances to justify the award of either form.

Not all forms of alimony are modifiable, nor are they necessarily modifiable for the same reasons. See the sections on each type of alimony for further discussion about modifiability.

2. PERIODIC ALIMONY

a. In General

S.C. Code Ann. § 20-3-130(B)(1) (Law. Co-op. Supp.) provides that the family court may award:

> Periodic alimony to be paid but terminating on the remarriage of the supported spouse or upon the death of either spouse (except as secured in subsection (D)) and terminable and modifiable based upon changed circumstances occurring in the future. The purpose of this form of support may include, but not be limited to, circumstances where the court finds it appropriate to order the payment of alimony on an ongoing basis where it is desirable to make a current determination and requirement for the ongoing support of a spouse to be reviewed and revised as circumstances may dictate in the future.

Permanent periodic alimony has been favored in South Carolina as a means of restoring a dependent spouse to the standard of living enjoyed during the marriage. Its purpose is to "place the supported spouse, as nearly as practical, in the position of support she enjoyed during the marriage." *Johnson v. Johnson*, 296 S.C. 289, 300, 372 S.E.2d 107, 114 (Ct. App. 1988).

The 1990 statute does not appear to have changed this preference. However, see the earlier discussion in this chapter about the purposes of alimony.

The cases which discuss periodic alimony are very fact specific and not altogether consistent. However, the three most significant factors are: (1) the duration of the marriage, (2) the overall financial situation of the parties, especially the ability of the supporting spouse to pay, and (3) whether either spouse was more at fault than the other. If the marriage was a long one, the parties have disparate career opportunities and the party with the higher earning ability is at fault, periodic alimony will almost always be awarded. On the other hand, if the marriage was brief, the parties have relatively equal earning abilities and neither party was more at fault than the other, no alimony should be awarded. The results in other types of cases are more difficult to predict, but almost all cases seem to turn on one or more of the three factors listed above.

A more detailed examination of the factors and some of the cases in which periodic alimony has been granted and denied are discussed in the section on determining entitlement and amount of alimony later in this chapter. Additional cases and discussion about periodic alimony can be found in the section on the purposes of alimony.

b. Termination, Modification, and Retroactivity

In addition to the section of the 1990 alimony statute set out above (S.C. Code Ann. § 20-3-130(B) (Law. Co-op. Supp.)), the modifiability of periodic alimony is also addressed in S.C. Code Ann. § 20-3-170 (Law. Co-op. Supp.):

> Whenever any husband or wife, pursuant to a judgment of divorce from the bonds of matrimony, has been required to make his or her spouse any periodic payments of alimony and the circumstances of the parties or the financial ability of the spouse making the periodic payments shall have changed since the rendition of such judgment, either party may apply to the court which rendered the judgment for an order and judgment decreasing or increasing the amount of such alimony payments or terminating such payments and the court, after giving both parties an opportunity to be heard and to introduce evidence relevant to the issue, shall make such order and judgment as justice and equity shall require, with due regard to the changed circumstances and the financial ability of the supporting spouse, decreasing or increasing or confirming the amount of alimony provided for in such original judgment or terminating such payments. Thereafter the supporting spouse shall pay and be liable to pay the amount of alimony payments directed in such order and judgment and no other or further amount and such original judgment, for the purpose of all actions or proceedings of every nature and wherever instituted, whether within or without this State, shall be deemed to be and shall be modified accordingly, subject in every case to a further

proceeding or proceedings under the provisions of this section in relation to such modified judgment.

This statute is generally consistent with the 1990 alimony statute, but it does not appear to serve any additional purpose in light of the amendments to S.C. Code Ann § 20-3-130.

The family court retains jurisdiction to modify periodic alimony unless the *Moseley* requirements have been met and a contract of nonmodifiability has resulted. In *Medlin v. King*, 294 S.C. 406, 365 S.E.2d 36 (Ct. App. 1988), the trial court had relieved the husband of all alimony obligations due to the remarriage of the wife. She claimed that their agreement for him to pay "support" controlled. The court held that the terms "support" and "alimony" are synonymous and, if the parties had intended for it to survive her remarriage, then she should have made certain that this was clear on the face of the agreement. Since it was not, the husband did not have to pay any more alimony.

Although the misconduct of a spouse following a divorce may not generally be considered as a ground for suspending alimony payments, a supporting spouse may be allowed to suspend payment of alimony during a period in which the supported spouse is guilty of contempt of court. In *Young v. Young*, 272 S.C. 433, 248 S.E.2d 588 (1978), the husband was allowed to suspend payment of alimony due to wife's failure to relinquish property to the husband pursuant to a court-ordered property settlement.

If a person's alimony obligations are reduced by the trial judge, but reinstated to their former level on appeal, the supporting spouse is responsible for the arrearages that accumulated while the case was on appeal. This issue was decided as a case of first impression in *Brown v. Brown*, 286 S.C. 56, 331 S.E.2d 793 (Ct. App. 1985). However, this will not be the result following an appeal of an initial award of alimony. In *Smith v. Smith*, 308 S.C. 492, 419 S.E.2d 232 (Ct. App. 1992), the wife had succeeded in having an award of rehabilitative alimony reversed in favor of periodic alimony. On remand, she had asked that the award be made retroactive to the time of the divorce decree. The trial court's denial of this request was upheld on appeal. The court held that the wife was not entitled to retroactive alimony as the case did not involve a reversal on appeal of a reduction or termination of support payments.

The *Brown* decision was revisited in *Christy v. Christy*, 317 S.C. 145, 452 S.E.2d 1 (Ct. App. 1994). While it is true as a general proposition of law, as stated in *Brown v. Brown*, 286 S.C. 56, 331 S.E. 2d 793 (Ct. App. 1985) (Brown II), that a party receiving payment under a judgment subsequently reversed on appeal must restore whatever advantage obtained thereby to his adversary, Brown II, and its predecessor *Brown v. Brown*, 278 S.C. 43, 292 S.E. 2d 297 (1982) (Brown I) involved situations where an existing award of alimony is modified by the trial court and the modification is then reversed or affirmed on appeal.

Different considerations are involved when an appellate court modifies an award of alimony than when a trial court does so. When an appeals court reverses a trial court's modification award, the parties are restored to their respective positions under the original award. Thus, the trial court's judgment of modification is vacated, and the party entitled to the benefits must restore those benefits. Also, where the appellate tribunal upholds a trial court judgment modifying an award, the modified award takes effect from its date of entry and not on the date of affirmance by the appeals court.

Conversely, where an appellate court modifies an award of alimony, the modified award is not as a matter of law entitled to retroactive application. Further, an appellate modification of alimony, whether an increase or a decrease, does not apply retroactively unless so directed by the appellate court. The Court of Appeals specifically held in *Christy* that the order of a lower court is effective until superseded or until the remittitur is filed directing the lower court otherwise, and any modification by the appellate court is to have prospective application from the date the remittitur is filed, unless otherwise directed by the appellate court.

If the trial judge awards alimony at the divorce hearing, and the appellate court remands for reconsideration of the amount of alimony without setting a new amount, the trial court may order that any increase or decrease in alimony will be retroactive. *Sexton v. Sexton*, ___ S.C. ___, 469 S.E.2d 608 (Ct. App. 1996)(finding that the trial court did not commit an error by ordering the wife to reimburse the husband for the overpayment of alimony after the trial court reduced the husband's alimony obligation on remand from Court of Appeals).

If the trial judge does not order alimony at the divorce hearing and an appellate court remands for reconsideration of alimony (but does not award alimony on appeal), the family court may award alimony retroactive to the date of the original hearing unless it would be an abuse of discretion. *Green v. Green*, ___ S.C. ___, 465 S.E.2d 130 (Ct. App. 1995) (finding no abuse of discretion in a retroactive award of alimony by the trial judge).

(1) Death

The provision in the 1990 alimony statute that periodic alimony terminates "upon the death of either spouse" is in accordance with the case law which preceded the enactment of the statute.

> We have previously held that the payment of alimony terminates at death unless affirmatively charged to the estate. *Jackson v. Jackson*, 279 S.C. 618, 310 S.E.2d 827 (Ct. App. 1983); and *Kennedy v. Kennedy*, 270 S.C. 358, 242 S.E.2d 417 (1978). By this opinion we seek to clarify our position.
>
> Alimony may be made by lump sum payments or periodic payments. If lump sum alimony is awarded, it is a debt owed and is properly chargeable to the estate if the obligor dies before full payment is made.
>
> Periodic payments of alimony are contingent in nature, usually extending until the receiving spouse's death or remarriage. . . . This support is owed by a divorced spouse, not a deceased spouse's beneficiaries or heirs at law.

> [I]f the obligation to pay installments of alimony is to be extended beyond the death of either party it must be done by an agreement of the parties, which is approved by the court and incorporated in the decree and *not* by the court decree alone.

McCune v. McCune, 284 S.C. 451, 455, 327 S.E.2d 340, 341-342 (1985).

Under *McCune*, only alimony payments accruing prior to death are enforceable against the payor's spouse's estate. However, under the 1990 alimony statute, periodic, rehabilitative and reimbursement alimony and separate maintenance accruing both before and after the death of the payor spouse would be enforceable to the extent that the family court makes provisions to secure the payment of the support under S.C. Code Ann. § 20-3-130(D) (Law. Co-op. Supp.). Security is discussed in an earlier section of this chapter.

(2) Remarriage

The provision in the 1990 alimony statute that periodic alimony terminates on the "remarriage of the supported spouse" is in accordance with the case law which preceded the enactment of the statute. *See also* S.C. Code Ann. § 20-3-150 (Law. Co-op. 1976), which provides that "in the event of the remarriage of the supported spouse [who is receiving periodic alimony] the amount fixed in such decree for his or her support shall forthwith cease and no further alimony payments shall be required from the supporting spouse."

Termination of alimony based on the remarriage of the supported spouse includes a finding that the supported spouse has entered into a common law marriage. In *Jeanes v. Jeanes*, 255 S.C. 161, 177 S.E.2d 537 (1970), the former wife's alimony was terminated because the facts were clearly sufficient to support a finding of a common law marriage to her boyfriend. They occupied the same house for two years, they shared expenses, the city directory listed them as husband and wife for two years, his employer listed her as his wife, she was described as his wife on a life insurance policy, and he claimed she was his wife on his state income tax forms. A request to terminate alimony due to the common law marriage of the supported spouse was rejected in *Jenkins v. Jenkins*, No. 93-UP-090 (S.C. Ct. App. 1993), because the facts did not support a conclusion that a common law marriage existed.

The trial court found that the supported spouse and her paramour were romantically and sexually involved, resided in the same home, and shared household expenses, including the mortgage payment, groceries and the gas bill. However, they never agreed to live together as man and wife, they never discussed marriage, and neither held the other out as a spouse. Further, they kept separate bank accounts and filed separate tax returns. The elements of a common law marriage were not established.

It is unclear whether the remarriage of the supporting spouse will justify a reduction of alimony, although it appears likely that it will not, absent other reasons to modify the award. It was not a factor, for example, in *Fender v. Fender*, 256 S.C. 399, 182 S.E.2d 755 (1971). Although the husband had remarried, this was not mentioned as a factor taken into account before deciding to increase his alimony payments to his first wife. In *Winterbottom v. Winterbottom*, 268 S.C. 361, 234 S.E.2d 14 (1977), the trial court had completely eliminated the husband's alimony obligations to his second wife and it had reduced his child support obligation from that marriage. The Court wrote:

> This is one of those unfortunate cases where a husband has a maximum obligation to three wives, with less than full ability to provide for them all. In such a case, the solution is never easy, but we think that a preference to the first and third wives, at the expense of the second, was not justified.

Id. at 365, 234 S.E.2d at 15.

*Winterbottom*was decided by a three to two vote, Justices Rhodes and Ness feeling that sufficient change in the circumstances was shown to warrant the modifications ordered. The modifications were a complete elimination of alimony payments of $100 every two weeks and a reduction in the amount of child support. The principal change in conditions seemed to be a combination of a remarriage and a move to Baltimore for a job relocation in Washington, D.C. The majority also wrote that "[i]f a reduction for the alimony and/or child support was justified, the amount of reductions was not, and we hold that the judge abused his discretion in completely eliminating alimony for June and reducing support for the daughter." *Id.*

In considering a request to reduce alimony payments due to the remarriage of the supporting spouse, the court must consider the supported spouse's income as well as the supporting spouse's expenses. In *Graham v. Graham*, 253 S.C. 486, 171 S.E.2d 704 (1970), the Supreme Court reversed the trial court for failing to consider the former wife's income. The ex-husband had requested a reduction in alimony. Although he was remarried, it was not clear whether his expenses had increased. The Court determined that the $350 per month support payment ($200 for child support and $150 for alimony) would take approximately 94% of his income. He would have $20.65 for his needs and his ex-wife would have $711.63 per month for herself and one child from the support and her earnings combined. Mr. Justice Bussey disagreed with the majority's arithmetic, and he wrote in dissent that "the husband's primary obligation and responsibility is to the wife and child whom he abandoned, and . . . any right or claim which his second wife might have, particularly under the circumstances of this case, is junior and secondary to such primary obligation." *Id.* at 501, 171 S.E.2d at 712. The Supreme Court has never adopted such a priority formulation on the whole, and the dissent cited no authority for its position.

Alimony may continue after remarriage if it is based upon an agreement of the parties, but only if the contract specifically requires it to continue. In *Medlin v. King*, 294 S.C. 406, 365 S.E.2d 36 (Ct. App. 1988), the Court of Appeals upheld the trial court's decision to relieve the husband of his obligation to pay alimony after the remarriage of his former wife because the agreement under which she claimed a right to continued alimony payments did not specifically provide that payments would continue after her remarriage. *See also Darden v. Witham*, 258 S.C. 380, 188 S.E.2d 776 (1972), in which the Supreme Court concluded that the periodic payments, which were being made by a man to his former wife pursuant to a property settlement agreement, were not alimony payments, although they were termed "alimony" in the agreement. Rather, they were actually installment payments arising out of a lump sum property agreement. The wife's remarriage, therefore, had no effect.

(3) Post-Divorce Paramours

A former spouse's relationship with a member of the opposite sex may warrant a change in alimony. In *Croom v. Croom*, 305 S.C. 158, 406 S.E.2d 381 (Ct. App. 1991), the ex-wife lived with a paramour and supported him, at least in part, with her alimony payments. There was evidence that they had decided not to marry so she could continue to receive alimony. The court said:

> South Carolina has not decided whether alimony should be terminated on the sole ground that the supported spouse is not entitled to alimony if he or she chooses to live in a continuing illicit relationship rather than remarry.
>
> Other courts have reasoned, however, that it is inequitable to allow the partners to the illicit relationship to benefit from alimony payments at the expense of the supporting ex-spouse by the simple expedient of choosing not to marry. The purpose of alimony is to provide the ex-spouse a substitute for the support which was incident to the former marital relationship. It is not awarded to support a live-in partnership between the supported ex-spouse and a third party. A rule requiring alimony to continue in these circumstances invidiously discriminates because it penalizes a divorced spouse for remarrying, but rewards one for cohabiting without benefit of marriage. Since the State has a compelling interest in promoting marriage and discouraging meretricious relationships, such a rule is also illogical and offensive to public policy.

Id. at 160, 406 S.E.2d at 382 (citations omitted).

This issue, however, has still not been resolved. The language quoted above is *dicta*, not the law of the case, because the decision of the court was that the wife was entitled to continue receiving alimony because it was being paid pursuant to a court approved agreement which specified only three events which would allow alimony to be modified or terminated. Living with a paramour was not one of them. *See also Friday v. Friday*, No. 95-UP-309 (S.C. Ct. App. 1995) (affirming the trial court's refusal to modify alimony because the separation agreement specified that alimony would continue until death or remarriage and the facts did not support a conclusion that the ex-wife had entered into a common law marriage).

The outcome of this issue is also clouded by the enactment of the 1990 alimony statute which states that, in determining whether or not to award alimony:

> [N]o evidence of personal conduct which may otherwise be relevant and material for the purpose of this subsection may be considered with regard to this subsection if the conduct took place subsequent to the happening of the earliest of (a) the formal signing of a written property or marital settlement agreement or (b) entry of a permanent order of separate maintenance and support or of a permanent order approving a property or marital settlement agreement between the parties.

S.C. Code Ann. § 20-3-130(C)(11) (Law. Co-op. Supp.). How the courts will interpret this provision when faced with evidence, as in *Croom*, that a former spouse and a paramour have decided not to marry so the supported spouse can continue to receive alimony payments. A couple of unpublished opinions mention this as a factor to be considered, although there was no evidence of such agreements in these cases. *Friday v. Friday*, No. 95-UP-309 (S.C. Ct. App. 1995) (finding no intent on the part of the wife not to remarry in order to continue to receive alimony); *Bryson v. Bryson*, No. 93-UP-215 (S.C. Ct. App. 1993) (finding the wife and her paramour had no scheme to remain unmarried so she could continue to receive alimony).

A supported spouse is at risk of losing alimony or having it modified if a paramour is providing support. In *Palmer v. Palmer*, 289 S.C. 216, 345 S.E.2d 746 (Ct. App. 1986), the trial court's termination of alimony was upheld when it was based on the wife having improved her overall financial status resulting from her relationship with a man who gave her automobiles, fur coats, paid many of her other expenses and with whom she traveled extensively. The court said:

> This court upheld a family court order substantially reducing a former wife's alimony based on her improved financial standing resulting from her cohabitation with a man. *Vance v. Vance*, 287 S.C. 615, 340 S.E.2d 554 (Ct. App. 1986). We agree with the reasoning expressed by the *Vance* court "Living with another, whether it is a live-in lover, a relative, or a platonic housemate, changes the wife's circumstances and alters her required financial support." 340 S.E.2d 554, 555 (Ct. App. 1986).

Id. at 218, 345 S.E.2d at 748.

The language quoted above may be broader than the court intended, for the reference to relatives contradicts earlier cases. In *Bailey v. Bailey*, 269 S.C. 1, 235 S.E.2d 801 (1977), the court found that it was "improper" for the family court to have expected an unmarried 19-year-old son and the widowed 66-year-old mother of the wife to pay her rent. The son and mother lived with the wife who did not require them to pay rent.

> Generally, because alimony is the replacement for the husband's duty to support his wife, the Court cannot consider the contributions of the wife's relatives to her support. The parents and emancipated children contribute to her welfare; the husband has a legal duty and children of a wife have only a moral duty and should not be relieved of that duty by the kindness of this wife's relations.

Id. at 6, 235 S.E.2d at 803. *Bailey* was cited with approval in *Prince v. Prince*, 285 S.C. 203, 328 S.E.2d 664 (Ct. App. 1985), in which the Court of Appeals concluded that the family court abused its discretion when it considered the contribution of the wife's emancipated daughter to the wife's support.

The *Palmer* court attempted to distinguish its facts from the *Prince* case by pointing out that the third party was a paramour in *Palmer* and a relative in *Prince*. However, it did not discuss the language quoted above from *Bailey*. If contributions of relatives are not to be counted because they only have a moral duty to provide support, not the legal duty of a husband, how can the court allow contributions to be counted from a paramour who has neither a legal nor a moral duty to provide support? Although it did not try to explain this conflict, the court was apparently aware of it, for it included this statement in the *Palmer* opinion: "As to the gratuitous nature of McKee's contributions, Diana can seek reinstatement of the alimony, if her financial condition deteriorates." *Palmer*, 289 S.C. at 219, 345 S.E.2d at 748. Perhaps the result in *Palmer* should be viewed more as an expression of the court's moral judgment than its legal judgment. Or, perhaps, *Bailey* and *Palmer* are best distinguished on the basis that the wife's needs were being met in *Bailey* but not in *Palmer*. However, neither of these possibilities was articulated in the opinions. For the time being at least, litigators will have difficulty predicting the results in similar cases.

A couple of unpublished opinions may help make these predictions, although they cannot be cited as precedent. In *Friday v. Friday*, No. 95-UP-309 (S.C. Ct. App. 1995), the husband claimed that the boyfriend was a "substitute husband" because they cohabited, he worked on her car and in the yard, and he gave her a little money to help pay for groceries. The court held that, even if true, the husband's contentions "show neither that the wife entered into a common law marriage nor that her paramour provided her a level of support sufficient to constitute a substantial change in her financial condition." In *Bryson v. Bryson*, No. 93-UP-215 (S.C. Ct. App. 1993), the Court of Appeals affirmed the trial court's refusal to modify alimony because the paramour's contributions "merely covered his share of the expenses" and the wife's "financial condition has not significantly improved as a result of cohabiting" with the paramour.

A final case to note on this topic is *Cartee v. Cartee*, 295 S.C. 103, 366 S.E.2d 269 (Ct. App. 1988). The husband sought to terminate or reduce his alimony payments on the basis that the wife was living with another man and enjoying the benefits of marriage. The trial court refused to terminate or reduce the payments as she was being paid by family members to live with this other man and ensure his safety. The weight of the evidence showed neither common law marriage nor sexual or romantic relations. The Court of Appeals affirmed the trial court.

(4) Changed Circumstances

Making periodic alimony "terminable and modifiable based upon changed circumstances occurring in the future" is also consistent with the prior version of S.C. Code Ann. § 20-3-130 and with case law.

The increased need of the supported spouse is among the more common bases for seeking a modification of an alimony award. *See Fender v. Fender*, 256 S.C. 399, 182 S.E.2d 755 (1971), where the husband's income tripled after the divorce and the wife's needs increased. Of course, any increase in payments ordered must be supported by an ability on the part of the supporting spouse to make them, and must be reasonable in light of all the circumstances. *Id.* However, the increased need must not stem from unreasonable activity on the part of the supported spouse:

> Unwarranted debts, without more, are insufficient to establish changed circumstances or justify an increase in alimony. The fact Mrs. Baker has gone further into debt merits only minimal consideration in light of the (1) court's observation some of her "obligations are a result of financial irresponsibility and foolish borrowing," (2) evidence she owes $1500 to clothing stores, and (3) lack of evidence her normal living expenses have increased. *See Von Herbers v. Von Herbers*, 6 Wash. 2d 100, 106 P.2d 737, 742 (1940); *Disney v. Disney*, 121 Cal. App. 2d 602, 263 P.2d 865, 873 (1953).

Inflation is not a basis for seeking modification of alimony. *See Calvert v. Calvert*, 287 S.C. 130, 336 S.E.2d 884 (Ct. App. 1985); *Baker v. Baker*, 286 S.C. 200, 332 S.E.2d 550 (Ct. App. 1985). In *Baker*, the court said this about inflation, emphasizing the need for "relative" postures to change in discounting inflation as a factor:

> Moreover, inflation, without more, is insufficient to establish changed circumstances or justify an increase in alimony. Inflation affects both spouses; when Mrs. Baker's cost of living increases, Mr. Baker's cost of living also increases. *See Goldberg v. Goldberg*, 30 Ill. App. 3d 769, 332 N.E.2d 710, 713 (1975); *Bellow v. Bellow*, 94 Ill. App. 3d 361, 419 N.E.2d 924, 929-930 (1981).

Id. at 203, 332 S.E.2d at 552.

According to *Baker*, while an increase in the income of the payor spouse may be grounds for seeking an increase in alimony, an increase may not be granted where the initial award of alimony was adequate to maintain the receiving spouse at the standard of living to which he or she was accustomed before the divorce. The court cited and adopted the following language: "alimony ... is ... based on the underlying principle that it is the duty of the husband to support his wife, not necessarily to endow her", and "(t)he purpose of alimony is to care for the wife's needs after divorce, not to provide her with a lifetime profit-sharing plan." *Id.* at 203, 332 S.E.2d at 552.

The court has not addressed a situation in which there was sufficient financial disparity between the parties to render the effect of inflation upon the parties' living standards grossly disproportionate. However, the dissent of Judge Gardner indicates that he felt *Baker* itself to be such a case. The disagreement between the majority and the dissent seems to be mainly one of point of view. Presumably the majority felt that Mrs. Baker, living on roughly $20,000.00 per year (combined earnings and alimony), did not fall into the class of persons whom inflation would affect disproportionately. At what point the disproportionality would occur will be determined by later cases.

Changes in circumstances which were expected or should have been anticipated by the parties at the time of the alimony award do not generally provide a basis for modifying alimony. *See Calvert v. Calvert*, 287 S.C. 130, 336 S.E.2d 884 (Ct. App. 1985). The parties' agreement contained a cost of living index as a means of determining periodic increases or decreases in alimony and child support payments. The possibility that the amounts could go up due to this was within the contemplation of the parties. *See also Diller v. Diller*, No. 92-UP-063 (S.C. Ct. App. 1992), an unpublished opinion. When the parties were divorced, the wife was attending a paralegal program. Less than a year after the divorce, the husband sought a reduction of alimony based on her completion of the paralegal course and finding a job as a receptionist/secretary where she worked thirty-two hours per week at minimum wage. The trial court reduced the amount of alimony, but the Court of Appeals reversed, finding that it was within the contemplation of the parties at the time of the divorce that she would complete her training and enter the work force. The court also noted that the husband's income had increased and that debts he had incurred in the purchase and renovation of a home and for investment purposes were matters he undertook voluntarily and did not constitute a material change in circumstances.

But see Brown v. Brown, 278 S.C. 43, 292 S.E.2d 297 (1982). The husband sought a reduction in alimony because his ex-wife became employed and because his salary was reduced when health problems forced a reduction in his work hours. The family court found that because the ex-wife's employment was anticipated, it was not a changed circumstance. The family court's finding that Mr. Brown's decreased salary was a change in circumstance requiring that the amount of alimony be calculated on a percentage of his income was reversed. The Supreme Court noted that "Mr. Brown knew at the time of the divorce his income would progressively decrease." *Id.* at 45, 292 S.E.2d at 297.

The Court of Appeals affirmed the proposition that anticipated increases in the incomes of supported spouses do not support alimony reduction requests in *Kelley v. Kelley*, ___ S.C. ___, 477 S.E.2d 727 (Ct. App. 1996). However, the reasoning of the Court of Appeals is a little hard to understand. The wife returned to full-time employment after the divorce. The court denied the husband's request to use her new income as a basis for reducing alimony payments due to changed circumstances. The court reasoned that her employment was anticipated by the parties at the time of the divorce. However, it does not appear from the opinion that the family court judge knew how much income she would earn or that he considered this anticipated income in determining her needs. If this is true, the husband should not have been barred on this basis from seeking a recalculation of her needs. Perhaps the case is best understood in light of its ultimate results: the husband obtained a reduction in his alimony obligation on the basis of his reduced income (see the following paragraph).

A reduction in salary can be used as a basis for reducing a person's alimony obligation, even if the person is voluntarily underemployed or unemployed, if the payor has a good-faith and reasonable explanation for the decreased income. *Kelley v. Kelley*, ___ S.C. ___, 477 S.E.2d 727 (Ct. App. 1996). The husband quit his accounting job at Michelin, participated in a real estate venture which failed, and was then only able to find a salaried job as a delivery manager of telephone directories. The reduction in his income was significant. The family court found that the husband was voluntarily underemployed but reduced his alimony obligation. The Court of Appeals inferred from the record that the trial court found the husband's explanation for his diminished salary to be in good faith and reasonable under the circumstances. The reduction of his alimony obligation was affirmed.

Requests for reductions in alimony based on reductions in income will be granted more easily than requests for reductions in child support payments. The Court of Appeals, in *Kelley*, *supra*, states that "[a]n even greater scrutiny is called for in cases where parents attempt to modify their child support obligations." *Id.* at ___ n.3, ___ S.E.2d at ___ n.3. The court did not explain the rationale behind this statement, but it probably included it because the result in *Kelley* does seem inconsistent with the case law involving requests to reduce child support obligations.

In seeking a modification of support on the basis of changed circumstances, the practitioner should keep in mind the holding in *Witt v. Witt*, 271 S.C. 541, 248 S.E.2d 494 (1978), that no showing of changed circumstances is necessary to request reconsideration of spousal support where there was no evidence introduced at the original trial about the husband's ability to pay support. If there has been no original condition established, it would be impossible for a person seeking a modification to ever establish changed conditions. The court emphasized that no decree should ever be issued without sufficient proof of the terms of the parties' agreement.

(5) Automatic Modification Provisions

Court-ordered automatic increases or decreases in alimony have not been allowed. In *Collins v. Collins*, 239 S.C. 170, 122 S.E.2d 1 (1961), it was pointed out that a child support and alimony order, which provided for an automatic increase tied to the cost of living index on a date certain in the future, was improper for want of proof of the betterment of the financial situation of the individual at that future date. The court found that "[t]o assume that the appellant will be able immediately after his graduation to pay or procure payment of a larger amount each month would be to indulge in speculation." *Id.* at 177, 122 S.E.2d at 4. The court pointed out that if an individual's financial situation improves at a later time so that payments from him should be increased, such increased payments could be ordered upon a proper showing. The same logic applies in regard to decreasing payments. *See Prince v. Prince*, 285 S.C. 203, 328 S.E.2d 664 (Ct. App. 1985) (holding that an order providing for sequential reductions in monthly alimony payments from $500 to $200 was improper). *But see Stevenson v. Stevenson*, 276 S.C. 475, 279 S.E.2d 616 (1981) (determining that the husband's income was "stale" and he was earning far below his potential, and ordering that his payments would increase in six months from $175 per month to $250 per month).

However, automatic increases are allowed if the parties agree to them and the court approves. In *Calvert v. Calvert*, 287 S.C. 130, 336 S.E.2d 884 (Ct. App. 1985), the court rejected the husband's request to modify the terms of the parties' court-approved agreement which used a cost of living index as a means of determining periodic increases or decreases in alimony and child support payments.

3. LUMP SUM ALIMONY

Lump sum alimony is provided for in S.C. Code Ann. § 20-3-130(B)(2) (Law. Co-op. Supp.):

> Lump sum alimony is a finite total sum to be paid in one installment, or periodically over a period of time, terminating only upon the death of the supported spouse, but not terminable or modifiable based upon remarriage or changed circumstances in the future. The purpose of this form of support may include, but not be limited to, circumstances where the court finds alimony appropriate but determines that such an award be of a finite and nonmodifiable nature.

Lump sum alimony was recognized prior to the enactment of the alimony statute, and the definition in the statute is consistent with the case law definition. Lump sum alimony was not modifiable under existing case law, either. *See Darden v. Witham*, 258 S.C. 380, 384, 188 S.E.2d 776, 778 (1972) (holding that where lump sum alimony has been awarded, the court "cannot modify the provision, even where it is payable in installments"); *Blakely v. Blakely*, 249 S.C. 623, 155 S.E.2d 857 (1967).

Lump sum alimony is to be considered only in exceptional circumstances and for compelling reasons where it appears that the payor may not live up to regular alimony obligations. *Millis v. Millis*, 282 S.C. 610, 320 S.E.2d 66 (Ct. App. 1984).

The 1990 statute does not appear to have had any impact on the approach taken by the courts with respect to awarding lump sum alimony.

> Lump sum alimony is appropriate upon finding of special circumstances. *Wingard v. Wingard*, 288 S.C. 644, 344 S.E.2d 191 (Ct. App. 1986). Lump sum awards are not favored and should be

> given only in exceptional cases or when consented to. Such an award must be supported by some impelling reason for its necessity or desirability. *Johnson v. Johnson*, 296 S.C. 289, 372 S.E.2d 107 (S.C. App. 1988).

Carroll v. Carroll, 309 S.C. 22, 23, 419 S.E.2d 801, 802 (Ct. App. 1992) (remanding the case for failing to designate which type of alimony had been awarded and for failing to make any finding of special circumstances).

The statute limits the application of "lump sum alimony" to circumstances where the court finds alimony appropriate but determines that such award should be of a finite and nonmodifiable nature. The circumstances that would justify a "finite and nonmodifiable" award are not set forth in the new alimony statute but are found in court decisions.

The principal justification which has been given for awarding lump sum alimony is the unwillingness of the spouse ordered to provide support to make regular payments of periodic alimony. See *Jones v. Jones*, 270 S.C. 280, 241 S.E.2d 904 (1978), where the husband drank a lot, was irregularly employed, and had moved to avoid making payments; and *Murdock v. Murdock*, 243 S.C. 218, 133 S.E.2d 323 (1963), where the husband moved to a different state and remarried. He was held in contempt for failing to make *pendente lite* payments. *See also Hendricks v. Hendricks*, 285 S.C. 591, 330 S.E.2d 553 (Ct. App. 1985), where the husband had not supported his family for nineteen years, and he was spending large sums to support a paramour. Arguably, a marriage of short duration ought also to give rise to contemplation of the lump sum alimony approach, since this minimizes the ties between the parties and frees them up more efficiently than would even designated short-term alimony.

An award of lump sum alimony based upon an agreement between the parties will be upheld. In *Richardson v. Richardson*, 309 S.C. 31, 419 S.E.2d 806 (Ct. App. 1992), the wife sought enforcement of the husband's agreement to pay lump sum alimony which had been incorporated into the divorce decree. Although the trial judge could not order the husband to comply specifically with the terms of the agreement to transfer title of the marital home to the wife (the house was titled in the husband's mother's name and she would not cooperate), the judge had ordered him to live up to the agreement by paying her the fair market value of the house. The Court of Appeals affirmed the trial court on the basis that the award was based upon an agreement of the parties, not findings by the court. However, the Court of Appeals also determined that the husband's uncertain medical condition also supported the award of lump sum alimony, stating that the special circumstances justifying a lump sum award include the need to continue support after the death of the supporting spouse.

4. REHABILITATIVE ALIMONY

Rehabilitative alimony was codified in 1990 with the enactment of the alimony statute. S.C. Code Ann. § 20-3-130(B)(3) (Law. Co-op. Supp.) provides:

> Rehabilitative alimony is a finite sum to be paid in one installment or periodically, terminable upon the remarriage of the supported spouse, the death of either spouse (except as secured in subsection (D)) or the occurrence of a specific event to occur in the future, or modifiable based upon unforeseen events frustrating the good faith efforts of the supported spouse to become self-supporting or the ability of the supporting spouse to pay the rehabilitative alimony. The purpose of this form of support may include but not be limited to circumstances where the court finds it appropriate to provide for the rehabilitation of the supported spouse, but to provide modifiable ending dates coinciding with events considered appropriate by the court such as the completion of job training or education and the like, and to require rehabilitative efforts by the supported spouse.

The option of making rehabilitative alimony modifiable is a substantial deviation from existing case law. Under prior case law rehabilitative alimony was nonmodifiable. The most recent statement of the prior case law is found in *Jordan v. Jordan*, 307 S.C. 407, 415 S.E.2d 424 (Ct. App. 1992). The wife petitioned for reconsideration of a rehabilitative alimony award, claiming that rehabilitation was not possible and she needed continual support. No appeal had been taken from the award of rehabilitative alimony, and the Court of Appeals found that it had no authority to modify rehabilitative alimony absent statutory authority or a reservation in the decree to allow change or review in the future. The Court noted that the 1990 amendments to section 20-3-130 would allow modification of rehabilitative alimony where "unforeseen events" frustrate the good faith efforts of the supported spouse to become self-supporting or the ability of the supporting spouse to pay the rehabilitative alimony. However, because the case at hand arose prior to the adoption and effective date of the statute, the court did not apply it to this case.

Otherwise, however, the 1990 statute has not had any impact on the approach taken by the courts with respect to awarding rehabilitative alimony. "The record must demonstrate the self-sufficiency of the recipient at the expiration date of the ordered payments and that the supported spouse will match the prior standard of living accustomed to during the marriage." *Belton v. Belton*, Op. No. 2613 (S.C. Ct. App. filed Jan. 13, 1997)(Davis Adv. Sh. No. 1 at 30).

> [R]ehabilitative alimony may be awarded only upon a showing of special circumstances justifying a departure from permanent, periodic support. There must be evidence demonstrating the self sufficiency of the supported spouse at the expiration of the ordered payments in order for rehabilitative alimony to be granted.

Carroll v. Carroll, 309 S.C. 22, 23, 419 S.E.2d 801, 802 (Ct. App. 1992) (remanding the case for failing to designate which type of alimony was awarded and for failing to make any finding of special circumstances).

The doctrine of rehabilitative alimony was not recognized in South Carolina until the Court of Appeals hinted that it might adopt it in *Millis v. Millis*, 282 S.C. 610, 320 S.E.2d 66 (Ct. App. 1984). However, it did not approve the concept in that case. Shortly thereafter, however, the Court of Appeals declared that South Carolina courts could award rehabilitative alimony in *Eagerton v. Eagerton*, 285 S.C. 279, 328 S.E.2d 912 (Ct. App. 1985); and it was acknowledged and cautiously adopted by the Supreme Court in *Herring v. Herring*, 286 S.C. 447, 335 S.E.2d 366 (1985), although it found the evidence insufficient to support an award of rehabilitative alimony.

The factors to be considered in awarding rehabilitative alimony are set forth in *Johnson v. Johnson*, 296 S.C. 289, 372 S.E.2d 107 (Ct. App. 1988), as:

1) duration of the marriage;

2) age, health, and education of the supported spouse;

3) financial resources of the parties;

4) parties' accustomed standard of living;

5) ability of the supporting spouse to meet his/her needs while meeting needs of supported spouse;

6) time necessary for the supported spouse to obtain job training or skills;

7) likelihood that the supported spouse will successfully complete retraining;

8) supported spouse's likelihood of success in the job market.

Id. at 301-302, 372 S.E.2d at 114. Only the final three factors are peculiar to rehabilitative alimony. The same factors were listed and applied in earlier cases. *See Toler v. Toler*, 292 S.C. 374, 356 S.E.2d 429 (Ct. App. 1987); *Crim v. Crim*, 289 S.C. 360, 345 S.E.2d 515 (Ct. App. 1986).

The 1990 statute does not define rehabilitation nor does it say what the goal of rehabilitation must be other than to allow the spouse to become self-supporting. However, the court should make factual findings as to what "rehabilitative goal" this type of alimony is to serve. *Shafer v. Shafer*, 283 S.C. 205, 209, 320 S.E.2d 730, 732 (Ct. App. 1984).

Practitioners should approach rehabilitative alimony with caution. The appellate courts have reversed many of the rehabilitative alimony cases they have considered, holding that rehabilitative alimony awards are only valid when established by evidence sufficient to support their temporary nature. They require a record that demonstrates the self-sufficiency of the recipient at the expiration date of the ordered payments. *See Belton v. Belton*, Op. No. 2613 (S.C. Ct. App. filed Jan. 13, 1997)(Davis Adv. Sh. No. 1 at 30) (reversing a rehabilitative alimony award because there were no exceptional circumstances and no evidence that the wife would succeed in her business venture); *Crawford v. Crawford*, 301 S.C. 476, 392 S.E.2d 675 (Ct. App. 1990) (holding that no evidence existed to demonstrate that the wife would be reasonably self-sufficient at the termination of the alimony payments); *Therrell v. Therrell*, 299 S.C. 210, 383 S.E.2d 259 (Ct. App. 1989) (holding that there must be evidence demonstrating the self-sufficiency of the supported spouse at the expiration of the ordered payments); *Hickman v. Hickman*, 294 S.C. 486, 366 S.E.2d 21 (Ct. App. 1988) (holding that the record did not show that after a period of time Ms. Hickman would become more self-sufficient than she was at the time of trial); *Toler v. Toler*, 292 S.C. 374, 356 S.E.2d 429, 431 (Ct. App. 1987) (holding that the purpose of this type of support is to encourage a dependent spouse to become self-supporting after divorce).

Although they have not been consistent, most of the cases have indicated that "self-sufficiency" means the ability to support oneself at the marital standard of living. *Cf. Eagerton v. Eagerton*, 285 S.C. 279, 328 S.E.2d 912 (Ct. App. 1985). In *Voelker v. Hillock*, 288 S.C. 622, 344 S.E.2d 177 (Ct. App. 1986), the Court of Appeals held that it was an abuse of discretion to award the wife rehabilitative alimony instead of periodic alimony. The marriage had lasted eleven years and had produced two children. The husband earned $100,000 per year and the wife anticipated earning up to $30,000 per year if she could successfully retrain in the field of secretarial science. *See also Crim v. Crim*, 289 S.C. 360, 345 S.E.2d 515 (Ct. App. 1986) (holding that an award of rehabilitative alimony was inappropriate because the husband's income potential vastly exceeded that of the wife, even if she became as rehabilitated as possible).

The test established by these cases is almost impossible to meet. Other states have resolved this problem by statute or case law that allows the court to review rehabilitative alimony after a set time period and determine if rehabilitation has taken place. Then, based on the facts in each case, alimony can be terminated or continued.

However, in *Bryan v. Bryan*, 296 S.C. 305, 372 S.E.2d 116, (Ct. App. 1988), the Court of Appeals allowed an award of rehabilitative alimony to stand, without discussing whether it would allow the wife to maintain the standard of living of the marriage. She was awarded $1700 per month rehabilitative alimony through August 1987. She was to complete her degree in May 1987. The award allowed reasonable time to find job. The wife's contention that she needed $2,500.00 per month and one year to secure a job was found unreasonable.

Some cases have begun considering the effect of periodic alimony on the supported spouse's motivation to earn independent income — that is, whether alimony, or a particular amount or form of it, serves as a disincentive for the supported spouse to work. The leading case on the disincentive topic is *Josey v. Josey*, 291 S.C. 26, 351 S.E. 2d 891 (Ct. App. 1986). The Court of Appeals reversed the trial court's award of $48,000 per year, agreeing with the husband that such an award could only serve to deter self-improvement by the wife and precluded any viable option of her remarriage. "The ultimate alimony award, based upon the reasonable needs of the wife, should not serve as a disincentive for her to make reasonable efforts to improve her employment potential or dissuade her, to the extent feasible from becoming self-supporting." Id. at 33, 351 S.E.2d at 896.

Even *Johnson v. Johnson*, 296 S.C. 289, 372 S.E.2d 107 (Ct. App. 1988), includes a statement that alimony should not serve as a disincentive for the supported spouse to improve her employment potential nor dissuade her from providing, to the extent feasible, for her own support. The Supreme Court noted in *Williamson v. Williamson*, 311 S.C. 47, 49, 426 S.E.2d 758, 760 (January 11, 1993), that "an alimony award should not serve as a disincentive for a spouse to make reasonable efforts to improve her employment potential or become self-sufficient." *Williamson* affirmed the trial court's denial of alimony on the basis that the wife had not presented sufficient evidence to establish the effect of her epilepsy on her ability to work.

If *Josey* becomes viewed as the more appropriate way to view the purposes of rehabilitative alimony (to provide an incentive to supported spouses to become self-sufficient), one could expect an increase in the use of rehabilitative alimony to provide an incentive for former spouses to rehabilitate themselves, perhaps in combination with smaller awards of periodic alimony.

However, in another case, the Court of Appeals found that periodic alimony did not provide a disincentive for the supported spouse to work. In *Curry v. Curry*, 309 S.C. 539, 424 S.E.2d 552 (Ct. App. 1992), the wife had not worked during the marriage at the husband's request. The husband was in the Navy and the wife had sole responsibility for raising their two children. The marriage lasted twenty-four years before the parties separated. The divorce was granted on the basis of the husband's adultery. At the time of the hearing, the husband had retired from the Navy, and he had a new job at which he was earning $29,000 annually and drawing retirement of $803 per month. The wife was earning $120 per month cleaning houses. The trial court's award of $719.10 per month in periodic alimony and 40% of the husband's retirement was upheld. The husband contended that the amount of alimony awarded served as a disincentive for the wife to work. "Under the circumstances, we find no disincentive for the wife to work and hold there was no abuse of discretion in the amount of alimony received." *Id.* at 541, 424 S.E.2d at 554.

5. REIMBURSEMENT ALIMONY

Reimbursement alimony is authorized by S.C. Code Ann. § 20-3-130(B)(4) (Law. Co-op. Supp.):

> Reimbursement alimony to be paid in a finite sum, to be paid in one installment or periodically, terminable on the remarriage of the supported spouse, or upon the death of either spouse (except as secured in subsection (D)) but not terminable or modifiable based upon changed circumstances in the future. The purpose of this form of support may include, but not be limited to, circumstances where the court finds it necessary and desirable to reimburse the supported spouse from the future earnings of the payor spouse based upon circumstances or events that occurred during the marriage.

The statute is consistent with prior case law. One purpose of reimbursement alimony is to compensate one spouse for the contribution to the professional degree of the other. *See Donahue v. Donahue*, 299 S.C. 353, 384 S.E.2d 741 (1989).

In *Donahue*, the Supreme Court stated, "where a partner to marriage takes the benefits of his spouse's support in obtaining a professional degree or license with the understanding the future benefits will accrue and inure to both of them, and the marriage is then terminated without the supported spouse giving anything in return, an unfairness has occurred that calls for a remedy." *Id.* at 363, 384 S.E.2d at 747. The court further stated that no mathematical formula is appropriate to setting a specific amount of "reimbursement alimony"; and the court approved an "all relevant factors" approach in which it considered the totality of the non-professional spouse's efforts in the family venture to obtain economic stability through education. The court specifically held that the "all relevant factors" approach includes consideration of the "amount of the supported spouse's contributions, his or her foregone opportunities to enhance or improve professional or vocational skills" and the "duration of the marriage following completion of the non-supporting spouse's professional education." *Id.* at 364, 384 S.E.2d at 747.

6. SEPARATE SUPPORT AND MAINTENANCE

The alimony statute provides for separate maintenance and support at S.C. Code Ann. § 20-3-130(B)(5) (Law. Co-op. Supp.):

> Separate maintenance and support to be paid periodically, but terminating upon the divorce of the parties, or upon the death of either spouse (except as secured in subsection (D)) and terminable and modifiable based upon changed circumstances in the future. The purpose of this form of support may include, but not be limited to, circumstances where a divorce is not sought, but it is necessary to provide for support of the supported spouse by way of separate maintenance and support when the parties are living separate and apart.

The statute conforms with previously recognized notions of separate maintenance and support under existing case law. Actions for separate support and maintenance are discussed in a separate chapter.

7. OTHER FORMS OF SPOUSAL SUPPORT

The alimony statute includes a catch-all category which permits the family court to award any form of alimony irrespective of whether it is specifically mentioned elsewhere in the statute. S.C. Code Ann. § 20-3-130(B)(6) (Law. Co-op. Supp.) provides that the family court may award: "Such other form of spousal support, under terms and conditions as the court may consider just, as appropriate under the circumstances without limitation to grant more than one form of support."

An important feature of this section is that more than one form of alimony may be ordered at the same time. However, no case has been located in which a South Carolina court has successfully awarded more than one form of alimony simultaneously.

This section, when read with the other provisions of the statute, also appears to allow the family court to alter the form or forms of alimony after the final hearing on the merits. That is, the court might decide to award one or more forms of alimony at the final hearing with a plan to change these at a point in the future. For example, rehabilitative alimony may be awarded at the divorce hearing, but periodic alimony would follow the end of the rehabilitative hearing (in cases where the supported spouse could become partially, but not fully, rehabilitated). Or perhaps the court might determine that it would be appropriate to award a portion of a retirement account in the form of alimony until a pension plan administrator receives a Qualified Domestic Relations Order and begins issuing a check directly to an alternate payee.

An award of alimony as an "other form of spousal support" was upheld in *C.A.H. v. L.H.*, 315 S.C. 389, 434 S.E.2d 268 (1993). The wife left the marital home after six years of marriage when her daughters from a previous marriage told her that her husband had sexually abused them, and she obtained a divorce on the ground of adultery based on that abuse. The wife sought "relocation alimony," and the trial judge awarded the wife "$105.00 per month as rehabilitative alimony for a period of one year." The husband appealed, arguing that the alimony award did not fall under S.C. Code Ann. § 20-3-130 (Law. Co-op. Supp.). The Supreme Court agreed that rehabilitative alimony may not have been appropriate under the circumstances, but it affirmed the award, finding "ample support in the record" for alimony under S.C.

Code Ann. § 20-3-130(B)(6) which authorizes the family court to award "such other form of spousal support, under terms and conditions as the court may consider just ...." *C.A.H.* at 391, 434 S.E.2d at 269.

The *C.A.H.* opinion does not specify what support the Court found in the record for the award of alimony. It appears to have been nothing other than the husband's misconduct. If so, the holding of this case is that, if a spouse engages in serious marital misconduct, a trial court is permitted to award temporary alimony. (One might assume that the Supreme Court would have affirmed an award of permanent periodic alimony, if the wife had requested it and the trial judge had awarded it.)

The section providing for "other forms of spousal support" does not allow the family court to award periodic alimony not terminable upon remarriage or modifiable upon changed circumstances. *Hazel v. Hazel*, ___ S.C. ___, 465 S.E.2d 776 (Ct. App. 1995).

> Under Respondent's innovative theory of the scope of subsection (6), any type of alimony which is by statute modifiable and terminable upon death or remarriage could be made non-modifiable and non-terminable if the family court judge considered it just. We do not believe that was the General Assembly's intent in creating subsection (6).

Id. at ___, 465 S.E.2d at 777.

I. DETERMINING ENTITLEMENT AND AMOUNT

1. DISCRETION OF THE TRIAL JUDGE

Where the parties have not settled the issue of alimony or otherwise agreed to limit the trial judge's authority, the alimony statute provides about as much discretion as possible. The intent of the legislature to provide greater flexibility to the trial judge appears in the first paragraph of S.C. Code Ann. § 20-3-130(A) (Law. Co-op. Supp.):

> In proceedings for divorce from the bonds of matrimony, and in actions for separate maintenance and support, the court may grant alimony or separate maintenance and support *in such amounts and for such term as the court considers appropriate* as from the circumstances of the parties and the nature of case may be just, *pendente lite*, and permanently. No alimony may be awarded a spouse who commits adultery before the earliest of these two events: (1) the formal signing of a written property or marital settlement agreement or (2) entry of a permanent order of separate maintenance and support or of a permanent order approving a property or marital settlement agreement between the parties. (emphasis added).

There is no set formula for determining whether a person is entitled to alimony nor for figuring out which type of alimony and how much of it should be awarded. While the statute provides more options to the trial judge, it also imposes a greater responsibility in that it requires the family court to consider all relevant factors before making its decision. The same obligation is set in section 20-3-130(C): "In making an award of alimony or separate maintenance and support, the court must consider and give weight in such proportion as it finds appropriate to all of the following factors. . . ."

If the trial judge fails to make it clear in the final order that all of the factors were considered before making an award of alimony, the odds of reversal appear to be very high. This is consistent with existing case law. *See Atkinson v. Atkinson*, 279 S.C. 454, 309 S.E.2d 14 (1983) (reversing for failing to make specific findings of fact about each factor).

2. AGREEMENTS

Spouses may decide alimony issues by mutual agreement, subject to review and approval by the trial judge. If a particular form of alimony is agreed to by the parties, the trial judge is not required to find any "special circumstances" in order to award it. *Richardson v. Richardson*, 309 S.C. 31, 419 S.E.2d 806 (Ct. App. 1992) (approving lump sum alimony as agreed to by the parties). S.C. Code Ann. § 20-3-130(G) (Law. Co-op. Supp.) provides:

> The Family Court may review and approve all agreements which bear on the issue of alimony or separate maintenance and support, whether brought before the court in actions for divorce from the bonds of matrimony, separate maintenance and support actions, or in actions to approve agreement where the parties are living separate and apart. The failure to seek a divorce, separate maintenance, or a legal separation does not deprive the court of its authority and jurisdiction to approve and enforce the agreements. The parties may agree in writing if properly approved by the court to make the payment of alimony as set forth in items (1) through (6) of subsection (B) nonmodifiable and not subject to subsequent modification by the court.

The statute makes it clear for the first time that an action to approve an agreement can be brought as an independent cause of action. However, the scope of the agreement which can be reviewed under this statute is limited to the issue of alimony or separate support and maintenance. Previously, the family court lacked jurisdiction to review and approve agreements except in the context of other marital litigation (additional discussion about subject matter jurisdiction is included in the separate chapter on subject matter jurisdiction).

The statute only allows the court to entertain such actions if "the parties are living separate and apart." Thus, it does not appear that it could review an agreement, under the authority of this statute, which has been made in contemplation of separation. It also appears doubtful that the statute would allow a family court to review prenuptial agreements dealing with alimony (however, the Equitable Apportionment of Marital Property Act appears to allow the family court to review prenuptial agreements that deal with property rights).

The statute also permits the parties to agree to make the payment of alimony "non-modifiable and not subject to subsequent modification by the Court." This codifies *Moseley v. Mosier*, 279 S.C. 348, 306 S.E.2d 624 (1983).

For further discussion about agreements, see the chapter on agreements.

3. FACTORS TO BE CONSIDERED

a. In General

S.C. Code Ann. § 20-3-130(C) (Law. Co-op. Supp.) provides: "In making an award of alimony or separate maintenance and support, the court must consider and give weight in such proportion as it finds appropriate to all of the following factors. . . ." All required statutory factors must be considered, and the trial court's findings with respect to each of them must be recited by the court pursuant to Rule 26(c), SCRFC. In *Epperly v. Epperly*, 312 S.C. 411, 440 S.E.2d 884 (1994), the trial judge held: "I find that alimony is not appropriate in this case due to the limited income of each party and that alimony is denied both parties." *Id.* at 415, 440 S.E.2d at 886. The Supreme Court remanded and directed the trial court "to redetermine alimony, considering all relevant factors, including the current and anticipated expenses of each spouse, and the fact that custody of the children has been placed with Wife." *Id.*

The statute lists thirteen factors to be considered in awarding alimony, including "such other factors as the court considers relevant." While the factors generally reflect the rules which were developed through case law before 1990, there are some notable exceptions.

Before the statute was enacted, the factors to be considered in awarding alimony were established by the Supreme Court. In *Lide v. Lide*, 277 S.C. 155, 283 S.E.2d 832 (1981), the Court indicated that the trial court should give consideration to each of the following factors before making its decision about alimony:

1) financial condition of the parties;

2) needs of the party seeking alimony;

3) age and health of the parties;

4) respective earning capacities and individual wealth;

5) contributions to the accumulation of their joint wealth;

6) conduct of the parties;

7) standard of living of the parties at the time of the divorce;

8) duration of the marriage;

9) ability to pay alimony; and

10) their actual incomes.

In *Atkinson v. Atkinson*, 279 S.C. 454, 309 S.E.2d 14 (Ct. App. 1983), the Court of Appeals repeated this list and added one more to be considered before the court could award some form of alimony other than periodic alimony:

11) special circumstances that might justify some other form of alimony (e.g. lump sum in *Atkinson*).

Curiously, neither case included two other factors that had been mentioned in earlier cases:

12) tax consequences (*Simonds v. Simonds*, 225 S.C. 211, 81 S.E.2d 344 (1954)); and

13) equitable distribution award (*Lee v. Lee*, 282 S.C. 76, 316 S.E.2d 435 (Ct. App. 1984); *Burgess v. Burgess*, 277 S.C. 283, 286 S.E.2d 142

(1982), citing to *Simmons v. Simmons*, 275 S.C. 41, 267 S.E.2d 427 (1980)).

The 1990 alimony statute substantially tracks the factors set forth in *Lide* and the other cases, but it adds a few and it describes some of them in greater detail. The factors listed in the statute are discussed below.

The cases which discuss periodic alimony are very fact specific and not altogether consistent. In South Carolina, the courts have set "maintaining the supported spouse in the standard of living enjoyed during the marriage" as the purpose for awarding alimony, not just a factor to be considered. Therefore, it has been given great weight in making alimony awards. (See the criticism of this practice in the section on purposes of alimony earlier in this chapter.)

Otherwise, the most significant factors to be considered in awarding alimony can be grouped under three topics:

1) the duration of the marriage;

2) the overall financial situation of the parties, especially the ability of the supporting spouse to pay; and

3) whether or not one of the parties was more at fault than the other.

It is important not to lose sight of the need to consider the overall financial situation of the parties and not focus too much on any particular factor listed in the statute. In *McMurtrey v. McMurtrey*, 272 S.C. 118, 249 S.E.2d 503 (1978), the court wrote:

> There is no limitation that alimony payments be made solely from current earnings. The undisputed evidence in this case is that the husband owns a 123 acre farm, which [he] leases out, on which is located an eight room brick house. The wife testified that the house was worth $40,000 and the land $1,000 per acre. The husband evaded questions on cross-examination as to his appraisal of the

> property, and never gave a valuation of this holding. There is no evidence of any encumbrance against this property and it is apparent to us that it affords a sufficient financial resource from which to generate the funds required to make the small monthly payment awarded the wife.

Id. at 121, 249 S.E.2d at 505.

The Court in *McMurtrey* cited *Eagerton v. Eagerton*, 265 S.C. 90, 217 S.E.2d 146 (1975), in which a reduction in income by a payor spouse was held insufficient to justify his failure to make proper payments during the period of the reduction. The evidence was that his income remained substantial and that he had sufficient property and means to meet the ordered payments, if he had a mind to do so. These cases thus stand clearly for the proposition that the overall net wealth of the paying spouse will be considered in determining his ability to pay.

Thus, it would seem clear that all assets of the supporting spouse and the supported spouse are to be taken into consideration in arriving at a determination of the proper amount of alimony in the first instance.

If the marriage was a long one, the parties have disparate career opportunities and the party with the higher earning ability is at fault, periodic alimony will almost always be awarded. On the other hand, if the marriage was brief, the parties have relatively equal earning abilities and neither party was more at fault than the other, no alimony should be awarded. The results in other types of cases are more difficult to predict, but almost all cases seem to turn on one or more of the three factors listed above.

Although it is impossible to distill a concise, cogent formula for determining whether and how much periodic alimony will be awarded, the following facts from a few fairly recent cases might provide some insights.

Permanent periodic alimony was allowed in *Hickman v. Hickman*, 294 S.C. 486, 366 S.E.2d 21 (Ct. App. 1988). The husband netted $2,870.56 per month. The parties had three children. The trial court awarded $333.33 per month permanent alimony, $666.67 per month unallocated child support, payment of tuition for two older children's high school, medical and hospitalization insurance for children, and medical, dental, orthodontic and periodontal expenses not covered by insurance. The trial court gave the wife the exclusive use and possession of the marital home for an indefinite period as an incident of support. It also ordered the husband to pay for the mortgage, taxes, insurance and all necessary repairs to the home (approximately $516.00 per month). The husband argued on appeal that rehabilitative alimony was more appropriate and that the entire award was excessive. The Court of Appeals affirmed.

Permanent periodic alimony was also awarded in *McDowell v. McDowell*, 300 S.C. 96, 386 S.E.2d 468 (Ct. App. 1989). The parties married in 1983 and separated in 1986. After the separation, the wife shot the husband. He was granted a divorce on the ground of physical cruelty, and he was awarded permanent periodic alimony of $200 per month due to the disabling injuries he sustained after his wife shot him. The wife appealed, but the Court of Appeals affirmed the award. The court considered the fact that before the shooting, the husband had worked for Frito-Lay earning $24,000.00. He had been unemployed since the shooting and his only income was $350.00 rental income, although he had applied for Social Security disability and was turned down. The wife earned $24,000.00 per year working for the U.S. Postal Service.

Permanent periodic alimony was also awarded in *Wood v. Wood*, No. 96-UP-124 (S.C. Ct. App. 1996). The parties were married in 1984 and separated in 1993. When they were divorced in 1994, the husband earned $103,000 per year; the wife $20,000. The wife did not have a college education and her potential for future earnings was not great. The wife's expenses exceeded her income by $1800 per month. The husband was solely responsible for the breakup of the marriage and admitted to committing adultery. The court held that the $800 per month awarded by the trial court was insufficient and modified the award to $2000 per month.

Permanent periodic alimony was not allowed in *Brandi v. Brandi*, 302 S.C. 353, 396 S.E.2d 124 (Ct. App. 1990). This was a ten year marriage. Ms. Brandi operated a typing business, and Mr. Brandi owned and operated convenience stores. During the marriage, she sold the typing business and worked in the convenience stores for the last two years of the marriage. They achieved an affluent lifestyle and a valuable marital estate. The trial judge granted the wife a divorce on the ground of adultery, and he awarded the wife $1500 per month in alimony and 30% of the marital estate. The Supreme Court remanded the case for reconsideration of the alimony award because Mrs. Brandi's expenses appeared excessive, she had not attempted to obtain employment despite her skills, and the trial judge should have considered the amount of marital property Ms. Brandi was to have received.

This type of alimony was also disallowed in *E.D.M. v. T.A.M.*, 307 S.C. 471, 415 S.E.2d 812 (1992). The Supreme Court denied the husband's request for an annulment on the basis that his wife had concealed her sexual incapacity, but the Court reversed the trial judge's award of periodic alimony. The marriage only lasted four and a half years. The parties were 31 years old and in good health. Both had college degrees and jobs: the husband was earning $48,000; the wife $20,000. The Court determined that alimony should be denied, stating that the "[w]ife made only minor contributions to the marriage and is able to support herself." *Id.* at 476, 415 S.E. 2d at 816.

b. Duration of the Marriage

S.C. Code Ann. § 20-3-130(C)(1) (Law. Co-op. Supp.) provides that, in making an award of alimony or separate maintenance and support, the court must consider and give appropriate weight to "the duration of the marriage together with the ages of the parties at the time of the marriage and at the time of the divorce or separate maintenance action between the parties."

In addition to considering the duration of the marriage, as required under *Lide*, the statute requires the Court to consider the "ages of the parties at the time of the marriage and at the time of the divorce or separate maintenance action between the parties."

The length of the marriage is usually the first factor examined by the courts. One would expect longer marriages to have a much higher probability of producing an alimony award than marriages of short duration. However, some relatively brief marriages have justified alimony awards in South Carolina. *See Johnson v. Johnson*, 296 S.C. 289, 372 S.E.2d 107 (Ct. App. 1988).

c. Physical and Emotional Condition

S.C. Code Ann. § 20-3-130(C)(2) (Law. Co-op. Supp.) provides that, in making an award of alimony or separate maintenance and support, the court must consider and give appropriate weight to "the physical and emotional condition of each spouse." This is consistent with *Lide*.

Considering the health of the parties helps evaluate other factors such as the needs of the parties and their earning capacities. A good example of the kind of attention the Court will pay to health factors may be found in *Bailey v. Bailey*, 269 S.C. 1, 235 S.E.2d 801 (1977). The Supreme Court felt that the trial judge had given insufficient consideration to the wife's impaired health:

> The record shows that Mrs. Bailey is in her mid-40's and has been afflicted with chronic and acute rheumatoid arthritis for about nine years. She has undergone surgery four times for this condition.
>
> Further surgery may be required. She is presently able to walk and get around by herself but is not able to do heavy housework; she needs the help of a maid. As far as it appears in the record, she has not been employed outside the home since her marriage in 1951 and is not now employable because of her severe physical impairment. Furthermore, she has no marketable skills.
>
> The $200 per month figure barely provides for the $175 the court found appellant needed for food, utilities and incidental medical expenses. The court made no allowance for clothing, travel, entertainment, emergencies, car, church, or other expenses.
>
> A review of the entire record convinces us that the alimony is not in keeping with the husband's assets, capacity to earn and ability to pay; the failing health of the wife, her needs and accustomed standard of living and her incapacity to earn and provide for herself. We find an abuse of discretion in the alimony award.

Id. at 5, 235 S.E.2d at 802.

The wife's health in *Bailey* clearly affected the following factors: her ability to earn, her ability to retrain, and her needs both in terms of maintaining her previous standard of living and in the abstract. Obviously, to the extent that impaired health affects the ability of a putative payor spouse to accomplish the payments in fact, it would be a factor. *See Smith v. Smith*, 260 S.C. 65, 194 S.E.2d 199 (1973). *See also Bugg v. Bugg*, 277 S.C. 270, 286 S.E.2d 135 (1982) (the husband was unable to work because of depression); *Deglman v. Deglman*, 276 S.C. 600, 281 S.E.2d 123 (1981) (the wife had physical and emotional problems and could not get health insurance); *Powers v. Powers*, 273 S.C. 51, 254 S.E.2d 289 (1979) (the wife had high blood pressure and diabetes).

An award of alimony to cover future medical needs of a spouse may be appropriate. Permanent alimony in the form of the wife's future medical expenses, including "all the hospital, medical, surgical, doctors, prescriptions, testing, and all other expenses the Plaintiff-wife has or will have aggravated by Herpes" was upheld in *Doe v. Doe*, 319 S.C. 151, 459 S.E.2d 892 (Ct. App. 1995). The husband had given the wife genital herpes before the marriage and lied to her about whether he was infected. The court said that the wife's extraordinary medical attention may well have justified an award of alimony without regard to the husband's fault.

A person seeking to use a physical disability to support a request for alimony has the burden of establishing the effect of the disability on the ability to work. In *Williamson v. Williamson*, 311 S.C. 47, 426 S.E.2d 758 (1993), the Supreme Court affirmed a denial of alimony to a wife who had epilepsy. The central question on appeal was whether the epilepsy rendered her disabled to the extent she could not work. It was undisputed at trial that she had epilepsy from birth. The wife had testified at trial that she had developed chronic seizures for the first time since early childhood after the parties were married. She presented no testimony other than her own to establish the extent of her disability. The wife had earned a master's degree in counseling before the marriage and the trial judge found that she had the ability to support herself, and that the extent of her disability had not been established by independent medical testimony. The Supreme Court affirmed the trial judge because the wife had failed to establish the extent of her medical condition with sufficient evidence, although it pointed out that the trial court's order did not constitute a ruling that expert medical testimony was required to establish the extent of a physical disability.

d. Educational Background

S.C. Code Ann. § 20-3-130(C)(3) (Law. Co-op. Supp.) provides that, in making an award of alimony or separate maintenance and support, the court must consider and give appropriate weight to "the educational background of each spouse, together with need of each spouse for additional training or education in order to achieve that spouse's income potential."

Lide did not specifically include educational background as a factor to be considered. There are not yet any cases in which this has been a significant factor, nor are there likely to be many. The importance of this factor, like health, is to aid the court in evaluating the parties' relative earning capacities and, perhaps, the appropriateness of rehabilitative alimony.

e. Employment History and Earning Potential

S.C. Code Ann. § 20-3-130(C)(4) (Law. Co-op. Supp.) provides that, in making an award of alimony or separate maintenance and support, the court must consider and give appropriate weight to "the employment history and earning potential of each spouse." *Lide* did not specifically include employment history as a factor to be considered, although earning potential was included.

If the parties are already equally capable of supporting themselves, there is no need for alimony. In *Trammell v. Trammell*, 268 S.C. 144, 232 S.E.2d 339 (1977), the Supreme Court held that the alimony awarded by the trial judge created a disproportionate income situation. The supporting spouse had $260 per month left after paying alimony, and the supported spouse had $650 per month after receiving alimony. The court remanded the case for reconsideration, apparently feeling that where income and asset postures were relatively equal between the parties, and fault played no major part, the parties should have been left where they were found. Also, in *Collins v. Collins*, 283 S.C. 526, 324 S.E.2d 82 (Ct. App. 1984), the Court of Appeals stated:

> We find that the court's denial of alimony and attorney's fees to the wife . . . is supported by the evidence. The husband earns approximately $740 monthly and the wife, $659 to $750. At the time

> of the separation, the husband had no separate assets. Both parties are able to work. An award of alimony is in the sound discretion of the trial judge, *McNaughton v. McNaughton*, 258 S.C. 554, 189 S.E.2d 820 (1972), upon a consideration of, among other things, the needs of the petitioner and the ability of the respondent to pay.

Id. at 531, 324 S.E.2d at 85. There was no discussion in *Collins* as to whether the wife's lifestyle after the divorce was going to be the same as it had been during the marriage. Thus, the objective of periodic alimony to maintain the marital standard of living, as discussed in *Johnson* and many other cases, was apparently not considered an important goal in this case.

The trial court must have sufficient evidence on which to base a determination of a person's earning potential. In *Sexton v. Sexton*, 298 S.C. 359, 380 S.E.2d 832 (Ct. App. 1989), an award of $375 per month in periodic alimony was reversed because, although there might have been a sufficient basis for the finding, there was nothing in the record on appeal to support the trial judge's conclusion that the husband had the potential to earn $500 per week. (The trial judge had also found that the husband's testimony concerning his earnings was not credible and that he had been deliberately keeping his income low in an attempt to reduce the amount of support he would be ordered to pay.)

f. Standard of Living During the Marriage

S.C. Code Ann. § 20-3-130(C)(5) (Law. Co-op. Supp.) provides that, in making an award of alimony or separate maintenance and support, the court must consider and give appropriate weight to "the standard of living established during the marriage." This is consistent with *Lide*.

As discussed earlier in the section on the purposes of alimony and in reference to rehabilitative alimony, South Carolina cases have set this as the primary goal for awarding periodic alimony, not just as a factor to be considered.

g. Earnings

The family court must consider and give appropriate weight to "the current and reasonably anticipated earnings of both spouses" in making an award of alimony or separate maintenance and support. S.C. Code Ann. § 20-3-130(C)(6) (Law. Co-op. Supp.). This factor is to be considered in conjunction with the other twelve factors. *Morehouse v. Morehouse*, 317 S.C. 222, 452 S.E.2d 632 (Ct. App. 1994).

This is consistent with *Lide*. This factor and others related to the assets and earning capacities of the parties are likely to become an even more important aspect of the decision-making process in recognition of the entry into the job market by an increasingly large percentage of women.

If the trial court does not obtain and record in its order information about the earnings and earnings potential of both parties, any award of alimony is likely to be reversed. In *Sexton v. Sexton*, 308 S.C. 37, 416 S.E.2d 649 (Ct. App. 1992), the alimony award was reversed because the court's finding regarding the husband's earning ability was unsupported by the record. Similarly, the absence of financial declarations caused *Jamar v. Jamar*, 308 S.C. 265, 417 S.E.2d 615 (Ct. App. 1992), to be remanded.

In *Lineburger v. Lineburger*, 303 S.C. 248, 399 S.E.2d 786 (Ct. App. 1990), the court determined that post-divorce bonuses are not marital property subject to equitable apportionment. Rather, they are ordinary income and can be considered by the trial court in awarding alimony. An award of 15% of the payor spouse's future bonuses to the payee as part of her alimony award was therefore affirmed.

h. Expenses and Needs

S.C. Code Ann. § 20-3-130(C)(7) (Law. Co-op. Supp.) provides that, in making an award of alimony or separate maintenance and support, the court must consider and give appropriate weight to "the current and reasonably anticipated expenses and needs of both spouses." This is consistent with *Lide*.

The family court may award less alimony to a mother when the father is solely responsible for a child's college expenses. *Doe v. Doe*, ___ S.C. ___, 478

S.E.2d 854 (Ct. App. 1996) (holding that an award of $300 per month was adequate in light of the fact that the father had been solely responsible for their son's college expenses).

i. Marital and Nonmarital Properties

S.C. Code Ann. § 20-3-130(C)(8) (Law. Co-op. Supp.) provides that, in making an award of alimony or separate maintenance and support, the court must consider and give appropriate weight to "the marital and nonmarital properties of the parties, including those apportioned to him or her in the divorce or separate maintenance action."

Under *Lide*, the trial judge was required to consider the "individual wealth" of each of the parties. Other cases were more explicit in stating that the court must consider the equitable division award. *See Lee v. Lee*, 282 S.C. 76, 316 S.E.2d 435 (Ct. App. 1984); *Burgess v. Burgess*, 277 S.C. 283, 286 S.E.2d 142 (1982); *Simmons v. Simmons*, 275 S.C. 41, 267 S.E.2d 427 (1980).

Under the alimony statute, the court must consider "the marital and non-marital property of the parties, including those apportioned to him or her in the divorce or separate maintenance action." Presumably, the court should make its equitable division award, determine and consider a spouse's potential earnings in relation to that award, and then make its decision about alimony.

j. Custody of the Children

S.C. Code Ann. § 20-3-130(C)(9) (Law. Co-op. Supp.) provides that, in making an award of alimony or separate maintenance and support, the court must consider and give appropriate weight to "custody of the children, particularly where conditions or circumstances render it appropriate that the custodian not be required to seek employment outside the home, or where the employment must be of a limited nature."

Under *Lide*, child custody was not a factor to be considered in the award of alimony. The alimony statute specifically makes custody of the children a factor to be considered, as well as any limited employment circumstances resulting from custodial responsibilities.

The most controversial element of this section will almost certainly be the determination of which conditions or circumstances make it "appropriate that the custodian not be required to seek employment outside the home." With the widespread availability of child care facilities, a case could be made that it should take a rare case to justify allowing a supported spouse to stay out of the job market to care for children. Of course, the other side of the coin is the value placed by our society in having mothers do exactly that, although the strength of the justification becomes increasingly weaker as the children become older. Perhaps one might begin to see awards of periodic alimony being set which decrease regularly as the children become older; or periodic alimony which decreases or terminates when the youngest child begins attending school.

In the short term, the impact of child custody on alimony awards will be determined by the personal beliefs of each family court judge. Eventually, the appellate courts will begin to define the parameters.

k. Marital Misconduct or Fault

(1) In General

S.C. Code Ann. § 20-3-130(C)(10) (Law. Co-op. Supp.) provides that, in making an award of alimony or separate maintenance and support, the court must consider and give appropriate weight to:

> [M]arital misconduct or fault of either or both parties, whether or not used as a basis for a divorce or separate maintenance decree if the misconduct affects or has affected the economic circumstances of the parties, or contributed to the breakup of the marriage, except that no evidence of personal conduct which may otherwise be relevant and material for the purpose of this subsection may be considered with regard to this subsection if the conduct took place subsequent to the happening of the earliest of (a) the formal signing of a written property or marital settlement agreement or (b) entry of a permanent

order of separate maintenance and support or of a permanent order approving a property or marital agreement between the parties.

Lide required that the "conduct of the parties" be considered. The 1990 alimony statute limits consideration of fault to misconduct which "affects or has affected the economic circumstances of the parties, or contributed to the breakup of the marriage." In no event may fault be considered unless it occurred before (a) the formal signing of a written property or marital settlement agreement or (b) entry of a permanent order of separate maintenance and support or of a permanent order approving a property or marital settlement agreement between the parties. This is a significant departure from existing case law.

The enactment of the 1990 alimony statute may have more impact on this factor than any other. However, it will require years of new appellate opinions to determine the extent of that impact. In the meantime, one can expect family court judges to interpret the statute in a variety of ways. Additional cases and discussion about the effect of marital misconduct can be found in the section on the purposes of alimony.

The statute does not change the rule that adultery must be affirmatively pled to bar an adulterous spouse from alimony. *Oyler v. Oyler*, 293 S.C. 4, 358 S.E.2d 170 (Ct. App. 1987).

If alimony is barred by adultery, the trial court is not allowed to use equitable apportionment to get around the bar. *Wannamaker v. Wannamaker*, 305 S.C. 36, 41, 406 S.E.2d 180, 183 (Ct. App. 1991). "The award that the trial judge made appears to be an attempt by the trial judge to compensate the wife for her failure to receive alimony, which was barred because of her adultery. Equitable distribution cannot be used because alimony is barred. *Berry v. Berry*, 294 S.C. 334, 364 S.E.2d 463 (1988)." *Id.* at 41, 406 S.E.2d at 183.

As indicated above, the factors to be considered in awarding alimony are exactly the same as those to be considered in awarding separate support and maintenance. The marital misconduct factor is discussed in both chapters because there has been a good bit of confusion historically between alimony and separate support and maintenance, particularly with regard to the rule of marital fault in making support decisions. The confusion has involved two separate but related issues: 1) the circumstance in which a spouse is barred from seeking support — that is, when a judge should not accept evidence about the factors set forth in section 20-3-130(C); and 2) the kinds of misconduct which will result in support being denied by the court after considering those factors.

The basic rule is that a *prima facie* case for support is established by showing that one spouse is in need of support and the other spouse is able to pay it. Once this has been established, the court looks to other relevant factors to decide whether to award support.

> Only an adulterous wife is statutorily denied alimony. Conversely, it is an irrefutable judicial principal that any alimony award rests in the sound discretion of the trial judge.
>
> Alimony is founded upon the legal duty of the husband to support his wife. It is not intended as a penalty against him nor as a reward to the wife. While the financial condition of the husband and the needs of the wife are important, they are not the only essentials to consider in determining the amount. There must also be considered all other circumstances of the particular case such as the age and health of the parties, their respective earning capacity, their individual wealth, the amount she contributed to the accumulation thereof and the conduct of the parties. *Graham v. Graham*, 253 S.C. 486, 171 S.E.2d 704 (1970).

Nienow v. Nienow, 268 S.C. 161, 170, 232 S.E.2d 504, 509 (1977) (holding that a wife was entitled to bring an action for alimony in South Carolina after her husband had obtained a divorce from her in Florida) (quoting *Beasely v. Beasely*, 264 S.C. 611, 612-613, 216 S.E.2d 535, 535-536 (1975)).

Marital fault has been one of the most important factors in determining whether a spouse is entitled to support, and it will continue to be a significant consideration. Under the 1990 alimony statute, however, fault is not to be considered in deciding whether to award support if the misconduct has neither affected the economic circumstances of the parties nor contributed to the breakup of the marriage.

See S.C. Code Ann. § 20-3-130(C)(10) (Law. Co-op. Supp.); *McKnight v. McKnight*, 283 S.C. 540, 324 S.E.2d 91 (Ct. App. 1984); *Welch v. Welch*, 250 S.C. 264, 157 S.E.2d 249 (1967) (this section of the Code and both cases are discussed below).

Misconduct of a spouse prior to the marriage may be considered in awarding alimony, if the misconduct extends to the marriage. *Doe v. Doe*, 319 S.C. 151, 459 S.E.2d 892 (Ct. App. 1995) (upholding an award of alimony to cover future medical expenses of wife who had been given genital herpes by the husband prior to the marriage. The court found that the husband's misconduct, "though originally premarital in nature, extended to the marriage when he continued to lie to the wife about his own medical condition and she proceeded to marry him in ignorance of the truth." *Id.* at 156, 459 S.E.2d at 895.).

(2) Misconduct Must be Substantial and Material to Bar Support

Courts have come to recognize that when a marriage has failed, both spouses were usually somewhat at fault in causing the deterioration of the marital relationship. However, a spouse will be denied support if he or she engaged in substantial misconduct which materially contributed to the failure of the marriage, unless the other spouse was equally at fault.

In holding that a wife was not absolutely barred from seeking support just because she removed herself from the marital home, the Supreme Court made the following observations in *McKnight v. McKnight*, 283 S.C. 540, 324 S.E.2d 91 (Ct. App. 1984):

> Her entitlement to separate maintenance and support is not affected "unless she is guilty of disqualifying fault in bringing about or causing the disruption of the marital relation, which her physical departure from the home merely signifies." *Welch v. Welch*, 250 S.C. [264] at 268, 157 S.E.2d 249 [1967].
>
> As to what constitutes fault which will bar a wife from separate maintenance and support, this Court in *Miller v. Miller*, 225 S.C. 274, 82 S.E.(2d)

> 119 [1954], recognized that most marital difficulties are to some extent the fault of both parties and approved the rule that the wife need not be blameless in order to recover. Relief should be denied to her on this ground only if she was guilty of substantial fault or misconduct "'which materially contributed to the disruption of the marital relation or induced the action by the husband upon which she relies to justify their separation . . . .' [citations omitted]."
>
> *Welch*, 250 S.C. at 251, 157 S.E.(2d) 249.
>
> The evidence in this case sheds little light on which of the parties, if either, engaged in substantial misconduct which materially contributed to the disruption of the marital relationship. What is clear is that Mrs. McKnight's departure was not the cause of but only signified that disruption.

Id. at 544, 324 S.E.2d at 93. *See also Doe v. Doe*, ___ S.C. ___, 478 S.E.2d 854 (Ct. App. 1996) (holding that the family court did not err in awarding alimony to a wife who allegedly abandoned her husband). *But see Brown v. Brown*, 239 S.C. 444, 123 S.E.2d 772 (1962), in which the court held, after reciting similar language as set forth above, that the wife was not entitled to support because she was substantially at fault in the separation and materially provoked the difficulties of which she had complained in her unsuccessful attempt to divorce her husband on the ground of physical cruelty.

Where marital misconduct exists but it is equally divided, support is not barred even if a divorce has been awarded to one spouse on the ground of misconduct by the other spouse. *Clardy v. Clardy*, 266 S.C. 270, 222 S.E.2d 771 (1976). In *Clardy*, the court determined that the trial court properly awarded alimony to a wife although the husband had been granted a divorce on the basis of her desertion. "Although the divorce was granted to the husband, it is inferable that fault is about equally divided. The divorce law of this State does not deny to a wife alimony except in case of adultery." *Id.* at 273, 194 S.E.2d at 772.

(3) Habitual Drunkenness Alone is Not a Bar to Support

Habitual drunkenness will not bar alimony unless misconduct resulting from the condition materially contributed to the disruption of the marital relationship. The Supreme Court held that the trial court properly awarded support in *Herbert v. Herbert*, 260 S.C. 86, 194 S.E.2d 238 (1973), after the husband had been granted a divorce on the ground of the wife's habitual drunkenness:

> Admittedly, the respondent is a chronic alcoholic and it was determined in this case that she was a habitual drunkard within the meaning of Section 20-101(4) of the Code.
>
> In the case of *DeSipio v. DeSipio*, D.C. Mun. App., 186 A.(2d) 624, the Court held that the wife's chronic alcoholism was not misconduct precluding separate support and maintenance and went on to say that "chronic alcoholism, although frequently a cause of much unhappiness in family relationships, is not to be equated with misconduct. It is a disease, difficult to control or permanently cure, and seriously affects the employability of the victim."
>
> . . .
>
> The record here shows that the trial judge took into consideration, in making an award of alimony to the wife, the fact that she was a habitual drunkard but that such addiction should not be "used as the basis for determining real moral wrongdoing on her part."

Id. at 91, 194 S.E.2d at 239.

(4) Adultery is Sometimes an Absolute Bar to Support

Adultery will be an absolute bar to alimony only if it is committed before the earliest of two events: (1) the formal signing of a written property or marital settlement agreement, or (2) entry of a permanent order of separate maintenance and support or of a permanent order approving a property or marital settlement agreement between the parties. S.C. Code Ann. § 20-3-130(A) (Law. Co-op. Supp.). This was not always the case. Until the statute was enacted, a spouse risked having support barred if he or she committed adultery at any time before the final divorce decree. In *Morris v. Morris*, 295 S.C. 37, 41, 367 S.E.2d 24, 26 (1988), the court stated: "We hold that she was no less a 'spouse' under the separate maintenance decree, her romantic interludes no less 'adulterous,' than as the parties had never separated."

The implications of the statutory language are potentially quite significant. A strict reading would appear to permit married couples to engage in adultery without fear of losing their rights to spousal support if they have signed a property agreement at any time during the marriage or, perhaps, even a premarital agreement. (One can expect our courts to be reluctant to interpret the statute so liberally.) The unanswered questions about this language pose risks for litigants, particularly since the statute does not define the parameters of "written property or marital settlement agreement." Does the agreement have to be complete — that is, does it have to settle every detail of every issue between the parties? Or could an agreement suffice which settles some or a significant portion of property or other issues? What if the agreement is found to be invalid, either in part or in its entirety, for any of the reasons discussed in the chapter on agreements? Could a spouse who commits adultery in reliance on the existence of the agreement be required to pay support due to some unknown and unintended defect in the agreement? For the answers to these questions, we will have to wait for legislative clarification or, more likely, for appellate case decisions.

Adultery which has been condoned or unconditionally forgiven cannot be used as a basis for denying alimony. *Grubbs v. Grubbs*, 272 S.C. 138, 249 S.E.2d 747 (1978) (reversing a denial of alimony where the wife's adultery occurred ten years before the parties' separation).

Adultery must be pled as a defense. If it is not raised in the pleadings, it cannot be proved at trial. *Doe v. Doe*, ___ S.C. ___, 478 S.E.2d 854 (Ct. App. 1996) (affirming the trial court's decision to bar the husband's attorney from cross-examining the wife about extramarital relationships). The court stated that the "[h]usband did not plead Wife's adultery and thus was not entitled to question her on the issue at trial. ... adultery is an avoidance to an action for alimony which must be pled under Rule 8(c), SCRCP." *Id.* at ___, 478 S.E.2d at 858.

(5) Desertion is Not Necessarily a Bar to Support

Under the common law, and for many years in South Carolina, desertion was an absolute bar to an award of spousal support, unless the abandonment was "justified." This is no longer the case.[11]

> Although in several jurisdictions, desertion absolutely bars a spouse from alimony, that is not the case in South Carolina. In *Welch v. Welch*, 250 S.C. 264, 157 S.E.(2d) 249 (1967), an action for separate support and maintenance, the Court stated that the fact that the wife removed herself from the marital home was entitled to little, if any, weight. Her entitlement to separate maintenance and support is not affected "unless she is guilty of disqualifying fault in bringing about or causing the disruption of the marital relation, which her physical departure from the home signifies." *Welch*, 250 S.C. at 268, 157 S.E.(2d) 249.
>
>> As to what constitutes fault which will bar a wife from separate maintenance and support, this Court in *Miller v. Miller*, 225 S.C. 274, 82 S.E.(2d) 119 [1954], recognized that most marital difficulties are to some extent the fault of both parties and approved the rule that the wife need not be blameless in order to recover. Relief should be denied to her on this ground only if she was guilty of substantial fault or misconduct "'which materially contributed to the

---

[11] The statute which makes child and spousal nonsupport a criminal offense, S.C. Code Ann. § 20-7-90 (Law. Co-op. 1976), provides in part: "A husband or wife abandoned by his or her spouse is not liable for the support of the abandoning spouse until such spouse offers to return unless the misconduct of the husband or wife justified the abandonment." While this language might help a nonsupporting spouse avoid going to jail, this statute has not been cited in a civil spousal support case and it appears to be irrelevant to marital litigation.

> disruption of the marital relation or induced the action by the husband upon which she relies to justify their separation . . . .' [citations omitted]."

Welch, 250 S.C. at 251, 157 S.E.(2d) 249.

> The evidence in this case sheds little light on which of the parties, if either, engaged in substantial misconduct which materially contributed to the disruption of the marital relationship. What is clear is that Mrs. McKnight's departure was not the cause of but only signified that disruption.

McKnight v. McKnight, 283 S.C. 540, 544, 324 S.E.2d 91, 93 (Ct. App. 1984). This statement essentially represents the current law codified in S.C. Code Ann. § 20-3-130(C)(10) (Law. Co-op. Supp), which provides that, in making an award of alimony or separate maintenance and support, the court must consider and give weight to "marital misconduct or fault of either or both parties whether or not used as a basis for a divorce or separate maintenance decree if the misconduct affects or has affected the economic circumstances of the parties, or contributed to the breakup of the marriage . . . ."

Many cases have struggled over the question of whether or not a spouse, usually the wife, was justified in leaving the marital home or otherwise at fault in bringing about the marital problems. A brief survey follows: *Machado v. Machado*, 220 S.C. 90, 80 S.E.2d 123 (1951), held that the wife was justified in leaving the marital home because of the husband's false accusations of marital infidelity while he flaunted his own love affair. In *Mincey v. Mincey*, 224 S.C. 520, 80 S.E.2d 123 (1954), the wife was found to have had just cause to leave her husband based on his "reprehensible conduct" which was not sufficient to serve as a ground for divorce. *Inabinet v. Inabinet*, 236 S.C. 52, 113 S.E.2d 66 (1960), determined that the wife was not required to live with her husband in his parents' home because they were rude and interfered. In *Brown v. Brown*, 239 S.C. 444, 123 S.E.2d 772 (1962), the Supreme Court determined that the wife was not entitled to a divorce on the ground of physical cruelty and should not receive any support because she had invited arguments with her husband and pursued them rather diligently and vigorously at times, thus substantially provoking the difficulties about which she complained (that is, she asked for it).

The modern rule began to take shape in the late 1960's in *Welch v. Welch*, 250 S.C. 264, 157 S.E.2d 249 (1967) (quoted at the beginning of this section in *McKenzie v. McKenzie*, 254 S.C. 372, 175 S.E.2d 628 (1970)) and other cases in the early to mid 1970's. This, of course, was the same period in our country's history when increased attention was beginning to be paid to women's rights in general. Although the husband had been granted a divorce on the ground of desertion in *Page v. Page*, 260 S.C. 298, 195 S.E.2d 613 (1973), the Supreme Court held that the trial court had erred in ruling that the wife's request for alimony was barred by a prior adverse ruling in an action brought by the wife charging the husband with physical cruelty and seeking separate support. A divorce had been awarded to the husband on the ground of desertion, and the wife's request for a divorce on the ground of physical cruelty had been denied.

> Regarding the former adjudication that the wife left the marital abode without just cause or excuse as conclusive against her claim to alimony in the divorce action, the court refused to hear her evidence relating to this claim. This was error. Only an adulterous wife is automatically barred from alimony by the terms of the statute. Sec. 20-113, Code of 1962. In all other cases, "the circumstances and conduct of an offending spouse might be such as to bar her from alimony but this is a matter solely for the trial judge, governed by equity and justice and the condition of both parties. The exercise of such a discretion will not be disturbed on appeal unless an abuse thereof is shown." *Herbert v. Herbert*, S.C., 194 S.E.2d 238, 239 (1973); *McKenzie v. McKenzie*, 254 S.C. 372, 175 S.E.2d 628 (1970).

Id. at 301, 195 S.E.2d at 614. The case was remanded for consideration of the wife's alimony claim.

The Supreme Court ruled that the wife should have been awarded alimony in *Clardy v. Clardy*, 266 S.C. 270, 222 S.E.2d 771 (1976), although the husband had been granted a divorce on the basis of her desertion. "Although the divorce was granted the husband, it is inferable that fault is about equally divided. The divorce law of this State does not deny to a wife alimony except in case of adultery . . . ." *Id.* at 273, 222 S.E.2d at 772.

As explained at the beginning of this section, the fact that one spouse abandons another is no longer significant in and of itself. The important issue is whether the act of abandonment caused the disruption of the marital relationship or only served as evidence that the marital relationship had already been disrupted. *McKnight v. McKnight*, 283 S.C. 540, 544, 324 S.E.2d 91, 93 (Ct. App. 1984). This essentially represents the law which is codified in S.C. Code Ann. § 20-3-130(C)(10) (Law. Co-op. Supp.).

l. Tax Consequences

S.C. Code Ann. § 20-3-130(C)(11) (Law. Co-op. Supp.) provides that, in making an award of alimony or separate maintenance and support, the court must consider and give appropriate weight to "the tax consequences to each party as a result of the particular form of support awarded."

*Lide*did not provide for consideration of tax consequences although *Simonds* did. As the alimony statute also contains specific provisions allowing the court to designate the spousal support as either deductible to the payor spouse and taxable to the supported spouse, or nondeductible to the payor spouse and nontaxable to the supported spouse, the court's involvement with the tax consequences resulting from support awards should increase under the alimony statute.

With this statutory mandate to consider tax consequences, the court should consider the tax consequence of the support award to both spouses, essentially with the court determining the net spendable income of both spouses after considering all sources of income, the payment and receipt of support, and the payment of taxes.

Tax considerations are discussed in the chapter on taxes.

m. Other Support Obligations

S.C. Code Ann. § 20-3-130(C)(12) (Law. Co-op. Supp.) provides that, in making an award of alimony or separate maintenance and support, the court must consider and give appropriate weight to "the existence and extent of any support obligation from a prior marriage or for any other reason of either party."

Lide did not include consideration of other support obligations. The alimony statute requires consideration of all other support obligations, although the statute does not inform the court how to treat them.

n. Other Relevant Factors

S.C. Code Ann. § 20-3-130(C)(13) (Law. Co-op. Supp.) provides that, in making an award of alimony or separate maintenance and support, the court must consider and give appropriate weight to "such other factors the court considers relevant."

Lide also includes a catch-all provision that gives the trial court the flexibility to consider additional relevant factors, even if the legislature did not think of them.

CHAPTER SEVEN
PROPERTY

CHAPTER SEVEN
PROPERTY

A. IN GENERAL

The division of marital property in South Carolina is governed by the Equitable Apportionment of Marital Property Act, S.C. Code Ann. §§ 20-7-471 through 20-7-479 (Law. Co-op. Supp.). The Act became effective on June 13, 1986, and codified much of the extensive case law covering property division in South Carolina. However, the legislation introduced new issues about the division of marital property, and it will be many years before all of these questions are answered.

S.C. Code Ann. § 20-7-470 (Law. Co-op. Supp.) defines marital property as: "[A]ll real and personal property which has been acquired by the parties during the marriage and which is owned as of the date of filing or commencement of marital litigation . . . regardless of how legal title is held . . . ."

The philosophy behind equitable apportionment is explained in *Walker v. Walker*, 295 S.C. 286, 368 S.E.2d 89 (Ct. App. 1988):

> Equitable distribution is based on a recognition that marriage is, among other things, an economic partnership. Upon dissolution of the marriage, property accumulated during the marriage should be divided and distributed in a manner which fairly reflects each spouse's contribution to its acquisition, regardless of which spouse owns legal title.

Id. at 288, 368 S.E.2d at 90.

The objective in dividing marital property is to sever all joint interests in the property as completely as possible, absent compelling reasons to retain joint ownership. The Court of Appeals outlined some basic principles in *Johnson v. Johnson*, 285 S.C. 308, 329 S.E.2d 443 (Ct. App. 1985):

> First, the family court must begin with the premise that division and distribution of the marital home should be accomplished at the time of entry of the judgment of divorce. If possible, all issues between the parties should be resolved at that point so that disputes and irritants do not linger and present further incentives to litigation. The family court's objective should be to dissolve the marriage, sever all entangling legal relations and place the parties in a position from which they can begin anew.

Id. at 311, 329 S.E.2d at 445.

Family courts should avoid awarding fractional interests in marital property. In *Shealy v. Shealy*, 280 S.C. 494, 313 S.E.2d 48 (Ct. App. 1980), the court reversed an award of the exclusive use of the marital home to the wife until her death or remarriage. The court noted:

> Due to their nature, domestic cases are difficult to end absolutely. Awarding fractional interests in real or personal property is not a satisfactory disposition to divorcing parties. It denies control of sale or encumbrances to both. Management, repairs, etc. are difficult to handle between persons at odds after divorce. Also, proven statistics have shown that women live longer than men thus furthering the uncertainty of an individual fractional interest. This could invite future litigation. In the future, Family Court judges are encouraged to make final dispositions of property interests where possible or, in the alternative, cite compelling reasons for awarding fractional or joint interests. Courts may determine incidental questions, afford complete justice and prevent multiplicity of litigation in divorce actions. *McLean v. McLean*, 273 S.C. 571, 257 S.E. 2d 751 (1979).

Id. at 498 n.1, 313 S.E.2d at 50, n.1. The Court of Appeals cited *Shealy* with approval in *Bass v. Bass*, 285 S.C. 178, 328 S.E.2d 649 (Ct. App. 1985), and added that if trial courts fail to make a final disposition of property interests, they "must state compelling reasons for leaving loose ends." *Id.* at 182, 328 S.E.2d at 352.

The family court is expected to follow four steps in deciding how to divide marital property:

(1) identify the marital property, real and personal, to be divided between the parties;

(2) determine the fair market value of the property so identified;

(3) identify the proportionate contributions, both direct and indirect, of each party to the acquisition of the marital property; and

(4) provide for an equitable division of the marital property.

Cannon v. Cannon, ___ S.C. ___, 467 S.E.2d 132 (Ct. App. 1996) (holding that it was error for the family court not to value the personal property in the marital home).

Equitable apportionment cannot be used in lieu of alimony where a spouse is not otherwise entitled to receive alimony.

> The award that the trial judge made appears to be an attempt by the trial judge to compensate the wife for her failure to receive alimony, which was barred because of her adultery. Equitable distribution cannot be used because alimony is barred.

Wannamaker v. Wannamaker, 305 S.C. 36, 41, 406 S.E.2d 180, 183 (Ct. App. 1991) (citing *Berry v. Berry*, 294 S.C. 334, 364 S.E.2d 463 (1988)).

Which spouse is entitled to income from marital property during an appeal is an open question. In *Hunt v. Hunt*, 311 S.C. 355, 428 S.E.2d 899 (Ct. App. 1993), the trial court awarded the wife earnings on a portion of the husband's pension fund. An appeal by both parties followed. After the Supreme Court affirmed the equitable distribution award and increased the alimony award, the trial court conducted a hearing to determine who was entitled to receive the earnings on the wife's portion of the pension during the pendency of the appeal. The family court ruled in favor of the wife. The husband appealed, arguing that, because the wife was the primary appellant in the appeal and because she was not successful in her appeal of the equitable distribution award, she was akin to a judgment creditor and therefore not entitled to any earnings, as an unsuccessful judgment creditor is not entitled to interest. The Court of Appeals rejected this position, but it did not rule directly on the merits of the husband's argument. It held that he had not preserved this question for appeal because he had not raised this argument with the trial court and there was no evidence that he made a SCRCP, Rule 59(e) motion. The court also found that the division of the pension was not an issue in the original appeal to the Supreme Court. The question is, therefore, still open.

B. JURISDICTION

1. IN GENERAL

Before 1976, South Carolina courts had no specific statutory authority to adjudicate the property rights of parties. In *Piana v. Piana*, 239 S.C. 367, 123 S.E.2d 297 (1961), the Supreme Court determined that the power to adjudicate property rights derived from section 20-105 of the 1952 Code (presently codified as S.C. Code Ann. § 20-3-50 (1976)) which states: "Actions for divorce from the bonds of matrimony shall, except as otherwise provided, be only in the equity jurisdiction of the court of common pleas"). *Piana* held that any property claims, whether real or personal, could be settled by the divorce court.

Perhaps the most unusual aspect of *Piana*, however, is that the family court did not grant a divorce to either party. The Supreme Court said that equity powers gave the trial court the right to adjudicate such claims even though the divorce was denied:

> While our divorce statute (Title 20, Chapter 2 of the 1952 Code) does not expressly authorize the Court in a divorce proceeding to settle disputed claims of the parties to real and personal property, yet such an action is in the equity jurisdiction of the Court (Section 20-105) and we find nothing in the statute undertaking to restrict the broad powers of a court of chancery. The Court having general

> jurisdiction when a divorce action is brought, such jurisdiction is not lost when a divorce is denied.

Id. at 375, 123 S.E.2d at 301.

In 1976, the South Carolina General Assembly, during its reorganization of the family court system, specifically granted the family court jurisdiction to deal with property claims. It amended S.C. Code Ann. § 14-21-1020 (1976) (now codified as S.C. Code Ann. § 20-7-420 (Law. Co-op. Supp.)) to provide that the family court shall have exclusive jurisdiction to hear and determine actions:

> For divorce *a vinculo matrimonii*, separate support and maintenance, legal separation[12], and in other marital litigation between the parties, and for settlement of all legal and equitable rights of the parties in such actions in and to the real and personal property of the marriage and attorney fees, if requested by either party in the pleadings.

The statute thus gave or confirmed in the family court the powers alluded to in *Piana*.

The family court can only apportion marital property if the apportionment is incident to: (1) a divorce *a vinculo matrimonii*, (2) an action for separate support and maintenance, (3) a proceeding to dispose of marital property after a prior decree of dissolution of a marriage by a court which lacked personal jurisdiction over the other spouse or which lacked jurisdiction to dispose of the property, or (4) other marital litigation between the parties. *Brown v. Brown*, 295 S.C. 354, 368 S.E.2d 475 (1988) (holding that the Equitable Apportionment of Marital Property Act did not allow a wife to seek a division of marital property while she was still living in the same house with her husband and was not seeking to alter the marital relationship).

---

[12] Despite its inclusion in the statute, South Carolina does not recognize actions for legal separation.

The family court may not adjudicate property interests between people who are living together but not married. The court of common pleas is the appropriate forum. *Hallums v. Bowens*, 318 S.C. 1, 428 S.E.2d 894 (Ct. App. 1993) (holding *ex mero motu* that, since the trial court determined that the parties had not established a valid common law marriage, "the family court did not have jurisdiction to allocate properties of this unmarried couple").

The family court may order equitable distribution of property following the annulment of a marriage. *Splawn v. Splawn*, 311 S.C. 423, 429 S.E.2d 805 (1993); *White v. White*, 283 S.C. 348, 323 S.E.2d 521 (1984) (both holding that the family court has jurisdiction to consider and rule on all matters in annulment actions). (See additional discussion about subject matter jurisdiction in Chapter One.)

The family court's authority over marital property includes contracts relating to such property. S.C. Code Ann. § 20-7-479 (Law. Co-op. Supp.) states that "[t]he family courts of this state have subject matter jurisdiction over all contracts relating to property which is involved in a proceeding under this article and over the construction and enforcement of those contracts." (See the chapter on agreements for additional discussion of the family court's jurisdiction over agreements.)

2. PROPERTY DIVISION MUST BE SOUGHT IN PLEADINGS

The family court only has the power to adjudicate real and personal property claims that are properly pleaded by the parties. S.C. Code Ann. § 20-7-420 (Law. Co-op. Supp.) This point is verified in case law. In *Loftis v. Loftis*, 286 S.C. 12, 331 S.E.2d 372 (Ct. App. 1985), the Court of Appeals found that the family court had no authority to order the sale of a house that was being used by the wife because such relief was not requested in the pleadings. Similarly, in *McCullough v. McCullough*, 271 S.C. 475, 248 S.E.2d 308 (1978), the Supreme Court held that while there was "authority to effectuate property settlements incident to a divorce [those] matters [must] properly [be] brought before the Court in the pleadings and stipulations of the parties." *Id.* at 477, 248 S.E.2d at 309.

The Supreme Court advised family court judges in 1996 that they do not have subject matter jurisdiction to equitably apportion marital property that is not listed in either party's financial declaration.

3. INDEPENDENT ACTIONS FOR PROPERTY DIVISION

The Equitable Apportionment of Marital Property Act gives the family court jurisdiction to hear actions for division of marital property as independent actions apart from any other marital litigation, but only following a divorce decree or other dissolution of the marriage by a court which lacked subject matter jurisdiction to divide the marital property. This is a change from prior case law.

This change in the law was recognized by the Court of Appeals in *Eckhardt v. Eckhardt*, 309 S.C. 225, 420 S.E.2d 875 (Ct. App. 1992). The parties were divorced through an action brought by the husband in North Carolina while the wife was living in Kentucky. Neither party requested division of the marital property. The wife later brought an action in South Carolina seeking a division of the marital property. The trial judge dismissed the action. The Court of Appeals ruled that an action for division of marital property can be maintained following a divorce under the provisions of the Equitable Apportionment Act of 1986.[13]

The court relied on the following language in S.C. Code Ann. § 20-7-472 (Law. Co-op. Supp.) in reaching its conclusion:

> In a proceeding for divorce a vinculo matrimonii or separate support and maintenance, or in a proceeding for disposition of

---

[13] Thus, it appears from *Eckhardt* that the enactment of the Equitable Apportionment of Marital Property Act overruled *Sims v. Sims*, 290 S.C. 190, 348 S.E.2d 835 (1986), which held that the family court had no subject matter jurisdiction to apportion marital property following a divorce action unless one of the parties requested a division of marital property in the divorce pleadings. In *Sims*, the husband sought to set aside a conveyance of property to a third party after the divorce was final, claiming that a predivorce agreement controlled the disposition of the property. The Supreme Court said the action belonged in circuit court, not family court.

property following a prior decree or dissolution of a marriage by a court which lacked subject matter jurisdiction to dispose of the property, and in other marital litigation between the parties, the court shall make a final equitable apportionment between the parties of the parties' marital property upon the request by either party in the pleadings.

4. OMITTED PROPERTY

If the family court can divide marital property following a divorce action in which it is not asked to divide any marital property (see preceding discussion), can it divide marital property after a divorce if the parities asked the family court to divide some, but not all of the marital property during the divorce proceeding? The answer to this question is not clear, but it appears unlikely. Therefore, practitioners representing clients who want the family court to divide only part of the marital estate during marital litigation, but might want it to divide more of it at a later time, should inform the court about the additional assets and ask it to reserve jurisdiction to divide them. *See Hayes v. Hayes*, 312 S.C. 141, 439 S.E.2d 305 (Ct. App. 1993); *Jordan v. Jordan*, 307 S.C. 407, 415 S.E.2d 424 (Ct. App. 1992) (both holding that "[a] family court order can be modified only when jurisdiction was specifically reserved in the decree or if allowed by statute").

An argument exists that the family court has jurisdiction to divide marital property that was omitted from the initial division of the marital estate under the Equitable Division of Marital Property Act, even if the family court does not specifically reserve jurisdiction to consider it. In *Brown v. Brown*, 295 S.C. 354, 368 S.E.2d 475 (1988), the Supreme Court indicated that one of the times when the family court can divide marital property under the Equitable Apportionment of Marital Property Act is incident to a proceeding to dispose of marital property after a prior decree of dissolution of a marriage by a court which lacked personal jurisdiction over the other spouse or which lacked jurisdiction to dispose of the property. Given the Supreme Court's advice to the family court judges that they lack subject matter jurisdiction to apportion marital property that is not listed on either party's financial declaration, one can argue that the family court can apportion omitted items of property even if it did not reserve jurisdiction because it did not have jurisdiction to allocate those items of property during the marital litigation.

5. PROPERTY OWNED BY THIRD PARTIES

Property owned by a third party can be equitably apportioned by the family court, if the husband or wife claims an equitable interest in the property and the third party is made a party to the action. In *Sexton v. Sexton*, 298 S.C. 359, 380 S.E.2d 832 (Ct. App. 1989), the sole issue on appeal was "whether the Family Court has subject matter jurisdiction to equitably apportion property owned by a third party." *Id.* The wife claimed that, although the marital home was titled in the husband's parents' names, she was entitled to an equitable apportionment of the property. The court found that S.C. Code Ann. § 20-7-470 (Law. Co-op. Supp.) defines marital property as:

> "[A]ll real and personal property which has been acquired by the parties during the marriage and which is owned as of the date of filing or commencement of marital litigation . . . regardless of how legal title is held . . . ." This section specifically provides for the possibility that marital property could be titled in a third party.
>
> In order to determine whether the property is marital property the Family Court has the authority to join the owner of the property as a necessary party to the action.
>
> . . .
>
> If the property is found to be marital property, the Court has the authority to apportion it among the parties.

Id. at 361, 380 S.E.2d at 834.[14] See also *Barnwell v. Barnwell*, ___ S.C. ___, 476 S.E.2d 492 (Ct. App. 1996), in which the Court of Appeals reversed the family court's ruling that the marital home was not marital property. The house and lot were titled to a company owned by the husband's father. The Court of Appeals concluded that the wife substantiated her claim of gift by clear, cogent, and convincing evidence.

A failure to join third-party property owners does not necessarily invalidate an apportionment order. In *Seawright v. Seawright*, 305 S.C. 167, 406 S.E.2d 386 (Ct. App. 1991), the Court of Appeals ruled that it was error for the family court to declare the husband to be the equitable owner of the marital home without the title owner of record (the wife's sister) being made a party to the suit. However, it allowed the division of property to stand because it found the division of marital property to be fair and equitable.

6. MODIFICATION

The general rule is that property divisions are not modifiable, unless the family court reserves jurisdiction to do so. *Hayes v. Hayes*, 312 S.C. 141, 439 S.E.2d 305 (Ct. App. 1993) (holding that "[a] family court order can be modified only when jurisdiction was specifically reserved in the decree or if allowed by statute") (citing *Jordan v. Jordan*, 307 S.C. 407, 415 S.E.2d 424 (Ct. App. 1992)). However, modification has been allowed to prevent inequitable results, although most cases conclude that the family court lacks subject matter jurisdiction to modify a property award. For example, in *Hayes v. Hayes*, 312 S.C. 141, 439 S.E.2d 305 (Ct. App. 1993), the Court of Appeals wrote:

> A family court order can be modified only when jurisdiction was specifically reserved in the decree or if allowed by statute. *Jordan v. Jordan*, 307 S.C. 407, 415 S.E.2d 424 (Ct. App. 1992).

---

[14] The same parties were involved in *Sexton v. Sexton*, 308 S.C. 37, 416 S.E.2d 649 (Ct. App. 1992) (discussed in the section on apportionment), which held that the trial judge could not rely on his apportionment of the personal property at the divorce hearing in making a subsequent determination of the relative equities of the parties in the marital home.

> There is no statutory authority for modifying an order of equitable distribution; nor is there a reservation of jurisdiction to modify the property in the original decree. Moreover, S.C. Code Ann. § 20-7-472 (Supp.) states, in pertinent part, "[the family] court's order as it affects distribution of marital property shall be a final order not subject to modification, except by appeal or remand following proper appeal." Therefore, there was no subject matter jurisdiction for the family court to consider this matter.

Id. at 144, 439 S.E.2d at 307.

In *Hayes*, the parties' property settlement agreement was approved by the family court. The wife subsequently contended that she should be allowed to seek a share of her former husband's military retirement because the law did not allow her to do so when the property was divided. The Court of Appeals affirmed the family court's refusal to modify the property division on the basis of *res judicata* and because the trial court did not have subject matter jurisdiction to consider the issue. See also, *Burns v. Burns*, ___ S.C. ___, 448 S.E.2d 571 (Ct. App. 1994), in which a former husband asked the family court to modify, on the basis of changed circumstances, those parts of a divorce decree that reflected his agreement to pay certain debts. The bankruptcy court had found that the debt obligations were non-dischargeable. The Court of Appeals held that the law was clear that the family court did not have the authority to modify property divisions, citing S.C. Code Ann. § 20-7-472 (Law Co-op. Supp.).

A modification was allowed, however, in *Fisher v. Fisher*, 319 S.C. 500, 462 S.E.2d 303 (Ct. App. 1995). The family court modified the terms of its property settlement order to reflect the wife's right to share in the husband's retirement income, although the income was from a voluntary separation incentive plan rather than the regular military pension that was contemplated at the time of divorce. The Court of Appeals affirmed this modification.

Although property settlement agreements are contractual in nature and therefore nonmodifiable, the courts will look at the "thrust" of such agreements rather than isolated provisions in determining their nature. In *Kane v. Kane*, 280 S.C. 479, 313 S.E.2d 327 (Ct. App. 1984), the Court of Appeals differentiated a "true" property agreement from one in which disposition of property is "merely incidental." In *Kane*, the parties entered into a separation and support agreement that included provisions for alimony, child support, and disposition of the marital home. The parties then obtained a divorce in the Dominican Republic. The husband, appealing the trial judge's finding that "the foreign divorce was void for lack of jurisdiction and . . . the agreement was unfair because [the wife] was unaware of her husband's financial status when she signed the agreement," argued that the agreement was a nonmodifiable property settlement. *Id.* at 480, 313 S.E.2d at 328-29. The Court of Appeals noted that, although the agreement contained certain provisions covering the disposition of property, "the primary thrust of the agreement was alimony and support and custody of the children." *Id.* at 481, 313 S.E.2d at 329.

C. IDENTIFICATION (WHAT IS IT?)

1. ACQUIRING AN INTEREST IN MARITAL PROPERTY

a. In General

A spouse seeking to claim an interest in marital property has the burden of proving that the property is marital property. "It is well settled that a spouse claiming an equitable interest in property upon dissolution of the marriage has the burden of proving the property is part of the marital estate." *Carroll v. Carroll*, 309 S.C. 22, 26, 419 S.E.2d 801, 803 (Ct. App. 1992) (citing *Roberts v. Roberts*, 296 S.C. 93, 370 S.E.2d 881 (Ct. App. 1988), *aff'd as modified*, 299 S.C. 315, 384 S.E.2d 719 (1989)).

Uncontradicted testimony by one spouse is sufficient to carry the burden of proving that property is nonmarital. *See Roe v. Roe*, 311 S.C. 471, 429 S.E.2d 830 (Ct. App. 1993) (holding that it was error to include an emerald ring in the marital estate in light of the uncontradicted testimony of the wife that it was her separate property).

Marital property is all property accumulated during the marriage that does not fall within some established exception. *Berry v. Berry*, 290 S.C. 351, 350 S.E.2d 398 (Ct. App. 1986). This includes marital debts as well as assets. (Cases related to marital debts are discussed in the section on apportionment: encumbrances on the property and other debts, later in this chapter.)

S.C. Code Ann. § 20-7-471 (Law. Co-op. Supp.) provides the basis on which a spouse is entitled to claim an interest in marital property:

> During the marriage a spouse shall acquire, based upon the factors set out in § 20-7-472, a vested special equity and ownership right in the marital property as defined in § 20-7-473, which equity and ownership right are subject to apportionment between the spouses by the family courts of this State at the time marital litigation is filed or commenced as provided in § 20-7-472.

Unfortunately, the statute does not define the term "special equity." The theory of division prior to the more modern decisions relied on a fiction designated "special equity." The use of the term in the statute may have resulted from an attempt by the drafters' to incorporate the concept into the legislation. Taken in the context of the whole act, however, it appears that a new specie of title or interest may have been created.

The concept of "special equity" is explained more fully in *Webber v. Webber*, 285 S.C. 425, 330 S.E.2d 79 (Ct. App. 1985). The Court of Appeals described the "special equity doctrine" as follows:

> "Where a wife has made a material contribution to the husband's acquisition of property during coverture, she acquires a special equity in the property." *Wilson v. Wilson*, 270 S.C. 216, 241 S.E.(2d) 566, 568 (1978) (quoting 27B C.J.S. *Divorce* § 293 (1950)). Therefore, one spouse acquires a special equity in the property of the other if (1) the property was acquired during coverture, (2) the spouse contributed to the acquisition of the property, and (3) the spouse's contribution was material.

Id. at 427-428, 330 S.E.2d at 81.

Property "acquired during coverture" includes appreciation in the value of nonmarital property. Thus, a "special equity" may be acquired in the nonmarital property of the other spouse by proving that a material contribution was made to any appreciation in its value. In *Webber*, the Court of Appeals affirmed an order giving the wife a "special equity" of one-third interest in the husband's electrical shop based on evidence that she contributed to its construction, helped build up the electrical business without compensation by keeping the books and occasionally accompanying her husband when he wired houses, and helped paint and wire the new shop. However, the court remanded the question of whether she was entitled to an interest in the appreciation of the marital home, although the evidence showed that the wife had helped make improvements to the marital home. The court could not determine from the record whether her contribution to the renovations was material.

There may be some question as to whether a "material" contribution is still required to create a special equity. "Material" is not used in S.C. Code Ann. § 20-7-472(3) (Law. Co-op. Supp.) which directs family court judges to consider the contributions of each spouse when determining the equities in marital property. The statute does, however, require the court to consider the "quality" of the contribution as well as its factual existence.

Support for the abandonment of the materiality requirement for creating a special equity is arguably found in *Murray v. Murray*, 312 S.C. 154, 439 S.E.2d 312 (Ct. App. 1993), although this would probably not be an accurate inference. In discussing a special equity award by the trial court, the Court of Appeals did not address the materiality aspect of the "special equity doctrine." The most likely reason for this omission is that the appropriateness of awarding the wife a special equity in the marital home (nonmarital property of the husband) does not appear to have been appealed by the deceased husband's estate. The primary issue before the court was the wife's claim that her deceased husband's real estate was transmuted into marital property. The court held that it was not transmuted. However, the language used by the court is subject to an interpretation that a material contribution is not required.

The court stated that the trial court "in accordance with *Webber*" awarded the wife a special equity of fifty percent of the appreciation in the marital home during their seventeen years of marriage. *Id.* at 159, 439 S.E.2d at 316. In fact, the award does not seem to be "in accordance with *Webber*," because it does not appear that the wife made a material contribution to the appreciation in the marital home. Although she helped maintain and improve the marital home during the marriage, the court said the record did not reflect how her contributions affected the value of the property. In fact, the court noted that the record showed that her efforts were largely routine duties such as cleaning and painting.

In comparison to the contributions of the wife in *Webber*, it is difficult to understand how the wife's efforts in *Murray* could possibly be considered to be "material" contributions. The most likely explanation for the differences between *Murray* and *Webber* is that the issue of the appropriateness of the award of a special equity in the marital home was not raised on appeal in *Murray* and the Court of Appeals did not intend implicitly to modify the special equity doctrine by its brief statement that the special equity award was "in accordance with *Webber*."

S.C. Code Ann. § 20-7-473 (Law Co-op. Supp.) defines marital property and nonmarital property as follows:

> The term "marital property" as used in this article means all real and personal property which has been acquired by the parties during the marriage and which is owned as of the date of filing or commencement of marital litigation as provided in § 20-7-472 regardless of how legal title is held, except the following, which constitute nonmarital property:
>
> (1) Property acquired by either party by inheritance, devise, bequest, or gift from a party other than the spouse;
>
> (2) Property acquired by either party before the marriage and property acquired after the happening of the earliest of (a) entry of a pendente lite order in a divorce or separate maintenance action; (b) formal signing of a written property or marital settlement agreement; or (c) entry of a permanent order of separate maintenance and support or of a permanent order approving a property or marital settlement agreement between the parties;

(3) Property acquired by either party in exchange for property described in items (1) and (2) of this section;

(4) Property excluded by written contract of the parties. "Written contract" includes any antenuptial agreement of the parties which must be considered presumptively fair and equitable so long as it was voluntarily executed with both parties separately represented by counsel and pursuant to the full financial disclosure to each other that is mandated by the rules of the family court as to income, debts, and assets;

(5) Any increase in value in nonmarital property, except to the extent that the increase resulted directly or indirectly from efforts of the other spouse during marriage.

Interspousal gifts of property, including gifts of property from one spouse to the other made indirectly by way of a third party, are marital property which is subject to division.

The court does not have jurisdiction or authority to apportion nonmarital property.

The language indicating that a gift from a third party is not marital property unless the gift has been transmuted into marital property is consistent with prior case law. In *Barr v. Barr*, 287 S.C. 13, 336 S.E.2d 481 (Ct. App. 1985), the Court of Appeals affirmed the trial court's finding that the husband's father's cancellation of a mortgage to his son and his daughter-in-law was a gift to his son only, not a joint gift. The father said the mortgage cancellation was intended as a gift to his son, although it happened six years before they separated. Judge Shaw dissented, saying he did not believe the father had such an intention at the time he canceled the mortgage.

Premarital gifts, including engagement rings, are non-marital property because they are acquired before the wedding. *See McClerin v. McClerin*, 310 S.C. 99, 425 S.E.2d 476 (Ct. App. 1992) (upholding the trial judge's decision that the ring in question was an engagement ring given to the wife before the wedding, not during the ceremony as the husband contended. No comment was made as to whether the result would have been different if the ring had been given to her during the ceremony, but before they were pronounced husband and wife).

Severance pay, unlike retirement benefits, is not marital property. *Fisher v. Fisher*, 319 S.C. 500, 462 S.E.2d 303 (Ct. App. 1995) (affirming family court's decision that voluntary separation incentive payments from the military are marital property because they are retirement benefits, not severance pay). *See also Mallett v. Mallett*, ___ S.C. ___, 473 S.E.2d 804 (Ct. App. 1996) (holding that potential termination payments for an insurance agent are not marital property).

Property acquired during the marriage and owned when the marital litigation commenced is presumed to be marital property and the party claiming otherwise has the burden of establishing the non-marital character of the property. *See* S.C. Code Ann. § 20-7-473(1) (Law. Co-op. Supp.); *Morehouse v. Morehouse*, 317 S.C. 222, 452 S.E.2d 632 (Ct. App. 1994); *Johnson v. Johnson*, 296 S.C. 289, 372 S.E. 2d 107 (Ct. App. 1988), *cert. den.* 298 S.C. 117, 378 S.E. 2d 445 (1989). In *Morehouse*, the husband appealed the equal division by the trial court of the stock in a business. He contended that the stock transfer to him was a gift from his father. However, he failed to prove his case. The corporate tax returns listed him as the one hundred percent owner of the stock and indicated he was the agent for service of process and the custodian of the books. The husband was also the sole owner of all outstanding voting stock. Additionally, the husband's father did not file any gift tax returns on the transaction.

A spouse will have an interest in property acquired in the name of the other spouse and a third party if marital funds are used to purchase the property, even if the purchase is made after marital litigation is filed. *Cannon v. Cannon*, ___ S.C. ___, 467 S.E.2d 132 (Ct. App. 1996). Similarly, a spouse may have an equitable interest in equipment purchased with marital funds for use in a business which is the other spouse's nonmarital property. *Pool v. Pool*, ___ S.C. ___, 467 S.E.2d 753 (Ct. App. 1996) (holding that the wife was entitled to an interest in the value of exercise equipment that was purchased for the husband's health club which was nonmarital property, and noting the husband's failure to establish that the equipment was nonmarital property where the parties' joint income tax refund showed they reported rental income from the health club for leased equipment).

b. Date of Acquisition and Valuation

Marital property is "acquired" on the date a spouse files a divorce complaint or initiates other marital litigation. This is mandated by statute and supported by case law. Specifically, the pertinent part of S.C. Code Ann. § 20-7-471 (Law. Co-op. Supp.) concerning the acquisition of marital property states that ". . . equity and ownership right [sic] are subject to apportionment between the spouses by the family courts of this state at the time marital litigation is filed or commenced as provided in § 20-7-472."

The date on which marital litigation is commenced is also the date on which the value of marital property is established. Although the equitable apportionment statutes do not say when marital litigation should be valued, the Court of Appeals reasoned in *Smith v. Smith*, 294 S.C. 194, 363 S.E.2d 404 (Ct. App. 1987), that the valuation date must be the date of filing or commencement of the action, ". . . since that is the time that property must now be owned to come within the meaning of the term 'marital property'" *Id.*, at 202, 363 S.E.2d at 409.

"The 'ownership right' in 'marital property' is acquired during marriage. 'Marital property' as such does not exist until the date when marital litigation is filed or commenced." *Prosser v. Pee Dee State Bank*, 295 S.C. 212, 214, 367 S.E.2d 698, 698 (1988). This chronological distinction was quite important to the appellant in *Prosser* who was attempting to acquire title to certain real estate she received in a property settlement agreement in her divorce action. She wanted the court to enjoin the respondent, Pee Dee State Bank, from enforcing a lien against her ex-husband regarding the subject property. The court held that the respondent's lien recorded in 1983 took precedence over the wife's marital property acquired three years later at the commencement of marital litigation. *See also United States v. Schifferli*, 895 F.2d 987 (4th Cir. 1990) (agreeing with the district court's denial of standing to a spouse who claimed an equitable interest in certain property, the court found that the spouse had not commenced marital litigation and, therefore, had not acquired marital property pursuant to sections 20-7-471 and 473); *Hardin v. Hardin*, 294 S.C. 402, 365 S.E.2d 34 (Ct. App. 1987) (holding that the trial court erred when it divided as martial property a life insurance policy which was acquired after the divorce proceeding commenced). *But see Hodge v. Hodge*, 305 S.C. 521, 409 S.E.2d 436

(1991) (determining that the wife's acquisition of marital property upon filing for divorce was not trumped by a prior recorded lien or encumbrance).

The Court of Appeals has also applied the date of acquisition test to gifts of money made to third parties during the marriage. In *Panhorst v. Panhorst*, 301 S.E. 100, 390 S.E.2d 376 (Ct. App. 1990), the court held that the family court did not have any jurisdiction to treat as marital property gifts of money that were made by the husband to his mother during the marriage, but without his wife's knowledge because they did not involve property that was "marital property" when marital litigation was commenced:

> The statute embodies the Legislature's decision that the marital estate must be identified on a fixed date. Given the vicissitudes of life, the parties' fortunes will change over the years of the marriage. Often the marital estate may have enjoyed a greater value in the past than it does at the dissolution of the marriage. It may be affected by changes in the incomes and earning capacities of the spouses, their spending habits, their savings and investments, and a host of other factors. By requiring the estate to be identified as of the date marital litigation is filed, the Legislature has elected to foreclose the spouses from litigating every expenditure or transfer of property during the marriage. One spouse or the other may have spent marital funds foolishly or selfishly or may have invested them unprofitably. The statute wisely prevents the other spouse from resurrecting these transactions at the end of the marriage to gain an advantage in equitable distribution. Were it to do otherwise, human greed and vindictiveness would transform the courts into "auditing agencies for every marriage that falters." *In re Marriage of Getautas*, 189 Ill. App. (3d) 148, 151, 136 Ill. Dec. 509, 513, 544 N.E. (2d) 1284, 1288 (1989).

Id. at 104-105, 390 S.E.2d at 378-379.

There are some circumstances in which expenditures that are made by one spouse prior to the commencement of marital litigation will be included in the marital estate, particularly transactions that are intended to benefit only one of the spouses in contemplation of marital litigation. In *Roe v. Roe*, 311 S.C. 471, 429 S.E.2d 830 (Ct. App. 1993), the Court of Appeals rejected a wife's claim that $5,500 she paid from her husband's funds to her attorney and investigator on the same day she filed the divorce complaint was no longer marital property subject to equitable apportionment.

The "marital estate" that comes into existence with the commencement of marital litigation ceases to exist if the marital litigation which that it is withdrawn or stricken before a final order is issued. In *Hickum v. Hickum*, 320 S.C. 97, 463 S.E.2d 321 (Ct. App. 1995), the wife filed an action for divorce and a *pendente lite* order was issued. The action was dismissed because it was not brought to trial in a timely manner. The husband then filed for divorce which was granted to the wife on her counterclaim for adultery. The husband appealed the trial court's ruling that the valuation date of the marital estate was the date on which the second case was filed. The Court of Appeals, citing *Shannon v. Shannon*, 301 S.C. 107, 390 S.E.2d 380 (Ct. App. 1990), affirmed the trial court's ruling, holding that it is not enough that the parties in the past engaged in some litigation if that litigation did not serve as the vehicle for equitable distribution.

Property becomes part of the marital estate if it is acquired by one spouse during marital litigation that does not bring about a division of marital property. In *Hickum, supra.*, the husband's retirement account increased substantially between the entry of a *pendente lite* order in a divorce brought by the wife on the ground of adultery (it was dismissed because it was not brought to trial within 270 days of the date of filing) and the filing of a divorce action a year later which dissolved the marriage and divided the marital estate. The husband argued that this property should have been excluded from the marital estate. The Court of Appeals disagreed and affirmed the trial court's decision to include it all. Judge Goolsby dissented from this portion of the opinion, interpreting S.C. Code Ann. § 20-7-473(2) (Law. Co-op. Supp.) as an unambiguous statement by the legislature that property is not marital property if it is acquired after the entry of a *pendente lite* order, whether or not the litigation in which the order is issued brings about a division of the marital estate.

Adherence to a strict rule about the valuation date can lead to inequitable results, for example, where marital property changes significantly in value due to the efforts of one party, the assets are purposefully dissipated by one party, or one party engages in bad faith efforts to delay divorce proceedings. The following comment appears in 24 Am. Jur. 2d *Divorce and Separation* § 939 (1983):

> But where marital assets are normally valued at the time of the filing of the complaint, it has been held that, in determining what is equitable, the trial judge must take into account any significant change in the valuation of marketable assets that occurs prior to final judgment.

The South Carolina appellate courts appear to recognize the potential inequities of adhering to a strict rule about the valuation date, but they have not yet provided clear guidance about acceptable variances. In *Smith v. Smith*, 294 S.C. 194, 363 S.E.2d 404 (Ct. App. 1987), the Court of Appeals acknowledged that the date of valuation was changed by legislation to the date on which marital litigation is filed.[15] The court made the following comments which suggest that family courts are not required to adhere strictly to the rule that the valuation date is when marital litigation commences:

> The husband levels one other complaint at the trial court's apportionment of the marital property. This complaint concerns 4,000 shares of Builders Mart of America stock and 3,675 shares of Tel/Man stock that trial court found were owned by the parties. The trial court directed either that the shares be divided in kind or that the wife be paid their fair market value at the time the parties separated, a value much less than it had on the date the trial court issued its order.
>
> *We know of no authority, and the husband does not cite any, that holds that only one spouse is entitled to any appreciation in marital assets that occurs after the parties separate and before the parties are divorced. We would think both parties would be entitled to any such appreciation.*

---

[15] Previously it was the date of separation. *See Anderson v. Anderson*, 282 S.C. 162, 318 S.E.2d 566 (1984).

> We also know of no South Carolina authority for the trial court to value marital property, including stocks, as of the date of dissolution of the marriage. The proper date would be "the time the marital litigation is filed or commenced," since that is the time the property must now be owned to come within the meaning of the term "marital property."

Id. at 203, 363 S.E.2d at 409 (emphasis added).

The result in *Smith* was that the Court of Appeals removed the buy-out option and ordered the stocks divided fifty-fifty as apportioned by the trial court. Thus, the court did not directly address the question. Nor did it suggest what family courts should do in similar cases, if a buy-out is not a viable option.

South Carolina has not yet articulated a distinction in its treatment of "passive" and "active" assets, as have some other states. *Cf. Greenwald v. Greenwald*, 164 A.D.2d 706, 565 N.Y.S. 494 (1991); *Scavone v. Scavone*, 230 N.J. Super. 482, 553 A.2d 885 (1988). A passive asset is one which increases or decreases in value without any activity by either party to a divorce proceeding, such as an IRA account or an inactive stock account, such as in *Smith.* It is fairer to value a passive asset at or near the time of the final hearing, because both parties are equally deserving to share in any increase or decrease. An active asset, on the other hand, increases or decreases in value due to the management or investment efforts of one party, such as a business in which only one spouse works. Active assets should be valued at the time of commencement of the marital litigation, so the person who causes the change in value receives the benefits of their labor and skills.

Although the distinction between "passive" and "active" assets is not articulated in any South Carolina case, the concept may be recognized in practice. In *Jamar v. Jamar*, 308 S.C. 265, 417 S.E.2d 615 (Ct. App. 1992), the Court of Appeals determined that the commencement date of marital litigation was the proper date for valuing marital bank accounts that had decreased in value due to the husband's withdrawal for personal expenditures. The analysis used by the court is similar to discussions of the distinctions between passive-active assets in other jurisdictions. Since the decrease in value of the bank accounts was due to the husband's withdrawals, but not the wife's, it was an active asset, and it would not have been fair to the wife to value the property at any time other than the commencement of litigation.

It may be the position of South Carolina courts that both parties must share in gains, but not losses, from investments made with marital funds during marital litigation. This is inconsistent with the idea that active assets are to be valued at the time of commencement of litigation. However, the Court of Appeals concluded in *Cannon v. Cannon*, ___ S.C. ___, 467 S.E.2d 132 (Ct. App. 1996), that the wife was entitled to share in the increased value of thirty-nine acres of land that the husband purchased with a third party after marital litigation was commenced. The husband used marital funds as the down payment on the property. The Court of Appeals found that the wife was entitled to share in the increased value of the land because she indirectly contributed to its acquisition, although the land was not titled in her name, she did not make any payments on the mortgage, and she did not participate in any decisions regarding the property's acquisition. "The increase in the value of the nonmarital thirty-nine acres would not have occurred but for the down payment made with marital funds which made acquisition of this land possible." *Id.* at ___, 467 S.E.2d at 136. It is not clear if the court would have reached the same conclusion if the husband had lost money on the investment, but it seems unlikely.

A valuation date other than the commencement of marital litigation may be used to avoid inequitable results when the parties are separated for a long time before commencing marital litigation. This was the result in *Wannamaker v. Wannamaker*, 305 S.C. 36, 406 S.E.2d 180 (Ct. App. 1991), where the Court of Appeals refused to allow the wife to share in the value of the husband's medical practice and other assets that were acquired eight or more years after the parties separated. This was also the result in *Shannon v. Shannon*, 301 S.C. 107, 390 S.E.2d 380 (Ct. App. 1990), where the wife made improvements to the marital home during a ten year period of separation that increased its value by $11,000 to $18,000 by the time marital litigation was commenced. The Court of Appeals remanded the case and stated: "In so doing, we point out to the trial court that some consideration should be shown the wife for her contribution to the increase in the value of the house after separation." *Id.* at 112, 390 S.E.2d at 383. In *Nemeth v. Nemeth*, Op. No. 2616 (S.C. Ct. App. filed Jan. 13, 1997)(Davis Adv. Sh. No. 1 at 47), however, a wife was awarded fifty percent of the value of the husband's retirement plan as of the date marital litigation was commenced, although the parties were separated five years before divorcing.

The Court of Appeals noted that there were numerous attempts at reconciliation during the first three years of separation.

In summary, neither party should be the sole beneficiary of changes in the value of marital property that occur during marital litigation unless the change is attributable to that party's efforts alone. Consideration should be given to the respective contributions of the parties to any change in value. However, the appellate courts have not yet provided clear guidance to the family courts.

2. TRANSMUTATION OF NONMARITAL INTO MARITAL PROPERTY

Property that is the individual property of a spouse may be transmuted into marital property. The concept of transmutation has been developed in case law in South Carolina.

Although the Equitable Apportionment of Marital Property Act does not expressly mention transmutation, transmutation is still considered a valid doctrine in South Carolina. *See Strickland v. Strickland*, 297 S.C. 248, 376 S.E.2d 268 (1989); *Kendall v. Kendall*, 295 S.C. 136, 367 S.E.2d 437 (Ct. App. 1988) (both holding that the enactment of the Equitable Apportionment of Marital Property Act did not abrogate or abolish the doctrine of transmutation).

Inherited property is not subject to equitable distribution, unless it becomes transmuted into marital property. Whether inherited property is the nonmarital and sole property of the inheriting spouse or marital property subject to equitable distribution was first addressed in *Hussey v. Hussey*, 280 S.C. 418, 312 S.E.2d 267 (Ct. App. 1984). The court held that inherited property is not subject to equitable distribution, but noted that:

> [I]n certain instances, where the nonmarital character of inherited property is lost, it may be equitably divided. This may occur when the property becomes so commingled as to be untraceable; is utilized by the parties in support of the marriage; or is titled jointly or

> otherwise utilized in such a manner as to evidence an intent by the parties to make it marital property.
>
> In addition, we hold that though inherited property is not marital property subject to equitable distribution, it may properly be considered as a factor in determining what constitutes an equitable division of the marital property.

Id. at 423, 312 S.E.2d at 270-271. *Hussey* was remanded due to the trial court's failure to adequately describe what part of Mr. Hussey's inherited property it had found to be his separate property.

Mere commingling of non-marital property does not automatically make such property marital in nature. In *Brooks v. Brooks*, 289 S.C. 352, 345 S.E.2d 510 (Ct. App. 1986), the wife inherited $16,000 from her father's estate of which she spent $1,000 on the marital home, then placed $1,500 in a savings account for one of the parties' sons, and used another $3,500 on behalf of the other son. The remaining $10,000 of her inheritance went into a savings account. The trial court granted the husband's request to treat this savings account as marital property, but the Court of Appeals reversed, holding that the savings account was not subject to equitable distribution. "The husband impliedly argues if any portion of an inheritance is used in the furtherance of the marriage, the entire sum loses its independent status and becomes marital property. We reject this argument as meritless." *Id.* at 355, 345 S.E.2d at 512.

If the parties treat a pension fund as if all of it is marital property, that portion which was earned prior to the marriage may be transmuted into marital property (the portion earned during the marriage is already marital property). In *Murphy v. Murphy*, 319 S.C. 324, 461 S.E.2d 39 (1995), the parties agreed upon a "game plan" following the husband's retirement to commingle the non-marital portion of the pension fund with the portion earned subsequent to the marriage, so that the entire fund was used to support the marriage. Furthermore, the wife waived her right to survivor's benefits in the whole pension fund so they could receive accelerated retirement payments during the marriage. The Supreme Court ruled that the portion of the retirement fund earned prior to the marriage was transmuted into marital property.

Funds belonging to one spouse retain their character as nonmarital property as long as they are traceable, irrespective of whether they are kept in separate or in joint accounts. In *Wannamaker v. Wannamaker*, 305 S.C. 36, 406 S.E.2d 180 (Ct. App. 1991), the wife asserted that the husband's stock was transmuted into the marital estate. The Court of Appeals held that, although the money used to purchase the stocks were commingled in the same account with funds used for marital purposes, the stock money was strictly accounted for and thus traceable. *See also Luthi v. Luthi*, 289 S.C. 489, 374 S.E.2d 102 (Ct. App. 1986) (holding that it was error for the trial court to conclude that a trust had become part of the marital estate because the husband had moved property in and out of the trust).

A finding of transmutation may depend on whether members of the family have actually used an asset, as opposed to merely receiving the income generated by it. In *Peterkin v. Peterkin*, 293 S.C. 311, 360 S.E.2d 311 (1987), the Supreme Court held that the use of income generated by the husband's pre-marital property for family purposes did not transmute the property into marital property. Prior to and during the marriage, the husband had acquired interests in land, a trust, and stocks by gifts and inheritance. His interests in two tracts of land, his vested interest in the trust, and the stocks were held to be his separate property. "Merely using the income derived from these items in support of the marriage does not transmute them into marital property." *Id.* at 313, 360 S.E.2d at 313.

However, the farm acreage in which he had a life estate, the farm house, its contents and the farm equipment lost their nonmarital character and became subject to equitable distribution when they were utilized in support of the marriage. "In contrast to the other properties the husband brought into the marriage, the Lang Syne Farm, and not merely the income the farm produced, was used in support of the marriage." *Id.*

The *Peterkin* court's determination that the farm property was transmuted appears to be at odds with two earlier cases. In *Walton v. Walton*, 282 S.C. 165, 318 S.E.2d 14 (1984), the court held that the wife had no equitable interest in the marital home or surrounding acreage which had been owned by the husband prior to the marriage. *Walton* was relied on in *Sauls v. Sauls*, 287 S.C. 297, 337 S.E.2d 893 (Ct. App. 1985), in which the court held that the marital home was not marital property where one spouse purchased and paid for the house before the marriage. (Actually, the property in *Sauls* was divided pursuant to an agreement that the wife was challenging. The court determined that the agreement was fair.)

Walton and *Sauls* are difficult to reconcile with *Peterkin*, but there are important factual differences. In *Sauls*, there is no report that the wife claimed that the value of the marital home and surrounding acreage were enhanced by her contributions to the marriage, whereas Mrs. Peterkin did make this claim. Also, the Waltons were only married eight years; the Peterkins were married for twenty-five years. In addition, Mrs. Sauls initially agreed to the division of property and received other real estate in the transaction.

Trimnal v. Trimnal, 287 S.C. 495, 339 S.E.2d 869 (1986), was decided after *Walton* and *Sauls* but before *Peterkin*. In *Trimnal* the husband acquired title in the marital home partly by gift and partly by purchase. The Supreme Court held that the gift portion was transmuted when the marital home was used to support the marriage. It also found that the wife obtained an equitable interest in the remainder of the property by contributing to mortgage payments and through other joint efforts during the marriage. In accord with *Trimnal* is *Barret v. Barret*, 290 S.C. 453, 351 S.E.2d 177 (Ct. App. 1986), in which the court found that 2.78 acres of land that were purchased by the wife prior to the marriage were transmuted into marital property. The court reached this conclusion based on the husband's two years of payments on the mortgage and the use of a mobile home on the land as their marital residence.

In 1988, the Court of Appeals indicated that it would be incorrect to interpret these earlier cases to mean that a house which was nonmarital property would be transmuted into marital property simply by allowing the family to live in it. In *Johnson v. Johnson*, 296 S.C. 289, 372 S.E.2d 107 (Ct. App. 1988), the court reaffirmed the rule that the intent of the spouse who initially owns the property is the most important factor to consider when the issue of transmutation is present: "As a general rule, transmutation is a matter of intent to be gleaned from the facts of each case. The spouse claiming transmutation must produce objective evidence showing that, during the marriage, the parties themselves regarded the property as common property of the marriage." *Id.* at 295, 372 S.E.2d at 110-111. *Johnson* further explains that any increase in the value of the marital home is also nonmarital property, except whatever part of the increase is attributable to the contributions of the nonowner spouse:

> [A]ny increase in the value of nonmarital property during the marriage is nonmarital property, except to the extent the increase resulted from the efforts of the other spouse during the marriage.
>
> If the opposing party shows that an item of property was either acquired before the marriage or falls within a statutory exception, this rebuts the prima facie case for its inclusion in the martial estate.

Id. at 294-295, 372 S.E.2d at 110.

Other cases also agree that the use of a house as the marital residence does not necessarily transmute it into nonmarital property. In *Ray v. Ray*, 296 S.C. 350, 372 S.E.2d 910 (Ct. App. 1988), the parties had moved into the marital home in 1971. They made extensive renovations to the structure. Later, in 1976, the husband acquired the house as a gift from his step-mother. The parties continued to live there until they separated in 1985. The Court of Appeals found that no transmutation had occurred. Furthermore, the wife was not entitled to a share of the increased value due to the improvements, because they had been made while the house was owned by the stepmother. See also *Carroll v. Carroll*, 309 S.C. 22, 419 S.E.2d 801 (Ct. App. 1992), in which the court found that the husband's condominium, purchased prior to the marriage and titled in his name only, was not transmuted into marital property. In fact, the court held no transmutation or intent to transmute existed during the marriage despite the fact that the couple lived in the condominium for approximately two years, beginning one month prior to the wedding.

Similar results were reached in cases involving a horse and silver. *See McDowell v. McDowell*, 300 S.C. 96, 386 S.E.2d 468 (Ct. App. 1989) (holding that the husband failed to carry the burden of proving that a horse owned by the wife prior to the marriage had been transmuted, although both parties cared for the horse and marital funds were used to support it); *Pappas v. Pappas*, 300 S.C. 62, 67, 386 S.E.2d 301, 304 (Ct. App. 1989) (holding that the wife's silver had not been transmuted by using it for family purposes or by insuring it under the same policy as marital property. "By its very nature, a silver service is something that will be used by the whole family, not one person").

Evidence of transmutation can include placing the property in joint names, transferring the property to the other spouse as a gift, using the property exclusively for marital purposes, commingling the property with marital property, using marital funds to build equity in the property, or exchanging the property for marital property. *Johnson v. Johnson*, 296 S.C. 289, 295, 372 S.E.2d 107, 111 (Ct. App. 1988). The ultimate holding in *Johnson* was that the property was not transmuted, based on the court's finding that the parties' unenforceable antenuptial agreement served as evidence of the husband's intent to maintain ownership of his nonmarital property.

The Court of Appeals similarly concluded that the husband's nonmarital property was not transmuted in *Murray v. Murray*, 312 S.C. 154, 439 S.E.2d 312 (Ct. App. 1993). The wife claimed that the trial court had erred in excluding the parties' marital residence and three rental properties from the martial estate. The real estate in question had been purchased by the husband prior to the marriage. The Court of Appeals ruled that the wife had failed to "produce affirmative objective evidence showing that, during the marriage, the parties themselves regarded the property as the common property of the marriage." *Id.* at 157, 439 S.E.2d at 315.

It was not enough to prove transmutation in *Murray* to show that the parties shared the marital home for seventeen years. "[T]he mere use of separate property to support the marriage, without some additional evidence of intent to treat it as property of the marriage, is not sufficient to establish transmutation." *Id.* at 157, 439 S.E.2d at 315. It was not enough to show that she contributed time and labor to the improvement and maintenance of the marital home and rental properties. "While improvements made by a spouse to nonmarital property may result in the spouse's receiving an equitable interest in the property, contributions of time and labor do not necessarily prove transmutation." *Id.* at 158, 439 S.E.2d at 315. It was not enough to show that income from the rental units was put into the parties' joint banking account. "[M]erely using income derived from nonmarital property in support of marriage does not transmute nonmarital property into marital property." *Id.* at 158, 439 S.E.2d at 315.

The *Murray* court not only concluded that the wife failed to carry her burden of proof, but it also found evidence of the husband's intent to retain the nonmarital nature of the property in his will, which provided that upon his death all of the property was to be liquidated and the wife could remain in the marital home only until the estate was settled. Using the same analysis, the court also ruled that two mortgages on nonmarital property payable to the husband were not transmuted into marital property. The court, however, did affirm the family court's award of a special equity to the wife in the marital home. It would not decide whether she was entitled to a special equity in the rental properties, however, because she raised that issue for the first time in her reply brief.

An intent to transmute nonmarital property into marital property will usually be found in cases where both spouses have assumed responsibility for debt attached to the property. It apparently does not matter whether the spouse who did not originally own the property has actually contributed toward discharging the debt. In *Frank v. Frank*, 311 S.C. 454, 429 S.E.2d 823 (Ct. App. 1993), the marital home was given to the wife by her parents before the marriage. However, the parties assumed joint responsibility for loans secured by the home during the marriage. The Court of Appeals held that the property had been transmuted:

> In the instant case the wife owned the marital home prior to the marriage. Both parties, however, signed a $30,000.00 promissory note securing a mortgage on the house, and, therefore, both parties are liable for the discharge of the debt. Even though the home equity loan had not been repaid and the husband contributed very little in the way of financial support to the marital home, he remains liable on the note. Accordingly, we hold that, to the extent that the husband is liable for the home improvement loan, the marital home is transmuted.

Id. at 457, 429 S.E.2d at 825.

The holding in *Frank* is an extension of the holdings in *Canady v. Canady*, 296 S.C. 521, 374 S.E.2d 502 (Ct. App. 1988) and *Wyatt v. Wyatt*, 293 S.C. 495, 361 S.E.2d 777 (Ct. App. 1987). The spouses in these cases participated more actively in helping pay off mortgages than the husband in *Frank*, and they also made improvements to the properties in question. The following language appears in both cases: "Though one spouse acquires legal title to property prior to marriage, the discharge of indebtedness by both the husband and wife may transmute the property into marital property." *Canady*, 296 S.C. at 524, 374 S.E.2d at 504; *Wyatt*, 293 S.C. at 497, 361 S.E.2d at 779.

*Frank*appears to mean that the existence of joint indebtedness will create a presumption of an intent to transmute the property, and it is not necessary to show that both parties contributed toward discharging the debt (of course, the relative contributions toward discharging debts may be taken into account by the trial judge in apportioning the property).

If property is determined to be transmuted by the creation of a joint debt obligation, all of the property that secures the debt is transmuted. In *Canady*, the court held that the marital home and the entire twenty-five acre tract on which it sat had been transmuted because the mortgage extended to the entire property, not just to the marital home.

Reconveying an interest in marital property to the other spouse is not by itself sufficient evidence for a court to determine whether the property is marital or nonmarital. In *Corbett v. Corbett*, 313 S.C. 184, 437 S.E.2d 136 (Ct. App. 1993), the husband had completed building a house about seven months before the marriage, financing it with a construction mortgage. The husband and wife alternated making payments on the house. A year after the marriage, he deeded the wife a one-half interest in the home; and, five months later, they took out a second mortgage on the property, which payments were all made by the husband. Shortly before the parties separated after three and one-half years of marriage, the wife deeded her one-half interest back to the husband (no reason for the transfer appears in the record, nor did it appear that the wife received any consideration or intended it as a gift). The trial judge found that the home was nonmarital property on the basis of the reconveyance. The Court of Appeals reversed, holding that "[t]he reconveyance places the wife in no different position than she would have been in had the husband never deeded her any interest in the property." *Id.* at 186, 437 S.E.2d at 138. According to the Court of Appeals, the trial judge should have specifically determined whether the property was transmuted, and if not, he should have considered the extent to which the wife's contributions enhanced the value of the home.

Money which one spouse lends to the other is not transmuted, if the transaction is arms-length. In *Freeman v. Freeman*, 318 S.C. 265, 457 S.E.2d 3 (Ct.

App. 1995), the court held that the trial judge erred in failing to address the issue of a promissory note which the wife claimed represented a loan which the husband was obligated to repay. The husband did not object to the admission of the note nor did he present any evidence to rebut the wife's testimony, but he admitted the note was not paid.

The burden of proof is on the party making the loan. In *Miller v. Miller*, 293 S.C. 69, 358 S.E.2d 710 (1987), the Supreme Court found that the wife presented no evidence about the nature of a loan to her husband and, therefore, she did not establish that it was an arms-length transaction. The court indicated that a loan of nonmarital property to another spouse under circumstances indicating a marital purpose would be transmuted, but it provided no guidance for determining what constitutes a "marital purpose." *Miller* also affirmed the trial court's ruling that the husband had to repay money he borrowed from his children during the marriage. *Id.* at 72, 358 S.E.2d at 712. In *Roe v. Roe*, 311 S.C. 471, 429 S.E.2d 830 (Ct. App. 1993), the wife argued unsuccessfully that she should not be required to repay a $15,000 loan from her husband that she used as down payment on a house. The Court of Appeals held that her reliance on *Panhorst v. Panhorst*, 301 S.C. 100, 390 S.E.2d 376 (1990), was misplaced because the wife retained the investment the $15,000 bought as equity in the home, which she did not dispute was marital property. The court similarly rejected her claim that $5,500 she had paid from her husband's funds to her attorney and investigator on the same day she filed the divorce complaint was no longer marital property subject to equitable apportionment, citing *Miller*.

3. RETIREMENT PENSIONS

a. In General

Retirement benefits, specifically civil service and military benefits, are marital assets subject to equitable division in South Carolina. *Ferguson v. Ferguson*, 300 S.C. 1, 386 S.E.2d 267 (Ct. App. 1989). Family court judges are statutorily required to consider and weigh retirement benefits when apportioning marital property. S.C. Code Ann. § 20-7-472(8) (Law. Co-op. Supp.) states: "In making apportionment, the court must give weight in such proportion as it find appropriate to all of the following factors: . . . the existence or nonexistence of vested retirement benefits for each or either spouse."

Vested retirement funds are considered marital property under the Equitable Apportionment of Marital Property Act, S.C. Code Ann. §§ 20-7-471 to 20-7-479 (Law. Co-op. Supp.), however, the portion of a pension attributable to the period of time that a spouse is employed before the marriage is non-marital property. *Noll v. Noll*, 297 S.C. 190, 375 S.E.2d 338 (1988); *Murphy v. Murphy*, 319 S.C. 324, 461 S.E.2d 39 (1995).

If the parties treat a pension fund as if all of it is marital property, that portion which was earned prior to the marriage is probably transmuted into marital property. In *Murphy*, the parties agreed upon a "game plan" following the husband's retirement to commingle the non-marital portion of the pension fund with the portion earned subsequent to the marriage, so that the entire fund was used to support the marriage. Furthermore, the wife waived her right to survivor's benefits in the whole pension fund so they could receive accelerated retirement payments during the marriage. The Supreme Court ruled that the portion of the retirement fund earned prior to the marriage was transmuted into marital property.

Both matured and unmatured retirement benefits are subject to equitable division in South Carolina. One issue facing the courts after the enactment of the Equitable Apportionment of Marital Property Act was whether retirement benefits to be paid in the future could be considered "vested" under S.C. Code Ann. § 20-7-473 (Law. Co-op. Supp.). This section defines "marital property" subject to equitable division as "all real and personal property which has been acquired by the parties *during the marriage* and which is owned as of the date of filing or commencement of marital litigation . . . ." (emphasis added). *Kneece v. Kneece*, 296 S.C. 28, 370 S.E.2d 288 (Ct. App. 1988), resolved this issue by agreeing with the overwhelming majority of states that have considered this issue that "no meaningful distinction between matured and unmatured retirement pensions" exists and thus unmatured retirement pensions may be classified as marital property. *Id.* at 33, 370 S.E.2d at 291. The *Kneece* court added that, despite the practical difficulties of dividing a pension that has yet to be distributed, such problems "present no justification for denying the wife an interest in the pension." *Id.* at 34, 370 S.E.2d at 291-92. In *Hardwick v. Hardwick*, 303 S.C. 256, 399 S.E.2d 791 (Ct. App. 1990), the court said, "where . . . it is evident an employer makes a contribution to a retirement fund as an employment benefit or as a form of additional compensation, as opposed to an outright gift to the employee, the contribution is marital property and subject to equitable division." *See also Ferguson v. Ferguson*, 300 S.C. 1, 386 S.E.2d 267 (Ct. App. 1989) (private business retirement plan); *Noll v. Noll*, 297 S.C. 290, 375 S.E.2d 338 (Ct. App. 1988) (federal civil service pension).

Future renewal commissions on insurance policies are considered marital property subject to equitable distribution. *Freeman v. Freeman*, 318 S.C. 265, 457 S.E.2d 3 (Ct. App. 1995), In *Freeman*, the wife claimed a percentage interest in future renewal commissions to be received by her husband for insurance sold by her husband or his agents during the time of the marriage. The evidence showed numerous contributions the wife had made to the development of her husband's business. The court agreed that the wife was entitled to a share of the commissions, stating "[l]ike military retirement benefits, renewal commissions are essentially compensation for past services, and those benefits accrued during marriage constitute a joint investment of both parties." *Id.* at 268, 457 S.E.2d at 5.

However, potential termination benefits that are intended to compensate insurance agents for lost renewal commissions are not marital property. *Mallett v. Mallett*, ___ S.C. ___, 473 S.E.2d 804 (Ct. App. 1996). At the time of the divorce, the husband was still employed by an insurance company. His contract provided that, if his employment was terminated prior to retirement, he would be entitled to 60 monthly installments based upon a specified percentage of his earnings during his final year of employment. The Court of Appeals decided that it would be impossible to put a present value on the possibility that he would receive termination payments before he reached retirement, especially since an undetermined portion of such payments would be earned after the commencement of marital litigation.

Contributions to individual retirements accounts (IRA's) are subject to equitable distribution. *Pool v. Pool*, ___ S.C. ___, 467 S.E.2d 753 (Ct. App. 1996).

South Carolina courts have not decided whether Social Security payments are subject to equitable apportionment. Other jurisdictions have held that the Social Security Act preempts state courts from treating Social Security benefits as property, thus exempting them from equitable distribution. *Cf. Kirk v. Kirk*, 577 A.2d 976, 980

(R.I. 1990); *Swan v. Swan*, 720 P.2d 747, 749 (Or. 1986); *Cruise v. Cruise*, 372 S.E.2d 882, 884 (N.C. Ct. App. 1989). Even if Social Security is not subject to equitable distribution, if is an economic factor to be considered in making decisions about property division. *Cf. Pongonis v. Pongonis*, 606 A.2d 1055, 1058 (Me. 1992); *Frederiksen v. Frederiksen*, 368 N.W.2d 769, 776 (Minn. App. 1985); *Rudden v. Rudden*, 765 S.W.2d 719, 720 (Mo. Ct. App. 1989).

b. Military Retirement Benefits

Military retirement benefits are marital property and are subject to equitable division in marital litigation. The Supreme Court ruled in 1983 that military retirement benefits should be treated only as income, not as marital property. *Brown v. Brown*, 279 S.C. 116, 302 S.E.2d 860 (1983). Although the Court did not feel that the Equitable Apportionment of Marital Property Act decided this issue, it overruled *Brown* in *Tiffault v. Tiffault*, 303 S.C. 391, 401 S.E.2d 157 (1991), stating:

> [W]e are now prepared to overrule *Brown* in light of the economic reality that military retirement benefits accrued during marriage constitute a joint investment of both parties. Typically, as in this case, a military spouse must move from place to place and consequently forfeit a separate career or make other outstanding contributions in support of the marriage. Military retirement pay is essentially compensation for past services. We conclude vested military retirement benefits constitute an earned property right which, if accrued during the marriage, is subject to equitable distribution.

Id. at 392, 401 S.E.2d at 158.

Thus, military retirement benefits are subject to distribution as marital property. The effective date on which military retirement benefits became subject to equitable division appears to be the date of the Court of Appeals decision in *Martin v. Martin*, 296 S.C. 436, 373 S.E.2d 706 (Ct. App. 1988). This is the holding of *Hamby v. Hamby*, 315 S.C. 518, 445 S.E.2d 656 (Ct. App. 1994).

It does not matter whether military retirement benefits have not yet vested. In *Ball v. Ball*, 312 S.C. 31, 430 S.E.2d 533 (Ct. App. 1993), *aff'd*, 314 S.C. 445, 445

S.E.2d 449 (1994), the husband had over eighteen years of active military service when the hearing was held. He argued that his military pension benefits were not subject to equitable distribution because they had not yet vested. The Court of Appeals rejected this argument, relying on *Kneece*. The court also rejected his argument that the apportionment was erroneous because the family court was unable to place a value on it. The court noted that the family court had considered the wife's interest in the retirement pension entirely separately from the rest of the marital estate and had deferred any payments to her until such time as Sgt. Ball received payments pursuant to the pension plan. The Supreme Court noted that Ms. Ball made contributions to the marriage that were significant in that she had moved with the Husband numerous times during the nine year marriage, cared for his children from a prior marriage, and provided other services of benefit to him and his children.

If all or a portion of military retirement pay has been waived by a retiree in order to obtain veterans' disability benefits, a state may not treat the waived pay as property divisible upon divorce. In *Mansell v. Mansell*, 490 U.S. 581, 109 S.Ct. 2023, 104 L.Ed.2d 675 (1989), the U.S. Supreme Court reached this result, conceding that the result might inflict economic harm on many former spouses. It felt bound by the clear language in Section 1408(c)(1) of the Former Spouses' Protection Act that excludes military retirement pay which has been waived to receive veterans' benefits from its definition of "disposable retired pay" which can be treated as marital property subject to division. The result on remand was not changed by this ruling because the husband agreed in the property settlement, which was approved at the final divorce hearing, to give his wife fifty percent of his retirement pay, including the portion that was waived. He was bound by his agreement and did not obtain a modification of the divorce decree. *See In re Marriage of Mansell*, 217 Cal. App.3d 219, 265 Cal. Rptr. 227 (1989).

A spouse cannot rely on the U.S. Supreme Court's decision in *Mansell* to avoid paying a former spouse a portion of military retirement benefits that include disability pay where the parties entered into a property settlement agreement that was approved by the family court after *Mansell* was decided. *Price v. Price*, ___ S.C. ___, 480 S.E.2d 92 (Ct. App. 1996) (holding that "[e]quity does not permit a party to defeat justice by asserting violation of public policy, statute, or illegality of agreement in order to insulate the party from his own wrong").

A spouse seeking a share of a military retirement fund must demonstrate making some contribution to its acquisition. In *Walker v. Walker*, 295 S.C. 286, 368 S.E.2d 222 (Ct. App. 1988), the Court of Appeals agreed with the trial judge that the wife made no direct or indirect contribution to the husband's retirement fund because they never established a marital home during the marriage (she lived with her parents while he traveled the world on assignments from the Navy) and they had produced no children.

The contribution can be indirect as well as direct. In *Curry v. Curry*, 309 S.C. 539, 424 S.E.2d 552 (Ct. App. 1992), the Court of Appeals stated that "a spouse need not prove that he or she made a material contribution to the acquisition of particular property in order to be entitled to an interest in it." *Id.* at 541, 424 S.E.2d at 554. *Curry* affirmed the trial judge's award to the wife of forty percent of the husband's retirement benefits from the Navy because she took care of the children and home while he was out to sea and she moved from place to place for the benefit of the husband's military career. The Court of Appeals considered a broader range of factors in a similar case and reached the same conclusion in *Connors v. Connors*, 310 S.C. 76, 425 S.E.2d 65 (Ct. App. 1992).

Contributions of a wife to the career of her military husband that are considered significant include moving with him several times during a nine year marriage, caring for his children from a prior marriage, and providing other services of benefit to him and his children. *Ball v. Ball*, 312 S.C. 31, 430 S.E.2d 533 (Ct. App. 1993), *aff'd* 314 S.C. 445, 445 S.E.2d 449 (1994).

An action to seek marital distribution of military retirement benefits may be brought after a divorce, if the court which heard the divorce did not have subject matter jurisdiction to divide the property. *Eckhardt v. Eckhardt*, 309 S.C. 225, 420 S.E.2d 875 (Ct. App. 1992). However, if the marital property was divided during the divorce proceeding, the family court does not have subject matter jurisdiction to reconsider a spouse's interest in a military retirement pension, even where the division of property occurred prior to *Tiffault* when military retirement pensions were not considered marital property subject to division. *Hayes v. Hayes*, 312 S.C. 141, 439 S.E.2d 305 (Ct. App. 1993).

4. PROFESSIONAL DEGREES

Professional degrees are not subject to equitable apportionment in South Carolina. Such degrees are considered "personal intellectual attainment, not marital property subject to equitable distribution." *Heath v. Heath*, 295 S.C. 312, 368 S.E.2d 222 (Ct. App. 1988) (quoting from *Helm v. Helm*, 289 S.C. 169, 345 S.E.2d 720 (1986)). Both *Helm* and *Heath* involved the attempted division of medical degrees and both attempts failed. These cases must be distinguished from *Donahue v. Donahue*, 299 S.C. 353, 384 S.E.2d 741 (1989), where the contribution of one spouse to the other spouse's established medical practice was proper ("here . . . we are concerned not with the appellant's degree, but with his *practice*, therefore *Helm* and *Heath* are inapplicable"). Also see the discussion of reimbursement alimony in the chapter on alimony.

5. WORKERS' COMPENSATION AND PERSONAL INJURY CLAIMS

Proceeds from employment claims or personal injury awards that come into existence before marital litigation is commenced are marital property subject to equitable division. Proceeds from personal injury claims are also subject to apportionment as marital property.

Whether workers' compensation or personal injury awards are marital property was first considered in South Carolina in *Orzula v. Orzula*, 292 S.C. 264, 356 S.E.2d 114 (1987). The Supreme Court determined that they are marital property because such awards fit none of the exceptions under S.C. Code Ann. § 20-7-473 (Law. Co-op. Supp.) which defines nonmarital property.

Orzula was challenged in *Marsh v. Marsh*, 308 S.C. 304, 417 S.E.2d 638 (Ct. App. 1992). The husband asked the Court of Appeals to analyze personal injury claims based on the purpose for which the award was made. He asserted that his personal injury settlement from an automobile accident was not "compensation for economic losses (i.e., reimbursement for lost wages and medical or other expenses) to the marital partnership, but rather represented uniquely personal losses to him for pain and suffering, mental anguish, disfigurement, and post-divorce loss of earning capacity." *Id.* at 305, 417 S.E.2d at 639. The Court of Appeals noted that a rapidly increasing number of courts, instead of taking an all or nothing approach, have "distinguished between losses suffered by the marital partnership and those suffered by the injured spouse. This approach is commonly referred to as the 'analytic approach.'" *Id.*

The Court of Appeals surmised in *Marsh* that the Supreme Court might want to revisit *Orzula* in view of the husband's argument, but it concluded that it was bound by *Orzula* and effectively locked into the "mechanistic approach." Although it conceded that the doctrine was subject to criticism, the Court of Appeals explained the justifications for South Carolina's adoption of this approach. First, the "mechanistic approach" is the easiest method for trial courts to apply. Second, most states with equitable distribution statutes follow this approach. Lastly, the all-or-nothing nature of the mechanistic approach is tempered by the fact that the Equitable Apportionment of Marital Property Act "gives family court judges sufficient latitude to make adjustments for personal injury awards that represent compensation for injuries uniquely personal to one spouse in dividing the marital estate." *Id.* at 308, 417 S.E.2d at 640.

Marsh was subsequently reviewed by the Supreme Court and it reaffirmed *Orzula* in *Marsh v. Marsh*, 313 S.C. 42, 437 S.E.2d 34 (1993). However, the Court stated:

> We emphasize the family court is not required to divide all marital property between the spouses based on the same percentage of division. For example, the court could divide the general marital property equally between the two but award the personal injury compensation entirely to the injured spouse. Classifying the property as marital merely gives the family court the authority to divide the award as the equities presented in the particular case may require."

Id. at 45, 437 S.E.2d at 36. Thus, *Orzula* and *Marsh* stand for the proposition that workers' compensation and personal injury awards are marital property in their entirety if the claim or right arose during the marriage, but the family court may consider the equities of dividing these awards separately from the rest of the marital estate.

In the second *Marsh* case, the Supreme Court overruled that portion of the Court of Appeals' opinion in *Mears v. Mears*, 305 S.C. 150, 406 S.E.2d 376 (Ct. App. 1991), which had remanded the case to the trial court for a determination of what portion of an employment claim settlement was marital property.

The primary holding of the first *Mears* case was not affected. In the 1991 case, the Court of Appeals considered the point in time at which a workers' compensation or personal injury claim becomes marital property. In affirming the Court of Appeals' disposition of this issue, the Supreme Court quoted the following from the Court of Appeals' opinion:

> [A]n unliquidated employment claim which accrues before and represents compensation for injuries suffered or property lost prior to commencement of marital litigation is marital property even though received after the valuation date .... We therefore hold that in the absence of fraud, deception or effort by one spouse to secrete or hide an unliquidated employment claim, the other spouse' right to share in such a claim asserted for the first time after a court ordered distribution will not be recognized.

Mears v. Mears, 308 S.C. 196, 197, 417 S.E.2d 574, 575 (1992) (quoting from *Mears v. Mears*, 305 S.C. 150, 156-157, 406 S.E.2d 367, 380 (Ct. App. 1991)).

In the 1992 *Mears* case the Supreme Court also affirmed the Court of Appeals' holding that employment claims are marital property subject to equitable distribution and stated that "the filing or commencement of litigation" is "the determinative date of whether an asset or right of action constitutes marital property." The Supreme Court also noted that the hearing on equitable distribution is the appropriate time for the family court to "ascertain whether such a right of action existed or had accrued at the time of commencement of litigation."*Id.*

6. EFFECT OF DEATH

The death of a spouse involved in marital litigation does not terminate proceedings to divide marital property. "With respect to the equitable division of marital property, marital litigation is not abated by the death of a spouse." *Hodge v. Hodge*, 305 S.C. 521, 524, 409 S.E.2d 436, 438 (Ct. App. 1991). In *Hodge*, the husband died while an appeal regarding the distribution of property was pending. The Court of Appeals reasoned that under S.C. Code Ann. § 20-7-471 (Law. Co-op. Supp.), the husband gained a "vested" property right during the marriage to certain property and this right was not abated by his subsequent death.

D. VALUATION

1. IN GENERAL

The Equitable Apportionment of Marital Property Act provides some guidance to the family court for determining the value of marital property:

> In determining the value of contributions prior to making an equitable apportionment, the court:
>
> (1) shall make findings of fact from credible evidence of the values of property and services, if any;
>
> (2) is empowered to take judicial notice of official reports of the federal and state governments, including official bulletins, publications, and reports of general public interest where these reports are made and published by authority of law or have been adopted by state statute;
>
> (3) has the authority to appoint experts as necessary for the purpose of valuation of property and contributions and to assess the cost against any or all parties is the action.

S.C. Code Ann. § 20-7-474 (Law. Co-op. Supp.).

Although the statute speaks in terms of valuing the "contributions" of the parties to the marital property, the Court of Appeals has interpreted this language to encompass placing a value on the marital property itself. In *Wood v. Wood*, 292 S.C. 43, 354 S.E.2d 796 (Ct. App. 1987), the court remanded the issue of equitable distribution to the trial court and noted about section 20-7-474 that "the trial judge has the authority to appoint experts as necessary for the purpose of valuation of *property and contributions* and to assess the cost against any or all parties to the action." *Id.* at 48, 354 S.E.2d at 799 (emphasis added).

The trial court is required to value all marital property of the parties. A failure to value some of the property may be reversible error. *Cannon v. Cannon*, ___ S.C. ___, 467 S.E.2d 132 (Ct. App. 1996)(remanding because the trial court did not value the personal property in the marital home).

The court's determination of the value of the marital property cannot be arbitrary. In *Ferguson v. Ferguson*, 300 S.C. 1, 386 S.E.2d 267 (Ct. App. 1989), the Court of Appeals reversed after both parties questioned the family court's valuation of their personal property. The court said: "While it is appropriate for a family court judge to select a value for property that falls within the range of values testified to, it is inappropriate to simply average the values testified to by the parties to arrive at a value." *Id.* at 5, 386 S.E.2d at 269.

A party may not complain on appeal that the trial court's valuation is unsupported by the evidence unless the party offered evidence about value at trial. In *Roe v. Roe*, 311 S.C. 471, 429 S.E.2d 830 (Ct. App. 1993), the wife appealed the trial judge's valuation of a train collection. The husband testified that it was worth $7,000, but the wife offered no evidence of its value. The Court of Appeals held that she could not complain on appeal, citing *Cox v. Cox*, 290 S.C. 245, 248, 349 S.E.2d 92,93 (Ct. App. 1986).

2. VALUATION OF BUSINESSES

a. Fair Market Value

When valuing a "going business" for purposes of equitable distribution in a divorce decree, the court should value the assets as those of an on-going business and not as liquidated assets. "Marital businesses are to be valued at fair market value as on going businesses." *R.G.M. v. D.G.M.*, 306 S.C. 145, 152, 410 S.E.2d 564, 568 (1991). *See also Roberson v. Roberson*, 296 S.C. 56, 370 S.E.2d 612 (1988) (holding that the family court erred in awarding wife $25,000 portion of husband's trucking business when the court failed to identify the business as marital property, value it, reasonably apportion it, or conclude what, if any, contributions the wife made to the "business"); *Woodward v. Woodward*, 294 S.C. 210, 363 S.E.2d 413 (Ct. App.

1987). The court in *Woodward* rejected the family court's valuation of the husband's professional association, stating:

> The trial judge apparently accepted the book value of the accounts receivable but made no deduction for uncollectibles and taxes. This was error in view of the uncontradicted evidence by both parties' experts that some deduction needed to be made for uncollectibles and taxes. When valuing business assets of a going business for equitable division purposes, the family court should value the assets as part of a "going business" not as liquidated assets. *Reid v. Reid*, 280 S.C. 367, 312 S.E.2d 724 (Ct. App. 1984). Although the trial judge was free to believe the valuation placed on the accounts receivable by the husband's expert represented the liquidated value of the assets and not their fair market value, the evidence does not support the value the trial judge placed on them.

Id. at 214, 363 S.E.2d at 416.

The court should accomplish its determination of the fair market value of the corporate property by considering the business' net asset value, the fair market value for its stock, and earnings or investment value. *See Reid v. Reid*, 280 S.C. 367, 312 S.E. 2d 724 (Ct. App. 1984) (office supply company); *Kirsch v. Kirsch*, 299 S.C. 201, 383 S.E.2d 254 (Ct. App. 1989) (pharmacy); *Brandi v. Brandi*, 302 S.C. 353, 396 S.E.2d 124 (Ct. App. 1990) (convenience stores. In addition to utilizing real estate appraisals offered by the wife, "[t]he valuation should also have considered other factors such as inventory, accounts payable and receivable, and other legitimate assets or liabilities." *Id.* at 357, 396 S.E.2d 126.).

The determination of the value of businesses of the type usually seen in domestic litigation, small and closely held, is no easy task, yet there are some guidelines discussed in the following cases: *Santee Oil Co., Inc. v. Cox*, 265 S.C. 270, 217 S.E.2d 789 (1975); *Metromont Materials Corp. v. Pennell*, 270 S.C. 9, 239 S.E.2d 753 (1977); *Dibble v. Sumter Ice and Fuel Co.*, 283 S.C. 278, 322 S.E.2d 674 (Ct. App. 1984).

b. Goodwill

Some practitioners may misinterpret the position of the appellate courts with respect to whether the goodwill of a business can be included in its valuation for purposes of dividing the marital property. The first case in which the value of goodwill was considered in marital litigation was *Casey v. Casey*, 293 S.C. 503, 362 S.E.2d 6 (1987), in which the Supreme Court considered the value of goodwill connected to a chain of retail fireworks stores. The court pointed out that other jurisdictions are split on this issue, but decided that: "When the goodwill in a business is *dependent on the owner's future earnings*, it is too speculative for inclusion in the marital business. Moreover, these future earnings are accounted for in an award of alimony." *Id.* at 504, 362 S.E.2d at 7 (citations omitted) (emphasis added). The Court of Appeals affirmed this position in two cases involving the valuation of medical practices. *Wood v. Wood*, 298 S.C. 30, 378 S.E.2d 59 (Ct. App. 1989) (medical practice); *Donahue v. Donahue*, 299 S.C. 353, 384 S.E.2d 741 (1989) (dental practice). In *Donahue*, the wife received nothing from the dental practice because the expert testified at trial that the only value of the practice was its goodwill.[16]

South Carolina appellate courts have not yet considered, in a case involving the division of marital property, the issue of goodwill in the valuation of a business in which goodwill is not dependent on the owner's future earnings. In *Hickum v. Hickum*, 320 S.C. 97, 463 S.E.2d 321 (Ct. App. 1995), the court denied the husband's request to place a higher value on a cosmetic business that the wife and her sister

---

[16] A majority of states does not agree with South Carolina's position on goodwill. Many allow consideration of goodwill in valuing professional practices. For information about the treatment of goodwill by other states in the context of marital litigation see the following annotations: Divorce and separation: goodwill in law practice as property subject to distribution on dissolution of marriage, 79 A.L.R.4th 171; Valuation of goodwill in medical or dental practice for purposes of divorce court's property distribution, 78 A.L.R.4th 853; Valuation of goodwill in accounting practice for purposes of divorce court's property distribution, 77 A.L.R.4th 609; Divorce and separation: goodwill in accounting practice as property subject to distribution on dissolution of marriage, 77 A.L.R.4th 645; Valuation of goodwill in law practice for purposes of divorce court's property distribution, 77 A.L.R.4th 683; Divorce and separation: goodwill in medical or dental practice as property subject to distribution on dissolution of marriage, 76 A.L.R.4th 1025; Accountability for good will on dissolution of partnership, 65 A.L.R.2d 521.

operated as equal partners. The opinion does not discuss whether the goodwill of the business depended on the future earnings of the spouse. The court noted in a footnote that "the courts of South Carolina have consistently held that the goodwill of a business is too speculative to be included in the marital estate." *Id.* at ___ n.5, 463 S.E.2d at ___ n.5. This is an overly broad statement of prior case law, and the goodwill issue was not determinative of the outcome of the case. The real thrust of the court's decision to affirm the family court's valuation of the business was that, even if goodwill was considered, it would not have affected the valuation of the business significantly. The court noted that the business' tax return from the prior year showed a net profit of $204 and its total assets were $7,250 in inventory.

The inclusion of goodwill in the value of businesses generally is an accepted practice in South Carolina. In *Dibble v. Sumter Ice and Fuel Co.*, 283 S.C. 278, 284, 322 S.E.2d 674, 677 (Ct. App. 1984), the court wrote, "[t]he principal question then becomes: what is the value of the Corporation's goodwill on the date of liquidation and what method or combinations of methods best accounts for that goodwill?" Ultimately, the goodwill in this company was valued at $360,000.

Thus, there is no reason to assume that the family courts should not include the value of a business' goodwill in dividing marital property in circumstances in which the goodwill is not based on the owner's future earnings.

3. VALUATION OF RETIREMENT BENEFITS

Two common methods recognized by South Carolina courts in valuing retirement benefits are: (1) present cash value, and (2) distribution from each payment.

> Two methods have generally been utilized in handling equitable division of a pension. The present cash value method was applied in this case. The trial court calculates, using actuarial evidence, the present value of the pension. The court further calculates the percentage of the present value attributable to the marriage and the appropriate equitable share of the other spouse. Usually, the pension is awarded to the employee spouse and there is

> an offset of other marital property to the nonemployee spouse. (citations omitted)
>
> The second approach is the reserve jurisdiction method. In such method, the trial court determines the formula for division but delays actual distribution until benefit payments are received.

Martin v. Martin, 296 S.C. 436, 440-441, 373 S.E.2d 706, 709 (Ct. App. 1988). The "reserve jurisdiction" method is also called "distribution from each payment." *Smith v. Smith*, 308 S.C. 372, 375, 418 S.E.2d 314, 316 (Ct. App. 1991).

The present cash method promotes finality and the severance of the entanglements between the parties, but its downside can be difficulty in valuation. There is no set rule for how to determine present cash value. Typically, for determinations involving defined benefit plans, the trial court "calculates the percentage of present value attributable to the marriage and the appropriate equitable share of the other spouse." *Belton v. Belton*, Op. No. 2613 (S.C. Ct. App. filed Jan. 13, 1997)(Davis Adv. Sh. No. 1 at 30) (quoting *Martin v. Martin*, 296 S.C. 436, 440-441, 373 S.E.2d 706, 709 (Ct. App. 1988)). In *Martin*, the trial court's use of the present value method was upheld although the husband argued that the method was unfair because it caused him to assume all the risk of not living to his estimated life expectancy.

Testimony from an actuary is required before the present value method can be used. In *Smith*, the Court of Appeals used the distribution from each payment method to correct what it held to be an erroneous valuation of the husband's civil service pension. The trial court undervalued the present cash value of the pension, apparently because no expert testimony was received from an actuary. The Court of Appeals noted that this is a prerequisite to being able to use the present value approach.

The court may consider the approximate gross monthly pension in calculating the value of retirement pensions. In *Martin v. Martin*, 296 S.C. 436, 378 S.E.2d 706 (Ct. App. 1988), the husband argued on appeal that the family court should have considered only the net monthly pension in determining the value of a military retirement pension. The court had considered the gross monthly pension. The Court of Appeals found no error.

If the value of a retirement pension cannot be calculated, it is appropriate for the trial court to consider the interests of each party in the retirement pension separately from the remainder of the marital estate and to defer any payments until payments begin under the pension plan. The Court of Appeals approved this practice in *Ball v. Ball*, 312 S.C. 31, 430 S.E.2d 533 (Ct. App. 1993), *aff'd*, 314 S.C. 445, 445 S.E.2d 449 (1994).

E. APPORTIONMENT

1. ALL RELEVANT FACTORS MUST BE CONSIDERED

The factors to be considered in apportioning marital property are set out in S.C. Code Ann. § 20-7-472 (Law. Co-op. Supp.), entitled "Equitable apportionment of marital property; criteria; finality of order." The statute requires that all factors be considered: "In making apportionments the court must give weight in such proportion as it finds appropriate to *all* of the following factors." (emphasis added).

The Court of Appeals in *Johnson v. Johnson*, 296 S.C. 289, 372 S.E.2d 107 (Ct. App. 1988), probably best summarized the purpose of the factors enumerated in S.C. Code Ann. § 20-7-472 (Law. Co-op. Supp.) when it wrote:

> These criteria guide the court in exercising its discretion over apportionment of the marital property. They are nothing more than equities to be considered in reaching a fair distribution of marital property. They subserve the ultimate goal of apportionment, which is to divide the marital estate, as a whole, in a manner which fairly reflects each spouse's contribution to the economic partnership and also the relative effect of ending that partnership on each of the parties.

Id. at 297, 372 S.E.2d at 112.

However, even if all relevant factors have not clearly been considered by the trial court, the appellate court may approve the division of marital property if it determines that the apportionment was fair despite this shortcoming. As the *Johnson* court stated in affirming the apportionment as "eminently fair":

> On review, this Court looks to the fairness of the overall apportionment. *See Morris v. Morris*, 295 S.C. 37, 367 S.E.2d 24 (1988). If the end result is equitable, it is irrelevant that this Court might have weighed specific factors differently from the trial judge.

296 S.C. at 300, 372 S.E.2d at 113. *See also Perry v. Perry*, 301 S.C. 147, 390 S.E.2d 480 (Ct. App. 1990) (holding that although the trial court failed to consider all relevant factors, the property division was affirmed as fair and equitable).

A person claiming that a division of marital property is incorrect has the burden on appeal of showing "not only error but prejudice." *West v. West*, 315 S.C. 44, 46, 431 S.E.2d 603, 604 (Ct. App. 1993) (quoting *Keller v. Pierce-Young-Angel Co.*, 253 S.C. 395, 399, 171 S.E.2d 352, 359 (1969). *West* held that the husband was correct in complaining that the trial judge should have specifically apportioned the personal property of the parties. It was harmless error, however, because the husband appeared to have benefited more than he was injured by this error, did not argue that the overall division was unfair, and did not argue what additional property should have been awarded to him.

The discretion to decide what weight should be assigned to the various factors in equitable apportionment is vested in the trial court, not the appellate court, by S.C. Code Ann. § 20-7-472 (Law Co-op. Supp.). *Morehouse v. Morehouse*, 317 S.C. 222, 452 S.E.2d 632 (Ct. App. 1994). Upon review, the appellate court looks to the fairness of the overall division and, if the end result is equitable, it is irrelevant that the appellate court might have weighed specific factors differently than the trial court. Even if the appellate court believes adjustments could be made, remand is unnecessary when the results reached at the trial level are fair and equitable. The family court's decision will be affirmed if the family court judge addresses the factors under § 20-7-420 with sufficiency for the appellate tribunal to conclude that the trial judge was cognizant of the required factors. *Id.*

An interesting issue that has not been fully explored by the appellate courts is the extent to which family courts are allowed or expected to apportion the entire marital estate as one unit, as opposed to considering the equitable interests of the parties in each item of property.

One might assume from the statute and some case decisions that the entire marital estate is to be considered, then apportioned as a unit on the basis of the parties' overall equities in it. However, it appears clear that family court judges are allowed, if not expected, to consider the equities in some specific items of property and to apportion them differently than the general marital estate. So far, unfortunately, no guidelines have been provided to help judges and practitioners identify which items may be considered separately and where the line is to be drawn.

A case which appears to say that the total marital estate is to be considered and apportioned as a unit is *Toler v. Toler*, 292 S.C. 374, 356 S.E.2d 429 (Ct. App. 1987), which states:

> [T]he court also failed to determine the proportionate shares of the *total estate* to which the parties were entitled *based on their respective contributions to the marriage and the acquisition of marital property*. The final cash distribution to the wife should have been determined by calculating her equitable percentage of the total marital estate and deducting therefrom the value of personal property she received in kind.

Id. at 380, 356 S.E.2d at 433 (emphasis added).

However, the Supreme Court has ruled that the family court may consider apportioning a personal injury award received by one spouse differently than the division of the general marital estate.

> We emphasize the family court is not required to divide all marital property between the spouses based on the same percentage of division. For example, the court could divide the general marital property equally between the two but award the personal injury compensation entirely to the injured spouse.

. . .

> Classifying the property as marital merely gives the family court the authority to divide the award as the equities presented in the particular case may require.

Marsh v. Marsh, 313 S.C. 42, 45, 437 S.E.2d 34, 36 (1993).

The Court of Appeals approved apportioning the equitable interests in a marital home by a different percentage than the rest of the marital estate in *Sexton v. Sexton*, 308 S.C. 37, 416 S.E.2d 649 (Ct. App. 1992).[17] There, the personal property was divided 50-50 at a prior hearing. In a subsequent proceeding, only the marital home was subject to division. The family court judge relied on the earlier decision in ruling that the wife was entitled to fifty percent of the parties' interest in the marital home, but he also stated that he had considered the statute and the case law in reaching this conclusion, although he did not make specific findings regarding any of the factors enumerated in the statute. The Court of Appeals was convinced by its independent review of the facts that the husband was entitled to more than fifty percent of the marital home because his family contributed to a substantial portion of the value of the home. It ruled that the trial judge could not rely on the prior determination of the percentage. The Court of Appeals held that, when additional marital assets are brought before the family court after other assets have been apportioned, the family court must explicitly reconsider all relevant factors before dividing the new asset, including direct and indirect contributions. It did not suggest, however, that the division of the entire marital estate should be reexamined.

The family court appears to have calculated one percentage for a retirement pension and another percentage for the other marital property in *Martin v. Martin*, 296 S.C. 436, 373 S.E.2d 706 (Ct. App. 1988), in which the Court of Appeals affirmed the family court's award to the wife of twenty percent of the husband's military pension and fifty five percent of the other marital assets.

---

[17] The same parties were involved in *Sexton v. Sexton*, 298 S.C. 359, 380 S.E.2d 832 (Ct. App. 1989) (discussed in the first section of this chapter) in which the court had ruled that the family court has subject matter jurisdiction to equitably apportion property owned by a third party.

Thus, it appears clear (especially from *Marsh*) that family court judges may separately consider the equitable apportionment of at least major assets such as retirement pensions, marital homes, and workers' compensation or personal injury awards. It is not yet clear how large the list of such major assets will become or whether the family court is also allowed to consider separately apportioning every item of marital property. It is also not clear why the appellate courts have encouraged this practice rather than requiring that the equities related to particular assets be considered in the process of dividing the total marital estate. Perhaps, the appellate courts are simply providing family court judges the flexibility to apportion items of property separately in cases where it would be more efficient and produce fairer results.

A spouse does not have to prove that he or she made a material contribution toward the acquisition of a particular asset in order to claim an interest in it. In *Reid v. Reid*, 280 S.C. 367, 312 S.E.2d 724 (Ct. App. 1984), the Court of Appeals said that "a spouse need not prove that he or she made a material contribution toward the acquisition of particular property in order to be entitled to an equitable interest in it." *Id.* at 376, 312 S.E.2d at 729. In *Walker v. Walker*, 295 S.C. 286, 368 S.E.2d 89 (Ct. App. 1988), Judge Goolsby wrote a concurring opinion to make the point that the court was not holding that a spouse must show that he or she contributed to the acquisition of particular property before being entitled to it (in *Walker* the husband's pension was the only item of marital property in the marital estate).

The fifteen factors enumerated in the statute are discussed below.

2. DURATION OF THE MARRIAGE

In making apportionment, the court must give weight in such proportions as it finds appropriate to "the duration of the marriage together with the ages of the parties at the time of the marriage and at the time of the divorce or separate maintenance or other marital action between the parties." S.C. Code Ann. § 20-7-472(1) (Law. Co-op. Supp.).

Although neither the case decisions nor the Equitable Apportionment of Marital Property Act say so directly, the results in cases involving long marriages would lead one to predict that, absent special circumstances, marital property will be divided on a 50-50 basis, at least where the wife has been a homemaker, and, perhaps, where she has made some other contribution to the accumulation of marital assets.

The following cases appear to support this conclusion: *Smith v. Smith*, 280 S.C. 257, 312 S.E.2d 560 (Ct. App. 1984), involved a thirty-year marriage. The husband complained on appeal about the wife receiving an undivided one-half interest in the marital home. The Court of Appeals, quoting from *Parrott v. Parrott*, 278 S.C. 60, 63, 292 S.E.2d 182, 182 (1982), said:

> [W]here, as here, one spouse has foregone career opportunities at the behest of the primary wage-earning spouse, and throughout a long marriage has remained in the home to rear children and provide a suitable environment for the family, the homemaker spouse shall have upon divorce an equitable interest in the real property acquired by the wage-earner spouse during the marriage.

Id. at 261, 312 S.E.2d at 563. The court affirmed the trial court, but noted that its ruling was supported by the wife's also contributing financially to its acquisition when proceeds realized from the sale of an earlier jointly owned marital home were used to purchase the property.

Additional cases that point to a 50-50 division of marital assets after long marriages include:

Doe v. Doe, ___ S.C. ___, 478 S.E.2d 854 (Ct. App. 1996), affirming a 50-50 division of marital property following a thirty-one year marriage.

Mallett v. Mallett, ___ S.C. ___, 473 S.E.2d 804 (Ct. App. 1996), affirming a 50-50 division of the marital estate following a twenty-one year marriage, although the Court of Appeals notes that the award was "generous."

Murray v. Murray, 312 S.C. 154, 439 S.E.2d 312 (Ct. App. 1993), affirming a wife's "special equity" of fifty percent of the appreciation in the marital home (which was the husband's nonmarital property) following a seventeen year marriage.

Harlan v. Harlan, 300 S.C. 537, 389 S.E.2d 165 (Ct. App. 1990), affirming a 50-50 division in a marriage which lasted 18 years. The wife worked a significant portion of that time and was the primary caretaker of the children.

Kirsch v. Kirsch, 299 S.C. 201, 383 S.E.2d 254 (Ct. App. 1989), affirming a 50-50 split. "This was a marriage of thirty years. While Mr. Kirsch provided the bulk of the income, Mrs. Kirsch was a homemaker and she also worked for approximately twelve years outside the home." *Id.* at 203, 383 S.E.2d at 255.

Martin v. Martin, 296 S.C. 436, 373 S.E.2d 706 (Ct. App. 1988), affirming an award of 55% of the marital assets to the wife, except 20% of the husband's military retirement pension.

> While the husband earned most of the marital income, the wife maintained the home. She was a frugal person and this trait helped in the accumulation of marital assets. The court found the wife has little job potential other than bartending, although she was doing well operating the lounge they had purchased.

Id. at 442, 373 S.E.2d at 710. Also, the husband's adultery had caused the breakup of the marriage.

Polis v. Polis, 295 S.C. 184, 367 S.E.2d 465 (Ct. App. 1988), remanding a division of 59% to the husband and 41% to the wife following a 41 year marriage because the family court had "emphasized the husband's financial input at her expense." The wife had worked some, contributed nonmarital assets, and been a homemaker who raised two children. The husband's drinking was the cause of the dissolution of the marriage.

Smith v. Smith, 294 S.C. 194, 363 S.E.2d 404 (Ct. App. 1987), affirmed a 50-50 split in an 18 year marriage in which the wife provided homemaker services and on occasion worked either part-time or full-time.

Leatherwood v. Leatherwood, 293 S.C. 148, 359 S.E.2d 89 (Ct. App. 1987), affirming a 50-50 award following a twenty-two year marriage. The wife was the primary caretaker and worked at the beginning of the marriage and later during the marriage as necessitated by her husband's indictment.

Other cases have held that something close to a 50-50 split is warranted in long marriages. *See Panhorst v. Panhorst*, 301 S.C. 100, 390 S.E.2d 376 (Ct. App. 1990) (affirming a division of 55% to the husband and 45% to the wife where the husband was granted a divorce after a long marriage due to the wife's adultery); *Josey v. Josey*, 291 S.C. 26, 351 S.E.2d 891 (Ct. App. 1986) (approving 55% to husband and 45% to wife. The marriage lasted over twenty years until the wife obtained a divorce due to the physician husband's adultery); *Stearns v. Stearns*, 284 S.C. 459, 327 S.E.2d 343 (1985) (reversing an award of 70% to the wife and 30% to the husband and ordering the marital property to be divided 55% to the wife and 45% to the husband, in a no fault divorce following thirty-one years of marriage).

One case is the exception that proves the rule. In *Brandi v. Brandi*, 302 S.C. 353, 396 S.E.2d 124 (Ct. App. 1990), the Court of Appeals affirmed an award of 30% to the wife and 70% to the husband, although the marriage lasted ten years and the wife was granted a divorce due to the husband's adultery.

3. MARITAL MISCONDUCT OR FAULT

S.C. Code Ann. § 20-7-472(2) (Law. Co-op. Supp.) provides that, in making apportionment, the court must give weight in such proportions as it finds appropriate to:

> [M]arital misconduct or fault of either or both parties, whether or not used as a basis for a divorce, if the misconduct affects or has affected the economic circumstances of the parties, or contributed to the breakup of the marriage; provided, that no evidence of personal conduct which would otherwise be relevant and material for purposes of this subsection shall be considered with regard to this subsection if such conduct shall have taken place subsequent to the happening of the earliest of (a) entry of a *pendente lite* order in a divorce or separate maintenance action; (b) formal signing of a written property or marital settlement agreement; or (c) entry of a permanent order of

> separate maintenance and support or of a permanent order approving a property or marital settlement agreement between the parties . . . .

Marital misconduct was the primary valuation factor used in *Sharpe v. Sharpe*, 307 S.C. 540, 416 S.E.2d 215 (Ct. App. 1992). In *Sharpe*, a 65-35 distribution was upheld in favor of the husband because the wife had unsuccessfully conspired to murder him. The Court of Appeals denied the husband's request that his wife receive nothing because the husband was also engaged in marital misconduct. Judge Cureton in a concurring opinion suggested a case-by-case approach stating:

> I . . . would not hold as a matter of public policy that in every case where one spouse participates in an attempt to murder the other spouse, the offending spouse should be barred from a property division. I would take the approach taken by the majority of the courts and evaluate the misconduct of the offending spouse in each case." *Id.* at 544, 416 S.E.2d at 217.

Unlike the murder conspiracy misconduct in *Sharpe*, most marital misconduct considered under S.C. Code § 20-7-472(2) (Supp.) involves adultery, habitual drunkenness, or physical cruelty. *Cf. R.G.M. v. D.E.M.*, 306 S.C. 145, 410 S.E.2d 564 (1991) (adultery consisting of homosexual affair deemed marital misconduct was considered and used in apportioning marital property); *Peirson v. Calhoun*, 308 S.C. 246, 417 S.E.2d 604 (S.C. Ct. App. 1992) (issue of husband's drinking was marital misconduct which damaged economic status of the parties; remanded to trial court for property revaluation); *Williams v. Williams*, 297 S.C. 208, 375 S.E.2d 349 (Ct. App. 1988) (physical cruelty).

The extent to which marital misconduct can affect a marital property division, especially when coupled with other equitable considerations, is illustrated in *Wannamaker v. Wannamaker*, 305 S.C. 36, 406 S.E.2d 180 (Ct. App. 1991):

> While we recognize the rule that a spouse need not prove that he or she made a material contribution to the acquisition of particular property in order to be entitled to an equitable interest in it, we hold in this case that the special circumstances of the long separation of the parties before initiation of marital litigation must be factored in as

> a special consideration. The husband's medical partnership began in 1985, some eight years after the parties' separated. The wife contributed nothing to either the acquisition or appreciation of the value of the partnership. We hold, under the special circumstances of this case, that the wife, whose adultery brought about the separation of the parties and the break up of this family, should not be apportioned an interest in the husband's medical partnership.
>
> The award that the trial judge made appears to be an attempt by the trial judge to compensate the wife for her failure to receive alimony, which was barred because of her adultery. Equitable distribution cannot be used because alimony is barred. *Berry v. Berry*, 294 S.C. 334, 364 S.E.2d 463 (1988).

Id. at 41, 406 S.E.2d at 183. Based on the same reasoning, the Court also held that the wife should not be allowed to claim an equitable interest in the husband's retirement account.

Another case in which marital misconduct was important is *West v. West*, 315 S.C. 44, 431 S.E.2d 603 (Ct. App. 1993). The Court of Appeals affirmed a 60-40 division in favor of the wife who had left the husband after five years of marriage due to his extreme physical and mental abuse. In rejecting the husband's appeal, the court noted the similarities of this case with *Johnson v. Johnson*, 296 S.C. 289, 372 S.E.2d 107 (Ct. App. 1988), in which a 50-50 division was approved although the marriage lasted only a little over a year and the wife did not contribute financially to the marriage. While the cases are similar, the opinion in *Johnson* did not mention fault as one of the factors justifying the 50-50 property division, although it was relied on as a significant justification for determining that periodic alimony should have been awarded.

Fault may be used to decrease an award, but not to increase it. In *Berry v. Berry*, 290 S.C. 351, 350 S.E.2d 398 (Ct. App. 1986), *aff'd*, 294 S.C. 334, 364 S.E.2d 463 (1988), the Court of Appeals held that "[w]hile it was proper for the trial judge to have disregarded the wife's fault, it was not proper for him to have increased her distributive share to make up for the alimony he could not award. Fault may be used to decrease an award, but never to increase it." 290 S.C. at 356, 350 S.E.2d at 401.

Marital misconduct will not be given weight, however, when it occurs after marital litigation commences. S.C. Code Ann. § 20-7-472(2) (Law. Co-op. Supp.). Also, fault will not be weighed if it did not lead to the dissolution of the marriage or adversely affect the financial status of the parties. In *Smith v. Smith*, 294 S.C. 194, 363 S.E.2d 404 (Ct. App. 1987), the wife's affair was accorded no weight since it did not cause the parties to separate (her affair "occurred well after parties separated"), and it did not damage the marriage economically.

The effect of marital misconduct on equitable distribution of property will not necessarily lead to a large award and may be mitigated by other factors. South Carolina opinions consistently include this quote from *Rampey v. Rampey* 286 S.C. 153, 332 S.E.2d 213 (Ct. App. 1985): "[A]lthough fault does not justify a severe penalty in making a division of marital property, it is a factor the court may consider in determining the equities between spouses." *Id.* at 156, 332 S.E.2d at 214. Mrs. Rampey conceded that she abandoned the marital home and was directly responsible for the breakup of the marriage. It was appropriate for the family court to consider her fault as a factor in the division of martial property. *Rampey* is cited in *Noll v. Noll* 297 S.C. 190, 375 S.E.2d 338 (Ct. App. 1988), in which the wife's adultery was ameliorated by "pre-existing marital discord." Thus, fault does not necessarily garner large awards and its presence may be counter-balanced by other factors. Its impact will depend on the facts of each case and the discretion of each trial judge.

4. CONTRIBUTIONS OF THE PARTIES

S.C. Code Ann. § 20-7-472(3) (Law. Co-op. Supp.) provides that, in making apportionment, the court must give weight in such proportions as it finds appropriate to:

> The value of the marital property, whether the property be within or without the State. The contribution of each spouse to the acquisition, preservation, depreciation, or appreciation in value of the marital property, including the contribution of the spouse as homemaker; provided, that the court shall consider the quality of the contribution as well as its factual existence.

The value of the property is not really a factor, although the statute says it is. Valuation of the marital property is a separate step in the process which must precede apportionment. While the value is relevant, it is really the contribution of each party to the value of marital property that is an important factor in deciding how to apportion the property.

The contributions of each party to the acquisition and value of marital property is the most important factor to be considered, except, perhaps, the duration of the marriage. In *Mobley v. Mobley*, 309 S.C. 134, 420 S.E.2d 506 (Ct. App. 1992), the issue of property division was remanded specifically because the trial court failed to properly consider § 20-7-472(3) of the Code. Most notably, the trial court concluded that no marital property existed, when in fact the husband conceded that all of their property, excluding AT&T stock, was marital property. Furthermore, the trial court also neglected to consider the wife's indirect contributions as a homemaker. Thus, section 20-7-472(3) is a factor which, if not considered fully by the court and counsel, may require the case to be remanded on appeal. *See also Rivenbark v. Rivenbark*, 301 S.C. 175, 391 S.E.2d 232 (1990) (holding that the trial court failed to consider all the factors listed in the statute, including the homemaker contribution by the wife); *Rowland v. Rowland*, 295 S.C. 131, 367 S.E.2d 434 (Ct. App. 1988) (remanding due to the failure of the family court to consider each party's contribution).

The contributions of a wife to the increased value of a business that was started by the husband with nonmarital property were considered in *McClerin v. McClerin*, 310 S.C. 99, 425 S.E.2d 476 (Ct. App. 1992). The Court of Appeals approved a 50-50 split of the increased value of the company's stock, supported by the trial judge's findings related to the direct and indirect contributions of the wife. The wife's indirect contributions included being involved at the inception of the business, working side by side with her husband building it to its present state, holding the title of Comptroller, and running the administrative aspects of the business.

5. INCOME OF EACH SPOUSE

In making apportionment, the court must give weight in such proportions as it finds appropriate to "the income of each spouse, the earning potential of each spouse, and the opportunity for future acquisition of capital assets." S.C. Code Ann. § 20-7-472(4) (Law. Co-op. Supp.).

The fact that the husband's earning potential far exceeded the wife's was an important factor among several the court considered in affirming the trial court's property division in the case of *Seawright v. Seawright*, 305 S.C. 167, 406 S.E.2d 386 (Ct. App. 1991). *See also Harlan v. Harlan*, 300 S.C. 537, 389 S.E.2d 165 (Ct. App. 1990) (affirming a 53% award of marital property to the wife based in part on the husband's greater earning potential); *Johnson v. Johnson*, 296 S.C. 289, 372 S.E.2d 107 (Ct. App. 1988) (considering the earnings potential and ability to acquire capital assets); *Woodside v. Woodside*, 290 S.C. 366, 350 S.E.2d 407 (Ct. App. 1986) (considering foregone career opportunities); *Kirsch v. Kirsch*, 299 S.C. 201, 383 S.E.2d 254 (Ct. App. 1984) (holding that the wife's monetary contributions as school teacher/homemaker offset husband's substantial income as a pharmacist and prompted a roughly even split of marital property).

6. HEALTH OF EACH SPOUSE

In making apportionment, the court must give weight in such proportions as it finds appropriate to "the health, both physical and emotional, of each spouse." S.C. Code Ann. § 20-7-472(5) (Law. Co-op. Supp.).

The ailing health of the wife was an important factor in the Court of Appeals' decision to remand the issue of equitable distribution in *Jamar v. Jamar*, 308 S.C. 265, 417 S.E.2d 615 (Ct. App. 1992) (the wife had asthma and heart disease, making her unemployable). *See also Brandi v. Brandi*, 302 S.C. 353, 396 S.E.2d 124 (Ct. App. 1990) (holding that, although the husband was in better health, the wife was only awarded 30% of the marital property due to other factors).

7. NEED FOR TRAINING AND EDUCATION

The court must also give weight in such proportions as it finds appropriate to "the need of each spouse or either spouse for additional training or education in order to achieve that spouse's income potential." S.C. Code Ann. § 20-7-472(6) (Law. Co-op. Supp.).

This factor is considered in *Coxe v. Coxe*, 294 S.C. 291, 363 S.E.2d 906 (Ct. App. 1987). The husband challenged the trial court's finding that he did not need additional training to achieve his income potential. The court reasoned that "[s]ince the husband ran a successful company for many years and has attended four and one half years of college, there is sufficient evidence to support the trial judge's finding." *Id.* at 293, 363 S.E.2d at 907.

8. NONMARITAL PROPERTY OF EACH SPOUSE

In making apportionment, the court must give weight in such proportions as it finds appropriate to "the nonmarital property of each spouse." S.C. Code Ann. § 20-7-472(7) (Law. Co-op. Supp.).

Although nonmarital property may not be distributed, it can be considered in apportioning the marital property. *Skipper v. Skipper*, 290 S.C. 412, 351 S.E.2d 153 (1986). In *Smith v. Smith*, 308 S.C. 372, 418 S.E.2d 314 (Ct. App. 1991), the husband withdrew $23,921 from his pension fund. The trial court ruled that this was nonmarital property and the wife failed to make a SCRCP, Rule 59(e) motion for reconsideration, thus precluding the Court of Appeals from reviewing the ruling. However, since the withdrawal had reduced the value of the pension fund, the court held that the husband was not entitled to an offset of $6,000 that he had contributed to the cost of his wife's education as a registered nurse.

9. RETIREMENT BENEFITS

In making apportionment, the court must give weight in such proportions as it finds appropriate to "the existence or nonexistence of vested retirement benefits for each or either spouse." S.C. Code Ann. § 20-7-472(8) (Law. Co-op. Supp.).

The equitable apportionment of retirement benefits is discussed in other sections of this chapter.

10. EXISTENCE OF SPOUSAL SUPPORT AWARD

In making apportionment, the court must give weight in such proportions as it finds appropriate to "whether separate maintenance or alimony has been awarded." S.C. Code Ann. § 20-7-472(9) (Law. Co-op. Supp.).

In *Seawright v. Seawright*, 305 S.C. 167, 406 S.E.2d 386 (Ct. App. 1991), the Court of Appeals held that it was proper to consider the nonexistence of alimony in valuing the marital estate even though the failure to give alimony was not based on a finding of adultery. *See also Smith v. Smith*, 294 S.C. 194, 363 S.E.2d 404 (Ct. App. 1987) (holding that "the fact of whether a spouse is awarded alimony is a proper matter for the trial court to consider in apportioning marital property". *Id.* at 202, 363 S.E.2d at 408).

11. USE OF THE MARITAL HOME

In making apportionment, the court must give weight in such proportions as it finds appropriate to "the desirability of awarding the family home as part of equitable distribution or the right to live herein for reasonable periods to the spouse having custody of any children." S.C. Code Ann. § 20-7-472(10) (Law. Co-op. Supp.).

The Court of Appeals has advised the family court judges for years to try not to award the use of the marital home as an incident of support. In *Shealy v. Shealy*, 280 S.C. 494, 313 S.E.2d 48 (Ct. App. 1980), the court reversed an award of the exclusive use of the marital home to the wife until her death or remarriage. In so doing, the court included the following comment in a footnote:

> Due to their nature, domestic cases are difficult to end absolutely. Awarding fractional interests in real or personal property is not a satisfactory disposition to divorcing parties. It denies control of sale or encumbrances to both. Management, repairs, etc. are difficult to handle between persons at odds after divorce. Also, proven statistics have shown that women live longer than men thus furthering the uncertainty of an individual fractional interest. This could invite future litigation. In the future, Family Court judges are encouraged to make final dispositions of property interests where possible or, in the alternative, cite compelling reasons for awarding fractional or joint interests. Courts may determine incidental questions, afford complete justice and prevent multiplicity of litigation in divorce actions. *McLean v. McLean*, 273 S.C. 571, 257 S.E. 2d 751 (1979).

Id. at 498 n.1, 313 S.E.2d at 50, n.1. The court cited *Shealy* with approval in *Bass v. Bass*, 285 S.C. 178, 328 S.E.2d 649 (Ct. App. 1985), and added that, if the family courts fail to make a final disposition of property interests, they "must state compelling reasons for leaving loose ends." *Id.* at 182, 328 S.E.2d at 652.

The considerations to be taken into account in determining the desirability of awarding the use of the marital home to one spouse are most comprehensively set forth in *Johnson v. Johnson*, 285 S.C. 308, 329 S.E.2d 443 (Ct. App. 1985):

> Beginning with the pronouncement in *Whitfield v. Hanks*, 278 S.C. 165, 293 S.E.(2d) 314 (1982), that family courts may grant a spouse possession of the marital home as an incident of support, our appellate courts have struggled to develop guidelines to aid the family court in determining the appropriate disposition to be made of the marital home. *See, e.g., Thompson v. Brunson*, 283 S.C. 221, 321 S.E.(2d) 622 (S.C. App. 1984); *Shafer v. Shafer*, 283 S.C. 205, 320 S.E.(2d) 730 (S.C. App. 1984); *Tucker v. Tucker*, 282 S.C. 261, 317 S.E.(2d) 764 (1984); *Jones v. Jones*, 281 S.C. 96, 314 S.E.(2d) 33

(S.C. App. 1984); *Smith v. Smith*, 280 S.C. 257, 312 S.E.(2d) 560 (S.C. App. 1984). These cases establish several basic principles.

First, the family court must begin with the premise that division and distribution of the marital home should be accomplished at the time of entry of the judgment of divorce. If possible, all issues between the parties should be resolved at that point so that disputes and irritants do not linger and present further incentives to litigation. The family court's objective should be to dissolve the marriage, sever all entangling legal relations and place the parties in a position from which they can begin anew. In most cases, the parting of the ways should be accompanied by clearly stated obligations for the future, put in monetary terms as far as possible.

Second, the court must carefully consider the claim of a party that the interests of that party or the children are so predominant, when balanced against the interests of the other, that an award of exclusive possession of the marital home is compelled. In *Thompson v. Brunson, supra*, and *Shafer v. Shafer, supra*, we noted some of the interests which may be considered compelling: (1) adequate shelter for minors; (2) suitable housing for a handicapped or infirm spouse; and (3) the inability of the occupying spouse to otherwise obtain adequate housing.

An award of exclusive possession to one party requires that the other defer the realization of the value of his share of the marital home. Such a requirement is usually a burden. Therefore, before the family court imposes such a burden, it should consider the size and expansiveness of the home in relation to the expected use and the cost of maintaining the home in comparison to the benefits received. Further, the court must consider the potential duration of the exclusive possession. The family court may not award exclusive possession of the marital home for an unlimited period of time. In the exercise of sound discretion, the court must make the award for a reasonable time based on the circumstances warranting the award in the first instance. *See Thompson v. Brunson*, 321 S.E.(2d) at 625.

> Finally, the family court must make some provision in its order for eventual distribution of the marital home and state the terms upon which such distribution will be made.

Id. at 311-312, 329 S.E.2d at 445-446.

"Special circumstances" must exist before a spouse is awarded the use of the marital home as an incident of support. In *Smith v. Smith*, 280 S.C. 257, 312 S.E.2d 560 (Ct. App. 1984), the Court of Appeals stated:

> A court should not give a spouse exclusive use possession of a residence as an incident of support where the evidence reflects that a substantial portion of the other spouse's assets are invested in the home and there is no evidence either that the spouse has custody of the parties' minor children, that the other spouse is severely handicapped, or that some other special circumstance exists which would warrant such an award.

Id. at 264, 312 S.E.2d at 565. *See also Leatherwood v. Leatherwood*, 293 S.C. 148, 359 S.E.2d 89 (Ct. App. 1987) (reversing an award of the exclusive use of the marital home for four years, holding that it was error to award it to the wife where "no special circumstances exist which would warrant such an award").

"Special considerations" were also found in *Harlan v. Harlan*, 300 S.C. 537, 389 S.E.2d 165 (Ct. App. 1990):

> The court should consider such factors as (1) the need for adequate shelter for minors; (2) suitable housing for a handicapped or infirm spouse; and (3) the inability of the occupying spouse to otherwise obtain adequate housing. In making an award the court must make the award for a reasonable time based on the circumstances warranting the award in the first instance.

Id. at 541, 389 S.E.2d at 168. In *Harlan*, the Court of Appeals affirmed an award of exclusive use of the marital home to the wife who had custody of four children ranging in age from 18 to 5. The court also ruled that the husband could petition for modification of this exclusive use provision after the two oldest children reached the age of majority.

12. TAX CONSEQUENCES

In making apportionment, the court must give weight in such proportions as it finds appropriate to "the tax consequences to each or either party as a result of any particular form of equitable apportionment." S.C. Code Ann. § 20-7-472(11) (Law. Co-op. Supp.).

If an asset has not been sold or its sale is not clearly imminent, the tax consequences of a potential sale of that asset should not be considered. In fact, it is an abuse of discretion for the family court to consider the tax consequences if the apportionment order does not contemplate the liquidation or sale of an asset. *Ellerbe v. Ellerbe*, ___S.C. ___, 473 S.E.2d 881 (1996) (reversing the family court's valuation of the parties' retirement accounts at 48% of their face values). See also *Josey v. Josey*, 291 S.C. 26, 351 S.E.2d 891 (Ct. App. 1986), in which the Court of Appeals held that the trial court properly rejected the husband's claim that his net worth should have been reduced by the estimated amount of capital gains taxes that he was expecting to pay when certain assets were sold. "While the decree requires a sale of some assets, we would be required to speculate as to what, if any, taxes would have to be paid by the husband. Moreover, any assets transferred to the wife as part of the division would not result in a transfer taxable to the husband." *Id.* at 31, 351 S.E.2d at 894.

However, where the assets in question are expected to be fully liquidated upon apportionment of the marital property, the family court should consider all tax consequences of that sale. *Graham v. Graham*, 301 S.C. 128, 390 S.E.2d 469 (Ct. App. 1990) (holding that the trial court improperly determined the present liquidated value of the husband's IRA account, by failing to factor in the $27,125 in state and federal taxes that would have to be paid if the IRA account was liquidated in addition to the penalty that would be imposed for an early withdrawal of funds).

If one party causes tax penalties and assessments to be levied, e.g., by not paying taxes on time, that party may have to bear the entire burden of paying those extra charges. In *Roe v. Roe*, 311 S.C. 471, 429 S.E.2d 830 (Ct. App. 1993), the wife claimed on appeal that she should not have to share equally in the tax liability on her husband's retirement, because there were things the husband could have done, but failed to do, to reduce the tax liability and because he had caused penalties and assessments to be levied by failing to pay the taxes on time. The husband argued that they should share the entire tax liability because they had agreed to share the retirement funds without benefit of legal or tax advice. The Court of Appeals agreed that the parties should equally share the tax liability, but it remanded the case to the trial court for a determination of the sum the wife owed, excluding penalties and assessments the husband could have avoided by timely payment of the taxes.

Funds which have already been used to pay taxes on marital property should be offset against the marital estate to be divided. *Cross v. Cross*, 296 S.C. 474, 374 S.E.2d 178 (1988) (holding that approximately $29,000 of a money market account that was used by the husband to pay taxes should have been offset, with the remainder being available for equitable distribution).

Of course, the party who wants the court to consider tax consequences has the burden of providing sufficient evidence to enable the court to do so. In *Hardwick v. Hardwick*, 303 S.C. 256, 399 S.E.2d 791 (Ct. App. 1991), the Court of Appeals held that the husband could not complain that the trial judge did not properly calculate the current liquidated value of his IRA's and retirement plan, including tax consequences and penalties for withdrawal, where the trial court valued them as stated on the husband's financial declaration and he offered no other values or evidence of the impact of liquidation on the assets.

13. SUPPORT OBLIGATIONS

S.C. Code Ann. § 20-7-472(12) (Law. Co-op. Supp.) provides that, in making apportionment, the court must give weight in such proportions as it finds appropriate to "the existence and extent of any support obligations, from a prior marriage or for any other reason or reasons, of either party." No cases have been discovered which discuss this factor.

14. ENCUMBRANCES ON THE PROPERTY AND OTHER DEBTS

In making apportionment, the court must give weight in such proportions as it finds appropriate to "liens and any other encumbrances upon the marital property, which themselves must be equitably divided, or upon the separate property of either of the parties, and any other existing debts incurred by the parties or either of them during the marriage." S.C. Code Ann. § 20-7-472(13) (Law. Co-op. Supp.).

For purposes of equitable distribution, "marital debt" is "debt incurred for the joint benefit of the parties regardless of whether the parties are legally jointly liable for the debt or whether one party is legally individually liable." *Hardy v. Hardy*, 311 S.C. 433, 436, 429 S.E.2d 811, 813 (Ct. App. 1993).

In *Hardy*, the Court of Appeals held that credit card charges made before marital litigation is commenced are part of the net estate which must be equitably apportioned by the family court. The court noted that "the trial judge failed to recognize that the law relating to marital debts was materially impacted by S.C. Code Ann. § 20-7-472 (Supp.)." *Id.* at 436, 429 S.E.2d at 813. It held that the statute, specifically sections 20-7-472 (13) & (15), creates:

> [A] presumption that a debt of either spouse incurred prior to marital litigation is a marital debt and must be factored in the totality of equitable apportionment. The presumption is rebuttable.[18]

---

[18] Thus, the adoption of the Equitable Apportionment of Marital Property Act which became effective on June 13, 1986, changed the law stated by the Supreme Court in *Levy v. Levy*, 277 S.C. 576, 291 S.E.2d 201 (1982):

> We refuse to hold, as a matter of law, that the judge must order the sharing of debts as well as the sharing of assets. At the same time, we point out that it is always proper for the judge to take into consideration the debts of both parties as well as the properties of both parties in decreeing equitable distribution. It is entirely conceivable that the distribution of the assets might have been decreed in different proportions had the Wife been required to absorb portions of the Husband's debts.

Id. at 578, 291 S.E.2d at 202. In *Levy*, the trial court did not require the wife to share fully in the

*Id.*at 436, 429 S.E.2d at 811. *See also Frank v. Frank*, 311 S.C. 454, 429 S.E.2d 823 (Ct. App. 1993) (filed on the same day that *Hardy* was refiled without change after the Court of Appeals denied a petition for rehearing) (holding that the trial court erred in failing to identify and apportion marital debts as it had done with the parties' marital property).

The burden of proving a spouse's debt as nonmarital rests upon the party who makes such an assertion. If the trial judge finds that a spouse's debt was not made for marital purposes, it need not be factored into the court's equitable apportionment of the marital estate, and the trial judge may require payment by the spouse who created the debt for nonmarital purposes. *Hickum v. Hickum*, 320 S.C. 97, 463 S.E.2d 321 (Ct. App. 1995).

Only debts that are incurred for marital purposes are subject to equitable distribution. "While it is proper to consider marital debts in making an equitable distribution of marital assets, it is also incumbent upon the court to ensure the debts were incurred for the benefit of both parties during the marriage." *Peirson v. Calhoun*, 308 S.C. 246, 253, 417 S.E.2d 604, 607 (Ct. App. 1992) (affirming the family court's conclusion that all the debts were incurred for family purposes because the husband's testimony to this effect was uncontradicted by the wife).

A husband's debt to an insurance agency of which he was part owner was held to be a marital debt in *Ellerbe v. Ellerbe*, ___ S.C. ___, 473 S.E.2d 881 (Ct. App. 1996).

The same husband's tax liability for the year was also held to be marital debt, although it was not payable until after the date of filing for divorce. *Id.* The court held that it was unfair to include the husband's income, but not the tax liability on the income.

---

marital debts in dividing the marital estate. The Supreme Court affirmed, but Justice Harwell dissented, explaining that he would have remanded the case for a determination of which debts were incurred for the mutual benefit of the parties during the marriage and ordered such indebtedness to be equitably divided.

At least with respect to debts on a marital home, "debts" was defined in an unpublished opinion as debts that are incurred and existing at the time a husband and wife enter into a separation agreement, unless they designate the specific debts they intend for the agreement to encompass. *Jenkins v. Jenkins*, No. 93-UP-090 (S.C. Ct. App. 1993) (holding that the parties' agreement that the husband would assume all responsibility for the debts associated with the marital home did not include ongoing, recurring expenses associated with the ownership of the marital home such as insurance and taxes).

A debt owed to the parties cannot be apportioned as a marital asset, if that debt has already been used in calculating the value of a particular marital asset. See *Roe v. Roe*, 311 S.C. 471, 429 S.E.2d 830 (Ct. App. 1993), in which the court held that the trial court erred by assigning to the wife as a marital asset a debt owed by a third party because the same debt had been considered by the appraiser and included in the value of a pizza parlor which had been apportioned to the wife.

15. CHILD CUSTODY OBLIGATIONS

S.C. Code Ann. § 20-7-472(14) (Law. Co-op. Supp.) provides that, in making apportionment, the court must give weight in such proportions as it finds appropriate to "child custody arrangements and obligations at the time of the order." No cases have been found which discuss this factor.

16. OTHER FACTORS

S.C. Code Ann. § 20-7-472(15) (Law. Co-op. Supp.) provides that, in making apportionment, the court must give weight in such proportions as it finds appropriate to "such other relevant factors as the trial court shall expressly enumerate in its order."

This factor is a "catch-all" that gives trial courts ample discretion to use any other information they deem relevant to apportion marital property appropriately.

Although not specifically held to be considered as an "other factor" under the statute, the cases of *Johnson v. Johnson*, 296 S.C. 289, 372 S.E. 2d 107 (Ct. App. 1988) and *Peirson v. Calhoun*, 308 S.C. 246, 417 S.E. 2d 604 (Ct. App. 1992), recognize the theory of a marriage as an "economic partnership." The essential element of the partnership theory is an understanding by the parties that the marriage will be treated as an economic entity. If this understanding is found to exist, the marital estate is subject to equal division.

F. DISTRIBUTION (HOW TO DIVIDE IT?)

1. ANY REASONABLE MEANS MAY BE USED

The family court "may utilize any other reasonable means to achieve equity between the parties." S.C. Code Ann. § 20-7-476 (Law. Co-op. Supp.).

Absent compelling reasons, the objective in dividing marital property should be to sever all joint interests in the property as completely as possible. The Court of Appeals described some basic principles in *Johnson v. Johnson*, 285 S.C. 308, 329 S.E.2d 443 (Ct. App. 1985):

> First, the family court must begin with the premise that division and distribution of the marital home should be accomplished at the time of entry of the judgment of divorce. If possible, all issues between the parties should be resolved at that point so that disputes and irritants do not linger and present further incentives to litigation. The family court's objective should be to dissolve the marriage, sever all entangling legal relations and place the parties in a position from which they can begin anew.

Id. at 311, 329 S.E.2d at 445.

The parties should not be left in a position where they will be in business together. The Supreme Court has ruled that it was an abuse of discretion to award the wife a percentage of a closely held corporation owned by the husband and his brothers, since this would allow the dissention and bitterness between the parties to spread to the business and might impede the success of the business. *Ducate v. Ducate*, 279 S.C. 246, 306 S.E.2d 218 (1983). The Court of Appeals ruled in *Hunn v. Hunn*, 289 S.C. 499, 347 S.E.2d 108 (Ct. App. 1986), that on remand the trial court should reconsider that part of its order which provided that the parties would have joint ownership of their restaurant businesses. The court said that this result should be avoided, absent compelling reasons.

The general rule is that the trial judge may employ any reasonable means to divide the property. In *Bass v. Bass*, 285 S.C. 178, 328 S.E.2d 649 (Ct. App. 1985), the Court of Appeals stated the rule as follows: "Broad jurisdiction is granted family court judges in matters of equitable distribution of marital assets in a divorce decree and is such that judges may employ any reasonable means to effectuate an equitable division." *Id.* at 182, 328 S.E.2d at 651. The *Bass* court based this rule on the general jurisdictional statute of the family court, S.C. Code Ann. § 20-7-420 (Law. Co-op. 1976). *See also Brandi v. Brandi*, 302 S.C. 353, 357, 396 S.E.2d 124, 126 (Ct. App. 1990).

The method used by the trial judge to divide marital property cannot be arbitrary. The Supreme Court reversed a division of marital property in *Bauer v. Bauer*, 287 S.C. 217, 337 S.E.2d 211 (1985), where the trial judge went down a numbered list of marital assets, giving even-numbered items to one party and odd-numbered items to the other.

2. SALE OF THE MARITAL PROPERTY

The family court has the power to require the sale of marital property and a division of the proceeds to effect an equitable apportionment. S.C. Code Ann. § 20-7-476 (Law. Co-op. Supp.). Case law indicates that a family court should first attempt an "in-kind" distribution of the assets before forcing a sale. *See Donahue v. Donahue*, 299 S.C. 353, 360, 384 S.E.2d 741, 745 (1989) (citing *Stevenson v. Stevenson*, 295 S.C. 412, 415, 368 S.E.2d 901, 903 (1988), for the proposition that an in-kind distribution, where feasible, is preferred over a sale of marital property); *Wyatt v. Wyatt*, 293 S.C. 495, 415, 361 S.E.2d 777, 779 (Ct. App. 1987) (holding that where an in-kind distribution is possible, the sale of marital assets is improper, but reversing due to insufficient evidence as to valuation).

A property distribution that required the husband to pay the wife most of her share in cash, rather than an "in kind" distribution, was upheld in *Hough v. Hough*, 312 S.C. 344, 440 S.E.2d 387 (Ct. App. 1994). The trial court determined that the husband should get sixty percent of the marital property, the wife forty percent. He gave the husband the marital home and the marital business, in addition to one car and his jewelry. He gave the wife the other car and her jewelry. He ordered the household goods sold at public auction because the parties had not been able to resolve the values or a method of distribution. He ordered the husband to make up the difference in cash. The husband appealed, but the Court of Appeals affirmed, finding no abuse of discretion "under the circumstances of this case in which the marital home is situated across from the husband's parents' home, and the jewelry business is operated by the husband." *Id.* at 346, 440 S.E.2d at 388.

3. DIVIDING RETIREMENT PENSIONS (QDRO's)

a. In General

The family court has several options for dividing retirement pensions. One way is to allow the person who has the pension to retain the full pension, offsetting other marital assets against it. The offset is easily done if there is an adequate amount of other marital property. Alternatively, the court may also consider utilizing the distribution from each payment method, and decide whether reserved jurisdiction or a QDRO is appropriate. *Belton v. Belton*, Op. No. 2613 (S.C. Ct. App. filed Jan. 13, 1997)(Davis Adv. Sh. No. 1 at 30).

If the court chooses to require a retirement plan administrator to make payments directly to the spouse instead of having the payments be made by the retiring spouse, this can be accomplished through a Qualified Domestic Relations Order (QDRO). A QDRO is a judgment, decree or order, issued for our purposes by a family court, which creates or recognizes the existence of an alternate payee's right to, or assigns to an alternate payee the right to, receive all or a portion of the benefits payable to a participant under a retirement plan. It includes any judgment, decree or order that relates to the provision of child support, alimony, or marital property rights of a spouse, former spouse, child, or other dependent of a participant and which is made pursuant to a state's domestic relations law. An "alternate payee" is any spouse, former spouse, child or other dependent of a participant who is recognized as having a right to receive all, or some portion of, the benefits payable under a plan. The full definition of QDRO can be found in the Employment Retirement Income Security Act (ERISA), 29 U.S.C. § 1056.

The reason why QDROs are important is that pension plans are generally restricted to making payments to one person, and they cannot be assigned or alienated. "Each pension plan shall provide that benefits provided under the plan may not be assigned or alienated." 29 U.S.C. § 1056(1) (Employee Retirement Income Security Act). Payments made from a pension to someone other than the person who earned the pension, other than a surviving spouse, would have tax consequences. However, the tax authorities have recognized that pensions are considered marital property which is subject to division upon divorce, and QDROs are the device which permits this exception to the rule. The tax regulations provide this exception at § 1.401(a)-13(g) of the federal tax code. (This section refers to the definition of QDRO contained in the tax code at 26 U.S.C. § 414(p) (1988). That definition is the same as the one set forth above from 29 U.S.C. § 1056(3) (Employee Retirement Income Security Act).

The IRS requires a QDRO to include specific information for it to qualify for recognition by a plan administrator and for it to effectively transfer retirement funds without immediate taxation. QDROs may be simple or complicated depending on the particular retirement plan and the plan administrator. A private retirement fund arrangement with a combination of deferred compensation, defined benefit funds, and/or profit-sharing needs the services of a CPA with experience in this area who will work with the plan administrator to fashion a QDRO that will be approved by the plan administrator.

A QDRO must provide at a minimum: a) the name and last known mailing address, if any, of the participant and the name and mailing address of each alternate payee; b) the amount or percentage of the benefits of the participant to be paid by the plan to each alternate payee, or the manner in which such amounts or percentage is to be determined; c) the number of payments or period to which such order applies; and d) each plan to which the order applies.

Further, the QDRO will meet the requirements necessary for its recognition only if it: a) does not require a plan to provide any type or form of benefit, or any option, not otherwise provided under the plan; b) does not require the plan to provide increased benefits; and c) does not require the payment of benefits to an alternate payee that are required to be paid to another alternate payee under another order previously determined to be a QDRO.

A QDRO shall not be treated as failing to meet these requirements solely because the order requires that payment of benefits be made to an alternate payee in the case of any payment before a participant separated from service, on or after the date on which the participant attains (or would have attained) the earliest retirement age, that is: a) the date on which the participant is entitled to a distribution under the plan, or b) the later of: (i) the date the participant attains age 50, or (ii) the earliest date on which the participant could begin receiving benefits under the plan if the participant separated from service.

Each retirement plan is required to establish reasonable procedures to determine the qualified status of domestic relations orders and to administer distributions under such qualified orders. Upon the receipt of a QDRO, the plan administrator is required to notify the participant and each alternate payee of the receipt of the order and of the plan's procedures for determining the qualified status of domestic relations orders. Within a reasonable period of time after receipt, the plan administrator is required to determine whether the order is a QDRO and to notify the participant and each alternate payee of such determination.

The procedures applicable to the plan administrator pending the determination of qualification are set forth below:

a) during the period in which the issue of whether a domestic relations order is a qualified domestic relation order is being determined, the plan administrator shall separately account for the amounts, referred as "segregated amounts," which would have been payable to the alternate payee during such period if the order had been determined to be a qualified domestic relations order;

b) if, within eighteen months, the order is determined to be qualified, the plan administrator shall pay the segregated amounts, including interest, to the persons entitled thereto;

c) if, within eighteen months, the order is determined not to be qualified or the issue is not resolved, the plan administrator shall pay the segregated amounts, including interest, to the person who would have been entitled to such amounts if there had been no order;

d) a determination that the plan qualifies after the close of the eighteen month period applies prospectively;

e) the eighteen month period begins with the date on which the first payment would be required under the domestic relations order.

It can take quite a long time to receive approval of a QDRO from a plan administrator. The preferred practice is to state in the decree the general provisions of the division of the retirement funds with leave to submit a Supplemental Decree which deals only with the requirements of a QDRO. This will simplify the process with a plan administrator.

The plan administrator plays a key role in insuring that the client receives the funds ordered by the court. With proper authorization from the spouse owning the retirement account, the plan administrator may also assist in the attorney's preparation for trial by relaying documents for review by the CPA in deter mining values and the specific provisions.

It is important to involve a CPA who is familiar in this area to assist in valuing the retirement accounts and transferring them by way of a QDRO to the receiving spouse. There are myriad technical details that may affect any given case, and the only way to be sure that the asset has actually been obtained for the client is to work with a CPA. The expense of a CPA will be small compared to the benefit received by the client.

Almost every retirement plan must provide a qualified joint and survivor annuity (QJSA) benefit to a participant who is married at the time of retirement. I.R.C. §§ 401(a)(11) and 417. The QJSA must pay the participant's surviving spouse at least fifty percent of the benefit payable to the participant during the participant's life. The plan must also provide a qualified pre-retirement survivor annuity (QPSA) if the participant dies while vested under the plan. I.R.C. § 401(a)(11). The surviving pre-retirement survivor annuity is not paid until the participant would have reached the earliest retirement age under the plan. I.R.C. § 417(c). The participant cannot elect a different form of benefit without the spouse's consent. I.R.C. § 417(a)(2). The spouse must consent in writing before the plan may pay benefits to the participant in any form other than a joint and survivor annuity. The spouse has a veto power over the participant's selection of any other benefit. The spouse must also consent to any plan loan for which the participant's benefits are used as security. I.R.C. § 417(a) (4).

One would be well-advised to write, on behalf of the spouse client, to the plan administrators of the participant's plans, stating that the spouse does not consent to any distribution from any tax-qualified retirement plan in which the participant has an interest, and that any prior consent is no longer valid and is revoked.

The only type of plan not subject to the rules is a defined contribution plan (profit-sharing plan) that pays the participant's full benefit at death to the participant's surviving spouse. I.R.C. § 401(a)(11)(B).

b. QDROs Under the South Carolina Retirement System

A qualified domestic relations order (QDRO) must be used to access retirement benefits payable through the South Carolina State Retirement System. S.C. Code Ann. §§ 9-18-10 through 9-18-100 (Law. Co-op. Supp.). A QDRO may require the South Carolina Retirement System to pay to the spouse of a member or retired member of the retirement system the following benefits: (1) retirement benefit, (2) withdrawal or refund of contributions, (3) disability benefit, or (4) death benefit. No other benefits may be paid to an alternate payee. S.C. Code Ann. § 9-18-10 (Law. Co-op. Supp.).

The administrator of the retirement system has the exclusive authority to determine if a judgment qualifies as a QDRO. S.C. Code Ann. § 9-18-30(A) (Law.

Co-op. Supp.). If the determination is negative, the aggrieved party may appeal to the Administrative Law Judge Division and may petition the court which issued the order to amend the order so that it will be qualified. S.C. Code Ann. § 9-18-30(B) (Law. Co-op. Supp.).

The statute is unduly restrictive to the point of defeating the purpose of a QDRO. For example, although a QDRO is typically used to equitably divide property of the parties, this cannot be fully accomplished under a South Carolina Retirement System QDRO because the statute does not allow an alternate payee to designate a beneficiary of the award in the event the alternative payee predeceases the plan's participant. In effect, in such a situation, a portion of the amount awarded to the alternate payee will revert to the plan's participant.

4. SEQUESTRATION, TRUSTEES, AND RECEIVERS

The family court has a broad array of tools at its disposal to aid it in identifying, protecting, and distributing the marital assets. S.C. Code Ann. § 20-7-475 (Law. Co-op Supp.) allows sequestration of marital property at any stage of the proceedings "where it appears to the court that personal jurisdiction may not be obtained over an absent party or where a party refuses to comply with an order of the court." Section 20-7-475 only applies to equitable division awards, not support orders. *See Lloyd v. Lloyd*, 295 S.C. 55, 367 S.E.2d 153 (1988) (reversing the sequestration of a husband's retirement account that was ordered by the trial judge to enforce a support order).

The trial judge has the inherent power to appoint a sequestrator *sua sponte* to protect the interests of the parties. This is part of the court's broad discretion to use "any other reasonable means to achieve equity between the parties." S.C. Code Ann. § 20-7-476 (Law. Co-op Supp.). *See Murphy v. Murphy*, 329 S.C. 324, 461 S.E.2d 39 (1995) (affirming the family court's *sua sponte* sequestration of the husband's investment account, although neither party petitioned for it, after concluding that the husband had not provided a proper accounting of the account and that substantial funds and stocks had been depleted from it).

In addition to the option of sequestration, the family court is empowered to appoint a trustee, or even a receiver, when the parties are having trouble agreeing how to divide the property and it appears that one of the parties may be trying to waste or hide marital assets. In *Whetstone v. Whetstone*, 309 S.C. 227, 420 S.E.2d 877 (Ct. App. 1992), the husband did not make a full disclosure of his assets and he failed to account for monies received in his business. He also appeared to be trying to avoid the orders of the family court and to be hiding marital assets. The family court initially appointed a trustee by consent order to oversee the marital assets, but eventually the court ordered that the husband's assets, including his business, be put under the control of a receiver.

5. NOTICES ABOUT PROCEEDINGS

Either party may record a notice of the pendency of domestic relations proceedings involving title to real estate pursuant to S.C. Code Ann. § 20-7-477 (Law. Co-op. Supp.).

The statute also provides that, once the decision of the court has been filed, it has the force and effect of a judgment of the court of common pleas. A form for the Transcript of Judgment that can be filed to alert title examiners about the family court's decision regarding real estate is provided in S.C. Code Ann. § 20-7-478 (Law. Co-op. Supp.).

6. INTEREST ON DISTRIBUTIONS

Fixed awards of money for equitable distribution shall accrue interest at the post-judgment rate from the date of the judgment or the date each payment of specified periodic payments becomes due. *Casey v. Casey*, 311 S.C. 243, 428 S.E.2d 714 (1993). However, an equitable division award which does not require a cash payment from one party to the other is not subject to interest. *Christy v. Christy*, 317 S.C. 145, 452 S.E.2d 1 (Ct. App. 1994).

When Mr. and Mrs. Christy divorced, the trial court divided the marital estate so that neither was required to make a cash payment to the other. Rather, the parties were to make appropriate transfers of titles to various properties. For example, the husband was awarded the business and the wife the marital home. The case was appealed and the husband claimed entitlement to interest from the date of entry of the trial court's decision, citing S.C. Code Ann. § 34-31-20(B) (Law. Co-op. 1976), which provides:

> All money decrees and judgments of courts enrolled or entered shall draw interest according to law, the legal interest shall be at the rate of fourteen percent per annum.

The Court of Appeals affirmed the denial of interest to the husband, noting that the equitable distribution award was not an order to make a cash payment, but merely a distribution of property.

CHAPTER EIGHT
PATERNITY

CHAPTER EIGHT
PATERNITY[19]

A. IN GENERAL

The issue of paternity is sometimes the threshold question in actions for child custody and support. For many years in South Carolina, the common law, as stated in *McGlohon v. Harlan*, 254 S.C. 207, 174 S.E.2d 753 (1970), prevailed:

> The common law recognized no legal duty on the part of a father to provide for the support of an illegitimate child. He was said to be a *filius nullius*, the child of nobody. There was no procedure for determining paternity. An illegitimate child had no rights against an asserted parent that could be enforced in court.

Id. at 211, 174 S.E.2d at 755.

Much has changed in paternity law since that time. Today, parents are obligated to support *all* of their children:

> Any able-bodied person capable of earning a livelihood who shall, without just cause or excuse, abandon or fail to provide reasonable support to his or her . . . minor unmarried *legitimate or illegitimate* child dependent on him or her shall be deemed guilty of a misdemeanor and upon conviction shall be imprisoned for a term of not exceeding one year or be fined not less than three hundred dollars, or both, in the discretion of the circuit court.

S.C. Code Ann. § 20-7-90(A) (Law. Co-op. 1976) (emphasis added).

---

[19] Parentage is the gender neutral term for paternity and maternity. There are rare cases when one must prove that a woman is the mother of a child. However, the reality is that men, not women, are the objects of most proceedings to determine parentage. "Paternity," "alleged father," and "putative father" are used in the text of this chapter rather than gender neutral terms to reflect this reality and to be consistent with the language used in most legislation.

Major changes in paternity law occurred in 1984 with the enactment of the Determination of Paternity Act (S.C. Code Ann. §§ 20-7-952 to 20-7-957 (Law. Co-op. 1976, Supp.)); in 1994 with the passage of the Uniform Interstate Family Support Act (UIFSA) (S.C. Code Ann. §§ 20-7-960 to 20-7-1170 (Law. Co-op. Supp.)); and in 1995 and 1996 with the enactment of and amendments to the Administrative Process for Establishing and Enforcing Paternity and Child Support Act (S.C. Code Ann. §§ 20-7-960 to 20-7-1170 (Law. Co-op. Supp.)).[20]

These sections of the Children's Code present specific rules and procedures for determining paternity, including standing, jurisdiction, venue, genetic testing, and special procedural and evidentiary rules for judicial and administrative determinations of paternity. This chapter provides an overview of South Carolina paternity laws, but many of the details are omitted and reference to specific statutes should be made by lawyers handling paternity cases.

B. JURISDICTION, VENUE AND STANDING

The family court and the Child Support Enforcement Division of the Department of Social Services (the Division) share jurisdiction over proceedings to determine paternity. Although S.C. Code Ann. § 20-7-420(7) (Law. Co-op. 1976) indicates that the family court has exclusive jurisdiction, other legislation gives the Division concurrent jurisdiction to determine paternity. S.C. Code Ann. § 20-7-9505 (Law. Co-op. Supp.) provides: "[n]otwithstanding Section 20-7-420 and any other provision of law, the Child Support Enforcement Division of the Department of Social Services also has jurisdiction to establish paternity ... in cases brought pursuant to Title IV-D of the Social Security Act in accordance with this article (the

---

[20] Additional legislative action can be anticipated as South Carolina responds to federal mandates contained in the Personal Responsibility and Work Opportunity Reconciliation Act of 1996, Pub. L. No. 104-193, 110 Stat. 2105 (1996). The legislation calls for improving the effectiveness of programs to encourage voluntary acknowledgments of paternity, streamlining the process for establishing paternity when it is denied, and enhancing the level of cooperation by welfare recipients in identifying and helping locate the fathers of their children. The specific changes contemplated by the Act are discussed in Legler, "The Coming Revolution in Child Support Policy: Implications of the 1996 Welfare Act," 30 *Fam. L. Q.* 519 (Fall, 1996).

Division assists people receiving public assistance and anyone else who requests its assistance upon payment of a nominal fee).

The Division is defined as a tribunal in the Uniform Interstate Family Support Act (UIFSA). "'Tribunal' means a court, administrative agency, or quasi-judicial entity authorized to establish, enforce, and modify support orders or to determine parentage." S.C. Code Ann. § 20-7-965(23) (Law. Co-op. Supp.). "The tribunals of this State are the family court and the support enforcement agency. For purposes of continuing exclusive jurisdiction under this subarticle, the tribunals of this State have concurrent jurisdiction to establish, modify, and enforce child support in cases being administered pursuant to Title IV-D of the Social Security Act." S.C. Code Ann. § 20-7-970 (Law. Co-op. Supp.). UIFSA specifically provides that "a tribunal of this State has jurisdiction, to the extent otherwise authorized by law, to ... (6) determine parentage." S.C. Code Ann. § 20-7-1025(B) (Law. Co-op. Supp.).

A very broad long arm jurisdiction statute asserts personal jurisdiction over nonresidents in paternity (and other) proceedings. An older statute gives the family court personal jurisdiction over "[a]ny person who has sexual intercourse in this State," for purposes of paternity proceedings "with respect to a child who may have been conceived by that act of intercourse." S.C. Code Ann. § 20-7-953(A) (Law. Co-op. 1976). UIFSA extends the concept of long arm jurisdiction as broadly as possible. The family court may exercise personal jurisdiction over a nonresident in a proceeding to establish, enforce, or modify a support order or to determine parentage if:

(1) the individual is personally served in South Carolina;

(2) the individual submits to the jurisdiction of this state by consent, by entering a general appearance, or by filing a responsive pleading having the effect of waiving any contest to personal jurisdiction;

(3) the individual resided with the child in South Carolina;

(4) the individual resided in South Carolina and provided prenatal expenses or support for the child;

(5) the child resides in South Carolina as a result of the acts or directives of the individual;

(6) the individual engaged in sexual intercourse in South Carolina and the child may have been conceived by that act of intercourse; or

(7) there is any other basis consistent with the constitutions of South Carolina or the United States for the exercise of personal jurisdiction.

S.C. Code Ann. § 20-7-980 (Law. Co-op. Supp.).

Paternity actions may be brought in the county in which the child or putative father resides or is found, or, if the putative father is dead, in the county where probate proceedings have been or could be brought. S.C. Code Ann. § 20-7-420 (Law. Co-op. 1976). In a case brought by an adult child to establish paternity and obtain support in the form of college expenses from her putative father, the putative father challenged venue, arguing that his county of residence had continuing jurisdiction over the action because of a prior proceeding there which included a paternity determination. *Jennings v. Dargan*, 308 S.C. 317, 417 S.E.2d 646 (Ct. App. 1992). The Court of Appeals held that the county of residence of the child was a proper venue for a paternity action even where a prior paternity proceeding had been initiated in another county. The court pointed out that the prior action had been dismissed by agreement of the mother and putative father; therefore, the county in which the first proceeding was brought maintained no continuing jurisdiction over the subsequent proceeding.

A paternity action may be brought by:

(1) A child;

(2) The natural mother of a child;

(3) Any person in whose care a child has been placed;

(4) An authorized agency, including, but not limited to, the Department of Social Services, pursuant to the provisions of

> Chapter 5 of Title 43, and any other person or agency pursuant to the provisions of §§ 20-7-435 [Persons who may institute proceeding respecting neglected or delinquent children] and 20-7-840 [Persons who may file petition for support]; or
>
> (5) A person who claims to be the father of a child.

S.C. Code Ann. § 20-7-952(C) (Law. Co-op. 1976).

In a UIFSA proceeding, an action on behalf of a minor's child can be maintained by the minor or by a guardian *ad litem* or other legal representative. S.C. Code Ann. § 20-7-1030 (Law. Co-op. Supp.).

This interaction of these statutes with other state law which requires minors to appear by guardian *ad litem* has not been considered in any appellate case. S.C. Code Ann. § 15-5-310 (Law. Co-op. 1976) ("When an infant is a party he must appear by guardian *ad litem* ....").

C. DETERMINING PATERNITY

1. PRESUMPTION OF LEGITIMACY; EVIDENCE

Children born during the course of a marriage are presumed to be the children of the husband and wife of that marriage. The Supreme Court reaffirmed this in *Chandler v. Merrell*, 291 S.C. 224, 353 S.E.2d 133 (1989). The facts involved an intervention in an adoption case by a man who claimed to be the real father of a child who had been conceived and born during the mother's marriage to another man. The intervenor offered evidence of his sexual access to the mother during the relevant period as well as evidence showing that the blood types presented a better-than-average possibility that he was the real father. The Supreme Court, however, upheld the trial judge's ruling that the child was not the child of the intervenor, saying:

> The presumption of legitimacy is one of the strongest known to law. Every child born in wedlock is presumed to be legitimate. *Hudson v. Blanton*, 282 S.C. 70, 316 S.E.2d 432 (Ct. App. 1984).
>
> . . .
>
> The presumption of a husband's access to his wife may be overcome only by the clearest of evidence that it was impossible for him to father his wife's child because of impotence or imbecility, or by reason of his entire absence during the period of conception.

Id. at 225-226, 353 S.E.2d at 134-135 (citations omitted). The Court concluded that mere proof of the intervenor's access is not enough to overcome the presumption and establish his paternity.

The testimony of a husband and wife as to "any relevant matter" is admissible at a paternity trial, including testimony regarding parentage and marriage. S.C. Code Ann. § 20-7-956(8) (Law. Co-op. 1976). Prior to the adoption of the Determination of Paternity Act the rule was that any evidence of a married couple's sexual non-access to each other during the time of conception was only admissible if offered by third parties. *Barr's Next of Kin v. Cherokee, Inc.*, 220 S.C. 447, 68 S.E.2d 440 (1951) (overturning for insufficiency of evidence the ruling of the trial court that a decedent's illegitimate daughter was entitled to all of the decedent's Workmen's Compensation benefits). Some cases have interpreted the statutory provision as allowing a husband and wife to testify about sexual non-access to each other during the time of conception, thereby expressly overruling the prior rule as stated in *Barr*. *See South Carolina DSS, on Behalf of Roseboro v. Burris*, 297 S.C. 537, 377 S.E.2d 578 (1989) (allowing testimony by the husband and wife of non-access and the putative father's testimony that he had sexual relations with the mother which supported the family court's finding that the putative father, not the husband, was the child's father).

Expert opinions as to time of conception and any other "relevant and competent" evidence the court deems admissible are admissible on the issue of paternity. S.C. Code Ann. § 20-7-956(A)(7) (Law. Co-op. Supp.).

Evidence of a mother's sexual activity is irrelevant and immaterial in a paternity proceeding, except for impeachment purposes, unless the specific instances of sexual activity are within the critical period of conception. *See South Carolina DSS v. Brown*, 272 S.C. 568, 569, 253 S.E.2d 100, 100 (1979). *See also Kennington v. Catoe*, 68 S.C. 470, 47 S.E. 719 (1904).

> It is manifest that mere reputation of the wife for unchastity, especially when such reputation was before marriage, or after birth of the child, would have no such tendency [to rebut the presumption that a child born during coverture is legitimate]; nor would her unchaste conduct with reference to other men have such tendency, unless it related closely to the period when the child was begotten.

Id. at 473, 47 S.E. 720.

The family court may examine a child for the absence or presence of similarities in appearance between the child and the putative father. S.C. Code Ann. § 20-7-956(B) (Law. Co-op. Supp.).

2. ADMINISTRATIVE PROCESSES FOR DETERMINING PATERNITY; GENETIC TESTING

Paternity determinations may be litigated in the family court or handled administratively by the Child Support Enforcement Division of the Department of Social Services. Although a statute provides that paternity actions are civil non-jury actions (S.C. Code Ann. § 20-7-953(C) & (D) (Law. Co-op. 1976)), the legislature approved in 1995 an administrative process for determining paternity (S.C. Code Ann. §§ 20-7-960 to 20-7-1170 (Law. Co-op. Supp.). UIFSA also provides an administrative process for establishing the paternity of South Carolina residents upon requests from mothers and children who live in other states. S.C. Code Ann. §§ 20-7-960 to 20-7-1170 (Law. Co-op. Supp.). The UIFSA procedures are explained in more detail for in the chapter on child support, to which they also apply.

The Administrative Process for Establishing and Enforcing Paternity and Child Support begins with a notice of financial responsibility from the Child Support

Enforcement Division to an alleged father. S.C. Code Ann. § 20-7-9515 (Law. Co-op. Supp.). The notice informs the father of the allegation of paternity and provides additional information, including the right to request a court hearing. An alleged father has thirty days to object to the notice of financial responsibility and make a written request for a court hearing. S.C. Code Ann. § 20-7-9540(A) (Law. Co-op. Supp.). If no request is made for a court hearing, the alleged father can be required to attend a "negotiation conference" with the Division to discuss the allegation of paternity. S.C. Code Ann. § 20-7-9515 (Law. Co-op. Supp.).

If an alleged father fails to attend the negotiation conference and does not make a timely written denial of paternity, the Division may enter an order declaring the alleged father to be the legal father of the child. S.C. Code Ann. § 20-7-9550(B) (Law. Co-op. Supp.). This order takes effect in fifteen days unless the alleged father shows good cause for missing the negotiation conference or not filing a written denial of paternity. There is no requirement that a default order declaring paternity be approved by a family court judge, although a default order setting child support must be approved by a family court judge. S.C. Code Ann. § 20-7-9530 (Law. Co-op. Supp.).

If an alleged father attends the negotiation conference and admits paternity, the Division can issue a consent order finding that the person is the father of the child and setting an agreed upon amount of child support (the amount must be consistent with the child support guidelines). S.C. Code Ann. § 20-7-9525 (Law. Co-op. Supp.). The consent order does not have to be approved by a family court judge. When the order is filed with the appropriate clerk of court, it has all the force, effect, and remedies of an order of the court. S.C. Code Ann. § 20-7-9525(B) (Law. Co-op. Supp.).

If an alleged parent attends the negotiation conference but denies paternity, the Division can issue a subpoena ordering the alleged parent to submit to paternity genetic testing, if the testimony and supplementary evidence presented at the negotiation conference "demonstrate a reasonable probability that the alleged father had sexual intercourse with the child's mother during the probable time of the child's conception or if the evidence shows a probable existence of a presumption." S.C. Code Ann. § 20-7-9550(A) (Law. Co-op. Supp.). "A reasonable probability of sexual intercourse during the possible time of conception may be established by affidavit of the child's mother." *Id.*

The Division may apply to the family court for an order compelling an alleged parent to submit to genetic testing, "if the rights of others and the interests of justice require." The family court must enter the order compelling the alleged parent to submit to genetic testing "if the court finds reasonable cause to believe that the alleged father is the natural or presumed father of the child. S.C. Code Ann. § 20-7-9550(C) (Law. Co-op. Supp.).

The family court has the power upon its own motion or that of any "interested party" to order the mother, the child, and the putative father to undergo genetic tests. S.C. Code Ann. § 20-7-954 (Law. Co-op. Supp.). The court may also order any "male witness [who] offers testimony indicating that his act of intercourse with the natural mother may have resulted in the conception of the child" to undergo genetic testing or other tests to determine whether he is the child's father. S.C. Code Ann. § 20-7-956(C) (Law. Co-op. Supp.).

Results of genetic tests or the refusal of a party to submit to such tests are admissible at a paternity hearing as are voluntary acknowledgments of paternity, foreign paternity determinations, and paternity indicated on birth certificates. S.C. Code Ann. § 20-7-956(A) (Law. Co-op. Supp.). Genetic test results must be "properly verified to show the chain of custody of blood specimens," and, unless challenged by a motion at least twenty days prior to the date of trial, the results "must be introduced and admitted without the foundation testimony or other proof of authority or accuracy." *Id.*

If the results of paternity tests exclude or tend to exclude the possibility that the witness is not the father, his testimony must be "stricken from the record and disregarded." S.C. Code § 20-7-956(C) (Law. Co-op. Supp.). Even where the tests show a substantial likelihood of paternity, the results must be weighed along with the other evidence. *Id.* The results are not to be "viewed as absolutely determinative of the issue of paternity" but rather as establishing a rebuttable *prima facie* case of paternity. *South Carolina DSS v. Bacot*, 280 S.C. 485, 489, 313 S.E.2d 45, 48 (Ct. App. 1984) (upholding the family court's finding that the appellant was the father of the child).

3. SETTLEMENTS AND VOLUNTARY AGREEMENTS

Paternity settlements should be handled with care. The child's current and potential interests should be considered. In order to strengthen the finding of paternity, the child should be represented by a guardian *ad litem*. Also, the guardian and the trial judge should also ensure that the settlement is in the best interests of the child and that it is properly reviewed by the court. In *Jennings v. Dargan*, 308 S.C. 317, 417 S.E.2d 646 (Ct. App. 1992), the Court of Appeals voided a settlement of a paternity action (which included no admission of paternity) between a mother and a putative father approximately twenty years after it was entered into because the family court had held no hearing after the settlement and had made no finding that the settlement was a fair one in the best interests of the minor. This was despite the fact that the child had been represented by a guardian *ad litem*. The twenty-year-old plaintiff in college was allowed to maintain the action to prove paternity and to seek assistance with college expenses.

The administrative process for determining paternity and child support does not provide for the safeguards suggested above. Also, UIFSA specifically allows interstate child support actions to proceed without joining the children as parties. S.C. Code Ann. § 20-7-1095 (Law. Co-op. Supp.). It is not clear that children will be bound by a determination of paternity in cases where they are not joined or do not have guardians *ad litem* appointed. If a child later learns that someone else is the father and wants to have the real father declared such by the court, will the child be bound by a determination of paternity via a proceeding in which they did not participate? One might safely predict future litigation resulting in a small percentage of cases.

4. FINALITY OF A PATERNITY DETERMINATION

If a finding of paternity is made, either by operation of law or court decree, it will be difficult to challenge at a later date. A foreign paternity determination whether established through administrative or judicial process is admissible at a hearing to determine paternity, and this determination "creates a conclusive presumption of paternity." S.C. Code Ann. § 20-7-956 (Law. Co-op. Supp.). One assumes a paternity determination made in a South Carolina judicial or administrative proceeding will be treated similarly. UIFSA specifically prohibits a party whose parentage of a child has been determined by law from pleading nonparentage as a defense to a proceeding under UIFSA. S.C. Code Ann. § 20-7-1095 (Law. Co-op. Supp.).

One cannot challenge on the basis of fraud a finding of paternity in a divorce proceeding if more than a year has passed since the hearing. *Mr. G v. Mrs. G*, ___ S.C. ___, 465 S.E.2d 101 (Ct. App. 1995). Two and a half years after his divorce, Mr. G sought an order declaring him not to be the father of the child for whom he was ordered to pay child support in the divorce decree. Mr. G alleged that his former wife repeatedly lied to him about his being the little girl's natural father and that he only recently learned of her deceit.

The Court of Appeals ruled that the former wife's fraud was intrinsic, not extrinsic, fraud and, therefore, he could not attack the judgment which was more than a year old. The court relied on the fact that Mr. G had an opportunity to deny paternity during the divorce proceedings, but he had admitted paternity and agreed to pay child support. Judge Hearn dissented from the majority opinion. She believes the fraud was extrinsic, not intrinsic, and she believes the extrinsic-intrinsic distinction should be discarded because of its propensity for confusion and inequity. Furthermore, she believes the trial court should not have granted the Rule 12(b)(6) motion to dismiss due to Rule 60(b)(5) which permits relief where "it is no longer equitable that the judgment should have prospective application." The majority did not consider the Rule 60(b)(5) issue because the family court never ruled on it.

D. ARTIFICIAL INSEMINATION

A husband who consents for his wife to conceive a child through artificial insemination with the understanding that the child will be treated as his own is the legal father of the child and will be charged with all of the legal responsibilities of paternity, including support. Written consent is not required. "Husband's consent to his wife's impregnation by artificial insemination may be express, or it may be implied from conduct which evidences knowledge of the procedure and failure to object." *In re Baby Doe*, 291 S.C. 389, 393, 353 S.E.2d 877, 879 (1987) (affirming the trial court's order holding the husband responsible for the support of a child born to his wife as a result of artificial insemination with sperm donated by an anonymous third-party donor) (citing *R.S. v. R.S.*, 9 Kan. App.2d 39, 670 P.2d 923 (1983)).

E. REQUIREMENT FOR A NEW BIRTH CERTIFICATE

Once paternity has been established, either by adjudication or acknowledgment, a new birth certificate which reflects the name of the father must be prepared for the child. In instances where the court has made a "determination of paternity pursuant to Section 20-7-952," the certificate is to reflect the name of the father determined by the court. S.C. Code Ann. § 44-63-163 (Law. Co-op. Supp.) states:

> If the surname of the child is not decreed by the court, the request for the certificate must specify the surname to be placed on the certificate. When an amended certificate is prepared, the original certificate and certified copy of the court order must be placed in a sealed file not to be subject to inspection except by order of the family court.

In cases in which the putative father admits his paternity:

> A certificate must be prepared for a child born out of wedlock in this State to include the name of the father upon receipt of a sworn acknowledgment of paternity signed by both parents to include the surname by which the child is to be known. However, if the reputed father or the mother is deceased, if another man is shown as the father of the child on the original birth certificate, or if the original birth certificate states that the mother was married, a new certificate may be prepared only when a determination of paternity is made by the family court pursuant to Section 20-7-952. A paternity acknowledgment is not subject to inspection except upon order of the family court.

S.C. Code Ann. § 44-63-165 (Law. Co-op. Supp.).

CHAPTER NINE
TERMINATION OF PARENTAL RIGHTS

CHAPTER NINE
TERMINATION OF PARENTAL RIGHTS

A. IN GENERAL

The family court may order the termination of parental rights for any of the following reasons:

1) abuse or neglect which is unlikely to stop[21];

2) the child has been removed from the home for at least six months and the parent has not remedied the conditions which caused the removal;

3) willful failure to visit for six months;

4) willful failure to provide support for six months;

5) a finding that the presumptive father is not the biological father and that the child's best interests will be served by such termination; or

6) the inability of the parent to care for the child due to a diagnosable condition that is unlikely to change within a reasonable time.

S.C. Code Ann. § 20-7-1572 (Law. Co-op. Supp.).

The South Carolina Code provides that termination of parental rights statutes are to be "liberally construed in order to ensure prompt judicial procedures for freeing minor children from the custody and control of their parents by terminating the parent-child relationship. The interests of the child shall prevail if the child's interest and the parental rights conflict." S.C. Code Ann. § 20-7-1578 (Law. Co-op. 1976). *See also Dorn v. Criddle*, 306 S.C. 189, 410 S.E.2d 590 (Ct. App. 1991)

---

[21] As this book does not cover actions for abuse or neglect, this chapter does not discuss termination cases based on abuse or neglect.

(holding that a father's abandonment was not excused by his drug and alcohol abuse); *South Carolina DSS v. Vanderhorst*, 287 S.C. 554, 340 S.E.2d 149 (1986) (refusing because of the "best interests of the child" to reverse the trial court's termination of parental rights).

In cases decided before and after the enactment of this legislation in 1984, South Carolina courts held that "statutes providing for the termination of parental rights are to be strictly construed in favor of the parent and the preservation of the relationship of parent and child. *Goff v. Benedict*, 252 S.C. 83, 165 S.E.2d 269 (1969)." *Leone v. Dilullo*, 294 S.C. 410, 413, 365 S.E.2d 39, 40 (Ct. App. 1988). In a dissenting opinion in *Hopkins v. South Carolina DSS*, 313 S.C. 322, 330, 437 S.E.2d 542, 546 (1993), Justice Toal cites § 20-7-1578 as controlling how termination of parental rights statutes are to be construed. The majority opinion does not discuss the applicability of § 20-7-1578, but states "[p]arental rights may be terminated only upon clear and convincing evidence" and "[t]he public policy of this State is to reunite parents and children." *Id.* at 326, 437 S.E.2d at 544.

Immoral conduct by a parent does not justify termination of parental rights, but it might justify not awarding custody and requiring supervised visitation. *Bevis v. Bevis*, 254 S.C. 345, 175 S.E.2d 398 (1970) (affirming family court's determination that the mother had not abandoned the children and that termination of her parental rights was not justified by her adultery and post-divorce immoral lifestyle).

B. APPOINTMENT OF COUNSEL AND GUARDIAN *AD LITEM*

As of January 1, 1997, family courts are required to appoint legal counsel for any person subject to a termination of parental rights proceeding who cannot afford legal representation, unless the defendant is in default. This includes parents, guardians, or any other persons whose parental rights are subject to termination. S.C. Code Ann. § 20-7-1570(A) (Law. Co-op. Supp.).

The family court is also required to appoint a guardian *ad litem* for any child who is the subject of termination proceedings. S.C. Code Ann. § 20-7-1570(B) (Law. Co-op. Supp.).

If a termination proceeding is contested, an attorney must be appointed for the child's guardian *ad litem*, whether or not the guardian *ad litem* is a lawyer. S.C. Code Ann. § 20-7-1570(B) (Law. Co-op. Supp.).

If the proceeding is not contested, an attorney must be appointed for a nonlawyer guardian *ad litem* if the guardian *ad litem* requests one after finding that appointment of counsel is necessary to protect the rights and interests of the child. S.C. Code Ann. § 20-7-1570(B) (Law. Co-op. Supp.).

The statute appears to give a nonlawyer guardian *ad litem*, not the family court judge, the power to decide if an attorney must be appointed. That is, it appears that a family court judge does not have any discretion to deny a nonlawyer guardian *ad litem*'s request for appointment of counsel. One might think that the family court has the inherent authority to review the need for appointed counsel and to reject a guardian *ad litem*'s request for appointment of legal counsel, if the court concludes that one is not needed to protect the interests of the child. However, it is clear from the statute that the legislature did not intend for the family court to have such discretion, because it specifically provides for the family court's case by case review of requests for appointment of counsel when the guardians *ad litem* are lawyers. S.C. Code Ann. § 20-7-1570(B) (Law. Co-op. Supp.). The statute does not provide for case by case review when the guardians *ad litem* are not lawyers.

C. STANDING

An action to terminate parental rights may be brought by a child protective services agency (typically DSS) or by "any interested party." S.C. Code Ann. § 20-7-1564 (Law. Co-op. 1976). This includes foster care review boards. *In re Lide*, 284 S.C. 419, 327 S.E.2d 70 (1985). It also includes foster parents. *Greenville County DSS v. Bowes*, 313 S.C. 188, 192, 437 S.E.2d 107, 109 (1993); *Hopkins v. South Carolina DSS*, 313 S.C. 322, 437 S.E.2d 542 (1993); *South Carolina DSS v. Pritchett*, 296 S.C. 517, 374 S.E.2d 500 (Ct. App. 1988); *Boyer v. Boyer*, 291 S.C. 183, 352 S.E.2d 514 (Ct. App. 1987).

D. WILLFULNESS

Determining whether a parent's failure to support or visit a child is willful within the meaning of the statute "is a question of intent to be determined in each case from all the facts and circumstances. *Berry v. Ianuario*, 286 S.C. 522, 335 S.E.2d 250 (Ct. App. 1985); *Bevis v. Bevis*, 254 S.C. 345, 175 S.E.2d 398 (1970)." *South Carolina DSS v. Broome*, 307 S.C. 48, 52, 413 S.E.2d 835, 838 (1992). (*Berry* upheld the termination of a natural father's parental rights where the father had failed either to provide support or to visit within the six months prior to the action for termination. *Bevis* upheld the family court's finding that a natural mother had not abandoned her children, but in fact had persistent and continued contacts with them over the years.) In making a determination of willfulness, the trial judge is given wide discretion.

Conduct stemming from drug or alcohol abuse is not excused because of its origin. In *Dorn v. Criddle*, 306 S.C. 189, 410 S.E.2d 590 (Ct. App. 1991), the father argued that his failure to pay support could not be considered willful because it was caused by drug and alcohol abuse. The Court of Appeals refused to recognize a *per se* rule that the abuse of drugs and alcohol negates willfulness in termination of parental right cases. However, it remanded the case for a trial *de novo* because the appeal took three years.

When a child has been taken into protective custody, a failure to follow a treatment plan established by DSS may be considered a willful failure to visit and serve as a basis for termination of parental rights. *South Carolina DSS v. Broome*, 307 S.C. 48, 52, 413 S.E.2d 835, 838 (1992), was a successful action by the Department of Social Services (DSS) to terminate the mother's parental rights for lack of visitation. DSS initially took emergency custody of the daughter two days after her birth because of a "threat of harm" by the mother. The treatment plan DSS developed for the mother's schizophrenia included attending Parents Anonymous, getting continuing mental health treatment, and taking medication. During the four years while DSS had custody of the child, DSS scheduled ninety-four visits. The mother actually visited only thirty-five times in those four years. Additionally, although support had been set at $30 per month, the mother paid only $250 in support payments in 1988. The Supreme Court determined that the mother's failure to follow any portion of the DSS plan constituted willfulness.

Parental rights may not be terminated if a court order prevents a parent from exercising visitation (S.C. Code Ann. § 20-7-1572(3) (Law. Co-op. 1976)). However, parental rights may be terminated for willful failure to visit if the order outlines a mechanism through which visitation can resume and the parent fails to comply with the requirements of the order. In *In re M.*, 312 S.C. 248, 439 S.E.2d 857 (Ct. App. 1994), the court upheld the termination of a father's parental rights for willful failure to visit his son although the father's visitation rights had been suspended by a court order following a finding that he had sexually abused his son. The father was ordered to participate in psychotherapy until his therapist determined that he no longer needed treatment. He made three brief visits to counselors, receiving treatment from none of them. The father stated that he did not need treatment and would not seek it even if it meant he could not resume visitation with his son. The Court of Appeals concluded that "[t]he father's defiant refusal to meet the reasonable conditions placed on his right to visitation was tantamount to an election not to visit M. unless he could do it on his own terms." *Id.* at 250, 439 S.E.2d at 859.

Failure to visit for more than six months due to incarceration is considered willful conduct. In *South Carolina DSS v. Richardson*, 298 S.C. 130, 378 S.E.2d 601 (Ct. App. 1989), the court affirmed the termination of a Florida prisoner's parental rights due to his failure to visit his daughter. The court also noted the absence of any evidence that he ever attempted to contact her.

"Conduct of the parent which evinces a settled purpose to forego parental duties may fairly be characterized as 'willful,' because it manifests a conscious indifference to the rights of the child to receive support and consortium from the parent." *Leone v. Dilullo*, 294 S.C. 410, 413, 365 S.E.2d 39, 40 (Ct. App. 1988) (affirming the termination of the mother's parental rights because of a pattern of indifference to her two children over a period of five years).

Conversely, "an act or course of conduct by a parent which is done through force of circumstances or dire necessity" is not 'willful.' *Hamby v. Hamby*, 264 S.C. 614, 617, 216 S.E.2d 536, 538 (1975) (upholding the family court's finding of willful abandonment where a father had not visited his child for several years, had never supported the child, and had willfully engaged in conduct resulting in his imprisonment). Parental conduct that can be reasonably explained will not be the basis for a finding of willful failure to visit. *See also Wilson v. Higgins*, 294 S.C. 300, 363 S.E.2d 911 (Ct. App. 1987) (reversing the family court's termination of parental rights of a mother who was prevented from visiting by the child's father).

The parental rights of the putative father of an illegitimate child should not be terminated for failure to visit where the father has not been allowed to visit the child. In *Hopkins v. South Carolina DSS*, 313 S.C. 322, 437 S.E.2d 542 (1993), the trial court found and the Supreme Court affirmed that there was no evidence that the putative father had abandoned the child by failing to visit for six months where the record showed that he was not permitted to visit the child which had been placed with foster parents by DSS until three months after the child's guardian *ad litem* had first sought termination and only two months before the foster parents filed their termination action.

E. FAILURE TO VISIT

The family court may order termination of parental rights upon a finding that:

> The child has lived outside the home of either parent for a period of six months, and during that time the parent has wilfully [sic] failed to visit the child. The court may attach little or no weight to incidental visitations, but it must be shown that the parent was not prevented from visiting by the party having custody or by court order. The distance of the child's placement from the parent's home must be taken into consideration when determining the ability to visit . . . .

S.C. Code Ann. § 20-7-1572(3) (Law. Co-op. 1976).

Incidental visitation is explained in *Horton v. Vaughn*, 309 S.C. 383, 423 S.E.2d 543 (Ct. App. 1992), as follows: "As used in a TPR statute, an 'incidental visitation' means that a parent may not rely upon fortuitous meetings between the parent and a child as a defense to an abandonment claim." *Id.* at 387, 423 S.E.2d at 545. However, in order for a court to find abandonment, the evidence must show that neither the custodian nor a court prevented the abandoning parent from visiting the child. *See Duck v. Jenkins*, 297 S.C. 136, 375 S.E.2d 178 (Ct. App. 1988), which noted that a "cause of action for termination cannot accrue based on abandonment if the mother is precluded by court order from visiting" her child. *Id.* at 140, 375 S.E.2d at 180. *See also Wilson v. Higgins*, 294 S.C. 300, 363 S.E.2d 911 (Ct. App. 1987), which reversed the family court's termination of parental rights of a mother who was prevented from visiting by the child's father.

The court is allowed to look beyond the six months prior to initiation of a termination action in determining whether an abandonment has taken place. *Abercrombie v. LaBoon*, 290 S.C. 35, 348 S.E.2d 170 (1986). In *Abercrombie*, the father had paid little child support, seldom visited the child, and sometimes secreted his whereabouts during the period between the divorce in 1978 and 1981. When the mother announced her intention to remarry, he returned to South Carolina to seek enforcement of his parental rights. The mother sought to have them terminated. The father argued that the critical period for determining abandonment is the six months immediately preceding the initiation of the termination action. The Supreme Court rejected this argument and held: "We are not persuaded that only the six month period prior to commencement of the actions may be considered by the court. The family court may consider *all* relevant conduct by the parent in determining whether abandonment has occurred." *Id.* at 37, 348 S.E.2d at 171.

The statute mandates that consideration be given to the distance of the child's placement from the parent's home when determining the ability to visit. S.C. Code Ann. § 20-7-1572(3) (Law. Co-op. 1976). The court weighed this factor in *Leone v. Dilullo*, 294 S.C. 410, 365 S.E.2d 39 (Ct. App. 1988), where the mother had not visited her children once in five years. Although the court noted that Connecticut is a considerable distance from South Carolina, it obviously considered the distance factor undeterminative. It found that the mother abandoned her children based on evidence of the mother's pattern of almost total indifference. She never wrote the children, seldom telephoned, and never attempted to provide even nominal amounts of money toward the children's support.

F. FAILURE TO SUPPORT

The family court may also order termination of parental rights upon a finding that:

> The child has lived outside the home of either parent for a period of six months, and during that time the parent has wilfully failed to support the child. Failure to support means that the parent has failed to make a material contribution to the child's care. A material contribution consists of either financial contributions according to the parent's means or contributions of food, clothing, shelter, or other necessities for the care of the child according to the parent's means. The court may consider all relevant circumstances in determining whether or not the parent has wilfully failed to support the child, including requests by the custodian and the ability of the parent to provide support.

S.C. Code Ann. § 20-7-1572(4) (Law. Co-op. Supp.).

This section of the statute was amended in 1992 by modifying the second sentence (which previously read: "Failure to support means that the parent has failed to make a material contribution to the child's care when contribution has been requested by the custodian of the child") and by adding the final sentence.

The 1992 amendment appears to have removed the possibility of successfully basing a defense to termination on the ground that no one asked the parent to provide child support. The probable failure of that line of defense was suggested under the prior wording of the statute in *Boyer v. Boyer*, 291 S.C. 183, 352 S.E.2d 514 (Ct. App. 1987), where the court indicated that the duty to support one's children is an independent obligation and suggested that nonsupport would not be excused just because a parent was not asked to provide it. However, the court did not need to reach the question because it found that a sufficient request was made to the father. Although he was never served with the support order, he was served with the support petition and the custodian read the support order to him over the telephone.

If a parent is able to pay child support, it appears unlikely that a failure to make some effort to pay child support will be excused. Even if a parent is virtually penniless, the parent is expected to share some of his or her income with the children. *See South Carolina DSS v. Phillips*, 301 S.C. 308, 391 S.E.2d 584 (Ct. App. 1990) (affirming the termination of the father's parental rights and holding that the father's incarceration did not relieve him of his duty to support his child even if he could only afford to send very little money out of his meager prison allowance).

Although the conclusiveness of the result in *Phillips* may be clouded somewhat by the Supreme Court's opinion in *Hopkins v. South Carolina DSS*, 313 S.C. 322, 437 S.E.2d 542 (1993), the unique facts of *Hopkins* make it more likely that no change of policy was intended. The possible confusion arises from the failure of the *Hopkins* Court to discuss more clearly why the father's parental rights should not have been terminated for failure to pay support. Part of the answer appears to be that neither the foster parents' nor the guardian's termination action asked that his rights be terminated for nonsupport, that is, the trial court had no authority to terminate for this reason. Another reason is that the termination hearing was held in 1989. Until S.C. Code § 20-7-1572(4) (Law. Co-op. Supp.) was amended in 1992, nonsupport could not serve as a basis for termination unless a "contribution has been requested by the custodian of the child." The mother never asked for support and the trial court found that the father paid all he could afford to pay after being asked by DSS to pay support, not many months before the termination actions were filed.

The Supreme Court's original opinion in *Hopkins* (filed on January 6, 1992, then withdrawn) concluded that the father's parental rights should be terminated for willful failure to pay child support as ordered by the family court (and the dissent continues to argue this in the 1993 opinion). Although it is not altogether clear in the opinion, it does not appear that the father was ordered to pay support until he was ordered to pay $20 per month in the order that was being appealed. Of course, the appellate court would have had no indication in its record about the father's degree of compliance with that order.

Another factor in the Court's decision to preserve the father's parental rights may have been that the father's paternity (which he was trying to establish, not avoid) was not conclusively determined by blood testing until shortly before the actions were brought to terminate his parental rights. Although this issue was not discussed, the Court may have felt that it would be unfair to terminate his rights for nonsupport given the short time in which he knew for sure that he was the father. It also appears that the majority of the Court was impressed by the father's persistence in trying to establish his paternal rights in the face of unwarranted difficulties caused by DSS. On the whole, it is unlikely that *Hopkins* should be read as indicating any change in the attitude of the appellate courts about terminating the rights of parents who do not support their children.

If a noncustodial parent's offer to pay child support is refused by the custodial parent, nonsupport cannot be used to permit an adoption without the consent of the non-supporting parent, or inferentially, as a basis for terminating parental rights, in general. In *Abernathy v. Baby Boy*, 313 S.C. 27, 437 S.E.2d 25 (1993), an unmarried father, who was stationed overseas in the military, objected to a proposed adoption of his infant child. The trial court considered S.C. Code Ann. § 20-7-1690 (A)(5)(b) (Law. Co-op. Supp.). This requires the consent of unmarried fathers if the child is placed with the prospective adoptive parents within six months of birth and "the father paid a fair and reasonable sum, based on the father's financial ability, for the support of the child or for expenses incurred in connection with the mother's pregnancy or with the birth of the child, including but not limited to, medical, hospital, and nursing expenses." The father claimed that he made a good faith effort to provide support for the child, but his attempts were frustrated by the mother. The trial judge agreed and granted the father custody, defeating the proposed adoption. The Supreme Court affirmed, holding that strict compliance with the language of the statute is not required when a father "undertakes sufficient prompt and good faith efforts to assume parental responsibility and to comply with the statute." *Id.* at 32, 437 S.E.2d at 29.

G. STANDARD OF PROOF

Termination of parental rights requires a showing of clear and convincing evidence. *See Hopkins v. South Carolina DSS*, 313 S.C. 322, 437 S.E.2d 542 (1992); *South Carolina DSS v. Broome*, 307 S.C. 48, 52, 413 S.E.2d 835, 838 (1992); *South Carolina DSS v. Brown*, 317 S.C. 332, 454 S.E.2d 335 (Ct. App. 1995) (all citing *Santosky v. Kramer*, 455 U.S. 745, 102 S. Ct. 1388, 71 L. Ed. 2d 599 (1982)).

The U.S. Supreme Court in *Santosky* held that in actions to terminate parental rights a standard any lower than clear and convincing violates the parent's right to due process under the Fifth and Fourteenth Amendments. The New York statute that was challenged in *Santosky* provided that the decision to terminate parental rights was to be based on a "fair preponderance" of the evidence presented. The Court held the statute invalid, stating that "[b]efore a State may sever completely and irrevocably the rights of parents in their natural child, due process requires that the State support its allegations by at least clear and convincing evidence." *Id.* at 747-748, 102 S. Ct. at 1392, 71 L. Ed. 2d at 603. The Court also declared that each state may determine its own standard of proof, which may be greater than clear and convincing. *Id.* Prior to *Santosky*, there was some authority that the standard in South Carolina was a preponderance of the evidence. *See Hamby v. Hamby*, 264 S.C. 614, 216 S.E.2d 536 (1975) (upholding the family court's finding that a father's consent was not needed in the child's adoption because he had not visited his child for several years, had never paid support, and had willfully engaged in conduct resulting in his arrest and imprisonment, thus abandoning the child).

A criticism of the procedures, if not the standard of proof, required by *Santosky* can be found in the dissenting opinion of Justice Toal, joined by Chief Justice Harwell, in *Greenville County DSS v. Bowes*, 313 S.C. 188, 437 S.E.2d 107, 112 (1993). The majority held that the trial judge erred in terminating a mother's parental rights for abuse. The judge had relied in part on an finding of abuse which had been made by a different judge in an earlier action to remove the child from the mother's home. In a removal action the standard of proof is preponderance of the evidence, and the trial judge should have heard evidence in the termination case independently to determine whether the evidence of abuse was clear and convincing. The Supreme Court also held that the trial judge had failed to make any determination the abuse was severe or repetitive, as required by S.C. Code Ann. § 20-7-1572(1) (Law. Co-op. 1976).

In order to terminate parental rights on the basis of child abuse, a direct evidentiary link between the child abuse and the parent whose rights are being terminated may be required to meet the clear and convincing evidence standard. In *South Carolina DSS v. Brown*, 317 S.C. 332, 454 S.E. 2d 335 (Ct. App. 1995), the Department of Social Services instituted an action to terminate the parental rights of James and Mattie Mae Brown to their child, Jenea. The family court terminated the Browns' parental rights based on a finding that Jenea's sibling was harmed within the meaning of § 20-7-490(C), and it was not reasonably likely that the home could be made safe within three months because of the severity of the abuse, which resulted in the death of the child, and the denial of any wrongdoing. The Court of Appeals held there was insufficient evidence to link the mother to the death of the child. On the date of the child's death Mrs. Brown was at work thirty miles away. The fatal injuries occurred within three or four hours of death, and there was no testimony that Mrs. Brown had ever abused the child. The Department of Social Services took the position that both parents were responsible as they shared custody, care and control of the child. The Court of Appeals ruled that this was not a sufficient basis for the termination of the parental rights of Mrs. Brown, absent clear evidence that she either participated in, acquiesced in, or had knowledge of the abuse.

H. AVOIDING TERMINATION BY REPENTANT CONDUCT

Once a court finds clear and convincing evidence of abandonment of a child for a period of six months, it must then examine the parent's subsequent conduct to determine whether abandonment has been cured. In *Abercrombie v. LaBoon*, 290 S.C. 35, 348 S.E.2d 170 (1986), the Supreme Court stated:

> Earlier conduct by a parent which may have warranted a finding of abandonment may be cured by the parent's subsequent repentant conduct. Once conduct warranting a finding of abandonment is shown to have existed, the court must then determine whether the parent's subsequent conduct was of a sufficient nature to terminate the earlier abandonment.

Id. at 37, 348 S.E.2d at 171 (citations omitted). However, the court in *Abercrombie* considered the timeliness of the parent's curative conduct. The father's attempt to remedy the abandonment occurred only after the passage of three years and the initiation of the termination action. The court held that such a "judicially-motivated repentance, standing alone" would rarely warrant a finding that an abandonment has been cured. *Id.* at 38, 348 S.E.2d at 172.

Slight attempts to remedy the earlier circumstances, if not actually successful, are not sufficient to preserve parental rights. *See South Carolina DSS v. Pritchett*, 296 S.C. 517, 374 S.E.2d 500 (Ct. App. 1988) (affirming termination of parental rights despite an eleventh-hour attempt by the parents to correct their history of a violent and unstable marriage and their failure to take advantage of recommended counseling services).

I. ADOPTION

Actions for termination of parental rights are closely linked with adoption. The purpose of the termination of parental rights subarticle of the South Carolina Code is:

> [T]o establish procedures for the reasonable and compassionate termination of parental rights where children are abused, neglected, or abandoned in order to protect the health and welfare of such children and make them eligible for adoption by persons who will provide a suitable home environment and the love and care necessary for a happy, healthful, and productive life.

S.C. Code Ann. § 20-7-1560 (Law. Co-op. 1976).

Consent to adoption must be obtained from a parent whose parental rights have not been terminated, even if the adoption would be beneficial to the child. *See Bevis v. Bevis*, 254 S.C. 345, 175 S.E.2d 398 (1970) (holding that a mother who refused to consent to her children's adoption by their step-mother had not abandoned the children); *Goff v. Benedict*, 252 S.C. 83, 165 S.E.2d 269 (1969) (holding that an adoption could not occur without the mother's consent).

In an adoption action in which termination of parental rights is requested, the jurisdiction of the family court may be defined by the Uniform Child Custody Jurisdiction Act (UCCJA). In a case of first impression in South Carolina, *Clark v. Gordon*, 313 S.C. 240, 437 S.E.2d 144 (1993), the Supreme Court noted that there is a split of authority around the country before it ruled that the UCCJA should be considered in actions for adoption and termination of parental rights in which the trial judge determines that the substantive controversy is one of custody. "If so, then the case should be treated as a custody case regardless of the name in which the controversy is cloaked." *Id.* at 243, 437 S.E.2d at 146.

Generally, persons who may petition for adoption are South Carolina residents. However, some provisions for nonresidents are in place, particularly for special needs children, relatives, where one parent is in the military, where the child or family is subject to notoriety, or where other unusual or exceptional circumstances exist. S.C. Code Ann. § 20-7-1670 (Law. Co-op. Supp.). Additionally, the family court must determine that the placement will be in compliance with the Interstate Compact on the Placement of Children. S.C. Code Ann. § 20-7-1980, *et seq.* (Law. Co-op. Supp.).

When out-of-state residents attempt to adopt a child in South Carolina, the family court must consider two competing interests: first, the finding of unusual or exceptional circumstances; and, second, the express and implied policy against "baby selling." *Adoptive Parents v. Biological Parents*, 315 S.C. 535, 446 S.E. 2d 404 (1994). Although it is *dictum* because the case was remanded due to insufficient facts, the Supreme Court's opinion agrees, in general, with the argument of the adoptive parents that the bonding between the adoptive parents and the child, the participation of the adoptive parents in the birth process, the selection of the adoptive parents by the biological parents, and the financial support for the biological parents' medical and living expenses, were sufficient to constitute unusual or exceptional circumstances.

No person may buy or sell a minor child for purposes of adoption. S.C. Code Ann. §§ 16-3-1060 and 20-7-1690 (Law. Co-op. Supp.).

J. EFFECTS OF TERMINATION OF PARENTAL RIGHTS

The only rights or obligations remaining between a parent and child after termination of the parent's parental rights is the child's right to inherit from the parent. That right is extinguished only by a final adoption of the child. S.C. Code Ann. § 20-7-1576 (Law. Co-op. Supp.) provides:

> (A) An order terminating the relationship between parent and child under this subarticle divests the parent and the child of all legal rights, powers, privileges, immunities, duties, and obligations with respect to each other, except the right of the child to inherit from the parent. A right of inheritance is terminated only by a final order of adoption.

> (B) The relationship between a parent and child may be terminated with respect to one parent without affecting the relationship between the child and the other parent.

A termination of parental rights also terminates all parental obligations. Thus, a parent's obligation to feed, clothe, and otherwise support a child, being correlative to the parent's rights in and to a child, are terminated if the rights to that child are terminated by a valid court order. *Coffey v. Vasquez*, 290 S.C. 348, 350 S.E.2d 396 (Ct. App. 1986).

CHAPTER TEN
CHILD CUSTODY

CHAPTER TEN
CHILD CUSTODY

A. IN GENERAL

1. BEST INTEREST OF CHILD IS CONTROLLING FACTOR

No area of law seems to operate under a single standard more than child custody. All jurisdictions recognize the principle that the best interest of the child is the controlling factor in custody cases. *Ingold v. Ingold*, 304 S.C. 316, 404 S.E.2d 35 (Ct. App. 1991). South Carolina recognized this standard even before the paramount right of the father was discredited. *Ex parte Schumpert*, 40 S.C.L. (6 Rich.) 344 (1853). Nonetheless, even though this area of the law is nominally governed by a single principle, it is muddled by difficulty of definition and explanation. As stated in *Ford v. Ford*, 242 S.C. 344, 130 S.E.2d 916 (1963), "[t]he difficulty is not in the recognition of the foregoing principles, but in the application thereof to the facts of the case, and determining what is for the best interests of the children involves a consideration of all of the circumstances of the particular case and, usually, many factors." *Id.* at 349-350, 130 S.E.2d at 920.

The best interest of the child as the controlling factor is included in S.C. Code Ann. § 20-7-100 (Law. Co-op. Supp.) which provides in part that "[t]he welfare of the minor shall be the first consideration and the court having jurisdiction shall determine all questions concerning the guardianship of the minor."

Custody cases in South Carolina must be viewed in two segments. The older cases were generally brought when a parent died. *See Williams v. Rogers*, 224 S.C. 426, 79 S.E.2d 464 (1954) (involving a mother's successful action to regain custody of her son from her late husband's parents); *Douglass v. Merriman*, 163 S.C. 210, 161 S.E. 452 (1931) (granting a father custody as against his late wife's parents); *Alewine v. McGill*, 141 S.C. 116, 139 S.E. 172 (1927) (finding the father of an infant to have the "highest claim" to its custody as against his late wife's parents); *Watson v. Watson*, 134 S.C. 147, 132 S.E. 39 (1926) (upholding custody of an infant in his late father's father to whom the child's mother had conveyed the child in a deed); *Busbee v. Reese*, 125 S.C. 121, 118 S.E. 185 (1923) (holding a fit father's right to custody superior to that of his late wife's mother). *Alewine v. McGill*, 141 S.C. 116, 139 S.E. 172 (1927), is a case representative of the older custody opinions. Custody was awarded to the father as opposed to the maternal grandfather shortly after the mother's death. The father's paramount claim founded in the common law overcame his previous transgressions.

The historical evolution of the law of child custody in South Carolina is important as some of the early principles continue to surface in the modern cases. Although South Carolina was early to recognize the best interest of the child standard, there are a number of cases in which great consideration is given to the rights of the parents. The paramount right of the father, while rejected in *Ex parte Schumpert*, 40 S.C.L. (6 Rich.) 344 (1853) (upholding custody in the mother), was the basis of the decision in *Ex parte Hewitt*, 45 S.C.L. (11 Rich.) 326 (1858). Custody was granted to the father even though the Court alluded to the best interest standard and the tender years doctrine ("age of nurture"). Priority of the father, in line with the general Anglo-American approach at the time (*see King v. DeManneville*, 102 Eng. Rep. 1054 (K.B. 1804) (holding that a father is entitled to custody even of an "infant at the breast of its mother")), was derived from the father's common law duty to support his children. In *Hewitt* and in *Busbee v. Reese*, 125 S.C. 121, 125, 118 S.E. 185, 186 (1923), language of the Court suggested that the father must have been found unfit before custody could be granted to another party. *See also Shelley v. Westbrooke*, 37 Eng. Rep 850 (Ch. 1817), in which Percy Bysshe Shelley, the famous poet, was denied custody of his children due to his immoral conduct and way of life (and, as well, due to his radical political and religious views). *See also Alewine v. McGill*, 141 S.C. 116, 139 S.E. 172 (1927); *Ex parte Davige*, 72 S.C. 16, 18, 51 S.E. 269, 270 (1905) (both upholding the paramount custody right of the father).

The more modern factual situation arises as child custody is part of a divorce or an ongoing dispute between divorced parents. No fine line separates the old and the modern cases, but the introduction of divorce made custody proceedings more complicated and more frequent. Today, neither the father nor the mother are entitled to a presumption in favor of one having custody over the other. The factors to be considered must focus primarily on the welfare of the children whose custody is in dispute.

2. NONJUDICIAL RESOLUTION OF CUSTODY DISPUTES

a. Agreements

Although most child custody issues arise in the context of marital litigation, many custody disputes do not require judicial intervention. If parents can agree what custody arrangement is in the best interests of their children, the judicial system will usually stay out of the matter. If the parents want custody agreements to be enforceable, however, their validity will depend on considerations discussed in the chapter on agreements as well as the court's consideration of the best interests of the children.

The Supreme Court first considered the effect of parental agreements concerning child custody in *Ford v. Ford*, 242 S.C. 344, 130 S.E.2d 916 (1963). The parents had settled child custody litigation in Virginia by agreeing that the father would have custody of the children. The mother moved to South Carolina and initiated litigation to change custody while the children were visiting her, relying primarily on the tender years doctrine. The father pleaded the agreement, but also claimed that he was more fit to have custody than the mother. The Court had this to say about the effect of the agreement:

> The general law on the subject of contracts or agreements as to custody of children is set forth in 17A Am. Jur. 17, Section 822, the concluding sentence of the text reading as follows: 'The rule is that contracts between spouses as to the custody of children will be recognized unless the welfare of the children requires a different disposition.'
>
> It seems to us that under this general rule it was incumbent upon the wife to show that the welfare of the children required the court to ignore and set aside the agreement of the parties.

Id. at 354, 130 S.E.2d at 922. The Court continued to consider the circumstances under which the agreement had been created and breached, and it described the factors to be considered in evaluating the agreement:

> Pertinent to the issue before us, we think, is whether the agreement entered into between the parties was fair, just, equitable and in the best interests of the children at the time it was entered into. If it was, another pertinent inquiry is whether there is any showing that there had been a sufficient change of conditions to indicate that the agreement was not, under the circumstances prevailing at the time of the trial, a proper one in the best interests of the children.

Id. at 355, 130 S.E.2d at 923. The Court determined that the agreement was fair and served the best interests of the children and that the wife had failed to carry her burden of showing that the agreement should be disregarded. The father retained custody, and the Court ordered the mother to return the children to him at the conclusion of the current school year.

The overall effect of the *Ford* decision is that the parent wishing to challenge an agreement about child custody has the burden of convincing a court either that 1) the agreement was improperly created; 2) it did not serve the best interests of the children at the time it was made; or 3) circumstances have changed which support a change of custody irrespective of the agreement. The principle that the party seeking to set aside the agreement has the burden of proving that the welfare of the children requires the agreement to be abrogated was affirmed in *Davenport v. Davenport*, 265 S.C. 524, 220 S.E.2d 228 (1975) (affirming an agreement giving a mother custody although the mother, now reformed, had committed adultery in her condominium while the children were there).

There is an interesting statute which permits parents to transfer custody of their children by deed or through a will. S.C. Code Ann. § 21-21-25 (Law. Co-op. 1976) is titled, "Manner in which custody of minors may be disposed of," and it reads in part:

> The father of any child under the age of twenty-one years and not married, if the mother is dead, or the mother of any such child, the father being dead . . . may by deed executed and recorded according to law or by last will or testament . . . dispose of the custody and tuition of the child while he remains under the age of twenty-one years to any other person, in possession or in remainder.

The practical effect of this statute appears to be small, for it also provides that deeds must be approved by a family court judge (except to an agency authorized to receive custody of children), and it further provides that "[n]othing in this section may be construed to abrogate, lessen, or interfere with the right and duty of a court of competent jurisdiction at any time to transfer and assign the custody of a child for its best interest." However, a will or deed intending to transfer the custody of a child would serve as evidence of the wishes of the parent or parents, and anyone trying to challenge the custody would presumably have the burden of proving that another arrangement would better serve the interests of the children. There do not appear to have been any cases involving this statute.

b. Child Snatching (and the PKPA)

For our purposes, child snatching is defined as the unapproved movement of a child from one location to another by one parent for the purpose of denying the other parent physical or legal custody or otherwise interfering with that parent's ability to exercise parental rights, such as visitation.

(1) When No Custody Order Exists

Absent an agreement or court order regarding child custody, both parents are equally entitled to the custody of their children. S.C. Code Ann. § 20-7-100 (Law. Co-op. Supp.) provides in part:

> The mother and father are the joint natural guardians of their minor children and are equally charged with the welfare and education of their minor children and the care and management of the estates of their minor children; and the father and mother have equal power, rights, and duties, and neither parent has any right paramount to the right of the other concerning the custody of the minor or the control of the services or the earnings of the minor or any other matter affecting the minor.

One exception for illegitimate children is created by S.C. Code Ann. § 20-7-953(B) (Law. Co-op. 1976) which says that, absent any court order to the contrary, custody of children born out of wedlock is solely in the mother. However, that statute also provides that an acknowledged father or one for whom paternity has been established may petition the court for custody or visitation in a proceeding other than the paternity proceeding. At such proceeding, one would assume that there would be no presumption in favor of the mother and that the best interest of the child would determine which parent should be awarded custody.

The consequence of both parents having equal rights to custody is that either one can move the children to another location without directly violating any law. For example, S.C. Code Ann. § 16-3-910 (Law. Co-op. Supp.) sets the penalty for kidnaping, but specifically excludes "when a minor is seized or taken by his parent."

The risk in moving a child from its usual environment is that, if a custody hearing is eventually held, the trial judge may conclude that the parent who moved the child acted contrary to the child's best interest, especially if the move was secret or otherwise interfered with the exercise of visitation or other parental rights by the other parent.

(2) When Custody Order Exists

This section discusses those times when the noncustodial parent obtains physical custody and refuses to return the child to the custodial parent. A parent who has been awarded legal custody may not be completely free to move whenever and wherever he or she wishes. However, the issues related to movements of children by custodial parents are discussed in the sections in this chapter on conditions of custody and modification of custody.

S.C. Code Ann. § 20-7-100 (Law. Co-op. Supp.) provides in part that "[n]either parent shall forcibly take a child from the guardianship of the parent legally entitled to custody of the child."

It is a criminal felony in South Carolina for any person, including a noncustodial parent, to take a child out of the state with an intent to violate a custody order. If the child is returned to South Carolina within seven days, the crime will be treated as a misdemeanor. S.C. Code Ann. § 16-17-495 (Law. Co-op. Supp.). Prosecutions under this statute appear to be rare, however, they do occur. *See State v. W.M.S.*, ___ S.C. ___, 465 S.E.2d 580 (Ct. App. 1995)(upholding a conviction for transporting a child under the age of sixteen outside the state with intent to violate a custody order. The court rejected the convicted mother's claim that she should have been allowed to present evidence needed to prove her defense of necessity (to protect the child from possible abuse by the custodial grandmother's husband). The court held that she failed to establish all the elements necessary to receive a jury charge for the defense.).

The more common consequence of violating a custody order is that the family court can hold the offending parent in contempt of court and impose a jail term of up to one year. This was the result in *Curlee v. Howle*, 277 S.C. 377, 287 S.E.2d 115 (1982), in which the Supreme Court affirmed the trial court's issuance of a contempt order and subsequent one-year imprisonment of a father who removed his child to another state in violation of the court-decreed custody of the mother. Whether or not punishment will be imposed is in the discretion of the trial judge, and it will depend on the particular circumstances of each case. For example, in *Scheibner v. Wonderly*, 279 S.C. 212, 305 S.E.2d 232 (1983), a father with custody was required to give the mother sixty days' notice before moving out of state. He gave her notice, but he moved on the fifty-seventh day. The mother had served him with a petition on the fifty-fifth day in which she sought to have him prevented from moving, although the pleadings had been signed a month earlier. The Supreme Court concluded that the father was technically in contempt of court, but it upheld the family court's decision to impose no sanction. The Court stated that in contempt proceedings the law does not require punishment but only permits it.

Perhaps the greatest deterrent to child snatching is that it is becoming much less likely that child snatching will result in a permanent change of custody. The Federal Parental Kidnaping Prevention Act of 1980 (PKPA) (28 U.S.C. § 1738A), which became effective on December 28, 1980, prevents the courts of one state from modifying a child custody determination of another state where the court making the original custody determination had jurisdiction under the laws of that state, and it was the home state of the child on the date of the commencement of the proceedings. The provisions of the PKPA relating to multi-state custody disputes are discussed in the section on jurisdiction later in this chapter.

The PKPA also makes child snatching a federal crime. 18 U.S.C. § 1073 provides in part:

> Whoever moves or travels in interstate or foreign commerce with the intent either (1) to avoid prosecution, or custody or confinement after conviction, under the laws of the place from which the fugitive flees, for a crime, or an attempt to commit a crime, punishable by death or which is a felony under the laws of the place from which the fugitive flees . . . shall be fined not more than $5,000 or imprisoned not more than five years, or both.

The Congress expressly declared its intent that the statute quoted above is to be applied to cases involving parental kidnaping and interstate or international flight to avoid prosecution under applicable state felony statutes. *See* 18 U.S.C. § 1073 notes. Thus, because S.C. Code Ann. § 16-17-495 (Law. Co-op. Supp.) makes it a felony to take a child across state lines in violation of a custody order, such actions become federal offenses under section 1073, and federal resources can be brought to bear in locating and prosecuting the offender. However, it is not yet clear how fully the federal law enforcement establishment will provide assistance in child napping cases.

The Parental Kidnaping Prevention Act also amended Section 454 of the Social Security Act to allow states to expand their parent locator services for use in child support proceedings to include searches for abducted children. Participation of the states is not mandatory; the states may enter voluntary agreements with the Secretary of the Department of Health and Human Services to allow access to the parent locator service. To date, a number of states have signed such agreements, including South Carolina.

Section 463 of the Social Security Act allows dissemination of information to locate a parent or child for the purpose of enforcing state or federal laws, presumably criminal laws, or for the purpose of making or enforcing child custody decrees. However, access is allowed only to those persons who are "authorized." Under the act, the definition of authorized persons extends primarily to agents or attorneys engaged in criminal or civil law enforcement, or courts and their agents, but not parents. This does not deny parents access but instead regulates it. Assistance can be obtained through the Child Support Enforcement Division of the Department of Social Services.

The parent locator service may prove helpful to a parent who is the victim of an abduction, but it is not a field investigation service. It is a computer search utilizing primarily the individual's Social Security number to conduct a search of a variety of federal records relating to wages and employment. Any such search may be frustrated by a change in the individual's identity or job. There is a nominal charge for processing a request.

c. International Child Snatching

Special problems are created when one parent takes a child outside of the United States in an effort to impede or defeat the other parent's right to visitation or custody. Obtaining relief within the judicial system is usually difficult, sometimes impossible. The *International Parental Kidnaping Crime Act of 1993* (IPKCA) provides some hope of a more effective remedy.

The Parental Kidnaping Prevention Act of 1980 (PKPA) applies the Federal Fugitive Felon Act (18 U.S.C. 1073 (1994)) to a parental kidnaping cases involving interstate or international flight, but it imposes no criminal sanctions beyond those provided by state law. State prosecutors are reluctant to spend resources seeking extradition from foreign countries of parents who have fled with children. Even when a state prosecutor is interested in going forward, the PKPA provides no remedy unless the other country has an extradition treaty with the United States.

The Hague Convention on the Civil Aspects of International Child Abduction, 51 Fed. Reg. 10494 (1986), is an international treaty which provides a useful civil remedy. It requires member states to return a wrongfully removed or retained child to the country of its habitual residence. However, the Hague Convention is useful only when the abducting parent and child are living in a country which is a signatory to the Hague Convention (most countries are not). Where it is available, the Hague Convention procedures should be the tool of first resort.

If the abducted child is not in a Hague Convention country, but is in a country which has an extradition treaty with the United States, employing the *International Parental Kidnaping Crime Act of 1993* (IPKCA) may be the best option. The IPKCA amended 18 U.S.C. § 1204, which makes international kidnaping a federal crime, to include parents. It provides for fines or for imprisonment up to three years for anyone who removes a child from the United States, or improperly retains a child outside the United States, with the intention of obstructing the lawful exercise of parental rights. A person with "parental rights" is a person who is entitled to physical custody of a child, whether the right is joint or sole, and whether the right arises by operation of law, court order, or legally binding agreement of the parties. It includes visitation rights.

The IPKCA provides a basis for the United States government to request extradition of the abducting parent from countries which have extradition treaties with the United States. The request will be made on the basis of federal, not state, warrants which carry more weight in the eyes of some foreign governments.

A left-behind parent should first report the missing child and abductor to the police and to the State Department in Washington, D.C., then to the FBI. One should also file a timely "Hague application" in the event the child appears in a Hague Convention country. More information can be obtained from the State Department which provides many informational forms, booklets, and service free of charge. Another source of helpful information is Mikeon, "International Parental Kidnaping: A New Law, a New Solution," 30 *Fam. Law Q.* 235 (Spring, 1996).

B. JURISDICTION

1. IN GENERAL

The family court has no jurisdiction over the custody of a child who has reached eighteen years of age. In *Holcombe v. Kennison*, 300 S.C. 479, 388 S.E.2d 807 (1990), the Supreme Court stated that "'Child' is statutorily defined as a person under eighteen years of age. S.C. Code Ann. §§ 20-7-390 and -490(A) (1985). The family court's jurisdiction to determine custody matters applies only to children. S.C. Code Ann. § 20-7-400(A)(1)(e) (1985)." *Id.* at 480, 388 S.E.2d at 808 (holding that, because the daughter had reached eighteen years of age, the issue was moot as to whether the family court had erred in declaring that the daughter's marriage was invalid and, therefore, she had not become emancipated as a result of getting married).

The family court has authority to hear and determine cases involving child custody issues pursuant to S.C. Ann. § 20-7-400(A) (Law. Co-op. 1976):

> Except as otherwise provided herein, the court shall have exclusive original jurisdiction and shall be the sole court for initiating action:
>
> (1) Concerning any child living or found within the geographical limits of its jurisdiction:
>
> . . .
>
> (e) Whose custody is the subject of controversy, except in those cases where the law now gives other courts concurrent jurisdiction. In the consideration of these cases, the court shall have concurrent jurisdiction to hear and determine the issue of custody and support.

Additional authority to decide custody issues in divorce cases is provided in S.C. Code Ann. § 20-3-160 (Law. Co-op. 1976):

> In any action for divorce from the bonds of matrimony the court may at any stage of the case, or from time to time after final judgments, make such orders touching the care, custody, and maintenance of the children of the marriage, and what, if any, security shall be given for the same as from the circumstances of the parties and the nature of the case and the best spiritual as well as other interests of the children may be fit, equitable and just.

The family court has been described as a court of "continuing jurisdiction" in custody matters. *Dent v. Dent*, 273 S.C. 387, 256 S.E.2d 743 (1979). This "continuing jurisdiction" has come to mean that the court which granted the divorce may alter these matters and that no other court may. This is the approach as well of the Uniform Child Custody Jurisdiction Act, discussed below.

2. MULTI-STATE CHILD CUSTODY DISPUTES (UCCJA and PKPA)

a. Legislation and Purposes

The family court may not have jurisdiction to decide a child custody dispute if the parents live in different states or if the child whose custody is in dispute has lived in South Carolina for less than six months. To determine whether South Carolina has jurisdiction either to make an award of child custody or to modify an existing child custody order from another state, one must consider legislation enacted by the South Carolina legislature (UCCJA) as well as by the United States Congress (PKPA). While the state and federal statutes are similar, there are some differences which could affect the outcomes of particular cases. The South Carolina Court of Appeals has acknowledged that "[w]here the provisions of the federal Parental Kidnaping Prevention Act of 1980 (PKPA), 28 U.S.C. § 1738A and state law conflict, the federal act controls." *Schwartz v. Schwartz*, 311 S.C. 303, 307-308, 428 S.E.2d 748, 750-751 (Ct. App. 1993) (citing *Marks v. Marks*, 281 S.C. 316, 315 S.E.2d 158 (Ct. App. 1984)).

The Federal Parental Kidnaping Prevention Act of 1980 (PKPA) (28 U.S.C. § 1738A), which became effective on December 28, 1980, prevents the courts of one state from modifying a child custody determination of another state where the court making the original custody determination had jurisdiction under the laws of that state, and it was the home state of the child on the date of the commencement of the proceedings. (The PKPA also makes child snatching a federal crime. This aspect of the PKPA is discussed in the section on child snatching earlier in this chapter.)

The purposes and legislative history of the PKPA are discussed in *Thompson v. Thompson*, 484 U.S. 174, 108 S. Ct. 513, 98 L. Ed.2d 512 (1988), in which the U.S. Supreme Court declared that the PKPA does not furnish an implied cause of action in federal court to determine which of two conflicting custody decisions is valid.[22]

---

[22] The Court's advice about how to resolve conflicts between states which issue conflicting custody orders in spite of the PKPA is not particularly helpful.

> The Parental Kidnaping Prevention Act (PKPA or Act) imposes a duty on the States to enforce a child custody determination entered by a court of a sister State if the determination is consistent with the provisions of the Act. In order for a state court's custody decree to be consistent with the provisions of the Act, the State must have jurisdiction under its own local law and one of five conditions set out in § 1738A(c)(2) must be met. Briefly put, these conditions authorize the state court to enter a custody decree if the child's home is or recently has been in the State, if the child has no home State and it would be in the child's best interest for the State to assume jurisdiction, or if the child is present in the State and has been abandoned or abused. Once a State exercises jurisdiction consistently with the provisions of the Act, no other State may exercise concurrent jurisdiction over the custody dispute, § 1738A(g), even if it would have been empowered to take jurisdiction in the first instance, and all States must accord full faith and credit to the first State's ensuing custody decree.

484 U.S. at 175-177, 108 S.Ct. at 514-515, 98 L. Ed. 2d at 517-519.

The opinion also explains the need for federal legislation in this area. Full faith and credit was not always being granted to child custody orders of other states because they were not considered by some states to be sufficiently "final" to trigger

---

> We note, as a preliminary response, that ultimate review remains available in this Court for truly intractable jurisdictional deadlocks. In addition, the unspoken presumption in petitioner's argument is that the States are either unwilling or unable to enforce the provisions of the Act. This is a presumption we are not prepared, and more importantly, Congress was not prepared, to indulge. State courts faithfully administer the Full Faith and Credit Clause every day; now that Congress has extended full faith and credit requirements to child custody orders, we can think of no reason why the courts' administration of federal law in custody disputes will be any less vigilant. Should state courts prove as obstinate as petitioner predicts, Congress may choose to revisit the issue.

484 U.S. at 187, 108 S.Ct. at 520, 98 L. Ed. 2d at 525.

full faith and credit requirements and because the custody orders were subject to change according to each state's views of the child's best interest.

> For these reasons, a parent who lost a custody battle in one State had an incentive to kidnap the child and move to another State to relitigate the issue. This circumstance contributed to widespread jurisdictional deadlocks like this one, and more importantly, to a national epidemic of parental kidnaping. At the time the PKPA was enacted, sponsors of the Act estimated that between 25,000 and 100,000 children were kidnaped by parents who had been unable to obtain custody in a legal forum.
>
> . . .
>
> A number of States joined in an effort to avoid these jurisdictional conflicts by adopting the Uniform Child Custody Jurisdiction Act (UCCJA), 9 U.L.A. §§ 1-28 (1979). The UCCJA prescribed uniform standards for deciding which State could make a custody determination and obligated enacting States to enforce the determination made by the State with proper jurisdiction. The project foundered, however, because a number of States refused to enact the UCCJA while others enacted it with modifications. In the absence of uniform national standards for allocating and enforcing custody determinations, noncustodial parents still had reason to snatch their children and petition the courts of any of a number of haven States for sole custody.

484 U.S. at 180-181, 108 S.Ct. at 517, 98 L. Ed. 2d at 521.

On July 1, 1980, six months after the enactment of the PKPA, South Carolina adopted a version of the Uniform Child Custody Jurisdiction Act (UCCJA), S.C. Code Ann. § 20-7-782 to 830 (Law. Co-op. 1976). Section 784 sets forth the purposes of the Act which, in summary form, are: first, to avoid jurisdictional conflict and promote cooperation between courts of different States; second, to make sure that litigation over child custody should take place in the State having the most intimate connection or closest relationship to the child; third, to attempt to make child custody determinations more binding so that there will be less temptation on the part of parents to engage in continuing litigation; and fourth, to penalize parents for so-called "child snatching."

b. Due Process and Other Procedural Matters

The UCCJA and the PKPA require a two-step proceeding under most circumstances. First, the court must determine whether it has jurisdiction. Second, the court must determine whether it is proper to exercise jurisdiction if it does have it. Only after making these two determinations may the court proceed to make a determination on the merits of the claim involved. These steps are discussed in subsequent sections.

However, in no case may a court rule on the merits of a multi-state custody dispute until all designated parties have been appropriately notified and given opportunities to be heard. Both the UCCJA (at S.C. Code Ann. § 20-7-790) and the PKPA (at 28 U.S.C. § 1738A(e)) require that "reasonable notice and opportunity to be heard shall be given to the contestants, any parent whose parental rights have not been previously terminated and any person who has physical custody of the child" (the PKPA adds "or of any contestant" to the end of this statement). The PKPA does not provide procedures for giving such notices, but the UCCJA, at section 20-7-792, provides that notice "shall be given in a manner reasonably calculated to give actual notice." This includes personal service outside the state, service by mail, or service as directed by the court, e.g., service by publication. Absent an emergency, at least twenty days notice is required. S.C. Code Ann. § 20-7-792(b) (Law. Co-op. 1976). No notice is required if a person submits to the jurisdiction of the court. S.C. Code Ann. § 20-7-792(d) (Law. Co-op. 1976).

A failure to provide the requisite notice and opportunity to be heard could result in another state refusing to recognize the validity of a custody order resulting from such a proceeding. South Carolina held in *Clark v. Gordon*, 313 S.C. 240, 437 S.E.2d 144 (1993), that a family court judge was not bound to give full faith and credit to a custody decree from Missouri unless notice and an opportunity to be heard had been given. This case involved an action for adoption and termination of the parental rights of the father. The father asserted that Missouri, not South Carolina, was the proper forum under the UCCJA, because a Missouri court had given him custody and he continued to reside in Missouri. After determining that this was an action for custody subject to the UCCJA, the Supreme Court held that the UCCJA gives the "the court that issues a custody decree continuing and exclusive jurisdiction as long [as] it can satisfy the jurisdictional requirements of § 20-7-788," but that "§ 20-7-808 does not require South Carolina courts to enforce custody orders of other states, where those orders are entered contrary to the requirements of the Act." *Id.* at 244, 437 S.E.2d at 147. The Court further held that full faith and credit should be given to custody orders of other states only if those orders are competently entered in accordance with standards set forth in the Children's Code, including notice and an opportunity to be heard. In that the mother had filed affidavits supporting her claim that she did not have notice of the Missouri hearing, the Supreme Court determined that the trial court had erred in finding as a matter of law that it had no authority to determine the validity of the Missouri order, and it remanded the case for findings of fact and conclusions of law on the notice issue.

In *Clark*, the Supreme Court cited *Purdie v. Smalls*, 293 S.C. 216, 359 S.E.2d 306 (Ct. App. 1987) as controlling. In *Purdie*, the Court of Appeals held that South Carolina had become the home state of the child under S.C. Code Ann. § 20-7-788 (Law. Co-op. 1976), and the family court could decide who should have custody, notwithstanding a New York decree awarding custody to the father. The court also found that the mother had not been given any notice of the New York proceeding.

The UCCJA requires very specific information to be provided to the court by way of pleading or affidavit at the outset of a custody action (and as an ongoing duty). Section 20-7-800 specifies that every party in a custody proceeding shall provide specific information with respect to the child's present and previous addresses, previous or ongoing custody litigation involving the same child, and the identity of any person who is not a party to the action who has custody of the child or who may claim custody or visitation rights with respect to the child.

Finally, there are other matters in the UCCJA having to do with the mechanisms for procuring the appearance of parties, taking testimony out-of-state, and the like. These are described clearly in the statute. Two items do deserve some emphasis, however. S.C. Code Ann. § 20-7-812 (Law. Co-op. 1976) provides for a somewhat URESA-like procedure for filing and enforcing custody decrees of other states. All that must be done is to file a certified copy of a custody decree of another state. Incidentally, although it was rather clearly the law of this state anyway (*see Curlee v. Howle*, 277 S.C. 377, 287 S.E.2d 115 (1982)), this section also gives the family court specific authorization to order payment of necessary travel and other expenses, including attorneys' fees, incurred by the party entitled to custody (or witnesses) when someone makes it necessary to enforce the custody decree of another state in the courts of this state.

The clerk of each family court is required to maintain a registry of certified copies of custody decrees of other states received for filing, communications as to the pendency of custody proceedings in other states, communications concerning a finding of inconvenient forum by courts of another state, and other communications or documents concerning custody proceedings in another state which may affect the jurisdiction of a court of South Carolina or the disposition to be made by it in a custody proceeding. S.C. Code Ann. § 20-7-814 (Law. Co-op. 1976).

c. Determining Whether Jurisdiction Exists

The PKPA and the UCCJA contain similar provisions for determining whether jurisdiction exists to make a child custody determination by initial or modification decree. The PKPA provides as follows at 28 U.S.C. § 1738A(c):

> d(c) A child custody determination made by a court of a State is consistent with the provisions of this section only if--
>
> (1) such court has jurisdiction under the law of such State; and
>
> (2) one of the following conditions is met:
>
> (A) such State (i) is the home State of the child on the date of the commencement of the proceeding, or (ii) had been the child's home State within six months before the date of the commencement of the proceeding and the child is absent from such State because of his removal or retention by a contestant or for

other reasons, and a contestant continues to live in such State;

(B) (i) it appears that no other State would have jurisdiction under subparagraph (A), and (ii) it is in the best interest of the child that a court of such State assume jurisdiction because (I) the child and his parents, or the child and at least one contestant, have a significant connection with such State other than mere physical presence in such State, and (II) there is available in such State substantial evidence concerning the child's present or future care, protection, training, and personal relationships;

(C) the child is physically present in such State and (i) the child has been abandoned, or (ii) it is necessary in an emergency to protect the child because he has been subjected to or threatened with mistreatment or abuse;

(D) (i) it appears that no other State would have jurisdiction under subparagraph (A), (B), (C), or (E), or another State has declined to exercise jurisdiction on the ground that the State whose jurisdiction is in issue is the more appropriate forum to determine the custody of the child, and (ii) it is in the best interest of the child that such court assume jurisdiction; or

(E) the court has continuing jurisdiction pursuant to subsection (d) of this section.

Thus, jurisdictional priority under the federal legislation goes to the "home State" of the child pursuant to subsection (A). Once a state is the "home state," it remains the "home state" for six months after the child leaves if a contestant remains there. Inquiry into "significant connections" or "substantial evidence" is only to be made pursuant to subsection (B) when there is no "home State" or no other state has jurisdiction otherwise, e.g., pursuant to subsections (C) or (D).

The UCCJA is a little different. It does not give clear priority to the "home State" but would also allow jurisdiction to be exercised under S.C. Code Ann. § 20-7-788(a)(2) (Law. Co-op. 1976) when:

> it is in the best interest of the child that a court of this State assume jurisdiction because (i) the child and his parents, or the child and at least one contestant, have a significant connection with such State and (ii) there is available in such State substantial evidence concerning the child's present or future care, protection, training and personal relationships;

These differences in the language of the two laws could lead to different results. For example, it is more likely under the wording of the UCCJA that two states could legitimately assert jurisdiction over the same case, one claiming jurisdiction as the "home State" and the other as the state with the more significant connections and substantial evidence. Of course, this conflict should be avoided so long as both states recognize the supremacy of the federal law under which it is clear that the "home State" has jurisdiction. However, the more liberal language in the UCCJA still may still be an important consideration where the question is whether a court retains jurisdiction to modify its own order. *See* the discussion of *Schwartz v. Schwartz*, 311 S.C. 303, 428 S.E.2d 748 (Ct. App. 1993), in the section on "modifying custody orders in multi-state cases" later in this chapter.

The definitions of "home State" are exactly the same in the UCCJA (S.C. Code Ann. § 20-7-786(5)) and the PKPA (28 U.S.C. § 1738A(b)(4)):

> "home State" means the State in which, immediately preceding the time involved, the child lived with his parents, a parent, or a person acting as parent, for at least six consecutive months, and

> in the case of a child less than six months old, the State in which the child lived from birth with any of such persons. Periods of temporary absence of any of such persons are counted as part of the six-month or other period;

The UCCJA, but not the PKPA, specifically states that mere physical presence of the child, or of the child and one of the contestants, is not alone sufficient to confer jurisdiction. S.C. Code Ann. § 20-7-788(b) (Law. Co-op. 1976). The UCCJA also provides that the physical presence of the child before the court is not a prerequisite for jurisdiction to determine his or her custody. S.C. Code Ann. § 20-7-788(c) (Law. Co-op. 1976).

The UCCJA and the PKPA include similar prohibitions against assuming jurisdiction when custody proceedings are already pending in another State. The PKPA provides at 28 U.S.C. § 1738A(g):

> A court of a State shall not exercise jurisdiction in any proceeding for a custody determination commenced during the pendency of a proceeding in a court of another State where such court of that other State is exercising jurisdiction consistently with the provisions of this section to make a custody determination.

The UCCJA provides at S.C. Code Ann. § 20-7-794:

> A court of this State shall not exercise its jurisdiction under this subarticle if at the time of filing the petition a proceeding concerning the custody of the child was pending in a court of another State exercising jurisdiction substantially in conformity with this subarticle, unless the proceeding is stayed by the court of the other state because this State is a more appropriate forum or for other reasons.

It is not likely that the differences in language would affect the outcome of a case. Both require not only that an action in the other state was initiated first but that the other State actually has jurisdiction. However, there is still a risk under both statutes that one state may declare that another state does not have jurisdiction, then proceed simultaneously with its own custody proceedings.

d. Modifying Custody Decrees in Multi-State Cases

The PKPA provides that a court which has made a child custody determination has continuing jurisdiction as long as it continues to have jurisdiction under the laws of its state and the child or any contestant continues to live there. This is found in 28 U.S.C. § 1738A(d) which says:

> The jurisdiction of a court of a State which has made a child custody determination consistently with the provisions of this section continues as long as the requirement of subsection (c)(1) of this section continues to be met and such State remains the residence of the child or of any contestant.

The UCCJA and the PKPA restrict the ability of one state's courts to modify the custody decrees of another state's courts. The PKPA (28 U.S.C. § 1738A(f)) permits one state to modify child custody decree by a court of another state, only if:

> (1) it has jurisdiction to make such a child custody determination; and
> (2) the court of the other State no longer has jurisdiction, or it has declined to exercise such jurisdiction to modify such determination.

The UCCJA describes the circumstances under which one state may modify a custody decree of another state in S.C. Code Ann. § 20-7-810 (Law. Co-op. 1976):

> If a court of another State has made a custody decree, a court of this State shall not modify that decree unless (1) it appears to the court of this State that the court which rendered the decree does not now have jurisdiction under jurisdictional prerequisites substantially in accordance with this subarticle or has declined jurisdiction to modify the decree and (2) the court of this State has jurisdiction.

In essence, the PKPA and the UCCJA both say that modification of another state's custody decree is only appropriate when the new state has jurisdiction and either the other state no longer has jurisdiction (see the earlier section on "determining whether jurisdiction exists") or when the other state has declined to exercise its jurisdiction (see the following section on "deciding whether to decline jurisdiction"). The danger inherent in this language is that it leaves it up to each state to determine whether the other state continues to have jurisdiction to modify its own orders.

This is exactly what happened in *Schwartz v. Schwartz*, 311 S.C. 303, 428 S.E.2d 748 (Ct. App. 1993), in which the Court of Appeals held that a California court improperly modified its own custody decree. Thus, a father was prevented from enforcing the modified custody decree in South Carolina. The parties were married in California and their daughter was born there. The mother eventually left because of physical abuse and took the child with her to live in South Carolina where her parents and other family members resided. A divorce was granted in California and joint child custody was ordered, with the mother having primary physical custody. The father later brought an action in California seeking sole custody. The mother wrote a letter, but did not file an answer; and the father was given sole custody. Eight months later, he sought enforcement of the modified custody order in South Carolina. The trial judge granted his request and ordered the mother to give custody of the child to the father at noon the following day. However, the Supreme Court granted a writ of *supersedeas*, then the Court of Appeals reversed the case on appeal, holding that the California decree could not be enforced in South Carolina.

The court cited *Marks v. Marks*, 281 S.C. 316, 315 S.E.2d 158 (Ct. App. 1984) for the proposition that "[w]here the provisions of the federal Parental Kidnaping Prevention Act of 1980 (PKPA), 28 U.S.C. § 1738A and state law conflict, the federal act controls." *Id.* at 307, 428 S.E.2d at 750.[23] The Court then considered the PKPA, finding that South Carolina, not California, was the "home State" when the decree was modified (thus, California could not assert jurisdiction pursuant to section 1738A(c)(2)(A)) and that the child was physically present in South Carolina and South Carolina had not declined to exercise jurisdiction (thus,

---

[23] *Schwarz* was the first South Carolina case since *Marks* to mention the PKPA. All cases during the interval had been decided under the UCCJA without referring to the PKPA.

California could not assert jurisdiction pursuant to section 1738A(c)(2)(B), (C) or (D)).

Finally, the *Schwartz* court considered whether California could assert continuing jurisdiction pursuant to section 1738A(d) on the basis that the father still resided in California and California still had jurisdiction under its state laws (i.e., the UCCJA). California's version of the UCCJA is the same as South Carolina's. Thus, either the "home State" or the "significant connections/substantial evidence" sections could serve as a basis for having jurisdiction. The court concluded that California did not have jurisdiction under its laws because: (1) the child no longer had a "significant connection" to California (it had only "slight contact" with California at the time that the father began his custody action); and (2) the record did not support a conclusion that there was in California "substantial evidence concerning the child's present or future care, protection, training and personal relationships" (in part because the California court had made no findings as to jurisdictional facts and there was a total absence of any findings concerning the child's present or future care, protection, training, and personal relations).

South Carolina found its role reversed in *Knoth v. Knoth*, 297 S.C. 460, 463, 377 S.E.2d 340, 342 (1988), when an Illinois court modified a custody decree from South Carolina. Although it appears that Illinois may have become the "home State" by the time it acted, the Supreme Court of South Carolina concluded that South Carolina courts retained jurisdiction pursuant to S.C. Code Ann. § 20-7-788(a)(2) (Law. Co-op. 1976) in light of the "significant contacts/substantial evidence" factors. The children had fairly recently moved to Illinois with their father and their mother still lived in South Carolina where the family court had initially decided child custody, visitation and support. Both parents had appeared in the other forum to contest jurisdiction, and both forums had assumed jurisdiction. The Supreme Court of South Carolina considered a string of cases from other jurisdictions before concluding:

> Although more than one state may meet these jurisdictional requirements, once a custody decree has been entered, the continuing jurisdiction of the decree state is exclusive. Exclusive continuing jurisdiction is not affected by the child's residence in another state.

> Illinois' action here created the very conflict the Act was designed to avoid.

Id. at 464, 377 S.E.2d at 342-343 (citations omitted). The Court then held the Illinois decree invalid and reinstated the previous South Carolina family court holding giving the mother extended visitation in the summer and on holidays, as well as whenever she visited Illinois.

The Court of Appeals held that South Carolina courts could modify a New Hampshire child support order in *Sinclair v. Albrecht*, 287 S.C. 20, 26, 336 S.E.2d 485, 488 (Ct. App. 1985). The mother and child had lived in South Carolina for more than a year, the husband had also left the decree state of New Hampshire, and there was no action pending there. The court concluded that, although the continuing jurisdiction of the decree state is exclusive once a custody decree has been issued, the decree state loses interstate jurisdiction "if all the parties have moved away or contact with the decree state has otherwise become slight." *Id.* at 20, 336 S.E.2d at 488. Although it appears that the case could have been more easily disposed of by referring to the "home State" priority recognized in the PKPA, the court made no reference to it.

The Court of Appeals relied on a significant connections analysis and did not refer to the PKPA or "home state" in reversing a family court judge's decision to assume jurisdiction over a visitation dispute involving a mother and a child who lived in Utah. *Smoak v. Wright*, 314 S.C. 325, 443 S.E.2d 920 (Ct. App. 1994). The facts that the child was conceived in South Carolina, he came to South Carolina on three occasions for short visits with his mother's parents, and his father, maternal grandparents, and paternal grandparents live in South Carolina were not enough to establish a "significant connection" with this State and give the family court jurisdiction to hear the case under the Uniform Child Custody Jurisdiction Act.

The Court of Appeals held that the PKPA prevented South Carolina courts from considering a child custody dispute in *Marks v. Marks*, 281 S.C. 316, 315 S.E.2d 158 (Ct. App. 1984). The initial litigation had taken place in West Virginia and the mother had been awarded custody. The father had moved to South Carolina, and he refused to return their son to West Virginia following a visit. He filed an action in West Virginia seeking to change custody in which he challenged the mother's fitness, presented the 10-year-old son's desire to live with him, and alleged physical and psychological abuse. However, the West Virginia court left custody with the mother. The father then fled to South Carolina with the child, and a South Carolina family court judge awarded him custody. While the appeal from this was pending, a West Virginia court granted a divorce and awarded custody to the mother after finding that she was a fit and proper person to have custody. This finding was not appealed.

The Court of Appeals ruled that the PKPA applied and that it preempted any state law that might have existed at the time (it had become effective on December 28, 1980, and the action in *Marks* had been commenced on January 8, 1981). It held that South Carolina could not reconsider the custody issue in light of the West Virginia court's decision and it reversed the family court's ruling. The court also determined that the common law result would have been the same (S.C. had not yet adopted the UCCJA).

e. Deciding Whether to Decline Jurisdiction (inconvenient forum and parental misconduct)

The issue of whether South Carolina should exercise jurisdiction usually centers on whether S.C. is an inconvenient forum. This has been a frequent issue of litigation under the UCCJA. S.C. Code Ann. § 20-7-796 (Law. Co-op. 1976) allows a court to decline to exercise jurisdiction "if it finds that it is an inconvenient forum to make a custody determination under the circumstances of the case and that a court of another state is a more appropriate forum." Subsection (c) of section 20-7-796 sets out factors to consider in determining whether South Carolina is an inconvenient forum.[24]

The Supreme Court explained the rules relating to claims that South Carolina is not a convenient forum in *Mansour v. Mansour*, 296 S.C. 215, 371 S.E.2d 537 (1988):

---

[24] The PKPA also anticipates in 28 U.S.C. § 1738A(c)(2)(D) that a state may decline to exercise jurisdiction on the basis that it is a less convenient forum than another state, but it provides no guidelines for determining how to make this decision.

> A *forum non conveniens* ruling was discretionary at common law and is discretionary under the UCCJA. *See Nienow v. Nienow*, 268 S.C. 161, 232 S.E.2d 504 (1977); *Oehler v. Clinton*, 282 S.C. 25, 317 S.E.2d 445 (1984); *McGee v. McGee*, 287 S.C. 644, 340 S.E.2d 571 (Ct. App. 1986). The UCCJA requires a judge confronting a forum convenience issue to consider, among other things, if: (1) another state recently was the child's home state; (2) another state has closer connection with the child and his family; and (3) if substantial evidence concerning the child's present or future care, protection, training and personal relationships is more readily available in another state.

Id. at 217, 371 S.E.2d at 538.

The Supreme Court determined that Connecticut was not the more convenient forum in *Mansour* in that the children had lived with the father in South Carolina for the entire school year after having left Connecticut. The Court relied on S.C. Code Ann. § 20-7-786(5) (Law. Co-op. 1976) which defines a child's "home State" as the state where the child has lived with a parent for the immediately preceding six months. In *McGee*, the Court of Appeals found that the family court properly declined to exercise jurisdiction over the question of custody under S.C. Code Ann. § 20-7-796(a) (Law. Co-op. 1976). The mother and one child lived in Georgia and she had filed an action in South Carolina seeking to hold the father in contempt over a dispute about visitation. The father had counterclaimed for custody of the son who was living with the mother.

The Supreme Court recognized that Delaware had become the "home State" of the child and was the more convenient forum to decide the parent's dispute over visitation issues in *Kirylik v. Kirylik*, 292 S.C. 475, 357 S.E.2d 449 (1987). The mother and child had moved to Delaware after the parties had separated. The family court in South Carolina had awarded her custody and support, and it had set a specified visitation schedule for the father. It subsequently issued a judgment of divorce. The mother had the custody award registered in Delaware pursuant to the UCCJA. The Court affirmed the trial judge's decision to decline jurisdiction when the father filed a petition in South Carolina seeking to hold the mother in contempt for refusing to permit him to exercise visitation on two occasions.

The Supreme Court ruled that South Carolina was the home state and most convenient forum in *Williams v. Williams,* 285 S.C. 270, 329 S.E.2d 751 (1985). The mother and child had been permanent residents here for seven years, and there was no apparent link to the original forum state of North Carolina, other than the fact of the father's residence there.

Perhaps the most controversial case involving an inconvenient forum claim under the UCCJA was the first one considered by the Supreme Court. In *Oehler v. Clinton*, 282 S.C. 25, 317 S.E.2d 445 (1984), the trial judge declined to exercise jurisdiction on the basis of inconvenient forum, and this was upheld by a 3-2 Court. The father had originally had custody, as ordered by a North Carolina court where he lived and the parties had resided. Some years later, the mother removed the child from the father's home on December 26, 1980, and took it to South Carolina where she then resided. On December 27, 1980, the father killed himself. On December 29, 1980, the paternal grandparents obtained in North Carolina an *ex parte* order awarding them emergency custody. On December 30, 1980, the mother obtained in South Carolina an *ex parte* order awarding her temporary custody. In February, 1981, the North Carolina court gave permanent custody to the grandparents. The mother ignored the North Carolina order, and when the grandparents asked a S.C. family court to enforce the order in September, 1981 (two months after S.C. had adopted the UCCJA), the mother sought to have the S.C. court decide the custody issue on the merits. The family court judge declined to exercise jurisdiction. The South Carolina Supreme Court indicated that it felt that either state could have exercised jurisdiction, but it decided against getting into competition with the North Carolina courts which had assumed jurisdiction first.

If the Supreme Court is presented with the same facts as *Oehler* today, one might expect it to employ the same analysis used by the Court of Appeals in *Schwartz v. Schwartz*, 311 S.C. 303, 428 S.E.2d 748 (Ct. App. 1993). If so, it would probably reach the same result. It would almost certainly conclude that the North Carolina court had primary jurisdiction to determine custody initially (custody litigation was filed there first, and it was the "home State" and would have also met the "significant connection/substantial evidence" test). The question as to whether a South Carolina court had jurisdiction to modify the custody order, would depend on whether North Carolina still had jurisdiction under its laws. South Carolina would have become the "home State," therefore the answer would depend on the Court's analysis of the "significant contact/substantial evidence" test and the Court would most probably conclude that South Carolina did not have jurisdiction to modify the North Carolina order. Given the *Oheler* Court's negative opinion of the mother's conduct in trying to avoid legal proceedings, it may have decided not to exercise jurisdiction in any event, if it concluded that the mother's conduct was "reprehensible." *See* S.C. Code Ann. § 20-7-798 (Law. Co-op. 1976), discussed later in this section. The *Oehler* dissenters make the point that it is difficult to understand how an "inconvenient forum" holding was justified given that the mother and child lived in Rock Hill, just across the state line from the grandparents' residence in Mecklenburg County.

An intriguing aspect of *Oehler* is that the Supreme Court did not address the issue of whether the mother had automatically become the child's custodian upon the death of the father by operation of law. If so, the grandparents' petition for custody would have been filed after the mother had obtained legal as well as physical custody, and South Carolina would have had primary authority to exercise jurisdiction over any subsequent custody dispute. This point was pressed by Justices Littlejohn and Gregory in a separate dissenting opinion written by Justice Littlejohn. The dissenters argued that the North Carolina court did not have initial jurisdiction to determine custody because the mother and the child were physically present and domiciled in South Carolina at the time of the father's death. Therefore, she had the right and duty to assume custody and control of their child until such time as someone challenged that right. If the grandparents wanted to seek custody of their grandchild, they should have been required to do so in South Carolina. According to the dissenters:

> [T]he only issue for our court to determine on this appeal is whether the mother should be permitted to litigate in her own state where both she and the child are domiciled, or if she should be required to litigate in California, Arizona, Michigan or even in the State of North Carolina, which happens to be close by, merely because that is where the grandparents happen to reside.

Id. at 31, 317 S.E.2d at 449. The majority of the Court did not address the merits of this issue because it had not been preserved for the appeal, briefed or otherwise mentioned until oral argument, and only two members of the Court were willing to raise it *ex mero motu.*

Although the reported cases dealing with whether or not South Carolina should exercise its jurisdiction have centered on the issue of inconvenient forum, the UCCJA, in section 20-7-798, also authorizes the court to decline jurisdiction if the person seeking custody has "wrongfully taken the child from another state or has engaged in similar reprehensible conduct." The statute requires the family court to not exercise its jurisdiction to modify a child custody order if the petitioner has "improperly removed the child from the physical custody of the person entitled to custody or has improperly retained the child after a visit or other temporary relinquishment of physical custody."

f. Attorneys' Fees and Litigation Expenses

The trial court can award attorneys' fees and litigation expenses to defendants in child custody cases pursuant to S.C. Code Ann. § 20-7-798 (Law. Co-op. 1976), if jurisdiction is declined because the person requesting custody has "wrongfully taken the child from another state or has engaged in similar reprehensible conduct." In *Wierszewski v. Tokarick*, 308 S.C. 441, 418 S.E.2d 557 (Ct. App. 1992), the husband had petitioned for custody under section 20-7-788(a)(3), alleging that his child had been physically abused by the mother. The family court declined to exercise jurisdiction. It found insufficient evidence of abuse and held that it was not the most convenient forum because the child had lived in Nevada for 14 months. The wife's request for fees and costs under section 20-7-798 was denied because the case did not fit the circumstances described in the statute. However, the Court of Appeals specifically did not decide whether fees and costs could have been awarded pursuant to S.C. Code Ann. § 20-7-420 (Law. Co-op. 1976), the general jurisdictional statute of the family court, because it had not been raised in the petition or addressed in the order.

Attorneys' fees and costs can be awarded to plaintiffs who have to enforce other states' custody orders in South Carolina pursuant to S.C. Code Ann. § 20-7-812 (Law. Co-op. 1976). However, in *Schwartz v. Schwartz*, 311 S.C. 303, 428 S.E.2d 748 (Ct. App. 1993), the Court of Appeals reversed an award of attorneys' fees, costs and guardian litem fees under this statute because the defendant prevailed on appeal.

The court also directed the unsuccessful plaintiff to pay the guardian ad litem's fees, but it cited no authority.

3. INDIAN CHILD WELFARE ACT

The Indian Child Welfare Act requires the family court to transfer jurisdiction to an Indian child's tribe in any proceeding for the foster placement of, or termination of parental rights to, an Indian child not domiciled or residing within the reservation of the tribe, absent good cause to the contrary. 25 U.S.C. § 1911(b).

The Indian Child Welfare Act probably applies only to cases where a Native American child is being removed from an existing Native American family. In *Rye (Weasel) v. Weasel*, ___ S.W.2d ___ (Ky. Sup. Ct. 1996), the Supreme Court of Kentucky agreed with courts in other states that Congress did not intend for the Indian Welfare Act to divest state courts of jurisdiction to decide custody cases regarding Native American children who have not lived for many years in an existing Native American family. The court noted that the child had no contact with her mother (the biological father was unknown) or her tribe since being placed with her aunt and uncle, and that she was raised in an non-Native American environment. Other cases that reach the same conclusion include *In re Adoption of Crews*, 825 P.2d 305 (Wash. Sup. Ct. 1992); *In re S.C.*, 833 P.2d 1249 (Okla. Sup. Ct. 1992); *In re D.S.*, 577 N.E.2d 572 (Ind. Sup. Ct. 1991); *S.A. v. E.J.P.*, 571 So.2d 1187 (Ala. Ct. Civ. App. 1990); *In re T.S.*, 801 P.2d 77 (Mont. Sup. Ct. 1990); *In re Adoption of TRM*, 525 N.E.2d 298 (Ind. Sup. Ct. 1988); *In re S.A.M.*, 703 S.W.2d 607 (Mo. Ct. App. 1986); *In re Adoption of D.M.J.*, 741 P.2d 1386 (Okla. Sup. Ct. 1985). No case was found which reaches any other conclusion.

Even in cases that fall within the scope of the Indian Welfare Act, good cause for retaining jurisdiction includes significant hardship for witnesses to travel to the reservation. *South Carolina DSS v. Coleman*, 303 S.C. 226, 399 S.E.2d 773 (1990) (reversing on the basis of *forum non conveniens* the family court's decision to transfer jurisdiction to the juvenile court of an Indian tribe in South Dakota).

C. CUSTODY DISPUTES BETWEEN NATURAL PARENTS

1. JOINT CUSTODY

It is not clear whether joint or divided custody can be awarded in South Carolina. In 1996, the legislature amended S.C. Code Ann. § 20-7-420 (Law. Co-op. Supp.) to give family court judges the authority "to order joint or divided custody where the court finds it is in the best interests of the child." (emphasis added) S.C. Code Ann. § 20-7-420(42) (Law. Co-op. Supp.) This seems to express a legislative policy in favor of joint custody, but the Supreme Court of South Carolina has consistently held that joint custody is not in the best interests of children. It will take a decision by the Supreme Court before one knows if the legislation changes anything. As explained below, however, the Supreme Court hints in a 1995 case that it may be willing to reconsider its position on joint custody.

Family court judges have been awarding joint custody for many years in cases in which both parents want it and the court is convinced that the parents are capable of cooperating sufficiently to make it work. There is little risk of reversal on appeal when judges give parties what they both want. With the 1996 legislation in place, family court judges may now begin awarding joint custody when they believe it would be better for children than awarding sole custody to one parent, even if one parent would rather have sole custody. However, family court judges have no power to award joint or divided custody unless it is requested in the pleadings of at least one of the parties. *See Parris,* 319 S.C. 308, 460 S.E. 2d 571 (1995).

For now, the Supreme Court's decisions establish a presumption that joint or divided custody is not in the best interests of children.

> The best interest and welfare of the children demand that divided custody should be avoided if possible, and it will not be approved except under exceptional circumstances or for strong and convincing reasons, 27B C.J.S. *Divorce* § 308d, p. 446. *See also* . . . 92 A.L.R.(2d) 695 [(1957)]. Divided custody is usually harmful to and not conducive to the best interest and welfare of the children.

In *Nelson on Divorce* (2nd Ed.), section 15.17, it is stated:

> The courts generally endeavor to avoid dividing the custody of a child between contending parties, and are particularly reluctant to award the custody of a child in brief alternating periods between estranged and quarrelsome persons. Under the facts and circumstances of particular cases, it has been held improper to apportion the custody of a child between its parents, or between one of its parents and a third party, for ordinarily it is not conducive to the best interests and welfare of a child for it to be shifted and shuttled back and forth in alternate brief periods between contending parties, particularly during the school term. Furthermore, such an arrangement is likely to cause confusion, interfere with proper training and discipline of the child, make the child the basis of many quarrels between its custodians, render its life unhappy and discontented, and prevent it from living a normal life.

The trial judge, without making any findings of fact, directed divided and alternate custody. We have carefully reviewed the entire record in this case and find no exceptional circumstances that would justify the direction made by the trial judge. It follows that the order of the trial judge granting divided and alternate custody should be reversed.

Mixson v. Mixson, 253 S.C. 436, 446, 171 S.E.2d 581, 586 (1969).

*Mixson*is cited in *Avin v. Avin*, 272 S.C. 514, 515, 252 S.E.2d 888, 888-889 (1979), in which the mother's "visitation" was so substantial that she had as much physical time with the child as did the legal custodian father. The Supreme Court viewed this order as an abuse of discretion. Similar holdings resulted in *Lassiter v. Lassiter*, 289 S.C. 341, 345 S.E.2d 504 (Ct. App. 1986) (rejecting 150 days per year as amounting to divided custody); *Courie v. Courie*, 288 S.C. 163, 341 S.E.2d 646

(Ct. App. 1986) (holding that 165 days was too much). *See also Sharpe v. Sharpe*, 256 S.C. 517, 183 S.E.2d 325 (1971) (disallowing custody in the father from June 15 to August 15).

As a measure of how much visitation is not too much, *see Johns v. Johns*, 309 S.C. 199, 420 S.E.2d 856 (Ct. App. 1992). The Court of Appeals determined that it did not amount to split custody for the father to have the following visitation rights: every other weekend from 6:00 p.m. Friday until 6:00 p.m. Sunday; the first two weeks of June, July and August; alternate Thanksgiving and spring break holidays; and one week at Christmas. The Court of Appeals noted that this was much less visitation than was rejected in *Lassiter* and *Courie*, involved much less shuttling of the children, and there had been no showing that the amount of visitation would have a detrimental effect on the children.

If joint custody is awarded but one of the parents later asks the family court to change it to sole custody, no case in South Carolina outlines criteria to be applied by the family court in deciding whether custody should be changed from joint to sole custody. *Wheeler v. Gill*, 307 S.C. 94, 413 S.E.2d 860 (Ct. App. 1992). In *Wheeler*, both parents agreed that joint custody was not working and both sought sole custody pursuant to the original order which required that the joint custody arrangement be reviewed in one year.

Some older cases allowed joint custody. These may have been overruled implicitly by the more recent cases. *See Sanders v. Sanders*, 232 S.C. 625, 630, 103 S.E.2d 281, 284 (1958) (affirming the trial court's order that the mother and father were each to have the children six months each year as it was in the best interest of the children (one was six years old, the other was seventeen months old) not to be separated from each other and to have the benefit of the love, affection, and care of both parents); *Koon v. Koon*, 203 S.C. 556, 560, 28 S.E.2d 89, 90-91 (1943) (affirming an award of joint custody of an infant to the maternal grandparents and paternal grandparents with the direction that it remain in the home of each of them one half of the time). The *Sanders* Court cited *Koon* in saying that "[d]ivided custody is probably not the perfect solution, for problems of this kind are rarely if ever susceptible of perfect solution; but in the circumstances of the instant case it seems the best one possible from the standpoint of the children's welfare." *Id.* at 633, 103 S.E.2d at 286.

The Supreme Court may have signaled a willingness to reconsider its position about joint custody in *Parris v. Parris*, 319 S.C. 308, 460 S.E.2d 571 (1995).

> *Parris* was a very close custody case in which both parents were almost equally fit to have custody. On appeal, the mother asked the Supreme Court to reconsider its rule against joint custody. The Court declined to address the issue because neither party asked for joint custody in their pleadings and the mother never moved to alter or amend the judgment of the trial court. Therefore, the issue was not preserved for review on appeal, and the Court wrote "Accordingly, we need not decide in the present case whether to reconsider our position on joint custody." *Id.* at ___, 460 S.E.2d at 573.

2. FACTORS CONSIDERED IN DETERMINING BEST INTERESTS OF CHILDREN

The factors to be considered include anything which might relate to the fitness of a parent or the best interest of a child. Seldom is any one factor determinative of the outcome. Most cases involve consideration of a wide range of topics, including who has been the primary caretaker; the conduct, attributes and resources of the parents; opinions of third parties (including guardians *ad litem*, expert witnesses and the child); and the age, health and sex of the child. In sum, what a court will find to be in the best interest of a child will depend on the particular facts of each case.

a. Fitness of Parents

In most child custody disputes which go to trial, the purpose of the litigation is to try to prove that the other parent is unfit (or at least less fit) to have custody. The reason is that most trial judges will rule that the best interest of a child is to award custody to the parent who is most fit to care for him or her. Although a lawyer is restricted by the facts of his or her case, proving unfitness of the opposing party virtually guarantees an award of custody to his or her client (unless also proven unfit). Fitness decisions normally turn on either of two considerations; whether either parent has been the primary caretaker, or whether either parent has engaged in conduct which would affect the welfare of the child.

Evidence of emotional problems and epilepsy was determined to be irrelevant where it was not shown that either condition would incapacitate the husband in his role as a father. *Thompson v. Brunson*, 283 S.C. 221, 228, 321 S.E.2d 622, 626 (Ct. App. 1984). *See also*, *Todd v. Todd*, 242 S.C. 263, 130 S.E.2d 552 (1963) (awarding custody to a parent who had recovered from mental illness after hospitalization).

(1) Primary Caretaker

There has been an assumption that custody will be awarded to the parent who has been the primary caretaker of the children, unless unfitness is proved or there is other evidence that the welfare of a child will be better served by awarding custody to the other parent. In modern society, however, it is becoming more and more common for both parents to work, thus making it more difficult to identify either one as the primary caretaker.

The primary caretaker was awarded custody in *Smith v. Smith*, 294 S.C. 194, 363 S.E.2d 404 (Ct. App. 1987), in which the children had lived with their mother since separation; and in *West v. West*, 294 S.C. 190, 363 S.E.2d 402 (Ct. App. 1987), where, although both parents had shared responsibility for rearing the children, the father had been the primary caretaker during the months just before the separation. In *Burns v. Burns*, 293 S.C. 1, 358 S.E.2d 168 (Ct. App. 1987), the mother failed to convince the court that she was still the primary caretaker, although she had been when the children were infants. In upholding an award of custody to the father, the court found that the father had contributed substantially to the care of the children. The Supreme Court reversed a custody award to the father and gave custody to the mother, whom it found to be the primary caretaker, in *Epperly v. Epperly*, 312 S.C. 411, 440 S.E.2d 884 (1994).

If one parent is the primary breadwinner and the other parent plays a more active role in the daily lives of the children, the family court may consider this as a factor in deciding custody.

> Although not the sole factor, the amount of time a parent spends with the child has traditionally been a relevant consideration in determining which of two fit parents receives custody. Work habits necessarily impact upon this consideration. Where, as here, the record reveals a pattern of one parent as primary caretaker and the other parent as the primary wage earner, it would be incomprehensible for a court to disregard this fact in awarding custody.

Parris v. Parris, 319 S.C. 308, 311, 460 S.E.2d 571, 573 (1995). This was an extremely close custody case and both parents were found to be fit custodial parents. However, the father was more actively involved in the child's daily life, taking him, or car pooling, to doctors, baseball, swimming, soccer, parent\teacher conferences, signing report cards, doing yard work together, birthday parties, getting the child up in the morning and off to school, making breakfast on weekends, cooking the family's Sunday dinner, etc.

The Court agreed with the mother, a realtor, that the fact she is "aggressive" and "career oriented" is not, standing alone, relevant to a determination of custody. However, it found her work habits highly relevant when considered in the context of the amount of time she spent with the child.

A more active social life by one parent coupled with the other parent being the primary caretaker will justify the court's award to the primary caretaker. In *The Husband v. The Wife*, 301 S.C. 531, 392 S.E.2d 811 (Ct. App. 1990), the Court of Appeals upheld the trial judge's award of custody to the husband who had been the primary caretaker for the children since the parties' separation. In addition, the court found that "[t]he wife has put her rather active social life first. Even before she took a night job, she stayed out several nights a week playing bridge." *Id.* at 534, 392 S.E.2d at 813. The Court of Appeals specifically found that the wife was also a fit parent, but it found no abuse of the trial court's discretion in awarding custody to the husband. One distinction in this case from the *Parris* case is that The Wife was found to have committed adultery. However, the Court of Appeals said this was not a factor in its decision about who should have custody. "In deciding who should have custody of the children, we have not considered the fact that the wife was determined to be guilty of adultery." *Id.* at 532, 392 S.E.2d at 812.

See also West v. West, 294 S.C. 190, 363 S.E.2d 402 (Ct. App. 1987); *Jones v. Jones*, 290 S.C. 49, 348 S.E.2d 178 (Ct. App. 1986). In *West*, the Court of Appeals affirmed an award of custody to the father, stating:

> The record reveals both parties shared the responsibility of rearing the children, however Mr. West was the primary caretaker during the months prior to the separation.
>
> . . .
>
> The record also reveals Mrs. West was a user of profane language around the children and that her lifestyle revealed she placed her personal and professional life above her care for the children and the home life.

Id. at 193, 363 S.E.2d at 403. In *Jones*, the Court of Appeals upheld a custody award to the father where the evidence showed he was the primary caretaker, and the mother had committed adultery and used drugs.

(2) Conduct

Cases involving questions of unfitness commonly focus on parental conduct which is considered "immoral." The issue of who was at fault in the breakup of a marriage has also been considered in determinations of unfitness, but increasingly to a lesser degree unless the marital fault also involves immoral conduct.

"Immoral" conduct, including exposing children to an adulterous relationship, has always been a significant factor in determining custody in South Carolina, but it is clearer today that the conduct must have some nexus to the welfare of the child before it will be relevant to child custody. The court had this to say about immoral conduct in *Shainwald v. Shainwald*, 302 S.C. 453, 395 S.E.2d 441 (Ct. App. 1990):

> In this state, conduct which is "immoral" must also be shown to be detrimental to the welfare of a child before it is of legal significance in a custody dispute. *Langston v. Langston*, 250 S.C. 363, 157 S.E.2d 858 (1967); *Stroman v. Williams*, 291 S.C. 376, 353

> S.E.2d 704 (Ct. App. 1987). We think the record supports the court's finding that the mother had exposed her adulterous relationship to the children.

Id. at 460, 395 S.E.2d at 445-446. There was no additional discussion in *Shainwald* about the resulting detriment to the welfare of the children; therefore, it appears that harm to the children will be assumed upon a showing that they have been "exposed" to an adulterous relationship or other immoral conduct. The court upheld the award of custody to the father.

However, custody was awarded to a child's aunt and uncle rather than to its mother, although there was no finding that the mother's conduct had been detrimental to the child nor that she was currently engaging in any improper conduct in *Kramer v. Kramer*, ___ S.C. ___, 473 S.E.2d 846 (Ct. App. 1996). The case probably turned more on questions of the mother's financial ability to provide a proper home for the child, but the opinion also states "we do not believe that Mother is a fit parent able to provide a good home for Daniel." *Id.* at ___, 473 S.E.2d at 849. The conduct of the mother that concerned the Court was that she abandoned the child and the father when the child was one year old, a previous child was born out of wedlock, the child involved in this case was born in a common law relationship [it is not clear why this concerned the Court], she moved around a bit and had various relationships, and she had two more children out of wedlock. Although she married the father of the two most recent children shortly before seeking custody of the child in this action, the court did not seem to believe the sincerity of her commitment to domestication.

"Flagrant promiscuity" will result in a change of custody even if children are not directly exposed to it. In *Boykin v. Boykin*, 296 S.C. 100, 370 S.E.2d 884 (Ct. App. 1988), the Court of Appeals reversed the trial judge and ordered custody changed to the father. The facts are that the mother worked at night, leaving the child with her maternal grandmother. She often went partying after work, drinking beer and, occasionally, smoking marijuana until the early morning hours. She admitted having sexual relations with at least five men during the preceding year. The court concluded:

> We hold that this and other evidence of record, together with the admittedly promiscuous lifestyle of the mother, requires the

> conclusion by this Court that Amanda's best interest will be served by changing custody to her father. Flagrant promiscuity on the part of a custodial parent will, we hold, inevitably affect the welfare of the child and establish a watershed in the court's quest to protect the best interest of a minor child.

Id. at 102, 370 S.E.2d at 886. The court noted that the mother was not entirely lacking in redeeming qualities, but also found that the decision was buttressed by the fact that the father was a person of high quality and had very acceptable parenting skills.

Although the Court of Appeals appears to place homosexual conduct in the category of "immoral" behavior, perhaps as it would with any out-of-wedlock sexual relationship, it held in *Stroman v. Williams*, 291 S.C. 376, 353 S.E.2d 704 (Ct. App. 1987), that homosexual conduct does not render a person unfit to have custody as a matter of law. The court wrote:

> Although the father claims the younger daughter has been substantially affected by the mother's lesbian relationship with the other woman, he points to no evidence that supports his claim. Our own examination of the record did not uncover any evidence that the daughter was being exposed to deviant sexual acts or that her welfare was being adversely affected in any substantial way.

Id. at 379, 353 S.E.2d at 705. The court went on to report the evidence which showed the daughter to be healthy and well-adjusted, including a note that she was heterosexual.

Boykin and *Stroman* may be a little inconsistent in that the mother in *Stroman* appears to have been living with her friend in a lesbian relationship in the same house with the children, while there is nothing in the opinion to indicate that the children were exposed to their mother's sexual activity. Probably, *Boykin* is better understood as a case in which the court disapproved of the mother's lifestyle altogether, whereas it was persuaded by the expert testimony in *Stroman* that the children were not being harmed by their mother's relationship.

Other cases standing for the principal that "the morality of a parent is a proper consideration in determining child custody but it is limited in its force to what relevancy it has, either indirectly or directly, to the welfare of the child" include *Davenport v. Davenport*, 265 S.C. 524, 527, 220 S.E.2d 228, 230 (1975); *Marshall v. Marshall*, 282 S.C. 534, 540-41, 320 S.E.2d 44, 48 (Ct. App. 1984).

Immoral conduct is less likely to be relevant to a custody decision if the trial judge is convinced that the conduct has ended and the moral lapse is not likely to be repeated. *Davenport v. Davenport*, 265 S.C. 524, 527, 220 S.E.2d 228, 230 (1975) (awarding custody to the mother although she admitted adultery during the divorce proceedings). *See also Bonnette v. Bonnette*, 276 S.C. 653, 281 S.E.2d 774 (1981) (holding that an award of custody to the father was in error where the mother's one adulterous act was not indicative of a continued course of conduct and the father had failed to prove that the welfare of the child required that custody be granted to him); *Linder v. Agnew*, 276 S.C. 153, 276 S.E.2d 774 (1981) (upholding custody in an adulterous mother whose conduct had been reformed); *Langston v. Langston*, 250 S.C. 363, 374, 157 S.E.2d 858, 863 (1967) (affirming an award of primary custody to a mother who'd had custody for 2 ½ years and who before and after her adulterous infatuation had been a loving and attentive mother). *But see Johnson v. Johnson*, 251 S.C. 420, 163 S.E.2d 229 (1968), in which the wife's adultery affected the outcome because the court found that her adultery would reduce the time she would have to spend with her children since she was ineligible for alimony and would have to work.

The Supreme Court did not find the mere fact of the existence of an illegitimate child in the household to cause any difficulty in *Dent v. Dent*, 273 S.C. 387, 256 S.E.2d 743 (1979). The family court had ordered a change of custody from the mother to the father, in large part because of the mother's sexual conduct which had resulted in an illegitimate child. The Supreme Court reversed, indicating that the sexual conduct of the wife was a fairly isolated incident and that her conduct had not, since the time of the alleged specific incident, been indicative of moral laxity which would adversely affect the welfare of the children. The Court also found that the mother had suffered temporary emotional distress at about the time of her separation from the husband and that there was nothing to indicate that it was of a permanent nature. Thus, it was not determinative.

Another case in which the Supreme Court was willing to overlook the temporary moral lapses of an emotionally troubled mother is *Cole v. Cole*, 274 S.C. 449, 265 S.E.2d 669 (1980). The Court reversed the trial court's initial custody determination that the two youngest children were to be moved from the mother's custody to the father's while the two oldest were to remain with the mother. The ages of the children were 6, 9, 16 and 17; and the older two children were biologically the mother's (adopted by the father), while the younger two were the biological children of both parties. The Supreme Court found that, although the wife had engaged in sexual relationships and adulterous conduct following the separation of the parties but prior to the divorce decree (the husband had been granted the divorce on the ground of adultery), the family court should consider such conduct only to the extent that it was relevant either directly or indirectly to the welfare of the children.

The Supreme Court said that neither the wife's prior emotional disturbance nor her adulterous conduct had a current effect upon her roles as mother and housekeeper. The Court found a degree of contradiction between the award of custody of the two older children to her and the family court's apparent belief that she was not a proper custodian for the younger children. Of substantial significance to the Supreme Court's decision was the fact that the younger children had remained in the mother's home and that they were "happy and well adjusted in this environment." *Id.*at 454, 265 S.E.2d at 671. There was conclusive evidence of the recuperation and present strength and stability of the mother, and there was inadequate support for the finding that the mother's moral lapse by way of post-separation adultery has adversely affected the welfare of the children. Probably significant as well is the fact that the Supreme Court viewed the father as being more or less on the same moral level as the mother.

There was no specific finding of unfitness, but the husband's conduct seemed to be the conclusive factor in awarding custody of one of the children to the mother in *Prather v. Prather*, 4 S.C. Eq. (4 Desaus.) 33, 43-44 (1809), where he beat up his wife for ruining a batch of whiskey and badgered his wife about his various lovers. The same holds true in *Graydon v. Graydon*, 150 S.C. 117, 147 S.E. 749 (1929), where the husband had a considerable drinking problem.

Specific conduct tending to prove unfitness includes: insanity (Dillon v. Dillon, 219 S.C. 255, 64 S.E.2d 649 (1951)); living with a married person other than one's spouse (*Stutz v. Funderburk*, 272 S.C. 273, 252 S.E.2d 32 (1979); *Pullen v. Pullen*, 253 S.C. 123, 169 S.E.2d 376 (1969)); improper association with the opposite sex (*Johnson v. Johnson*, 251 S.C. 420, 163 S.E.2d 229 (1968); *Cook v. Cobb*, 271 S.C. 136, 245 S.E.2d 612 (1978); *Peay v. Peay*, 260 S.C. 108, 194 S.E.2d 392 (1973)); drug abuse (*Moorhead v. Scott*, 259 S.C. 580, 193 S.E.2d 510 (1972), although no evidence of drug abuse was found in this case; *Skinner v. King*, 272 S.C. 520, 252 S.E.2d 891 (1979)); association with homosexuals and general nomadic nature (*Cook v. Cobb, supra*); emotional instability, current psychiatric care, and attempted suicide (*Peeples v. Peeples*, 270 S.C. 116, 241 S.E.2d 159 (1978); *Murray v. Murray*, 271 S.C. 62, 244 S.E.2d 538 (1978)).

Any one of these factors standing alone may not be sufficient to constitute unfitness, but the frequency of the misconduct and the relevance it has to a child's welfare will be important.

Is it appropriate for the family court to consider whether a parent smokes tobacco in deciding child custody disputes? Although this issue has been raised at the trial level, no reported cases have considered this question in South Carolina. However, the legislature appears to have enunciated a public policy against smoking around children when it amended S.C. Code Ann. § 44-95-20 (Law. Co-op. Supp.) in 1994 to prohibit smoking "in child care facilities, as defined in Section 20-7-2700, which are licensed pursuant to Subarticle 11, Article 13, Chapter 7, Title 20." S.C. Code Ann. § 44-95-20(2) (Law. Co-op. Supp.). Given the growing medical evidence about the harmful effects of second hand smoke, it seem appropriate for a court to consider whether one of the parents in a custody dispute is a smoker.

The effect of reformation by a parent after the initial custody award, is discussed in the section on modification of custody: rehabilitation of unfitness.

b. Attributes and Resources of Parents

A separate issue from the fitness of the parents is consideration of what the parents will be able to provide for children who are placed in their custody. This can involve a wide range of issues, such as financial and physical resources, free time to spend with the children, access to friends and relatives, the availability of child care, tenderness, caring and religious training.

A person's race cannot be the only factor considered in determining child custody issues, but it may be a factor which can be considered, particularly if a nexus can be established between the person's race and the best interests of the child. The United States Supreme Court considered the general issue in *Palmore v. Sidoti*, 466 U.S. 429, 104 S. Ct. 1879, 80 L. Ed. 2d 421 (1984), in which the non-custodial father was seeking a change of custody based on his ex-wife's cohabitation with an African American, whom she subsequently married. The trial court had ordered that custody be changed from the mother to the father, solely considering the fact that the paramour was of a different race than the child. The U.S. Supreme Court held that "[t]he effects of racial prejudice, however real, cannot justify a racial classification removing an infant child from the custody of its natural mother found to be an appropriate person to have such custody." *Id.* at 434, 104 S. Ct. at 1882, 80 L. Ed. 2d at 426. The Court further stated that, while the Constitution cannot control such prejudice, it cannot thereby tolerate the prejudice. The law cannot directly or indirectly give an effect to private biases. The case does not state that race cannot be considered at all in deciding custody cases, but it is likely that some nexus between a person's race and the best interest of the child would have to be proven before it would be relevant.

The father's superior financial ability and the network of support available to him were the primary factors considered in reversing an award of custody to the mother in *Radtke v. Radtke*, 297 S.C. 260, 376 S.E.2d 275 (1989). This was consistent with the recommendations of a child psychologist and the guardian *ad litem*. The Supreme Court felt the family court had given too much weight to the tender years doctrine, although the children were both young females.

Concerns about a parent's financial ability to provide a good home for a child can result in a denial of custody, particularly where there is no father from whom child support can be collected. The Court of Appeals awarded custody of a child to its aunt and uncle, following the death of the child's father, largely because of its concerns about the mother's ability to provide a good home in *Kramer v. Kramer*, ___ S.C. ___, 473 S.E.2d 846 (Ct. App. 1996). The mother was not working, had few job skills, and was financially dependent on her new husband (the father of her two subsequent children). Although the new husband testified that he would support the child, the Court found this testimony questionable in light of evidence that he was $16,000 in arrears on child support owed to a former wife.

A finding that the father's home would provide a better environment for the daughter was the primary reason for awarding him custody in *Wheeler v. Gill*, 307 S.C. 94, 413 S.E.2d 860 (Ct. App. 1992), where the father's environment included an apparent loving extended family, attentiveness to the daughter's interest in outdoor activities, and the provision of a more stable and consistent home environment.

The education and parenting skills of a parent are legitimate factors to consider. *See Davenport v. Davenport*, 265 S.C. 524, 220 S.E.2d 228 (1975), where the mother's education included a degree in elementary education and eighteen hours of graduate study in early childhood development. She was employed as a sixth grade teacher. In *Morehouse v. Morehouse*, 317 S.C. 222, 452 S.E.2d 632 (Ct. App. 1994), one factor in favor of giving custody to the father was that he was the more tender, caring parent.

Further, the special attention necessitated by learning difficulties or poor performance in school are considerations to be taken into account in changing custody. The daughter of George and Amy Gilbert developed a learning disability near the time the Gilbert's were divorced and by agreement she went to live with her father in Atlanta in order to attend a special school. Subsequently the father instituted an action for a change of custody in *Gilbert v Gilbert*, 270 S.C. 202, 241 S.E.2d 559 (1978). He was awarded custody based, in part, on the testimony by experts that the child was at a critical stage in her language development. The Supreme Court held that the deterioration in the child's condition and manifestation of language impediment subsequent to the original custody award to the mother, combined with the school in Atlanta, constituted a sufficient change of circumstances to justify the modification of the custodial arrangement from the mother to the father. However, the court called for an annual review. The trial judge found both parents to be "fit and proper" and concerned for their daughter.

Consistently, a mother lost the primary placement of her son under a joint custodial arrangement because of lack of proper attention to the learning difficulties of her son in *Glanton v. Glanton*, 314 S.C. 58, 443 S.E.2d 810 (Ct. App. 1994). Upon entering the fourth grade the boy's grades plummeted and he was tested and found to be performing at a second grade level. Despite an indication that he might be dyslexic, the mother refused to allow the completion of the necessary testing, preferring to blame the father and the teachers. The trial court changed the primary placement of the boy from the mother to the father. On appeal the placement was affirmed. The educational deterioration with the mother, as opposed to the progress following the *pendente lite* transfer, were such significant changes of circumstances to justify the modification of the custody arrangement. While careful to point out that grades were not the only factor for the change of custody, the court cites the inability or unwillingness of the mother to appreciate the child's difficulties at school and her increasingly adverse effects on the child as an important issue.

The amount of time a parent has to spend with the children has frequently been a consideration, but it appears to be less important than it once was, probably due to the proliferation of two-income (two-job) families and the widespread acceptance of day care for young children. For example, it was noted in *Radtke* that the father had to rely on child care outside the home, but the father retained custody because a child psychologist and the guardian *ad litem* reported that the children were well cared for and happy after six months in full-time day care while living with the father temporarily in Scotland.

However, in situations in which there is a notable distinction between the parties in the amount of time they will be able to devote to being with the children, a clear advantage appears to lie with the parent able to spend more time. This may hold true even in the face of misconduct by the more available parent:

> While we do not condone the conduct of the mother in certain respects, the record shows that she is not employed, gives the children her full attention, and has apparently done an acceptable job in caring for the needs of the children on the small amount of $20.00 per week contributed by the father. She lives in a two bedroom trailer located in the yard of her parents whose helpful interest in the children is shown by the record. The father works, lives alone, and would have to leave the children with others while he is away from home.

Miller v. Sammons, 255 S.C. 487, 488, 179 S.E.2d 724, 725 (1971).

Other cases in which the time available to spend with the child was important in awarding custody include: *Bonnette v. Bonnette*, 276 S.C. 653, 281 S.E.2d 790 (1981) (reversing an award of custody to father because his irregular work schedule kept him from spending time with the child); *Davenport v. Davenport*, 265 S.C. 524, 220 S.E.2d 228 (1975) (granting custody to the mother who was a teacher and could be home by 3:30 p.m.); *Ford v. Ford*, 242 S.C. 344, 130 S.E.2d 916 (1963) (awarding custody to the father based partly on his willingness to work fewer hours in order to spend more time with his children); *Shainwald v. Shainwald*, 302 S.C. 453, 456, 395 S.E.2d 441, 443 (Ct. App. 1990) (upholding an award of custody based largely on the father's ability to spend time with the children); *Sealy v. Sealy*, 295 S.C. 281, 368 S.E.2d 85 (Ct. App. 1988) (affirming custody to the mother where she operated a day care center from her home and where the husband was in the Navy and the children would be living with his parents if he was awarded custody); *Thompson v. Brunson*, 283 S.C. 221, 321 S.E.2d 622 (Ct. App. 1984) (denying the mother custody partly because of her intention to accept employment that would require frequent overnight travel).

In *McCoy v. McCoy*, 283 S.C. 383, 323 S.E.2d 517 (1984), the Court noted that a child's best interests would be served by changing custody to the father, noting that with the father having remarried, the child would benefit from the care of the stepmother:

> The record reflects the husband is a career soldier with a stable financial future. He has remarried and has two small children by his present wife. His second family joins him wholeheartedly in his desire to raise his daughter. In his home she will have her own bedroom and the benefit of her stepmother's constant care and supervision.
>
> The wife also remarried but is now divorced. She is employed as a night waitress earning a low income, and now lives with a friend where her daughter must share a bedroom with two other children. Having not lived in one place more than six months since the divorce, she has no permanent home though she says she intends to find one. She has left the child on more than one occasion at a babysitter's home for the evening but failed to pick her up for several days. Under

> our view of the evidence, we agree the child's interests are best served by changing custody to the husband.

Id. at 386, 323 S.E.2d at 519.

In general, the availability of relatives to help take care of the children is considered a plus. However, the court will give preference to the parent who is willing to spend more time personally caring for the child, especially if it considers the involvement of relatives or other third parties excessive. In *Gandy v. Gandy*, 297 S.C. 411, 377 S.E.2d 312 (1989), the Supreme Court remanded the case for further findings of fact. However, the Court questioned the correctness of giving custody to the father, who relied on his parents for primary child care, in light of court appointed expert testimony that the children should be placed with the parent who was willing to stay with them and not rely on babysitters, even relatives. The expert determined that the parents' over reliance on their parents as caretakers of the children had resulted in "cross-generational parenting," "mixed messages," and "general identity confusion for Brad and Rusty." The expert noted that, while the grandparents should continue to maintain an ongoing relationship with their grandchildren, they should be restored to a secondary as opposed to primary role in Brad and Rusty's lives. He recommended that custody be given to the parent most able to set up a domicile away from his or her own parents.

Religious beliefs and practices could be significant factors in custody decisions, but there have not been many cases in which religion has been mentioned. South Carolina law, in S.C. Code Ann. § 20-7-1520 (Law. Co-op. 1976), creates a preference for custody in someone of the same religious faith as the parents or the child. There have been no reported case decisions specifically relying on this statute.

The father's concern about the religious and educational needs of the children was a factor considered in *Shainwald v. Shainwald*, 302 S.C. 453, 395 S.E.2d 441 (Ct. App.1990), although the court noted that "[a]s to the father's religious beliefs, the record leaves much to be desired in terms of the sincerity of his religious commitment and especially the regularity of church attendance." *Id.* at 460, 395 S.E.2d at 446. In *Driggers v. Hayes*, 264 S.C. 9, 212 S.E.2d 579 (1975), the Court noted that the grandparents had provided love and religious training in ruling that the trial court had properly denied the parents' request to return custody of their daughter to them. (The case really turned on the fact that the nine-year-old girl had spent her entire life with the grandparents.)

c. Opinions of Third Parties

The trial judge is entitled to hear the opinions of anyone who has something relevant to say about the welfare of children whose custody is in dispute. It is common for the court to consider the recommendations of guardians *ad litem* and expert witnesses such as child psychologists. It is less common, but sometimes determinative, to consider the opinions of the children themselves.

When the surviving parent is unable to take custody of the child, the trial court may consider the surviving parent's desires as to who should have custody, but it is not required to do so. The Court stated in *Linder v. Agnew*, 276 S.C. 153, 276 S.E.2d 774 (1981), answering the appellant's argument that the surviving parent's desire was for her to have custody of the child, that "[a] father who is currently serving time in prison for killing the child's mother is not in a position to decide custody." *Id.* at 155, 276 S.E.2d at 775.

The Supreme Court has directed attention to 42 Am. Jur. 2d 34 *Infants* §§ 31, 32, (1969), and to 35 A.L.R. 2d 612 (1954), and 99 A.L.R. 2d 954 (1965), cited in *Crowe v. Lowe*, 256 S.C. 321, 182 S.E.2d 310 (1971), for the role of interviews by family court judges with children and for the relevancy of outside investigations into the parties' homes.

(1) Guardians and Experts

The opinions of guardians *ad litem* and other expert witnesses play an increasingly important role in child custody disputes. The presumable objectivity of these reports, especially from guardians or experts appointed by the court, makes them highly valuable to both the court and the favored party.

How to regulate properly the influence of the guardian *ad litem* in child custody cases has been the issue in several appellate decisions. In *Collins v. Collins*, 283 S.C. 526, 324 S.E.2d 82 (Ct. App. 1984), the Court of Appeals implicitly approved the trial court's use of a guardian *ad litem*'s report, but held that the parties were entitled to cross examine the guardian and any witnesses on whose testimony the guardian relied as a basis for making recommendations. *Richmond v. Tecklenberg*, 302 S.C. 331, 396 S.E.2d 111 (Ct. App. 1990), held that the report of a guardian *ad litem* could be admitted into evidence.

The court rejected the mother's argument that a guardian *ad litem* should not be allowed to give opinions regarding custody in *Shainwald v. Shainwald*, 302 S.C. 453, 395 S.E.2d 441 (Ct. App. 1990). The guardian *ad litem* had testified at the hearing, then submitted a written report which was not shared with the parties. "A guardian ad litem is a representative of the court appointed to assist it in properly protecting the interests of an incompetent person." *Id.* at 457, 395 S.E.2d at 444. Although the court held that the extent to which a guardian *ad litem* is permitted to testify and give an opinion or recommendation is left to the trial judge's discretion, it cautioned judges to be mindful of the guardian's role as an advocate and of the need for a guardian to perform his or her duties properly.

The *Shainwald* court also held it was improper for the trial judge to receive and utilize a written report from the guardian *ad litem* after the hearing without first giving the parties a chance to see the report and, likewise, providing them with an opportunity to examine the guardian and other witnesses who furnished facts in the report. *Id.* at 458, 395 S.E.2d at 444, 445. Ultimately, however, the court concluded that the trial judge's use of the report was harmless error.

In other cases, the courts have considered the suggestions of social service agencies, hospital professionals, and family court officials. *McSwain v. Holmes*, 269 S.C. 293, 237 S.E.2d 363 (1977) (Department of Social Services (DSS)); *Ex parte Soles*, 267 S.C. 29, 225 S.E.2d 859 (1976) (DSS); *Jones v. Ard*, 265 S.C. 423, 219 S.E.2d 358 (1975) (DSS); *Ex parte Roper*, 254 S.C. 558, 176 S.E.2d 175 (1970) (mental health center); *Cutshaw v. Harvey*, 223 S.C. 276, 75 S.E.2d 602 (1953) (guardian *ad litem*; Department of Public Welfare).

The potential importance of expert witness testimony was affirmed in *Wheeler v. Gill*, 307 S.C. 94, 413 S.E.2d 860 (1992). In that custody dispute, the father's psychotherapist testified that "the father was the emotional and psychological parent" and that an award of custody to the mother would damage the child. *Id.* at 97, 413 S.E.2d at 862. She also testified that she was helping the father develop parenting skills. Custody was retained in the father, based on stability and family environment, and his attentiveness to the child.

(2) Child's Preference

Age and maturity are the two factors which determine what weight will be given to a child's preference. The leading case is *Guinan v. Guinan*, 254 S.C. 554, 176 S.E.2d 173 (1970), where it was held that:

> Ordinarily, the wishes of a child of this boy's age [sixteen], intelligence, and experience, although probably not controlling, *Ex parte Reynolds*, 73 S.C. 296, 53 S.E. 490 (1906), are entitled to great weight in awarding his custody as between estranged parents. Annot., 4 A.L.R.3d 1396, 1434 (1965). The court made no finding of fact tending to offset this important factor in awarding custody, and the record before us is bare of any evidence tending to do so. Absent any evidence tending to establish that the best interest of the boy would be served by awarding his custody to the mother, the court erred in failing to allow him to live with the parent of his choice.

Id. at 557-558, 176 S.E.2d at 174.

In *Moorhead v. Scott*, 259 S.C. 580, 193 S.E.2d 510 (1972), in which the wishes of children of ages 9, 11 and 12 to live with their father were not granted in light of a finding that it would be far more beneficial for the children to live with their mother and her new husband. The Supreme Court said this about consideration of children's wishes:

> Our court has given little significance to the wishes of a six year old child. *Poliakoff v. Poliakoff*, 221 S.C. 391, 70 S.E.2d 625 (1952). On the other hand, our Court has given great weight to the wishes of a child sixteen years of age. *Guinan v. Guinan*, 254 S.C. 554, 176 S.E.2d 173 (1970). It is clear that the wishes of a child of any age may be considered under all the circumstances, but the

> weight given to those wishes must be dominated by what is best for the welfare of the children.

Id. at 585, 193 S.E.2d at 513.

It is unclear how much deference appellate courts will give to a trial judge's decision to change custody based on the preferences of the child. For example, compare *Bolding v. Bolding*, 278 S.C. 129, 293 S.E.2d 699 (1982), with *Aiken v. Nelson*, 292 S.C. 400, 356 S.E.2d 839 (1987). In *Bolding*, the trial court's decision to change custody was reversed because the Supreme Court held that proof of the eleven-year-old son's desire to live with the father was not by itself sufficient proof that the best interest of the child would be served by changing custody from the mother to the father. However, Justice Ness dissented because he believed the trial judge was in a better position to make the decision. He noted that the trial judge had conducted a lengthy private interview with the child before concluding that uprooting the child could affect him for the rest of his life (and he noted that none of this testimony was included in the record). Justice Ness also noted that both parents were fit and that the son wanted not only to live with his father but also to be able to attend school and live in the neighborhood with his lifelong friends. In *Aiken*, the trial court had changed custody to the father largely based on the wishes of a fourteen-year-old son. In reviewing the matter, the court concluded that "[b]ased on the totality of the evidence and the broad discretionary powers of the trial court, absent a showing of abuse in making such determinations, we conclude that the transfer and award of custody to respondent should be affirmed." *Id.* at 403, 356 S.E.2d at 841.

While these cases could be read as revealing different approaches to reviewing the decisions by a trial judge, they could also be explained as indicating that greater weight should be given to the wishes of a fourteen-year-old than an eleven-year-old child. In *Aiken*, the court noted that the family court judge had considered the existence of a Georgia law which gives a child fourteen years of age certain preferential rights with respect to custody. O.C.G.A. §§ 19-9-1 and 19-9-3 (1982), as amended (1984). Judging from the handful of South Carolina cases on children's preferences, it appears that somewhere between 12 and 14 may well be the ages at which the wishes of the child will be given serious consideration.

Custody will not be changed if the court views a child's preference as the result of permissiveness by the non-custodial parent. If the court finds this, or pressure from the parent, then the child's preference will carry little weight. *See Smith v. Smith*, 261 S.C. 81, 198 S.E.2d 271 (1973) (finding that a seven-year-old child's preference to live with his father may have been influenced by his father's permissiveness, and leaving custody with the mother).

Statements made by a guardian *ad litem* about children's preferences will serve as adequate notice to the trial court of the children's wishes, especially if counsel fails to request that the judge take testimony from the children. *See Perry v. Perry*, 315 S.C. 373, 433 S.E.2d 911 (1993), in which the Supreme Court held that it was not error to fail to take testimony from children (ages 12, 8, and 5) where trial counsel did not request it and the guardian *ad litem* told the trial judge that the children desired to live with their mother (who was denied custody). The Supreme Court also noted that the weight given to a child's wishes "must be dominated by what is best for the welfare of the child," and it found ample support for placing the children with their father. *Id.* at 375, 433 S.E.2d at 912.

d. Age, Health and Sex of Child (Tender Years Doctrine)

There used to be a strong preference in favor of awarding custody of young children to their mothers. This is referred to as the Tender Years Doctrine. The doctrine was expressly abolished by statute effective May 18, 1994. S.C. Code Ann. § 20-7-1555 (Law. Co-op. Supp.). Since that date, the Tender Years Doctrine can no longer be considered as a factor in deciding child custody cases in South Carolina. *Cash v. Cash*, ___ S.C. ___, 465 S.E.2d 371 (Ct. App. 1995).

Historically the mother was preferred for custody if the child was within the age of nurture, although such a claim was defeated in *Ex parte Hewitt*, 45 S.C.L. (11 Rich.) 326 (1858), by the father's "paramount" common-law right. As the Court read the father's priority out of the common law — *Koon v. Koon*, 203 S.C. 556, 28 S.E.2d 89 (1943) (awarding custody to the grandparents as against the father); *Driggers v. Hayes*, 264 S.C. 69, 212 S.E.2d 579 (1975) (awarding custody to the grandparents as against the parents) — the mother's right to custody strengthened. By 1926, in *Watson v. Watson*, 134 S.C. 147, 132 S.E. 39 (1926), the Court said that there must be some legal obstacle to prevent awarding custody to a "pure young woman, of high Christian character." *Id.* at 154, 132 S.E. at 41. This movement continued and probably reached a pinnacle in *Ex parte Atkinson*, 238 S.C. 521, 121 S.E.2d 4 (1961), where the Court cited with approval 17A Am. Jur. *Divorce and Separation* § 819 (1957):

> In a few cases it is said that neither parent has a paramount right over the other to the custody of a minor child. But it must be evident that this is a theoretical proposition which generally gives way, in the case of children of tender years, to a preference for the mother.

Id. at 531, 121 S.E.2d at 9.

The decline of the Tender Years Doctrine began in the late 1950's and early '60's in cases in which the doctrine was cited matter-of-factly after the custody decision has been made on other grounds. *Todd v. Todd*, 242 S.C. 263, 130 S.E.2d 552 (1963); and *Dobson v. Atkinson*, 232 S.C. 12, 100 S.E.2d 531 (1957), are two of many examples. The appropriate role of the Tender Years Doctrine was considered in a well-reasoned opinion in *Ford v. Ford*, 242 S.C. 344, 130 S.E.2d 916 (1963). The Court enumerated the factors to be considered in custody cases. Tender years was one of a number of factors that included the residence and surroundings of the home, the opportunities available to the child, financial fitness, the conduct of the parent, and possession of the child prior to the proceeding. *Id.* at 352, 130 S.E.2d at 921. In *Ford* the mother failed in her bid for custody because it rested solely on the Tender Years Doctrine, which was not enough to effect a change of custody pursuant to an agreement which settled prior divorce litigation in Virginia.

In the 1970's, the Tender Years Doctrine continued to have some effect, but only in initial determinations of custody. For example, mothers were turned down in their attempts to regain custody although they argued the Tender Years Doctrine in *Jones v. Ard*, 265 S.C. 423, 219 S.E.2d 358 (1975), and *Green v. Loveday*, 270 S.C. 410, 242 S.E.2d 441 (1978). The mother in *Jones* was denied custody after expressly being found fit. This result may have been a little unexpected because of the ruling earlier that year in *Simons v. Simons*, 263 S.C. 509, 211 S.E.2d 555 (1975), in which the Court said, *inter alia*, that the mother should be awarded custody if proved fit.

The distinction between the cases is that *Jones* involved an attempt to regain custody, while *Simons* was an initial custody determination.

It was not long before the flat statement of a preference for the mother in *Simons* was further eroded. Both *Ex parte Soles*, 267 S.C. 29, 225 S.E.2d 859 (1976), and *Collins v. Collins*, 283 S.C. 526, 324 S.E.2d 82 (Ct. App. 1984), held that the Tender Years Doctrine did not require that the mother be awarded custody if deemed fit. In *Soles*, the Supreme Court found that evidence of violence in the mother's home was sufficient to warrant a change in custody to the father. *Collins* held that both parties were fit to assume custody of their child but the father was "able and willing to provide a more stable home for his daughter," while the mother's "primary present interests are her social and career endeavors." *Id.* at 528, 324 S.E.2d 84. The main problem the court found with the mother's schedule was that she frequently remained away from her home at night, often leaving her daughter overnight with persons who did not give their prior approval, while the father was "settled and mature." *Id. See also Marshall v. Marshall*, 282 S.C. 534, 540, 320 S.E.2d 44, 48 (Ct. App. 1984), which held that the Tender Years Doctrine does not create any presumption as to which parent should have custody of the child and that the trial judge cannot interpret the doctrine so as to create a presumption. For a mother to receive custody under the doctrine she must also be a competent, fit and proper person to have custody.

By the late 1980's, the Tender Years Doctrine had become virtually negligible as a factor to be considered in awarding custody. In *Radtke v. Radtke*, 297 S.C. 260, 376 S.E.2d 275 (1989), the Supreme Court reversed an award of custody to the mother, in part because it felt the family court had given too much weight to the Tender Years Doctrine, although the children were both young females. "Moreover, the family court erred in holding the tender years doctrine mandates that custody be given the mother because the children are young females. *Alligood v. Hunt*, 291 S.C. 368, 353 S.E.2d 699 (1987)." *Id.* at 263, 376 S.E.2d at 276.

Wheeler v. Gill, 307 S.C. 94, 413 S.E.2d 860 (Ct. App. 1992), made it clear that the Tender Years Doctrine could only be applied where there was no other factor on which to base a custody decision. The parents were relatively equal in all respects, and the mother argued on appeal that she was the primary caretaker and that the Tender Years Doctrine should have caused the trial judge to award her custody. The court wrote:

> The age, health and sex of a child, often referred to as the tender years doctrine, are factors to be considered in awarding custody of a young child. *Ford v. Ford*, 242 S.C. 344, 130 S.E.2d 916 (1963). However, the doctrine creates no presumption as to which parent is entitled to custody. *Marshall v. Marshall*, 282 S.C. 534, 320 S.E.2d 44 (Ct. App. 1984). The cases are legion that the controlling consideration in making a custody award is the welfare and best interest of the child.

Id. at 99, 413 S.E.2d at 683. The court went on to find that the trial judge had considered the age, sex and health of the child and there was no abuse of discretion, although the case was an admittedly close one.

The court said this about the modern utility of the tender years doctrine: "The tender years doctrine has evolved over the years to the point that its present utility is most apparent in those cases where parents are found to be equally fit and the doctrine is applied as a tie breaker determinant." *Id.* at 100, 413 S.E.2d at 684. The court did not feel that the parties' relative fitness was so equal in *Wheeler* that the application of the doctrine mandated an award of custody to the mother. It upheld the trial court's finding that the father's home provided the better environment for their daughter. In *Woodall v. Woodall*, ___ S.C. ___, 471 S.E.2d 154 (1996), however, the Supreme Court concluded that the relative merits of the parties were so equal that it was appropriate for the trial judge to rely on the Tender Years Doctrine in awarding custody of the mother. The Court noted that the Tender Years Doctrine had been legislatively abolished at the time of its decision, but it was still viable when the trial judge issued his ruling.

The Supreme Court appeared to breathe fresh life into the Tender Years Doctrine in *Epperly v. Epperly*, 312 S.C. 411, 440 S.E.2d 884 (1994). However, this was probably not intended, for reliance on the Tender Years Doctrine was unnecessary to its decision. The Court reversed an award of custody to the father. A clear basis for doing this was its determination that the mother had been the primary caretaker of the children. Rather than relying on this factor alone, however, the Court also cited the Tender Years Doctrine as a reason for its decision, saying that it "militates in favor of awarding custody to Wife." *Id.* at 415, 440 S.E.2d at 886. The following statement appears in the opinion: "Further, the 'tender years doctrine,' which creates a preference for the mother of young children, should also be a factor weighed by the Family Court in determining custody." *Id.* at 415, 440 S.E.2d at 886. The Court cites *Collins v. Collins*, 283 S.C. 526, 324 S.E.2d 82 (Ct. App. 1984), in support of this statement, although *Collins* held that a mother is not entitled to custody just because of the Tender Years Doctrine. The Court did not mention any of the more recent cases on the issue, most notably the Court of Appeals' 1992 decision in *Wheeler v. Gill*, which indicates that the Tender Years Doctrine should only be considered when the parents are both equally fit, presumably not when one can be identified as the primary caretaker.

The Court of Appeals' opinion in *Cash v. Cash*, ___ S.C. ___, 465 S.E.2d 371 (Ct. App. 1995), makes it clear that the Tender Years Doctrine can no longer be considered in awarding custody, even in close cases. The court notes that the family court judge found child custody to be a very difficult decision because both parties were head and shoulders above most parents and either would have been fit to provide custodial care for the child. However, the court states, "the tender years doctrine has now been statutorily abolished. [citation omitted] It follows that to the extent prior case law interprets and applies the doctrine, the case law is no longer applicable." *Id.* at ___, 465 S.E.2d at 373.

3. RESTRICTIONS (NOT TO MOVE CHILD OUT-OF-STATE)

Although the family court appears to have the power to impose conditions and restrictions on custody awards, it is not clear what situations warrant the use of this power. For example, the question of whether the custodial parent should be allowed to move with the children to an out-of-state location is being resolved on a case-by-case basis. The issue more commonly arises in actions brought by noncustodial parents trying to prevent the other parent from moving, or to obtain custody if the custodial parent does move.

The legislature clarified the family court's power with respect to moves within South Carolina in 1996 by adding the following language to S.C. Code § 20-7-420(30) (Law. Co-op. Supp.): "however, the court may not issue an order which prohibits a custodial parent from moving his residence to a location within the State unless the court finds a compelling reason or unless the parties have agreed to such a prohibition."

Cases in which a noncustodial parent seeks to modify a custody award based on the custodial parent's move or desire to move to another location are discussed in the section of this chapter on modification of custody.

The Supreme Court sustained a restraining order to prevent the mother from moving the child out of South Carolina in *McAlister v. Patterson*, 278 S.C. 481, 299 S.E.2d 322 (1982). The order further provided for a change of custody from her to the father if the mother did remove the child. The Court wrote:

> As a rule, the presumption is against removal of the child. *Koon v. Koon*, 203 S.C. 556, 28 S.E.2d 89 (1943); *King v. King*, 202 Ga. 838, 44 S.E.2d 791 (1947); *In re DeFord*, 226 N.C. 189, 37 S.E.2d 516 (1946); *Pugh v. Pugh*, 133 W. Va. 501, 56 S.E.2d 901 (1949). In situations where removal will benefit the child, removal has been allowed. *See, e.g., Watkins v. Rose*, 115 S.C. 370, 105 S.E. 738 (1921); *Duncan v. Duncan*, 293 Ky. 762, 170 S.W.2d 22 (1943); *D'Onofrio v. D'Onofrio*, 144 N.J. Super. 200, 365 A.2d 27 (1976); *Arnold v. Arnold*, 67 Ohio App. 282, 36 N.E.2d 430 (1941); *Bennett v. Bennett*, 228 Wis. 401, 280 N.W. 363 (1938).
>
> While this Court is free to find facts based on our view of the preponderance of the evidence, *Brown v. Brown*, 278 S.C. 43, 292 S.E.2d 297 (1982), the trial judge, who observes the witnesses and is in a better position to judge their demeanor and veracity, is given broad discretion. *Peay v. Peay,* 260 S.C. 108, 194 S.E.2d 392 (1973).
>
> We agree with the trial judge that removal of the child from his familiar surroundings to a place where he would be among strangers would not benefit the child. Rather, it would be detrimental not only to the healthy father-son relationship but also to the relationships with his great grandmother, who has vested visitation rights, his grandparents and his great aunt.

> The trial judge found the best interest and welfare of the minor child would best be served by his remaining in Laurens County with his father, friends and other relatives. His judgment is surely a reasonable one which is amply supported by the evidence in the record. We find no abuse of discretion. Therefore, the order of the family court is affirmed.

Id. at 483, 299 S.E.2d at 323-24. In another 1982 case, *Curlee v. Howle*, 277 S.C. 377, 287 S.E.2d 115 (1982), the propriety of imposing a requirement that the custodial parent had to give the mother sixty days' notice of his intention to move was not discussed, although the case involved whether to hold the father in contempt for moving only fifty-seven days after giving the required notice.

The presumption against moving a child out-of-state is restated in *Sealy v. Sealy*, 295 S.C. 281, 368 S.E.2d 85 (Ct. App. 1988), but it has also been noted that "a parent cannot be denied custody just because that parent intends to take the child to another state." *Marshall v. Marshall*, 282 S.C. 534, 541, 320 S.E.2d 44, 49 (Ct. App. 1984). In *Sealy*, the mother won custody from the paternal grandmother who was asking that permanent custody be given to the husband who also lived in another state within twenty minutes' driving distance of the mother. The *Marshall* court found that, although the mother admitted to engaging in adulterous behavior, the father was not the proper parent to have custody due to his lack of independence from his parents and because he had always turned over custody of the children to other members of his family, and on one occasion he had hidden the children from their mother. *Id.* at 320, 320 S.E.2d at 48. The court allowed the mother to take the children back to Louisiana because all of her family and friends were there, despite the presumption that children should not be taken out of the state. The court stated that removal of the child is only one condition the trial judge should consider, and no abuse of discretion had occurred. *Id.* at 541, 542, 320 S.E.2d at 49.

Recognition of the *McAlister* presumption against moving a child out of state did not prevent the Court of Appeals from reversing a family court order which prohibited the mother from moving more than 250 miles from Spartanburg in *Eckstein v. Eckstein*, 306 S.C. 167, 410 S.E.2d 578 (Ct. App. 1991). There had been no finding of fact that the restriction would serve the best interests of the children, the mother needed to move to Alabama to find work, and neither the father nor mother had any other family in South Carolina.

If a move out-of-state is contemplated at the time of the custody award, the family court is not likely to prohibit the move in a subsequent proceeding. In *VanName v. VanName*, 308 S.C. 516, 419 S.E.2d 373 (Ct. App. 1992), the Court of Appeals affirmed the trial judge's refusal to restrain the mother from moving to Virginia to take a better job, or to award custody to the father. It found that this move was contemplated at the time of the original custody award and that the change was not sufficient to warrant a change of custody. Judge Goolsby dissented because he thought it was unfair to require the father to drive that far to maintain a relationship with his children, especially when the mother had made no effort to find a new job in the Greenville area. He would have ordered the mother to return to South Carolina or lose custody to the father.

Whether the result in *VanName* would have been different if the move had not been contemplated at the time of the initial award of custody is not clear. Nor is the result if the father had raised the issue at the initial hearing and sought a restraining order prohibiting the move. If the presumption against removal stated in *McAlister* is still the law of South Carolina, as it appears to be, the result may well have been different at trial and on appeal.

However, the issues of law presented in such cases are far from resolved, for there are no clear criteria on which a trial judge can rely in deciding whether a move should be permitted or enjoined. In *Dobson v. Atkinson*, 232 S.C. 12, 100 S.E.2d 531 (1957), the Supreme Court upheld a family court's decision to deny a father's request to enjoin the mother from taking their child to Taiwan for two years. The mother had become remarried to a doctor in the military service who had been ordered overseas. It is doubtful that a modern court would rely on the presumption against moving the child and compel the mother to choose either to live apart from her husband for two years or to give up custody of her child, at least not unless the trip presented some real danger to the welfare of the child other than the possible harm to her relationship with her father.

4. MODIFICATION OF CUSTODY

a. Standing

No statute defines who has standing to bring issues of child custody before the family court. However, the Supreme Court seems to have held that any person who can give good reason to show interest in the welfare of a child, particularly one having had physical custody of the child, has standing to present issues involving child custody.

The paternal grandparents brought suit against the child's mother, seeking custody and an adoption order in *Cook v. Cobb*, 271 S.C. 136, 245 S.E.2d 612 (1978). They were denied adoption, but obtained custody, and the mother appealed. She claimed that the grandparents had no standing to seek custody, although they had physical custody of the child for four and one-half years by the time the Supreme Court got the case; and she argued that she should prevail based on her natural parental rights over the child as against a non-parent. (She coupled with that a constitutional claim that her constitutional rights as a parent were infringed by the lower court's order.) On the issue of standing, the Court said:

> Normally, grandparents have no standing to claim entitlement to the custody of their grandchildren. The mother and father are the joint natural guardians of their minor children and are charged with their welfare. See § 21-21-10, *Code of Laws of South Carolina* (1976). Nevertheless, it is provided by statute that "[t]he welfare of the minor shall be the first consideration" concerning the custody of the minor. § 21-21-10. We therefore base our conclusion affirming custody in the grandparents, not on any inherent or statutory right that they might have to the custody of grandchildren, but rather on what we regard to be in the best interests of the child under the facts of this case.

Id. at 142, 245 S.E.2d at 616.

b. Factors

(1) Changed Circumstances Must Be Shown

No custody determination is final. The family court retains jurisdiction to reconsider the best interests of the children in the event that circumstances change and their welfare would be served by changing custody. The Court wrote, in *Wolfe v. Wolfe*, 220 S.C. 437, 68 S.E.2d 348 (1951), that a parent could apply to the court for an order transferring custody "in the event of changed conditions, or for other valid reasons." *Id.* at 441, 68 S.E.2d at 350. However, in the absence of a change of circumstance which affects the welfare of the child, it will usually be inappropriate to order a change of custody.

The Supreme Court reviewed the general nature of changes in custody awards in *Moss v. Moss*, 274 S.C. 120, 262 S.E.2d 11 (1980):

> The change of conditions necessary to transfer custody must normally occur before the date of the petition requesting custody. *Cook v. Cobb*, 271 S.C. 136, 245 S.E.2d 612 (1978). Being of the opinion that respondent failed in her burden of proving a change in conditions substantially affecting the interest and welfare of the children, we reverse. *Green v. Loveday*, 270 S.C. 410, 242 S.E.2d 441 (1978); *Jones v. Ard*, 265 S.C. 423, 219 S.E.2d 358 (1975).
>
> In support of a change of conditions, respondent asserts the children had been residing with her since the May 2, 1977, order granting appellant custody. However, the record shows the reason for this was because respondent, in violation of the order, removed the children from the State and rightful custody of appellant and remained in hiding with the children in Florida until appellant was able to locate the children and return them to South Carolina in May of 1978 just five days before this present petition was dated.
>
> Considering respondent's action in terms of the children's welfare, *Smith v. Smith*, 261 S.C. 81, 198 S.E.2d 271 (1973), we are of the opinion that such was not in the children's best interests.

> Moreover, respondent's action negates removal of the impediment to her previous quest for custody, namely her nomadic lifestyle. *See Stutz v. Funderburk*, 272 S.C. 273, 252 S.E.2d 32 (1979).
>
> Respondent further relies on her engagement to remarry and consequent stabilization of her once nomadic lifestyle as supportive of a change of custody. We disagree that her change of marital status, which occurred eleven days after the date of respondent's petition for change of custody, demonstrates the substantial change of circumstances required. *Green v. Loveday*, supra; *Cook v. Cobb*, supra. Further, the record reflects a previous remarriage by respondent which was annulled.
>
> Lastly, respondent contends appellant's present wife's pregnancy is a change of circumstances warranting transfer of custody. Appellant remarried in 1973. We do not view the pregnancy as a circumstance in and of itself sufficient to compel the transfer. Not every change of circumstance will justify a change of custody. *Jones v. Ard*, supra; *Stutz v. Funderburk*, supra (dissenting opinion).
>
> Furthermore, there is no finding by the lower court, nor do we adduce any evidence from the record before us, of the custodial parent's unfitness or of the children's unhappiness with appellant and his present wife. *Green*, supra. Likewise, there is no evidence of respondent's unfitness.
>
> There being insufficient evidence of a substantial change of conditions, the order of the lower court is reversed. The order of May 2, 1977, awarding appellant custody and granting respondent liberal visitation privileges remains in effect.

Id. at 121, 262 S.E.2d at 12.

From *Moss*, we thus see (1) that a modification of a custody order may be had only upon a showing of substantially changed circumstances; (2) that the circumstances must have changed (ordinarily, prior to the date of the filing of the petition); (3) that the change in conditions must substantially affect the interest and welfare of the child(ren) in question; (4) that it would be relevant to show that the custodial parent had become unfit; (5) that "child snatching" is not in the best interests of the children "snatched" so that a "snatching" parent may not profit from it; and (6) that the court wishes to see convincing evidence of a change in lifestyle when the previous custody determination has been based in part on a perceived disadvantage to the child(ren) stemming from lifestyle choice.

In sum, the same considerations go into determining whether to change custody as the court considers in making an initial award. The only difference is that the moving party has the burden of proving that sufficient circumstances have changed since the initial award to make it in the best interests of the children to change custody.

Immoral conduct does not preclude a change in custody at a later date if the custodial spouse has begun engaging in more immoral conduct than the noncustodial spouse. In *Branham v. Branham*, 266 S.C. 581, 225 S.E.2d 343 (1976), the Court changed custody to the father although the mother had been granted initial custody pursuant to a divorce on ground of the father's adultery. The changed circumstances were that the wife and child were found living in Atlanta with an unmarried black singer. Also, the Court made a finding as to the father's fitness in light of the mother's current unfitness. *See also* Annotation, *Custodial Parent's Sexual Relations with Third Party as Justifying Modification of Child Custody Order*, 100 A.L.R.3d 625 (1980).

Failing to comply with the terms of a custody order is not a sufficient change of circumstance on which to change custody, unless it reflects on the custodial parent's fitness as a parent. In *Pinckney v. Hudson*, 294 S.C. 332, 364 S.E.2d 462 (1988), the trial judge had ordered custody changed from the mother to the father for failing to comply with the custody arrangements as ordered. The Supreme Court reversed, finding that the change had not remained constant and there had been no showing that the change was in the best interests of the child. "The alleged violations have no affect [sic] on appellant's fitness as a parent." *Id.* at 333, 364 S.E.2d at 462.

If the custodial parent ceases to be the child's primary caretaker, it will depend on the facts of each case as to whether this constitutes abandonment or whether it is in the best interests of the child to change custody. In *Brown v. Starnes*, No. 92-UP-137 (S.C. Ct. App. 1992), the Court of Appeals overruled a family court's transfer of custody to the father where it was shown that the custodial parent, Vassey, had allowed the child to live next door with Vassey's mother. Vassey's mother and the child's father sought custody. The trial court awarded custody to the father, finding that the mother had "abandoned" her custodial rights. The Court of Appeals disagreed, holding that the evidence that Vassey let the child live nearby with Vassey's own mother was not sufficient to establish that Vassey intended completely to relinquish parental control over the child and, therefore, to abandon the child. The court explained that the mother remained involved with the child in a variety of ways and had not abandoned her. It also pointed out that the practical effect of the custody change in this case was to substitute the paternal grandmother for the maternal grandmother as the child's primary caretaker. As there had been no showing that this was in the best interest of the child, custody was returned to the mother.

Remarriage can amount to a circumstance justifying a change of custody. However, "remarriage alone is an insufficient basis for changing custody. *Fisher v. Miller*, 288 S.C. 576, 344 S.E.2d 149 (1986)." *Sealy v. Sealy*, 295 S.C. 281, 284, 368 S.E.2d 85, 87 (Ct. App. 1988). Remarriage is normally relevant to show improved circumstances on the part of a remarried spouse seeking to obtain custody, not to show a deterioration of the circumstances of a custodial parent. As Mr. Justice Bussey wrote for the Court in *Barrett v. Barrett*, 261 S.C. 111, 198 S.E.2d 532 (1973):

> The only change of circumstance of any substance whatever disclosed by the evidence in this case is that fact that the wife, approximately one month after the divorce decree, intermarried with one John Kelly Bowser. The record disclosed that Mr. Bowser was 48 years of age, while Mrs. Bowser was 28. He had been previously married and divorced, with children by his first marriage, all of whom were grown or nearly so. Bowser had had the Barrett children with him in his home for a little over a month before they departed for Greenville. He testified in this proceeding, expressing his interest in the children and his willingness to help his wife rear them. He was regularly employed, with his income being approximately the same as that of the respondent.

> The record is devoid of any evidence even tending to prove that Mr. Bowser is of a character that would be detrimental in any manner to the children's best interest. As aptly pointed out in the recent case of *Moorhead v. Scott*, 259 S.C. 580, 193 S.E.2d 510 [1972], remarriage is of course a change of condition but such "is not ordinarily of an adverse character and is most often used as a basis to gain custody rather than a reason to lose it."

Id. at 115, 198 S.E.2d at 534. However, in *Raven v. Cecil*, 262 S.C. 509, 205 S.E.2d 837 (1974), the Court upheld an order returning custody to the natural mother in part on the basis of evidence that, despite the best efforts and intentions of the new stepmother for the child, the child was not adjusting properly to the home his father and his stepmother had established.

Custody is not to be changed unless a betterment to the child will result. Remarriage is often not a sufficient change in circumstance for the court to reverse custody. In *Green v. Loveday*, 270 S.C. 410, 242 S.E.2d 441 (1978), a few days after the divorce the father of the child visited his ex-wife's house and found a man under the bed, and the child was also present. The family court subsequently awarded custody to the father. The mother soon thereafter married the man found under the bed and petitioned the same court for custody based on this change of circumstance. The court denied her petition stating, "We do not believe the remarriage of the mother is such a substantial change of condition to warrant the transfer of Heather's custody to her. There was no showing that the respondent father was an unfit parent, or that the child's welfare depended on her placement with the mother." *Id.* at 412, 242 S.E.2d at 442. *Jones v. Ard*, 265 S.C. 423, 219 S.E.2d 358 (1975), held that since the child had a good relationship with his father and his stepmother, who provided a stable home for him, the mere fact that his natural mother was now remarried did not entitle her to a change in custody.

The "snatching" of a child from its usual environment even when the "snatcher" is the custodial parent (at least when the departure cuts off visitation and removes the child from regular association with close relatives) can serve as a ground for changing custody:

> The conduct of the mother, as shown by this record, in *secretly and suddenly taking the child from familiar surroundings and close relatives to accompany her in the pursuit of her illicit affair with the singer* was sufficient to sustain the finding of a change in conditions affecting the best interests of the child and to justify placing custody with the father.
>
> The continuing jurisdiction of the lower court in matters of this kind assures periodic review of the father's conduct and discharge of his parental duties and such action by the lower court from time to time as may be for the child's best interest.

Branham v. Branham, 266 S.C. 581, 583-84, 225 S.E.2d 343, 344 (1976) (emphasis supplied).

However, *Branham* is probably better understood as another case in which the mother's "immoral" conduct caused her to lose custody, because South Carolina courts have generally not modified custody solely on the basis that the custodial parent moved to another location. *See Smith v. Smith*, 261 S.C. 81, 198 S.E.2d 271 (1973), in which the mother had moved with the child to Texas without telling the father. The trial court ordered that the father was to have custody from June 15 to August 15; but the Supreme Court reversed, holding that the move was in the best interests of the mother and child and was not made for the purpose of depriving the father of any rights. *See also Sharpe v. Sharpe*, 256 S.C. 517, 183 S.E.2d 325 (1971), which reversed the trial court's finding of contempt by the custodial mother. In the absence of an order restricting where a custodial parent can live, the mere fact that the mother went to another state to live with relatives without the knowledge or permission of the father did not constitute a material change of conditions justifying a transfer of custody to the father, even though the move violated the court's order by interfering with the exercise of the father's visitation rights.

(2) Rehabilitation of Unfitness

Where custody has been awarded to one parent because the other parent was determined to be unfit, rehabilitation of the unfit parent is a changed circumstance which sometimes has resulted in a change of custody. However, the only effect of proving rehabilitation is to remove the bar to that parent being considered for custody. The court must still make an independent determination about the best interests of the children, and it will often leave custody undisturbed unless there is a showing that the custodial parent is not doing a good job or the change would otherwise be in the best interest of the child.

Although remarriage alone is an insufficient basis for changing custody, "remarriage which restores 'moral fitness' has been recognized as a factor to be considered in awarding change of custody." *Sealy v. Sealy*, 295 S.C. 281, 284, 368 S.E.2d 85, 87 (Ct. App. 1988). In *Sealy*, the mother won a change of custody of her two daughters from the paternal grandmother upon a showing that she had restored her moral fitness by marrying her paramour, establishing a quiet and respectable home, operating a day care center in her home, and by showing that she had become more responsible than she was at the time of the divorce hearing. However, in *Alligood v. Hunt*, 291 S.C. 368, 353 S.E.2d 699 (1987), the Supreme Court denied the mother's request for a change of custody. Although the mother had remarried, the Court held that it was proper to consider the mother's prior adultery as a factor in considering the parties' relative stability. Considering that the mother had been married three times and had four adulterous relationships during her first two marriages, the Court found that her morality was a proper consideration and left custody in the father.

Thus, the test today seems to be that a reformed parent must not only show present fitness, but also must carry the burden of proving other changed circumstances which make it in the best interests of the children to change custody. Otherwise, there appears to be a presumption that the children should remain with the custodial parent.

The need to show changed circumstances beyond the restoration of fitness has not always been so clear. Some of the earlier cases which considered the effect of a parent's rehabilitation created an impression that a reformed mother was presumptively entitled to custody, especially of young children. The results in these cases may have been brought about more by the vestiges of the Tender Years Doctrine than anything else. They are probably not currently valid predictors of results to expect today, at least to the extent they indicate that an independent determination of the welfare of the children is not as important as a finding that the mother has been rehabilitated.

One of the cases which was often cited for the proposition that a rehabilitated mother should be given custody is *Stutz v. Funderburk*, 272 S.C. 273, 252 S.E.2d 32 (1979). The father had originally consented to custody going to the mother, once she became financially able to care for their young son. This was incorporated into the divorce decree, and she was subsequently deemed to have met this condition and received custody. Eight months later, the court granted custody to the father, largely based on a finding that the mother was then living with a man while she was married to another person. She later sought to regain custody based on the fact that she had married her paramour and on the Tender Years Doctrine. The following language appears in the opinion:

> Appellant correctly argues that, if the illicit affair constituted a change of circumstances sufficient to justify depriving appellant of custody, then her marriage to her paramour and otherwise restoration of her moral fitness should constitute a strong factor in establishing a sufficient change of condition to require restoration to the appellant-mother of her prior conceded and court-sanctioned right to custody of her child, then and now, of tender years.

Id. at 277, 252 S.E.2d at 34. Justices Ness and Littlejohn strongly dissented, focusing on factors which are given prominence in modern cases. They noted that although the mother had remarried and moved to a nice home, the husband had also remarried and lived in a nice home. "Most importantly, all indications are that Jason is happy and content in his present environment." *Id.* at 278, 252 S.E.2d at 35. Perhaps *Stutz* should be distinguished from later cases because the husband originally agreed that the mother should have custody and because of the Tender Years Doctrine.

Subsequent cases revealed some confusion about the degree of weight to be given to the moral rehabilitation of mothers. In *Moss v. Moss*, 274 S.C. 120, 262 S.E.2d 11 (1980), the mother's change in marital status that ended her nomadic lifestyle was held not to be enough to regain custody, especially since she had removed the children from South Carolina and hidden with them in Florida. Nor was the mother able to regain custody in *Rodgers v. Gray*, 285 S.C. 111, 328 S.E.2d 478

(1985), by marrying one of her former paramours and ceasing her promiscuous lifestyle for eight months.

However, the mother did obtain a ruling that her prior moral unfitness should not be considered in her bid to have custody changed from the father in *Ewing v. Baumrind*, 283 S.C. 461, 322 S.E.2d 696 (Ct. App. 1984). The husband was initially awarded custody, due in part to the wife's continuing course of immoral behavior (which had also been the cause of the divorce). After two years, the wife married her lover and petitioned for custody using her marriage as a change of circumstances. The family court judge nonsuited her, but the Court of Appeals reversed and remanded the case for a full hearing, holding that the family court could not determine what was in the best interest of the child without allowing evidence to be presented. The court stated:

> In the case of *Baer v. Baer*, [282 S.C. 362,] 318 S.E.2d 582 (S.C. App. 1984), this Court held:
>
> If the mother's affair constituted a change of circumstances sufficient to justify depriving her of the children's custody, then the mother's marriage to her paramour should require that her right of custody be reinstated because the marriage restored her moral fitness.
>
> . . .
>
> We hold that Linda's remarriage, under the peculiar circumstances of this case, restored her moral fitness and negates consideration of her past conduct in the decisionmaking of this case.
>
> . . .
>
> The trial judge erred in holding that in order for him to change custody, Linda must show, in addition to a change of circumstances on her part, that Baumrind had engaged in conduct that adversely affected the welfare of the children.

Id. at 463-464, 322 S.E.2d at 696-697.

The trial judge had written that he thought the transfer of custody from father to mother would be "detrimental to the children," presumably because the father had them so long. *See Ford v. Ford*, 242 S.C. 344, 130 S.E.2d 552 (1963). However, there was no evidence in the record to support this opinion of the trial judge, and since he had in fact placed an improper burden on the wife in not letting her have her day in court once she properly pleaded changed circumstances, the case had to be remanded.

D. CUSTODY DISPUTES BETWEEN PARENTS AND THIRD PARTIES

There is a presumption in favor of awarding custody to the biological parents. In *Kay v. Rowland*, 285 S.C. 516, 331 S.E.2d 781 (1985), the Supreme Court stated flatly that, in a custody dispute between a natural parent and a third party, "[o]nce the natural parent is deemed fit, the issue of custody is decided." *Id.* at 517, 331 S.E.2d at 782. *Kay* relied on *McDowell v. Richardson*, 279 S.C. 268, 305 S.E.2d 577 (1983), in which the Court found it was error to award custody to a grandparent absent a finding that the natural parent was unfit. That is, the court recognized the superior rights of a natural parent in a custody dispute with a third party.

Other blood relatives do not enjoy the same preference, however. In *McCutchon v. Charleston County DSS*, 302 S.C. 338, 396 S.E.2d 115 (Ct. App. 1990), the natural parents' rights were terminated to allow an adoption by foster parents, and the paternal grandparents' request for custody was denied. The court wrote:

> The McCutcheons, as grandparents, are not entitled to any preferences. *Dunn v. Dunn*, 298 S.C. 365, 380 S.E.2d 836 (1989). Their status as blood relatives is but one factor in determining the child's best interests. *Kemry v. Fox*, 273 S.C. 268, 255 S.E.2d 836 (1979). While the judge did not find the McCutcheon home unsuitable, he determined Kimberly's best interests would be served by staying with the family she has known for nearly all her life. We agree.

Id. at 347, 396 S.E.2d at 120.

In *Dunn*, a mentally deficient mother, who relinquished custody of her two-year old son to the Department of Social Services, joined DSS in a suit to prevent her parents from adopting her son. The Supreme Court denied the grandparents' adoption petition after considering the fact that the grandparents were both physically disabled, were entirely dependent upon Social Security which barely exceeded their expenses (without the grandson), and that they and five of their six children did not graduate from high school. *Kemry* held that "[w]hile, in a contest for custody of a child between a grandparent and a party not related to the child, some weight should be given to the grandparent's status as a relative. *See* 30 A.L.R.3d 290, the welfare and best interests of the child are determinative." *Kemry* at 269, 255 S.E.2d at 837. The unmarried mother in *Kemry* had been killed in a car accident, and a couple who had been her good friends received temporary custody of her small child. The child's father and maternal grandmother both petitioned the Court for custody, but they lost. The father failed to appeal and, upon the grandmother's appeal, the Court simply stated that after "reviewing the record and briefs in this matter, we conclude that the lower court properly awarded custody. . . ." and gave no further reasons for failing to give the grandmother custody. *Id.*

Curiously, there is no mention of the presumption in favor of the biological parent either in *Bramlett v. Davis*, 289 S.C. 85, 344 S.E.2d 867 (Ct. App. 1985) (granting a mother a change of custody from her mother and step-father based on a showing that she had changed her Bohemian lifestyle, rehabilitated herself and established a stable marriage and home life), or in *Mann v. Walker*, 285 S.C. 194, 328 S.E.2d 659 (Ct. App. 1985) (holding that, although the child had been with its paternal grandparents for two years and both parents agreed for them to have custody, the mother should have custody based upon her showings that she had established a suitable home and had a good relationship with the child and that the grandparents' house was less than satisfactory to the welfare of the child).

The apparently clear rule in favor of biological parents was modified slightly in *Moore v. Moore*, 300 S.C. 75, 386 S.E.2d 456 (1989). While it continued to recognize a rebuttable presumption that the child's best interests are served by placing custody with a biological parent, it reminded the family courts that they must treat the welfare of the child as the paramount consideration. *Moore* described four factors for the trial judge to examine:

(1) The parent must be fit and able to properly care for the child and provide a good home;

(2) The amount of contact, as measured by visitation, financial support, or both, which the parent had with the child while in the care of a third party;

(3) The circumstances under which the temporary relinquishment occurred; and

(4) The degree of attachment between the child and the temporary custodian.

Id. at 79, 386 S.E.2d at 458. In *Moore*, the Supreme Court affirmed the trial judge's determination that the father's custody rights were superior to those of the Sanderses (a husband and wife) who had voluntarily offered to help care for one of the father's children when he separated from his wife and moved in with his parents while commuting to an Air Force base in another town. The child was seven years old and was in the custody of the Sanderses for approximately four years when the order under appeal was issued. The father maintained contact with the child, but he faced several impediments to his ability to assume full responsibility for this child, including the Sanderses refusal to allow the father to have overnight visits or to visit the child anywhere except in their home.

In considering the four factors listed above, the *Moore* Court concluded there was no dispute as to the father's fitness, his ability to provide proper care and a home for the child nor as to the circumstances surrounding his temporary relinquishment of custody. The remaining issues were (1) the amount of contact by the natural parent with the child, and (2) the degree of attachment between the child and the third parties. The trial court had found that the father had abandoned the child, but the Supreme Court disagreed, holding that the father had maintained contact with his son and his attempts to have more contact had been impeded by the Sanderses. Regarding the degree of attachment between the Sanderses and the child, the Court said "[e]ven though there may exist a psychological parent-child relationship, the mere existence of such a bond is inadequate ground to justify awarding permanent custody to the Sanderses; particularly in an instance where such a relationship was built on the foster parents' overt acts which inhibited the development of a normal relationship between the natural parent and his child." *Id.* at 80-81, 386 S.E.2d at 459.

The *Moore* factors were applied by the Court of Appeals in *Shake v. Darlington County DSS*, 306 S.C. 216, 410 S.E.2d 923 (Ct. App. 1991), in which the court upheld the trial judge's decision not to terminate the parental rights of the natural mother, but reversed the trial court's decision to return custody to the natural mother. In ordering that the foster parent should retain custody of the four year old child who had been living with her for virtually his entire life, the Court of Appeals determined that, unlike in *Moore*, the natural mother did not have the ability to provide proper care and a good home to the child. Among the facts supporting this, the court found that the natural mother gave higher priority to her own sexual desires than to her son's need for a stable environment. The court also noted that the child had been removed from the mother's home pursuant to an emergency protective order due to the threat of harm. The court further determined that the child and the foster parent had established a close bond and that removal from the foster parent's care would have been very traumatic for the child.

The biological mother recovered custody of her son from her parents in *Malpass v. Hodson*, 309 S.C. 397, 424 S.E.2d 470 (1992), upon showing that she was a fit parent and had a strong attachment to her son. The grandparents had received custody of the child when he was nine months old. He was six years old when the appeal was decided. The mother had given him up when she was in an abusive marriage and could not care for him. She remarried after divorcing the abusive husband, and she had been seeking full custody of her son during the five years since her divorce. The Supreme Court considered the *Moore* factors. The grandparents tried to prove that the mother was unstable, but the Court discounted their evidence because the events they relied on were too dated to be relevant to her present fitness, which was established in the record. Although the Court found the degree of attachment between the child and the grandparents to be very close, it also found a strong attachment between the mother and the child. The other factors were met without challenge.

An award of custody to a third party over the objection of a natural parent will not be upheld unless the order indicates that the trial judge considered each of the *Moore* factors. *See Hogan v. Platts*, 312 S.C. 1, 430 S.E.2d 510 (1993), in which the Supreme Court held that the failure of the trial judge's order to indicate that the *Moore* factors had been considered required the case to be remanded. The trial judge had awarded custody of a twenty-two month old child (at the time of trial; four and a half years old when the Supreme Court's opinion was filed) to her aunt and uncle-in-law with whom she had been placed by the father following the death of the mother in an automobile accident. The mother and father had been separated when the mother was killed and the daughter, who was seriously injured in the accident, was only a week old. Although the father had obtained court-ordered visitation rights, he testified that the had never exercised them because he did not have the time.

The *Moore* factors may not serve as a basis for awarding custody to a third party where facts which weigh against the natural parent were beyond that parent's control and the parent has made a good faith attempt to exercise parental responsibility. Also, the closeness of the relationship between a child and a third party will apparently not be a significant consideration if the parent also has a close relationship with the child or if one can be created through a reunion plan. In *Hopkins v. South Carolina DSS*, 313 S.C. 322, 437 S.E.2d 542 (refiled October 23, 1993), the Supreme Court reaffirmed the rebuttable presumption that a fit natural parent should have custody as against a third party, stating that "[t]he public policy of this State is to reunite parents and children." The Court considered the *Moore* factors in affirming the trial court's refusal to terminate the parental rights of an unwed father of a nine year old child whom he had never lived with or established any parental relationship. The Court found that the child's mother had misled the father about his paternity and had lived for years in locations unknown to the father, following which the father's efforts to establish his paternity and establish a relationship with his son had been frustrated by "unreasonable conditions imposed by DSS."

In considering the *Moore* factors, the *Hopkins* Court found the father to be a fit parent.[25] It also found that he was not responsible for the circumstances which required the exercise of DSS' emergency protective services (the mother had

---

[25] Justice Toal argues in a dissenting opinion that the child will be traumatized by the separation from his foster parents and especially from his half-sister and that "the natural father ... appears to be distinctly unqualified to heal any emotional scars borne by the minor child." *Id.* at 333, 437 S.E.2d at 547. However, she does not specifically take issue with the majority's conclusion that the father is fit to have custody.

neglected and abused the children, later kidnaping them from a foster home, and her parental rights had been terminated). The father's limited contact with the child was caused by the mother's conduct and by the conditions imposed by DSS, and the Court concluded that the father's efforts to have contact with the child were "admirable." The final factor, the extent of the child's attachment to his foster parents, was "clearly the sticking point," for the foster parents had taken the child in believing he could become their child (DSS had incorrectly allowed the child to be placed with potential adoptive parents). The Court determined that "it is only fair to recognize the strong bond which has been established" between the foster parents and the child. It concluded that the family court judge had struck a proper balance by allowing the child to continue to reside with the foster parents until he had developed a close relationship with his father, if the plan for reunion which DSS was ordered to establish succeeds.

Thus, *Hopkins* appears to stand for the proposition that the existence of, or even the potential for, a close relationship between a biological parent and a child is a more important consideration than the extent of the child's attachment to third parties such as foster parents. If a bond exists between the parent and the child, or if one can be established, it does not appear that the child's relationship with a third party will be given much weight, irrespective of how strong or close it is.

The theme of biological preference was sounded in *Sanders v. Emery*, 317 S.C. 230, 452 S.E.2d 636 (Ct. App. 1994). A child was born in December, 1988. The next year, the parents separated and the father pled guilty to criminal sexual conduct with a fourteen year old and served three months in jail. During the separation, the mother tried to give the child to neighbors because she could not care for her alone. DSS intervened, placing the child with her paternal grandparents. Thereafter, the maternal grandmother and the great-grandparents sought custody of the child. The trial court found the mother to be borderline mentally retarded, emotionally immature and not capable of taking care of the child. The court also found that the mother was working with DSS by attending parenting classes and educational programs. The father, who had reconciled with his wife, was also attending parenting classes.

In 1992, the parents secured an order granting them unsupervised visitation with their daughter. They instituted a custody action when the maternal grandmother was hospitalized for psychiatric reasons. However, the trial court awarded custody to the great-grandparents.

The Court of Appeals determined that the trial judge gave too much weight to the relationship between the great grandparents and the child and too little weight to the strong presumption favoring the return of custody to fit biological parents. "In child custody matters, the public policy of this state is to reunite parents and children." *Id.* at 233, 452 S.E.2d at 638. In applying the *Moore* criteria, the Court of Appeals noted that the family court specifically declined to find the parents unfit (the parents had taken steps to rehabilitate themselves and the supervising DSS authorities had determined that neither parent posed a threat of abuse or neglect). In considering the degree of attachment between the child and the custodian the court noted that a close attachment should be expected since the child had been in the daily care of the great grandparents for two years, and it disregarded this attachment, quoting *Moore* for the proposition that "custody should not be subject to change because of adverse possession." *Id.* at 236, 452 S.E.2d at 639. The court also noted the advanced ages of the great grandparents and the young age of the child in deciding that the best interests of the child were served by returning her to her biological parents.

The first case following *Moore* in which a biological parent lost a custody dispute with a third party is *Kramer v. Kramer*, ___ S.C. ___, 473 S.E.2d 846 (Ct. App. 1996). Following the death of the child's father, the child's paternal aunt and uncle filed for custody and the biological mother also sought custody. The trial court awarded custody to the mother, but the Court of Appeals reversed and awarded custody to the aunt and uncle. Applying the *Moore* factors, the court said it did not believe the mother was a fit parent able to provide a good home for the children. It based this conclusion on concerns about the mother's past conduct and doubts about her financial ability to support the child. The conduct that concerned the court was that she abandoned the child and the father when the child was one year old, a previous child was born out of wedlock, the child involved in this case was born in a common law relationship [it is not clear why this concerned the court], she moved around a bit and had various relationships, and she had two more children out of wedlock. Although she married the father of the two most recent children shortly before seeking custody of the child in this action, the court did not seem to believe the sincerity of her commitment to domestication. Doubts about her financial ability to support the child were based on the facts that the mother was not working, had few job skills, and was financially dependent on her new husband (the father of her two subsequent children). Although the new husband testified that he would support the child, the court found this testimony questionable in light of evidence that he was $16,000 in arrears on child support owed to a former wife.

The Court of Appeals also found that the other three *Moore* factors supported its decision. The mother had minimal contacts with the child during the four years between her abandonment and the custody action, seeing him only once or twice a year, and she failed to send Christmas presents or provide financial support. The circumstances surrounding relinquishment of custody were that she abandoned the child and pursued a life of her own, showing little regard for the welfare of her son. There was a high degree of attachment between the child and his aunt and uncle. Even during the time the father had custody, the aunt and uncle were acting as the boy's parents. Thus, the Court of Appeals determined that the presumption in favor of biological parents was rebutted and it changed custody from the mother to the aunt and uncle. However, the ultimate outcome of the case is not certain. The Court of Appeals noted that its decision was based on facts as they existed at the time of the custody trial and the mother, who had custody of the child while the appeal was pending, may petition the family court for custody based upon a change in conditions since the prior decree.

Cases decided before *Kay*, *McDowell*, *Moore*, and *Sanders* appear to have given less weight to the presumption in favor of the natural parents. In a case decided ten years before *Moore*, the Supreme Court allowed custody to remain with the maternal grandparents although both natural parents separately requested custody and claimed that changed circumstances warranted the change. In *Skinner v. King*, 272 S.C. 520, 252 S.E.2d 891 (1979), the Court wrote:

> While we recognize that a preference should be given to the parents as against others in child custody disputes, the claim of a parent to the custody of a son or daughter must yield to the best interest of the child. *Cook v. Cobb*, 271 S.C. 136, 245 S.E.2d 612 (1978). The paramount consideration in custody cases is the welfare of the child. *Davenport v. Davenport*, 265 S.C. 524, 220 S.E.2d 228 (1975).

Id. at 523, 252 S.E.2d at 892. The father's only change was that he had become employed. The mother, on the other hand, had remarried and was active in her church. However, both were employed and away from the home during the day. The Court concluded:

> Mrs. Skinner's circumstances have changed more than Mr. Skinner's circumstances, but as with Mr. Skinner, we are not convinced that Mrs. Skinner's circumstances have improved sufficiently to warrant the conclusion that it would be Stephanie's best interest to upset the present custody arrangement.
>
> Stephanie should be returned to either her father or mother as soon as practicable, but not until it appears that a transfer of custody would be in her best interests. *Cook v. Cobb*, *supra*. Neither parent has made a showing sufficient to convince this Court that it would be in Stephanie's best interests to remove her at this time from the custody of Rev. and Mrs. King.

Id. at 523-24, 252 S.E.2d at 892-93. *Cook v. Cobb*, 271 S.C. 136, 245 S.E.2d 612 (1978), affirmed the trial judge's decision to award custody of a child to the paternal grandparents instead of to the mother who had remarried and was living in New Jersey. After obtaining a custody order by agreement with her husband, the mother had left the child with the paternal grandparents while she went to New York to pursue a theatrical career. She did not try to regain custody for three years. The Court based its decision to leave custody with the grandparents on a finding of changed circumstances: the mother's three-year absence, the close relationship between the child and the grandparents, the mother's move to New York, and the mother's "bohemian lifestyle."

It is impossible to determine if the results in these cases would have been different if they had been decided after *Kay*, *McDowell*, *Moore*, and *Sanders*, but it is possible.

CHAPTER ELEVEN
VISITATION

CHAPTER ELEVEN
VISITATION

A. IN GENERAL

Ordinarily the noncustodial parent is entitled to visitation. The privilege of visitation, and its determination, is within the broad discretion of the trial court. The visitation must be organized in the best interest of the child. These principles are stated most succinctly in *McGregor v. McGregor*, 255 S.C. 179, 177 S.E.2d 599 (1970):

> Where the custody of a minor child is awarded to one parent by a divorce decree, it is the prevailing practice to insert in the decree a provision granting visitation rights to the parent who does not have custody. Of course, a court, in granting the custody of a minor child to one parent, has the power to deny visitation rights to the other parent when the circumstances justify such, and the rights of visitation should not be denied unless the court is convinced that such are detrimental to the best interest of the child. The estrangement of child and parent should be avoided whenever possible. In determining whether the parent who does not have custody should be given visitation rights, the welfare and best interest of the child are the primary considerations. *Mixson v. Mixson*, 253 S.C. 436, 171 S.E.2d 581 [1969].
>
> The general rule is that minor children, notwithstanding the divorce, are entitled to the love and companionship of both parents, and the well rounded development of a normal child demands an association with both parents. The decree, within the discretion of the court, may and, under normal circumstances, should include a provision permitting the parent deprived of their custody to visit or communicate with the children under such restrictions as the circumstances may warrant. 27B C.J.S. *Divorce* § 312, at page 478.

> The question of determining and limiting visitation rights is one addressed to the broad discretion of the trial judge and in the absence of a clear abuse of such, the order granting, denying or limiting visitation rights will not be disturbed. *Graham v. Graham*, 253 S.C. 486, 171 S.E.2d 704 [1970]. However, a judicial award of the custody of a child and the fixing of visitation rights is not final and changed circumstances may authorize the change of custody or visitation rights in the future. *Porter v. Porter*, 246 S.C. 332, 143 S.E.2d 619 [1965].

Id. at 182-183, 177 S.E.2d at 600-601. This language from *McGregor* was quoted with approval in *King v. Gardner*, 274 S.C. 493, 265 S.E.2d 260 (1980).

Appellate courts have consistently held there is no relationship between visitation rights and child support payments. "A custodial parent cannot withhold visitation because of a non-custodial parent's failure to make child support payments." *Garris v. McDuffie*, 288 S.C. 637, 643, 344 S.E.2d 186, 190, n. 1 (Ct. App. 1986). The Court of Appeals reversed the trial court's ruling that the issue of the mother's contempt had become moot when the parents reached an agreement about future visitation. The mother indicated she had been reluctant to cash support checks because she thought she might have to allow the father to resume visitation if she did. *See also Anderson v. Anderson*, 282 S.C. 162, 318 S.E.2d 566 (1984) (reversing an order conditioning the father's obligation to make child support payments on continued visitation by the children).

Even if the custodial parent improperly prevents visitation, child support payments must continue to be made. In *Garris v. Cook*, 278 S.C. 622, 300 S.E.2d 483 (1983), the trial judge held that it would be inequitable to make the father pay arrearages since he could not restore his lost visitation. The father had stopped making support payments because the mother would not let him visit the children. The Supreme Court reversed, saying "[w]e find no authority making the duty of child support contingent on visitation, and find it difficult to conceive of a case in which a parent's act should be allowed to prejudice the child's right to support." *Id.* at 623, 300 S.E.2d at 484.

The custodial parent has no obligation to pay child support to the noncustodial parent during periods of visitation. In *Avin v. Avin*, 272 S.C. 514, 252 S.E.2d 888 (1979), the trial court had ordered the custodial father to pay child support to the mother when the child was visiting her. The Supreme Court reversed. "The fixed obligation of a custodial parent to provide for the necessities of life for the children is a continuing one and does not cease during the temporary absences of the children while on visitation. To require that he pay child support to the noncustodial parent during such temporary periods, in addition to maintaining at all times a permanent home for the children, is against the weight of reason." *Id.* at 516, 252 S.E.2d at 889.

Each parent, whether the custodial or noncustodial parent of the child, has equal access and the same right to obtain all educational records and medical records of their minor children. S.C. Code Ann. § 20-7-100 (Law. Co-op. Supp.).

B. JURISDICTION

There is no specific statutory authorization for the family court to award visitation to a noncustodial parent. As mentioned in the preceding section, the court's authority to award visitation derives from its power to decide custody matters. That is, visitation is an encroachment into the otherwise exclusive right of the custodial parent to control who the child will be exposed to and under what circumstances.

The family court can *sua sponte* order parties joined to marital litigation if necessary for a complete determination of the issues being heard by the court. *Frye v. Frye*, ___ S.C. ___, 448 S.E.2d 586 (Ct. App. 1994) (citing as authority Rule 19(a), SCRCP which allows the court to order a person to be made a party where the person is subject to service of process and, in the person's absence, complete relief cannot be accorded among those already parties and also citing S.C. Code Ann. § 20-7-420(19) (Law. Co-op. 1976), which permits a family court judge to bring in and make parties to any proceeding pending before the court any person whose presence to the proceedings may be found necessary to a complete determination of the issues therein or the relief to which the parties are entitled.). However, such parties are entitled to an opportunity to be heard and to present evidence on issues related to their interests. *Id.*

The family court retains the power to enforce compliance with its visitation orders through civil contempt, even if it has lost the jurisdiction to modify such judgments under the Uniform Child Custody Jurisdiction Act. Of course, it is within the family court's discretion whether to exercise its contempt power. In *Kirylik v. Kirylik*, 292 S.C. 475, 357 S.E.2d 449 (1987), a family court judge had awarded custody to the mother and set visitation rights for the father. The mother had moved to Delaware where she sought modification of the father's visitation. Delaware had declared itself to be the home state and assumed jurisdiction. Thereafter, the father asked the family court in South Carolina to hold the mother in contempt, alleging that she had twice refused to let him visit the child. The South Carolina trial judge had declined to exercise jurisdiction or to consider holding the wife in contempt because the modification petition was pending in Delaware at the time. The Supreme Court held that it was within the trial judge's discretion to exercise or to decline to exercise jurisdiction. *Id.* at 477, 357 S.E.2d at 450.

The family court may not delegate its authority or responsibility for protecting the interests of minors involved in litigation. In *Stefan v. Stefan*, ___ S.C. ___, 465 S.E.2d 734 (Ct. App. 1995), the family court suspended the visitation rights of a father and, in its final order, it appointed a guardian *ad litem* for the children and directed that the approval of the guardian was required before visitation resumed. The trial judge also ordered the father to complete parenting skills classes and such other testing or training as a parenting professional deemed appropriate. The Court of Appeals held that the family court judge abused his discretion by delegating judicial authority to the parenting specialist and the guardian and by authorizing the guardian to recommend the time for the resumption of visitation.

The *Stefan* opinion also holds that it is error to appoint a guardian *ad litem* for children at the end of litigation when one is not appointed during the pendency of the proceedings. "A guardian *ad litem* in a custody or visitation case represents the interests of the children <u>during the litigation</u>." *Id.* at ___, 465 S.E.2d at 736 (emphasis supplied by the court).

The family court's jurisdiction to modify visitation is discussed in the section on modification of visitation.

C. NONPARENTAL VISITATION

1. GRANDPARENTS

a. Standing

A grandparent has standing to seek visitation only when one of the following situations exist: either or both parents of a minor child are dead; the parents are divorced; or the parents are living separate and apart in different habitats regardless of a court order or agreement. S.C. Code Ann. § 20-7-420(33) (Law. Co-op. Supp.).

Grandparents usually have no right to seek visitation when the family court terminates the parental rights of a child's parents. S.C. Code Ann. § 20-7-1770 (Law. Co-op. 1976). However, they continue to have standing to seek visitation even if the child in question has been adopted, if their son or daughter has not consented to the adoption or otherwise lost parental rights. In *Chavis v. Witt*, 285 S.C. 77, 328 S.E.2d 74 (1985), the Supreme Court held that the adoption statute did not preclude grandparents from seeking visitation although their son (the child's father) had died. The mother remarried and her new husband adopted the child. The Court upheld the family court's determination that the best interests of the child were served by allowing her to visit with the grandparents.

Grandparents have standing to seek visitation even if there is no pending divorce, child custody, or child support issue before the court. *Chavis*.

b. Entitlement

Although grandparents may have standing to seek visitation, this does not mean they are entitled to it.

In determining whether visitation rights should be granted to a grandparent, the best interests of the grandchild are always paramount. *Chavis v. Witt*, 285 S.C. 77, 328 S.E.2d 74 (1985). Before awarding visitation rights to grandparents, the family court must make a written finding that court ordered visitation is in the best interests of the grandchild and will not interfere with the parental/child relationship. S.C. Code Ann. § 20-7-420 (33) (Law. Co-op. Supp.).

It is usually not in the best interests of a grandchild to order visitation with grandparents if the parent who is the child of the grandparents is the custodial parent or has visitation rights.

> [I]t would seldom, if ever, be in the best interests of the grandchild to grant visitation rights to grandparents when their child, the parent, has such rights . . . . [V]isitation by grandparents should be derivative; otherwise the child might have four, or even six people competing for his company: father, mother, paternal grandparents and maternal grandparents.

Brown v. Earnhardt, 302 S.C. 374, 376-377, 396 S.E.2d 358, 359 (1990). *Brown* goes on to say:

> [O]rdinarily it is not conducive to the best interests and welfare of a child for it to be shifted and shuttled back and forth in alternate brief periods between contending parties, particularly during the school term. Furthermore, such an arrangement is likely to cause confusion, interfere with the proper training and discipline of the child, make the child the basis of many quarrels between its custodians, render its life unhappy and discontented and prevent it from living a normal life.

Brown v. Earnhardt, 302 S.C. 374, 377-378, 396 S.E.2d 358, 359-360 (1990) (quoting from *Avin v. Avin*, 272 S.C. 514, 252 S.E.2d 888 (1979)).

Grandparents will not be awarded autonomous visitation privileges absent a showing of exceptional circumstances. In *Brown* the Supreme Court found that the bond of love and affection existing between grandparents and a child does not, in and of itself, justify carving out of the custody and visitation rights of the natural parents another visitation right and vesting it in the grandparents. In this instance, since the father maintained strong parental ties with the child, the grandparents would be able to continue providing a "stabilizing influence" in their granddaughter's life without court-ordered visitation. *See also Horton v. Vaughn*, 309 S.C. 383, 423 S.E.2d 543 (Ct. App. 1992) (finding no special circumstances warranting court-ordered visitation rights to the paternal grandmother with a child who was living with the maternal grandparents).

c. Constitutionality Issues

The constitutionality of South Carolina's statute permitting court-ordered visitation by grandparents has not yet been challenged. Other states have considered the constitutionality of their grandparent visitation statutes and most, but not all, have upheld them. In deciding these cases, the courts consistently find that the right to raise one's children is a fundamental liberty interest protected by the Fourteenth Amendment to the United States Constitution. They also acknowledge that court-ordered grandparent visitation necessarily interferes with parental authority and may erode the fundamental autonomous relationship between parent and child. The central issue is whether the balancing of the rights of grandparents, parents, and children warrants the state's intrusion into parental autonomy. Most cases conclude that ordering "reasonable" grandparent visitation following a finding that it is "in the best interests of the children" is not a constitutionally prohibited intrusion. *Cf. Campbell v. Campbell*, 896 P.2d 635 (Utah Ct. App. 1995); *Sketo v. Brown*, 559 So.2d 381 (Fla.App. 1990); *Bailey v. Menzie*, 542 N.E.2d 1015 (Ind. App. 1989); *Spradling v. Harris*, 13 Kan.App.2d 595, 778 P.2d 365 (1989); *King v. King*, 828 S.W.2d 630 (Ky.), cert. den., 506 U.S. 941, 113 S.Ct. 378, 121 L.Ed.2d 289 (1992); *Herndon v. Tuhey*, 857 S.W.2d 203 (Mo.1993) (en banc); *Roberts v. Ward*, 126 N.H. 388, 493 A.2d 478 (1985); *People ex rel. Sibley v. Sheppard*, 54 N.Y.2d 320, 445 N.Y.S.2d 420, 429 N.E.2d 1049 (1981); *Deweese v. Crawford*, 520 S.W.2d 522 (Tex.App.1975).

Some courts have concluded that court-ordered grandparent visitation is unconstitutional. These rulings are based on the premise that, even assuming grandparent visitation promotes the health and welfare of children, the state may only impose that visitation over the parents' objections on a showing that failing to do so would be harmful to the children. *Brooks v. Parkerson*, 265 Ga. 189, 454 S.E.2d 769 (1995) (holding that Georgia's grandparent visitation statute was unconstitutional under the Georgia Constitution and the Constitution of the United States because it failed to require a showing of substantial harm before grandparent visitation could be ordered); *Hawk v. Hawk*, 855 S.W.2d 573 (Tenn. 1993) (holding that court-ordered grandparent visitation violated Tennessee's Constitution because under Tennessee law the state's interest must be "sufficiently compelling" to overcome a fundamental constitutional right, and absent a threat of substantial harm to a child's welfare the state lacks a significant compelling justification for the infringement on the fundamental right of parents to raise their children as they see fit).

2. OTHERS

There is no statute in South Carolina which specifically grants visitation rights to other people with close ties to the child such as surrogate parents, foster parents, or homosexual partners. Nor have there been any cases on this matter. One should examine the following annotations for information about how other jurisdictions have handled these issues: Annotation, *Visitation Rights of Homosexual or Lesbian Parent*, 36 A.L.R.4th 997 (1985); Annotation, *Visitation Rights of Persons Other Than Natural Parents or Grandparents*, 1 A.L.R.4th 1270 (1980).

D. TERMS AND CONDITIONS OF VISITATION

1. IN GENERAL

Courts do not get involved in setting terms or conditions on child visitation unless they are asked to do so. First, they lack subject matter jurisdiction until a litigant puts visitation in issue. Second, most judges prefer for the parties to work out suitable arrangements between themselves. It is very difficult to set visitation terms and conditions which will suit both parents for as long as their children are minors.

A potentially important issue for practitioners (and one which has seen surprisingly little judicial attention) is that the custodial parent has the inherent authority to set terms and conditions of visitation when children are temporarily in the custody of other people, such as baby sitters, school officials, and others with whom the children spend the night or travel. *See* 67A C.J.S. *Parent & Child* § 10 (1978).

What is less clear is the extent to which the custodial parent is permitted to set terms and conditions of visitation when the children are temporarily in the care of the noncustodial parent. It does not seem that it would be in the best interest of a child to allow the noncustodial parent to have complete liberty to ignore the custodial parent's wishes and the normal rules for the child (e.g., about not handling firearms, or not watching violent or sexual or horror movies). *See* Annotation, *Interference by Custodian of Child with Noncustodial Parent's Visitation Rights as Ground for Change of Custody*, 28 A.L.R.4th 9 (1984).

There are surprisingly few cases in South Carolina involving attempts by custodial parents to regulate the actions of noncustodial parents. *Wheeler v. Gill*, 307 S.C. 94, 413 S.E.2d 860 (Ct. App. 1992), suggests how appellate courts will decide cases in which the custodial parent wants to place reasonable terms and conditions on the non-custodial parent's visitation. The court upheld the family court's granting a father's request to prohibit the mother from making unauthorized visits to their daughter's day care center:

> There was testimony that her visits *were not welcomed by the father* and had the *potential* for disruption. The final amended order on this issue prohibits the mother from visiting Lindsey at the day care, except when invited, when "volunteers are allowed to participate in activities with a class," or on special occasions "when parents are normally allowed to attend." We do not view these prohibitions as overly oppressive and find support in the record for the restrictions. However, to the extent the restrictions prohibit the mother from responding to a genuine emergency at the day care center when the father is otherwise unavailable, we accordingly modify the trial court's order.
>
> There is no merit to the wife's contention that South Carolina law prohibited the placing of such restrictions on the mother because the father did not request that relief in his pleadings. Of course, the prohibitions were simply a term of the visitation order which the court was requested to establish in the event it awarded sole custody to the father.

Id. at 101, 413 S.E.2d at 864-865 (emphasis added). Although this case really involves limiting the amount of visitation allowed for the non-custodial parent, it appears to give great weight to the wishes of the custodial parent. It remains to be seen whether similar weight will be given to the custodial parent's wishes when cases involving disputes about how to raise children come before the appellate courts.

2. NORMAL TERMS AND CONDITIONS

There is no statute setting forth "official terms and conditions of visitation" in South Carolina, but the cases identify some fairly clear parameters. The amount of visitation awarded is a matter left to the trial judge's discretion. *Hyde v. Hyde*, 302 S.C. 280, 395 S.E.2d 186 (1990).

Visitation arrangements are not allowed which involve excessive shuttling of the children between parents. In *Mixson v. Mixson*, 253 S.C. 436, 446, 171 S.E.2d 581, 586 (1969), the trial court modified the wife's sole custody of the children to provide for divided and alternate custody. The children were to sleep at the mother's home from Monday to Friday. She was to deliver the child who was not in school to the father's house by 9:00 a.m. each morning. The two older children would be picked up by the father after school and stay with him until the mother picked them up at 7:00 p.m. Summers and weekends were similarly divided. In reversing the custody award, the Supreme Court wrote:

> The best interest and welfare of the children demand that divided custody should be avoided if possible, and it will not be approved except under exceptional circumstances or for strong and convincing reasons. 27B C.J.S. *Divorce* § 308d, p. 447. See also the annotation in 92 A.L.R.(2d) 695. Divided custody is usually harmful to and not conducive to the best interest and welfare of the children.
>
> In *Nelson on Divorce* (2d), section 15.17, it is stated:
>
> > 'The courts generally endeavor to avoid dividing the custody of a child between contending parties, and are particularly reluctant to award the

> custody of a child in brief alternating periods between estranged and quarrelsome persons. Under the facts and circumstances of particular cases, it has been held improper to apportion the custody of a child between its parents, or between one of its parents and a third party, for ordinarily it is not conducive to the best interests and welfare of a child for it to be shifted and shuttled back and forth in alternate brief periods between contending parties, particularly during the school term. Furthermore, such an arrangement is likely to cause confusion, interfere with the proper training and discipline of the child, make the child the basis of many quarrels between its custodians, render its life unhappy and discontented, and prevent it from living a normal life.'
>
> The trial judge, without making any findings of fact, directed divided and alternate custody. We have carefully reviewed the entire record in this case and find no exceptional circumstances that would justify the direction made by the trial judge. It follows that the order of the trial judge granting divided and alternate custody should be reversed. *Id.* at 446-447, 171 S.E.2d at 586.

*Mixson*is cited in *Avin v. Avin*, 272 S.C. 514, 515, 252 S.E.2d 888, 888-889 (1979), in which the mother's "visitation" was so substantial that she had as much physical time with the child as did the legal custodian father (the mother had the child forty weekends per year). This order was viewed by the Supreme Court as an abuse of discretion. Similar holdings resulted in *Sharpe v. Sharpe*, 256 S.C. 517, 183 S.E.2d 325 (1971) (disallowing custody in father from June 15 - August 15); *Courie v. Courie*, 288 S.C. 163, 341 S.E.2d 646 (Ct. App. 1986) (holding that visitation totaling 165 days was too much); and *Lassiter v. Lassiter*, 289 S.C. 341, 345 S.E.2d 504 (Ct. App. 1986) (rejecting visitation of 150 days per year (every other weekend, every Wednesday evening, six weeks in summer, and alternating major holidays) as amounting to divided custody). However, in *Ingold v. Ingold*, 304 S.C. 316, 404 S.E.2d 35 (Ct. App.1991), the Court reversed a trial judge's reduction of the father's summer visitation from six weeks to three weeks because there had been no showing that the six weeks visitation was detrimental to the best interest of the child. *Ingold* can be distinguished from *Lassiter* in that the father in *Ingold* lived in California and was unable to visit the children frequently.

As a measure of how much visitation is not excessive, *see Woodall v. Woodall*, ___ S.C. ___, 471 S.E.2d 154 (1996). The Supreme Court described the following visitation schedule as "standard": every other weekend, from 6:00 p.m. Friday until 6:00 p.m. Sunday; four weeks during the summer months, to consist of consecutive week periods; alternate Easter, July 4th, Labor Day, Thanksgiving, and Christmas Holidays; the husband was awarded visitation with the son every Father's Day; and the wife could have the son every Mother's Day. *See also Johns v. Johns*, 309 S.C. 199, 420 S.E.2d 856 (Ct. App. 1992), which holds that it does not amount to split custody for a noncustodial parent to have the following visitation rights: every other weekend from 6:00 p.m. Friday until 6:00 p.m. Sunday; the first two weeks of June, July and August; alternate Thanksgiving and spring break holidays; and one week at Christmas. The Court noted that this was much less visitation than was rejected in *Lassiter* and *Courie*, involved much less shuttling of the children, and there was no showing that the amount of visitation would have a detrimental effect on the children.

It is not clear whether any of the rulings on visitation will be affected by the legislature's 1996 amendment of S.C. Code Ann. § 20-7-420 which authorizes the family court "to order joint or divided custody where the court finds it is in the best interest of the child."

3. EXTRAORDINARY TERMS AND CONDITIONS

The courts will uphold restrictions on visitation beyond those normally imposed on noncustodial parents only if they are reasonable and protect the welfare of the child.

> A family court may impose upon a noncustodial parent such conditions and restrictions on [a parent's] visitation privileges as the court, in its discretion, thinks proper. [citation omitted] The privilege of visitation must yield to the best interests of the children and may

> be denied or limited if the best interests of the child will be served thereby.

Frye v. Frye, ___ S.C. ___, ___, 448 S.E.2d 586, 588 (Ct. App. 1994).

A restriction which allowed visitation only as long as the child was not exposed to persons not related to the father by blood or marriage was held to be overly broad and unreasonable in *Jackson v. Jackson*, 279 S.C. 618, 310 S.E.2d 827 (Ct. App. 1983). Conversely, in the same case, the Court of Appeals upheld a requirement that the father would have to post a $10,000 bond to see the child. The bond was based on threats the father had made concerning removing the child from this country and the strong ability of the father to accomplish the threat.

A limitation of the father's visitation to only six hours per month based on evidence of his irrational rage and uncontrollable temper and that he had physically and mentally abused both the wife and child was upheld in *Hyde v. Hyde*, 302 S.C. 280, 395 S.E.2d 186 (Ct. App. 1990). Restricting a father's visitation with his daughter to his parents' home was upheld in light of the fact that two small children from former marriages had died accidentally while in their father's sole custody within months of each other in *Hartley v. Hartley*, 292 S.C. 245, 355 S.E.2d 869 (Ct. App. 1987). The Supreme Court upheld a restriction of visitation to eight hours (10:00 a.m. to 6:00 p.m.) on one day each week (alternate Saturdays and Sundays) in *Simons v. Simons*, 263 S.C. 509, 211 S.E.2d 555 (1975). Although there were no special facts cited in this case, the Court may have been influenced by the fact that the wife had obtained a divorce on the basis of physical cruelty, even though the divorce was reversed and remanded because the appellate record was insufficient to permit appellate review. In *Frye v. Frye*, ___ S.C. ___, 448 S.E.2d 586 (Ct. App. 1994), certain conditions on the father's visitation rights were allowed following harassment of the former wife by the new wife. The husband, while not participating in the actions of his new wife, was aware of the actions and took no steps to stop her.

Restricted or supervised visitation may be ordered where one of the parents is involving the child in disputes with the custodial parent. In serious cases of misbehavior, the visitation rights of the non-custodial parent may even be suspended. In *Nash v. Byrd*, 298 S.C. 530, 381 S.E.2d 913 (Ct. App. 1989), *e.g.*, the court approved the trial court's decision to suspend the father's visitation rights until he obtained counseling and reestablished his relationship with the child. For a more complete discussion of *Nash*, see the section on termination of visitation rights.

A case showing extreme deference to the trial court's discretion is *Graham v. Graham*, 253 S.C. 486, 171 S.E.2d 704 (1970), in which the Supreme Court upheld a North Carolina trial court's order that the father's visitation with his daughter was restricted to Mecklenburg County. Although the Court decided to let the restriction stand, the only justification it gives is that the trial court apparently considered the father's conduct in deserting his wife and child and committing adultery. There is no analysis of how the best interest of the child is served by this restriction. One might expect courts in North and South Carolina to reach a different conclusion today, absent additional justifications. Similarly, one might question the current validity of the result in *Porter v. Porter*, 246 S.C. 332, 143 S.E.2d 619 (1965), in which the Court held that it was an abuse of discretion for the circuit court judge, on appeal from the Juvenile and Domestic Relations Court of Greenville County, to expand the father's visitation from 2:00-5:00 p.m. in his residence on Sunday to allowing the father to visit from 2:00 p.m. Saturday until 5:00 p.m. Sunday on alternate weekends. As in *Graham*, the conduct that justified such restricted visitation was that the father deserted his family and committed adultery. It is difficult to understand how this conduct justifies restrictions on the fathers' visitation rights, absent some showing that it affected the children or that it was not otherwise in the children's best interests to have normal visitation with their fathers. The results in these cases appear to be punishment for the fathers' misconduct.

A child's need to attend Sunday School or, presumably, to participate in other scheduled activities will not justify placing extraordinary limits on the noncustodial parent's visitation rights. In *Matthews v. Matthews*, 273 S.C. 130, 254 S.E.2d 801 (1979), the Court reversed the trial court's decision to reduce the father's visitation from every Saturday at 10:00 a.m. through Sunday at 5:00 p.m. to only one day of visitation every other week. The trial court's only stated reason for the reduction is to allow the child to be regular in its attendance of Sunday school and church. There is no discussion of whether the father's visitation was so excessive as to be tantamount to divided custody.

Some additional cases in which restrictions have been permitted are discussed in the section on suspension or termination of visitation.

E. MODIFICATION AND TERMINATION OF VISITATION

1. MODIFICATION OF VISITATION

The family court has continuing jurisdiction to modify visitation if a showing can be made that the best interest of the child will be served by modifying visitation rights:

> Absent an appeal of the original decree fixing the visitation rights of the non-custodial parent, visitation is still subject to the continuing jurisdiction of the family court to modify rights previously established upon a showing that such modification would serve the best welfare and interests of the child. *Porter v. Porter*, 246 S.C. 332, 143 S.E.2d 619 (1965); *McGregor, supra* [255 S.C. 179, 177 S.E.2d 599 (1970)].

King v. Gardner, 274 S.C. 493, 495, 265 S.E.2d 260, 262 (1980). In *King*, however, the Supreme Court overruled the family court's award of expanded visitation rights to the mother. The trial judge's determination that the visitation set in the unappealed order was "unreasonable" was unsupported in the order or in the testimony, and there was no showing of changed circumstances nor any showing that the child would benefit from more visitation with the mother.

A change in visitation can be awarded upon a showing of changed circumstances. *King v. Gardner*, 274 S.C. 493, 265 S.E.2d 260 (1980) (quoting *McGregor v. McGregor*, 255 S.C. 179, 177 S.E.2d 599 (1970)): "'A judicial award of the custody of a child and the fixing of visitation rights is not final and changed circumstances may authorize the change of custody or visitation rights in the future. (citations omitted)'" *Id.* at 183, 177 S.E.2d 600-601.

In *Ingold v. Ingold*, 304 S.C. 316, 404 S.E.2d 35 (Ct. App. 1991), the Court of Appeals found that the trial court had erred in reducing the father's visitation from six weeks to three weeks. There was no change of circumstances, for the parties' visitation agreement contemplated that they would live thousands of miles apart, and the mother did not show any adverse impact on the child. *Fisher v. Miller*, 288 S.C.

576, 344 S.E.2d 149 (1986), denied a request to reduce the mother's visitation since there was no showing of changed circumstances to warrant the reduction and the mother faithfully exercised her visitation rights. Although there were problems with implementation of the order, there was no showing or finding as to which of the parties was responsible for the implementation problems. Nor was there a finding of changed circumstances or that a reduction in visitation was in the best interest of the child.

The family court may not modify visitation unless such relief is specifically requested in the pleadings. In *Aiken v. Aiken*, 289 S.C. 370, 345 S.E.2d 710 (1986), the Supreme Court reversed the trial court's modification of visitation, stating that "a party may not receive relief not contemplated in the pleadings. *See Gainey v. Gainey*, 279 S.C. 68, 301 S.E.2d 763 (1983)." *Id.* at 371, 345 S.E.2d at 711. In *Aiken*, the wife brought an action for contempt for failure to pay child support and alimony and the husband counterclaimed for a change of custody. Neither party's pleadings asked the court to modify visitation.

2. TERMINATION OR SUSPENSION OF VISITATION

The family court may terminate or suspend the visitation privileges of a parent if it is in the child's best interests.

> The privilege of visitation must yield to the best interests of the children and may be denied or limited if the best interests of the child will be served thereby.

Frye v. Frye, ___ S.C. ___, ___, 448 S.E.2d 586, 588 (Ct. App. 1994).

The decision to terminate visitation between parent and child is a drastic one. While the family court has the power to absolutely forbid visitation in an extreme case, that power has been and should be used sparingly. After all, there are very few parental rights left if a noncustodial parent loses visitation privileges.

There are no reported cases in which the visitation rights of a parent have actually been terminated, apart from cases involving adoptions or other terminations of parental rights. (Cases involving termination of parental rights due to a parent's willful failure to visit a child for six months are discussed in the section on termination of parental rights in this chapter.) One unpublished opinion affirmed the family court's denial of visitation. *Cleveland v. Cleveland*, No. 96-UP-433 (S.C. Ct. App. 1996). The father had been convicted on the charge of solicitation to commit the murder of his wife and he was incarcerated. The children were six and eight. Even under these circumstances, however, the court pointed out that the father could file a petition to seek visitation as circumstances change. The court did not specify whether the changed circumstances on which visitation could be reinstated might be his release from incarceration, the maturation of the children, or something else.

Some cases involve fact situations in which the courts have come close to terminating visitation, and suspensions of fathers' visitation rights have been upheld. In serious cases of misbehavior involving the child, the visitation rights of the non-custodial parent may be suspended. In *In re M*, 312 S.C. 248, 439 S.E.2d 857 (Ct. App. 1994) (affirming the termination of a father's parental rights for lack of visitation), the Court of Appeals noted that the family court suspended a father's visitation rights upon concluding that the father sexually abused his son. In *Nash v. Byrd*, 298 S.C. 530, 381 S.E.2d 913 (Ct. App. 1989), the Court of Appeals approved the trial court's decision to suspend the father's visitation rights until he obtained counseling and reestablished his relationship with the child. The Court found that the father engaged in a course of conduct calculated to harass the mother and to gain information to support a change of custody. He made derogatory comments about the mother in the child's presence. He parked near her home and lurked about. He followed the mother and child to and from work and school blowing his horn and maneuvering around her vehicle. Although he was given visitation for virtually the entire summer, his visitation was creating physical and emotional anxiety for the child.

After the father was enjoined from coming around the mother's home or the school, the father's family became involved. His mother and brother questioned the son about alleged acts of abuse or neglect; they reported false allegations of neglect to DSS; the grandmother made the child feel compelled to write letters to the court and DSS falsely expressing dissatisfaction with his mother and alleging abuse and neglect; and the father's brother prowled the halls at school and followed the mother's car. The father's mother and brother disparaged the child's mother in the child's presence and used various means to intimidate the child. Ultimately, the child refused to visit his father. The Court of Appeals agreed that he should not be forced to do so and found that the trial judge properly held the father in contempt and suspended his visitation privileges:

> We find no error in the judge's determination that the problems were caused by Nash's [the father's] conduct and that Byrd [the mother] took all reasonable steps to resolve the problems. The record is replete with evidence as to the father's fault. For example, during visitations, Nash did not protect Jason from harassment by Nash's mother and brother. Also, it was Nash who precipitated the suspension of visitation by telling Jason that, if he did not want to, he did not have to visit anymore.
>
> . . .
>
> In determining visitation rights, the welfare of the child is the paramount consideration. *Grimsley v. Grimsley*, 250 S.C. 389, 158 S.E.2d 197 (1967). The child is an innocent victim of the broken home and at best has a most difficult time in adjusting to the separation of the parents. It is therefore the duty of the parents, irrespective of other considerations, to lend their aid in creating an atmosphere that will foster the best interests of the child. Neither parent has a right to use the child as a pawn or club in dealing with the other and, where such is done to the detriment of the child, it affords proper ground to deny or limit visitation privileges. *Id.*
>
> In this case, Nash has refused to work to resolve the visitation problems. Nash has spurned Dr. Price's [his son's psychologist] invitations to meet with him to attempt to resolve the visitation conflicts. He has simply demanded his visitation rights without regard for the feelings and sensitivities of the child. In effect, Nash has used the prior visitation order as a weapon to place Byrd [his wife] in the dilemma of either subjecting Jason to potential emotional harm by forcing him into visits or subjecting herself to contempt sanctions by not insisting that Jason visit Nash.

> The record amply supports the need for supervision and counseling.

Id. at 534-536, 381 S.E.2d at 916-917.

The Supreme Court described a situation in *Venable v. Venable*, 273 S.C. 96, 254 S.E.2d 309 (1979), in which it found the facts to be almost sufficient, but not quite, to justify termination of a father's visitation rights. The sole issue before the Court was whether the father should be allowed visitation:

> The parties were married in March of 1975 and had one child who is now approximately four years old. The father admitted committing various acts of physical cruelty against appellant and the child, and a divorce was granted to the wife on that ground in May of 1978.
>
> In recognition of respondent's impulsive and violent temper, both judges concluded he could visit with his son only at the residence of the mother, providing he is on good and proper behavior. The appellant has returned to her hometown in Connecticut, and seeks to prohibit respondent from exercising the visitation privileges granted him by the special referee and the trial judge.
>
> The decision to terminate visitation between parent and child is a drastic one. *Grimsley v. Grimsley*, 250 S.C. 389, 158 S.E.2d 197 (1967). While the court certainly has the power to absolutely forbid visitation in an extreme case, that power should be sparingly used. *Grimsley, supra; Porter v. Porter*, 246 S.C. 332, 143 S.E.2d 619 (1965).
>
> Respondent has acknowledged his explosive personality and has admitted abusing his son. While we decline to deny him the right to visit his child, that right should be restricted in order to ensure the safety of appellant and her son. Therefore, we hold that prior to visiting with the boy in appellant's home in Connecticut, respondent must notify appellant and her attorney, and must obtain permission

> from the family court to exercise his privilege of visitation. With this modification, the order of the trial court is affirmed.

Id. at 96-97, 254 S.E.2d at 310.

The *Grimsley* case cited in *Venable* involves the use of a child as a pawn in an ongoing struggle between the parents. Although the Court refused to end visitation on the part of the allegedly manipulative father, it delivered a clear warning to him not to continue in a detrimental course of conduct:

> While we are not too favorably impressed with some of the actions of the father, we cannot say that the lower court abused its discretion in continuing his visitation privileges. We are satisfied, as was the lower court, that a recognition in the future by the parties of the mutual rights of each other and the welfare of the child will eliminate as far as possible problems concerning the child's emotional adjustment. However, a continued failure of the parties to reconcile themselves to the situation that exists and to attempt to live with the situation without further harassment may necessitate the drastic action of denying visitation privileges to the offending parent. We are confident that the lower court in the exercise of its continuing jurisdiction in the matter will enter, when necessary, such future orders respecting custody and visitation as will assure that the child will not be subjected to a continuing tug-of-war between the parents.

Grimsley at 393, 158 S.E.2d at 199. In *Grimsley*, the mother was alleging that the father was trying to use the child to accomplish his goal of reconciliation. He had communicated his beliefs regarding divorce to induce the child to believe that the mother was committing a sin by continuing to refuse to live with him.

The courts remain reluctant to suspend visitation privileges, even when the parent engages in egregious behavior. In *Stefan v. Stefan*, ___ S.C. ___, 465 S.E.2d 734 (Ct. App. 1995), the Court of Appeals held that the family court erred in suspending a father's visitation rights even though the family court found that the father almost totally disregarded court orders related to visitation during the pendency of the action. Facts which were not disputed on appeal included findings by the family court that the father was:

> guilty of, *inter alia*: entering the wife's home uninvited in violation of the Order; refusing to leave when told to do so; making disparaging remarks about the wife in front of the children; splintering the door to the wife's home; engaging in immature and threatening behavior in the presence of the wife and children; committing other various acts of harassment; wilfully violating the Temporary Order which prohibited him from assaulting, harassing, annoying or interfering with the wife; again making disparaging remarks about the wife in front of the children; repeatedly calling the wife's home and making disparaging and harassing remarks to the wife; calling the wife's mother and making disparaging and harassing remarks to the wife; calling the wife's mother and making disparaging and harassing comments to her; refusing to tell the wife the general whereabouts of the children during visitation; and refusing to return the children's clothes after visitation.

Id. at ___, 465 S.E.2d at 734-736. The Court of Appeals' opinion states:

> While the husband's conduct and disregard for court orders caused the family court justifiable concern, it was not sufficient to serve as a basis for suspending his visitation rights, particularly in the absence of a guardian's recommendation that it would be in the children's best interest. We find the husband is entitled to visitation.

Id. at ___, 465 S.E.2d at 737. The apparent significance attributed by the Court to the absence of a recommendation of a guardian *ad litem* is puzzling. There was no guardian *ad litem* for the child from which such a recommendation could come. It is probably reading too much into this comment to interpret it to mean that a family court judge cannot find that it is in the best interest of a child to suspend the visitation rights of a parent absent a recommendation of a guardian *ad litem* to do so. No other case has suggested this.

CHAPTER TWELVE
CHILD SUPPORT

CHAPTER TWELVE
CHILD SUPPORT

A. IN GENERAL

1. NEW ERA IN CHILD SUPPORT LAW

Existing and future legislative changes "promise to spur a revolution in child support policy and associated family law." Legler, "The Coming Revolution in Child Support Policy: Implications of the 1996 Welfare Act," 30 *Fam. L. Q.* 519, 520 (Fall, 1996). This article describes federal mandates contained in the Personal Responsibility and Work Opportunity Reconciliation Act of 1996, Pub. L. No. 104-193, 110 Stat. 2105 (1996).

Private lawyers will become less frequently involved in establishing and enforcing child support orders as a result of the establishment of an administrative process for establishing and enforcing child support and the existence of powerful enforcement tools that are available only to the Child Support Enforcement Division of the Department of Social Services (the Division). (These developments are discussed later in this chapter.)

It may violate the Rules of Professional Conduct for a lawyer to charge a client to help establish or enforce child support, if the lawyer has not informed the client of the availability of assistance from the Division and counseled the client about this option. Although clients can still choose to use private lawyers to establish and collect child support, only the wealthiest clients are likely to select this option.

This new era in child support law began in South Carolina on May 25, 1990, when the South Carolina Child Support Guidelines became effective. Previously, child support awards in South Carolina were determined on a case-by-case basis, and there were no standard criteria for making such determinations.

The promulgation of the guidelines coincided with aggressive federal initiatives to force states to get tough on nonsupporting parents. The ultimate goal of federal activities in the area of child support enforcement is to make the payment of child support automatic and inescapable. In furtherance of this goal, federal legislative requires state legislatures to enact laws that enhance child support collection by improving the ability of state child support collection agencies to: (1) locate individuals and assets - access to information; (2) work cases in volume using computers, automation, and information technology - mass case processing; and (3) take enforcement action automatically, preferably administratively, without reliance on a complaint-driven process - pro-active enforcement. Legler, "The Coming Revolution in Child Support Policy: Implications of the 1996 Welfare Act," 30 *Fam. L. Q.* 519, 538 (Fall, 1996).

The Child Support Enforcement Division of the Department of Social Services (the Division) is a state program mandated by Title IV-D of the Social Security Act, 42 U.S.C. §§ 651-669. The Division's objective is to establish paternity and to establish and enforce child support orders for individuals receiving its services.[26]

Any person can receive assistance from the Division. Individuals who are not receiving public assistance benefits can secure the Division's services by completing and submitting an application form and paying a $1.00 fee. The services of the Division are available to both custodial and noncustodial parents. A person may request the Division's full services or may just request a specific service such as assistance in locating an absent parent (the Division has access to myriad federal, interstate, state, and local sources to locate absent parents).

The Division has extensive weapons to establish and enforce child support claims which are not available to private attorneys (see the sections in this chapter on UIFSA, Administrative Process for Establishing and Enforcing Child Support, and Civil Enforcement of Child Support). Until similar remedies are available to private lawyers, lawyers with clients who have paternity or child support claims

---

[26] The Division must also provide assistance with the enforcement of an existing order for spousal support when that order is incident to an order for child support. 42 U.S.C. § 654(6).

(particularly those seeking to enforce existing orders in difficult cases) should consider referring those clients to the Division for assistance.

If a lawyer represents a client who assigned child support rights to the Division (e.g., AFDC recipients are required to do so as a condition of receiving AFDC payments), any action involving child support issues, including divorce cases, should be coordinated with the Division. The family court should make any child support awards in such cases payable to the Department of Social Services, unless the Division agrees to some other arrangement.

It is unlikely that private lawyers will be able to match the effectiveness of the Division in extracting agreements to pay child support or in enforcing existing support orders. It is certain that private lawyers will not be able to assist clients with these problems at a lower cost to the client than the Division. Where a private lawyer is assisting a client with multiple marital problems, e.g., divorces in which child support is among the issues to be decided, it is possible that the client's best interests will be served by including child support among the issues handled by the private lawyer. In many situations, however, a private lawyer should consider referring the client to the Division and should not represent the client for a fee unless the client insists after being fully counseled.

Lawyers almost certainly have a duty to inform prospective and existing clients about more efficient and inexpensive ways to resolve their legal problems, although there is no express provision requiring this in the Rules of Professional Conduct. There is a fiduciary relationship between lawyers and clients, and the Rules of Professional Conduct impose a duty to render candid advice to a client on matters concerning the client's economic interests as well as the client's economic interests. Rule 2.1, SCACR 407 (Law Co-op. 1990). A lawyer is also required to "explain a matter to the extent reasonably necessary to permit the client to make informed decisions regarding the representation." Rule 1.4, SCACR 407 (Law Co-op. 1990). Agency law imposes a duty to convey to clients relevant information which the principal would desire to have. *Restatement (2nd) Agency* § 381 (1958). Finally, a lawyer is required to charge reasonable fees. Rule 1.5, SCACR 407 (Law Co-op. 1990). In light of the above, a lawyer who fails to inform a client of the availability of the services of the Division with child support problems will risk malpractice and disciplinary charges.

2. PERSONS RESPONSIBLE FOR CHILD SUPPORT

Mothers and fathers are required to support their children, both legitimate and illegitimate. S.C. Code Ann. § 20-7-90 (Law. Co-op. 1976) provides in part:

> (A) Any able-bodied person capable of earning a livelihood who shall, without just cause or excuse, abandon or fail to provide reasonable support to his or her spouse or to his or her minor unmarried legitimate or illegitimate child dependent on him or her shall be deemed guilty of a misdemeanor . . . .
>
> . . .
>
> As used in this section "reasonable support" means an amount of financial assistance which, when combined with the support the member is reasonably capable of providing for himself or herself, will provide a living standard for the member substantially equal to that of the person owing the duty to support. It includes both usual and unusual necessities.

Grandparents can be held responsible for supporting grandchildren born to unmarried minors under a statute enacted in 1995. S.C. Code Ann. § 20-7-936 (Law. Co-op. Supp.) provides:

> When a child is born to parents, either or both of whom are unmarried and under eighteen years of age, the Child Support Enforcement Division of the State Department of Social Services may pursue support and maintenance of that child from one or both of the child's maternal and paternal grandparents as long as the parent of the child is under eighteen years of age.

This legislation is particularly useful to the Department of Social Services when unmarried minors with children receive AFDC payments even though their parents are capable of contributing to the support of their grandchildren. However, the statute presents a number of issues to be resolved by the courts. It makes no exception for unmarried minors who are emancipated. The statute covers all child support cases in which assistance is sought from the Department of Social Services, not just those in which AFDC is being provided. The statute does not require a determination that the child's parents are unable to provide adequate support before grandparents can be pursued. It is also unclear whether a grandparent with an adult child can be pursued under this statute if the adult child has a baby with a minor (the concluding phrase, "as long as the parent of the child is under eighteen years of age," could be interpreted to exclude grandparents of adult children or to allow them to be pursued as long as either parent is under eighteen).

South Carolina statutes have been amended to bring the state's statutory scheme into compliance with the decision in *Orr v. Orr*, 440 U.S. 268, 99 S.Ct. 1102, 59 L.Ed.2d 306 (1979), which successfully challenged an Alabama statute providing that husbands, but not wives, could be required to pay alimony. The U.S. Supreme Court held that gender-based statutory schemes for allocation of family responsibilities violate equal protection under the Fourteenth Amendment to the U.S. Constitution.

A father is not responsible after divorce for the support of his wife's illegitimate child(ren) by another man, who was born before the marriage, unless he has formally adopted the child. *Walton v. Walton*, 282 S.C. 165, 318 S.E.2d 14 (1984).

A husband who consents for his wife to conceive a child through artificial insemination with the understanding that the child will be treated as his own is the legal father of the child and will be charged with all of the legal responsibilities of paternity, including support. "Written consent is not required. Husband's consent to his wife's impregnation by artificial insemination may be express or it may be implied from conduct which evidences knowledge of the procedure and failure to object." *In re Baby Doe*, 291 S.C. 389, 392-392, 353 S.E.2d 877, 878-798 (1987) (citing *R.S. v. R.S.*, 9 Kan. App.2d 39, 670 P.2d 923 (1983)). *Doe* affirmed the trial court's order holding the husband responsible for the support of a child born to his wife as a result of artificial insemination with sperm donated by an anonymous third-party donor.

It is inappropriate to require a custodial parent to pay child support to a non-custodial parent while the child is in the physical custody of the non-custodial parent, as during extended visitation. *Avin v. Avin*, 272 S.C. 514, 252 S.E.2d 888 (1979) (reversing the trial court's award of support to the non-custodial parent during periods of visitation). The rationale is that the custodial parent has the fixed obligation to maintain a place of residence, which obligation does not materially diminish due to the temporary absence of the child.

3. CONSEQUENCES OF NONSUPPORT

Nonsupport of a child is a basis for terminating parental rights. See the chapter on termination of parental rights.

A parent who does not provide support for a child may be denied a share of an intestate child's estate. S.C. Code Ann. § 62-2-114 (Law. Co-op. Supp.) allows the probate court to deny or limit either or both parent's entitlement to a share of the proceeds of an intestate child's estate "if the court determines, by a preponderance of the evidence, that the parent or parents failed to reasonably provide support for the decedent as defined in Section 20-7-40 and did not otherwise provide for the needs of the decedent during his or her minority."

A parent who does not provide support for a child may be denied a share of damages awarded by a jury in a wrongful death action arising from the death of a child. S.C. Code Ann. § 15-51-40 (Law. Co-op. Supp.) allows the probate court to deny or limit either or both parents' entitlement for a share of the damages awarded by a jury in a wrongful death action "if the court determines, by a preponderance of the evidence, that the parent or parents failed to reasonably provide support for the decedent as defined in Section 20-7-40 and did not otherwise provide for the needs of the decedent during his or her minority."

A parent who does not provide support for a child may be denied workers' compensation death benefits upon the death of the child. S.C. Code Ann. § 49-40-140 (Law. Co-op. Supp.) allows the Workers' Compensation Commission to deny or limit either or both parents' entitlement for a share of workers' compensation benefits which would otherwise be payable to the mother and father of a deceased worker "if the commission determines, by a preponderance of the evidence, that the parent or parents failed to reasonably provide support for the decedent as defined in Section

20-7-40 and did not otherwise provide for the needs of the decedent during his or her minority."

The three statutes mentioned above were enacted in response to *Adkins, et al. v. Comcar Industries, Inc.*, 316 S.C. 149, 447 S.E.2d 228 (Ct. App. 1994), *aff'd* ___ S.C. ___, 475 S.E.2d 762 (1996). Section 49-40-140 effectively annuls the holding of *Adkins*, in which a deceased child's mother disputed the father's entitlement to share in workers' compensation death benefits. The father paid only $20.00 in child support during his son's life (the parties separated a year after his birth), he had minimal contact with his son, and admitted he had seen his son only three times over the last twelve years of his son's life. However, no legal action had been taken to terminate his parental rights. The Workers' Compensation Commission ruled that the man was not a "father" within the meaning of S.C. Code § 42-9-140 (Law. Co-op. Supp.) and, consequently, he was not entitled to receive any benefits. The circuit court and the Court of Appeals disagreed. The Court of Appeals held that the father was entitled to claim benefits for himself. The Court further ruled that the commission did not have the discretion to apportion the benefits based on the facts of the case and the father was, therefore, entitled to 50% of the benefits.

B. JURISDICTION

1. IN GENERAL

The family court and the Child Support Division of the Department of Social Services have concurrent jurisdiction over child support cases. S.C. Code Ann. § 20-7-420 (Law. Co-op. 1976) says that the family court has exclusive jurisdiction in child support matters; but, notwithstanding section 20-7-420, UIFSA and other legislation gives concurrent jurisdiction and confers limited judicial powers in child support matters to the Child Enforcement Division of the Department of Social Services. S.C. Code Ann. § 20-7-965(23), -970, & -9505 (Law. Co-op. Supp.).

The pertinent jurisdictional provisions of S.C. Code Ann. § 20-7-420 (Law. Co-op. 1976) provide that the family court has jurisdiction:

(1) To hear and determine matters which come within the provisions of the Uniform Reciprocal Enforcement of Support Act.[27]

. . .

(11) To hear and determine proceedings within the county to compel the support of a spouse or child, whether legitimate or illegitimate.

. . .

(14) To order the support of a spouse or child, or both, irrespective of whether they are likely to become a public charge.

. . .

(16) To require of persons legally chargeable with the support of a spouse or child, who are possessed of sufficient means or who are able to earn such means, the payment weekly, or at other fixed periods, of a fair and reasonable sum for such support, or as a contribution toward such support, according to the means of the persons so chargeable.

. . .

(21) To determine the manner in which sums ordered paid for support shall be paid and applied, whether to a person through the court or through the clerk of court.

. . .

---

[27] This should be amended to substitute the Uniform Interstate Family Support Act.

(30) To make any order necessary to carry out and enforce the provisions of this chapter, and to hear and determine any questions of support, custody, separation or any other matter over which the court has jurisdiction, without the intervention of a jury.

S.C. Code Ann. § 20-7-934 (Law. Co-op. Supp.) grants the family court authority to enforce or modify support orders transferred to the family court from "any other court":

> Any family court has jurisdiction and authority to enforce or modify an order or decree of any other court respecting support of wife or children subject to the limitations contained in § 20-7-933, custody of children and visitation upon an order from the court of original jurisdiction, transferring jurisdiction to the family court. Petition may be made by either party to the original action to transfer the cause to the family court of the county where the other party resides, or petition may be made by the family court of the county to which transfer is sought, if it appears that the transfer will serve the ends of justice. The court of original jurisdiction may transfer the cause in its discretion.

Child support cannot be modified unless such relief is requested in the pleadings. *Dake v. Painter*, 288 S.C. 118, 341 S.E.2d 620 (1986) (reversing reduction in child support from $260 every two weeks to $225 two times per month).

The family court can acquire jurisdiction to decide child support matters upon the filing of either a summons and complaint or the filing of a rule to show cause. S.C. Code Ann. § 20-7-860 (Law. Co-op. 1976) provides:

> The court shall in a proper case issue a summons or rule to show cause, requiring the respondent to appear at the court at a time and place named, to show cause why the order for support prayed for by the petition shall not be granted. A summons or rule to show cause shall not be refused without giving the petitioner an opportunity to present witnesses and be heard by the court.

An Attorney General's Opinion (1980 Op. Att'y Gen. No. 80-100, p.152) determined that this section's predecessor, Section 14-21-860, resulted from the legislature's intention to provide the family court with an alternative method for acquiring jurisdiction in actions for child support by allowing such actions to proceed based either on the filing of a summons and complaint or a rule to show cause, notwithstanding other provisions found in the general law and rules of court.

The family court is permitted to issue *ex parte* orders for temporary child support where conditions warrant when the following circumstances exist:

(1) The summons or rule to show cause cannot be served; or

(2) The defendant has failed to obey the summons or rule to show cause; or

(3) The defendant is likely to leave the jurisdiction; or

(4) A summons or rule to show cause would be ineffectual; or

(5) The safety of the plaintiff is endangered; or

(6) A defendant on bond or on probation has failed to appear.

S.C. Code Ann. § 20-7-880 (Law. Co-op. 1976).

The family court is required to segregate alimony from child support. S.C. Code Ann. § 20-3-150 (Law. Co-op 1976) provides in part: "In the event the court shall award custody of the children to the spouse receiving alimony the court shall, by its decree, unless good cause to the contrary be shown, allocate any award for permanent alimony and support between the supported spouse and the children . . . ."

2. RETROACTIVE CHILD SUPPORT

If a parent is failing to support children adequately, he or she can be ordered to do so at any time and can be ordered to pay support retroactively to make up for previous inadequacies. In theory, a parent can be forced to pay retroactive child support from the time he or she stopped providing adequate support for the child, or at least from the time the parent stopped living with the child.

The failure of one parent to request support from the other is not an excuse for not supporting a child. In *Major v. Major*, 277 S.C. 318, 286 S.E.2d 666 (1982), the Court made the following statement about retroactive child support:

> It is implied by respondent that the mother's failure to request assistance waived her claim to retroactive relief. We reject any suggestion that a parent may waive a child's right to support by agreement or otherwise.
>
> The issue of retroactive support is to be resolved in accordance with the evidence presented. *McSwain v. Holmes*, 269 S.C. 293, 237 S.E.2d 363 [1977]. *Id.* at 321, 286 S.E.2d at 668 (citation omitted). The Court interpreted the divorce decree to require the husband to pay support from the time the older child had begun living with the mother (sixteen months earlier) until his eighteenth birthday. In *Sutton v. Sutton*, 291 S.C. 401, 353 S.E.2d 884 (Ct. App. 1987), the Supreme Court affirmed the trial court's order which awarded an increase in child support retroactively to the date of the filing of the modification petition, even though retroactive child support had not been specifically requested in the pleadings.

However, the chances of obtaining retroactive child support diminish with time. In *McSwain v. Holmes*, 269 S.C. 293, 237 S.E.2d 363 (1977), the Supreme Court considered the possibility of imposing a retroactive support obligation, but it decided that it was not appropriate under all the facts of the case. The wife had remarried within five days of the divorce and had waited three years before seeking child support. The husband was a laborer and the court determined that it would work a hardship on him if he was ordered to pay retroactive child support. The case was remanded for the family court to issue a support order for future support based on his increased earnings. In *Hallums v. Hallums*, 296 S.C. 195, 371 S.E.2d 525 (1988), the mother petitioned for sixteen years of retroactive child support for a child who was now twenty-four years old. As it had in *McSwain*, the Court determined that it would be inequitable to require the father to pay child support. The Court also determined that the mother's action was barred by laches which it defined as "neglect for an unreasonable and unexplained length of time, under circumstances affording opportunity for diligence, to do what in the law should have been done. *Byars v. Cherokee County*, 237 S.C. 548, 118 S.E.2d 324 (1961)." *Id.* at 198, 371 S.E.2d at 527. The Supreme Court determined that the father established the necessary elements of delay, unreasonable delay and prejudice.

Where the spouse seeking retroactive support can justify the delay, it is less likely that the defense of laches will apply. *South Carolina DSS, et al. v. Holden*, 319 S.C. 72, 459 S.E.2d 846 (1995). Here, the action for child support was filed nine years after the divorce. The divorce decree ordered the father to pay child support but he had paid none. The mother, by affidavit, testified that she had continually asked for child support, but the father had refused. She had twice contacted the Attorney General's office but could not afford to pursue the action. The Supreme Court held the record did not support the defense of laches because the mother had justified the delay in seeking arrearages and, further, because the father had failed to show prejudice by the delay since he was ordered to repay the arrearages at the rate of $25 per month, rather than in a lump sum.

Even though a child has reached eighteen, the custodial parent is still allowed to seek child support from the other parent for the period before the child reached majority. *See Holcombe v. Hardee*, 304 S.C. 522, 405 S.E.2d 821 (1991) (reversing and remanding the trial court's finding that the mother could not afford to contribute to private school expenses of the dyslexic son under eighteen because of the trial court's failure to make specific findings with respect to each factor and the absence of financial declarations in the record).

Once a parent has made a *prima facie* case of nonsupport against the other parent, the burden is on the parent wishing to prove support payments to produce evidence of such payments. An award of retroactive child support in the amount of $4,000 was upheld in *Wint v. Wint*, 310 S.C. 48, 425 S.E.2d 48 (Ct. App. 1992). The parents had agreed that the father would pay child support in a separation agreement which was subsequently submitted to the family court but not approved. However, the court determined that the husband was estopped from denying his obligation to support his children during the period of separation. Although the father claimed that he had been paying some child support, he failed to include any evidence of payments in the record. Thus, it was impossible for the Court of Appeals to determine how much support he actually paid, and he failed to prove any abuse of discretion in being ordered by the trial judge to pay the full amount owed.

The family court may award retroactive child support if the supporting parent is found to have failed to disclose income or assets at the time of the initial award, even in cases brought pursuant to a RURESA [today, UIFSA] action. This is to prevent manifest injustice and possible condonation of a fraud perpetrated upon the court by the parent. *Harris v. Harris*, 307 S.C. 351, 415 S.E.2d 391 (1992).

C. ADMINISTRATIVE PROCESS FOR ESTABLISHING AND ENFORCING CHILD SUPPORT[28]

Powerful administrative procedures are available for establishing and enforcing child support.[29] The Child Support Enforcement Division of the Department of Social Services (the Division) is authorized to use administrative procedures to establish child support obligations, including binding child support orders, without tying up family court resources. If a person properly objects to this administrative process, the normal family court process is used.

Limited judicial powers are granted to the Child Support Enforcement Division. "Notwithstanding Section 20-7-420 and any other provision of law, the Child Support Enforcement Division of the Department of Social Services also has jurisdiction to establish paternity and to enforce child support in cases brought

---

[28] Amy B. Rothschild, Chief Attorney of DSS's Child Support Enforcement Division, reviewed and made helpful comments about a draft of the 1996 revisions concerning UIFSA and the Child Support Enforcement Division's powers and procedures.

[29] Additional legislative action can be anticipated as South Carolina responds to federal mandates contained in the Personal Responsibility and Work Opportunity Reconciliation Act of 1996, Pub. L. No. 104-193, 110 Stat. 2105 (1996). The legislation calls for improving access to information about nonsupporting fathers, implementing procedures to make it easier to process masses of cases, and making enforcement more automatic and effective. The specific changes contemplated by the Act are discussed in Legler, "The Coming Revolution in Child Support Policy: Implications of the 1996 Welfare Act," 30 *Fam. L. Q.* 519 (Fall, 1996).

pursuant to Title IV-D of the Social Security Act and in accordance with this article." S.C. Code Ann. § 20-7-9505 (Law. Co-op. Supp.). Everyone is eligible for the Division's services (individuals not receiving public assistance must pay a $1.00 fee).

The process begins with the Child Support Enforcement Division's issuance of a "notice of financial responsibility" to a person who is responsible for the support of a child on whose behalf the child's custodian is receiving support enforcement services from the Division pursuant to Title IV-D of the Social Security Act. The statute prescribes seventeen specific points of information which must be included in the notice. S.C. Code Ann. § 20-7-9515 (Law. Co-op. Supp.).

The notice invites the person to attend a negotiation conference to determine the obligor's duty of support. If a stipulation about the person's duty of support is agreed on at the negotiation conference, the Division issues a support order. S.C. Code Ann. § 20-7-9525(A) (Law. Co-op. Supp.). If no stipulation is agreed upon at the negotiation conference, the Division files the notice of financial responsibility and proof of service in the county in which the obligee resides and the matter is set for a hearing in the family court. S.C. Code Ann. § 20-7-9525(C) (Law. Co-op. Supp.).

If the person does not attend or try to reschedule the negotiation conference after proper service and does not file a written request for a hearing before the time scheduled for the conference, the Division issues an order of default setting forth the amount of the obligor's duty of support. The default order must be approved by the family court. S.C. Code Ann. § 20-7-9530(A) (Law. Co-op. Supp.). Once approved and filed with the clerk of the family court along with proof of service and an affidavit of default, a default order has all the force, effect, and remedies of an order of the family court. S.C. Code Ann. § 20-7-9535(B) (Law. Co-op. Supp.). If the person makes a timely written request for a court hearing to the Division, the Division files the request for a hearing and matter is set for a hearing in the family court. S.C. Code Ann. § 20-7-9540 (Law. Co-op. Supp.).

The amount of the child support obligation, whether established through negotiation or in the default order, must be based upon the child support guidelines. S.C. Code Ann. § 20-7-9525(D) & -9530(C) (Law. Co-op. Supp.).

A similar procedure is available for modifying existing child support orders. S.C. Code Ann. § 20-7-9565 (Law. Co-op. Supp.).

D. INTERSTATE SUPPORT ORDERS (UIFSA)

1. IN GENERAL

South Carolina adopted the Uniform Interstate Family Support Act (UIFSA) in 1994 (S.C. Code Ann. §§ 20-7-960 through 20-7-1220 (Law. Co-op. Supp.)). UIFSA replaces the Revised Uniform Reciprocal Enforcement of Support Act of 1984 (RURESA). The basic purpose of UIFSA is to improve the enforcement of child support by reciprocal legislation among the states. UIFSA provides jurisdiction to establish and enforce support obligations when a party defendant is not within the territorial jurisdiction of a state's courts. Although a person may still use private counsel to pursue child support, UIFSA provides a mechanism whereby a public agency (in South Carolina, the Child Support Enforcement Division of the Department of Social Services) can represent the interests of an individual seeking to establish or enforce of a support obligation.

UIFSA applies to the establishment and enforcement of paternity and spousal and child support obligations and to the modification of child support. UIFSA proceedings may be used when a resident or agency of South Carolina wants to establish or enforce the support obligation of a person who lives in another state, in which case a South Carolina tribunal[30] is the "initiating tribunal." UIFSA can also be used when a nonresident or a child support enforcement agency of another state wants to establish or enforce the support obligation of a South Carolina resident, in which case a South Carolina tribunal is the "responding tribunal." UIFSA procedures do not provide an exclusive remedy. A person may elect to hire private counsel to litigate support issues in the state where the defendant resides.

---

[30] UIFSA and other legislation define the Child Support Enforcement Division of the Department of Social Services as a "tribunal" and give it limited judicial powers and concurrent jurisdiction in paternity and support matters with the family court. S.C. Code Ann. § 20-7-965(23), -970, & -9505 (Law. Co-op. Supp.).

In a UIFSA proceeding, a tribunal may do one or more of the following, if it has jurisdiction under UIFSA and to the extent it is otherwise authorized by law:

> (1) modify an order of child support or spousal support issued by a tribunal of this State;
>
> (2) establish an original order for spousal or child support;
>
> (3) enforce a support order and income withholding order of another state without registration;
>
> (4) register a spousal support order or child support order of another state for enforcement;
>
> (5) register a child support order of another state for modification; and
>
> (6) determine parentage.

S.C. Code Ann. § 20-7-1025 (Law. Co-op. Supp.).

The family court does not have jurisdiction to modify a spousal support order of another state, unless it has obtained continuing, exclusive jurisdiction. S.C. Code Ann. § 20-7-1005(C) (Law. Co-op. Supp.).

2. JURISDICTION

a. Continuing, Exclusive Jurisdiction

A tribunal which issues a support order consistent with UIFSA has continuing, exclusive jurisdiction over support as long as that state remains the residence of the obligor, the individual obligee, or the child for whose benefit the support order is issued. S.C. Code Ann. § 20-7-1000(A) (Law. Co-op. Supp.). A temporary support order issued ex parte or pending resolution of a jurisdictional conflict does not create continuing, exclusive jurisdiction in the issuing tribunal. S.C. Code Ann. § 20-7-1000(E) (Law. Co-op. Supp.).

Once a support order has been issued, no tribunal other than the tribunal with continuing, exclusive jurisdiction may modify the order unless: (1) neither the obligor, the individual obligee, nor the child currently resides in the issuing state and South Carolina has personal jurisdiction over the respondent (S.C. Code Ann. § 20-7-1146 (Law. Co-op. Supp.)); (2) each individual party has filed written consent for the tribunal to modify the order and assume continuing, exclusive jurisdiction (S.C. Code Ann. § 20-7-1000(C) (Law. Co-op. Supp.)).

A state loses its ability to modify its own support order if the order is modified by a tribunal of another state pursuant to a law substantially similar to UIFSA (e.g., RURESA or URESA). S.C. Code Ann. § 20-7-1000(B)(1) (Law. Co-op. Supp.). This might occur, for example, in a responding state which has not yet enacted UIFSA. Under URESA, child support is modifiable by the state in which enforcement is sought. In *Deltoro v. McMullen*, ___ S.C. ___, 471 S.E.2d 742 (Ct. App. 1996), the Court of Appeals held that the savings clause in the legislation enacting UIFSA preserved the family court's jurisdiction to modify a Virginia support order in a case which was pending when UIFSA was adopted, although the family court's order was issued two weeks after the adoption of UIFSA. [Presumably, this modification gave South Carolina continuing, exclusive jurisdiction over child support.]

To determine whether a tribunal has the authority to hear a support case, the following analysis is used:[31]

1. Is there an existing support order? If not, the South Carolina tribunal can become the tribunal with continuing, exclusive jurisdiction, assuming it otherwise has jurisdiction to act. (If proceedings to establish a support order have been filed in more than one state, the state which is the "home state" of the child has priority to assume jurisdiction, if the proceeding is filed in the "home state" before the expiration of time for filing a responsive pleading challenging the exercise of jurisdiction by the other state and the contesting party timely challenges the exercise of jurisdiction by the other state. S.C. Code Ann. § 20-7-995 (Law. Co-op. Supp.).

---

[31] This analysis is adapted from materials prepared for a S.C. Bar CLE seminar, "Family Law Update," September, 1994, by Gale R. DuBose, Esq., and Christene M. Brogdon.

The "home state" of the child is the state in which the child has lived for at least six months immediately preceding the filing of a proceeding for support, and if a child is less than six months old, the state in which the child lived from birth. S.C. Code Ann. § 20-7-965(4) (Law. Co-op. Supp.).)

2. If there is an existing support order, how many? If only one, the South Carolina tribunal must recognize that order and its authority is limited to enforcement only, unless the South Carolina tribunal becomes the tribunal with continuing, exclusive jurisdiction. S.C. Code Ann. § 20-7-1000 & -1010(A)(1) (Law. Co-op. Supp.).

3. If there are more than one existing support orders, does a tribunal in another state exercise continuing, exclusive jurisdiction? If not, the South Carolina tribunal may enforce the orders, and it becomes the tribunal with continuing exclusive jurisdiction by issuing an order.

4. If there are more than one existing support orders and there is a tribunal in another state which can exercise continuing, exclusive jurisdiction, how many? If only one, the South Carolina tribunal must recognize that order and its power is limited to enforcement only, unless South Carolina becomes the tribunal with continuing, exclusive jurisdiction. S.C. Code Ann. § 20-7-1010(A)(2) (Law. Co-op. Supp.).

5. If there are more than one existing support orders and there is more than one tribunal in another state which can exercise continuing, exclusive jurisdiction, is one of those states the child's "home state"? If it is, the South Carolina tribunal must recognize the "home state" tribunal's order and its power is limited to enforcement only, unless South Carolina becomes the tribunal with continuing, exclusive jurisdiction. S.C. Code Ann. § 20-7-1010(A)(3) (Law. Co-op. Supp.).

6. If there are more than one existing support orders and there is more than one tribunal in another state which can exercise continuing, exclusive jurisdiction, but none of them is the child's "home state," the South Carolina tribunal must recognize the most recent order, and its power is limited to enforcement only,

unless South Carolina becomes the tribunal with continuing, exclusive jurisdiction. S.C. Code Ann. § 20-7-1010(A)(4) (Law. Co-op. Supp.).

UIFSA does not grant general jurisdiction to decide issues such as custody or visitation. *Hoover v. Hoover*, 271 S.C. 177, 246 S.E.2d 179 (1978) (although the case interprets URESA, there is no reason to expect a different result under UIFSA). The wife and husband were married in South Carolina. She left with their only child and moved to Michigan where she filed a motion for support through URESA. The father remained in South Carolina. The trial court ordered the father to pay child support and established visitation rights for the father. The court further determined that, while the husband would have to pay support for the period preceding the wife's move to Michigan, he did not have to pay for the period of time after then because his visitation privileges had been denied by the wife. The Supreme Court reversed, citing a variety of cases holding that URESA did not give the court subject matter jurisdiction to deal with visitation. *Id.* at 181, 246 S.E.2d at 181. [UIFSA specifically provides that a responding tribunal may not condition the payment of a support order upon compliance by a party with provisions for visitation. S.C. Code Ann. § 20-7-980 (Law. Co-op. Supp.).]

b. Long Arm Personal Jurisdiction

UIFSA extends the concept of long arm jurisdiction as broadly as possible. A South Carolina tribunal may exercise personal jurisdiction over a nonresident in a proceeding to establish, enforce, or modify a support order or to determine parentage if:

(1) the individual is personally served in South Carolina;

(2) the individual submits to the jurisdiction of this state by consent, by entering a general appearance, or by filing a responsive pleading having the effect of waiving any contest to personal jurisdiction;

(3) the individual resided with the child in South Carolina;

(4) the individual resided in South Carolina and provided prenatal expenses or support for the child;

(5) the child resides in South Carolina as a result of the acts or directives of the individual;

(6) the individual engaged in sexual intercourse in South Carolina and the child may have been conceived by that act of intercourse; or

(7) there is any other basis consistent with the constitutions of South Carolina or the United States for the exercise of personal jurisdiction.

S.C. Code Ann. § 20-7-980 (Law. Co-op. Supp.).

3. SPECIFIC APPLICATIONS

a. Establishing Support Obligations

UIFSA proceedings to establish support obligations are initiated by filing a complaint in an initiating tribunal for forwarding to a responding tribunal or by filing a complaint directly in an appropriate tribunal of another state which has or can obtain jurisdiction. S.C. Code Ann. § 20-7-1025(C) (Law. Co-op. Supp.). The complaint must be verified and must contain information specified in the statute. S.C. Code Ann. § 20-7-1075 & -1080 (Law. Co-op. Supp.). Filing fees cannot be required. S.C. Code Ann. § 20-7-1085(A). (Law. Co-op. Supp.).

Private counsel may be used (S.C. Code Ann. § 20-7-1065 (Law. Co-op. Supp.), or assistance can be obtained from the Child Support Enforcement Division of the Department of Social Services (S.C. Code Ann. § 20-7-1055 (Law. Co-op. Supp.)). Attorneys' fees may be awarded by the family court. If attorneys' fees are awarded, they may be ordered paid directly to the attorney and collected in the attorney's own name. S.C. Code Ann. § 20-7-1085(B) (Law. Co-op. Supp.). The court must award costs and attorneys' fees if it determines that a hearing was requested primarily for delay (in cases arising from requests to register foreign support orders, courts are required to presume that a hearing is requested primarily for delay if a registered support order is confirmed or enforced without change). S.C. Code Ann. § 20-7-1085(C) (Law. Co-op. Supp.).

Upon the filing of an UIFSA proceeding, the family court or the Child Support Enforcement Division as an initiating tribunal forwards the complaint and its accompanying documents to the responding tribunal or appropriate enforcement agency in the responding state, or, if the address of the respondent is unknown, to the state information agency of the responding state. S.C. Code Ann. § 20-7-1040 (Law. Co-op. Supp.). The powers of the responding tribunal are set forth in S.C. Code Ann. § 20-7-1045(B) (Law. Co-op. Supp.). They include the typical powers to enforce support orders as well as, *inter alia*, the authority to order income withholding; set aside property for support satisfaction; place liens and order executions against property; and require the obligor to seek work.[32]

If South Carolina establishes personal jurisdiction over the noncustodial parent, it will apply South Carolina procedural and substantive law and determine the duty of support and the amount payable in accordance with the law and guidelines of South Carolina. S.C. Code Ann. §§ 20-7-985 and 20-7-1035 (Law. Co-op. Supp.). The order must include the calculations on which the support order is based. § 20-7-1045 (Law. Co-op. Supp.).

The physical presence of the plaintiff in the responding tribunal is not required for the establishment, enforcement, or modification of a support order or the determination of parentage. Special rules of evidence are described in the legislation to facilitate the admission of certain documents. For example, UIFSA allows the verified petition and verified testimony of the custodial parent to be admitted into evidence without the custodial person being present. S.C. Code Ann. § 20-7-1100 (Law. Co-op. Supp.).

Special discovery rules permit a tribunal to: (1) communicate with a tribunal of another state in writing, by telephone or otherwise to obtain information concerning the laws of that state, the legal effects of judgments, decrees, or orders, and the status of proceedings there; (2) request a tribunal of another state to assist in

---

[32] The powers set forth in section 20-7-1045(B) can be employed by the family court, but only some of them are available to the Child Support Enforcement Division since it is not "otherwise authorized by law" to use them. For example, the Child Support Enforcement Division cannot order temporary child support, it cannot set aside property for support satisfaction, and it cannot execute against property.

discovery; and (3) compel a person over whom it has jurisdiction to respond to discovery issued by a tribunal of another state. S.C. Code Ann. §§ 20-7-1105 & -1110 (Law. Co-op. Supp.).

b. Enforcing Support Orders Via Registration Process

An alternative procedure for enforcing existing support and income withholding orders is provided in UIFSA. A party may register for enforcement another state's support order, income withholding order, or both, by sending the documents required for registering the order to the Child Support Enforcement Division of the Department of Social Services. S.C. Code Ann. § 20-7-1130 (Law. Co-op. Supp.).[33]

Upon receipt of the documents, the Child Support Enforcement Division, without initially seeking to register the order, is required to use any administrative procedure available to reach an understanding with the obligor in an attempt to expedite the proceedings and avoid involving the court. If the obligor does not contest administrative enforcement, the support order need not be registered. S.C. Code Ann. § 20-7-1130(B) (Law. Co-op. Supp.).

Once a foreign order is registered in the Registry of Foreign Support, it has the same effect and is subject to the same procedures and defenses as an order of a South Carolina court and it may be enforced and satisfied in the same manner. S.C. Code Ann. § 20-7-1136(B) (Law. Co-op. Supp.). A registered order of another state

[33] If the order includes a provision for income withholding, the registration procedure is not the most efficient tool available. An employer is required to comply with an income withholding order from another state "as if the order had been issued by a tribunal of this State" under a statute enacted in 1996. S.C. Code Ann. § 20-7-1125(A) (Law. Co-op. Supp.). All that is required is to mail two copies of the order to the employer by first class mail. There is no requirement to file a proceeding or register the order. S.C. Code Ann. § 20-7-1125(B) (Law. Co-op. Supp.). If the other state's withholding order appears regular on its face, the employer must: (1) give a copy of the order to the employee; (2) follow the procedure for withholding income as if the order was issued by a South Carolina court; and (3) distribute the funds as directed in the withholding order. S.C. Code Ann. § 20-7-1125(C) (Law. Co-op. Supp.). An obligor may object to the validity or enforcement of an income withholding order from another state by requesting a hearing in family court not later than twenty days after the first payment is withheld. S.C. Code Ann. § 20-7-1125(C) (Law. Co-op. Supp.).

must be enforced by South Carolina courts, but it may not be modified, if the issuing court had jurisdiction. S.C. Code Ann. § 20-7-1136(C) (Law. Co-op. Supp.). The law of the issuing state governs the nature, extent, amount and duration of current payments and arrearages, except that the longer statute of limitations in the two states applies. S.C. Code Ann. § 20-7-1138 (Law. Co-op. Supp.).

Notice of the registration of a support or income withholding order must be given to the nonregistering party. The notice must contain specified information, including information about how to contest the validity or enforcement of the order. S.C. Code Ann. § 20-7-1138 (Law. Co-op. Supp.). If the nonregistering party does not contest the validity or enforcement of a registered order within twenty-one days, the order is confirmed by operation of law. S.C. Code Ann. § 20-7-1138 (Law. Co-op. Supp.). Confirmation of a registered order, whether by operation of law or after notice and hearing, precludes further contest of the order with respect to any matter that could have been asserted at the time of registration. S.C. Code Ann. § 20-7-1146 (Law. Co-op. Supp.).

c. Modifying Child Support Orders Via Registration Process

A party or support enforcement agency seeking to modify, or to modify and enforce, a child support order issued in another state is required to register that order in the same manner as described above. A complaint setting forth the grounds for modification with specificity may be filed at the same time as a request for registration and enforcement or at a later time. S.C. Code Ann. § 20-7-1146 (Law. Co-op. Supp.).

A registered child support order can only be modified if, after notice and hearing, a tribunal of this state finds that:

> (1) neither the child, the obligee, nor the obligor reside in the issuing state, the nonresident plaintiff seeks modification, and the defendant is subject to the jurisdiction of a tribunal of this state; or
>
> (2) a party who is a natural person (not an agency) or the child is subject to the personal jurisdiction of a tribunal of this state and all the parties who are natural persons have filed an agreement in the

> issuing tribunal providing that the tribunal may modify the support order and assume continuing, exclusive jurisdiction over the order.

S.C. Code Ann. § 20-7-1152(A) (Law. Co-op. Supp.).

A South Carolina tribunal may not modify any aspect of a child support order that may not be modified under the law of the issuing state. S.C. Code Ann. § 20-7-1152(C) (Law. Co-op. Supp.). On issuance of an order modifying a child support order issued in another state, the South Carolina tribunal becomes the tribunal of exclusive, continuing jurisdiction. S.C. Code Ann. § 20-7-1152(D) (Law. Co-op. Supp.). The tribunal is required to recognize modifications of child support orders by tribunals of other states which have assumed jurisdiction and it is required to enforce such orders. S.C. Code Ann. §§ 20-7-1152 & 20-7-1154 (Law. Co-op. Supp.).

E. STANDING

Any interested person has standing to petition the family court for child support. S.C. Code Ann. § 20-7-840 (Law. Co-op. 1976) provides: "Any interested persons may file a petition to the court requesting the court to order persons legally chargeable to provide support as provided by law."

Presumably this might include any person who is concerned about whether children are receiving sufficient support. It clearly includes parents, guardians, people, and agencies such as DSS to which a parent has assigned child support rights, and the children themselves. Other than parents, the Department of Social Services is most likely to pursue child support.

F. PURPOSES AND DURATION

1. IN GENERAL/EMANCIPATION

Parents are obligated to provide "reasonable support" for their children. (The meaning of "reasonable support" is discussed in the section of this chapter on amount.) This support obligation usually terminates when the child reaches eighteen years of age, unless: 1) the child becomes emancipated sooner; 2) the parents agree to continue providing support; or 3) special circumstances exist which justify requiring parents to continue providing support for their children.

Absent an agreement to the contrary specifying an age in years, or a court order also specifying conditions justifying support beyond the age of majority, the support obligation terminates at the age of eighteen. *Cason v. Cason*, 271 S.C. 393, 247 S.E.2d 673 (1978) (finding that the legislature's action in reducing the age of majority from twenty-one to eighteen had the effect of reducing the age of emancipation, despite the fact that the age of emancipation had been twenty-one when the father's liability for child support was determined). "An ex-spouse's duty to support a child of the marriage ends by operation of law when the child turns eighteen. *Spires v. Higgens*, 271 S.C. 530, 248 S.E.2d 488 (1978)." *Bull v. Smith*, 299 S.C. 123, 125, 382 S.E.2d 905, 906 (1989).

The holdings of these cases have been modified by legislation. S.C. Code Ann. § 20-7-420(17) (Law. Co-op. Supp.) provides that "orders of support run until further order of the court, except that orders of child support run until the child is eighteen years of age or until the child is married or becomes self-supporting, as determined by the court, whichever occurs first." The remainder of the statute provides for the continuation of child support beyond the age of eighteen while the child remains in high school or when the child has physical or mental disabilities or other exceptional circumstances that warrant the continuation of support beyond the age of eighteen.

Whether a child has been emancipated depends upon the facts and circumstances of each case:

> In the absence of infirmity of mind or body rendering the child unable to take care of itself, and requiring it to remain with the parent, emancipation is effected by operation of law when the child attains majority. Emancipation during minority results not from any act of the child alone, but primarily from agreement of the parent, which may be either express or implied. It may be either partial or complete. If partial, it frees the child for only a part of the period of its minority, or from only a part of the parent's rights, or for some special purpose, such as the right to earn and spend its own wages. If complete, it completely severs the parental relationship so far as legal rights and liabilities are concerned. Whether or not a minor child has been emancipated depends upon the particular facts and circumstances of each case, and is, therefore, generally a question for the jury. Emancipation of a minor child is never presumed, and the burden of proof is upon him who alleges it.

Parker v. Parker, 230 S.C. 28, 31, 94 S.E.2d 12, 13 (1956) (holding that the plaintiff, as an unemancipated minor, could not be sued for causing his father's death by negligent operation of an automobile). *See also Timmerman v. Brown*, 268 S.C. 303, 233 S.E.2d 106 (1977) (holding that where a father and daughter agreed to the daughter leaving home, she became emancipated. Therefore, the father was not responsible for medical expenses or other debts incurred by her).

Even if a child has become emancipated, the parents may be required to resume paying child support if the child becomes dependent again. *See Crenshaw v. Thompson*, 280 S.C. 203, 311 S.E.2d 742 (Ct. App. 1984) (holding that a father should be required to continue making support payments for a child who, shortly after graduating from high school and becoming eighteen years old, was severely injured in an automobile accident which rendered him totally disabled). The power of the family court to require parents to provide child support beyond the age of eighteen due to physical or mental disabilities is codified in S.C. Code Ann. § 20-7-420(17) (Law. Co-op. Supp.).

The fact that one of several children has reached majority does not affect a parent's child support obligation, absent a family court order modifying the amount of support owed. In *Bull v. Smith*, 299 S.C. 123, 382 S.E.2d 905 (1989), one daughter reached majority and went to college. The other daughter remained a minor at home with the mother. The Supreme Court noted in the opinion that the father's obligation to continue paying the same amount of child support remained unchanged unless he sought a modification of the order. *See also Stroman v. Williams*, 291 S.C. 376, 353 S.E.2d 704 (Ct. App. 1987), holding that "[w]here a support order 'provides for payments for the benefit of two or more children, the marriage or emancipation of one minor child does not automatically affect the liability of the father for the full sum prescribed in the order.' 24 Am. Jur.2d *Divorce and Separation*, § 1050 at 1041 (1983)." *Id.* at 380, 353 S.E.2d at 706.

Child support payments are ordinarily terminated by the death of the party making the payments or of the child. *See Kennedy v. Kennedy*, 270 S.C. 358, 242 S.E.2d 417 (1978) (holding that an order for a father to pay alimony and child support and provide a home for his wife and children until she died or remarried or until the children reached majority did not affirmatively charge his estate with the affirmative responsibility of continuing these payments after his death).

2. BASIC NECESSITIES

It is impossible to create a complete list of all the things which a parent is required to provide for a minor child. However, the South Carolina Child Support Guidelines are intended to provide for expenditures in the following categories:

-food at home;
-food away from home;
-shelter;
-utilities;
-household goods (furniture, appliances, linens, floor coverings, and housewares);
-clothing;
-transportation (other than visitation related);
-ordinary health care; and
-recreation.

South Carolina Child Support Guidelines Handbook (DSS, May, 1994), p. 1. Other possible expenditures which are not accounted for in the guidelines include child care and extraordinary medical expenses as well as personal life or disability insurance, gifts, contributions, and savings. *Id.*

A supporting spouse should not be ordered to pay medical or dental expenses not otherwise covered by insurance if the spouse's share would be less than $250 per child per year. The Child Support Guidelines are based on an assumption that the custodial parent will be responsible for up to $250.00 per year in uninsured medical expenses. *Lovett v. Lovett*, 311 S.C. 279, 428 S.E.2d 874 (1993), affirms this and points out that the custodial spouse may petition for additional support based on a change of circumstances if the children suffer any extraordinary medical expenses. *Id.* The guidelines define extraordinary medical expenses as those that are reasonable and necessary uninsured medical expenses in excess of $250.00 per year per child. The guidelines leave it to the court's discretion to determine whether extraordinary medical expenses such as orthodoniture and professional counseling are reasonable and necessary.

3. HEALTH INSURANCE AND QMCSOs

The South Carolina Child Support Guidelines require the family court to consider provisions for adequate health insurance coverage for children in every child support order. S.C. Code Regs. § 114-4720(F) (Law. Co-op. Supp.). This regulation further provides, *inter alia*, "[o]rdinarily, the court should require coverage by that parent who can obtain the most comprehensive coverage through an employer, or otherwise, at reasonable cost."

A parent whose income is being withheld is required to notify the clerk of court of the availability of any health insurance for whom support is ordered within seven days after beginning work or changing jobs. S.C. Code Ann. § 20-7-1315(H)(3) (Law. Co-op. Supp.).

Legislation now enables the family court to order employers to include children who might not otherwise be eligible for coverage under a group health plan. Family court judges faced a significant problem in trying to order noncustodial parents to provide health insurance coverage for children when the group health plans only allowed coverage for children living with a parent who was covered by the health plan. This problem is resolved by legislation which allows courts to require health insurance coverage for dependent children under a group health plan in which either parent is covered (the Medical Child Support and Income Withholding Act, S.C. Code Ann. §§ 20-7-1200 through 20-7-1280 (Law. Co-op. Supp.)). This legislation was mandated by the Omnibus Budget Reconciliation Act of 1993, which added § 609 to the Employees Retirement Income Act of 1974 (ERISA). This section requires states to enact a Qualified Medical Child Support Act (QMCSO).

Each group health plan is required to provide benefits in accordance with the applicable requirements of any qualified medical child support group. A qualified medical support order from the family court is an order which creates or recognizes the right of an alternate recipient to receive benefits under a group health plan. An order requiring a parent to provide health coverage for a child must:

> (1) clearly specify:
>
> (a) the name, social security number, and last known mailing address, if any, of the parent and each child covered by the order;
>
> (b) a reasonable description of the type of coverage to be provided by the plan or the manner in which the type of coverage is to be determined;
>
> (c) the period to which the order applies;
>
> (d) each plan to which the order applies; and
>
> (2) not require a plan to provide a type or form of benefit or an option, not otherwise provided under the plan, except to the extent necessary to meet the requirements of this part of Subarticle 6.

S.C. Code Ann. § 20-7-1200 (Law. Co-op. Supp.).

Each employer is required to establish procedures to determine whether the order is a qualified order. Upon receipt of a qualified order, the employer must permit the parent to enroll an otherwise eligible child, without regard to any enrollment restrictions; or, if the parent is enrolled and fails to make application for the child, enroll the child upon application of the other parent, or an appropriate state agency.

The employer is required to continue coverage unless it is provided with written evidence that the order is no longer in effect or that the child is enrolled in a comparable program, or it has eliminated health coverage for all employees.

Within thirty days after receipt of an order requiring the obligated parent to provide health care coverage for a child, the parent or employer must provide the other parent written proof that the coverage has been obtained or that application has been made. Proof of coverage consists of, at a minimum: the name of the insurer, the policy number, an insurance card, the address to which claims must be mailed, a description of any restrictions on usage, description of any deductibles, and five claim forms.

4. EDUCATIONAL EXPENSES

a. In General

The family court has the authority to include in a support order "the expense of educating his or her child." S.C. Code Ann. § 20-7-420(15) (Law. Co-op. 1976). Such expenses are also listed as a possible reason for deviation from the child support guidelines. S.C. Code Regs. § 114-4710(B) (Law. Co-op. 1976). Parents can also be required to help pay high school or college expenses for a child who has reached majority, to support children with mental or physical disabilities, or if other exceptional circumstances exist. S.C. Code Ann. § 20-7-420(17) (Law. Co-op. Supp.).

Parents who are still married to each other may have the same responsibilities to pay educational expenses as divorced parents. Judge Goolsby commented in a footnote in *Wagner v. Wagner*, 285 S.C. 430, 433, 329 S.E.2d 788, 790, n.1 (Ct. App.

1985), that he was not sure of the constitutionality of the approach to child support outlined in *Risinger v. Risinger*, 273 S.C. 36, 253 S.E.2d 652 (1979), if it is limited to benefiting only the children of divorced parents. This interesting question was once presented to the Supreme Court, but there ruled on, if at all, only *sub silentio*. In *Cato v. Cato*, 276 S.C. 41, 276 S.E.2d 290 (1981), the Court rejected a constitutional challenge to *Risinger*, sustaining a lower court order which held that no denial of equal protection was involved because "the South Carolina Supreme Court in *Risinger* was not limiting its holding to divorcing or separating families but was speaking to the support obligation all parents owe all children when it wrote that 'we hold that a Family Court judge may require a parent to contribute that amount of money necessary to enable a child over 18 to attend high school and four years of college'. . . ." (*Cato* Transcript of Record at 19).

b. High School/Private School

Parents are required to support their children in high school, even after they reach eighteen years of age. S.C. Code Ann. § 20-7-420(17) (Law. Co-op. Supp.), requires parents, *inter alia*, to provide for child support past the age of eighteen:

> if the child is in high school and is making satisfactory progress toward completion of high school, not to exceed the nineteenth birthday unless exceptional circumstances are found to exist or unless there is a preexisting agreement or order to provide for child support past the age of eighteen years.

Both cases which considered this question before section 20-7-420(17) was enacted required support for children over the age of eighteen until graduation from high school. In *Cato v. Cato*, 276 S.C. 41, 276 S.E.2d 290 (1981), the Supreme Court issued a very brief opinion upholding the family court's determination, in light of *Risinger*, that the father should provide $35 per week support to his emancipated eighteen year old daughter until her graduation from high school. In *Garrett v. Garrett*, 288 S.C. 26, 339 S.E.2d 510 (1986), another very brief opinion, the Court did not even mention *Risinger* (or the age of the child) in holding that a supporting parent should pay child support until the child completed high school.

The propriety of ordering parents to pay private schooling expenses for children under eighteen has not yet been completely settled. It is clear that parents can be ordered to pay for private schools for children under eighteen when special circumstances show the need for it. In *Holcombe v. Hardee*, 304 S.C. 522, 405 S.E.2d 821 (1991), the mother was required to contribute to private school expenses for a dyslexic child who needed to attend school where he could obtain intensive instruction. *Holcombe* was remanded because the trial judge did not make specific findings with respect to each factor and there were no financial declarations in the record. In *Weil v. Weil*, 299 S.C. 84, 382 S.E.2d 471 (Ct. App. 1989), the Court of Appeals upheld the obligation of the father to pay private school tuition where the agreement of the parties expressly provided for such payment by the father, and where the school in question was a private school for the learning disabled.

A valid agreement to pay for a private school will be enforced, even absent special circumstances. In *Nelson v. Merritt*, 281 S.C. 126, 314 S.E.2d 840 (Ct. App. 1984), the divorce decree incorporated a prior agreement of the parties providing that the husband, Merritt, would "pay the school tuition for each child at 'an appropriate private institution' with standards similar to those at either Porter-Gaud or Ashley Hall, two private schools in Charleston." *Id.* at 128, 314 S.E.2d at 841. The wife brought an action to require the husband to pay the tuition of the children at a school of a similar nature in Virginia. The Court of Appeals found that the tuition at the new school was only about $500 per year higher than at Porter-Gaud, and that the schools were substantially similar. The court ordered the father to pay the higher amount.

A parent might be required to pay for private school if the court determines that it would be in the best interest of the child to attend a private school, even absent special circumstances. In *Rabon v. Rabon*, 288 S.C. 338, 342 S.E.2d 605 (1986), the Supreme Court affirmed a family court order which required the supporting spouse to pay for private elementary and secondary schooling for the children. The mother had enrolled the children in an exclusive private school without the consent of the father. The Court held that the mother was unable to make significant contributions towards the tuition costs, and it found that the enrollment in private school was in the best interests of the children. *See also Grubbs v. Grubbs*, 272 S.C. 138, 249 S.E.2d 747 (1978), in which the Court noted that a child support order of $592 per month plus the expenses of the daughter at private school was not excessive. It is not clear from the opinion whether the husband was contesting the order to pay for the private school.

c. College[34]

At the present time, it appears that children will not be able to force their parents to help them pay for college unless they first exhaust all other avenues of raising the money to go to college without such assistance and, of course, only if the parent can afford to provide assistance. However, the circumstances under which a parent should be required to help support a child in college have taken a great deal of judicial time and effort to define, and all questions have not yet been fully answered. A review of the major cases on this topic is useful in understanding the development of law in this area.

The responsibility of parents to provide support for the education of their children who have reached eighteen years of age was initially addressed in *Risinger v. Risinger*, 273 S.C. 36, 253 S.E.2d 652 (1979). The Supreme Court held that it was proper under some circumstances to order payment of child support for purposes of high school or higher education beyond the age of 18 years:

> Without holding that these are the only circumstances under which a Family Court's award is proper, we hold that a Family Court judge may require a parent to contribute that amount of money necessary to enable a child over 18 to attend high school and four years of college, where, as here, there is evidence that: (1) the characteristics of the child indicate that he or she will benefit from college; (2) the child demonstrates the ability to do well, or at least make satisfactory grades; (3) the child cannot otherwise go to school; and (4) the parent has the financial ability to help to pay for such an education.

Id. at 39, 253 S.E.2d at 653.

---

[34] Issues arising in connection with agreements by parents to pay for college education are discussed in the section on the effect of agreements in this chapter.

The Supreme Court wrote in *Kerr v. Kerr*, 278 S.C. 191, 293 S.E.2d 704 (1982), that a precarious financial state on the part of an emancipated child would suffice to meet the "otherwise unable" criterion:

> We find that there is the requisite evidence in this case to support the lower court's order. Counsel for the father concedes that most anyone would benefit from a higher education. The daughter in this case has not shown scholarly ability but has made overall passing and satisfactory grades.
>
> The daughter asserts that she cannot otherwise go to school without her father's assistance. She has apparently been able to go to school prior to this action and during the pendency of its appeal through a combination of activities on her part. The daughter has been living on her mother's monthly $456 disability check. They have been sharing the same living quarters and expenses. The daughter has worked part-time and has received some tuition grants. These facts and others contained in the record support the lower court's finding that the daughter's "obtaining a college education is in great jeopardy because of the lack of money."
>
> The father asserted that he did not have the financial ability to help pay for such an education. He testified that since he had remarried, he and his second wife had spent more money each year than they had earned. These "deficits" were possible by reason of gifts from his new wife's parents.
>
> It is apparent from the record that his opposition to the support payments was not based on financial considerations solely. On cross-examination, he stated:
>
> > Q. Well, you can't deny that according to the record here which has been established of your financial declaration and your examination?

> A. That's the past, I can make one statement: That if I have to support a child by a previous marriage into a college, I promise you there will be no gifts. There will be no deficits made up, that this ship will sink, because my mother-in-law will not pay for college tuition for a child by a previous marriage.
>
> Emancipated children who no longer have the benefit of a conventional home while attempting to further their education, have a severely restricted ability to earn adequate amounts to provide their own education during this crucial period. Exceptional circumstances were present, such as to warrant the mandate of the lower court.

Id. at 193-4, 293 S.E.2d at 706.

The Court of Appeals began to explain more fully the extent of an emancipated child's duty to help minimize college expenses in *Hughes v. Hughes*, 280 S.C. 388, 313 S.E.2d 32 (Ct. App. 1984). The Court of Appeals listed two additional factors for consideration: (1) the availability of loans and grants to the student, and (2) the ability of the child to earn income during the school year and on vacation. These factors are essentially elaborations of the third *Risinger* criterion: whether the child otherwise can attend school. *Hughes* held that if a child could obtain loans, grants and work, and does not, the child could "otherwise" attend school and aid from the sued parent should be minimal or non-existent. The court found that the Hughes' daughter had fulfilled her duty to help minimize the cost of college:

> Robin industriously sought to defray her college expenses in most every respect. She was able to finance the bulk of her expenses through loans and a scholarship earned as a result of her fine high school record, but there still remained an annual shortfall of approximately $700 in the cost of tuition and board. Although in the summer prior to matriculation she refused employment at a hospital because of her strong aversion to such facilities, she thereafter made a diligent effort to find summer work which was better suited for her. Also, in her final year of high school she secured part-time employment even though this required her to work at unreasonable

> hours. Furthermore, she made substantial contributions toward maintenance of her mother's household and cared for her younger brother, thereby eliminating the expense of day care. The evidence of Robin's industry is plainly more significant than any showing of indolence towards the fulfillment of her obligation to help defray expenses. The record therefore supports the finding that the father's assistance was necessary for Robin to attend college.

Id. at 391-392, 313 S.E.2d at 34. The court applied the *Hughes* factors again in *Wagner v. Wagner*, 285 S.C. 430, 329 S.E.2d 788 (Ct. App. 1985) in finding that the father should help pay for college. In *Hickman v. Hickman*, 294 S.C. 486, 366 S.E.2d 21 (Ct. App. 1988), the Court of Appeals found that a trial judge had erred in requiring a father to pay for his son's college education by not making findings regarding the son's ability to attend without his father's assistance, the availability of grants and loans, the son's ability to earn money during vacation time, or the reasonable costs of the son's education. The court remanded the case for these findings. In *Nicholson v. Lewis*, 295 S.C. 434, 369 S.E.2d 649 (Ct. App. 1988), the Court of Appeals affirmed an award of college expenses not only because it was what the father had agreed to pay but also because it met the standards set forth in *Risinger* and *Wagner*, i.e., he had the ability to pay and the child could not otherwise attend.

The Court of Appeals took an unusual approach to the issue of a parent's responsibility to help pay for college in *Patterson v. Patterson*, 288 S.C. 282, 341 S.E.2d 819 (Ct. App. 1989). It said in a footnote without further explanation that the continuation of child support for one daughter who had reached eighteen was "justified due to the fact the child was in college, and the evidence meets the criteria set out in *Lafitte v. Lafitte*, 280 S.C. 473, 313 S.E.2d 41 (Ct. App. 1984)." *Patterson*, at 285, 341 S.E.2d at 821, n.1. In fact, *Lafitte* cited the *Risinger* factors, but found that the wife was not entitled to be reimbursed for one half of the college expenses she had paid for their emancipated son. The *Lafitte* court wrote:

> The parties in this case entered no contractual agreement to support the older child beyond the age of eighteen. The record contains no evidence of any exceptional circumstances. There are no findings of fact by the court in its order as to any; rather, the order contains mere conclusions of law. Accordingly, the issues of

> reimbursement of past college expenses and payment of further college expenses are remanded for a determination as to the existence of any circumstances which would justify the payment of those expenses. The fact that the child was living at home and that Mr. Lafitte had, by consent, contributed to his college expenses in the past are but two factors under *Risinger* to be considered.

Lafitte at 477, 313 S.E.2d at 44.

It is puzzling why the *Patterson* court did not mention *Risinger*. Also worth noting is the notion expressed in *Lafitte* that the father was not bound to continue paying college expenses although he had voluntarily begun providing such assistance. Thus, a child has no guarantee that a parent's voluntary contributions to college will continue through the full term of the college experience.

A child's ability to attend college without parental assistance is a more important factor than whether the parent can afford to pay for college. In *Kelly v. Kelly*, 310 S.C. 299, 423 S.E.2d 153 (Ct. App. 1992), the Court of Appeals said that the "otherwise unable" factor, along with the parent's ability to pay, was determinative. However, the court called the son's ability to go to college without his mother's help more important than her ability to pay. The mother was not required to help pay for her son's college expenses where he had a car, was living with his father and was working.

If a parent agrees to pay for college expenses, on the other hand, the child has no duty to work, seek scholarships or otherwise attempt to minimize costs, unless such duties are specifically included in the agreement. In *McDuffie v. McDuffie*, 313 S.C. 397, 438 S.E.2d 239 (1993), the Supreme Court held that a daughter was under no obligation to minimize her college expenses where the father had agreed to pay "all college expenses." (Overruling that portion of the Court of Appeals' opinion in *McDuffie v. McDuffie*, 308 S.C. 401, 418 S.E.2d 331 (Ct. App. 1992), which concluded that the daughter in college had not fulfilled her "duty to help minimize college expenses" despite her working during summer months and also earning tuition scholarships.) Also see the section which addresses agreements to pay more than required by law later in this chapter.

The decision reached in *Ellis v. Taylor*, 316 S.C. 245, 449 S.E.2d 487 (1994), is consistent with *McDuffie*. The father agreed in a separation agreement which was incorporated into the divorce decree:

> ...to pay <u>all reasonable expenses</u> for college education for the children of the parties, including tuition, room and board, books, materials, and supplies <u>to the extent that such expenses are not provided by any scholarship, grant or other assistance available to the children</u>. (emphasis supplied by the court).

The Supreme Court held that, since nothing in the agreement required the children to minimize expenses, they were not required to do so.

The Supreme Court has not yet squarely addressed the question of whether a child must seek to minimize college expenses before parents are obliged to provide support, nor has it explored the extent of debt which a child must incur before parents will be required to contribute to educational expenses. The Court of Appeals, in *Hughes* and *Kelly*, makes it appear unlikely that parents will be required to support children in college absent truly exceptional circumstances. Federal and other loan programs make it possible for most college students to finance their own education, although they can incur substantial debt along the way.

However, the Supreme Court has not ruled on these questions since *Hughes* was decided. In *McDuffie v. McDuffie*, 313 S.C. 397, 438 S.E.2d 239 (1993), the Supreme Court included the following comment in a footnote: "Although this Court has recognized, *as factors*, the availability of grants and the ability of a child to earn income, *Bull v. Smith* [299 S.C. 123, 382 S.E.2d 905 (1989)], we have never held that there is a *duty* under *Risinger* for a child to minimize college expenses." *Id.* at 400, 438 S.E.2d at 241, nt. 4 (emphasis supplied by the Court).

Notwithstanding the Supreme Court's comment in *McDuffie*, the Court of Appeals did not change its position about the importance of a child's ability to borrow money, obtain loans, or earn income in *Doe v. Doe*, ___ S.C. ___, 478 S.E.2d 854 (Ct. App. 1996). However, *Doe* did not give the court an opportunity to address the question directly because the father failed to present any evidence to indicate whether the son was able to earn income during the school year or on summer vacations, and there was only minimal testimony as to the availability of grants and loans.

5. MENTAL OR PHYSICAL DISABILITIES

The family court may order parents to provide support past age eighteen "where there are physical or mental disabilities of the child ... that warrant the continuation of child support beyond age eighteen for as long as the physical or mental disabilities ... continue." S.C. Code Ann. § 20-7-420(17) (Law. Co-op. Supp.).

The language in this statute appears to reflect a clear legislative choice that, between parents and society as a whole, it is preferable for parents to be charged with the long-term support obligation for physically or mentally disabled children, at least to the extent that they are able to undertake it.

Even when a child has become emancipated, a subsequent physical disability may justify requiring parents to resume providing support. In *Crenshaw v. Thompson*, 280 S.C. 203, 311 S.E.2d 742 (Ct. App. 1984), a child attained the age of eighteen while still in high school. Shortly after graduating, he was severely injured in a car accident which resulted in his total disability. The trial judge interpreted section 14-21-210 (B)(4) (now S.C. Code Ann. § 20-7-420(17) (Law. Co-op. Supp.)) as empowering the court "to make all orders for support run . . . where there are physical or mental disabilities of the child . . . during any period and beyond the child's majority as such physical or mental disabilities may continue." The Court of Appeals affirmed the judgment.

6. OTHER EXCEPTIONAL CIRCUMSTANCES

The family court may order parents to provide support past eighteen "where there are ... other exceptional circumstances that warrant the continuation of child support beyond age eighteen for as long as the ... exceptional circumstances continue." S.C. Code Ann. § 20-7-420(17) (Law. Co-op. Supp.). Although this statutory language has existed for some time, no exceptional circumstances other than those described above have been reported in appellate court opinions.

G. EFFECT OF AGREEMENTS

1. IN GENERAL

The general topic of agreements is discussed in the chapter on agreements.

Some statutes specifically encourage agreements about child support. However, case law suggests that such agreements should not be approved and will not be enforced if the agreement is that a parent will be allowed to pay less than provided by law. S.C. Code Ann. § 20-7-840 (Law. Co-op. 1976) provides:

> Except where the circumstances indicate it to be undesirable, in all cases where an application for support has been made, an effort should be made by the judge to restore harmonious relations between the husband and wife and to adjust the issues raised by the application through conciliation and agreement. Where an agreement for the support of the petitioner is brought about, it must be reduced to writing and submitted to the court for approval. Where possible, the court shall see both parties and shall inquire of each whether the agreement, which he must state to them, is what they have agreed to. If it is, and the court shall approve it, the court without further hearing may thereupon enter an order for the support of the petitioner by the respondent in accordance with such agreement, which shall be binding upon the respondent and shall in all respects be a valid order as though it had been made after process has been issued out of the court. The court record shall show that such order was made upon agreement.

The wording of this statute is odd, for it sounds more like it was written with respect to spousal support, not child support. However, it is in the Children's Code, and it is the second section in Subarticle 3, Child Support. Although one must assume that this statute is related somehow to child support, its application is unclear.

The South Carolina Child Support Guidelines contain this statement about the effect of agreements in the section discussing justifications for deviating from the Guidelines:

> Agreements reached between the parties. The court may deviate from the guidelines based on an agreement between the parties if both parties are represented by counsel or if, upon a thorough examination of any party not represented by counsel, the court determines the party fully understands the agreement as to child support. The court still has the discretion and the independent duty to determine if the amount is reasonable and in the best interest of the child(ren).

S.C. Code Regs. § 114-4710(B)(13) (Law. Co-op. Supp.). (The same statement appears at S.C. Code Ann. § 20-7-852(13) (Law. Co-op. Supp.).)

Segments of the Uniform Enforcement of Family Support Act (UIFSA) require the Child Support Enforcement Division of the Department of Social Services to attempt to negotiate child support obligations with noncustodial parents of children whose custodial parent is receiving services pursuant to Title IV-D of the Social Security Act (AFDC). S.C. Code Ann. §§ 20-7-9515 & 20-7-9525 (Law. Co-op. Supp.). Any agreements reached with respect to child support must be based on the child support guidelines. This topic is discussed in more detail in the section on Interstate Support Orders earlier in this chapter.

In matters affecting the welfare of children, the family court's authority cannot be limited by any agreement between the parents. In *Moseley v. Mosier*, 279 S.C. 348, 306 S.E.2d 624 (1983), the wife argued that the child support terms which her husband had violated arose out of an agreement which were incorporated but not merged in the decree and, therefore, the agreement could not be judicially altered. The Supreme Court rejected this argument: "Family courts have continuing jurisdiction to do whatever is in the best interests of the child irregardless [sic] of what the separation agreement specifies. Therefore, on remand, the court has jurisdiction to determine what is in the best interests of the child." *Id.* at 351, 306 S.E.2d at 626. (The trial judge in *Moseley* had determined that the husband should not be held in contempt because child support was set by agreement, not by court order.)

In *Martin v. Ross*, 286 S.C. 43, 331 S.E.2d 785 (Ct. App. 1985), the Court of Appeals stated:

> At trial the judge ruled he had no jurisdiction to consider the issues of child support, visitation, custody, or property, by virtue of the settlement agreement. An agreement entered into upon divorce cannot prejudice the rights of the children. *Lunsford v. Lunsford*, 277 S.C. 104, 282 S.E.2d 861 (1981). Therefore, the judge erred in ruling that he had no jurisdiction.

Id. at 45, 331 S.E.2d at 786.

The authority of the family court to disregard agreements of parents when considering the interests of children extends only to matters which directly affect children's interests, not those that may incidentally or indirectly affect them. *Robinson v. Tyson*, 319 S.C. 360, 461 S.E.2d 397 (Ct. App. 1995). There, the Court of Appeals held that the modification of an agreed tax exemption does not fall within the ambit of the pervasiveness of the Supreme Court's statement in *Moseley* that family courts shall have "continuing jurisdiction to do what is in the best interest of the child regardless of what the separation agreement specifies." The opinion states:

> Certainly, almost any aspect of a divorce settlement could indirectly affect a child. Undisputably, the Supreme Court did not intend for issues of alimony and equitable distribution to be modifiable irrespective of the terms of the separation agreement, although they may most certainly indirectly affect children caught up in divorce proceedings.

Id. at 365, 461 S.E.2d at 400.

2. AGREEMENTS TO RELIEVE OR REDUCE SUPPORT OBLIGATION

An agreement entered into upon divorce cannot prejudice the rights of children. *See Martin v. Ross*, 286 S.C. 43, 331 S.E.2d 785 (Ct. App. 1985), which reversed the trial court's decision that it had no jurisdiction to consider the issues of child support, visitation, custody, or property because the parties had reached a settlement agreement before their divorce. The case was remanded with instructions to set a structured visitation schedule for the father.

If parents agree to an amount of child support which the family court should order, the trial judge must review any such agreement to determine whether it is reasonable and in the best interest of the children. *Price v. Ozment*, 318 S.C. 168, 456 S.E.2d 427 (Ct. App. 1995).

Even though an agreement might be enforced with respect to those provisions involving the parents' rights, any provision which adversely affects the right of minor children to support cannot be enforced. In *Forsythe v. Forsythe*, 290 S.C. 253, 349 S.E.2d 405 (Ct. App. 1986), the court upheld portions of an agreement which involved the wife's rights (she had freely and voluntarily entered it and it was fair within the bounds of reasonableness), but it remanded for reconsideration those provisions of the agreement involving child support (after making the mortgage payment, the wife would have been left with $269.00 a month for all living expenses for herself and the children, including the children's educational expenses).

Agreements which purport to release a parent from child support obligations are not binding on the family court. In *Lunsford v. Lunsford*, 277 S.C. 104, 282 S.E.2d 861 (1981), the Supreme Court ruled that an agreement between parents which provided that the custodial parent would not seek collection of past-due child support did not bar that parent from enforcing an existing support order. In *Peebles v. Disher*, 279 S.C. 611, 310 S.E.2d 823 (Ct. App. 1983), the mother had promised not to seek past-due support in consideration for the father's agreeing to allow her new husband to adopt their son. The Court of Appeals held that, where the court has set the amount of child support, the parties cannot reduce either parent's duty to support the child. As long as a person remains a minor child, the parents are obligated to support that child. *Id.* at 613-614, 310 S.E.2d at 825.

Two cases that were decided on the same day reached different results about the entitlement of children to support for college and about the effect of their participation in the negotiation of agreements between their parents. In *Jennings v Dargan*, 308 S.C. 317, 417 S.E.2d 646 (Ct. App. 1992), the daughter's paternity action was allowed and she was awarded support for her college expenses. The agreement between her parents which purported to relieve the father from responsibility for college expenses was not binding on her because it was not reviewed or approved by the trial court and, therefore, there had been no determination that it was in the daughter's best interest. The fact that the child had been represented by a guardian *ad litem* made no difference. In *McDuffie v. McDuffie*, 308 S.C. 401, 418 S.E.2d 331 (Ct. App. 1992), the father had agreed to pay for all college expenses, but the agreement provided that he would be relieved from his obligation to pay for college for any child who failed "to maintain an overall cumulative 'B' average for all courses." *Id.* at 407, 418 S.E.2d at 335. The trial court ruled that this escape clause was not enforceable because the daughters had neither been joined as parties nor participated in the action which produced the agreement. The Court of Appeals said this was an error because the language in the agreement was plain and unambiguous and the wife, not the daughter, was seeking reimbursement and she had entered the agreement freely and voluntarily. The case was remanded for a determination of how much reimbursement the wife was entitled to for the semesters in which a 'B' average had been maintained.

3. AGREEMENTS TO PAY MORE THAN REQUIRED BY LAW

a. In General

Parents can contractually obligate themselves to pay more child support than required by law.

> Where there is an agreement regarding the support of an adult child, the family court should not decide support issues as though there were no agreement. Parents can contractually obligate themselves beyond the support required by law. *Ratchford v. Ratchford*, 295 S.C. 297, 368 S.E.2d 214 (Ct. App. 1988); *Stanaland v. Jamison, supra*. [275 S.C. 50, 268 S.E.2d 578 (1980)]

> Under *Stanaland*, a parent can contractually obligate himself to support or pay the educational expenses of a child past majority. We hold such an agreement is not modifiable by the court without the consent of the parties. The court may order specific performance of such an agreement in the absence of a showing that the party sought to be charged is unable to perform.

In re White, 299 S.C. 406, 413-414, 385 S.E.2d 211, 215 (Ct. App. 1989) (citations omitted) (reversing a decision that a father who agreed to pay for college only had to pay half of the child's college and holding that the child had to seek grants and so forth to offset the expenses).

An agreement to pay more child support than required by law creates a contractual obligation that is enforceable in the circuit court and not the family court unless it is incorporated into an order of the family court. *Treadaway v. Smith*, Op. No. 2600 (filed Dec. 9, 1996)(Davis Adv. Sh. No. 33 at 23). In *Treadaway*, the Court of Appeals found that the intent of the parties was for an agreement to pay for college expenses to maintain its contractual nature and not to be merged into the order of the family court.

> When the language of a contract is plain and capable of legal construction, that language alone determines the instruments force and effect. *Jordan v. Security Group, Inc.*, 311 S.C. 227, 428 S.E.2d 705 (1993). The court's duty is to enforce the contract made by the parties regardless of its wisdom or folly, apparent unreasonableness, or the parties' failure to guard their rights carefully. *Id.*

Id. at ___, ___ S.E.2d at ___. The court found that the father did not believe at the time of contracting that he was legally obligated to provide support for college (the agreement was made before *Risinger v. Risinger*, 273 S.C. 36, 253 S.E.2d 652 (1979) was decided). Since the obligation was to pay more than required by law, it was not an obligation to pay child support which is exclusively in the family court's jurisdiction, and, therefore, the circuit court properly exercised its jurisdiction in deciding the case.

b. Agreements To Pay Educational Expenses

Where a valid agreement exists, the parent may be bound to pay for college without regard to the child's ability to otherwise attend. As mentioned above, *In re White* upheld an agreement in which the father had agreed to pay all expenses for college, and the court ruled that it was error for the trial judge to require the child to seek grants and so forth to offset the expenses. The Supreme Court reached the same conclusion in *McDuffie v. McDuffie*, 313 S.C. 397, 438 S.E.2d 239 (1993), holding that a daughter was under no obligation to minimize her college expenses where the father had agreed to pay "all college expenses," although this language was ambiguous as to the extent of the father's obligation. (Thus overruling the relevant portion of the Court of Appeals' opinion in *McDuffie v. McDuffie*, 308 S.C. 401, 418 S.E.2d 331 (Ct. App. 1992)). *See also Nicholson v. Lewis*, 295 S.C. 434, 369 S.E.2d 649 (Ct. App. 1988) (affirming the trial court's order that the father had to pay half of his daughter's college expenses as he had agreed).

A clear agreement may also bind a parent to pay college expenses without regard to the parent's financial ability or the child's ability to minimize college expenses. An agreement considered by the Supreme Court in *Ellis v. Taylor*, 316 S.C. 245, 449 S.E.2d 487 (1994), called for the father:

> to pay <u>all reasonable expenses</u> for college education for the children of the parties, including tuition, room and board, books, materials, and supplies <u>to the extent that such expenses are not provided by any scholarship, grant or other assistance available to the children</u>. (emphasis supplied by the court).

The Supreme Court held that nothing in the agreement required consideration of the father's ability to pay or the children's ability to minimize expenses, therefore, it overruled that portion of the Court of Appeals' decision in *Ellis v. Taylor*, 311 S.C. 66, 427 S.E.2d 678 (Ct. App. 1992), which held otherwise.

The Supreme Court also overruled that part of the Court of Appeals's decision which held that loans available from the child's college constituted "other assistance" that reduced the father's obligation to pay.

> When words of particular and specific meaning are followed by general words, the general words are construed to embrace only persons or things of the same general kind or class as those enumerated. [citation omitted] The forms of "assistance" enumerated in the agreement are all within the same general class of programs that do not require repayment. We find "other assistance" does not include loans which require repayment.

Ellis v. Taylor, 316 S.C. 245, 248, 449 S.E.2d 487, 488 (1994).

A contract provision leaving material terms open for future agreement is void for indefiniteness. *Ellis v. Taylor*, 316 S.C. 245, 449 S.E.2d 487 (1994). The parties' agreement regarding the father's obligation to pay for college expenses provided that "[a]s each child begins college, the parties shall agree to an amount for support of the home while the said child is in college." The Supreme Court found this provision too indefinite and uncertain to be enforceable, thus, it affirmed the Court of Appeals' termination of child support when the child entered college.

When an agreement to pay educational expenses is ambiguous, the court should seek to determine the intent of the parties. In *McDuffie v. McDuffie*, 313 S.C. 397, 438 S.E.2d 239 (1993), the Supreme Court concluded that a father's agreement to pay "all college expenses" for his daughter was patently ambiguous. It noted that the mother, in testifying on behalf of the daughter, had defined college expenses as "tuition, room, and board ... books or supplies." *Id.* at 400, 438 S.E.2d at 241. Therefore, having ascertained the intent of the parties from the record before it, the Court held that the father was not required by the terms of his agreement to pay for transportation and incidental expenses or spending money. (This affirmed the relevant portion of the Court of Appeals opinion in *McDuffie v. McDuffie*, 308 S.C. 401, 418 S.E.2d 331 (Ct. App. 1992).)

A paying parent is not required to give a "free ride" to a child. In *Bearden v. Bearden*, 272 S.C. 378, 252 S.E.2d 128 (1979), the Court pointed out that both the child and the parent usually have obligations under an agreement:

> Concomitant with Dr. Bearden's obligation, however, is the obligation of the child to apply himself to his college education. The

> lower court found that the child in question, Emmett, Jr., had attended Clemson University for a period of two years; that a normal course load for that period would have been sixty (60) semester hours; that Emmett, Jr., had attempted only thirty-one (31) semester hours and had passed only twenty (20) semester hours with a below average grade average. Emmett, Jr.'s last grade report shows the following courses taken and grades earned: Chemistry, F; English, D.; Psychology, F; Math, W (Withdrawn).
>
> The record reflects that Dr. Bearden paid his son's college expenses until it was demonstrated that the son was not doing acceptable college level work. By doing so Dr. Bearden satisfied his obligation under the property settlement agreement, and the lower court correctly found that Dr. Bearden was justified in refusing to spend any additional sums for Emmett, Jr.'s college expenses.

Id. at 382, 252 S.E.2d at 130-31.

However, a parent cannot arbitrarily terminate child support ordered under *Risinger* guidelines just because a child makes bad grades for one semester. In *Acrey v. Acrey*, 292 S.C. 387, 356 S.E.2d 430 (Ct. App. 1987), the father agreed to pay $500 per month as long as the son was pursuing a normal full-time course load and maintaining passing grades. The agreement was by the family court. The father sought relief when the son received grades below passing one semester. The trial court relieved him from his obligation for that one semester, with instructions that the payments were to resume if the son's performance complied with the terms of the agreement in the future. The father appealed and the Court of Appeals affirmed, distinguishing *Acrey* from *Bearden.* In *Acrey*, the judge relied on his interpretation of ambiguous language of the agreement to indicate a semester by semester determination of compliance. The father had not carried his burden of proof by introducing extrinsic evidence to explain or supplement the ambiguous agreement.

An agreement to pay for up to four years of college also encompasses two years of technical education. In *Cathcart v. Cathcart*, 307 S.C. 322, 414 S.E.2d 811 (Ct. App. 1992), the father had agreed to pay the costs of each of the parties' two daughters at four-year colleges. The trial judge held that the father was not responsible for his daughter's two-year course of study at Midlands Technical College. The Court of Appeals determined that his agreement had been to pay for any post high school education up to a four-year commitment, which included obligating him to pay for two years of technical education.[35]

An agreement calling for a parent to pay "reasonable college expenses" does not necessarily require a child to attend a state-supported school. *Ellis v. Taylor*, 311 S.C. 66, 427 S.E.2d 678 (Ct. App. 1992).

H. AMOUNT

1. IN GENERAL

The amount of support depends on the parents' income and assets or their ability to earn the means to provide child support. S.C. Code Ann. § 20-7-40 (Law. Co-op 1976) provides:

---

[35] For an interesting lesson in learning to keep one's mouth shut, see *Major v. Major*, 277 S.C. 318, 286 S.E.2d 666 (1982), in which the Supreme Court said:

> In reviewing the amount of child support, we take note of respondent's offer, made during oral argument, to assume present and future support of the older child as well as the expense of his college education. Although this offer does not bear directly on the amount of child support awarded below, we find that this admirable and voluntary assumption of post-emancipation support and educational costs, taken together with the father's continuing custody of the younger child, works a fair balance between the parties. We, therefore, do not reach the issue of the amount of pre-emancipation support granted by the decree, but instead we affirm the holding and modify the decree of divorce to direct that the respondent shall pay two hundred fifty ($250.00) dollars monthly together with all expenses of a four-year college education to the older child of the parties commencing with the eighteenth birthday of said child.

Id. at 321-322, 286 S.E.2d at 668-669. (In the same case, the court ordered the father to pay sixteen months of retroactive child support.)

> A husband or wife declared to be chargeable with the support of his or her spouse and children, if possessed of sufficient means or able to earn such means, may be required to pay for their support a fair and reasonable sum according to his or her means, as may be determined by the court.

Today, the amount of child support to be awarded is usually based on the South Carolina Child Support Guidelines, codified at S.C. Code Regs. §§ 114-4710 to-4750 (Law Co-op. Supp.). The primary factors to be considered under the guidelines are the actual gross incomes and earning potential of both parties. However, the family court is still required to consider a wider range of factors:

> The factors to be considered by the court in establishing the amount of child support obligations are both parents' income, ability to pay, education, expenses, and assets and the facts and circumstances surrounding each case. *Mitchell v. Mitchell*, 283 S.C. 87, 320 S.E.2d 706 (1989). The court is to award support in an amount sufficient to provide for the needs of the children and to maintain the children at the standard of living they would have been provided but for the divorce. The award should be an amount the parent can pay and still meet his or her own needs. *Smith v. Delaney*, 286 S.C. 583, 334 S.E.2d 821 (Ct. App. 1985).
>
> The Family Court judge did not address any of these factors beyond the income and expenses of the parents. Instead, the family court judge, by his own admission, relied entirely upon the South Carolina Child Support Guidelines.

Miller v. Miller, 299 S.C. 307, 312, 384 S.E.2d 715, 717-718 (1989). *See Holcombe v. Hardee*, 304 S.C. 522, 405 S.E.2d 821 (1991) which recites the same list of factors from *Miller*. Additional factors mentioned in other cases include: (1) the needs of the children; and (2) the health and general physical conditions of both parents. *See also Bradley v. Bradley*, 285 S.C. 170, 328 S.E.2d 647 (Ct. App. 1985); *Peebles v. Disher*, 279 S.C. 611, 310 S.E.2d 823 (Ct. App. 1984).

When the parents' combined incomes are so high that the guidelines do not cover the case, the amount of child support should reflect that "a child is entitled to live and be supported in a life style commensurate with the current income of his parents." *Mallett v. Mallett*, ___ S.C. ___, ___, 473 S.E.2d 804, 809 (Ct. App. 1996). The court affirmed a child support award of $2000 per month "considering the husband's income and the life style the child has enjoyed and is entitled to enjoy in the future." *Id.*

South Carolina courts have not yet considered a case in which the parents' combined incomes are unusually high, but only temporarily, for example, professional athletes whose prime earning years are not likely to last through a young child's minority. The issue then becomes whether the child is entitled to be supported at the standard of living before the parent began earning a large salary, whether the child should receive very high child support only so long as the parent is receiving a high income, or whether a trust or other mechanism should be used to ensure that the child will receive an adequate, and stable, amount of support during its minority. Other states have explored several options, most seeking in some way to preserve the extraordinary assets so the child will benefit throughout its minority. For example, the Supreme Court of Wisconsin applied that state's percentage standards in fashioning the child support obligation of a well-paid professional football player. Although it acknowledged that the 17% award exceeded the current needs of the child, it approved the family court's solution which was to provide for a monetary award to the mother covering the child's present needs, with the remainder of the monthly payment going into a trust fund. *Mary L.O. v. Tommy R.B.*, 544 N.W.2d 417 (Wis. 1996).

Although *Miller*, *Mallett*, and *Beinor v. Beinor*, 282 S.C. 181, 318 S.E.2d 269 (1984), say the objective in awarding child support is to allow the child to live at the standard of living to which he or she has become accustomed, this appears to be inconsistent with S.C. Code Ann. § 20-7-90(A) (Law. Co-op 1976), which provides in part:

> Any able-bodied person capable of earning a livelihood who shall, without just cause or excuse, abandon or fail to provide reasonable support to his or her spouse or to his or her minor

> unmarried legitimate or illegitimate child dependent on him or her shall be deemed guilty of a misdemeanor . . . .
>
> . . .
>
> As used in this section "reasonable support" means an amount of financial assistance which, when combined with the support the member is reasonably capable of providing for himself or herself, will provide a living standard for the member substantially equal to that of the person owing the duty to support. [emphasis added]

A court wishing to make a child support award under the statute would want to investigate the living conditions of both parents and try to fashion a child support award which would equalize them. Under the *Miller*, *Mallett*, and *Beinor* standard, a court might seek to award an amount of child support sufficient to make the child's lifestyle better than that of the paying parent (assuming both parents' incomes were used to support the family while they were living together).

However, it appears that the objective of child support awards under the guidelines is inconsistent with the standards mentioned above and, to the extent that they result in smaller awards of child support than would have been awarded previously, application of the guidelines would not benefit the children. According to the *South Carolina Child Support Guidelines Workbook*, "[t]he Income Shares Model calculates child support as the share of each parent's income which would have been spent on the children if the parents and children were living in the same household. The shares are based on the amount of money ordinarily spent on children by their families living in the United States and adjusted to South Carolina cost of living levels." *South Carolina Child Support Guidelines Workbook* (DSS May, 1994), p. 1.

If the average amount spent on children in South Carolina as prescribed in the guidelines is less than sufficient in a particular case, either because it does not maintain the children in the style to which they had been accustomed or it results in unequal lifestyles for the parents, application of the guidelines would appear to be open to challenge in such cases. After all, the guidelines were intended to set minimum levels of child support, not maximums.

2. CHILD SUPPORT GUIDELINES

a. In General

The South Carolina Department of Social Services has been required by state law since 1978 to promulgate child support guidelines in the context of obtaining support for children who are receiving aid to families with dependent children (AFDC). S.C. Code Ann. § 43-5-220 (Law. Co-op. 1976). However, the statute specifically provides that "[i]t is intended that the scale formulated pursuant to this section be optional, and that no court or support official be required to use it."

In 1988, the United States Congress enacted legislation which mandated the states to formally enact child support guidelines. 42 U.S.C. § 667 as amended by Pub. L. 100-485, Title 1, § 103(a), (b), (f), effective October 13, 1989. Section 667 provides in part:

> (a) Establishment of guidelines; method.
>
> Each State, as a condition for having its State plan [for AFDC] approved under this part, must establish guidelines for child support award amounts within the State. . . .
>
> . . .
>
> (b) Availability of guidelines, rebuttable presumption.
>
> (2) There shall be a rebuttable presumption, in any judicial proceeding for the award of child support, that the amount of the award which would result from the application of such guidelines is the correct amount of child support to be awarded. . . .

In 1989, the legislature amended S.C. Code Ann. § 43-5-580(b) (Law. Co-op. Supp.) to provide for mandatory child support guidelines:

> The department shall promulgate regulations which establish guidelines for minimum contributions which must be applied by the

> courts in determining the amount that an absent parent is expected to pay toward the support of a dependent child. Copies of the guidelines must be made available to courts, district attorneys, and to the public. The guidelines formulated pursuant to this section must be applied pursuant to the provisions of Section 20-7-852.

At the same time, the legislature amended S.C. Code Ann. § 20-7-852 (Law. Co-op. Supp.) to provide that:

> (A) In any proceeding in which child support is in issue, the amount of the award which would result from the application of those guidelines required under Section 43-5-580(b) is the amount of the child support to be awarded. However, a different amount may be awarded upon a showing that application of the guidelines in a particular case would be unjust or inappropriate. When the court orders a child support award that varies significantly from the amount resulting from the application of the guidelines, the court shall make specific, written findings of those facts upon which it bases its conclusion supporting that award.
>
> (B) Application of these guidelines to an existing child support order, in and of itself, is not considered a change in circumstances for the modification of that existing order.
>
> (C) Pursuant to Section 43-5-580(b), the department shall promulgate regulations which include addressing child support guidelines. The department shall review these regulations at least once every four years to insure that their application results in appropriate child support award amounts.

Although these sections became effective on January 31, 1990, they were not fully effective until the Department of Social Services promulgated regulations through the State Register. However, in *Miller v. Miller*, 299 S.C. 307, 384 S.E.2d 715 (1989), the Supreme Court held that the family courts could take judicial notice of the proposed guidelines and apply them before they had been approved as regulations, so long as they applied them properly.

The guidelines were eventually promulgated as regulations and are codified as part of the regulations of the Department of Social Services at S.C. Code Regs. §§ 114-4710 to-4750 (Law Co-op. Supp.).

The guidelines may be used in setting child support for children who have reached the age of majority but who have not yet become emancipated. *See Peterson v. Smith*, 307 S.C. 418, 415 S.E.2d 431 (Ct. App. 1992), in which the Court of Appeals held that the guidelines could be applied even after a child reached 18, as the child was disabled. The court also found that the needs of the child had increased since the previous order when she was four. She was twenty at the time of this order.

The guidelines rely primarily on the incomes of both parents in calculating child support awards. Income is defined to include the actual gross income of the parent, if employed to full capacity, or potential income if unemployed or underemployed. S.C. Code Regs. § 114-4720(A)(1) (Law. Co-op. Supp.).

b. Gross Income

Gross income is defined in S.C. Code Regs. § 114-4720(A)(2) (Law. Co-op. Supp.):

> Gross Income. Gross income includes income from any source including salaries, wages, commissions, royalties, bonuses, rents (less allowable business expenses), dividends, severance pay, pensions, interest, trust income, annuities, capital gains, social security benefits (but not Supplemental Security Income), worker's compensation benefits, unemployment insurance benefits, disability insurance benefits, Veteran's benefits and alimony, including alimony which a party received as a result of another marriage and alimony which a party receives as a result of the current litigation. Unreported cash income should also be included if it can be identified.
>
> (a) The court may also take into account assets available to generate income for child support. For example, the court may determine the reasonable earning potential of any asset at its market value and assess against it the current treasury

> bill interest rate or some other similar appropriate method of computing income.
>
> (b) In addition to determining potential earnings, the court should impute income to any non income producing assets of either parent, if significant, other than a primary residence or personal property. Examples of such assets are vacation homes (if not maintained as rental property) and idle land. The current rate determined by the court is the rate at which income should be imputed to such non performing assets.

"The court should count as income expense reimbursements or in-kind payments received by a parent from self-employment or operation of a business if they are significant and reduce personal living expenses, such as company car, free housing, or reimbursed meals." S.C. Code Regs. § 114-4720(A)(3)(c) (Law. Co-op. 1976). See *Mobley v. Mobley*, 309 S.C. 134, 420 S.E.2d 506 (Ct. App. 1992), in which the father's financial declaration included only his income from salary, dividends, and rents. The court rejected his argument that the other benefits, including a truck allowance and a house in which he lived free of charge, should be excluded because he had no tax liability for those benefits. Citing 27C C.J.S. *Divorce* § 674 (1986), the court held that child support awards may be based on income not reported for tax purposes.

Social Security disability payments being received by children are a substitute for their disabled parent's loss of earning power, therefore, such payments should be considered as income to the disabled parent in calculating the appropriate child support award. *Lovett v. Lovett*, 311 S.C. 279, 428 S.E.2d 874 (1993) (holding that the trial judge erred in reducing the husband's child support obligation by the amount of money the children were receiving from Social Security as a result of the mother's disability).

Whether or not Social Security benefits are includable in a parent's gross income for the purpose of calculating child support has not been addressed by a South Carolina appellate court. Most other jurisdictions have decided that Social Security benefits, including disability benefits, should be included if they are being received under Title II of the Social Security Act, 42 U.S.C. §§ 401-433, entitled

"Federal Old-Age, Survivors, and Disability Insurance Benefits." *Tienne v. Tienne*, 815 F. Supp. 394 (D. Kan. 1993); *Shepard v. Shepard*, 467 N.W.2d 237 (Iowa, 1991); *Kirk v. Kirk*, 577 A.2d 976 (R.I. 1990); *Mariche v. Mariche*, 243 Kan. 547, 758 P.2d 745 (1988) (all holding that Title II Social Security Benefits are subject to attachment for child support). These cases found that, although 42 U.S.C. § 407(a) provides that "none of the monies payable ... under [subchapter II] shall be subject to execution, levy, attachment, garnishment, or other legal process," 42 U.S.C. § 659(a) makes an exception for child support and alimony.

However, it appears likely that Federal Supplemental Security Income (SSI) benefits awarded pursuant to subchapter XIV of the Social Security Act, 42 U.S.C. §§ 1381-1383d, should not be included in a parent's gross income in calculating child support, nor can they be garnished or otherwise attached for payment of child support. *Becker County Human Servs. v. Peppel*, 493 N.W.2d 573 (Minn. App. 1992) (adopting the reasoning of *Tennessee Dept. of Human Servs. ex rel. Young v. Young*, 802 S.W.2d 594 (Tenn. 1990)). In *Becker*, the court pointed out that SSI benefits are given to people who are aged, blind, or disabled and who have incomes below a certain level. They are a form of public assistance, unrelated to past earnings. The court noted that 42 U.S.C. § 407(a) provides that "none of the monies payable ... under [subchapter II] shall be subject to execution, levy, attachment, garnishment, or other legal process," and that this protection is extended to SSI benefits by operation of 42 U.S.C. § 1383(d)(1).

Before the guidelines, the full assets of the parties were to be considered in making child support awards. In *McLean v. McLean*, 273 S.C. 571, 257 S.E.2d 751 (1979), the mother challenged the award of $41.20 per month as inadequate, and the court pointed out that it was error to refuse to consider in awarding child support monies the corpus of a spendthrift trust (estimated to be roughly $700,000) created by the father for his own benefit. *Id.* at 575-576, 257 S.E.2d at 753. There appears to be no reason why *McLean* would not still be valid.

Assets other than current income were allowed under prior case law to be used in calculating child support obligations. It is not clear whether or how they would be calculated under the guidelines. In *Tilghman v. Tilghman*, 315 S.C. 76, 431 S.E.2d 622 (Ct. App. 1993), the Court of Appeals found that the trial court had not considered the value of the father's assets which he had not, but could have, used to produce income for child support. However, in *dicta*, the court expressed its agreement with the trial judge that "the father's failure to use the assets to produce income does not preclude any consideration of them." *Id.* at 77, 431 S.E.2d at 623. In *Sutton v. Sutton*, 291 S.C. 401, 353 S.E.2d 884 (Ct. App. 1987), the husband claimed that he could not afford to pay increased child support payments and that his income did not justify the increased award. The court pointed out that "'[t]here is no limitation that child support payments be made solely from current earnings.' *Hughes v. Hughes*, 280 S.C. 388, 392, 313 S.E.2d 32, 34 (Ct. App. 1984)." *Sutton* at 406, 353 S.E.2d at 887. The court then affirmed the increased amount of child support awarded in light of the husband's 100% ownership of a meat company that was not in as bad financial condition as the husband wanted the court to believe, and especially in light of the fact that the company was paying a salary of $50,000 per year to his new wife who had not made more than $10,000 per year at the company before she married Mr. Sutton. The court found that he was intentionally manipulating his own income.

Although it is logical that some credit should be given for the use of assets belonging to the paying spouse, it is not clear how credit for such use is to be given under the guidelines. For example, in *Chastain v. Chastain*, 289 S.C. 281, 345 S.E.2d 737 (Ct. App. 1986), the use of the marital home was awarded as an incident of support based on special circumstances. The son suffered from Down's syndrome. The home was located in a secluded neighborhood and the neighbors knew the son and accepted him and would look after him on those occasions when he wandered off. On balance, the special needs outweighed the husband's interest in his equity in the marital home. It is not clear that the father was given any relief in the amount of child support he had to pay as a result of the house being awarded as an incident of child support.

c. Potential Income

If a parent is unemployed or underemployed, that parent's potential or prospective income should be considered. Potential income is defined in S.C. Code Regs. § 114-4720(A)(5) (Law. Co-op. Supp.):

> Potential Income. If the court finds that a parent is voluntarily unemployed or underemployed, it should calculate child support

> based on a determination of potential income which would otherwise ordinarily be available to the parent. However, the court may take into account the presence of young children or handicapped children who must be cared for by the parent, necessitating the parent's inability to work.
>
> (a) The court may also wish to factor in considerations of rehabilitative alimony in order to enable the parent to become employed.
>
> (b) In order to impute income to a parent who is unemployed or underemployed, the court should determine the employment potential and probable earnings level of the parent based on that parent's recent work history, occupational qualifications, and prevailing job opportunities and earning levels in the community.

Family courts in South Carolina were allowed to consider the earning potential of parents in calculating child support long before the guidelines were adopted. In *Camp v. Camp*, 269 S.C. 173, 236 S.E.2d 814 (1977), the husband had voluntarily depressed his income by not continuing to engage in the private practice of psychiatry. The Supreme Court said: "This matter is discussed in 24 Am. Jur. 2d *Divorce and Separation* § 632: 'When the husband has voluntarily relinquished a well-paying practice and has taken a position at a modest salary, the court may base the amount of alimony upon his capacity to earn money, or upon his prospective earnings.'" *Id.* at 175, 236 S.E.2d at 815. The Court concluded that he could be forced to pay the same amount he had agreed to pay before his change of employment.

The Court of Appeals reached the same conclusion when a father gave up a good job and enrolled in law school.

> When the husband elected to attend law school full-time, he voluntarily removed himself from the job market. Under these circumstances, the judge properly considered the husband's earning potential rather than simply his current income and properly disallowed the husband's diminished

> income as an excuse either for relieving the husband from any child support obligations at all or for reducing the amount the husband should otherwise pay in child support.

Chastain v. Chastain, 289 S.C. 281, 283, 346 S.E.2d 33, 35 (Ct. App. 1986). *See also R.G.M. v. D.E.M.*, 306 S.C. 145, 410 S.E.2d 564 (1991), in which the Supreme Court affirmed the trial court's award of child support based on its determination that the wife was capable of earning $15,000 per year. The wife had presented no evidence to the contrary.

One consequence of the guidelines' expectation of pro-rated equal financial contributions by both parents to child support may be to force more mothers to enter the work force. An apparent exception to this is when a mother is the custodial parent of young or handicapped children. In *Woodall v. Woodall*, ___ S.C. ___, 471 S.E.2d 154 (1996), a father complained on appeal that his wife voluntarily left the work force and the child support calculation should have been based on her potential income. The Supreme Court rejected this position, citing 27 S.C. Code Ann. Reg. § 114-4720(A)(5) (Law. Co-op. Supp.) for the proposition that the family court may take into account the presence of young or handicapped children who must be cared for by the parent necessitating the parent's inability to work. The mother in *Woodall* was the custodial parent for the parties' six year old child.

The result in *Woodall* is inconsistent with the result in *Eckstein v. Eckstein*, 306 S.C. 167, 410 S.E.2d 578 (Ct. App. 1991), which is not mentioned in *Woodall*. In *Eckstein* the Court of Appeals rejected a mother's argument that it was error to consider her earning potential in applying the guidelines when she was responsible for the care of two children, ages 5 and 7. The mother had a B.S. degree in engineering and was unemployed at the time of the decree. The family court calculated her potential earnings at $2,833.33 per month. The Court of Appeals said the trial judge committed no error in using her potential income, and noted that the judge had specifically included child care costs in making his determination of support.

The guidelines allow child care costs to be offset, but they make no allowance for the custodial parent's services. Under pre-guidelines case law, courts were permitted to consider the in-kind contributions of mothers who did not work.

> Financial assistance is just one aspect of a support obligation. Another aspect of support includes the services parents provide for a child. Respondent is the custodial parent and has the responsibility of performing the daily services the child requires, i.e., preparing meals, helping with homework, and washing clothes. *Smith v. Smith*, 294 S.C. 194, 363 S.E.2d 404 (Ct. App. 1987).

Cross v. Cross, 296 S.C. 474, 476, 374 S.E.2d 178, 179 (1988). *Smith* affirmed a child support order requiring the father to make all the financial contributions and allowing the wife's services to be considered in calculating her fair share of contributions to child support. It characterized the husband's contention that it was an abuse of discretion to not require the wife to contribute to the support of their children as "manifestly without merit." *Smith* at 198, 363 S.E.2d at 406.

d. Proof of Income

S.C. Code Regs. § 114-4720(A)(6) (Law. Co-op. Supp.) provides:

> Verification of Income. Ordinarily the court will determine income from verified financial declarations required by the Family Court rules. However, in the absence of any financial declaration or where the amounts reflected on the financial declaration may be in issue, the Court may rely on suitable documentation of current earnings, preferably for at least one month, using such documents as pay stubs, employer statements, or receipts and expenses if the parent is self-employed. Verification of current earnings, whether reflected on a financial declaration or not, can be supported with copies of the most recent tax returns filed by the payor. Income can also be verified through the Employment Security Commission or through the State Tax Commission.

If there is no evidence of the parties' income in the record on appeal, an appellate court cannot evaluate whether the trial judge abused his discretion in making a child support award. In *Abbott v. Gore*, 304 S.C. 116, 403 S.E.2d 821 (1991), the trial court increased the child support to the mother from $250 to $700. The father appealed the amount as excessive. The mother complained that the child support guidelines should have been used, even though they had not been mandatory at the time. The Supreme Court determined that neither party had carried the burden of proving abuse of discretion because there were no financial declarations in the record from which it could evaluate the father's complaint and because there was no child support guidelines worksheet in the record to demonstrate whether the mother had been prejudiced by the trial judge's failure to apply the guidelines.

Even where an appellate court determines that the trial judge made an error, it cannot determine the proper amount of child support without financial declarations in the record, and must remand such cases for further proceedings. *See Holcombe v. Hardee*, 304 S.C. 522, 405 S.E.2d 821 (1991) (reversing the trial court's finding that the mother could not afford to contribute to private school expenses of the dyslexic son under eighteen and remanding the case because of the trial court's failure to make specific findings with respect to each factor and the absence of financial declarations in the record); *Peebles v. Disher*, 279 S.C. 611, 310 S.E.2d 823 (Ct. App. 1984) (remanding the case because neither party filed a financial declaration and there was no other basis in the record on which to determine the income and assets of the parents such as tax returns, wage statements, loan applications, or testimony).

e. Deviation From the Guidelines

In all cases in which child support is an issue, the court must consider the guidelines. The guidelines are intended to cover all actions involving questions of child support. The family court does not have discretion in choosing whether or not the guidelines are applicable. *Price v. Ozment*, 318 S.C. 168, 456 S.E.2d 427 (Ct. App. 1995) (reversing a family court judge's decision that he could choose whether or not to award child support, and, if he chose not to award child support, the guidelines did not have to be utilized).

Although application of the guidelines is mandatory, the trial judge still has a certain amount of discretion and an award of support will not be overturned absent a showing of abuse of that discretion. S.C. Code Ann. § 20-7-852 (Law. Co-op. Supp.) states in part:

> (A) In any proceeding for the award of child support, there is a rebuttable presumption that the amount of the award which would

> result from the application of the guidelines required under Section 43-580(b) is the correct amount of child support to be awarded. A different amount may be awarded upon a showing that application of the guidelines in a particular case would be unjust or inappropriate.

The statute also provides that, if the court orders a child support award that "varies significantly" from the guidelines, it is required to make "specific, written findings of those facts upon which it bases its conclusion supporting that award." The statute leaves much discretion in the court to determine what "varies significantly." A variance of forty dollars has been held not to be a significant variance for which the court must provide its basis. *Sherman v. Sherman*, 307 S.C. 280, 414 S.E.2d 809 (Ct. App. 1992). The award in *Sherman* was $475 per month, rather than the $435 indicated by the guidelines. Because the family court did not consider the amount of deviation significant, it gave no explanation for that deviation. The Court of Appeals upheld the award despite the absence of any explanation for the deviation. *Id.* at 282, 414 S.E.2d at 810.

A failure to consider factors which that warrant deviation from the guidelines may be reversible error. In *White v. Cook*, 312 S.C. 352, 440 S.E.2d 391 (Ct. App. 1994), the Court of Appeals remanded a case in which the trial judge had believed that strict application of the guidelines was mandatory and had refused to consider whether a father's support obligation to his two additional children warranted deviation from the guidelines. The Court of Appeals noted that it was not commenting on whether or not, or how much, the family court should deviate from the guidelines on remand.

The factors which a court may consider as possible reasons for deviating from the guidelines are set forth in S.C. Code Ann. § 20-7-852(C) (Law. Co-op. Supp.) (they also appear at S.C. Code Regs. § 114-4710(B) (Law. Co-op. Supp.)):

(1) educational expenses for the child or children or the spouse, to include those incurred for private, parochial, or trade schools, other secondary schools, or post-secondary education where there is tuition or related costs;

(2) equitable distribution of property;

(3) consumer debts;

(4) families with more than six children;

(5) unreimbursed extraordinary medical or dental expenses for the noncustodial or custodial parent;

(6) mandatory deduction of retirement pensions and union fees;

(7) support obligations for other dependents living with the noncustodial parent, or non-court ordered child support from another relationship;

(8) child-related unreimbursed extraordinary medical expenses;

(9) monthly fixed payments imposed by court or operation of law;

(10) significant available income of the child or children;

(11) substantial disparity of income in which the noncustodial parent's income is significantly less than the custodial parent's income, thus making it financially impracticable to pay what the guidelines indicate the noncustodial parent should pay;

(12) alimony. Because of their unique nature, lump sum, rehabilitative, reimbursement, or any other alimony that the court may award, may be considered by the court as a possible reason for deviation from these guidelines; and

(13) agreements reached between the parties. The court may deviate from the guidelines based on an agreement between the parties if both parties are represented by counsel or if, upon a thorough examination of any party not represented by counsel, the court determines the party fully understands the agreement as to child support. The court still has the discretion and the independent

> duty to determine if the amount is reasonable and in the best interest of the child or children.

The court is also expected to consider the existence of additional dependents. The court is often faced with the task of balancing the needs of the noncustodial parent's additional dependents with those of the children in the action before the court, while also trying to encourage parental responsibility. Though the court may elect to deviate from the guidelines in such cases, the child support guidelines suggest a method of adjustment which allots equitable shares of support to the noncustodial parent's dependents. S.C. Code Reg. § 114-4720(I) (Law. Co-op. Supp.).

I. MODIFICATION OF CHILD SUPPORT

1. JURISDICTION

The family court has the authority to modify child support awards as the circumstances warrant, but usually only upon a showing of changed circumstances.

> The issue of child support is subject to the continuing review of the family court. *Stevenson v. Stevenson*, 276 S.C. 475, 279 S.E.2d 616 (1981). Child support may be modified upon a proper showing of a change in either the child's needs or the supporting parent's financial ability. *Calvert v. Calvert*, 287 S.C. 130, 336 S.E.2d 884 (Ct. App. 1985). The amount of child support awarded is within the sound discretion of the trial judge whose decision will not be disturbed on appeal absent an abuse of discretion. *Millis v. Millis*, 282 S.C. 610. 320 S.E.2d 66 (Ct. App. 1984).

Nicholson v. Lewis, 295 S.C. 434, 436, 369 S.E.2d 649, 650 (Ct. App. 1988). S.C. Code § 20-7-933 (Law. Co-op. Supp.) provides:

> The family court has the authority to enforce the provisions of any decree, judgment, or order regarding child support of a court

of this State, including cases with jurisdiction based on the revised Uniform Reciprocal Enforcement of Support Act[36], provided that personal jurisdiction has been properly established. This authority includes the right to modify any such decree, judgment, or order for child support as the court considers necessary upon a showing of changed circumstances. No such modification is effective as to any installment accruing prior to filing and service of the action for modification. Additionally, the family court has the right to hold any arrearage in child support in abeyance.

The general rule on modification is that it is necessary to show a "sufficient" change in conditions or circumstances of one or more of the parties or principals. In *Calvert v. Calvert*, 287 S.C. 130, 336 S.E.2d 884 (Ct. App. 1985), the court stated: "Generally, to warrant a modification in either alimony or child support, the change of circumstances must be either substantial or material." *Id.* at 38, 336 S.E.2d at 888-889. It is not yet clear whether the guidelines have changed this rule.

A child support order issued by another state can be can be modified by a South Carolina court only if it is registered pursuant to the Uniform Interstate Family Support act and, after notice and hearing, the court finds that:

(1) neither the child, the obligee, nor the obligor reside in the issuing state, the nonresident plaintiff seeks modification, and the defendant is subject to the jurisdiction of the family court; or

(2) a party who is a natural person (not an agency) or the child is subject to the personal jurisdiction of the family court and all the parties who are natural persons have filed an agreement in the issuing tribunal providing that the family court may modify the support order and assume continuing, exclusive jurisdiction over the order.

---

[36] This needs to be amended to the Uniform Interstate Family Support Act.

S.C. Code Ann. §20-7-1146 (Law. Co-op. Supp.). See additional discussion about the modification of support orders from other states in the section on interstate support orders earlier in this chapter.

The promulgation of the child support guidelines is not a sufficient change in circumstances to modify child support. S.C. Code Ann. § 20-7-852(B) (Law. Co-op. Supp.) says: "Application of these guidelines to an existing child support order, in and of itself, is not considered a change in circumstances for the modification of that existing order." *See also Tilghman v. Tilghman*, 315 S.C. 76, 431 S.E.2d 622 (Ct. App. 1993) (stating that the mere application of the guidelines was not a sufficient change in circumstances to increase child support, but holding that the increase in the father's income was a sufficient change in circumstances to do so).

Notwithstanding the above, all child support orders which are enforced by the Child Support Enforcement Division of the Department of Social Services (the Division) must be reviewed not later than thirty-six months after the establishment of the order or the most recent review unless, 1) in an AFDC case, neither party has requested a review and the Department of Social Services has determined that a review is not in the child's best interests; or 2) in a non-AFDC case, neither party has requested a review." S.C. Code Regs. § 114-4740 (Law. Co-op. Supp.).

Thus, in cases being enforced by the Division, there is no need to consider including an "escalator clause" to avoid the need to come back to court to obtain modifications of child support awards. South Carolina courts have consistently rejected the use of escalator clauses. In *Condon v. Condon*, 280 S.C. 357, 312 S.E.2d 588 (Ct. App. 1984), the court struck down an order providing that "the amount of child support to be paid by Mr. Condon should automatically increase from $390 per month to $540 after twenty-four months." The court held there was no precedent for this type of award and considered it an abuse of discretion. *Id.* at 360, 312 S.E.2d at 589. *See also Calvert v. Calvert*, 287 S.C. 130, 336 S.E.2d 884 (Ct. App. 1985), in which the court held that child support increases or decreases cannot be tied to cost of living indexes. "An inflationary increase in the cost of living does not amount, at least by itself, to a change in circumstances. Inflation affects everyone, father, mother, and child." *Id.* at 139, 336 S.E.2d at 889. The Court of Appeals had this to say about the impact of inflation on child support awards in *Nelson v. Merritt*, 281 S.C. 126, 314 S.E.2d 840 (Ct. App. 1984):

> Regarding inflation, we recognize that it has had a negative effect on the husband's buying power; however, no one is immune from inflation's cutting edge. Inflation reduces the buying power of little children too, including, we would think, Merritt's son and daughter. When the costs of food, clothing, shelter, transportation, and other necessaries increase, they go up for everybody, adults and children alike. The fact of inflation can scarcely be used, then, as a justification for reducing child support obligations particularly when, as here, the parent's income has increased more than nominally since the last child support order.

Id. at 444, 314 S.E.2d at 842 (citations omitted).

Matters which were (or should have been) within the contemplation of the parties when the child support award is made cannot serve as a basis for seeking a modification of support. *See Kneece v. Kneece*, 296 S.C. 28, 370 S.E.2d 102 (Ct. App. 1988) (finding no changed circumstances because the effect of the division of marital property in a divorce action, less land to farm, was an anticipated change at the time of the support award); *Thornton v. Thornton*, 294 S.C. 512, 366 S.E.2d 37 (Ct. App. 1988) (denying a request for additional support for orthodontic work because the need for the work was known at the time of the award and there was no evidence that the anticipated costs had increased and because the custodial parent's income had gone up since the support award while the noncustodial parent's income had gone down).

The fact that one of several children has reached majority does not affect a parent's child support obligation, absent a family court order modifying the amount of support owed. In *Bull v. Smith*, 299 S.C. 123, 382 S.E.2d 905 (1989), one daughter reached majority and went to college. The other daughter remained a minor at home with the mother. The Supreme Court noted in the opinion that the father's obligation to continue paying the same amount of child support remained unchanged unless he sought a modification of the order.

2. CHANGED CIRCUMSTANCES

a. Changes in the Child's Needs

Extraordinary medical expenses which were not provided for or anticipated at the time of the child support award constitute changed circumstances on which an adjustment of child support can be based. *Marsh v. Hancock*, 288 S.C. 341, 342 S.E.2d 607 (1986);

A need for orthodontic work or other special medical care might justify an increase in child support under some circumstances. By the same token, however, it might not. In *Smith v. Smith*, 262 S.C. 291, 204 S.E.2d 53 (1974), appeal after remand, 264 S.C. 624, 216 S.E.2d 541 (1975), the Supreme Court emphasized the relatively modest financial condition of the husband in holding eventually that there was no abuse of discretion on the part of the trial court in refusing an award for the dental expenses of one child. The father had already paid for orthodontic work for the oldest child. Thus, it would seem to follow that a need for orthodontic work is a legitimate consideration in a petition for increased child support; but it will not, any more than any other factor, be considered in isolation. A request for additional support for psychiatric care was handled similarly in *Campbell v. McPherson*, 268 S.C. 444, 234 S.E.2d 774 (1977). The Court required further proceedings to determine the actual need and hence justification for the psychiatric treatment.

A change in the mental condition of a supported child might constitute a sufficient change in conditions to warrant a modification of child support. *Grout v. Alexander*, 260 S.C. 655, 197 S.E.2d 826 (1973). In order to secure modification of an existing order with mental illness as the reason, however, it appears necessary to show in some detail the "financial, mental and physical burdens upon the custodian" which have become more substantial as a result of the change in mental condition of the child." *Id.* at 659, 197 S.E.2d at 827. The Supreme Court also found that the 1970 determination of child support payments was inadequate to meet the reasonable then current needs of the minor daughter, listing among the reasons for its conclusion the increased cost of living and the increased cost of maintaining a child of high school age as compared to a younger child. The Supreme Court also noted the more than doubling of the father's net income between 1970 and 1975. As the rather pointed dissent of Justice Ness highlights, the approach the majority took seemed to give short shrift to the fact that the wife had a substantial dividend income and that she engaged in major investing activities. The gravamen of the dissent was that the majority was failing to balance properly the needs and ability to pay of the two parents, even assuming a genuine need on the part of the child for increased expenditures on her behalf. (The dissent also noted that in its opinion some of the expenditures for the child were not in fact reasonably necessary in light of the financial posture of the parents, emphasizing items like $20 per month for fish and guinea pigs and a $900 annual item for domestic help "for the daughter" even though the wife was unemployed, supported in substantial part by her generous dividend income, and well-educated.)

If a disabled child is in need of child support beyond the age of eighteen, the child support guidelines may still be used by the court in determining the amount to award. *See Peterson v. Smith*, 307 S.C. 418, 415 S.E.2d 431 (Ct. App. 1992) (finding that the guidelines may be applied even after a child reaches 18, as the child was disabled. The court also found that the needs of the child had increased since the previous order when she was four. She was twenty at the time of this order.).

Other cases have also allowed increases in child support in recognition of the fact that teenagers cost more to support than younger children. *See Abbott v. Gore*, 304 S.C. 116, 403 S.E.2d 154 (1991); *Campbell v. McPherson*, 268 S.C. 444, 234 S.E.2d 774 (1977); *Grout v. Alexander*, 260 S.C. 655, 197 S.E.2d 826 (1973). However, the guidelines do not take the age of children into account, so any attempt to secure a change in child support on this basis will require convincing the trial judge to deviate from the guidelines.

The coming of a child into a substantial separate estate will not necessarily free the parents of their joint obligation to support him or her. *Greenville Hospital System v. Smith*, 269 S.C. 653, 239 S.E.2d 657 (1977), holds that a child's estate cannot be charged for necessary expenses unless the parents are unable to pay.

b. Changes in the Parents' Finances

While a substantial improvement in the earning capacities of a supporting spouse will generally justify some increase in the support award, it does not mandate it. Nor will a reduction in the earning power of the supporting spouse necessarily require a reduction in the amount of support. *See Hicks v. Hicks*, 280 S.C. 378, 312 S.E.2d 598 (Ct. App. 1984), in which the Court of Appeals held that the father should not be held in contempt. The decline in his real estate business had caused his support shortfall. *See also Camp v. Camp*, 269 S.C. 173, 236 S.E.2d 814 (1977); *Eagerton v. Eagerton*, 265 S.C. 90, 217 S.E.2d 146 (1975).

The burden of establishing a significant reduction in income is on the person seeking the reduction in child support. "A downward modification of child support based upon a decrease in the noncustodial parent's income is not warranted absent a strong showing by the person seeking the change that he is no longer in a condition to make the support payments prescribed by an earlier Family Court order." *Miller v. Miller*, 299 S.C. 307, 310-11, 384 S.E.2d 715, 717 (1989) (finding that the changes since the previous award were not substantial and that the father's financial declaration did not show he was incapable of paying the support ordered previously).

See also Pirkle v. Pirkle, 303 S.C. 266, 399 S.E.2d 797 (Ct. App. 1990) (denying father's request for reduction of child support because he did not prove that his financial situation was worse than it was when the original order was issued); *Justice v. Scruggs*, 286 S.C. 165, 332 S.E.2d 106 (Ct. App. 1985) (allowing reduction because the father had been advised to stop work because of congestive heart condition and high blood pressure).

c. Remarriage

The remarriage of a spouse in and of itself is not a change of conditions sufficient to justify a decrease in the amount of child support. *Sanders v. Sanders*, 230 S.C. 263, 95 S.E.2d 440 (1956). However, as is illustrated by *Lunsford v. Lunsford*, 277 S.C. 104, 282 S.E.2d 861 (1981), remarriage can be considered.

Remarriage of the custodial spouse does not ordinarily terminate child support which has been paid from the other spouse. The reason for this is simple: the new spouse of the custodial spouse has no obligation to maintain the new stepchildren. *McElrath v. Walker*, 285 S.C. 439, 330 S.E.2d 313 (Ct. App. 1985). In *Sanders v. Sanders*, 230 S.C. 263, 95 S.E.2d 440 (1956), the husband was ordered pay child support, and the wife subsequently remarried. The husband petitioned for a reduction in the amount of child support, claiming that the wife was in a better economic position as a result of the remarriage, and that this change of circumstance should free up some of his income so that he might put it to work in bettering the position of the other child of the marriage who remained with him. The Supreme Court wrote: "Nor does the betterment of the divorced wife's financial condition as the result of her remarriage require such modification of the decree where, as here, there is no proof of assumption by the second husband of obligation to support the child or children of the first marriage." *Id.* at 268, 95 S.E.2d at 442-43.

It is interesting to note that the 1962 Code contained the following language in section 15-1231: "The step-parent of a child is declared legally chargeable with the support of a step-child likely to become a public charge provided it is shown to the satisfaction of the Court that such step-parent had knowledge of the child's existence at the time of such step-parent's marriage." This section is now viewed as having been repealed, but the fact that it was put into the Code (applicable to counties having a population of between 60,000 and 70,000 according to the 1940 census, or a population of over 70,000 according to the census) indicates an awareness on the part of the legislature that, absent some such provision, step-parents are not to be charged with the duty of support.

South Carolina apparently does subscribe to the doctrine of *in loco parentis* with regard to step-children and step-parents. Essentially, the doctrine states that a step-parent may be held liable for the support of a step-child when the step-parent has voluntarily taken the child into the family and has assumed the duty of support. However, this is a difficult obligation to enforce, since the step-parent may end his obligation of support at will. *Chestnut v. Chestnut*, 247 S.C. 332, 147 S.E.2d 269 (1966). However, a duty of support may conceivably arise out of the factual relationship existing at a given time between a step-parent and a step-child.

Ordinarily, though, since no obligation of support exists between the step-parent and the step-child (absent adoption, of course), it logically follows that the support obligation of the natural parent is not affected by the remarriage of the custodial parent. However, in a somewhat ambiguous opinion in *Bryan v. Bryan*, 275 S.C. 289, 270 S.E.2d 623 (1980), the Supreme Court interpreted *Sanders* as implicitly standing for the proposition that "ordinarily, the income of a new spouse should not be considered in determining the question of support of children of a former marriage." *Id.* at 290, 270 S.E.2d at 623-24. The Court then went on to point out that the possibility nonetheless existed that it would be appropriate under some circumstances to consider the betterment of a divorced spouse's financial condition as a result of remarriage in modifying child support payments. In *Bryan* the husband was seeking a reduction in the amount he was paying for child support. The family court refused to reduce his obligation, apparently considering the income of his new wife as being a relevant factor. The Supreme Court's bottom line was that there was insufficient evidence in the record to justify this consideration. Therefore, the case was remanded for a redetermination by the family court of the propriety of reducing child support payments absent any information regarding the new wife's income or, interestingly, any obligation on the part of the husband to provide support for the children of the new wife.

It is not clear if the income of a new spouse can be considered in setting child support. It was allowed under prior case law, but it does not appear to have been done very often. In *Broome v. Larkin*, 295 S.C. 498, 369 S.E.2d 153 (Ct. App. 1988), the Court of Appeals held that family courts have the discretion to consider the income of a new spouse, but it also noted that it did not appear to have been a factor relied upon by the judge. "In determining whether to modify a parent's child support obligation, the trial judge has the discretion to consider the income of a new spouse, depending on the facts of each particular case. *Sutton v. Sutton*, 291 S.C. 401, 353 S.E.2d 884 (Ct. App. 1987)." *Broome* at 499, 369 S.E.2d at 154.

In this same connection, it is worth noting that in *Schadel v. Schadel*, 268 S.C. 50, 232 S.E.2d 17 (1977), the Supreme Court explicitly noted that a husband seeking reduction in child support payments had remarried and that his new wife had an annual net income that was substantial in relation to his own annual net income. It refused to order any reduction in the child support payment after so noting.

J. CIVIL ENFORCEMENT OF CHILD SUPPORT[37]

1. CONTEMPT

a. In General

If a valid court order exists, the parent who is obligated to pay child support can be held in contempt of court for not paying the required amount on time.

The family court has general authority to hear and decide cases or proceedings "against persons charged with failure to obey an order of the court made pursuant to authority conferred by law." S.C. Code Ann. § 20-7-420(13) (Law. Co-op. 1976). *See also* S.C. Code Ann. § 20-7-1350 (Law. Co-op. 1976) which allows the court to hold in contempt any adult who willfully violates, neglects or refuses to obey or perform any order or who violates any provision of the Children's Code.

There is a specific provision for holding someone in contempt for failing to pay child support after agreeing to do so or being ordered to do so. S.C. Code Ann. § 20-7-870 (Law. Co-op. 1976) provides:

> Where a respondent shall neglect or refuse to obey an order for support or upon agreement signed by the respondent and approved by the court, and the court is satisfied thereof by competent proof, it may, with or without notice, issue a warrant to commit the respondent to jail until the order is obeyed or until the respondent is discharged by law.

Other statutes describe additional specific situations in which the family court is authorized to hold someone in contempt. A person can be held in contempt for

---

[37] Establishing and enforcing child support obligations against people in the military involve special considerations beyond the scope of this book. The S.C. Bar has some helpful CLE materials on this topic: D. Strom, "Child Support Enforcement Against Military Personnel," *Domestic Practice: "Hot Tips From the Experts" Rides Again*, May 15, 1992, pp. 293-326.

failing to give security by written undertaking as ordered by the court. S.C. Code Ann. § 20-7-420(22) (Law. Co-op. 1976). Also, a parent can be held in contempt for refusing to comply with an order to provide support during the commitment of a child to the custody of someone other than his or her parents. S.C. Code Ann. § 20-7-1340 (Law. Co-op. 1976).

The family court cannot modify past due child support, but it may hold arrearages in abeyance. S.C. Code Ann. § 20-7-933 (Law. Co-op. 1976) provides in part: "No such modification [of child support] is effective as to any installment accruing prior to filing and service of the action for modification. Additionally, the family court has the right to hold any arrearage in child support in abeyance."

The primary purpose of civil contempt is to exact compliance with the court's orders, not to punish the contemnor. *Moseley v. Mosier*, 279 S.C. 348, 306 S.E.2d 624 (1983). "When the parent is *unable* to make the required payments, he is not in contempt. The record in this case reveals that the respondent faithfully paid each week as much child support as he could afford." *Id.* at 351, 306 S.E.2d at 626 (emphasis supplied). Although *Moseley* was reversed primarily because the husband had not violated any order (his support obligation arose out of a separation agreement, not a court order), the Court also held that the trial judge had not made a specific finding that the father had not willfully violated the terms of the agreement (he claimed he was unable to pay).

The burden is on the moving party to prove that the supporting parent is in contempt of court. *Brasington v. Shannon*, 288 S.C. 183, 341 S.E.2d 130 (1986). Before a person can be held in contempt, the record must be clear and specific as to the acts and conduct upon which the finding is based.

> Contempt results from the willful disobedience of a court order. Before a court finds a person in contempt, the record must clearly and specifically reflect the contemptuous conduct. In a proceeding for contempt for violation of a court order, the moving party must show the existence of the order and the facts establishing the respondent's noncompliance. The burden then shifts to the respondent to establish his defense and inability to comply with the order.

> In a Rule 53 [now Rule 24, SCRFC] proceeding, the clerk of court must identify the court order which the respondent has allegedly violated, and must identify the specific acts or omissions which constitute noncompliance. These facts must be alleged in the affidavit which supports the rule.

Id. at 184, 341 S.E.2d at 131 (citations omitted). In *Brasington*, the affidavit did not identify the order or the manner in which it had been violated; therefore, the finding of contempt was reversed. The party claiming that arrearages are owed must present evidence of the amount of arrearage in the record or the court cannot award it. *Taylor v. Taylor*, 294 S.C. 296, 363 S.E.2d 909 (Ct. App. 1987).

If a child support obligation is based on an agreement and the child's needs have not changed, the court's only inquiry should be whether the father has the ability to pay. *Ratchford v. Ratchford*, 295 S.C. 297, 368 S.E.2d 214 (Ct. App. 1988), involved an agreement about child support. The court wrote: "Nothing indicates the child's needs have changed. The only relevant inquiry by the Family Court, therefore, is whether or not the father can comply. If the father can comply, he must do so; if not, then the Court may judicially set a smaller amount of temporary child support." *Id.* at 299-300, 368 S.E.2d at 215.

b. Defenses/excuses

The court must find willful contempt. *Curlee v. Howle*, 277 S.C. 377, 287 S.E.2d 115 (1982) (finding willful contempt for failing to return child after visitation). Further, the party may not be convicted of contempt for violation of a court order that "fails to tell him in definite terms what he must do." *Welchel v. Boyter*, 260 S.C. 418, 196 S.E.2d 496 (1963).

When the contemnor is unable to pay, he is not to be held in contempt. The Supreme Court stated in *Hicks v. Hicks*, 280 S.C. 378, 312 S.E.2d 598 (1984), that:

> It is generally recognized that where a contemnor is unable, without fault on his part, to obey an order of the court, he is not to be held in contempt. *Brooks v. Brooks*, 277 S.C. 322, 286 S.E.2d 669 (1982). A determination of contempt should be imposed sparingly

> and within sound discretion of the trial judge. *Jackson v. Jackson*, 241 S.C. 1, 126 S.E.2d 855 (1962). Yet, the trial court's determination is subject to reversal where it is based on a finding without evidentiary support. *Bearden v. Bearden*, 272 S.C. 378, 252 S.E.2d 128 (1979).

Id. at 381, 312 S.E.2d at 599. *Hicks* reversed a finding of contempt for one period during which the father had been unemployed but actively seeking employment, but it upheld a separate finding of contempt for failure to pay during another period of time.

The Supreme Court has indicated a preference that a parent's support obligation should be reduced rather than send the supporting parent to jail if the parent is unable to pay the amount ordered. In *Moseley v. Mosier*, 279 S.C. 348, 306 S.E.2d 624 (1983), the Supreme Court noted that the mother's cause of action was one based on contract. The Court wrote that if she prevailed and the husband was ordered to pay but did not, the trial court could hold him in contempt.

> On the other hand, if the court determines that respondent cannot comply with the agreement, it may judicially set a smaller amount of temporary child support. In those circumstances, we believe the child's best interests are met by setting a smaller amount than by sentencing the child's supporter for contempt.

Id. at 351-352, 306 S.E.2d at 626.

Contempt will not be found if the conduct of one parent prevents the other parent from complying with the support order. In *Garris v. McDuffie*, 288 S.C. 637, 344 S.E.2d 186 (Ct. App. 1986), the Court of Appeals relieved the husband of his responsibility under the order to pay $749.69 for the children's medical expenses because the mother had failed to supply the bills to him promptly, as required in the child support order. The mother's delay had prevented him from filing a timely claim with his health insurance carrier.

The defense of laches may apply if the parent seeking support arrearages waits an unreasonable period of time before seeking to enforce a support order.

South Carolina DSS, et al. v. Holden, 319 S.C. 72, 459 S.E.2d 846 (1995) (holding that the mother had justified her nine year delay in seeking to enforce the support order). For more discussion of this defense, see the section earlier in this chapter on jurisdiction: retroactive child support.

If the parties agree at the time of divorce that the custodial parent will not seek child support, the custodial parent may be estopped from seeking back child support for the period between the divorce and the filing of an action for child support if the noncustodial parent can establish the elements of equitable estoppel:

1. a lack of knowledge and the means of knowledge of truth as to the facts in question;

2. justifiable reliance upon the conduct of the party estopped; and

3. prejudicial change in the position of the party claiming estoppel.

Id. It is unlikely that these conditions will be met very often, if ever. The Supreme Court held that the mother in *Holden* was not equitably estopped from seeking child support and arrearages because (1) there was evidence that the mother consistently asked the father for child support since the divorce; (2) there is no evidence the father changed his position in reliance of the alleged agreement to not pay child support; and (3) the father was not prejudiced by the payment of arrearages which were set at only $25 per month.

The *Holden* Court did not discuss whether the children could be equitably estopped from seeking back child support by an agreement between their parents. Such a holding would seem inconsistent with other rulings of South Carolina courts. *Cf. Martin v. Ross*, 286 S.C. 43, 331 S.E.2d 785 (Ct. App. 1985) (holding that an agreement entered into upon divorce cannot prejudice the rights of children). The section on agreements contains additional discussion of this issue.

Although the "compulsion of circumstances" rule has not yet been applied in South Carolina, it might be under appropriate circumstances. In *Foster v. Foster*, 294 S.C. 373, 364 S.E.2d 753 (Ct. App. 1988), the father alleged that the mother had agreed to allow him to suspend child support payments while he paid down a loan.

The mother said he had agreed to transfer title to the house in exchange for letting him suspend child support payments, but he had reneged. The court noted that:

> Situations may arise in which equitable considerations may permit an obligor spouse to be given credit against support payments for voluntary expenditures made on behalf of a minor child. Such credit has been allowed in a number of cases under a theory termed a "compulsion of circumstances." Consent or agreement by the custodial spouse to accept certain alternative methods of discharge of a support obligation is one of the circumstances often giving rise to the application of this rule. This rule, however, has never been applied by the courts of this State.

Id. at 376, 364 S.E.2d at 754 (citation omitted). The court determined that the mother and children had been prejudiced while the husband had obtained an economic advantage. It refused to apply the "compulsion of circumstances" rule, recognized the validity of *Grout*, and ordered the father to pay the arrearages.

Voluntary payments of cash or gifts which do not conform to the terms of the support order will not be credited against arrearages and will not serve as a defense to a contempt action. In *Grout v. Alexander*, 260 S.C. 655, 197 S.E.2d 826 (1973), the Supreme Court required the father to abide by the terms of the support order. The fact that he had made some expenditures for the son, some of which were required by the order, some of which were not, did not excuse his failure to make required weekly payments to the mother. *See also Mixson v. Mixson*, 253 S.C. 436, 171 S.E.2d 581 (1969) (holding that a parent under a support order is required to pay the required amounts according to the terms of the order).

A pending appeal does not suspend an order to pay child support. S.C. Code Ann. § 20-7-2220 (Law. Co-op. 1976) provides in part: "[t]he pendency of an appeal or application therefore shall not suspend the order of the family court regarding a child . . . nor shall it suspend payments for support and maintenance of the wife and child." The court relied on Section 20-7-2220 in *Kirsch v. Kirsch*, 299 S.C. 201, 383 S.E.2d 254 (Ct. App. 1989), in holding that a parent's appeal does not automatically stay payment of college expenses (the case was remanded for consideration of the factors set forth in *Risinger v. Risinger*, 273 S.C. 36, 253 S.E.2d 652 (1979) and other cases).

Adoption of a child does not relieve the supporting parent's responsibility to pay arrearages which accrue before the child is adopted. *Napier v. Kilgore*, 284 S.C. 313, 326 S.E.2d 171 (Ct. App. 1985) (affirming judgment that the father had to pay arrearages which accrued before his former wife's second husband adopted their child).

An order granting temporary custody of a child to its maternal grandparents does not affect a parent's support obligation under an earlier order unless it specifically addresses the issue. *Henderson v. Puckett*, 316 S.C. 171, 447 S.E.2d 871 (Ct. App. 1994). A divorce decree dated April 11, 1978, granted the mother custody of the four year old daughter of the parties, with the requirement that the father pay child support in the sum of $40.00 per week. About one year later, the maternal grandparents filed an action for temporary custody of the child and were successful. The order changing custody did not mention child support. On November 10, 1992, the family court granted a petition by the clerk of court to restore the 1978 support case to the active roster on the ground that the mother had furnished a new address for husband. The trial court refused to hold him in contempt on the basis that the order for temporary custody superseded the prior support order. The Court of Appeals remanded, holding that a temporary order addressing only the issue of custody has no effect on a prior order for child support.

Child support obligations are ordinarily terminated by the death of the party making the payments or of the child. *Kennedy v. Kennedy*, 270 S.C. 358, 242 S.E.2d 417 (1978) (holding that an order for a father to pay alimony and child support and provide a home for his wife and children until she died or remarried or until the children reached majority did not affirmatively charge his estate with the affirmative responsibility of continuing these payments after his death). The language used by the Supreme Court suggests that an order which shows a clear intent on the part of the trial judge to bind the father's estate after his death might be effective.

The issue of contempt becomes moot when a person complies with the order for which he or she has been held in contempt. This precludes appellate review. *Jordan v. Harrison*, 303 S.C. 522, 402 S.E.2d 188 (Ct. App. 1991); *Frye v. Frye*, ___

S.C. ___, 448 S.E.2d 586 (Ct. App. 1994). In *Jordan*, the father lost one job due to dishonesty and found a lower paying job. He obtained a reduction in his child support from $150.00 per week (which he had originally agreed to pay) to $76.26 per week and the trial court held his $850 arrearage in abeyance. He subsequently fell behind and was held in contempt. On appeal, the court found that the issue was moot because he had paid the arrearage (although they also found that he had committed willful contempt). The court noted that the payment of a fine imposed for contempt would also moot the issue of contempt and waive the right of appellate review. The facts of *Frye* are substantially similar to those of *Jordan* and support the identical results.

c. Rule To Show Cause Issued By Clerk

Into the 1980's, contempt proceedings had to be initiated by the person who was entitled to the support payments. For many people this was an inadequate remedy because they did not have sufficient funds to hire an attorney or they did not want to create trouble with the supporting parent. Today, automatic enforcement of child support is provided for in Rule 24, SCRFC, for orders which require support payments to be made through the family court:

> (a) Determination of arrearage. Clerks of court shall review all child support accounts paid through the clerk of court. This review shall be conducted at least once a month. An account shall be considered in arrears if a scheduled payment has not been received when review is made, and at least five (5) working days have passed.
>
> (b) Rule to Show Cause and Affidavit. Whenever an account is in arrears, the clerk of court shall issue a rule to show cause and an affidavit identifying the order of the court which requires such payment to be made and the amount of arrears, directing the party in arrears to appear in court at a specific time and date. This rule shall have the same force and effect as a rule to show cause issued by a judge.

The need to comply fully with the requirements of this statute was demonstrated in *Brasington v. Shannon*, 288 S.C. 183, 341 S.E.2d 130 (1986), in which a finding of contempt was reversed because the affidavit supplied by the clerk of court did not identify the order or the manner in which it had been violated (see the first section of this chapter for additional discussion of this case).

2. INSURANCE OR OTHER SECURITY

The family court has the authority to require a supporting spouse to maintain life insurance or to provide other security to guarantee the payment of child support. However, the standard for determining if security should be required makes it unlikely that it can be justified in cases other than those being handled by the Child Support Enforcement Division of the Department of Social Services.

Federal law requires South Carolina to have procedures for requiring an absent parent (a parent not living in the same home as the child) to give security, post a bond, or give some other guarantee to secure payment of overdue support. 42 U.S.C. § 666(a)(6).

S.C. Code Ann. § 20-7-420(22) (Law. Co-op. 1976) authorizes the family court "to require a person ordered to support another to give security by a written undertaking that he will pay the sums ordered by the court for such support . . . ."

S.C. Code Ann. § 20-3-160 (Law. Co-op. 1976) provides that in any action for an absolute divorce or after the divorce is final, the family court may:

> Make such orders touching the care, custody and maintenance of the children of the marriage and what, if any, security shall be given for the same as from the circumstances of the parties and the nature of the case and the best spiritual as well as other interests of the children may be fit, equitable and just.

The standard for determining whether to require insurance to guarantee child support was stated in 1971 as requiring a showing that it was reasonably necessary. "In order, however, to justify a requirement that security be given, the record must show that it was reasonably necessary to assure compliance with the order of the court." *Fender v. Fender*, 256 S.C. 399, 406, 182 S.E.2d 755, 758 (1971) (relieving father of obligation to make regular savings account deposits for his son, but upholding a requirement imposed by the trial court that he was to maintain a life insurance policy with the child as the beneficiary for the purpose of assuring that funds would be available for college education if the father died).

This standard appears to have been stiffened in subsequent cases to require that it be based on "justice, equity and compelling reasons." *See Harlan v. Harlan*, 300 S.C. 537, 335 S.E.2d 366 (1985) (overturning the family court's order that the mother had to maintain a life insurance policy "until no child was receiving support or engaged in his or her college education" because the husband had sufficient resources to meet his obligation and the arrearages did not amount to enough to justify it. The court also noted that the court had ordered that the wife, not the child, should be the beneficiary.); *Ivey v. Ivey*, 286 S.C. 315, 334 S.E.2d 123 (Ct. App. 1985) (reversing an order requiring the child to be named as beneficiary of the father's life insurance policy because he had sufficient resources to meet his obligation).

The need for "compelling reasons" is affirmed as the appropriate standard in more recent cases: "[t]he law requires a compelling reason, amounting to necessity, before maintenance of life insurance will be required of the supporting spouse," *Shambley v. Shambley*, 296 S.C. 408, 409, 373 S.E.2d 689, 690 (Ct. App. 1988); "While the court may require a supporting parent to maintain life insurance for the benefit of a minor child, there must be a compelling reason to do so," *Mallett v. Mallett*, ___ S.C. ___, 473 S.E.2d 846 (Ct. App. 1996) (holding that it was improper to require insurance where the father had adequate income to support his support obligations and there was no indication that he had shunned his child support obligation in any way).

Under the "compelling circumstances" standard, it will be rare that a court can justify requiring insurance or other security to guarantee child support. Presumably, justifications would include a history of reluctance to comply with court orders, an unstable financial history, or other indications of a potential problem in actually having the money paid on time over a period of time.

3. INCOME WITHHOLDING

The most effective way to enforce a support obligation of someone who has a regular job is to garnish his or her wages, that is, to have the employer take it out of the person's check and send it directly to the family court.

Each state is required by federal law to have "income withholding" or garnishment statutes or lose certain federal funding. 42 U.S.C. § 666(a)(1), -(a)(8)(B), & -(b). South Carolina's income withholding statute is S.C. Code Ann. §§ 20-7-1315 to -1329 (Law. Co-op. Supp.). This withholding statute grants the family court authority to garnish the salaries (or other income) of anyone who is behind on their support payments.

The statute was amended in 1994 to provide that, as of January 3, 1994, income is subject to immediate withholding when a child support order is issued or modified, without waiting for an arrearage to accumulate. S.C. Code Ann. § 20-7-1315(C)(4) (Law. Co-op. Supp.). The statute provides that wages are not subject to withholding only if: "(a) one of the parties demonstrates and the court finds that there is good cause not to require immediate income withholding; or (b) a written agreement is reached between both parties which provides for an alternative arrangement." (Previously, income withholding could not be required unless child support payments were a month late.)

The income withholding legislation grants the family court authority to direct a person's employer (or other payor) to withhold from the person's monthly pay an amount equal to one month's regularly scheduled support payment, plus costs, and plus an additional amount toward any arrearage owed. S.C. Code Ann. § 20-7-1315(F)(2) (Law. Co-op. Supp.).

The amounts which may be withheld for both current payments and arrearages must not exceed the rather generous limits set forth by the Federal Consumer Credit Protection Act (15 U.S.C. § 1673(b)). An obligor (person whose wages are being garnished) may not be fired or otherwise subjected to job discrimination because of the withholding, and an employer who violates that prohibition may be civilly fined by the court. An employer may also be subject to contempt proceedings and civil suits by a wrongfully terminated employee and the person to whom payments were to be made.

Income withholding for health insurance premiums may be required. Subject to certain limitations, if a court requires a parent to provide and maintain health care coverage for a child, and the parent is eligible for family health coverage through an employer, the order must include a provision directing the employer to withhold an amount sufficient to pay the premiums for the coverage offered by the employer. S.C. Code Ann. §§ 20-7-1230 *et seq.* (Law. Co-op. Supp.).

An employer is required to comply with an income withholding order from another state "as if the order had been issued by a tribunal of this State" under a statute enacted in 1996. S.C. Code Ann. § 20-7-1125(A) (Law. Co-op. Supp.). All that is required is to mail two copies of the order to the employer by first class mail. There is no requirement to file a proceeding or register the order. S.C. Code Ann. § 20-7-1125(B) (Law. Co-op. Supp.). If the other state's withholding order appears regular on its face, the employer must: (1) give a copy of the order to the employee; (2) follow the procedure for withholding income as if the order was issued by a South Carolina court; and (3) distribute the funds as directed in the withholding order. S.C. Code Ann. § 20-7-1125(C) (Law. Co-op. Supp.). An obligor may object to the validity or enforcement or an income withholding order from another state by requesting a hearing in family court not later than twenty days after the first payment is withheld. S.C. Code Ann. § 20-7-1125(C) (Law. Co-op. Supp.).

There are two alternative procedures for enforcing income withholding orders from other states, although neither is as efficient as the process provided in S.C. Code Ann. § 20-7-1125 (Law. Co-op. Supp.). One option is to file the order and submit specified documentation to the appropriate South Carolina clerk of court. Upon receipt of the out-of-state order and the required documentation, the clerk of court must order wage garnishment without any further action by a South Carolina judge. S.C. Code Ann. §§ 20-7-1315 *et seq.* (Law. Co-op. Supp.). Once wage withholding is initiated, the obligor's rights with respect to an out-of-state order are limited under § 20-7-1323(b) to contesting the existence or amount of the arrearage. *Shinn v. Kreul*, 311 S.C. 94, 427 S.E.2d 695 (Ct. App. 1993) (reversing the family court's refusal to issue an order of income withholding for child support based on an Iowa order which modified child support, holding that no new personal jurisdiction was needed by the Iowa court to modify child support (the garnishee had ignored notice of the Iowa proceedings), and that, even if it had needed personal jurisdiction, sufficient contacts of the garnishee with Iowa existed for it to have exercised personal jurisdiction).

The second alternative enforcement procedure is to register the order pursuant to the Uniform Interstate Family Support Act. S.C. Code Ann. § 20-7-1130 *et seq.* (Law. Co-op. Supp.). See the discussion of this procedure in the section on interstate support orders earlier in this chapter.

4. LIENS AGAINST PROPERTY

When a child support arrearage occurs, a lien may be recorded, after notice to the obligor. Upon recording, the arrearage has the same force and effect as a judgment and it is cumulative to the extent of any and all past due support, until the arrearage is paid in full. S.C. Code Ann. § 20-7-1316 (Law. Co-op. Supp.).

The statute also provides that the arrearage lien is not dischargeable in bankruptcy, but that is a matter of federal law. Child and spousal support obligations are not dischargeable under bankruptcy laws. 11 U.S.C. § 523(5). Also, 42 U.S.C. § 565 provides that support obligations which are assigned to the state are not dischargeable in bankruptcy.

5. DSS CHILD SUPPORT ENFORCEMENT DIVISION CASES

a. In General

Some powerful enforcement tools are available to people who use the services of the Child Support Enforcement Division of the Department of Social Services (the Division) that are not available to clients of private lawyers.[38] This is

[38] Additional enforcement tools can be anticipated as South Carolina responds to federal mandates contained in the Personal Responsibility and Work Opportunity Reconciliation Act of 1996, Pub. L. No. 104-193, 110 Stat. 2105 (1996). The legislation calls for improving access to information

because federal legislation requires states to provide these weapons to state agencies which provide child support services using federal funds. Anyone is eligible to receive the services of the Division for a $1.00 application fee. Lawyers with clients who have or expect to have difficulty collecting child support should consider advising such clients to seek assistance from the Division.

b. License Revocation

If a defendant in a case being administered by the Division is more than sixty (60) days behind on child support payments, the Division must request licensing authorities to revoke any certificates or licenses held by the defendant, unless the defendant within ninety (90) days of receiving notice has paid the arrearages owed or has signed a consent agreement with the Division establishing a schedule for payment of the arrearage. Revocation is accomplished simply by giving notice to the licensing entity that the license should be revoked. S.C. Code Ann. §§ 20-7-940 through -948 (Law. Co-op. Supp.). "License" is defined very broadly to include any "authorization issued by a licensing entity that allows an individual or is required of an individual to engage in a business, occupation, or profession." This includes business licenses, teaching certificates, driving licenses, hunting licenses, and professional licenses, including medical licenses (licenses to practice law are excluded, since the South Carolina Supreme Court regulates the practice of law).

Upon revocation, a defendant may appeal the revocation, but is limited to contesting only two issues: whether he is the obligor and whether he is in compliance with the support order. The license will only be reissued when the defendant has either paid the arrearage in full or established a plan with the Division for the payment of the arrearage. S.C. Code Ann. § 20-7-945(G) (Law. Co-op. Supp.).

Applicants for licenses are required to provide their Social Security numbers. S.C. Code Ann. § 20-7-949 (Law. Co-op. Supp.).

---

about nonsupporting fathers, implementing procedures to make it easier to process masses of cases, and making enforcement more automatic and effective. The specific changes contemplated by the Act are discussed in Legler, "The Coming Revolution in Child Support Policy: Implications of the 1996 Welfare Act," 30 *Fam. L. Q.* 519 (Fall, 1996).

c. Federal and State Income Tax Refund Interception

Federal income tax refunds may be withheld for past due child support. 42 U.S.C. § 664. Such withholding is triggered by a report from the Division.

State income tax refunds may be pursued and withheld for past due child support and health care expenses. S.C. Code Ann. § 43-5-220 (Law. Co-op. Supp.). Such withholding is triggered by a request from the Division. The debt for past due child support must be at least sixty (60) days in arrears and must be in excess of twenty-five dollars ($25.00). Tax refunds can be intercepted even if the parent is making periodic payments toward the arrearage pursuant to a court order or even if the delinquent amount has been placed in abeyance by court order. S.C. Code Ann. § 43-5-220(j) (Law. Co-op. Supp.).

d. "Full Collection" by Internal Revenue Service

The Division may request assistance from the Internal Revenue Service (IRS) to enforce support obligations. 45 CFR § 303.71. This is a particularly effective tool against self-employed people who have assets. The effect of the process is the creation of a tax lien and treatment of the support judgment as an equivalent to back taxes owed to the federal government. Certified claims will be treated by the IRS as any other tax delinquency. "Full collection" assistance from the IRS is available where reasonable efforts have been made to collect the support owed and the arrearage is at least seven hundred and fifty dollars ($750.00).

e. Unemployment Insurance Benefits Interception

The Division is authorized to intercept unemployment insurance benefits if the recipient is behind on child support payments. S.C. Code Ann. § 20-7-1315(F)(11) (Law. Co-op. Supp.).

f. Employer New Hire Reporting Program

A New Hire Reporting System established by the Division in 1996 provides a means for employers to voluntarily assist in the state's efforts to locate parents who owe child support by reporting information each month concerning newly hired and rehired employees directly to the Division. S.C. Code Ann. § 20-7-1315(L) (Law. Co-op. Supp.).[39]

g. Mandatory Job Training or Public Service Employment in AFDC Cases

A noncustodial parent who is unemployed or underemployed, and who is the parent of a child receiving Aid to Families with Dependent Children benefits can be ordered to participate in an employment training program or public service employment. S.C. Code Ann. § 20-7-873 (Law. Co-op. Supp.).

h. Authority to Pursue Grandparents

The Division can seek support from grandparents of grandchildren born to unmarried minors under a statute enacted in 1995. S.C. Code Ann. § 20-7-936 (Law. Co-op. Supp.) provides:

> When a child is born to parents, either or both of whom are unmarried and under eighteen years of age, the Child Support Enforcement Division of the State Department of Social Services may pursue support and maintenance of that child from one or both of the child's maternal and paternal grandparents as long as the parent of the child is under eighteen years of age.

This legislation is particularly useful to the Department of Social Services when unmarried minors with children receive AFDC payments even though their parents are capable of contributing to the support of their grandchildren. However, the statute presents a number of issues to be resolved by the courts. It makes no exception for unmarried minors who are emancipated. The statute covers all child support cases in which assistance is sought from the Department of Social Services,

---

[39] It may be among the inherent powers of the family court to order a nonsupporting parent to get a job or to get a better job. It is clearly an option when the family court is asked to enforce a child support order from another state. S.C. Code Ann. § 20-7-1045(B)(10) (Law. Co-op. Supp.) (a tribunal of this state may "order the obligor to seek appropriate employment by specified methods").

not just those in which AFDC is being provided. The statute does not require a determination that the child's parents are unable to provide adequate support before grandparents can be pursued. It is also unclear whether the grandparent whose child is an adult who has a child with a minor can be pursued under this statute (the concluding phrase, "as long as the parent of the child is under eighteen years of age," could be interpreted to exclude grandparents of adult children or to allow them to be pursued as long as either parent is under eighteen).

i. Consumer Credit Reporting

The Division is required to provide consumer credit reporting agencies a monthly report of parents who are two months behind in their child support payments. This only applies to those support orders which are being enforced by the Division. S.C. Code Ann. § 43-5-585 (Law. Co-op. Supp.).

6. DENIAL OF FEDERAL LOANS

President Clinton signed an executive order on September 28, 1996, ordering federal agencies to deny government loans - such as small business loans, farm loans, home loans - to parents who owe past due child support. He also said the government will create a computer system to locate delinquent support obligors who receive federal payments and will deduct child support debts from fees paid to government consultants and vendors and from benefits paid to retired federal workers. "The Treasury Department estimates that some $800 million in payments go to these deadbeat parents," he stated.

K. ENFORCEMENT VIA CRIMINAL PROSECUTION

1. STATE LAW

Nonsupport of a spouse or a child is a criminal offense in South Carolina. S.C. Code Ann. § 20-7-90 (Law. Co-op 1976). However, prosecutions are rare because the family court's contempt powers can also produce a fine and a jail term, and it is easier to have someone held in contempt by the family court than it is to have them convicted of criminal nonsupport. However, the risk of criminal prosecution does exist and a brief mention of it in this chapter is warranted, although criminal law issues are beyond the scope of this work.

The circuit court has jurisdiction over criminal charges for nonsupport:

> (A) Any able-bodied person capable of earning a livelihood who shall, without just cause or excuse, abandon or fail to provide reasonable support to his or her spouse or to his or her minor unmarried legitimate or illegitimate child dependent on him or her shall be deemed guilty of a misdemeanor and upon conviction shall be imprisoned for a term of not exceeding one year or be fined not less than three hundred dollars nor more than one thousand five hundred dollars, or both, in the discretion of the circuit court. . . . As used in this section "reasonable support" means an amount of financial assistance which, when combined with the support the member is reasonably capable of providing for himself or herself, will provide a living standard for the member substantially equal to that of the person owing the duty to support. It includes both usual and unusual necessities.
>
> (B) Any person who fails to receive the support required by this section may petition to a circuit court of competent jurisdiction for a rule to show cause why the obligated person should not be required to provide such support and after proper service and hearing the circuit court shall in all appropriate cases order such support to be paid. Any such petition shall in all appropriate cases order such support to be paid. Any such petition shall specify the amount of support required. Compliance with the circuit court order shall bar prosecution under the provisions of subsection (A) of this section.

S.C. Code Ann. § 20-7-90 (Law. Co-op 1976).

The statute was substantially rewritten in 1979 to render it sex-neutral and to provide that payment under court order will bar prosecution for criminal nonsupport.

The section applies to spouses and to minor unmarried legitimate or illegitimate children who are dependent upon the person charged with nonsupport.

Although *State v. Hellams*, 209 S.C. 141, 39 S.E.2d 212 (1946), held that the defense of "just cause or excuse" was applicable in prosecutions for nonsupport of children as well as for nonsupport of spouses,[40] the continued validity of this ruling is doubtful given the modern handling of child support matters. *Hellams* was based in part on the common law notions that the husband had the absolute right to custody of his children and the clear impropriety of his wife's leaving him without just cause and keeping the children away from him. Although *Hellams* has not been specifically overruled, it has not been cited in any other South Carolina case since it was decided.

The Governor is authorized to demand the extradition from another state of an individual who is charged criminally in South Carolina with failing to provide support for a child. The Governor is also required to comply with extradition requests from other states in such cases. S.C. Code Ann. §§ 20-7-1160 *et seq.* (Law. Co-op. Supp.).

2. FEDERAL LAW

The Child Support Recovery Act of 1992 makes it a federal crime for a person to fail to pay a past due support obligation created by a court order to a child who resides in another state, if the support has remained unpaid for a period longer than one year or if the amount owed is greater than $5000. The penalty for a first offense is a fine or six months, or both; for a second or subsequent offense, the penalty is a fine or two years, or both. The court is also required to order restitution equal to the amount of child support owed at the time of sentencing. 18 U.S.C.§ 228.

---

[40] "The established law in this State Carolina is that where a husband is providing a home, and the necessaries of life therein for his wife and minor, unmarried children, and the wife without just cause or excuse leaves that home and takes such minor children with her, and without just cause or excuse refuses the husband the custody of the children, then the duty no longer devolves upon him to support either." *State v. Hellams*, 209 S.C. 141, 147, 39 S.E.2d 212, 215 (1946) (holding that the trial judge's charge deprived the husband of his defense that he had a just cause or excuse for not supporting his minor children).

The constitutionality of the Child Support Recovery Act (commonly known as the "deadbeat dad" statute) is being challenged around the country with differing results. Some courts are holding that Congress exceeded its power under the commerce clause. *Cf. United States v. Mussare*, 894 F.Supp. 1360 (D. Ariz, 1995); *U.S. v. Parker*, 911 F.Supp. 830 (E.D. Pa. 1995). Other courts are deciding that Congress did not exceed its power and the Act is constitutional, including the only court in the Fourth Circuit which has considered the question as of June 30, 1996. *Cf. United States v. Murphy*, 893 F.Supp. 614 (W.D. Va. 1995); *U.S. v. Sage*, 906 F.Supp. 84 (D. Ct. 1995), *aff'd* 92 F.3d 101 (2d Cir. 1996); *U.S. v. Sims*, ___ F.Supp. ___ (N.D. Okla. 1996).

CHAPTER THIRTEEN
ATTORNEYS' FEES AND LITIGATION EXPENSES

CHAPTER THIRTEEN
ATTORNEYS' FEES AND LITIGATION EXPENSES

A. IN GENERAL

The family court is authorized by a variety of statutes to award attorneys' fees and litigation expenses to either party, both *pendente lite* and permanently. If the client is unable to pay his or her own attorneys' fees and the other party has adequate assets, the client can seek temporary fees and expenses for work performed prior to the filing of marital litigation as well as the amount of projected fees and expenses needed to prepare the case for trial.

A helpful perspective on attorneys' fees is provided in *Anderson v. Tolbert*, ___ S.C. ___, 473 S.E.2d 456 (Ct. App. 1996).

> Ordinarily, unless otherwise provided by contract or statute, the responsibility of paying attorney fees falls upon the party contracting for the services. *Blumberg v. Nealco, Inc.*, 310 S.C. 492, 427 S.E.2d 659 (1993). At common law, a spouse had no right to recover attorney fees from an adversary spouse. *Collins v. Collins*, 239 S.C. 170, 122 S.E.2d 1 (1961); *Brunner v. Brunner*, 296 S.C. 60, 370 S.E.2d 614 (Ct. App. 1988). In this state, S.C. Code Ann. §§ 20-3-120 through 20-3-140 (1985 & Seep. 1995) provide for statutory entitlement to attorney fees from an adversary spouse in domestic litigation. In this connection, S.C. Code Ann. § 20-3-145 (1985) mandates that an award of attorney fees shall constitute a lien on the property of the person ordered to pay the fee. The fact that attorney fees and costs are provided for in the same statutory sections as alimony is not mere coincidence. The American legal system's practice of imposing a duty on a husband to pay his wife's attorney fees in marital litigation rests solely on the husband's duty to provide necessary support for his wife and children. Homer H. Clark, Jr., *The Law of Domestic Relations in the United States* § 17.2 (2d ed. 1987). Matrimonial litigation statutes require the husband to pay the wife's

> attorney fees for reasons similar to those underlying temporary alimony. *Id.* Historically, the prevailing view was that when a wife became involved in litigation, legal services were as necessary an element of her support as food and lodging. *Id.* It was not until *Orr v. Orr*, 440 U.S. 268 (1979) was decided that this obligation was made to apply to both spouses in order to satisfy the demands of the Fourteenth Amendment's Equal Protection Clause. *See Armaly v. Armaly*, 274 S.C. 560, 266 S.E.2d 68 (1980).

Id. at ___, 473 S.E.2d at 457.

The equitable principles the trial judge considers are the same for awarding either fees or expenses. These factors are described in appellate court opinions. *Glasscock v. Glasscock*, 304 S.C. 158, 403 S.E.2d 313 (1991), is the leading case. It makes it clear that, if a court decides to award attorneys' fees, the award is to be based on a reasonable number of hours billed at a reasonable hourly rate. Fees tied to the amount in controversy or the amount won for the client are not allowed in marital litigation. Attorneys seeking fees and expenses are required to offer sufficient evidence of their time and effort to support the award.

This is consistent with the S.C. Rules of Professional Conduct which provide in Rule 407 1.5(d)(1), SCACR:

> (d) A lawyer shall not enter into an arrangement for, charge, or collect:
>
> > (1) Any fee in a domestic relations matter, the amount of which is contingent upon the securing of a divorce or upon the amount of alimony or support, or property settlement in lieu thereof, provided that a lawyer may charge a contingency fee in collection of past due alimony or child support;

As indicated in the rule, the prohibition against contingency fees in domestic matters does not extend to actions to collect arrearages after the divorce is final. As discussed by Professor Robert Wilcox in *South Carolina Legal Ethics* (S.C. Bar-CLE

Division, 1992) at page 4-3, the rule barring contingency fees is intended to prevent inconsistency "with state interests in encouraging reconciliation and in providing fair support for families." However, "[s]ince those interests are less at stake once the divorce is final and the support amounts have been fixed, a lawyer hired to collect past due alimony or child support may charge a contingency fee." *Id.* The rule appears to prohibit contingency fees with respect to property settlements, even in actions to enforce post-divorce property settlements, but this is not totally clear.

A contingency fee may also be charged by a lawyer representing the parents of one spouse in an alimony dispute when the parents are defending their title to property against a claim that the asset is marital property of the divorcing couple. S.C. Ethics Advisory Opinion 93-13 (June, 1993).

Trial judges have a great deal of discretion in making awards of attorneys' fees. In many situations, it is difficult to predict whether the judge will award any fees. If the court does make an award, it is unlikely that the full amount of attorneys' fees or expenses will be awarded in most cases. However, it is difficult to predict how much a judge will award in a particular case.

B. JURISDICTION

1. AWARDING FEES AND EXPENSES

There is no shortage of statutes authorizing the award of attorneys' fees and litigation expenses. However, "[a]ttorney's fees are not recoverable unless authorized by contract or statute. *Hegler v. Gulf Ins. Co.*, 270 S.C. 548, 243 S.E.2d 443 (1978)." *South Carolina DSS v. Tharp*, 312 S.C. 243, 245, 439 S.E.2d 854, 856 (1994) (the holding is discussed below).

The general jurisdictional statute for the family court authorizes it to award attorneys' fees in one section and litigation expenses in another. Attorneys' fees are authorized in S.C. Code Ann. § 20-7-420(2) (Law. Co-op. 1976) which states that the family court has exclusive jurisdiction:

> To hear and determine actions: For divorce *a vinculo matrimonii*, separate support and maintenance legal separation, and in other marital litigation between the parties, and for settlement of all legal and equitable rights of the parties in the actions in and to the real and personal property of the marriage and attorney's fees, if requested by either party in the pleadings.

Litigation expenses are authorized in S.C. Code Ann. § 20-7-420(38) (Law. Co-op. Supp.) which states that the family court has exclusive jurisdiction:

> To hear and determine an action where either party in his or her complaint, answer, counterclaim, or motion for *pendente lite* relief prays for the allowance of suit money *pendente lite* and permanently. In this action the court shall allow a reasonable sum for the claim if it appears well-founded. Suit money, including attorney's fees, may be assessed for or against a party to an action brought in or subject to the jurisdiction of the family court. An award of temporary alimony or suit costs must not be stayed by appeal of the award.

The family court may also award fees and expenses incurred after the entry of judgment. S.C. Code Ann. § 20-3-130(H) (Law. Co-op. Supp.) provides:

> The court, from time to time after considering the financial resources and marital fault of both parties, may order one party to pay a reasonable amount to the other for attorney fees, expert fees, investigation fees, costs, and suit money incurred in maintaining an action for divorce from the bonds of matrimony, as well as in actions for separate maintenance and support, including sums for services rendered and costs incurred before the commencement of the proceeding and after entry of judgment, pendente lite, and permanently.

This includes fees and expenses for services rendered in the trial court as a result of a case being remanded on appeal. *Bowen & Smoot v. Plumlee*, 308 S.C. 325, 417 S.E.2d 855 (Ct. App. 1992) (affirming award of attorneys's fees incurred in connection with hearing on remand to trial court for determination of attorneys' fees incurred by the children of divorcing parents in defending unsuccessfully suit by attorneys for attorneys' fees as third party beneficiaries of their parents' divorce).

Statutes which contain more specific language about attorneys' fees prevail over the general provisions in section 20-7-420. For example, the Supreme Court held in *South Carolina DSS v. Tharp*, 312 S.C. 243, 439 S.E.2d 854 (1994), that the more specific provisions of S.C. Code Ann. § 15-77-300 (Law. Co-op. Supp.) prevail over the general provisions of section 20-7-420(8),[41] and it reversed the trial court's award of attorneys' fees against DSS.

Attorneys' fees may not be taxed as court costs against a state agency if the agency initiated the litigation and was the prevailing party. S.C. Code Ann. § 15-77-300 (Law. Co-op. Supp.) provides:

> In any civil action brought by the State, any political subdivision of the State or any party who is contesting state action, unless the prevailing party is the State or any political subdivision of the State, the court may allow the prevailing party to recover reasonable attorney's fees to be taxed as court costs against the appropriate agency if:
>
> (1) The court finds that the agency acted without substantial justification in pressing its claim against the party; and
>
> (2) The court finds that there are no special circumstances that would make the award of attorney's fees unjust.
>
> The provisions of this section do not apply to civil actions relating to the establishment of ... child support actions, except as otherwise provided for herein, and child abuse and neglect actions.[42]

---

[41] The reference in the Court's opinion to subsection 420(8) appears to be a typographical mistake because that particular subsection does not speak to attorneys' fees.

[42] As of March, 1994, a bill was pending in the South Carolina Legislature to delete the words "and child abuse and neglect actions."

The Supreme Court relied on this statute in reversing an attorneys' fees award against DSS in *South Carolina DSS v. Tharp*, 312 S.C. 243, 439 S.E.2d 844 (1994). DSS had successfully terminated the parental rights of the parents, and the family court had ordered DSS to pay their attorneys' fees and the fees of the guardian *ad litem* (GAL) who was appointed to represent the mother. The Court reversed the award of attorneys' fees. However, it upheld the award of GAL fees as authorized under § 20-7-420(37), citing *Dunn v. Dunn*, 298 S.C. 365, 380 S.E.2d 836 (1989) (holding that assessment of GAL fees against DSS is not limited to cases in which DSS is the losing party). The issue of taking was raised by the attorney appointed to represent the defendant mother in this termination of parental rights case. No taking was found, however, in that the attorney had entered the cause at a very late stage of the proceedings.

If attorneys' fees and litigation expenses are not requested in the pleadings, the court might be able to award them anyway, if the other party does not make a timely objection to the introduction of evidence about them. Both of the statutes quoted above specifically require attorneys' fees and costs to be requested in the pleadings. However, in *Sherman v. Sherman*, 307 S.C. 280, 414 S.E.2d 809 (Ct. App. 1992), the court allowed an award of costs to the wife to stand, although it had not been requested in the pleadings, because the husband did not object to the introduction of evidence of legal research costs or deposition costs.

The *Sherman* court relied on Rule 15(b), SCRCP, which says that "[w]hen issues not raised by the pleadings are tried by express or implied consent of the parties, they shall be treated in all respects as if they had been raised in the pleadings." The facts provided in the opinion suggest that the trial judge made the award *sua sponte* without a specific request in the pleadings or in open court. Apparently, the judge received the unobjected to introduction of evidence about costs and ordered the other party to pay them. In the absence of additional facts about the circumstances of this award, it takes a rather strained interpretation of Rule 15(a), SCRCP, to convert the failure to object to the introduction of evidence about costs into a trial by "implied consent" of matters not requested in the pleadings. This ruling also appears to be contrary to other appellate decisions about subject matter jurisdiction (see Chapter One on subject matter jurisdiction). However, practitioners should exercise caution in scrutinizing evidence that is submitted by opposing parties in support of attorneys' fees and costs.

A statement in a pretrial order that attorneys' fees sought by both parties will be considered at the merits hearing does not give the court jurisdiction to award attorneys' fees unless the parties have requested them in their pleadings. *Pool v. Pool*, ___ S.C. ___, 467 S.E.2d 753 (Ct. App. 1996) (affirming an award of attorneys' fees under the Frivolous Civil Proceedings Act although there was no proper request by the husband for attorneys' fees).

Attorneys' fees and litigation expenses are recoverable by either party regardless of which party instigates the action. In *Golden v. Gallardo*, 295 S.C. 393, 368 S.E.2d 684 (Ct. App. 1988), the court upheld an award of $3,136.05 in attorneys' fees and $4,655.36 in costs and expenses to a mother after her ex-husband brought suit to enforce his visitation rights and she counterclaimed for back child support. The court held that "[r]egardless of which party brought the action, attorney fees, costs and expenses are recoverable." *Id.* at 395, 368 S.E.2d at 685.

*Golden*also cites S.C. Code Ann. § 20-7-804 (Law. Co-op. 1976) to support its holding that the trial judge had the authority to require the father to pay travel and other necessary expenses for the mother and children. Section 804(c), "Appearance of parties and the child," states:

> If a party to the proceeding who is outside this State is directed to appear . . . or desires to appear personally before the court with or without the child, the court may require another party to pay to the clerk of the court travel and other necessary expenses of the party so appearing and of the child if this is just and proper under the circumstances.

Three additional statutes authorize attorneys' fees and litigation expenses. S.C. Code Ann. § 20-3-120 (Law. Co-op. 1976) relates specifically to divorce actions:

> In every divorce action from the bonds of matrimony either party may in his or her complaint or answer or by petition pray for the allowance to him or her of alimony and suit money and for the allowance of such alimony and suit money pendente lite. If such

> claim shall appear well-founded the court shall allow a reasonable sum therefor.

Although included in a statute dealing primarily with alimony, S.C. Code Ann. § 20-3-130(H) (Law. Co-op. Supp.) appears to provide fairly broad authorization to award attorneys' fees and litigation expenses:

> The court, from time to time after considering the financial resources and marital fault of both parties, may order one party to pay a reasonable amount to the other for attorney fees, expert fees, investigation fees, costs, and suit money incurred in maintaining an action for divorce from the bonds of matrimony, as well as in actions for separate maintenance and support, including sums for services rendered and costs incurred before the commencement of the proceeding and after entry of judgment, pendente lite, and permanently.

However, in *Brunner v. Brunner*, 296 S.C. 60, 370 S.E.2d 614 (Ct. App. 1988), the court limited attorneys' fees awards under S.C. Code Ann. § 20-3-130(H) (Law. Co-op. Supp.) to those actions related to divorce, separate maintenance and support, and alimony. The court in *Brunner* held that the ex-wife was not entitled to bring an action to recover attorneys' fees she paid while protecting her previous alimony and attorneys' fees awards in her ex-husband's bankruptcy proceedings.

Although S.C. Code Ann. § 20-3-140 (Law. Co-op. 1976) appears to have been designed primarily to provide for *pendente lite* litigation expenses in actions for separate support and maintenance, its language actually encompasses all forms of marital litigation: "In all actions for separate support and maintenance, legal separation, or other marital litigation between the parties, allowances of alimony and suit money *pendente lite* shall be made according to principles controlling such allowance and actions for divorce *a vinculo matrimonii*."

The family court cannot award attorneys' fees based on an action brought in another court. In *Burns v. Burns*, ___ S.C. ___, 448 S.E.2d 571 (Ct. App. 1994), the Court of Appeals ruled that the family court erred when it awarded attorneys' fees in a divorce case based in part on attorneys' fees expended by the wife for representation in the husband's bankruptcy proceeding.

Special provisions for attorneys' fees and expenses are contained in the Uniform Interstate Family Support Act (UIFSA).[43] Private counsel may be used to establish and enforce interstate child support obligations (S.C. Code Ann. § 20-7-1065 (Law. Co-op. Supp.) or assistance can be obtained from the Child Support Enforcement Division of the Department of Social Services (see the chapter on child support for more information about UIFSA and assistance provided by the Department of Social Services). Attorneys' fees may be awarded by the family court in UIFSA proceedings. If attorneys' fees are awarded, they may be ordered paid directly to the attorney and collected in the attorney's own name. S.C. Code Ann. § 20-7-1085(B) (Law. Co-op. Supp.). The court must award costs and attorneys' fees if it determines that a hearing was requested primarily for delay (in cases arising from requests to register foreign support orders, courts are required to presume that a hearing is requested primarily for delay if a registered support order is confirmed or enforced without change). S.C. Code Ann. § 20-7-1085(C) (Law. Co-op. Supp.).

2. FRIVOLOUS LITIGATION

If the family court concludes that marital litigation is frivolous, attorneys' fees may be awarded pursuant to the South Carolina Frivolous Civil Proceedings Sanctions Act, S.C. Code Ann. § 15-36-10, *et seq.* (Law. Co-op. Supp.).

If marital litigation is initiated before a client's claims have been investigated, attorneys' fees can be awarded to the defendant if the claims are not supported by the facts. In *Kilcawley v. Kilcawley*, 312 S.C. 425, 440 S.E.2d 892 (Ct. App. 1994), the Court of Appeals affirmed an award of attorneys' fees to a defendant when the defendant's former wife decided to dismiss her motion to vacate their divorce decree. The court found that the plaintiff's lawyer had filed the motion to reopen without conducting any investigation regarding his client's claims. Once the claims were

---

[43] South Carolina adopted the Uniform Interstate Family Support Act (UIFSA) in 1994 (S.C. Code Ann. §§ 20-7-960 through 20-7-1220 (Law. Co-op. Seep. 1996)). UIFSA replaces the Revised Uniform Reciprocal Enforcement of Support Act (RURESA) of 1984.

investigated, the plaintiff decided to dismiss her motion to reopen, but the defendant refused to consent to the dismissal unless the plaintiff paid him $1000 in attorneys' fees. The trial judge awarded the requested fees, relying on the Frivolous Civil Proceedings in Sanctions Act, which provides in section 15-36-10:

> Any person who takes part in the procurement, initiation, continuation, or defense of any civil proceeding is subject to being assessed for payment of all or a portion of the attorney's fees and court costs of the other party if:
>
> (1) he does so primarily for a purpose other than that of securing the proper discovery, joinder of parties, or adjudication of the claim upon which the proceedings are based; and
>
> (2) the proceedings have terminated in favor of the person seeking an assessment of the fees and costs.

As noted by the Court of Appeals, the act also states a person has acted with a proper purpose where the person reasonably believes the existence of the underlying facts of the claim and:

> (1) reasonably believes that under those facts his claim may be valid under the existing or developing law; or
>
> (2) relies upon the advice of counsel, sought in good faith and given under full disclosure of all facts within the knowledge and information which may be relevant to the cause of action; or
>
> (3) believes, as an attorney of record, in good faith that his procurement, initiation, continuation, or defense of a civil cause is not intended to merely harass or injure the other party.

S.C. Code Ann. § 15-36-20 (Law. Co-op. Supp.).

The Court of Appeals agreed with the trial court's finding that the plaintiff's "primary purpose for initiation this proceeding was 'other than that of securing proper adjudication of the claim,'" citing facts which tended to show that the plaintiff did not believe the existence of the underlying facts of the claim. *Kilcawley*, at 428, 440 S.E.2d at 894.

The Court of Appeals also reminded the bar of the significance of an attorney's signature on a pleading or motion under Rule 11 (a), SCACR: "The signature of an attorney constitutes a certificate by him that he has read the pleading, motion or other paper; that *to the best of his knowledge, information and belief there is good ground to support it*; and that it is not interposed for delay." *Kilcawley*, at 427, 440 S.E.2d at 893, nt. 2 (emphasis added by the Court of Appeals).

See also Pool v. Pool, ___ S.C. ___, 467 S.E.2d 753 (Ct. App. 1996) in which the Court of Appeals affirmed an award of attorneys' fees to the husband upon a finding that the wife's claim of physical abuse was frivolous pursuant to the South Carolina Frivolous Civil Proceedings Act, S.C. Code Ann. § 15-36-10 through -50 (Law. Co-op. Seep. 1994), although attorney's fees were not requested in the husband's pleadings.

The results in *Kilcawley* and *Pool* are consistent with the Court of Appeals' position before the enactment of the Frivolous Civil Proceedings Sanctions Act. In *Rish v. Rish*, 296 S.C. 14, 370 S.E.2d 102 (Ct. App. 1988), the Court of Appeals held that it is an abuse of discretion to deny a request for attorneys' fees and costs when a plaintiff brings a frivolous case. In *Rish*, the husband filed for divorce on the ground of one year's separation in spite of the fact that existing case law "clearly stands for the proposition that the husband in this case is not entitled to a divorce on the ground of one year separation." *Id.* at 16, 370 S.E.2d at 103-104. His wife was permanently hospitalized in a mental institution, with no income or property, and her family had to furnish the funds to hire an attorney on her behalf. The Court of Appeals denied the husband a divorce, and it stated that the trial court judge committed an abuse of discretion in failing to order the wife's attorneys' fees to be paid in full by the husband.

3. DISCRETION OF TRIAL JUDGE

In general, the awarding of attorneys' fees is left to the discretion of the trial judge and will not be disturbed absent abuse of that discretion. *See Smith v. Smith*, 308 S.C. 492, 419 S.E.2d 232 (Ct. App. 1992).

It is not clear how the appellate courts decide whether an abuse of discretion has occurred. *Johnson v. Johnson*, 296 S.C. 289, 304, 372 S.E.2d 107, 115 (Ct. App. 1988), explains that "a decision lacking a discernable reason is arbitrary and constitutes an abuse of discretion." Thus, family court orders which do not adequately address the factors to be considered in awarding fees and costs, or which otherwise fail to adequately explain their decisions, are subject to being reversed on appeal. In *Darden v. Witham*, 263 S.C. 183, 209 S.E.2d 42 (1974), the Supreme Court quoted from 5A C.J.S. *Appeal and Error* § 1583b (1958) when it wrote:

> A reviewing court is never justified in substituting its discretion for that of the trial court; in determining whether the lower court has abused its discretion, the question is not whether the reviewing court agrees with the court below, but, rather, whether it believes that a judicial mind, in view of the relevant rules of law applicable to the particular case and on due consideration of all the circumstances, could reasonably have reached the conclusion of the court below, of which complaint is made.

Id. at 194, 209 S.E.2d at 46.

A later court took a different view of the relevance of its disagreement with the court below. Former Chief Justice Littlejohn made the following observations in an opinion he wrote while sitting as a special judge with the Court of Appeals:

> It is not always easy to determine when and if a trial judge has abused his discretion. Overly simplified, abuse of discretion involves the extent of disagreement. When an appellate court is in agreement with a discretionary ruling or is only mildly in disagreement, it says that the trial judge did not abuse his discretion. On the other hand,

> when the appellate court is in substantial or violent disagreement, it says that there has been an abuse of discretion.

Rish v. Rish, 296 S.C. 14, 15-16, 370 S.E.2d 102, 103 (Ct. App. 1988).

The following cases illustrate some of the situations in which the family court has been held to have abused its discretion with respect to attorneys' fees and litigation expenses.

When a plaintiff brings a frivolous case, the responding party should receive fees and costs. In *Rish*, the husband filed for divorce on the ground of one year's separation in spite of the fact that existing case law "clearly stands for the proposition that the husband in this case is not entitled to a divorce on the ground of one year separation." *Id.* at 16, 370 S.E.2d at 103-104. His wife was permanently hospitalized in a mental institution, with no income or property, and her family had to furnish the funds to hire an attorney on her behalf. The Court of Appeals denied the husband a divorce, and it stated that the trial court judge committed an abuse of discretion in failing to order the wife's attorneys' fees to be paid in full by the husband.

In certain situations, it is an abuse of discretion to refuse to order one party to fully reimburse the other for litigation expenses and attorneys' fees. In *Johnson v. Johnson*, 296 S.C. 289, 303-304, 372 S.E.2d 107, 115 (Ct. App. 1988), there was no question about the husband's ability to pay, but the wife had no means to pay for the defense of the divorce action. (It would have reduced her marital property award by 15% to pay her attorneys' fees out of it.) The court found that Mr. Johnson had initiated the litigation, and his attempt to enforce an invalid antenuptial agreement had made it more difficult to defend. He also failed to furnish discovery information and to file a proper financial declaration, which further increased the time and expense of litigation for Mrs. Johnson. However, the trial court, without giving any reason to justify its action, did not award full fees. The Court of Appeals held that the court abused its discretion in awarding attorneys' fees in an amount less than actually incurred.

The Court of Appeals held as inadequate an attorneys' fees award of only $650 of the actual $4,200 incurred in a child custody case in *Johns v. Johns*, 309 S.C. 199, 420 S.E.2d 856 (Ct. App. 1992). Although the parents' common law marriage was found to be void, the court ruled that the mother was still entitled to $2,000 of the $4,200 incurred in keeping custody of the child. She was unemployed and had worked only temporary jobs since the birth of their child. She had developed osteoporosis in the ankles and legs following an accident, which made it difficult for her to obtain work. She was living in subsidized housing. Her attorneys' fees were incurred in defending the custody action brought by the father.

The court in *Marks v. Marks*, 281 S.C. 316, 315 S.E.2d 158 (Ct. App. 1984), found a fee award of $500 to be inadequate due to the time necessarily devoted to investigation, three different appearances at hearings and preparation of briefs, and the necessary expenditures in bringing the husband, child, and witnesses from West Virginia to South Carolina.

4. ENFORCING AWARDS OF FEES AND EXPENSES

Once an attorneys' fees award has been made, the family court is authorized to enforce it. Although it would seem to clearly be within the authority of any court to enforce its own orders, there is a specific statute on the issue of attorneys' fees. S.C. Code Ann. § 20-3-125, (Law. Co-op. 1976), "Petition to enforce award of attorney fee," states: "Any attorney whose client has been awarded an attorney fee by the family court may petition the family court for the circuit in which the order was filed to enforce the payment of such fee."

There is an additional statute which provides that attorneys' fees constitute liens on the estates of the people who have been ordered to pay them, but apparently only in divorce actions. S.C. Code Ann. § 20-3-145 (Law. Co-op. 1976), "Attorney fee to constitute lien; payment to estate." S.C. Code Ann. § 20-3-145 provides:

> In any divorce action any attorney fee awarded by the court shall constitute a lien on any property owned by the person ordered to pay the attorney fee and such attorney fee shall be paid to the estate of the person entitled to receive it under the order if such person dies during the pendency of the divorce action.

This statute only authorizes the filing of a lien where the family court actually makes an award of attorneys' fees. It does not authorize filing a lien against the client's or jointly owned property where the family court orders both parties to be responsible for their own attorneys' fees. *Huff v. Jennings*, 319 S.C. 143, 459 S.E.2d 886 (Ct. App. 1995). In this case, the court allowed the a former husband to sue his former wife's attorney for slander of title. The attorney had filed a lien for attorneys' fees on the marital house and lot following a divorce. The trial court had ordered that both parties be responsible for their own attorneys' fees. The husband elected to purchase the wife's interest in the property as allowed in the divorce decree, but he had to pay the attorney's lien before he could sell the property. The court held that the lawyer had improperly filed the lien. It allowed the husband's slander of title action to go forward on his allegation that the attorney knew or should have known she had no valid lien against the property and that filing the lien created a cloud on the husband's property.

The family court has no jurisdiction to resolve a fee dispute between an attorney and his client over matters based on a contract. *Elliott v. Green*, 274 S.C. 348, 263 S.E.2d 650 (1980), held that the family court judge did not have jurisdiction to decide attorneys' fees where the fee arises from legal representation which was independent of the divorce action.

The family court has no jurisdiction to enforce an award of attorneys' fees if an application for a resolution of disputed fees has been filed with the Resolution of Fee Disputes Board of the South Carolina Bar. In *Bailey v. Bailey*, 312 S.C. 454, 441 S.E.2d 325 (1994), the Supreme Court held that the filing of an application for resolution of disputed fees gives exclusive jurisdiction of the issue of attorneys' fees to the Resolution of Fee Disputes Board pursuant to Rule 9 of the Resolution of Fee Disputes Board and Rule 407, SCACR.

Bailey also addresses the issue of whether attorneys are real parties in interest in marital litigation in which a request has been made for one party to pay the other party's attorneys' fees. The Supreme Court concluded that attorneys are not real parties in interest and, therefore, have no standing to intervene in the litigation, at least where no award of attorneys' fees has been made. It is less clear whether an attorney would be allowed to intervene as a real party in interest once the trial court has ordered one party to pay the other's fees.

The facts of *Bailey* are fairly unique. The husband and wife had reached an agreement on all issues except attorneys' fees. The court issued a settlement agreement order which required the husband to pay a sum of money to the wife, in care of her attorneys, in satisfaction of any obligation by the husband for the wife's attorneys' fees. This was never paid. Subsequently, the wife dismissed her two attorneys and negotiated a new agreement with her husband without the attorneys' knowledge. The new agreement was approved by the family court without notice to the attorneys. It required the husband to pay the wife a smaller sum of money in satisfaction of all his marital obligations. The attorneys moved to intervene and to set aside the new agreement, claiming that they had interests which had been negatively affected by the new settlement. The trial court granted their motion to intervene and it set aside the order approving the new settlement agreement. The Supreme Court reversed, finding that the original order approving the settlement agreement did not instruct the husband to pay attorneys' fees, rather it contemplated the attorneys' serving as a mere conduit for the transmission of the money to the wife. The Court wrote:

> In this instance, the real interest lies with the parties in the divorce action - the appellants - and they alone have a real proprietary interest in the subject matter of the proceedings. We find that respondents' interest as claimants asserting a right to attorney fees is peripheral and not the real interest at stake. Therefore, we hold that respondents lack standing to intervene in appellants' lawsuit.

Bailey at, 441 S.E.2d at 327. As mentioned earlier, the Court does not squarely address the question of whether attorneys may intervene after one of the parties has been ordered to pay the other's attorneys' fees.

An attorney may not maintain an action for attorneys' fees against his client's children on the theory that they benefitted from a judgment awarding child support. It is not proper for an attorney to attempt to take part of the awarded child support to satisfy attorneys' fees incurred by the mother of the children. *Bowen v. Plumlee*, 308 S.C. 325, 391 S.E.2d 559 (1990). In this case the plaintiff's attorneys had represented the defendant's mother in several domestic and bankruptcy matters. When it became apparent that she might not pay the attorneys, they instituted an action against her children on the theory that the children had benefitted from the attorneys' services because they had received a judgment for child support.

A final award of attorneys' fees is stayed by an appeal, but a *pendente lite* award is not. *Woodside v. Woodside*, 290 S.C. 366, 350 S.E.2d 407 (Ct. App. 1986), held that Supreme Court Rule 41 § 1(A) applies to attorneys' fees in domestic cases; therefore, the husband could not be held in contempt for not paying them while the appeal was pending. The court found that "[h]istorically, in this state an order for attorney fees has not been treated as a judgment that can be executed upon until it has at least been settled on appeal. Until then it is more in the nature of a disbursement." *Id.* at 378-379, 350 S.E.2d at 414-415. An award of temporary suit costs, including attorneys' fees, is not stayed on appeal by virtue of S.C. Code Ann. § 20-7-420(38) (Law. Co-op. Supp.), which states, in part: "An award of temporary attorney's fees or suit costs must not be stayed by an appeal of the award."

C. ENTITLEMENT TO ATTORNEYS' FEES AND AMOUNT

1. IN GENERAL

The factors to be considered in determining whether and how much attorneys' fees are to be awarded were clarified by the Supreme Court in *Glasscock v. Glasscock*, 304 S.C. 158, 403 S.E.2d 313 (1991). The major point of *Glasscock* is that "a fee award must be based upon a reasonable hourly fee." *Id.* at 161, 403 S.E.2d at 315. Although they are not presented in the opinion as clearly as they might have been, the factors to be considered with respect to attorneys' fees are provided in *Glasscock*. In deciding whether to award any attorneys' fees, the court is to consider:

(1) the contingency of compensation,

(2) the beneficial results obtained,

(3) the abilities of the parties to pay,

(4) their respective financial conditions, and

(5) the effect of the attorneys' fees on each party's standard of living.

This list was repeated by the Supreme Court in *E.D.M. v. T.A.M.*, 307 S.C. 471, 475, 415 S.E.2d 812, 816 (1992), but without "contingency of compensation." This is probably a reflection of the fact that "contingency of compensation" simply duplicates "the abilities of the parties to pay" their own attorneys' fees (see the following discussion of this factor).

The Supreme Court has stated that two "essential" factors in determining whether to award attorneys' fees are "the beneficial result obtained" and "a party's ability to pay." *Sexton v. Sexton*, 310 S.C. 501, 427 S.E.2d 665 (1993). In *Sexton*, the Supreme Court reversed *Sexton v. Sexton*, 308 S.C. 37, 416 S.E.2d 649 (Ct. App. 1992), to the extent that it had affirmed the trial court's award of attorneys' fees. It gave three reasons: 1) some of the beneficial results obtained at trial had been lost on appeal; 2) the husband's earning capacity had not been determined; and 3) a portion of the fee was incurred in litigation with a third party. The Court cited *Glasscock* for the proposition that the two factors mentioned were "essential." One can probably assume that the Supreme Court considers all factors listed in *Glasscock* to be essential.

It is interesting to note that "quality of services rendered" is not listed as a factor. Apparently, this is to be measured primarily by reference to results obtained. However, the court in *Johnson v. Johnson*, 296 S.C. 289, 304, 372 S.E.2d 107, 115 (Ct. App. 1988), regarded the "excellence of [the wife's] attorney's work in briefing and presenting the case" as one of several important factors which called for a full awarding of attorneys' fees for the wife.

Attorneys' fees requested for time spent on witnesses who are not used may be disallowed. *Mallett v. Mallett*, ___ S.C. ___, 473 S.E.2d 804 (Ct. App. 1996). Although the court upheld the trial court's decision to disallow attorneys' fees and costs incurred on witnesses whose testimony was not used, it provided no reasoning behind its decision. It is difficult to imagine that the court intended to signal that attorneys' fees may only be recovered for work which is ultimately used in the trial of the case.

The court may also disallow an attorneys' fees request for two attorneys, when only one attorney is necessary. *Id.* "This court will not criticize a party for hiring more than one attorney, provided their work is not duplicated and the complexity of the case demands it. Except for the personalities involved here, we are not convinced the case otherwise demands the attention of two attorneys." *Id.* at ___, 473 S.E.2d at 812. It is not clear to what extent this factor affected the court's adjustment of the attorneys' fees award on appeal. Nor is it evident from the opinion why the complexity of the case is a relevant consideration if the attorneys' work is not duplicated. *See also Anderson v. Tolbert*, ___ S.C. ___, 473 S.E.2d 456 (Ct. App. 1996) (criticizing the wife's hiring of two attorneys at $300.00 and $200.00 per hour to handle a case which the Court did not consider complex).

A failure to make specific findings with respect to each factor does not require reversal of an attorneys' fees award if the record on appeal is sufficient to support the trial judge's award. *See Golden v. Gallardo*, 295 S.C. 393, 368 S.E.2d 684 (Ct. App. 1988), in which the record was sufficient due to the inclusion of affidavits concerning costs and fees.

However, a family court order which contains only vague estimations of the time and labor devoted to the case and the extent of the legal services rendered is not sufficient to support a large award of attorneys' fees. In *Johnson v. Johnson*, 288 S.C. 270, 341 S.E.2d 811 (Ct. App. 1986), the wife was ordered to pay half of her husband's $35,000 attorneys' fees. The order failed to set forth specific findings of fact concerning all of the appropriate factors: "it merely states that the hotly contested issues in this case demanded considerable time from Mrs. Johnson's attorney. The vague estimations of time and labor devoted to the case and extent of legal services rendered do not support an award of $35,000 in attorneys' fees." *Id.* at 278, 341 S.E.2d at 816. The Court of Appeals remanded the case for specific findings of fact.

One exception to the need to make specific findings with respect to each factor is when the court is awarding fees and costs for compensatory contempt, not as costs of litigation. *See Whetstone v. Whetstone*, 309 S.C. 227, 420 S.E.2d 877 (Ct. App. 1992). The husband complained on appeal that the trial judge should have allocated attorneys' fees according to the criteria listed in *Darden v. Witham*, 263 S.C. 183, 209 S.E.2d 42 (1974), overruled *sub nom.* in *Glasscock*. However, the court said: "The *Darden* case is not applicable here. In the *Darden* case, the judge awarded the wife attorney's fees as costs of the litigation. Here, the judge awarded the fees as reimbursement for Mr. Whetstone's contempt." *Id.* at 235, 420 S.E.2d at

881. The court continued to explain that compensatory contempt is money awarded to a party who is injured by a contemnor's action to restore the party to his original position. Here, the court only awarded the wife litigation fees and costs which had been incurred as a result of his refusal to obey prior court orders. Thus, it was unnecessary to consider the factors in *Glasscock* and other cases.

2. ENTITLEMENT FACTORS

a. Contingency of Compensation and Beneficial Results Obtained

"Contingency of compensation" relates to the issue of whether the attorney for one party would be paid if the other spouse is not ordered to pay attorneys' fees. "While 'contingency of compensation' is an appropriate factor considered in awarding attorneys' fees, the contingency to be considered is whether the party on whose behalf the services were rendered will be able to pay the attorneys' fee if an award is not made." *Glasscock v. Glasscock*, 304 S.C. 158, 161, 403 S.E.2d 313, 315 (1991). Thus, as mentioned earlier with regard to *E.D.M. v. T.A.M.*, this factor simply duplicates the "abilities of the parties to pay" factor.

Even when the court determines that both parties can afford to pay for their own attorneys it may still award attorneys' fees to one spouse, if it concludes that the other spouse was uncooperative and prolonged and hampered a final resolution of the case. *Anderson v. Tolbert*, ___ S.C. ___, 473 S.E.2d 456 (Ct. App. 1996) (affirming an award of attorneys' fees related to those hearings caused by the husband's misconduct, although the wife's income was larger than the husband's).

If one spouse receives sufficient assets to pay attorneys' fees from the equitable division of property, the family court is justified in denying that spouse's request for attorneys' fees. *Cannon v. Cannon*, ___ S.C. ___, 467 S.E.2d 132 (Ct. App. 1996) (affirming trial court's refusal to award attorneys' fees on the basis that the wife had received sufficient assets in the equitable distribution of property to provide her with funds to pay her own attorney's fees).

"The factor 'beneficial results obtained' merely aids in determining whether an award is appropriate when considering whether the services of a lawyer facilitated a favorable result." *Glasscock v. Glasscock*, 304 S.C. 158, 161, 403 S.E.2d 313, 315 (1991).

Contingency fees are not allowed in divorce cases. "Neither of these factors [contingency of compensation and beneficial results obtained] endorses the use of a percentage fee." *Id.* In case there was any doubt remaining, the Court stated: "We expressly disapprove any percentage fee agreement in a domestic case." *Id.* The facts in *Glasscock* are that an attorney claimed a fee of $150,000, justifying the amount in excess of his hourly rate as an allowable increase for the beneficial results accomplished for his client. The Supreme Court cited Rule 407(1.5)(d)(1), SCACR, which prohibits "any fee in a domestic relations matter, the payment or amount of which is contingent upon . . . the amount of alimony or support, or property settlement in lieu thereof. . .," and Rule 407(1.5)(d)(1), SCACR, which "expressly forbids a fee made proportionate to the amount recovered for the client." *Id.* The Court agreed with the husband that a domestic lawyer's fee may not be contingent upon the amount recovered on the client's behalf.

The prohibition against contingency fees does not extend to actions to collect arrearages after the divorce is final. Rule 407 1.5(d)(1), SCARC provides:

> (d) A lawyer shall not enter into an arrangement for, charge, or collect:
>
> > (1) Any fee in a domestic relations matter, the amount of which is contingent upon the securing of a divorce or upon the amount of alimony or support, or property settlement in lieu thereof, provided that a lawyer may charge a contingency fee in collection of past due alimony or child support;

As discussed by Professor Robert Wilcox in *South Carolina Legal Ethics* (S.C. Bar-CLE Division, 1992) at page 4-3, the rule barring contingency fees is intended to prevent inconsistency "with state interests in encouraging reconciliation and in providing fair support for families." However, "[s]ince those interests are less at stake once the divorce is final and the support amounts have been fixed, a lawyer hired to collect past due alimony or child support may charge a contingency fee." *Id.* The rule appears to prohibit contingency fees with respect to property settlements, even to enforce post-divorce property settlements, but this is not totally clear.

In *Glasscock*, the Supreme Court specifically overruled *Darden v. Witham*, 263 S.C. 183, 209 S.E.2d 42 (1974), to the extent that it is inconsistent with *Glasscock.* In *Darden*, the trial court had awarded $175,000 in attorneys' fees, justifying the award in part on the testimony of expert witnesses (other attorneys) who said that the appropriate amount of fees was in the range of $75,000 to $350,000. The Supreme Court approved the award, although Justices Littlejohn and Brailsford dissented in separate opinions because they thought the award was too high. Justice Littlejohn pointed out that the fee amounted to $233 per hour. Justice Brailsford noted that "the record brings conviction that this conception of the amount involved in the controversy and of the benefits resulting to Mrs. Witham dominated the evaluation of the expert witnesses and the court of the legal services furnished her." *Id.* at 197, 209 S.E.2d at 48. However, no member of the Court said that it was inappropriate to consider the benefits obtained in setting the fee award. This led to some confusion, which *Glasscock* ended by making it clear that beneficial results do not warrant charging a percentage fee.

However, obtaining beneficial results is an essential factor in determining whether to award attorneys' fees, and, if beneficial results at trial are lost on appeal, the attorneys' fee award will be reconsidered. *Epperly v. Epperly*, 312 S.C. 411, 440 S.E.2d 884 (1994) (holding that the reversal on appeal of beneficial results obtained for wife at trial necessitated remand to the family court for reconsideration of the attorneys' fees award). As mentioned earlier, in *Sexton v. Sexton*, 310 S.C. 501, 427 S.E.2d 665 (1993), the Supreme Court reversed *Sexton v. Sexton*, 308 S.C. 37, 416 S.E.2d 649 (Ct. App. 1992), to the extent that it had affirmed the trial court's award of attorneys' fees, in part because some of the beneficial results obtained at trial had been lost on appeal. "The beneficial result obtained by counsel is a factor essential to determining whether an attorney's fee should be awarded. Husband argues that this factor is now undetermined since the issues of alimony and equitable distribution have been remanded for reconsideration. We agree." *Id.* at 503, 427 S.E.2d at 666.

Some additional guidance about how to apply the "beneficial results obtained" factor is found in a landlord/tenant case, *Prevatte v. Asbury Arms*, 302 S.C. 413, 396 S.E.2d 642 (Ct. App. 1990). This case was a statutory action to recover a security deposit. The Court of Appeals relied on a family law case in describing the proper factors to consider in deciding whether to award attorneys' fees. It had this to say about the "beneficial results obtained" factor:

> If a party is not the primary prevailing party or prevails only partially, the factor of beneficial results accomplished will weigh in favor of reducing the fee, since the time and labor devoted to the issues he lost should not, in equity, be charged against the opposing party who prevailed on those issues.

Id. at 417, 396 S.E.2d at 644.

Where both parties prevail on some issues, the family court may still choose to award attorneys' fees. In *Golden v. Gallardo,* 295 S.C. 393, 368 S.E.2d 684 (Ct. App. 1988), the court upheld an award of $3,136.05 in attorneys' fees and $4,655.36 in costs and expenses to a mother after her ex-husband brought suit to enforce his visitation rights, and she counterclaimed for back child support. The father claimed that the award was an abuse of discretion given his success at trial in having his visitation rights enforced, but the court found that the mother had not asked to terminate his rights but only to restrict them, which she succeeded in doing.

b. Financial Situations of the Parties

Three factors can be grouped under the heading of "financial situations of the parties." These are: abilities of the parties to pay, the parties' respective financial conditions, and the effect of fees on the parties' standard of living. *Glasscock* at 161, 403 S.E.2d at 315, nt. 1.

If one spouse receives sufficient assets to pay attorneys' fees from the equitable division of property, the family court is justified in denying that spouse's request for attorneys' fees. *Cannon v. Cannon,* ___ S.C. ___, 467 S.E.2d 132 (Ct. App. 1996) (affirming trial court's refusal to award attorneys' fees on the basis that the wife had received sufficient assets in the equitable distribution of property to provide her with funds to pay her own attorney's fees).

The financial disparity between divorcing spouses was a consideration in *Nienow v. Nienow*, 268 S.C. 161, 232 S.E.2d 504 (1977). A master recommended $5,000 in attorneys' fees. The trial judge found that none were due. The Supreme Court ruled that attorneys' fees and costs may be awarded if the burden of paying the fees would otherwise decrease the spouse's standard of living, taking into consideration the standard of living to which the spouse had become accustomed. The Court held that for the wife to pay her own attorneys' fees and costs would be a burden which would "necessarily decrease her standard of living," and she was therefore entitled to have her fees and costs paid by her husband, who could afford to do so. *Id.* at 172, 232 S.E.2d at 510.

The Court of Appeals also cited the lowered standard of living which the wife would have to bear if she faced the burden of paying her own attorneys' fees and costs in *Johnson v. Johnson*, 296 S.C. 289, 372 S.E.2d 107 (Ct. App. 1988). The court held that, since the wife quit her job to marry the husband, he had total assets of $653,773, and her modest alimony award would be reduced by fifteen percent if she had to pay her own fees and costs, the husband should pay her full fees and costs. *Id.*

The court will also weigh the spouses' individual earning potential, using either their present salaries or their educational levels. In *Eckstein v. Eckstein*, 306 S.C. 167, 410 S.E.2d 578 (Ct. App. 1991), the court refused to award more than $1,000 to the wife where her potential earning power as an engineer with a master's degree was $2,8333.33 a month, which was more than her husband's income, despite the fact that she had won a divorce on the ground of post-separation adultery.

The court will not award fees merely on a claim of inability to pay fees, especially where the other spouse is equally or more unable to pay. In *Peirson v. Calhoun*, 308 S.C. 246, 417 S.E.2d 604 (Ct. App. 1992), the wife sought to recover attorneys' fees of $19,000 as well as costs by claiming she had limited resources. The trial court denied the request because both parties had incurred substantial fees and costs and the wife clearly had more available cash than the husband. *See also Miller v. Miller*, 280 S.C. 314, 313 S.E.2d 288 (1984) (holding that it was proper for the trial court to deny a spouse attorneys' fees where the only evidence of the spouses's inability to pay was the bare assertion of inability to pay the fees otherwise); *R.G.M. v. D.E.M.*, 306 S.C. 145, 410 S.E.2d 564 (Ct. App. 1991) (denying wife's request for attorneys' fees because the wife provided no reasons for not being able to pay fees). In *Anderson v. Anderson*, 282 S.C. 162, 164, 318 S.E.2d 506, 507 (1984), the Supreme Court ordered the fees awarded to two attorneys reduced from $73,500 to $48,500, and it cautioned the attorneys and parties that continued litigation was unnecessarily depleting the assets of both parties.

c. Misconduct of a Party

Attorneys' fees may be awarded on the basis on a party's misconduct irrespective of any other factors, if the other party is required to incur attorneys' fees due to uncooperative, unreasonable, and contumacious conduct which disrupts, prolongs, or hampers the resolution of issues in marital litigation. However, the fees awarded should reflect only those extra fees and costs caused by the misconduct, if attorneys' fees would not otherwise be awarded.

The Court of Appeals remanded for a determination of attorneys' fees on this basis in *Anderson v. Tolbert*, ___ S.C. ___, 473 S.E.2d 456 (Ct. App. 1996), although the wife earned more money than the husband and the beneficial results obtained were unclear. Specifically, the Court held that the wife was entitled to attorneys' fees related to proceedings to enforce valid court orders and to emergency hearings designed to protect her and the children. The Court acknowledged that it would not have otherwise approved an award of attorneys' fees to the wife, but it held that an adversary spouse should not be rewarded for misconduct and, in equity, the husband should be required to pay for the expenses his misconduct created.

3. AMOUNT FACTORS

In deciding how much to award, the court is to consider:

1. the reasonableness of the hourly rate (which shall be determined according to (a) the professional standing of the counsel; and (b) the customary legal fees for similar services), and

2. the reasonableness of the hours billed (which shall be determined according to (a) the nature, extent and difficulty of the case; and (b) the time necessarily devoted to the case).

Glasscock v. Glasscock, 304 S.C. 158, 161, 403 S.E.2d 313, 315 (1991).

a. Reasonableness of Hours Billed

The reasonableness of the number of hours billed is to be determined according to (1) the nature, extent and difficulty of the case, and (2) the time necessarily devoted to the case.

The existence of novel questions of law is a basis on which an increased amount of time can be justified. In *Donahue v. Donahue*, 299 S.C. 353, 384 S.E.2d 741 (1989), the Court characterized the case as a "complex divorce action involving several difficult issues, some of them novel in this jurisdiction." *Id.* at 304, 384 S.E.2d at 748.

An attorney can justify billing a higher number of hours if the case is particularly complex or difficult. The *Donahue* Court noted that the wife's attorney "faced difficulty and lack of cooperation from the husband, which serves as an additional basis for the award of attorneys' fees." *Id.* In *Johnson v. Johnson*, 296 S.C. 289, 372 S.E.2d 107 (Ct. App. 1988), the husband argued that Mrs. Johnson's attorney spent too many hours preparing her case and that the fee was therefore excessive. The court held that the thirty-five hours spent by the wife's attorney on the pretrial brief, as well as the thirteen hours spent in conference with the client and four hours in trial preparation, were all necessary, considering the complicated issues and the vigorous manner in which the husband contested every issue. *Id.* at 304, 372 S.E.2d at 115. The court found no evidence of inflated hours.

The concept that it is appropriate to award higher attorneys' fees when the losing party has vigorously litigated the case or otherwise caused the attorney for the prevailing side to spend extra time and energy preparing the case was reaffirmed in *Perry v. Perry*, 315 S.C. 373, 433 S.E.2d 911 (Ct. App. 1993). The wife complained about being ordered to pay $14,000 of the $19,500 in fees and costs incurred by her husband. The Court of Appeals affirmed the award, noting that the wife had forced her husband to prove her adultery and had made a meritless claim of physical cruelty, thus contributing to her husband's fees and costs. The court also noted that the most time-consuming issue was custody, on which the husband had prevailed, and that the husband alone had presented evidence on the issue of equitable distribution, thus incurring significant costs for such preparation.

b. Reasonableness of Hourly Rate

The reasonableness of the hourly rate is to be determined according to (1) the professional standing of counsel, and (2) the customary legal fees for such services.

This recognizes that an appropriate attorneys' fees award for legal services is ordinarily based on an hourly rate which reflects a particular attorney's professional standing, but it also recognizes that the total fees must be in line with the range of fees which can be justified for handling a case with particular characteristics.

"Customary legal fees" must be based on the number of hours worked on the case. In *Glasscock*, three expert witnesses testified at trial that a reasonable fee for the services rendered by the wife's attorney was in a range between $150,000 and $173,000. This was based on his obtaining over $1.6 million for his client. The trial court awarded $150,000. The Supreme Court found that an award of $51,998.75 was reasonable in light of the lawyer's hourly rates and the time he had spent on the case.

c. Sufficiency of Proof of Fees

In determining the amount of attorneys' fees to be awarded, the court must make findings about the reasonableness of the number of hours billed and the hourly rate. *Glasscock v. Glasscock*, 304 S.C. 158, 403 S.E.2d 313 (1991), established that the reasonableness of the hourly rate is to be determined according to the professional standing of the counsel and customary fees for similar services. *Id.* at 161, 403 S.E.2d at 315. The reasonableness of hours billed is to be determined by the nature, extent, and difficulty of the case, and the time necessarily devoted to the case. *Id.* Thus, evidence must be offered to support the court's ruling on these factors. The most common way to do this is for the attorney to submit an affidavit detailing the work done and the charges made. Affidavits from other attorneys attesting to the professional standing of the attorney and the reasonableness of the hours billed are also sometimes used, particularly to support large claims in complex or difficult case.

A properly documented attorneys' fees award will be upheld on appeal. In *Sexton v. Sexton*, 308 S.C. 37, 416 S.E.2d 649 (Ct. App. 1992), the Court of Appeals upheld the trial court's award of $9,000 of the $12,000 requested in attorneys' fees, stating:

> The attorney fee affidavit was submitted into the record without objection. The affidavit addresses most pertinent attorney fee factors. A detailed statement of time and charges is attached to the affidavit. . . . The husband now claims proper findings were not made, or if made, they lacked support in the evidence. We disagree. The record adequately supports the award.

Id. at 44, 416 S.E.2d at 654. (It should be noted that the award of attorneys' fees in *Sexton* was reversed by the Supreme Court on a writ of *certiorari*, and the issue was remanded to the trial court for reconsideration. *Sexton v. Sexton*, 310 S.C. 501, 427 S.E.2d 665 (1993). The Court specifically expressed no opinion whether $9,000 was an appropriate amount to award, and the reasons for the reversal were unrelated to the sufficiency of the proof of the fees.)

Even if the trial judge's order does not adequately address the appropriate factors, the appellate court can uphold the award if it was properly documented at trial and the documentation is included in the record on appeal. The court in *Golden v Gallardo*, 295 S.E.2d 393, 396, 368 S.E.2d 684, 685 (Ct. App. 1988), found that the trial judge did not comply with Family Court Rule 27(c), but it sustained the attorneys' fees on the record before it because the attorneys had submitted affidavits regarding costs and fees which were included in the appellate record.

Inadequate documentation may result in no fees being awarded at all. In *Strickland v. Strickland*, 297 S.C. 248, 376 S.E.2d 268 (1989), the Supreme Court found:

> The record does not support the award of attorney's fees. The only evidence introduced was an affidavit stating that more than 20

> hours had been spent on the preparation of the case. Therefore, the factors cited above could not have been considered by the court because of the lack of evidence.

Id. at 253, 376 S.E.2d at 270. The Court concluded that the trial court had no choice but to let each party pay for his or her own legal expenses.

The effect of failing to file an affidavit at the merits hearing is unclear. In *Green v. Green,* ___ S.C. ___, 465 S.E.2d 130 (Ct. App. 1995), the wife's attorney did not file an affidavit at the hearing, but asked the court for permission to file an affidavit within a reasonable time after the hearing. There was no affirmative response from the court. The attorney subsequently submitted an affidavit with a copy of the proposed order. In its final order, however, the trial court ruled that it was unable to consider the award of attorneys fees because neither party presented evidence as to the amount of fees incurred. The wife appealed this finding. The Court of Appeals did not decide this question. Rather, it affirmed the refusal to award attorneys' fees on the basis that the wife had received sufficient assets in the equitable distribution of property to provide her with funds to pay her own attorneys' fees. When this question is decided, one might predict that courts will not award attorneys' fees on the basis of affidavits filed after the merits hearing unless an opportunity is provided for opposing counsel to conduct an examination about the attorneys' fee request.

A nonrefundable retainer must be reported in the fees affidavit. *In re Anonymous Member of the Bar,* 310 S.C. 10, 451 S.E.2d 391 (1994). This private reprimand was issued when an attorney filed a fees affidavit in which he indicated that his client had not paid him any fees or costs when, in fact, her mother had given the attorney a $5000 non-refundable advance retainer fee. The Court concluded that the lawyer misrepresented to the court that he had not received any payment for his services. (Note: South Carolina courts have not yet ruled whether nonrefundable retainer agreements are permitted in divorce cases. Some other states do not allow them. The practice of asking for nonrefundable retainers would seen inconsistent with the factors listed in *Glasscock v. Glasscock*, 304 S.C. 158, 403 S.E.2d 313 (1991).

D. LITIGATION EXPENSES

Fairly broad authorization to award attorneys' fees and litigation expenses is provided in S.C. Code Ann. § 20-3-130(H) (Law. Co-op. Supp.):

> The court, from time to time after considering the financial resources and marital fault of both parties, may order one party to pay a reasonable amount to the other for attorney fees, expert fees, investigation fees, costs, and suit money incurred in maintaining an action for divorce from the bonds of matrimony, as well as in actions for separate maintenance and support, including sums for services rendered and costs incurred before the commencement of the proceeding and after entry of judgment, pendente lite, and permanently.

The same considerations that apply to awarding attorneys' fees also apply to awarding litigation expenses. *Nienow v. Nienow*, 268 S.C. 161, 173, 232 S.E.2d 504, 510 (1977), established the general rule that "[t]he same equitable considerations apply to the issue of the costs of this action" as to the attorneys' fees. As indicated by the language quoted above, almost any reasonable expense can be claimed.

Reimbursable expenses include the reasonable and necessary expenses incurred in obtaining evidence of a spouse's infidelity. *See Stevenson v. Stevenson*, 295 S.C. 412, 368 S.E.2d 901 (1988), in which the wife disputed this expense, claiming that proof of her adultery was unnecessary because she had admitted it. However, because she had refused to admit the adultery until she took the stand, the court held that she should reimburse her husband for investigator fees.

Travel expenses may be claimed when a parent must travel a distance to protect visitation or custody rights. S.C. Code Ann. § 20-7-804(c), "Appearance of parties and the child," provides that:

> [I]f a party to the proceeding who is outside this State is directed to appear . . . or desires to appear personally before the court with or without the child, the court may require another party to pay to the clerk of the court travel and other necessary expenses of the

party so appearing and of the child if this is just and proper under the circumstances.

In *Ingold v. Ingold*, 304 S.C. 316, 404 S.E.2d 35 (Ct. App. 1991), the father, who lived in California, was forced to travel to South Carolina in order to protect his Christmas and summer custody of his daughter. The court upheld his custody rights and found that the mother, who had filed a complaint to modify the custody agreement, owed the father some reimbursement of attorneys' fees, travel expenses and costs to be decided by the trial court on remand. *See also Golden v. Gallardo*, 295 S.C. 393, 396, 368 S.E.2d 684, 685 (Ct. App. 1988), in which the father brought suit to enforce his visitation rights and the mother countered for child support arrearage. Each won a partial victory: she received back support and reduced visitation, and he was able to enforce his (reduced) visitation rights. Although remanded for further findings of fact, the mother's award of expenses due to traveling from New Mexico to South Carolina was upheld. The court did not penalize her for denying the father visitation because of his arrearage, and the court did not accept the father's argument that she could have filed suit for support rather than wait for him to file for visitation.

Expert witness fees are also recoverable. *Peirson v. Calhoun*, 308 S.C. 246, 255, 417 S.E.2d 604, 609 (Ct. App. 1992), held that the wife, although not at fault in the divorce (her husband's drinking was to blame), was still responsible for paying $400 to her husband's expert witness, whom she had deposed twice. The Court states that the family court has the authority to order payment of the fee under Rule 26(b)(4)(c), SCRCP: "the court may require the party seeking discovery to pay the other party a fair portion of the fees and expenses reasonably incurred by the latter party in obtaining facts and opinions from the expert."

E. INTEREST ON FEES

Attorneys' fees awards are "money decrees" or "judgments of courts" which draw interest under S.C. Code Ann. § 34-31-20(B) (Law. Co-op. 1976) which reads, "[a]ll money decrees and judgments of courts enrolled or entered shall draw interest according to law. The legal interest shall be the rate of fourteen percent per annum." *Christy v. Christy*, 317 S.C. 145, 452 S.E.2d 1 (Ct. App. 1994). The Court of

Appeals saw no reason to distinguish an award of attorneys' fees from a fixed equitable distribution award, and it held that interest on the attorneys' fee award was due for the time the case was on appeal.

CHAPTER FOURTEEN
AGREEMENTS

CHAPTER FOURTEEN
AGREEMENTS[44]

A. IN GENERAL

Agreements between husbands and wives are as common as marriage itself. For the most part, the law plays no role in marital agreements unless they violate criminal laws or public policy, were entered fraudulently, or are contrary to the best interests of the parties' children. The state has been described as a "silent but not by any means an inactive third party." *Fogel v. McDonald*, 159 S.C. 506, 512, 157 S.E. 831, 833 (1931). Questions of law become involved ordinarily only when one or both spouses wish either to formalize or enforce their agreements — that is, when there is a need to determine whether the parties have established valid, enforceable contracts.

The family court practitioner must pay particular attention to the subject matter jurisdiction of the family court, for it does not have authority to decide issues arising from all contracts between spouses, only certain ones. Once subject matter jurisdiction is established, the general rules of contract interpretation apply for the most part, but there are some special considerations to take into account in determining the validity and enforceability of agreements between spouses.

B. JURISDICTION

1. IN GENERAL

The family court does not have jurisdiction over all agreements between married people. For example, the family court lacks subject matter jurisdiction to

---

[44] Special procedures and rules governing agreements about paternity and child support between parents and the Child Support Enforcement Division of DSS are discussed in the chapters on paternity and child support, respectively.

decide general contractual disputes between spouses or former spouses unless they are incident to marital litigation or otherwise specifically authorized by legislation.

Public policy considerations may invalidate some agreements. There are certain incidents to marriage that "are deemed so important to its preservation and stability until any agreement which has the effect of materially varying or altering them, as a condition of the relationship, is ordinarily considered against public policy and, therefore, void." *Towles v. Towles*, 256 S.C. 307, 311, 182 S.E.2d 53, 54 (1971). In *Towles*, a divorce action was withdrawn, and the reconciliation agreement provided that the wife would never bring an action against her husband again. This was held to be against public policy and void, because it was so broad that it would have released the husband from one of his basic obligations as a husband: the duty to support his wife.

The family court can review agreements related to spousal support at any time.

> The Family Court may review and approve all agreements which bear on the issue of alimony or separate maintenance and support, whether brought before the court in actions for divorce from the bonds of matrimony, separate maintenance and support actions, or in actions to approve agreement [sic] where the parties are living separate and apart. The failure to seek a divorce, separate maintenance, or a legal separation[45] does not deprive the court of its authority and jurisdiction to approve and enforce the agreements. . . .

S.C. Code Ann. § 20-3-130(G) (Law. Co-op. 1976). However, the court does not have jurisdiction to review an agreement about spousal support, if the agreement clearly indicates that it is not subject to the jurisdiction of the family court. *Ratchford v. Ratchford*, 295 S.C. 297, 253 S.E.2d 652 (Ct. App. 1988).

---

[45] Despite its inclusion in the statute, there is no cause of action in South Carolina for a "legal separation."

The family court can also review agreements relating to child support and custody at any time, and the parties cannot divest the family court of this power. *Treadaway v. Smith*, Op. No. 2600 (filed Dec. 9, 1996)(Davis Adv. Sh. No. 33 at 23) (holding that the circuit court, not the family court, had jurisdiction to enforce a father's agreement to pay for college expenses because the agreement was not one to pay child support because he took on a greater obligation than imposed by law); *Ratchford v. Ratchford*, 295 S.C. 297, 253 S.E.2d 652 (Ct. App. 1988) (holding that the family court retains jurisdiction over child support irregardless of any agreement between the parties); *Sattler v. Sattler*, 284 S.C. 422, 423, 327 S.E.2d 71, 71 (1985) (holding that the family court had jurisdiction to modify child support and custody, notwithstanding the parties' agreement); *Moseley v. Mosier*, 279 S.C. 348, 306 S.E.2d 624 (1983) (reaffirming the principle that, despite the broad range of issues that may be agreed to or waived, the family court always has continuing jurisdiction as to issues affecting the interests of children).

The family court does not have jurisdiction to equitably apportion property that has been designated as nonmarital in a property settlement agreement:

> The term "marital property" as used in this article means all real and personal property which has been acquired by the parties during the marriage and which is owned as of the date of filing or commencement of marital litigation as provided in § 20-7-472 regardless of how legal title is held, except the following, which constitute nonmarital property:
>
> . . .
>
> (4) property excluded by written contract of the parties. "Written contract" includes any antenuptial agreement of the parties which must be considered presumptively fair and equitable so long as it was voluntarily executed with both parties separately represented by counsel and pursuant to the full financial disclosure to each other that is mandated by the rules of the family court as to income, debts, and assets . . . .

> The court does not have jurisdiction or authority to apportion nonmarital property.

S.C. Code Ann. § 20-7-473 (Law. Co-op. Supp.). Proposed legislation to enact the Uniform Premarital Agreement Act is discussed in the section of this chapter on premarital agreements.

If an agreement encompasses either real or personal property issues, attention must be given to S.C. Code Ann. § 20-5-50 (Law. Co-op. 1976). This is an older statute enacted to deal with issues related to marriage contracts, not agreements between spouses in general. However, it is still in the Code and its language is broad enough to encompass all settlement agreements. None of the cases dealing with marital agreements refer to it; therefore, its applicability is doubtful, but not certain. The statute requires specific documentation on penalty of declaring the marriage contract, deed or settlement null and void with respect to creditors and bona fide purchasers or mortgagees:

> All marriage contracts, deeds and settlements shall therein describe, specify and particularize the real and personal estate thereby intended to be included, comprehended, conveyed and passed or shall have a schedule thereto annexed containing a description and the particulars and articles of the real and personal estate intended to be conveyed and passed by such marriage contracts, deeds and settlements. Any such schedule shall be annexed to the contracts, deed or other settlement paper, signed, executed and delivered by the parties therein interested at the time of the signing, executing and delivering the marriage contract, deed or settlement, be subscribed by the same witness who subscribed the marriage contract, deed or settlement and be recorded therewith; otherwise, and in default of such schedule and recording thereof as aforesaid, the marriage contract, deed or settlement shall be deemed and declared to be fraudulent, null and void with respect to and against creditors and bona fide purchasers or mortgagees.

2. CONSIDERATION OF AGREEMENTS DURING MARITAL LITIGATION

If either party to marital litigation asks the family court to consider an agreement that is relevant to issues pending before the court, the family court should exercise jurisdiction over the agreement and consider it. *Funderburk v. Funderburk*, 286 S.C. 129, 332 S.E.2d 205 (1985) (citing S.C. Code Ann. § 20-7-420 (Law. Co-op. 1976) for the proposition that the family court is required to assert jurisdiction over an agreement which one party claimed was unfair and the other wanted upheld).

The factors to be used by the court in determining the validity of agreements are discussed later in this chapter.

3. POST DIVORCE MODIFICATION OR ENFORCEMENT

The family court's jurisdiction to modify or enforce agreements depends in part on what subjects are covered in the agreements. For example, property settlement agreements are generally not modifiable. Therefore, the sections about jurisdiction in other relevant chapters should also be read.

In *Moseley v. Mosier*, 279 S.C. 348, 306 S.E.2d 624 (1983), the Supreme Court went a considerable distance in clarifying the state of the law with regard to the enforcement and modification of marital agreements. Because of the importance of the *Moseley* decision, this section is divided into two subparts: pre-*Moseley* and post-*Moseley*.

a. Pre-*Moseley*

The family court does not have jurisdiction to enforce or modify agreements that were executed before *Moseley* was decided on August 30, 1983, unless they were "merged" into the family court's order. The distinction between "incorporation" and "merger" remains significant for such orders.

"Incorporation" means that, although an agreement is referenced by the decree, it retains its separate identity and is litigated as a separate contract, probably not in the family court. *Bryant v. Varat*, 278 S.C. 77, 292 S.E.2d 298 (1982). Before *Moseley*, if an agreement was merely incorporated but not merged, the family court had no continuing subject matter jurisdiction except as to child support. *Kelly v. Edwards*, 276 S.C. 368, 278 S.E.2d 773 (1981).

Prior to *Moseley*, "incorporation" occurred where the terms of the agreement specifically stated that the agreement should not become merged in the decree but should survive the decree. In *Kelly v. Edwards*, 276 S.C. 368, 278 S.E.2d 773 (1981), the Supreme Court held that the family court did not have subject matter jurisdiction over an agreement that was incorporated but not merged into the court's order. Despite the fact that the contractual provision at issue was to pay child support, the court held that "the issue of child support was not before the family court, only the interpretation of the contract." *Id.* at 370, 278 S.E.2d at 774. *See also Zwerling v. Zwerling*, 273 S.C. 292, 255 S.E.2d 850 (1979) (holding that there was no subject matter jurisdiction in the family court over an agreement that was neither incorporated nor merged into a divorce decree from another state (New York). The court explained that "any obligation arising under the agreement would be a contractual obligation and would be enforceable only by resort to ordinary contract remedies." *Id.* at 295, 255 S.E.2d at 852).

"Merger," on the other hand, means that an agreement loses its separate identity and the decree alone is subject to further litigation, with jurisdiction continuing in the family court. Whether an agreement was incorporated or merged often turned on the court's interpretation of the parties' intent.

It can be difficult to determine whether "merger" has occurred, however. In *Jeanes v. Jeanes*, 255 S.C. 161, 162, 177 S.E.2d 537, 537 (1970), the parties were granted a divorce, and although the decree "relieved the husband of any obligation for the support and maintenance of the wife," it left the division of the property to be decided by the parties and their attorneys. An agreement was reached calling for the husband to pay the wife $75.00 per month support and maintenance which would end upon the wife's death or remarriage. A supplemental order was issued containing the terms of the parties' agreement. The husband sought to have this modified, successfully claiming that his former wife had entered a common law marriage. The Court held that "[t]he agreement of the parties here as to alimony became merged in the supplemental decree and, therefore, lost its contractual nature, at least to the extent that the court has the power to modify the decree, if such modification be warranted." *Id.* at 164, 177 S.E.2d at 538. Although the Court held that merger had occurred, it did not give any analysis as to why it reached that conclusion.

Evidence of an intention to merge an agreement into the decree was found to exist where the terms of the agreement included language to the effect that the judicial decree would "embody the substance" of the agreement and "adjudge" the obligations of the parties. *Ex parte Jeter*, 193 S.C. 278, 8 S.E.2d 490 (1940). The decree in *Jeter* contained the following language:

> The said written agreement is hereby confirmed and is adjudged to be fully binding and enforceable against each of the parties herein insofar as it applies to each of them respectively, and the same is hereby made a part of this decree and judgment, with the same force and effect as though it were incorporated verbatim.

Id. at 281, 8 S.E.2d at 491. The Supreme Court held that the "agreement of the parties becomes merged in the decree, and therefore loses its contractual nature, at least to the extent that the Court has the power to modify the decree when changed circumstances so justify." *Id.* at 285, 8 S.E.2d at 493.

These pre-*Moseley* rules continue to apply, if the agreement was executed prior to *Moseley*. *See Treadaway v. Smith*, Op. No. 2600 (filed Dec. 9, 1996)(Davis Adv. Sh. No. 33 at 23) (finding that the circuit court had jurisdiction to enforce a pre-*Moseley* separation agreement because the document clearly indicated that the intent of the parties was that the agreement would not be merged into the divorce decree, but would remain contractual and survive incorporation); *Austelle v. Austelle*, 294 S.C. 19, 21, 362 S.E.2d 181, 183 (1987) (holding that the parties intended to withhold from the court the authority to determine the rights and obligations created by their agreement; therefore, the agreement retained its separate contractual nature, and it could not be enforced in the family court); *Roberts v. Roberts*, 293 S.C. 439, 361 S.E.2d 341 (Ct. App. 1987) (holding that the family court lacked subject matter jurisdiction to decide issues related to a property settlement agreement that was neither incorporated nor merged into the divorce decree and that the proper forum for deciding disputes related to such agreements is the circuit court); *Coble v. Coble*, 293 S.C. 434, 361 S.E.2d 339 (1987) (distinguishing "approval" from "adoption" and holding that a pre-*Moseley* agreement could not be enforced in the family court, although "[t]he family court found the agreement fair and equitable and 'approved' it" during the divorce proceedings).

b. Post-*Moseley*

The family court has broader jurisdiction to enforce or modify agreements that were executed after August 30, 1983. On that date, the Supreme Court addressed three important aspects of marital agreements in *Moseley v. Mosier*, 279 S.C. 348, 306 S.E.2d 624 (1983).

First, the Supreme Court held that "jurisdiction for all domestic matters, whether by decree or by agreement, will vest in the family court." *Id.* at 353, 306 S.E.2d at 627. Parties can still divest the family court of jurisdiction to review agreements that are not related to child custody or child support by clearly indicating this intent in their agreements. *Cf. Austelle v. Austelle*, 294 S.C. 19, 21, 362 S.E.2d 181, 183 (1987). However, once an agreement is submitted for review by the family court and approved, the family court has exclusive jurisdiction, even after a divorce action has ended, to determine whether to enforce or modify its terms. *Terry v. Lee*, 308 S.C. 459, 419 S.E.2d 213 (1992) (holding that the family court had exclusive jurisdiction to decide whether to divide retirement benefits where the action was grounded upon a property settlement agreement that was incorporated into the divorce decree).

Second, the *Moseley* court held agreements about property and alimony will not be enforceable in the family court until they have been approved by the family court. The court overruled cases turning on the use of words of art. In *Moseley*, a separation agreement was incorporated but not merged into the decree. In finding that the family court had jurisdiction to settle a dispute about the agreement, the Supreme Court said:

> Words of art such as "ratified," "adopted," "approved," "incorporated and merged" and "incorporation without merger" consistently have confused attorneys, judges and laymen in this state.
>
> . . .

> The parties' intent is rarely revealed from the agreement's words of art. Generally, those terms are used without intending or implying any particular legal consequences. Later, courts impose the consequences upon the unsuspecting parties. Today we overrule those cases which hold that words of art make a major distinction in the operation of divorce law. . . . In all decrees entered after their [sic] decision, the parties may contract concerning their property settlement and alimony, but the submitted agreement must be approved by the family court.

Id. at 352-353, 306 S.E.2d at 626-27.

Third, the Supreme Court held that parties can limit the jurisdiction of the family court to modify or enforce their alimony and property settlement agreements, if the family court approves such limitations. An approved agreement "unambiguously stipulating that the terms may not be enforced by contempt and/or that they may not be altered, binds the court, as well as the parties, to those terms." *Moseley v. Mosier*, 279 S.C. 348, 353, 306 S.E.2d 624, 627 (1983).

> The parties may specifically agree that the amount of alimony may not ever be modified by the court; they may contract out of any continuing judicial supervision of their relationship by the court; they may agree that the periodic payments or alimony stated in the decree shall be judicially awarded, enforceable by contempt, but not modifiable by the court; they may agree to any terms they wish as long as the court deems the contract to have been entered fairly, voluntarily and reasonably. With the court's approval, the terms become a part of the decree and are binding on the parties and the court. However, unless the agreement unambiguously denies the court jurisdiction, the terms will be modifiable by the court and enforceable by contempt.

Id. at 352-353, 306 S.E.2d at 626-627.

Any question about whether parties really can restrict the jurisdiction of the family court was put to rest in *Cathcart v. Cathcart*, 307 S.C. 322, 414 S.E.2d 811 (Ct. App. 1992), in which the Court of Appeals held that, where a merged agreement expressly deprives the court of jurisdiction, the family court is without jurisdiction to consider a request for reduction in alimony, either because of changed circumstances or because of the mother's meretricious relationship with another man. *See also Croom v. Croom*, 305 S.C. 158, 406 S.E.2d 381 (Ct. App. 1991), in which a merged agreement provided that alimony would terminate upon the occurrence of any of three specific events and that it would be nonmodifiable by the court. The former wife's living with another man was not one of the three conditions specified in the agreement; therefore, the court could not consider terminating or modifying alimony.

Any provision in a settlement agreement that purports to deny the court jurisdiction must be "explicit, clear, and plain." *Robinson v. Tyson*, 319 S.C. 360, 365, 461 S.E.2d 397, 400 (Ct. App. 1995). Although the former husband argued that the family court did not have subject matter jurisdiction to modify the tax exemption status of the parties because the court order was based on the agreement of the parties, the Court of Appeals found no provision in the parties' agreement which excluded the family court of jurisdiction to modify the tax deduction status of the parties. Thus, it upheld the trial court's decision to modify the divorce decree and grant the dependent tax deduction for the daughter to the mother.[46]

The rules of interpretation announced in *Moseley* apply only to decrees entered after *Moseley* in which agreements have been approved by the family court. For agreements that were made before *Moseley*, the earlier rules of interpretation, which emphasized the use of terms of art, will continue to be applied. Although there

---

[46] A curious aspect of *Robinson* is that it leaves open the question of whether the tax deduction status award is an incident of spousal support or equitable division. The court specifically found that it is not an issue directly related to the best interests of the children and the court was not authorized to modify it on that basis. Therefore, one might infer that the court's power to modify the tax status arose from its character as spousal support (although the opinion does not say so) because property divisions are not modifiable. However, there was no finding of changed circumstances to justify a modification of spousal support, and the court refused to address the question of whether the trial judge abused his discretion in modifying the tax deduction award because it was not asked to decide that issue.

will be fewer and fewer instances in which agreements signed before *Moseley* will be presented for judicial interpretation, such instances will occur and will have to be analyzed accordingly.

Parties may make agreements that contain provisions contrary to statutory law, as long as the terms do not violate public policy. In *Sattler v. Sattler*, 284 S.C. 422, 423, 327 S.E.2d 71, 71 (1985), an agreement provided unallocated support and included a provision that "[i]t was to be approved by the court for enforcement purposes only." The husband contended that the statutory bar of alimony for a spouse guilty of adultery controlled over the agreement. The court rejected this argument, and it found that the terms of the agreement were contractual in nature and, therefore, controlling. *Accord*, *Darden v. Witham*, 263 S.C. 183, 209 S.E.2d 42 (1974) (discussed in greater detail in the chapter on alimony). The agreement in *Sattler* had been "approved" but not "merged," and the court noted that the result would be the same under a *Moseley* analysis, although *Moseley* was not controlling because *Moseley* applies prospectively only. The agreement was both executed by the parties and approved by the trial court prior to *Moseley*.

3. OUT-OF-STATE AGREEMENTS

South Carolina gives full faith and credit to agreements that have been approved by courts in other states. *Marshall v. Marshall*, 282 S.C. 336, 318 S.E.2d 133 (Ct. App. 1984) (upholding a Florida divorce decree which had incorporated the parties' agreement providing that future child support would be based on a percentage of the divorced husband's income).

Presumably, agreements that have been entered into out-of-state, but not yet reviewed by any court, would be treated the same as agreements entered into in South Carolina, and South Carolina law would control.

C. DETERMINING THE VALIDITY OF AGREEMENTS

1. IN GENERAL: BASIC ELEMENTS OF A CONTRACT MUST BE MET

Ordinarily, a marital agreement must meet the basic requisites of a contract. In *Caulder v. Knox*, 251 S.C. 337, 162 S.E.2d 262 (1968), the Supreme Court set out the elements of a contract in a case which involved a contract to dispose of property by will. The Court described the essential elements of any contract as "a contractual intent, followed by an actual meeting of the minds of the parties and accompanied by a valid consideration. The terms of the contract must be definite and certain." *Id.* at 344, 162 S.E.2d at 266. The Court went on to note that intent "should be determined from the surrounding circumstances, as well as from the testimony of all witnesses; and subsequent acts are relevant to show whether a contract was intended." *Id.* at 345, 162 S.E.2d at 266. In *Caulder*, the plaintiff relied solely on parol evidence to prove that an oral contract was made to leave property to the plaintiff in exchange for the plaintiff's care for the couple who raised her. The Court held that the plaintiff did not meet the burden of proof with clear and convincing evidence.

If the language in an agreement is clear and unequivocal, the court must construe the agreement accordingly and not look to ancillary evidence of its meaning. In *White v. White*, 210 S.C. 336, 42 S.E.2d 537 (1947), the Supreme Court affirmed the trial court's construction of the terms of a separation agreement as requiring alimony to be paid by the husband's estate. The master's report, which is set out in the opinion, quotes extensively from a partnership contract case that did not involve domestic relations and applies the same principles to the domestic action:

> 'In construing and determining the effect of a written contract, the intention of the parties and the meaning are gathered primarily from the contents of the writing itself, or, as otherwise stated, from the four corners of the instrument, and when such contract is clear and unequivocal, its meaning must be determined by its contents alone; and a meaning cannot be given it other than that expressed. Hence words cannot be read into a contract which import an intent

> wholly unexpressed when the contract was executed. Where the contract evidences care in its preparation, it will be presumed that its words were employed deliberately and with intention.'

Id. at 342, 42 S.E.2d at 538 (relying on *McPherson v. J. E. Sirrine & Co.*, 206 S.C. 183, 33 S.E.2d 501 (1945)).

If an agreement cannot be enforced because it is beyond the ability of one of the parties to perform what is required, the family court should examine the intent of the parties and try to effect compliance as best as possible. In *Richardson v. Richardson*, 309 S.C. 31, 419 S.E.2d 806 (Ct. App. 1992), the husband could not transfer the marital home as agreed because it was owned by his mother. The Court of Appeals held that the family court had properly determined that the agreement was essentially one for lump sum alimony, and it had properly ordered the husband to pay the wife the fair market value of the marital home.

Some cases say that the duty of the court is to enforce the contract made by the parties regardless of its wisdom or folly, apparent unreasonableness, or the parties' failure to guard their rights carefully. *Cf. Ellis v. Taylor*, 316 S.C. 245, 449 S.E.2d 487 (1994). However, many other cases illustrate that the special nature of family court proceedings requires courts to give additional scrutiny to agreements between spouses because of public policy concerns, reciprocal fiduciary duties, children's interests, and general principles of equity.

2. WRITING

The general rule is that agreements between spouses must be in writing to be enforceable, but some exceptions exist.

Agreements based on the consideration of marriage [premarital agreements] are specifically within the Statute of Frauds, which provides that no action shall be brought whereby: "To charge any person upon any agreement made upon consideration of marriage; . . . Unless the agreement upon which such action shall be brought or some memorandum or note thereof shall be in writing and signed by the party to be charged therewith or some person thereunto by him lawfully authorized." S.C. Code Ann. § 32-3-10 (Law. Co-op. 1976).

Agreements about real or personal property are required to be in writing by S.C. Code Ann. § 20-5-50 (Law. Co-op. 1976) which is discussed in the section on jurisdiction earlier in this chapter.

Agreements for spousal support are covered by S.C. Code Ann. § 20-7-850 (Law. Co-op. 1976) which says:

> Where an agreement for the support of the petitioner is brought about, it must be reduced to writing and submitted to the court for approval. Where possible, the court shall see both parties and shall inquire of each whether the agreement, which he must state to them, is what they have agreed to. If it is, and the court shall approve it, the court without further hearing may thereupon enter an order . . . in accordance with such agreement. . . .

Despite these statutory provisions, there are some exceptions. For example SCRCP, Rule 43(k) provides:

> No agreement between counsel affecting the proceedings in an action shall be binding unless reduced to the form of a consent order or written stipulation signed by counsel and entered in the record, or *unless made in open court and noted upon the record.* (emphasis added).

An agreement made in open court and noted upon the record is not binding unless it includes the terms of the settlement. *Ashfort Corp. v. Palmetto Construction Group, Inc.*, 318 S.C. 492, 458 S.E.2d 533 (1995). In this case, the attorneys advised the circuit court judge that the case had been settled and the case was dismissed. Subsequently, a dispute arose over the terms of the settlement. One of the parties moved to reinstate the case; the other moved to compel settlement. The Supreme Court affirmed the circuit court's decision to reinstate the case, specifically holding that Rule 43(k), SCRCP is applicable to settlement agreements.

Once an agreement is read into the record, the parties may not rescind it, even prior to entry of final judgment.[47] In *Small v. Small*, 286 S.C. 87, 332 S.E.2d 769 (1958), the parties were engaged in settlement negotiations for several hours on the day of the divorce hearing. An agreement was reached, which was then read into the record. The wife attempted to have the agreement rescinded prior to the decree being entered, claiming that she had been in a "distraught emotional state [and] had not fully comprehended the settlement terms." *Id.* at 89, 332 S.E.2d at 770. The Court considered the relationship between S.C. Code Ann. § 20-7-850 and then Rule 14 of the Circuit Court Practice Rule (now SCRCP, Rule 43(k)). It held that the provisions of section 20-7-850, which say that out of court agreements "must be reduced to writing and submitted to the court for approval," complement rather than supersede the applicable procedural rules. *Id.* at 89, 332 S.E.2d at 771. With a few exceptions, the South Carolina Rules of Civil Procedure are made applicable to domestic relations actions by virtue of Family Court Rule 2.

The validity of the *Small* opinion was reaffirmed in *Jenkins v. Jenkins*, No. 86-MO-013 (S.C. Ct. App. 1986), an unpublished opinion in which the court wrote: "We hold that Mr. Jenkins cannot disavow the settlement after he orally ratified it in court. It became binding on both parties when it was read into the record, ratified by both parties and accepted by the court. *See Liles v. Liles*, 272 S.C. 511, 252 S.E.2d 886 (1979)." In *Liles*, the husband was intentionally absent from court, and his attorney orally ratified the agreement as he had been authorized to do. The husband was not allowed to disavow the agreement.

The court may be willing to enforce an oral agreement if it finds that the parties never intended the oral agreement to be reduced to writing before becoming effective. On the other hand, if the court finds that the parties did intend a written agreement to be a condition precedent to effectiveness, then the oral agreement will be a nullity. In *Bugg v. Bugg*, 272 S.C. 122, 249 S.E.2d 505 (1978), the parties, through their attorneys, had reached an oral agreement. The agreement was written up but Mrs. Bugg refused to sign it. The Supreme Court held that the agreement was unenforceable, reversing the trial court. The Supreme Court noted that "[w]hether the

---

[47] However, a person may rescind a request for divorce between the final hearing the filing of a divorce decree. "A moving party may rescind his divorce action even after the order is orally rendered." *Liles v. Liles*, 272 S.C. 511, 512, 252 S.E.2d 886, 887 (1979).

parties to an oral or informal agreement became bound prior to the execution of a contemplated formal writing is a question depending largely upon their intention," and it concluded that "the signing of the written agreement was a condition precedent to its effectiveness. Where it is determined that the parties intended not to be bound until the written contract is executed, no valid and enforceable obligation will be held to arise." *Id.* at 125-126, 249 S.E.2d at 507. Because the written agreement was ineffective, it was incapable of being incorporated into the divorce decree. *But see Sanchez v. Tilley*, 285 S.C. 449, 330 S.E.2d 319 (Ct. App. 1985) (enforcing the oral modification of a support agreement despite a requirement in the original agreement that any modifications must be in writing, where the oral agreement reduced child support and the payor spouse sought to avoid payment at all); *Caulder v. Knox*, 251 S.C. 337, 162 S.E.2d 262 (1968) (allowing parol evidence to establish a contract to dispose of property by will).

In the final analysis, principles of equity may prevail over rules of contract construction, especially where children's interests are involved. In *Clark v. Jones*, 272 S.C. 456, 252 S.E.2d 564 (1979), the Supreme Court upheld the lower court's enforcement of a verbal agreement the husband had made several years earlier that he would begin saving to help pay college expenses for his daughters if the wife would abandon her petition for increased child support. In reliance on this verbal promise, the wife abandoned her petition seeking an increase in child support. The trial court ordered the father to pay one-half of his daughter's college expenses, among other things. The Supreme Court affirmed, reasoning that the husband had benefited by paying lower child support over the years and should be required to comply with his obligations as well.

3. CONSIDERATION

Consideration "may consist either in some right, interest, profit or benefit accruing to the one party, or some forbearance, detriment, loss of responsibility given, suffered or undertaken by the other." *Sanchez v. Tilley*, 285 S.C. 449, 330 S.E.2d 319, 320 (Ct. App. 1985). In *Sanchez*, an agreement provided $750 per month child support for five children (two of whom were the husband's by a previous marriage) and waiver of alimony. The agreement also required modifications to be in writing. After the agreement was executed, the two children from the previous marriage moved in with their father, and an oral agreement was made that reduced child support to $450 per month. In enforcing the oral modification, the court said that the husband "benefitted by the oral contract, and the [wife] suffered a detriment," and that the oral agreement was "between two competent persons to do a lawful act and it was based upon a lawful and recognized consideration." *Id.* at 452, 330 S.E.2d at 320.

4. AMBIGUITY

All marital agreements are contracts. The examination of ambiguous terms of marital agreements is similar to that of any contract: parol evidence will be allowed for the limited purpose of clearing up ambiguity. Conversely, if the terms of the agreement are unambiguous, parol evidence will not be allowed. The family court's review for fairness, as discussed in the next section, extends to unambiguous agreements. *McKinney v. McKinney*, 274 S.C. 95, 261 S.E.2d 526 (1980). In *McKinney*, the parties had entered into a "property settlement agreement" which was incorporated into the divorce decree. The husband argued successfully at trial that "the agreement settled all issues arising out of the marital relationship, including alimony and attorney fees," and the judge refused to hear testimony on those issues. *Id.* at 97, 261S.E.2d at 527. The Supreme Court reversed, holding that the agreement "[did] not clearly treat and dispose of the issues" of alimony and attorneys' fees and that it was error for the judge to have excluded extrinsic evidence about the parties' intentions concerning these issues.

When the language of a contract is plain and capable of legal construction, that language alone determines the instrument's force and effect. *Ellis v. Taylor*, 316 S.C. 245, 449 S.E.2d 487 (1994). Whether ambiguity exists, however, must be determined by the four corners of the instrument. *See* the discussion of *White v. White*, 210 S.C. 336, 42 S.E.2d 537 (1947), in the section on determining the validity of agreements in general.

A contract provision leaving material terms open for future agreement is void for indefiniteness. Such was the result in *Ellis v. Taylor*, 316 S.C. 245, 449 S.E.2d 487 (1994). The specific language in question was: "as each child begins college, the parties shall agree to an amount for support of the home while said (sic) child is in college." The Supreme Court found the language too indefinite and uncertain to be enforceable.

However, when an agreement is generally clear and valid, except for nonmaterial terms which are necessary for a complete understanding of the parties' intention, the court can consider parol evidence to determine those missing or unclear terms.

> [W]here an agreement is silent as to a particular matter and because of the nature and character of the transaction an ambiguity arises, parol evidence may be admitted in order to supply a deficiency in the language of the contract. In such instance, parol evidence is admissible not to contradict the terms of the written agreement, but to determine the intent of the parties as to that particular matter.

Ebert v. Ebert, 320 S.C. 331, 339, 465 S.E.2d 121, 126 (Ct. App. 1995) (remanding to the family court to determine a reasonable date by which the wife must sell the marital home).

When an agreement is ambiguous, the court should seek to determine the intent of the parties. In *McDuffie v. McDuffie*, 313 S.C. 397, 438 S.E.2d 239 (1993), the Supreme Court concluded that a father's agreement to pay "all college expenses" for his daughter was patently ambiguous. It noted that the mother, in testifying on behalf of the daughter, had defined college expenses as "tuition, room, and board ... books or supplies." *Id.* at 399, 438 S.E.2d at 241. Therefore, the father was not obligated under the terms of his agreement, as defined by the testimony of his wife, to pay for transportation and incidental expenses or spending money.

McDuffie relied on *Mattox v. Cassady*, 289 S.C. 57, 344 S.E.2d 620 (Ct. App. 1986). In *Mattox*, the Court of Appeals reversed and remanded for a determination of the parties' intentions in using the phrase "gross alimony" in a settlement agreement. The decision was based entirely on pre-*Moseley* law because the divorce decree incorporating the settlement agreement had been entered prior to *Moseley*. The husband sought an end to alimony payments, claiming the alimony was periodic and therefore modifiable upon the wife's remarriage. The wife contended that the alimony was either in gross or that the payments were actually part of a disposition of property, which in either event would mean that the payments were non-modifiable upon a showing of changed circumstances. The court summarized the procedure for examining ambiguity in this manner:

> Like any other agreement, when the language of a settlement agreement is susceptible of more than one interpretation, it is the duty of the court to ascertain the intentions of the parties. The intentions of the parties to a settlement agreement must be determined as far as possible from the terms of the contract and once determined, they must be given effect by the court. It is the general rule that parol evidence is admissible to show the true meaning of an ambiguous written contract. The purpose of all rules of contract construction is to determine the parties' intentions. The courts, in attempting to ascertain this intention, will endeavor to determine the situation of the parties, as well as their purposes at the time the contract was entered.

Id. at 60-61, 344 S.E.2d at 622 (citations omitted).

The Court went on to note that "evidence of negotiations and other relevant contemporaneous agreements" would be admissible because the wife "did not seek to contradict or vary the terms of their or [the] agreement by parol evidence, but rather sought only to apprise the court of its terms." *Id.* at 62-63, 344 S.E.2d at 623. *See also McKinney v. McKinney*, 274 S.C. 95, 97, 261 S.E.2d 526, 527 (1980) (holding that, as with any other contract, where the language of the agreement is susceptible of more than one interpretation, the family court judge must first ascertain the intention of the parties by examining the extrinsic circumstances surrounding the agreement and the parties).

In construing an ambiguous order or decree into which the trial judge merged an agreement of the parties, the determinative factor is the intention of the judge. *Eddins v. Eddins*, 304 S.C. 133, 135, 403 S.E.2d 164, 166 (Ct. App. 1991). In determining the intention of the judge when construing an order which incorporates an ambiguous settlement agreement, it is not improper for an appellate court to consider the intention of the parties. *See Ratchford v. Ratchford*, 295 S.C. 297, 368 S.E.2d 214 (Ct. App. 1988). Ordinarily, when incorporating a settlement agreement negotiated by the parties, the family court judge cannot be held to intend one thing and the parties another. *McDuffie v. McDuffie*, 308 S.C. 401, 418 S.E.2d 331 (Ct. App. 1992).

If the language of an agreement is unambiguous, however, the family court should not accept testimony about the intention of the parties. In *Stanaland v. Jamison*, 275 S.C. 50, 51, 268 S.E.2d 578, 578 (1980), the disputed portion of the agreement provided that "[t]he husband shall pay the sum of $500.00 per month beginning September 1, 1976, for the support and education of each child. . . ." In response to the husband's claim that this provision meant a total of $500.00 for two children rather than $500.00 each, the trial judge agreed with the husband but stopped short of holding whether an ambiguity existed. The Supreme Court reversed, finding the provision unambiguous and stating that "[i]t was error to consider oral testimony and exhibits in an effort to prove that the parties intended something other than that which was written into the agreement." *Id.* at 53, 268 S.E.2d at 579. The Court noted:

> [T]he trial judge erred in undertaking to interpret the provisions of a contract which were not ambiguous. Its terms are clear, and if the parties did not intend to be bound by that which they included in the contract, they should have said so. Oftentimes it becomes the duty of the court to construe a contract which is subject to more than one interpretation, but when the terms of a contract are clear, there is no room for interpretation and the parties must live with the agreement which was made.

Id. at 52-53, 268 S.E.2d at 579.

The Court of Appeals relied on *Stanaland* in its holding in *Ex parte White*, 299 S.C. 406, 385 S.E.2d 211 (Ct. App. 1989). In *White*, the dispute arose over the terms of a settlement agreement which had been incorporated into the divorce decree providing that the husband would pay college expenses "at any State university in the State of South Carolina or any other equivalent school with equivalent costs." *Id.* at 409, 385 S.E.2d at 213. Because the daughter was a resident of North Carolina by the time she began college at Clemson, the father objected to paying out-of-state tuition. The court held that the agreement was unambiguous and that an agreement to pay post-secondary educational expenses for a child past the age of majority is non-modifiable absent the consent of the parties. *Id.* at 412-413, 385 S.E.2d at 215.

5. VOLUNTARINESS

Agreements must be entered into freely and voluntarily. "When approving a settlement agreement, a family court judge must, first, determine if assent to the agreement is voluntarily given ...." *Blejski v. Blejski*, Op. No. 2617 (S.C. Ct. App. filed Jan. 13, 1997)(Davis Adv. Sh. No. 1 at 54) (holding that remarks by the trial judge and alleged pressure from her attorney were insufficient as a matter of law to vitiate the settlement agreement and grant a new trial). *Accord*, *Doe v. Doe*, 286 S.C. 507, 334 S.E.2d 829 (Ct. App. 1985) ("Where one party seeks Family Court approval of a settlement agreement between a husband and wife and the other party repudiates it, the court must first determine if the agreement was freely and voluntarily entered into ...." *Id.* at 514, 334 S.E.2d at 834.)

Doe is a curious case. The wife admitted to committing a single act of fellatio on a man who was not her husband. The court, while refusing either to define fellatio[48] or to decide whether it constitutes adultery, held that her misconduct was condoned by the husband and, therefore, the statutory bar to alimony was unavailable to him. She had signed an agreement to divide the marital property and to waive alimony, but she later repudiated the agreement, claiming that she had signed it only because her husband had threatened to take the children and to "have [her] name drug through the mud all over town." *Id.* If the court had agreed with her that the agreement had not been freely and voluntarily entered into, the entire agreement should have been voided. However, the trial court apparently ignored this facet of her claim and went on to a consideration of whether the agreement was substantively fair, ruling that it was fair with respect to property division, but that it was not fair with respect to her waiver of alimony. The Court of Appeals upheld the trial judge without discussing the question of voluntariness, despite the language quoted above.

---

[48] "Definitions of fellatio are available from a number of sources, but not this opinion." *Id.* at 509, 334 S.E.2d at 831.

Overreaching by an attorney could result in a ruling that an agreement was not voluntarily entered. *Doe* relies on *Funderburk v. Funderburk*, 286 S.C. 129, 332 S.E.2d 205 (1985), for its language about the need to consider voluntariness before reaching the question of fairness. In *Funderburk*, the trial court refused to consider an agreement although both parties asked the court to rule on its validity. Mrs. Funderburk wanted the agreement upheld, but Mr. Funderburk asked the court to void the agreement on the basis of overreaching by his wife's attorney. The Supreme Court did not discuss what conduct would amount to "overreaching," but remanded the case, saying that "[o]n remand, the court shall first determine whether to void the agreement on the basis of overreaching by the wife's attorney. If the judge concludes that the husband entered the contract freely and voluntarily, he shall next examine the agreement's fairness under all the circumstances." *Id.* at 131, 332 S.E.2d at 206.

Something "other than the stress normally attendant to the breakup of a marriage" must be shown in order to prove that an agreement was not entered into freely and voluntarily. In *Burnett v. Burnett*, 290 S.C. 28, 30, 347 S.E.2d 908, 909 (Ct. App. 1986), the Court of Appeals held that Mrs. Burnett had entered the agreement fairly and voluntarily based on evidence that she chose not to consult her own lawyer after being advised to, negotiated a modification, had full knowledge of her husband's income and assets, and did not change her mind about the agreement for over a year. The agreement to divide marital property and for her to waive alimony was also held to be fair, procedurally and substantively.

6. FAIRNESS

"When approving a settlement agreement, a family court judge must, first, determine if assent to the agreement is voluntarily given, and, second, determine if the agreement is 'within the bounds of reasonableness from both a procedural and substantive perspective.'" *Blejski v. Blejski*, Op. No. 2617 (S.C. Ct. App. filed Jan. 13, 1997)(Davis Adv. Sh. No. 1 at 54) (quoting *Burnett v. Burnett*, 290 S.C. 28, 347 S.E.2d 908 (Ct. App. 1986)). *Accord Doe v. Doe*, 286 S.C. 507, 334 S.E.2d 829 (Ct. App. 1985) ("Where one party seeks Family Court approval of a settlement agreement between a husband and wife and the other party repudiates it, the court must first determine if the agreement was freely and voluntarily entered into and next determine if it is fair under all the circumstances." *Id.* at 514, 334 S.E.2d at 834.

The courts look at many factors in evaluating fairness, and although they are not all enumerated in any one case, there are several common threads throughout the cases by which one can predict how the court's analysis will proceed.

The role of the family court in assessing fairness is discussed in *Burnett v. Burnett*, 290 S.C. 28, 347 S.E.2d 908 (Ct. App. 1986):

> In deciding whether an agreement is fair, it is not the task of the Court to decide the rights of the husband and wife as if there had been no agreement. . . . Rather, the Court must decide if the agreement is within the bounds of reasonableness from both a procedural and substantive perspective.

Id. at 30, 347 S.E.2d at 909.

The family court is required to examine an agreement in light of the economic circumstances and contributions of each party. In *Drawdy v. Drawdy*, 275 S.C. 76, 268 S.E.2d 30 (1980), the Court found it "incumbent on the family court, where one party seeks to enforce and the other to repudiate a property settlement agreement to be incorporated into a subsequent divorce decree, to . . . examin[e] the agreement in light of the economic circumstances and contributions of each party." *Id.* at 77, 268 S.E.2d at 30. This duty to rule upon fairness "is especially critical where . . . one of the parties contests an agreement which was hastily drawn, contains no specific provision for or waiver of alimony and was admittedly not reached in contemplation of a final divorce." *Id.*

Thus, a property settlement agreement should bear some relationship to the contributions made by the parties. In *Lucas v. Lucas*, 279 S.C. 121, 302 S.E.2d 863 (1983), the Supreme Court held that an agreement in which the wife relinquished her claim to alimony, the marital home, and a majority of the personal property was not fair and equitable and should be voided. The wife had signed the agreement, which was drawn up by husband's attorney, without independent counsel. The agreement was signed two days after the parties' separation. The Supreme Court found that the wife's contribution was "substantial[ly] over and above normal wifely duties in the home," yet the agreement left her with virtually nothing. *Id.* at 23, 302 S.E.2d at 864.

However, "[a]n agreement shall not be voided as unfair merely because [it] did not divide the property on the basis of the parties' relative incomes and contributions to the marriage. All of the relevant factors must be weighed." *Funderburk v. Funderburk*, 286 S.C. 129, 131, 332 S.E.2d 205, 205 (1985). In other words, it is perfectly acceptable for a party's generosity to arise from a desire "to quickly get out of the marriage or to atone for past wrongs." *Id.*

An agreement may be declared unfair if one party appears to have dominated the will of the other. In *Jackson v. Jackson*, 279 S.C. 618, 310 S.E.2d 827 (Ct. App. 1983), the Court of Appeals upheld the family court's finding that an agreement was invalid despite the parties having been represented by an attorney of the wife's choosing. The agreement was written by the husband; the wife had "recently been beaten by her husband and was subject to constant mental abuse;" and she was, at the time the agreement was entered into, taking "large doses of sedatives and other medications to combat her illness." *Id.* at 620-621, 310 S.E.2d at 828. The court found undue influence and overreaching, noting that, although the parties were represented by a single attorney, the attorney never discussed the agreement with the wife alone nor made any inquiry as to the facts.

If both parties are represented by independent counsel, it is likely that their agreement will be found to be fair. *See Sauls v. Sauls*, 287 S.C. 297, 337 S.E.2d 893 (Ct. App. 1985) (upholding an agreement which the wife had challenged although it had been drafted by her attorney, and the husband had been represented by independent counsel).

Apparently, an agreement will be held to be unfair unless there has been adequate mutual disclosure about the financial status of the parties. The confidential relationship between parties to a postnuptial agreement imposes an affirmative duty upon each party transcending that which is normally required for a commercial transaction. *Geddings v. Geddings*, 319 S.C. 213, 460 S.E.2d 376 (1994).[49] This case upholds the circuit court's affirmance of the probate court's conclusion that a

---

[49] In *Geddings*, the Court consistently refers to the Geddings' agreement as an antenuptial (premarital) agreement and cites cases referring to premarital agreements, although the Geddings' agreement was made nine years into their marriage. There is no reason to believe the Court would apply a different standard in a case involving a premarital agreement.

wife's waiver of her elective share in her husband's estate was void because there had not been fair disclosure. The evidence showed that the wife had no real or general knowledge of the total extent of her husband's assets. The attorney preparing the waiver document testified that he did not discuss assets with the wife when it was executed. There was evidence that the husband was secretive about his financial affairs.

In defining for the first time in South Carolina what constitutes "fair disclosure" in the context of postnuptial agreements in which inheritance rights are waived, the Court states:

> 'Fair disclosure contemplates that each spouse should be given information, of a general and approximate nature, concerning the net worth of the other. Each party has a duty to consider and evaluate the information received before signing an agreement.' *In re Estate of Lopata*, 641 P.2d 952 (Colo. 1982); *In re Estate of Hill*, 335 N.W.2d 750 (Neb. 1983).
>
> > Fair disclosure means that before signing an antenuptial agreement, each party must disclose to the other the facts that exist at the time of the agreement and which, in the absence of the antenuptial agreement, affect or determine the prospective intestate share of a surviving spouse in the disclosing party's estate or which otherwise affect or determine distribution of property at the disclosing party's death.
>
> *In re Estate of Stephenson*, 503 N.W.2d 540 (Neb. 1993).

Id. at 215, 460 S.E.2d at 378. The result in *Geddings* is consistent with *Kane v Kane*, 280 S.C. 479, 313 S.E.2d 327 (Ct. App. 1984), in which the court let stand a family court determination that an agreement was unfair because the wife was unaware of her husband's financial status when she signed an agreement, and there was no information in the record from which the family court could have determined what financial information had been made available to the wife before she signed the agreement.

The family court's review of fairness is to include an examination of plain, unambiguous agreements. See *McKinney v. McKinney*, 274 S.C. 95, 261 S.E.2d 526 (1980). The review of ambiguous agreements, however, requires that the intent of the parties be determined by examining extrinsic circumstances before making a ruling as to fairness. (See the discussion about ambiguity in another section of this chapter.)

One instance of marital misconduct probably does not justify the execution of a one-sided settlement agreement in which the misbehaving spouse waives alimony. In *Doe v. Doe*, 286 S.C. 507, 334 S.E.2d 829 (Ct. App. 1985) (more facts of which are discussed in the section on voluntariness), the Court of Appeals affirmed the trial court's finding as to the unfairness of a settlement agreement waiving alimony. Although the parties entered into a settlement agreement waiving alimony, the trial judge found that the agreement was unfair. Despite the wife's marital misconduct, the trial judge found that she had been a good wife and mother for ten years and that the marital relationship had only begun to deteriorate when one of the parties' children was seriously injured in an accident. Additionally, the court noted that "[t]he wife testified about her repentant and remorseful attitude." *Id.* at 512, 334 S.E.2d at 832. The husband, while not admitting any marital misconduct, testified that he had treated the wife "like a recalcitrant child," which included taking away her driver's license and "taking the wheels off her car on other occasions." *Id.* at 513, 334 S.E.2d at 833. The finding of unfairness was made:

> 'with full recognition and appreciation by the court of [wife's] acts which contributed substantially to the breakup of the marriage and which would normally bar her from alimony, as well as her express waiver of alimony in the agreement and her full understanding of same at the time she entered into it.'

Id. at 514, 334 S.E.2d at 833 (quoting the trial judge's findings).

The holding in *Doe* is probably restricted to the facts, which were very sympathetic to the wife despite her admitted marital misconduct, but the case does illustrate the breadth of the court's discretion in findings as to fairness.

The family court's duty to rule on fairness must be accomplished during the term of court in which the merits of the case are heard. In *Michel v. Michel*, 289 S.C. 187, 345 S.E.2d 730 (Ct. App. 1986), the Court of Appeals refused to allow the trial court judge to vacate his own order when, two years after the order was entered, he discovered that it was not fair to one of the parties. The facts in *Michel* are unique. The settlement agreement was entered as result of the parties reaching an agreement that the wife and daughter would not pursue a claim against the husband for sexual battery of the daughter. The agreement called for the husband to pay $42,500 and the wife to release all claims for support, alimony, or equitable distribution, but it did not refer to the daughter's possible claim. The husband sought to have the settlement agreement voided upon learning that its main purpose in his view, protecting his reputation, had not been achieved because the wife had allegedly discussed the sexual battery with others. The trial judge held that he would not have approved the settlement if he had known the true facts surrounding it. He "further concluded that he had failed to discharge his responsibilities because he did not follow the requisite procedures in approving the agreement." *Id.* at 189, 345 S.E.2d at 731. The Court of Appeals held that the trial judge "loses jurisdiction to modify an order at the end of the term during which it is issued" and that only clerical errors that do not "[involve] the exercise of judgment or discretion on the merits of an action" may be corrected. *Id.* at 190, 345 S.E.2d at 732 (citations omitted).

The ruling on fairness must come at the time the case is heard on the merits. In *Fischl v. Fischl*, 272 S.C. 297, 251 S.E.2d 743 (1979), the wife sought a divorce on grounds of adultery. A temporary order was entered by agreement in court which provided for child custody and support, visitation, and property division, with the wife dropping the adultery action and the husband agreeing to allege desertion as grounds for divorce. He later changed his mind, stating that he wanted no divorce. No written agreement or order had been signed. Nevertheless, the trial judge ordered enforcement of the in-court agreement. The Supreme Court reversed, finding that "[i]n the last analysis, the court may direct the settlement which was agreed upon, but a determination of the issues which the court has already attempted to settle should await a hearing of the application for divorce on its merit." *Id.* at 300, 251 S.E.2d at 744. The Supreme Court noted that the husband did have a right to withdraw his claim for divorce. This meant that, although the judge has a duty "to rule upon the fairness of the settlement in light of the showing which [is] made," the showing must be made at the appropriate time. *Id.* at 300, 251 S.E.2d at 745.

7. CHILDREN'S INTERESTS

The family court always has continuing subject matter jurisdiction as to child support and custody. In *Moseley v. Mosier*, 279 S.C. 348, 351, 306 S.E.2d 624, 625 (1983), the Court affirmed that "[f]amily courts may always modify child support upon a proper showing of a change in either the child's needs or the supporting parent's financial ability" (citing *Smith v. Smith*, 275 S.C. 494, 272 S.E.2d 797 (1980)). The Court went on to "clarify the issue by stating that family courts have continuing jurisdiction to do whatever is in the best interests of the child regardless of what the separation agreement specifies." *Moseley* at 351, 306 S.E.2d at 625.

In *Johnson v. Johnson*, 251 S.C. 420, 163 S.E.2d 229 (1968), the Supreme Court noted, "It is academic that the interest of the children is the paramount issue." The Court ordered custody changed to the father, reversing the trial court on the basis of the wife's adultery, despite the parties' having made an agreement which provided that "the parties hereto shall have the privilege of having such friend or friends as he or she may desire without the right on the part of the other party to object thereto." *Id.* at 425, 163 S.E.2d at 231. The Court held:

> In spite of the August 1965 agreement she remained a married woman with obligations to her children, and even if one assumes that the husband, by reason of the agreement, had less than full right to complain of her associations, the facts remain: 1. that the agreement does not excuse adultery; 2. that the State has an interest in all marriage contracts and in the custody of the children; 3. that her conduct has been inconsistent with the best interest of the children; 4. no agreement can prejudice the rights of the children.

Id. at 428, 163 S.E.2d at 233.

It is hard to predict whether the result in *Johnson* would be stated so directly today, but the impact of marital misconduct on the Court's calculus, as discussed in greater detail in the chapter on alimony, is still a consideration.

The parties in a marital dispute may contract as to child custody and support, but the court will not hesitate to set aside the agreement upon a showing that the best interest of the child is not served by the terms of the agreement. In *Powell v. Powell*, 256 S.C. 111, 181 S.E.2d 13 (1971), the Supreme Court remanded a case for specific findings of fact concerning the lower court's award of custody. The parties had made a written agreement, the terms of which were included in the divorce decree, that custody of one of their two children would be with the paternal grandparents. Custody of the second child was with the mother. Later, the mother sought and was awarded custody of first child as well. The Supreme Court held:

> 'The rule is that contracts between spouses as to the custody of children will be recognized unless the welfare of the children requires a different disposition.' Under this rule it was incumbent upon the respondent to show that the welfare of [the child] required the court to ignore and set aside the agreement of the parties.

Id. at 116, 181 S.E.2d at 15 (quoting from *Ford v. Ford*, 242 S.C. 344, 130 S.E.2d 916 (1963)). *See also Sattler v. Sattler*, 284 S.C. 422, 327 S.E.2d 71 (1985) (refusing to give effect to the parties' agreement as to child support while enforcing provisions giving the wife alimony despite the fact that the wife's adultery was later proven); *South Carolina DSS v. Fingerlin*, 285 S.C. 73, 328 S.E.2d 71 (1985) (holding that jurisdiction to enforce child support provisions is properly with the family court even where a decree was entered by the court of common pleas).

8. PRESENCE OF PARTIES MAY BE REQUIRED

S.C. Code Ann. § 20-7-850 (Law. Co-op. 1976) includes the following language concerning attendance of the parties: "Where possible, the court shall see both parties and shall inquire of each whether the agreement, which he must state to them, is what they have agreed to." S.C. Code Ann. § 20-7-850 (Law. Co-op. 1976).[50]

---

[50] The Supreme Court advised family court judges in 1996 that, when one party is not present for a hearing at which approval of a settlement is being considered, they should follow this procedure: the trial judge should require an affidavit from that party to be a part of the record before the settlement agreement can be approved. The affidavit should make affirmative statements as to the questions that the judge would ask of the party if the party was personally present in the courtroom.

The presumption that the parties' presence is required may be overcome where one party intentionally stays away from the hearing. In *Liles v. Liles*, 272 S.C. 511, 252 S.E.2d 886 (1979), the Supreme Court refused to allow the husband to rescind a settlement agreement, when he was intentionally absent from the hearing. His attorney appeared and represented to the court that the husband had "authorized [the attorney] to accept the settlement agreement on his behalf." *Id.* at 513, 252 S.E.2d at 887. The Court noted that although "[a] moving party may rescind his divorce action even after the order is orally rendered," a different result occurs where only the settlement agreement and not the divorce itself is at issue. *Id.* at 512, 252 S.E.2d at 887 (citations omitted). The Court distinguished *Bugg v. Bugg*, 272 S.C. 122, 249 S.E.2d 505 (1978), on the basis of the parties' intent. In *Bugg*, the Court held that the parties intended the execution of the agreement to be a condition precedent to its becoming effective. On the other hand, in *Liles* the Court found "nothing to indicate the parties envisioned the execution of a more formal document prior to the finality of the settlement agreement." *Liles*, 272 S.C. at 513, 252 S.E.2d at 887.

An attorney may settle litigation on behalf of a client, and absent fraud or mistake, such a settlement is binding on the client. *Cf. Poore v. Poore*, 105 S.C. 206, 89 S.E. 569 (1916); *Arnold v. Yarborough*, 281 S.C. 570, 316 S.E.2d 416 (Ct. App. 1984); *Crowley v. Harvey & Battey, P.A., et al.*, Op. No. 24237, (S.C. Sup. Ct. filed April 17, 1995)(Davis Adv. Sh. No. 9 at 24). However, an attorney who settles litigation on behalf of a client may be subject to a malpractice lawsuit, even if the client accepts the benefits of the agreement. If the client ratifies the attorney-agent's acts by accepting the benefits of the settlement with knowledge of a problem, the client cannot maintain a malpractice suit. *Shelton v. Bressant*, 312 S.C. 208, 439 S.E.2d 833 (1993) (the attorney exceeded his authority when he agreed to the settlement and, knowing this, the client accepted the benefits of the agreement). However, where the settlement itself cannot be attacked and the issue is not one of agency but of negligence, the fact that the client has accepted the benefits of the settlement and judicially sought to enforce its terms are not bars to maintenance of a malpractice claim. *Crowley, supra.* (reversing a summary judgment in a legal malpractice suit in which a former client alleged that her attorneys negligently advised her in settling the property division issues in her divorce action).

D. CONSIDERATIONS RELATED TO SPECIFIC TYPES OF AGREEMENTS

1. IN GENERAL

Some special considerations may depend on the marital status of the parties when an agreement is made as well as whether they are living together or planning to resume living together. Generally speaking, similar public policy considerations come into play irrespective of the type of agreement, but some variations exist.

The practitioner must keep in mind that the family court does not have subject matter jurisdiction over all types of agreements between spouses. Some disputes may belong in the circuit court. *See Fielden v. Fielden*, 274 S.C. 219, 262 S.E.2d 43 (1980) (holding that family courts have no subject matter jurisdiction over actions in contract). Subject matter jurisdiction is discussed earlier in this chapter and in the chapter on subject matter jurisdiction.

2. PREMARITAL AGREEMENTS

a. In General

Premarital agreements have long been recognized as valid in South Carolina, but they have not been used extensively. Legislative activity may lead to more extensive utilization. Practitioners should approach premarital agreements with caution, for there are many unanswered questions about the extent of their enforceability.

A premarital (antenuptial or prenuptial) agreement is an agreement between prospective spouses made in contemplation of marriage. Because the agreement is executory, it becomes effective only upon marriage. *South Carolina Loan & Trust Co. v. Lawton*, 69 S.C. 345, 48 S.E. 282 (1904). The consideration for a premarital agreement is the marriage itself. In *South Carolina Loan & Trust Co.*, the parties executed a premarital agreement which provided that property would be held in trust for the wife and children. The husband's creditors were trying to reach the property.

Before their marriage, the parties had executed a second document that gave priority to existing creditors of the husband. The Supreme Court, in upholding the validity of the premarital agreement, stated:

> There is not complete execution of such instruments until actual marriage, and it does not matter how many changes may be made, and how many different instruments may be signed, the settlement, in the last form it assumes before marriage, is the real contract supported by the consideration of marriage.

Id. at 349, 48 S.E. at 283.

Of the few South Carolina cases involving premarital agreements, most dealt with whether or not a woman could waive her dower rights. After these cases were decided, dower rights were held to be an unconstitutional violation of equal protection in *Boan v. Watson*, 281 S.C. 516, 316 S.E.2d 401 (1984). However, the cases are instructive regarding the Supreme Court's approach to premarital agreements. In *Stork v. First National Bank of South Carolina*, 281 S.C. 515, 316 S.E.2d 400 (1984), the Supreme Court held that an antenuptial agreement can act as a bar to a wife's action to claim her dower rights in the estate of the husband. It noted that premarital agreements "are not opposed to public policy but are highly beneficial to serving the best interest of the marriage relationship." *Id.* at 516, 316 S.E.2d at 400. The Court said that for the agreement to be enforced it must be voluntarily made, in good faith, and be fair and equitable. It also commented that such agreements were to be encouraged. A distinction must always be made, however, between premarital agreements dealing with the disposition of property upon death versus those that anticipate divorce or separation.

Two older cases had determined that premarital agreements to release dower were not, in fact, releases which would by themselves bar dower for, at the time of contracting, the wives had no existing interest to relinquish in their future husband's estates. The agreements, however, were viewed as valid agreements not to claim or demand dower. In *Gelzer v. Gelzer*, 8 S.C. Eq. (3 Bailey Eq.) 387 (1831), the obligation imposed by the agreement was enforced; but in *Spiva v. Jeter*, 30 S.C. Eq. (9 Rich. Eq.) 434 (1857), the obligation was not enforced, because "[t]he obligation of the plaintiff to release any interest she might acquire, rested in contract, and depended on the fidelity with which the conditions of the contract were fulfilled by her future husband." *Id.* at 438-39. The Supreme Court found in *Spiva* that the failure of the husband to provide for his wife during the marriage, a part of his marital obligation, precluded performance of the agreement by the wife. The husband had left the wife in order to "go West." He neither sent for her nor provided for her during the following ten years. The wife had remained willing to accompany him.

Public policy prohibits premarital agreements that presuppose a future separation. *Campbell v. Moore*, 189 S.C. 497, 1 S.E.2d 784 (1937) (also discussed in the chapter on annulment), involved the execution of both a premarital agreement and a separation agreement. The premarital agreement was allegedly used to persuade the minor father of an illegitimate unborn child to marry the mother. The contract promised that a formal instrument (subsequent agreement or contract) would be entered into after the marriage ceremony. In return for $300, the wife would relieve the husband from any child support or maintenance obligations and renounce her dower interest. In addition, she would not claim any interest in the husband's estate. This document also contained a provision allowing the father to seek an annulment without objection from the wife. The second agreement was entered into after the marriage and contained substantially the same provisions contained in the premarital contract. It also put a nine month hold on any attempt by the father to seek an annulment or divorce and specified that the father would have no control (custody rights) over the upbringing of the child. This case came before the Court pursuant to the husband's action for an annulment on the grounds that the marriage was entered into under duress. The wife, in her counterclaim, asked for child support and maintenance. As an affirmative defense, she claimed that a valid marriage ceremony took place. The opinion of the special referee and the subsequent order of the court were affirmed by the Supreme Court.

The findings of the special referee are set forth in the opinion. He first detailed the necessity of consent in a valid marriage contract, the existence of which overcomes any question of legality, including provisions in the contract (post or prenuptial) that regulate cohabitation. After discussing the public policy behind the prohibition of antenuptial contracts which have in mind a future separation, the referee found that the contracts did presuppose separation and, thus, had no legal effect. Considering the interests of the minor child, the referee refused to allow the annulment. As this case exemplifies, public policy is of major importance when the validity of a prenuptial agreement is under the court's consideration. The state has an interest in matters such as marriage, child support, and legitimacy, as well as contracts entered into by minors, and it has established a protective policy concerning such matters.

The above cases are the only South Carolina cases that directly address the subject of premarital contracts. Nonetheless, it is clear that they are recognized and enforced at least as to disposition at death, and in all likelihood with regard to disposition on separation so long as the agreements do not promote separation or divorce.

Premarital contracts are increasingly being enforced in other jurisdictions, even if they anticipate the possibility of divorce. Yet, these agreements can be altered, rescinded or revoked as can any contract; and, to avoid inequity, the court itself can modify them under some conditions if there have been changed circumstances. The courts retain this power because of the strong state interest in the institution of marriage.

Premarital agreements which presuppose a divorce are probably not enforceable. In *Campbell v. Moore*, 189 S.C. 497, 1 S.E.2d 784 (1937), the Supreme Court held an agreement invalid in which the parties agreed to become divorced and this intent was readily ascertainable from the contract. In other words, it held that a premarital agreement cannot be a contract to breach another contract (that of marriage) which has yet to come into existence. At the same time, there would appear to be no reason why they cannot be made in contemplation of the modern reality that divorce is not an uncommon event. Aside from this limitation, premarital contracts are useful in detailing the property divisions between a couple in an effort to preclude litigation at a future stage.

b. Usefulness for Defining "Marital Property"

Prospective spouses may agree before marriage what property will be defined as "marital property" in the event of a divorce. The family court will not have jurisdiction to equitably apportion property that has been properly designated as nonmarital property in such agreements:

> The term "marital property" as used in this article means all real and personal property which has been acquired by the parties during the marriage and which is owned as of the date of filing or commencement of marital litigation as provided in § 20-7-472 regardless of how legal title is held, except the following, which constitute nonmarital property:
>
> . . .
>
> (4) property excluded by written contract of the parties. "Written contract" includes any antenuptial agreement of the parties which must be considered presumptively fair and equitable so long as it was voluntarily executed with both parties separately represented by counsel and pursuant to the full financial disclosure to each other that is mandated by the rules of the family court as to income, debts, and assets . . . .
>
> . . .
>
> The court does not have jurisdiction or authority to apportion nonmarital property.

S. C. Code Ann. § 20-7-473 (Law. Co-op. Supp.).

c. Uniform Premarital Agreement Act

Legislation was proposed, but not passed, during the 1992 session that would have codified the Uniform Premarital Agreement Act (with significant modifications). If submitted again and enacted, this legislation would have an impact on the law concerning premarital agreements and, perhaps, expand their utilization. Although it is not yet the law in South Carolina, the Act provides helpful guidelines that may help avoid some of the potential pitfalls lurking in premarital agreements. Significant provisions of the Act include:

- A premarital agreement must be in writing, and have financial declarations attached.

- It must be signed by both parties after each has consulted with independent counsel.

- The family court should have jurisdiction to approve premarital agreements [which it does not presently have unless the agreement is involved in "marital litigation"].

- Consideration is not necessary.

- The subject matter over which parties may contract is broad, and includes a list of specific property rights and a catchall provision of "any other matter, including their personal rights and obligations, not in violation of public policy." [Although spousal support was included as one of the specific areas of coverage, the recommendation of the Family Law Section of the S.C. Bar was to delete the subsection.]

- The agreement may not adversely affect the right of a child or spouse to support.

- A written agreement is necessary to amend or revoke a premarital agreement after the parties are married.

- The standard of proof to set aside an agreement is preponderance of the evidence, and involuntariness, unconscionability, lack of full disclosure, inadequate knowledge, or lack of independent counsel must be shown.

- A premarital agreement made in contemplation of a marriage that is determined to be void will be enforced only to the extent necessary to avoid an inequitable result.

Both the Equitable Apportionment of Marital Property Act (S.C. Code Ann. § 20-7-473 (Law. Co-op. Supp.)) and the Uniform Premarital Agreement Act call for a written agreement, signed by both parties, after independent consultation with counsel. Both further require financial disclosure through the use of financial declarations. Neither, of course, allows parties to include contract provisions which would be against their children's best interests.

3. AGREEMENTS MADE WHILE MARRIED, BUT LIVING APART

a. In General

There are basically three types of agreements which can be made while the parties are married, but living apart: (1) settlement agreements (these settle existing marital litigation but do not contemplate resumption of cohabitation); (2) reconciliation agreements (these may or may not end existing marital litigation, but they do contemplate resumption of cohabitation by spouses who are living apart); and (3) separation agreements (these do not involve existing marital litigation and may be created whether or not the parties are living apart at the time the agreement is reached).[51]

b. Settlement Agreements

As mentioned above, settlement agreements are defined for our purposes as agreements which settle existing marital litigation and do not contemplate resumption of cohabitation. If they do, they are reconciliation agreements. In general, there are not any special considerations about them that are not discussed elsewhere in this chapter.

c. Reconciliation Agreements

Reconciliation agreements are a somewhat different species, however, because in addition to the general considerations which apply to all marital agreements, drafters of reconciliation agreements must consider the strong public policy in favor of marriage, which translates into a policy that promotes

---

[51] These terms are frequently used interchangeably in practice. The definitions are provided for the purpose of this book.

reconciliation. In *Brown v. Brown*, 243 S.C. 383, 134 S.E.2d 222 (1963), the Supreme Court stated: "It has long been settled that the public policy of this state relating to marriage is to foster and protect it, to make it a permanent and public institution, to encourage the parties to live together, and to prevent separation." *Id.* at 387, 134 S.E.2d at 224. It would seem that the considerations discussed earlier with respect to premarital agreements would apply equally to reconciliation agreements. After all, a decision to resume living together is similar to a decision to become married in the first place.

It has long been held that public policy forbids any agreement that operates in derogation of marriage. In *Towles v. Towles*, 256 S.C. 307, 182 S.E.2d 53 (1971), the wife and husband executed a reconciliation agreement whereby the wife promised to "never again bring any suit at law or in equity against the [husband] for any reason whatsoever." The Supreme Court wrote:

> The marriage contract is one in which the State has a vital interest. Once entered into, the law imposes upon the parties certain mutual obligations and liabilities which have long been considered essential incidents to the marital relationship. These incidents to marriage are deemed so important to its preservation and stability until any agreement which has the effect of materially altering them, as a condition of the relationship, is ordinarily considered against public policy and, therefore, void.
>
> . . .
>
> [T]he agreement by the wife that she would never bring an action against her husband again, as a condition of the resumption of the marriage relationship, is against public policy and therefore void. The right of the wife to support from her husband must be determined without regard to the agreement not to sue.

Id. at 312, 182 S.E.2d at 55.

4. AGREEMENTS MADE WHILE MARRIED AND LIVING TOGETHER

As defined earlier for our purposes, separation agreements do not involve existing marital litigation (if they did they would be settlement or reconciliation agreements), and they may be created whether or not the parties are living apart at the time the agreement is reached. There is nothing wrong with two married people entering into a contract with each other, but similar public policy considerations will apply as to premarital and reconciliation agreements.

Property settlement agreements between spouses who are contemplating divorce are encouraged, if the agreements do not relieve the parties of their marital obligations but, rather, define these obligations. In *Drawdy v. Drawdy*, 275 S.C. 76, 268 S.E.2d 30 (1980) (discussed earlier in this chapter in the section on fairness), the Court noted that "[p]roperty settlement agreements are praiseworthy products of cooperation between parties seeking a divorce" and that they "serve to decrease the workload on our family courts and thereby enhance judicial efficiency." *Id.* at 78, 268 S.E.2d at 31. *Drawdy* was remanded because the family court judge did not made a finding as to fairness before incorporating the parties' agreement into the divorce decree.

The confidential relationship between parties to a postnuptial agreement imposes an affirmative duty upon each party transcending that which is normally required for a commercial transaction. *Geddings v. Geddings*, 319 S.C. 213, 460 S.E.2d 376 (1994).[52] This case upholds the circuit court's affirmance of the probate court's conclusion that a wife's waiver of her elective share in her husband's estate was void because there had not been fair disclosure. The evidence showed that the wife had no real or general knowledge of the total extent of her husband's assets. The attorney preparing the waiver document testified he did not discuss assets with the wife when it was executed. There was evidence that the husband was secretive about his financial affairs.

---

[52] In *Geddings*, the Court consistently refers to the Geddings' agreement as an antenuptial (prenuptial) agreement and cites cases referring to antenuptial agreements, although the Geddings' agreement was made nine years into their marriage.

In defining for the first time in South Carolina what constitutes "fair disclosure" in the context of postnuptial agreements in which inheritance rights are waived, the Court states:

> 'Fair disclosure contemplates that each spouse should be given information, of a general and approximate nature, concerning the net worth of the other. Each party has a duty to consider and evaluate the information received before signing an agreement.' *In re Estate of Lopata*, 641 P.2d 952 (Colo. 1982); *In re Estate of Hill*, 335 N.W.2d 750 (Neb. 1983).
>
>> Fair disclosure means that before signing an antenuptial agreement, each party must disclose to the other the facts that exist at the time of the agreement and which, in the absence of the antenuptial agreement, affect or determine the prospective intestate share of a surviving spouse in the disclosing party's estate or which otherwise affect or determine distribution of property at the disclosing party's death.
>
> *In re Estate of Stephenson*, 503 N.W.2d 540 (Neb. 1993).

Id. at 213, 460 S.E.2d at 378.

5. EFFECT OF RECONCILIATION

By definition, the reconciliation of spouses should have no impact on a reconciliation agreement since such agreements contemplate the reconciliation and define some of the terms under which the parties will live following the reconciliation. *See, e.g., Cook v. Cook*, No. 82-MO-244 (S.C. 1982), an unpublished opinion in which the Supreme Court affirmed the trial court's distribution of property pursuant to a reconciliation agreement. The husband had agreed to execute a deed as to his interest in the marital residence which was to be held in trust and delivered to the wife only if the husband left again. When this event occurred, the deed was delivered to the wife. The Court held the husband had no cause to complain, noting:

"The family court order dismissing Wife's first action for divorce upon the parties' reconciliation was made subject to the terms and conditions of reconciliation . . . . When this order was not appealed, it became the law of the case, and as such remains binding on Husband." *Id.* at 2.

The effect of an unanticipated reconciliation upon a settlement or separation agreement will depend on whether particular provisions have been fully executed. As to provisions that were executed, such as completed property transfers, the reconciliation has no effect. As to executory provisions, such as those pertaining to support, a reconciliation has the effect of nullification. In *Crawford v. Crawford*, 301 S.C. 476, 392 S.E.2d 675 (Ct. App. 1990), the court addressed the issue of "whether the public policy of this state precludes the enforcement of the terms of the property settlement agreement after the parties have reconciled pursuant to a reconciliation agreement which expressly sanction[s] the prior property settlement agreement." *Id.* at 480, 392 S.E.2d at 678. The Court of Appeals noted that although "[t]he general law in South Carolina, at least as to matters of support, is that a separation agreement is annulled by the subsequent reconciliation of the parties," a different result occurs when the property agreement has been court approved. *Id.* (citing *Machado v. Machado*, 220 S.C. 90, 66 S.E..2d 629 (1951)). *Crawford* also held that the public policy of South Carolina recognizes that the reconciliation of the parties nullified the provisions of the separation and reconciliation agreements regarding the parties' agreements not to be liable for the support of each other, and it allowed the family court's award of alimony to stand.

CHAPTER FIFTEEN
BANKRUPTCY

CHAPTER FIFTEEN
BANKRUPTCY

A. IN GENERAL

The purpose of this chapter is to give family court practitioners a basic understanding of bankruptcy law and procedure. Bankruptcy practice is a specialty field in which local rules and unpublished opinions play important roles. Family court practitioners who believe their client or their client's spouse may file bankruptcy should consult a bankruptcy specialist. The materials in this chapter will help identify potential bankruptcy issues in domestic proceedings. Lawyers should draft agreements and orders with the possibility in mind that they may be scrutinized at a later time in the bankruptcy court. These documents should clearly show the parties' intentions about the nature of any interspousal debts, and they should discuss property division and support issues in distinctly separate sections.

The purpose of bankruptcy proceedings is to offer debtors opportunities for fresh starts. The Bankruptcy Code gives debtors two ways to deal with debt loads that are too heavy for them to manage: 1) by providing a structure for paying off the debts or part of them without losing ownership of their property (reorganization), or 2) by employing a procedure through which they are discharged from responsibility for their debts by selling the debtors' assets, even if this does not produce enough cash to fully pay off the debts (liquidation). The Bankruptcy Code is divided into chapters, with Chapters 11, 12, and 13, being concerned with rehabilitation, and Chapter 7 with liquidation.

Debts and other obligations that are excepted from discharge will survive a bankruptcy case, that is, the debtor will not be relieved of responsibility for them. Therefore, bankruptcy litigation often involves disputes over the dischargability of particular debts.

Although exceptions to discharge are to be narrowly construed, so as to effect the "fresh start" purpose of bankruptcy, bankruptcy laws favor enforcement of familial support obligations over a "fresh start" of the debtor. *In re Miller*, 55 F.3d

1487 (10th Cir. 1995), *cert. den.* 116 S.Ct. 305. Bankruptcy proceedings under Chapters 7, 11, 12, or 13 do not release debtors from alimony or support obligations owed to a spouse, former spouse, or child if the obligation arose from a separation agreement, judgment of divorce, or property settlement and the debt has not been assigned to a third party other than the government. The spouse, former spouse, or child has priority over some other unsecured creditors. Until 1994, debts created by property divisions between spouses were dischargeable in bankruptcy. Today, it is possible in many circumstances to prevent these debts from being discharged.

The bankruptcy process cannot be used as a device for defrauding creditors. The Fourth Circuit Court of Appeals affirmed the dismissal of a bankruptcy petition where the debtor's sole purpose for filing bankruptcy was to favor certain creditors and defraud his former wife. *Kestell v. Kestell (In re Kestell)*, ___ F.2d ___ (4th Cir. 1996). More than half of the man's debt was a dischargeable lump sum owed to his former wife pursuant to their divorce decree. He tried to use a check from his employer for accrued sick leave to reimburse creditors he thought worthy of priority, while ignoring the debt to his wife (and without informing the bankruptcy trustee). The court concluded that the debtor's actions constituted "substantial abuse" of the bankruptcy process. *See also In re Prosser*, 87-1185, C-89-8061 (Bankr. D.S.C. 1989) (an unpublished opinion of the South Carolina bankruptcy court),[53] in which the debtor transferred property to his ex-wife pursuant to a property settlement and divorce decree. He later remarried his former spouse. The bankruptcy court ruled that these transfers were done with the intent to defraud creditors and ordered that the transfers be rescinded and the property turned over to the Chapter 7 trustee.

---

[53] Copies of unpublished opinions can be obtained from the bankruptcy court. Family court practitioners should be aware that there is no rule against citing unpublished opinions in the South Carolina bankruptcy court, and many bankruptcy practitioners are familiar with the unpublished opinions and frequently refer to them in briefs and arguments.

B. OVERVIEW OF THE BANKRUPTCY CHAPTERS

1. CHAPTER 7

Chapter 7 (11 U.S.C. § 701 *et seq.*) bankruptcies involve the liquidation of the debtors' assets. An individual, a husband and wife together, a business, or a partnership may elect to file for liquidation under Chapter 7. As with all chapters, debtors report all assets and liabilities and claim exemptions pursuant to S.C. Code § 15-41-30 (Law. Co-op. Supp) which protects certain property from creditors. A Chapter 7 trustee is appointed to determine whether there is equity in the debtor's property which is available for distribution to creditors. If there is, the case is deemed an "asset case" and the trustee liquidates the estate.

Any assets produced by liquidating the estate are first applied to administrative expenses. Secured creditors have priority over unsecured creditors up to the value of the assets which serve as collateral for their claims. Priority creditors are paid next. This includes debts such as tax claims, unpaid wages, most alimony, and other support obligations. Unsecured creditors share any remaining assets on a *pro rata* basis.

Most cases filed under Chapter 7 are "no asset" cases due to liens which encumber the debtor's property and due to the debtor's exemptions. Creditors will not receive a distribution from the bankruptcy court in a "no asset" case, and the debtor will retain all property, subject to the claims of secured creditors.

2. CHAPTER 13

Chapter 13 (11 U.S.C. § 1301 *et seq.*) bankruptcies are also known as "wage earner" plans, and they may be filed by an individual, or a husband and wife together, provided the debtor has a regular source of income. Businesses cannot file Chapter 13 bankruptcies. The debtor proposes a plan to repay creditors over a three to five year period by making payments to a Chapter 13 trustee, who in turn distributes the money to creditors. Only the debtor may propose a plan in a Chapter 13, not the creditors. There are limits on how much a person can owe and still seek Chapter 13 protection. Unsecured debts must total less than $250,000, and secured debts must total less than $750,000. 11 U.S.C. § 109.

Long term secured debt such as mortgage indebtedness will continue to be paid outside the plan. Pre-bankruptcy arrearages on long term debt must be paid through the Chapter 13 trustee. All short term secured debt (less than five years), all tax debt, and all unsecured debt must be paid through the plan.

Secured debt, with the exception of mortgages secured by the debtor's residence, may be modified by reducing the interest rate and by extending the number of payments. By utilizing this option, many Chapter 13 plans result in payments to all creditors in an amount equal to or less than a prebankruptcy payment. Under 11 U.S.C. § 506(a), a secured creditor (other than a mortgagee) is entitled to receive only the value of the secured property. (However, if the creditor is over-secured, the creditor can continue to receive interest.) The remainder of the debt is unsecured, and the secured creditor will share the remaining assets on a *pro rata* basis with the unsecured creditors. This could be paid at 100% or anything less, depending on the debtor's ability to pay. Any amount not paid to unsecured creditors through the plan will be discharged by the bankruptcy. A debtor is required to pay priority claims, such as alimony and child support, in full. However, the claims of the unsecured creditors can be compromised.

3. CHAPTER 11

Individuals and businesses may file under Chapter 11 (11 U.S.C. § 1101 *et seq.*), which is commonly known as a reorganization. It is more expensive than Chapter 13 and may take longer. People who do not qualify for Chapter 12 or 13 file Chapter 11 bankruptcies if they want to reorganize as do businesses that want to reorganize.

A debtor in a South Carolina Chapter 11 case is given a period of 180 days in which to propose a plan to pay creditors. This chapter empowers a debtor to modify the rights of all creditors, including secured creditors. The debtor's plan may reduce the interest rate on secured debt and may provide for a longer period in which to pay the secured claims. Unsecured debt may be compromised in a Chapter 11 case.

In addition to paying a greater filing fee than in the other chapters, a debtor in a Chapter 11 case is required to file monthly operating reports with the court and to pay quarterly fees to the office of the United States Trustee. The debtor also must open separate bank accounts, and the words "debtor-in-possession" must appear on the account. The debtor remains in possession of the funds unless a trustee is appointed for grounds such as incompetence or mismanagement.

Due to the administrative requirements, as well as the nature of Chapter 11 cases, a Chapter 11 case can be burdensome and very expensive. For this reason, most individuals do not elect to file a Chapter 11 action. Chapter 11's chief advantage is that it does not have limits on the amount of debt owed by the debtor. Its chief disadvantage, other than the expense, is that the creditors must vote on the plan.

4. CHAPTER 12[54]

A Chapter 12 (11 U.S.C. § 1201 *et seq.*) proceeding is a farm bankruptcy case. This type of bankruptcy is very similar to a Chapter 13 action. However, to qualify for a Chapter 12 filing, the debtor must be a family farmer with regular annual income. A family farmer can be an individual, a husband and wife, a corporation, or a partnership. The debtor must have debts of less than $1,500,000, of which 80% of the noncontingent liquidated debts (excluding the principal residence) must arise out of the farming operation (excluding a debt for the principal residence). In addition, 50% of the individual's or individual and spouse's gross income for the taxable year preceding the filing of the case must have been generated from farming operations.

---

[54] Chapter 12 was repealed on October 1, 1993 but extended to October 1, 1998, Pub.L. 99-554, Title III, § 302(f), Oct. 27, 1986, 100 Stat. 3124. All cases commenced or pending under Chapter 12, and all matters and proceedings in or relating to such cases, are to be conducted and determined under Chapter 12 as if it had not been repealed. The substantive rights of parties in connection with such cases shall continue to be governed under the laws applicable to such cases as if Chapter 12 had not been repealed. 11 U.S.C. § 1201, notes.

A Chapter 12 debtor must file a reorganization plan no later than 90 days after the filing of the bankruptcy petition. This plan must provide for payments to a Chapter 12 trustee for a period of three to five years. Through this plan, a debtor may modify the rights of secured creditors by reducing the interest rate and stretching out the number of payments. Priority claims must be paid in full. The claims of unsecured creditors can be compromised.

C. PROPERTY OF THE BANKRUPTCY ESTATE

1. INCLUDED ASSETS

The property of the bankruptcy estate is all property in which the debtor has a legal or equitable interest as of the filing of the bankruptcy petition. This includes proceeds, products, offerings, rents, or profits from such property. Property becomes property of the bankruptcy estate by operation of 11 U.S.C. § 541(a) which provides that all legal or equitable interests of the debtor in property becomes property of the bankruptcy estate immediately upon the filing of the petition. Property acquired within 180 days of the filing of the petition by bequest, devise, or inheritance, as a result of a marital property settlement agreement or divorce decree, or as a beneficiary of a life insurance policy or death benefit plan, will also become property of the estate.

Bankruptcy law determines what constitutes property of the bankruptcy estate. The bankruptcy estate's rights in the property are no greater than those which the debtor holds in the property on the date of filing. Earnings from services performed by an individual Chapter 7 or Chapter 11 debtor that are received after the filing date are not property of the estate. However, in Chapter 12 or Chapter 13 cases, property of the estate also includes post petition income and property obtained after the bankruptcy petition is filed. A debtor's interest in property is determined under state law, although the Bankruptcy Code determines what constitutes property of the estate. *Cf. Butner v. U.S.*, 440 U.S. 48, 99 S. Ct. 914, 59 L. Ed. 2d 136 (1979) (holding that a dispute between a bankruptcy trustee and a second mortgage holder over the right to the rents collected during the period between the mortgagor's bankruptcy and the foreclosure sale was a question to be decided by reference to state law).

The certain exceptions which give the bankruptcy estate a greater interest in the property consist of the trustee's avoiding powers, that is, the trustee's powers to demand the return of the debtor's property from a third party. For example, a trustee may possess avoiding powers to set aside preferential transfers or fraudulent conveyances, or to demand the turnover of property from a creditor that repossessed property prior to bankruptcy. These rights would not be available to a debtor outside of bankruptcy, but they are granted to the trustee by the Bankruptcy Code.

There are limits to the extent domestic transfers can be avoided. For example, a trustee may not avoid a transfer if the transfer is a *bona fide* alimony or support payment to a spouse, former spouse, or child of the debtor, and if it was made pursuant to a valid separation agreement, divorce decree, or other order of a court of record, and it has not been assigned. 11 U.S.C. § 547(c)(7).

Whether or not an item is property of the estate may affect the nondebtor spouse's interest in the property. Reference must be made to state law to determine the interest of the debtor. For example, if real estate was awarded by a court to the nondebtor spouse as part of an equitable division of property and the decree awarding the property has become final, the bankruptcy estate's interest in the property is limited to bare legal title, not the ownership interest which was awarded to the non-debtor spouse. This is true even if the real estate is titled in the name of the debtor. *See* 11 U.S.C. § 541(d); *In re Smith*, 123 B.R. 856 (Bankr. D. Neb. 1990).

The *Smith* case involves a land sale contract which was awarded to the wife as part of a divorce proceeding. The real estate remained titled in the name of the debtor and the wife. The debtor, a Chapter 11 debtor-in-possession, claimed a legal interest in the land because the title was still in his name and the name of the wife. The court ruled that under the state judgment the wife was awarded all rights in the land sale contract for her share of marital property. Therefore, the debtor retained nothing upon which his creditors could levy, and he could not exercise the trustee's strong arm powers of Section 544 to avoid the wife's interest in the property.

Section 544 empowers the trustee with the rights and powers of (1) a creditor who has a judicial lien on all property of the debtor; (2) a creditor holding an execution returned unsatisfied; and (3) a bona fide purchaser of real estate other than fixtures from the debtor. This section allows a trustee to defeat the rights of creditors who fail to perfect their interests in property of the estate. *See* 4 *Collier on Bankruptcy* ¶544.02 (1992).

A trustee's strong arm powers must be read in conjunction with S.C. Code Ann. § 20-7-471 (Law. Co-op. Supp.), which provides that a spouse acquires a vested special equity and ownership right in property acquired during the marriage. Although a spouse is granted a special equity and ownership right in marital property acquired during the marriage, the ownership right in marital property cannot attach until that property is created by the filing of marital litigation. The filing of a bankruptcy petition by a spouse prior to the commencement of the marital litigation may result in the non-debtor spouse's loss of property rights as a result of the trustee's strong arm powers. A nonfiling creditor should consider filing a lis pendens upon the prepetition commencement of marital litigation.

The former wife in *Prosser v. Pee Dee State Bank*, 295 S.C. 212, 367 S.E.2d 698 (1988), sought a declaration that a 1983 judgment obtained by the Pee Dee State Bank against the husband was subordinate to the wife's "vested special equity" and ownership right in marital property which she acquired under S.C. Code Ann. § 20-7-471 (Law. Co-op. Supp.). The wife initiated a divorce proceeding in 1986, and a divorce was granted in 1986. The court ruled that the wife's "ownership right" did not attach until 1986 when she filed the divorce petition. The bank's judgment lien attached when it was recorded three years earlier and was superior to the wife's interest in certain real estate owned by the parties. The application of this authority in a bankruptcy case could result in defeating the non-debtor spouse's ownership rights in the marital property if a domestic action is not commenced before bankruptcy.

The rights of third parties are affected only when notice of pendency of action is filed. S.C. Code Ann. § 20-7-477 (Law. Co-op. Supp.). Thus, it is strongly recommended that a *lis pendens* be filed in all counties in which the parties own real estate and in the county in which the domestic action is proceeding, and that it be filed immediately upon the filing of the domestic action, provided that the domestic action is initiated prior to the bankruptcy filing. This will prevent a trustee from raising the issue that his or her rights in marital property are not affected by the marital litigation due to the failure to file a *lis pendens*.

2. EXEMPTED ASSETS

South Carolina "opted out" of the federal exemptions provided by 11 U.S.C. § 522(d). Therefore, South Carolina debtors must claim exemptions under state law or other federal laws. Exemptions allow debtors to prevent some property from being used to satisfy their debts. Property exempted by state law is listed in S.C. Code Ann. § 15-41-30 (Law. Co-op. Supp.). Other exemptions are scattered throughout a variety of other statutes. Practitioners should obtain a copy of the bankruptcy court form titled "Debtor's Claim for Property Exemption," which lists all exemptions and provides citations to the specific legislative provisions which authorize them. A few examples of exempted property include: homestead, $5,000.00; motor vehicle, $1,200.00; household furnishings and goods, clothing, appliances, books, animals, crops, musical instruments, $2,500.00; jewelry, $500.00; professionally prescribed health aids, no limit; tools of the trade, $750.00; and state employee retirement system benefits, no limit. S.C. Code Ann. §§ 9-1-1680 & 15-41-30 (Law. Co-op. Supp.).

Of particular importance to family court practitioners is the provision which exempts an unlimited amount of alimony, support, and separate maintenance payments. S.C. Code Ann. § 15-41-30(10)(D)(Law. Co-op. Supp.).

The exemptions apply in all individual bankruptcy cases, and they apply whether or not a debtor is involved in a bankruptcy proceeding. The debtor is entitled to avoid certain liens which impair the debtor's right to claim an exemption.

D. EXCEPTIONS TO DISCHARGE

1. SPOUSAL AND CHILD SUPPORT CANNOT BE DISCHARGED

a. In General

Alimony and child support are generally nondischargeable. 11 U.S.C. § 523(a) provides that a bankruptcy discharge does not discharge the debtor's obligation:

> (5) to a spouse, former spouse, or child of the debtor, for alimony to, maintenance for, or support of such spouse or child, in connection with a separation agreement, divorce decree or other order of a court of record, determination made in accordance with state or territorial law by a governmental unit, or property settlement agreement, but not to the extent that
>
> > (A) such debt is assigned to another entity, voluntarily, by operation of law, or otherwise (other than debts assigned pursuant to section 408(a)(3) of the Social Security Act, or any such debt which has been assigned to the Federal Government or to a State or any political subdivision of such State); or
> >
> > (B) such debt includes a liability designated as alimony, maintenance, or support, unless such liability is actually in the nature of alimony, maintenance, or support; or of any debt;

An order for payment of support must satisfy a two prong test before the debt will be declared nondischargeable by the bankruptcy court: first, the obligation must be payable on behalf of a spouse, former spouse or child; and, second, the obligation must be in the nature of alimony, maintenance, or support. *In re Scott*, 194 B.R. 375

(Bankr. D.S.C. 1995); *In re Burns*, 186 B.R. 637 (Bankr. D.S.C. 1992); *Cribb v. Cribb (In re Cribb)*, 34 B.R. 862 (Bankr. D.S.C. 1983).

The fact that "alimony" is waived by a spouse in a divorce proceeding and the debtor's obligation to the spouse is described as a "property settlement" does not mean that a bankruptcy court is bound by this label. *In re Carrig*, 14 B.R. 658, 8 Bankr. Ct. Dec. (CRR) 330, 5 Collier Bankr. Cas. 2d (MB) 446 (Bankr. D.S.C. 1984) (holding that in the absence of any evidence of collusion, the payments to be made by the husband to the wife to provide her with a place to live in consideration for her giving up her residence in the marital home were in the nature of alimony and were not dischargeable). Legislative history makes it clear that bankruptcy law and not state law determines whether a debt is alimony, maintenance or support. H.R. Rep. No. 595, 95th Cong., 1st Sess. 363 (1977); S. Rep. No. 989, 95th Cong., 2d Sess. 77-79 (1978). However, bankruptcy courts most often look to state law in formulating this determination.

The burden of proving nondischargability of an obligation under 11 U.S.C. § 523(a)(5) rests with the creditor. *Carrig*. However, the failure of a former spouse to file a timely objection to discharge does not make such a debt dischargeable. *In re Campbell*, 30 B.R. 664 (Bankr. D.S.C. 1983) (holding that, to the extent that a debt is for support, it is not dischargeable regardless of whether a challenge is filed as to its dischargeability).

Fees and costs awarded by the family court in addition to direct payments of spousal or child support may be nondischargeable if they are considered in the nature of support. For example, attorneys' fees awarded pursuant to a divorce decree are nondischargeable if they are in the nature of support. In *In re Brown*, Op. No. 81-00585 (Bankr. D.S.C. 1982), the bankruptcy judge found in light of the debtor's wife's waiver of alimony that the family court's award of fees to the wife's attorney was in the nature of support and, therefore, nondischargeable. The bankruptcy court noted that the family court judge "had information regarding the financial condition of both parties before him at the time of his ruling, and determined the financial needs of the wife and her children were such that the burden of attorney's fees incurred by the wife should be borne by the husband." *Brown* (citing *In re French*, 9 B.R. 464, Bankr. L. Rep. (CCH) ¶68207, 4 Collier Bankr. Cas. 2d (MB) 263 (Bankr. S.D. Cal. 1981), which held that such payments are in the nature of support payments and, thus, nondischargeable). *See also In re Brunner*, 84-01428 (Bankr. D.S.C. 1985), which reached the same conclusion in view of the wife's financial needs.

A debtor's obligation to pay joint debts of himself and wife, including credit cards debts or a home mortgage, are nondischargeable if the debt is in the nature of support. *In re Burns*, 186 B.R. 637 (Bankr. D.S.C. 1992). Although the obligation was not directly payable to the wife, it was on her behalf and the debts were household obligations and routine living expenses which, if not assumed by the husband, would diminish the wife's and child's standard of living. It also appeared that the wife would not have relinquished her right to alimony and child support but for the debtor's assumption of responsibility for these joint debts.

A debt created by an order to pay part of the fees for a psychologist and a guardian *ad litem* in a divorce case may be nondischargeable in bankruptcy. In *In re Miller*, 55 F.3d 1487 (10th Cir. 1995), *cert. den.* 116 S.Ct. 305, the court determined that these fees were in the nature of support and the wife was not allowed to discharge them, even though she was awarded alimony and child support in the divorce proceeding. *Accord, Pauley v. Sprong*, 661 F.2d 6 (2d Cir. 1981). Similarly, a guardian *ad litem*'s attorneys fees and the moving party's attorneys fees in a termination of parental rights case may be nondischargeable as support. *Matter of Dvorak*, 986 F.2d 940 (5th Cir. 1993) (holding that the proceedings were for the benefit and support of the child).

b. If Assigned, Support Obligations Can be Discharged

A debt for alimony, maintenance, or support which is nondischargeable under 11 U.S.C. § 523(a)(5) becomes dischargeable if it is assigned to another entity voluntarily, by operation of law, or otherwise except child support which has been assigned to a state in exchange for Aid to Families with Dependant Children. It is permissible for the debtor to pay third parties directly. For example, the debtor can make mortgage payments to the mortgage holder rather than giving the spouse money for the mortgage payment. Thus, for example, some courts have held that, if a spouse who wins an award of past due child support assigns this right to her attorney, the debt becomes dischargeable in bankruptcy. *Cf. In re Mozingo* 153 B.R. 276 (Bankr. W.D.Mo. 1993) (holding that the public policy supporting nondischargeability was no longer served the moment the former spouse's attorney became entitled to receive the benefit of the debt rather than the former spouse).

c. A Spouse's Lien on Marital Property May Be Nondischargeable

A lien on marital property which is created by a court order at the same time the marital property is divided by the court is nondischargeable if its purpose is to provide child or spousal support and it has not been assigned. Most liens, including judicial liens, can be avoided by filing bankruptcy. However, 11 U.S.C. § 522(f)(1)(A) provides that a debtor may not avoid the fixing of a lien on an interest of the debtor in property to the extent that such lien impairs an exemption to which the debtor would have been entitled, if such lien is a judicial lien that secures a debt:

> (i) to a spouse, former spouse, or child of the debtor, for alimony to, maintenance for, or support of such spouse or child, in connection with a separation agreement, divorce decree or other order of a court of record, determination made in accordance with State or territorial law by a governmental unit, or property settlement agreement; and
>
> (ii) to the extent that such debt (I) is not assigned to another entity, voluntarily, by operation of law, or otherwise; and (II) includes a liability designated as alimony, maintenance, or support, unless such liability is actually in the nature of alimony, maintenance or support.

2. INTERSPOUSAL DEBTS ARISING FROM PROPERTY DIVISION MAY BE NONDISCHARGEABLE

Debts arising from property divisions between divorcing spouses are nondischargeable unless the debtor spouse cannot otherwise support himself or his dependents or continue operating his business, or unless the detriment to him of paying the debt outweighs the detriment to the spouse of nonpayment. 11 U.S.C. § 523(a) provides that a debt is not dischargeable if it is a debt:

> (15) not of the kind described in paragraph (5) [alimony and child support] that is incurred by the debtor in the course of a divorce or separation or in connection with a separation agreement, divorce decree or other order of a court of record, a determination made in accordance with State or territorial law by a governmental unit unless--
>
> > (A) the debtor does not have the ability to pay such debt from income or property of the debtor not reasonably necessary to be expended for the maintenance or support of the debtor or a dependent of the debtor and, if the debtor is engaged in a business, for the payment of expenditures necessary for the continuation, preservation, and operation of such business; or
> >
> > (B) discharging such debt would result in a benefit to the debtor that outweighs the detrimental consequences to a spouse, former spouse, or child of the debtor.

The factors to be examined in determining whether the benefits of discharging the debtor's property related divorce debts outweigh the detrimental consequences to the nondebtor spouse include, but are not limited to: the incomes and expenses of both parties; whether the nondebtor spouse is jointly liable on the debts; the number of dependents; the nature of the debts; reaffirmation of any debts; and the nondebtor spouse's ability to pay. *In re Campbell*, 198 B.R. 467 (Bankr. D.S.C. 1996); *In re Scott*, 194 B.R. 375 (Bankr. D.S.C. 1995).

The statute only protects property divisions resulting from a separation agreement, divorce decree, or property settlement agreement. Mere common law liability is insufficient to invoke this exception to discharge. 3 *Collier on Bankruptcy* ¶523.15[2] (1992).

A complaint objecting to the discharge of a property division debt division must be filed within 60 days of the date scheduled for the first meeting of creditors. 11 U.S.C. Bankruptcy Rules (Supp.), Rule 4007(c).

A property division debt arising from a divorce is still dischargeable if the debtor files a Chapter 13 bankruptcy, which provides for a restructuring of debt. However, the nonfiling spouse has the protections of any other Chapter 13 creditor. The debt repayment plan must be proposed in good faith and provide for payment in full of debts for child or spousal support.

E. AUTOMATIC STAY

1. IN GENERAL

An automatic stay is imposed when a bankruptcy action is filed. This prohibits any disposition of or collection attempts against property of the bankrupt person's estate. The stay takes effect immediately upon the filing of a bankruptcy petition, and without notice. 11 U.S.C. § 362. This can impede marital litigation unless relief from the stay is granted by the bankruptcy court.

A good example of the potential impact of the automatic stay is provided by *In re McWhorter*, 37 B.R. 742 (Bankr. D.S.C. 1984). Later on the same day he filed a bankruptcy petition, the debtor was ordered by the family court to immediately transfer legal title to an automobile to his former wife. This order was issued because the family court awarded the former wife all interest in the automobile in its divorce decree which was filed prior to date on which the bankruptcy petition was filed. However, because the debtor held legal title to the automobile at time he filed for Chapter 7 bankruptcy, the automobile became property of the bankruptcy estate, and the family court's order was ineffective against the estate.

The automatic stay specifically bars the following activities:

-the commencement or continuation of judicial, administrative or other actions against the debtors that could have been commenced prepetition to recover a prepetition claim;

-the enforcement against the debtor or against property of the estate of a judgment obtained before the commencement of the case;

-any act to obtain possession of property of the estate or to exercise control over property;

-any act to create, perfect or enforce any lien against property of the estate;

-any act to create, perfect, or enforce against property of the debtor any lien that secures a claim that arose before the commencement of the case;

-any act to collect, assess or recover a claim against the debtor that arose before the commencement of the case;

-the set off of any debt owing to the debtor that arose before the commencement of the case; and

-the commencement or continuation of a United States Tax Court proceeding.

11 U.S.C. § 362(a).

The automatic stay does not stay the commencement or continuation of an action or proceeding to establish paternity, establish or modify alimony, maintenance or support, or to collect alimony, maintenance and support from property that is not part of the bankrupt estate. 11 U.S.C. § 362(b)(2). However, it may be prudent to seek relief from the stay before proceeding in such actions.

A violation of the automatic stay which is knowing and willful may result in an award of damages, including punitive damages, and the party violating the stay may be held in contempt of the bankruptcy court. 11 U.S.C. § 362(h).

Actions taken in violation of the automatic stay are probably void. In *In re Stringer*, 847 F.2d 549 (9th Cir. 1988), the court stated: "Any proceedings in violation of the automatic stay in bankruptcy are void. The automatic stay is subject, however, to several narrow exceptions including 'the collection of alimony, maintenance, or support.' 11 U.S.C. § 362(b)(2)." *Id.* at 551. *Stringer* held that a state court order modifying a prior child support order was void because the modification order could not be considered "collection" of child support and was, therefore, in violation of the stay and void.

However, in *In re Brooks*, 79 B.R. 479, 16 Bankr. Ct. Dec. (CCH) 992 (Bankr. 9th Cir. 1987), the husband filed for bankruptcy, during which a transfer of property was made despite the stay, without objection from the husband's trustee. The husband and the wife later divorced. Subsequently, she filed for bankruptcy and her trustee claimed that the transfer during the husband's bankruptcy was void. The U.S. Court of Appeals held that "a post-petition transfer in violation of a stay is not absolutely void once committed, but rather voidable." *Id.* at 480. The court determined that the husband's trustee had discretion under 11 U.S.C. § 549 to choose whether to avoid the transfer of property which occurred after the commencement of the bankruptcy action. As the trustee had chosen not to object, the transfer was valid and the wife's trustee's claim was rejected.

Co-debtors are also protected by the automatic stay in Chapter 12 or Chapter 13 cases. This stay protects co-debtors from collection efforts by creditors on consumer debts. The co-debtor stay may be important in a domestic proceeding. The stay protects the non-debtor spouse from the claims of creditors on joint debts. For example, a creditor cannot proceed against a spouse who co-signed loan agreements with the bankruptcy petitioner, even though the spouse has not filed for bankruptcy protection.

A creditor subject to the co-debtor stay may get relief from the co-debtor stay, if the Chapter 12 or Chapter 13 plan does not propose to pay the co-debtor obligation in full. A debtor or another creditor must respond to a creditor's motion for relief within twenty days or the stay will be lifted.

2. DURATION OF AUTOMATIC STAY

The duration of the automatic stay is controlled by 11 U.S.C. § 362(c) which provides that, except as otherwise provided in section 362 (d), (e), and (f):

(1) the stay of an act against property of the estate under subsection (a) of this section continues until such property is no longer property of the estate; and

(2) the stay of any other act under subsection (a) of this section continues until the earliest of:

(A) the time the case is closed;

(B) the time the case is dismissed; or

(C) if the case is a case under chapter 7 of this title concerning an individual or a case under chapter 9, 11, 12, or 13 of this title, the time a discharge is granted or denied.

Property ceases to be property of the estate if it is exempted by the debtor, sold by the trustee, or abandoned. Of course, it is not possible to pursue collection of alimony or support from property which is sold by the bankruptcy trustee. Property which is claimed as exempt or which is abandoned is property of the debtor protected by the stay of 11 U.S.C. § 362(a)(5).

In a Chapter 11 case, property of the estate vests in the debtor upon confirmation of the plan, and the order of confirmation also acts as a discharge to the debtor.

3. OBTAINING RELIEF FROM AUTOMATIC STAY

a. In General

Depending on the nature of the proceeding, it may be possible to obtain relief from the automatic stay in order to continue an action against a debtor who files for bankruptcy. Immediately upon learning of a bankruptcy filing by a spouse involved in a domestic proceeding an assessment should be made to determine whether the continuation of the domestic proceeding violates the stay.

Relief from the automatic stay shall be granted for cause, including the lack of adequate protection of a person's interest in the property. 11 U.S.C. § 362(d)(1). Relief may also be granted if the debtor does not have any equity in the property and the property is not necessary to an effective reorganization. 11 U.S.C. § 362(d)(2). The party requesting relief has the burden of proof on the issue of the debtor's equity in the property, and the debtor has the burden of proof on other issues. 11 U.S.C. § 362(g).

When relief is granted to pursue the collection of debts outside of the bankruptcy proceedings, one can only collect from post petition property (property acquired after the bankruptcy action was commenced) or property which is not property of the bankruptcy estate. Property of the estate in a Chapter 12 or Chapter 13 case may include post petition property or post petition earnings. Care should be taken to define and pursue only the relief granted by the bankruptcy court.

b. Relief Related to Paternity or Support

The automatic stay does not operate as a stay of the commencement or continuation of an action or proceeding for the establishment of paternity, the establishment or modification of an order for alimony, maintenance or support, or the collection of alimony, maintenance, or support from property that is not property of the estate. 11 U.S.C. § 362(b)(2). However, due to the difficulty of proceeding against property which is not property of the estate without also proceeding against the debtor, a safer practice is to obtain relief from the automatic stay to pursue such matters. One should also seek a declaration from the bankruptcy court that the nondebtor spouse has authority to proceed against the debtor and the estate as well as against property which is not included in the bankruptcy estate.

A nondebtor spouse who wishes to pursue modification of spousal or child support should seek relief from the stay under 11 U.S.C. § 362(d)(1), which allows relief "for cause." *See In re Harrell*, 105 B.R. 751 (Bankr. M.D. Ga. 1989) (allowing relief from the stay for a mother to seek modification of spousal support in state court); *In re McDonald*, 755 F.2d 715 (9th Cir. 1985) (allowing relief from the stay for a mother to seek modification of spousal support in state court).

A nonfiling spouse can obtain relief to pursue payment of support arrearages where the debtor has not proposed a plan to pay prebankruptcy support arrearages. However, if a Chapter 11, 12, or 13 plan provides for payment of the arrearages, a bankruptcy court may find that "cause" does not exist and deny the motion. Debts to a spouse or a child for alimony, maintenance, or support must be included in a Chapter 13 plan, and the plan must provide for full payment. 11 U.S.C. § 1322(a)(2); § 507(a)(7) (Supp.).

c. Relief to Pursue Division of Marital Property

Equitable distribution proceedings are stayed by the filing of a bankruptcy petition. However, relief from stays can be obtained. Bankruptcy courts recognize that state courts have special expertise in equitable distribution disputes to which the federal courts owe significant deference. *Robbins v. Robbins (In re Robbins)*, 964 F.2d 342, 345-346 (4th Cir. 1992). *Robbins* considers whether the stay should be lifted to allow an ongoing equitable distribution proceeding to continue. It holds that the stay should be lifted in such cases.

Whether a spouse should be allowed to imitate an equitable distribution proceeding after a bankruptcy petition is filed is addressed in *Roberge v. Roberge (In re Roberge)*, 188 B.R. 366 (Bankr. E.D.Va. 1995). The husband filed for bankruptcy protection after obtaining an *ex parte* divorce without notice to the wife. The divorce court did not have jurisdiction to divide the marital property. The wife initiated an equitable distribution proceeding and, upon learning the husband had filed for bankruptcy, she requested relief from the stay. Relying on the reasoning of the Fourth Circuit in *Robbins*, the *Roberge* court held that it was appropriate to lift the stay and allow the wife to proceed with her equitable distribution action. It said the question of whether a creditor's lien against marital assets after vesting of equitable distribution rights, but before an equitable distribution award is made, cuts off those equitable rights is a matter of state law best left to state courts. The court also noted that it was unlikely under the facts of that case that the husband and wife would engage in collusion to the detriment of the creditors. *Roberge* notes that the case law on this issue is evenly divided around the country.

The factors that the bankruptcy court should consider in deciding whether to lift a stay are set forth in *Robbins*: (1) whether the issues in the pending litigation involve only state law, so the expertise of the bankruptcy court is unnecessary; (2) whether modifying the stay will promote judicial economy and whether there would be greater interference with the bankruptcy case if the stay were not lifted; and (3) whether the estate can be protected properly by a requirement that creditors seek enforcement of any judgment through the bankruptcy court. A request for relief from the stay was denied without prejudice in *In re Ackerman*, 194 B.R. 404 (Bankr. D.S.C. 1996), because the bankruptcy court would probably hear the matter within a few months while the family court would probably not get to it for a year (judicial economy) and in part because the case involved an issue of fraudulent conveyance which must be heard in the bankruptcy court (the issues did not involve only state law).

Other factors the court will consider are (1) which court is likely to reach the matter first, and (2) whether the case involves issues which must be resolved by the bankruptcy court.

If relief is granted for the family court to determine the division of marital property, the bankruptcy court retains jurisdiction over the debtor's property once the debtor's interest is determined. *Robbins* at 346; *In re White*, 851 F.2d 170 (6th Cir. 1988) (holding that the bankruptcy court did not abuse its discretion in permitting a state court divorce action, pending at the time of bankruptcy, to decide how the marital property would be divided. The bankruptcy court allowed the family court to determine the division of marital property, but retained exclusive jurisdiction over the debtor's property once the debtor's interest was determined.).

d. Procedures for Obtaining Relief from Stay

The procedures for obtaining relief from the automatic stay, other than relief to pursue collection of child support, are contained in Rule 4001-1 of the Local Rules of the United States Bankruptcy Court for the District of South Carolina, December 1, 1996 (Local Rules). A nondebtor spouse who desires relief from a stay must file a motion for relief from the stay with the bankruptcy court and pay a filing fee. A form entitled "Certification of Facts" setting out the facts and grounds supporting the request for relief should be included with the motion. The moving party selects a hearing date from a list of available dates provided by the clerk of court, typically within 30 days of the filing of the motion. The court will provide a notice of the hearing on the motion. The moving party must serve, at least 15 days before the hearing date, the following documents on the debtor, the debtor's attorney, and the trustee if one has been appointed: the § 362 motion, the certification of facts, the notice of hearing, a blank certification of facts, and a certification of service of the preceding items. These documents, except the blank certification, must be simultaneously filed with the clerk.

Anyone who wishes to object to a motion for relief from the stay must file an objection within 10 days after being served. Each objecting party must serve on the moving party and file with the clerk an objection to the motion, a certification of facts, and a certification of service.

If no objection is filed and served on the moving party within 10 days, the moving party shall file: a certificate indicating that no objection has been served, and a proposed order granting the relief sought by the moving party. If these documents are filed more than 48 hours before the scheduled hearing date, the hearing may be canceled by the court. Otherwise, the moving party must appear at the hearing and present the certificate and proposed order to the court.

In a Chapter 11 case, the pleadings must also be served on the unsecured creditor's committee, unless a committee has not been appointed. If a committee has not been appointed, the motion must be served on the twenty (20) largest unsecured creditors in the Chapter 11 case.

In cases involving child support obligations, there are special provisions which make it easier to obtain relief from the stay. Child support creditors or their representatives are permitted to appear and intervene without charge and without meeting any special local court rule requirement for attorney appearances. A lawyer does not have to be admitted to practice in federal court to seek a relief from a stay to pursue collection of a child support obligation. If the debtor does not object, relief can be granted without a hearing.

The specific procedures for obtaining relief from the stay to pursue the collection of child support are contained in Local Rule 4001-3. The custodian of a child who is owed child support by the debtor must file a motion of intent to collect child support. In addition to an executed notice of motion and motion of intent to collect child support, the moving party must also simultaneously submit to the clerk of court a copy of the child support order or child support agreement; a certificate of service by first class mail of the notice of motion and motion upon the debtor, the debtor's attorney, and the bankruptcy trustee, if one has been appointed; and a proposed order. The bankruptcy court provides straightforward forms for this purpose.

If the debtor properly objects within 20 days of the mailing of the motion of intent to collect child support, a hearing will be scheduled on the matter.

If the debtor, debtor 's attorney, or trustee does not file an objection to the motion of intent to collect child support, the court may enter the order filed with the motion, and the moving party may proceed to collect the child support. Collection of child support under Rule 4001-3 is limited to collection from the debtor's post-petition wages, earnings, or income. In a chapter 13 case in which relief is granted under Rule 4001-3, any right to collect child support from post-petition wages of the debtor is subordinated to, and subject to, any order to pay trustee issued by the bankruptcy court and such child support may be collected only to the extent there are excess monies remaining after payment of the order to pay the trustee.

CHAPTER SIXTEEN
TAXATION

CHAPTER SIXTEEN
TAXATION[55]

A. IN GENERAL

The purpose of this chapter is to present the essential and basic federal income tax rules that directly relate to divorce, separation, child support, property and other concerns in the divorce context. It is not an exhaustive compilation. During the initial drafting of this chapter, over 1,700 pages of code provisions, regulations and statutes relating to taxes were generated. This summary description of tax law is intended to help the practicing lawyer recognize the need for further research or for the employment of an expert.

Lawyers practicing in this area will often say, "I'll rely on the C.P.A. to advise me and my client on tax matters." However, the lawyer needs to understand the tax laws well enough to know when to refer matters to a C.P.A. In many cases, of course, there is not enough money to justify using a C.P.A. Very few accountants or family court lawyers are well-versed in the tax laws relating to divorce. However, all practitioners need some basic understanding of tax law to function appropriately in advising their clients.

The format of this chapter presents the tax rules related to each area which were in effect before the Domestic Relations Tax Reform Act of 1984, followed by the rules presently in effect. The "old law" is presented for an important reason: these rules remain in effect for orders and agreements issued or entered into prior to 1984/1985. Current actions involving cases with orders in effect before the effective dates for the new rules will be governed by prior tax law. Examples of such actions include contempt, change of economic circumstances, child support changes and proceedings for enforcement. In dealing with such prior orders, the practitioner should consider whether to "elect into" the new rules or whether it would be

[55] Dennis L. Dabney, C.P.A., helped write this chapter. Mr. Dabney and Raymond E. McKay, Jr., Esquire, reviewed the 1995 supplement and provided helpful suggestions, additions and deletions to the materials.

beneficial to the parties to continue the applicability of the "old rules" to the situation. In the area of alimony, there exist three separate sets of rules for deductibility qualification, depending on the execution date of the original judgment of the court.

B. CHILDREN

1. CHILD SUPPORT

Child support payments are nondeductible to the payor and not taxed as income to the person receiving the payments if (1) they are fixed by a "decree," instrument or agreement in effect at the time the payments are made and (2) the payments are for the support of the children of the payor. I.R.C. §§ 71(a), (b)(2), (c); § 262.

2. DEPENDENCY EXEMPTIONS

a. Dependency Exemptions Prior to DRTRA (1984)

Generally, a divorced or separated parent who had custody of a child for a greater part of the year was entitled to claim the exemption for the child, if the parents together had custody of the child for more than one-half of the year and provided more than one-half of the child's support. A special rule provided that the non-custodial parent could claim the dependency exemption if (1) a decree or written agreement allocated the exemption to the non-custodial parent and such parent paid at least $600 for the support of the child during the calendar year and (2) the non-custodial parent provided at least $1,200 for the support of the child during the year and the custodial parent did not clearly establish proof of providing a greater portion of support than the non-custodial parent. Special "multiple support" agreements between divorced spouses overrode all of the above rules.

b. Dependency Exemptions Under DRTRA (1984)

The Domestic Relations Tax Reform Act of 1984 (DRTRA (1984)) established new dependency exemption rules which apply to tax years beginning after December 31, 1984. The rules apply to parents living apart at all times during the last six (6) months of the calendar year. Parents living apart for the last six (6) months of the year may qualify under the more favorable head-of-household filing status if other eligibility tests are met (see below). A child is treated as a dependent of both parents for purposes of medical expenses.

Under the DRTRA (1984), the custodial parent (divorced or separated) is entitled to the dependency exemption so long as both parents contribute at least half the child's support. However, the custodial parent may assign his or her right to the dependency exemption as custodial parent, provided he or she completes IRS Form 8332, "Release of Claim to Exemption for Child of Divorced or Separated Parents." The form must be attached to the non-custodial parent's tax return each and every year for which the exemption is assigned.

A decree of divorce or separation instrument which was executed before January 1, 1985, and which provides that the non-custodial parent is entitled to the dependency exemption will be honored, provided that at least $600 in support is provided for the child during the year by such parent. A pre-1985 instrument may be modified to adopt the new rules. The modification must expressly state that the provisions of the Domestic Relations Tax Reform Act of 1984 will apply. *See* I.R.C. § 152(a), (e).

Family court judges have the authority to allocate the right to claim the dependency exemption to either parent pursuant to the Internal Revenue Code and corresponding state tax provisions and to require the execution and delivery of all necessary documents and tax filings in connection with the exemption. *See* S.C. Code Ann. § 20-3-130(F) (Law. Co-op. Supp.). If the parties wish to restrict the court's ability to allocate the dependency exemption, "any provision in the settlement agreement denying the court jurisdiction must be 'explicit, clear, and plain.'" *Robinson v. Tyson*, 319 S.C. 360, 365, 461 S.E.2d 397, 400 (Ct. App. 1995) (quoting *Moseley v. Mosier*, 279 S.C. 348, 353, 306 S.E.2d 624, 627 (1983)). Although the former husband argued that the family court did not have subject matter jurisdiction to modify the tax exemption status of the parties because the court order was based on the agreement of the parties, the court could find no provision in the parties' agreement which excluded the family court's jurisdiction to modify the tax deduction status of the parties. Thus, it upheld the trial court's decision to modify the court decree and grant the dependent tax deduction for the daughter to the mother.

A curious aspect of ***Robinson*** is that it leaves open the question of whether the tax deduction status award is an incident of spousal support or equitable division. The court specifically finds that it is not an issue directly related to the best interests of the children and the court was not authorized to modify it on that basis. Therefore, one might infer that the court's power to modify the tax status arises from its character as spousal support (although the opinion does not say so) because property divisions are not modifiable. However, there was no finding of changed circumstances to justify a modification of spousal support, and the court refused to address the question of whether the trial judge abused his discretion in modifying the tax deduction award because it had not been asked to decide that issue.

3. DEDUCTIONS FOR CHILD-RELATED EXPENSES

Certain medical care costs paid for a dependent child by a parent may be deducted, to the extent the expenses, combined with the allowable medical expenses of the parent, exceed seven and a half percent (7.5%) of adjusted gross income. This deduction is not limited to the custodial parent and cannot have been reimbursed, e.g., by insurance. I.R.C. §§ 105, 213.

There is also a tax credit allowed for a portion of the expenses related to child care costs in certain situations. For individuals who maintain a household which includes one or more "qualifying individuals," there is a tax credit equal to the "applicable percentage" of the "employment-related expenses" paid by such individual. A "qualifying individual" can be either (1) a dependent of the taxpayer who is under the age of fifteen and who can be claimed as a dependent by the taxpayer under I.R.C. § 151(c); (2) a dependent of the taxpayer who is physically or mentally incapable of caring for himself or herself; or (3) the spouse of the taxpayer, if the spouse is physically or mentally incapable of caring for himself or herself. "Applicable percentage" means thirty percent (30%) reduced (not below twenty percent (20%)) by one percentage point for each $2,000 (or fraction thereof) by which the taxpayer's adjusted gross income for the taxable year exceeds $10,000. "Employment-related expenses" are the amounts paid for household services and for the care of a qualifying individual, if such expenses are incurred to enable the taxpayer to be gainfully employed for any period for which there are one or more qualifying individuals. *See* I.R.C. § 21.

C. ALIMONY

1. ALIMONY PRIOR TO DRTRA (1984)

Payments of alimony pursuant to a decree of divorce or separate maintenance, a written separation agreement or decree for support or maintenance were deductible by the payor spouse and includible in the income of the recipient spouse. The amount of payment was allowable as a deduction whether or not the payor itemized his or her deductions. In order to be treated as alimony, a payment had to meet several requirements. First, the payment must have been imposed under the decree of divorce or separate maintenance or under a written instrument incident to the divorce or separation. Second, the payment must have been in discharge of a legal obligation based on a family or marital relationship. Third, the payment had to qualify as "periodic." A payment would not qualify as "periodic" if it discharged a principal sum, unless the sum could be paid over a period exceeding ten (10) years from date of the providing instrument, and the annual amount could not exceed ten percent (10%) of the principal sum. A contingent payment was not a payment in discharge of a principal sum.

2. ALIMONY UNDER DRTRA (1984) AND TRA (1986)

The Domestic Relations Tax Reform Act of 1984 (DRTRA (1984)) repealed prior alimony law tax requirements. The provisions changing alimony requirements are applied to instruments executed after December 31, 1984. Instruments which were executed before January 1, 1985, can be modified to be subject to these new provisions.

In general, the Tax Reform Act of 1986 (TRA (1986)) did not change the rules governing the federal income tax treatment of alimony and separate support and maintenance payments. However, the new law removed certain limitations regarding spousal support payment qualifications. These changes make certain payments qualify as alimony or separate maintenance under the Tax Reform Act of 1986 that would not have qualified under prior law.

a. Alimony Criteria Unaffected by TRA (1986)

The general rule is that alimony and separate support payments are taxed to the recipient and deducted by the payor, if the payments meet the criteria set by the tax laws. The DRTRA (1984) provided the following criteria for alimony qualification, which were not changed by the TRA (1986):

1) Payments must be made in cash.

2) Payor and payee may not be members of the same household at time of payment.

3) The parties (or the court) may designate the payment or a portion of the payment to be tax free.

4) If any amount specified in the instrument will be reduced on the happening of a contingency relating to a child, then an equal amount will be treated as child support (not deductible) rather than alimony.

b. Minimum Term and Front-Loading Provisions

The DRTRA (1984) provided that alimony payments in excess of $10,000 per year would be deductible only if the instrument provided that the payor spouse was required to make alimony payments for at least six (6) years. The DRTRA (1984) also provided that, in order to be deductible, alimony payments could not vary by more than $10,000 during any of the required six (6) years. To the extent that prior year payments exceeded the current year's payment by more than $10,000, such amounts for the prior years had to be recaptured as income to the payor and as a deduction to the payee.

The TRA (1986) repealed the six (6) year minimum term rule and the six (6) year ("front-loading") recapture rule and replaced them with a three (3) year ("front-loading") recapture rule. The TRA (1986) also increased the amount of annual payments that are exempt from any front-loading limitation from $10,000 to $15,000. All recaptured amounts occur in the third "post-separation" year. "Post-separation" is defined in I.R.C. § 71(f)(6) as follows:

> For purposes of this subsection, the term "1st post-separation years" means the first calendar year in which the payor spouse paid to the payee spouse alimony or separate maintenance payments to which this section applies. The second and third post-separation years shall be the first and second succeeding calendar years, respectively.

The recomputation occurs only in the third year. I.R.C. § 71(f)(1)(A); Temp. Treas. Reg. § 1.71-1T(Q-26). Under the DRTRA (1984), the recomputation occurred whenever payments in early years were substantially larger than payments in later years.

The DRTRA (1984) recapture rule was retroactively amended by the TRA (1986) to shorten the recapture period to three (3) years for divorce or separation instruments executed after December 31, 1986. However, the 1986 law continues the $10,000 computation base for instruments executed in 1985 and 1986. The six (6) year minimum term rule under DRTRA (1984) is not affected unless the instrument is modified. Instruments executed under the DRTRA (1984) between January 1, 1985, and December 31, 1986, may be expressly modified to have the new rules applied. Such amendments apply for the taxable year in which the modification is made and all subsequent taxable years.

The DRTRA (1984) also included the following provisions which were not changed by the TRA (1986):

1) In applying the "recapture rules," years beginning with the tax year of the death of either spouse or the remarriage of the payee spouse will be ignored, if death or remarriage terminates the payments.

2) Payments to be made over a period of at least six (6) years which fluctuate (beyond the control of payor) as a result of a continuing liability to pay a fixed percentage of income from the earnings of a business, property or services are not taken into account in applying these rules.

3) Support amounts provided under a temporary support order or agreement are not to be considered for purposes of recapture.

c. Termination At Death Provisions

The DRTRA (1984) required the divorce or separation instrument to state that there was no liability to make payments for any period after the death of the payee spouse. This rule also applied to temporary orders.

The TRA (1986) continues the rule that payments may qualify as alimony or separate maintenance payments only if the payor spouse's liability terminates upon the death of the payee spouse. However, the law no longer requires the instrument to expressly so state, if alimony terminates under state law upon the death of the recipient spouse. This provision is retroactive to overrule the DRTRA (1984) and is therefore effective for instruments executed after December 31, 1984. *See* I.R.C. §§ 71, 215, 422(a); Temp. Treas. Reg. § 1.71-1T(Q-26). Modifications are permitted to instruments executed before January 1, 1987. Pub. L. 99-514, I.R.C. § 1843(c)(2). Under South Carolina law, spousal support usually terminates upon death. S.C. Code Ann. § 20-3-130(B) (Law. Co-op. Supp.).

3. DESIGNATING DEDUCTIBILITY/TAXABILITY OF ALIMONY

The Internal Revenue Code provides that the parties and courts issuing support orders, i.e., family courts, have the ability to designate the deductibility and taxability of alimony. In doing so, all or part of an alimony payment may be designated as deductible to the payor spouse and taxable to the recipient spouse (deductible/taxable), or as non-deductible to the payor and non-taxable to the recipient (non-deductible/non-taxable). The tax free alimony provision has been frequently used in agreements but less frequently used by family court judges.

Internal Revenue Code section 71(b)(1)(B) provides that, in order to qualify as deductible/taxable alimony, the instrument must not "designate such payment as a payment which is not includible in gross income under this section and not allowable as a deduction under section 215."

The Internal Revenue Regulations additionally deal with such designation in a temporary order by stating: "If the spouses are subject to temporary support orders, the designation of otherwise qualifying alimony or separate payments as non-deductible and excludable must be made in the original or a subsequent temporary support order." Temp. Treas. Reg. § 1.71-1T(Q-8).

This approach is very useful in instances where it is desirable to assure that recipient spouse will receive a specified sum. Frequent changes in tax law have demonstrated the difficulties in estimating net after-tax results of support payments. This approach may be particularly useful in matters of "rehabilitative" or "reimbursement" alimony. *See* I.R.C. §§ 71, 215.

The South Carolina alimony statute, S.C. Code Ann. § 20-3-130(C)(11) (Law. Co-op. Supp.), requires the family court to consider and give weight to the tax consequences to each party as a result of the particular form of support awarded. S.C. Code Ann. § 20-3-130(F) provides in part: "The court may elect and determine the intended tax effect of the alimony and separate maintenance and support as provided by the Internal Revenue Code and any corresponding state tax provisions." Under this statute the family court has the discretion to designate alimony as deductible to the payor spouse and taxable to the payee spouse. *Wood v. Wood*, No. 96-UP-124 (S.C. Ct. App. 1996).

4. TRUST INCOME AS ALIMONY

A trust may be used to provide payments to a spouse. Payments do not have to end at the payee's death and recomputation does not apply to such payments. The recipient is taxed on the income received and section 71 does not apply. I.R.C. § 682.

Appreciated property can be transferred into a § 682 alimony trust without recognition of capital gains. I.R.C. § 1041.

D. PROPERTY

1. PROPERTY PRIOR TO DRTRA (1984)

Under prior law, transfers of property between divorcing spouses were taxed in two circumstances. The first was pursuant to *U.S. v. Davis*, 370 U.S. 65, 82 S.Ct. 1190, 8 L.Ed.2d 335 (1962), which provided that an exchange of property for a release of the recipient's marital rights was a taxable event for the property transferor. Gain was recognized to the extent that the fair market value of the property exceeded the adjusted basis (usually cost) of the property. Such transferor's gain was calculated separately for each transferred asset. *McKinney v. Commissioner*, 64 T.C. 263 (1975). The recipient took a basis in the property equal to its fair market value at the time of transfer (Rev. Rul. 67-221, 1967-2 C.B. 63) and reported no gain on the release of marital rights in exchange for the property.

The second circumstance occurred when the divorcing spouses exchanged properties which they owned jointly or separately, other than an equal division of co-owned property which is non-taxable (Rev. Rul. 76-83, 1976-1 C.B. 213). Calculation of the transferor's taxable gain and the recipient's acquired basis was subject under this circumstance to a lengthy and complicated formula approach, resulting in a taxable event for the spouse who received the smaller portion of the property.

2. PROPERTY UNDER THE DRTRA (1984)

New rules apply to property transfers made after the date of enactment (July 18, 1984) of the Domestic Relations Tax Reform Act of 1984. These provisions do not apply to transfers pursuant to instruments in effect before date of enactment unless both spouses elect to have the provisions apply. Elections of this sort usually take the form of a prescribed affirmative statement filed with each spouse's tax return. The parties may elect to have the provision apply only to transfers after December 31, 1983. *See* I.R.C. § 1041.

Section 421 of the DRTRA (1984), 26 U.S.C. § 421, provides that the transfer of property to a spouse incident to a divorce will be treated in the same manner as a gift for income tax purposes. There will be no gain or loss recognized to the transferor, and the recipient will receive the property at a carry-over basis (transferor's basis or, most often, cost). A transfer will be treated as incident to a divorce if the transfer occurs within one year after the parties cease to be married or if it is related to the divorce and takes place not more than six years after the marriage ceases. This non-recognition rule applies whether the transfer is for the relinquishment of marital rights, for the assumption of liabilities in excess of basis, for cash or other property, or for other consideration and is intended to apply to any indebtedness which is discharged. Temp. Treas. Reg. § 1.1041-1T(b)(Q7). The transfer does not qualify if it is to a nonresident alien. I.R.C. § 1041(d). This non-recognition rule also applies in the case of transfers of property between spouses during the marriage.

Even though there is no income tax consequence incident to property settlements as discussed above, there may be a gift tax issue. Transfers pursuant to a written agreement concerning marital and property rights are exempt from gift taxes only if the divorce occurs within three years starting one year prior to the date of the agreement. I.R.C. § 2516.

The basis of the transferee in the property is the adjusted basis of the transferor. I.R.C. § 1041(b)(2). The transferor is required to give to the transferee records on the basis, holding period and investment tax credit on the property. Temp. Treas. Reg. § 1.1041-1T.

3. TAX CONSIDERATIONS RELATED TO SALE OF RESIDENCE

If property (old residence) used by the taxpayer is sold and property (new residence) is purchased and used by the taxpayer as the principal residence within a period beginning two years before the date of such sale and ending two years after such date, any gain shall be recognized only to the extent that the taxpayer's adjusted sales price of the old residence exceeds the cost of the new residence. I.R.C. § 1034. The gain not recognized may be allocated between the taxpayer and the taxpayer's spouse based on their respective title interest. I.R.C. § 1034(g).

An individual's income does not include any gain up to $125,000 from the sale or exchange of property if: (1) the person has attained the age of fifty-five before the date of the sale or exchange, and (2) during the five year period ending on date of the sale or exchange, such property has been owned and used as the person's principal residence for periods aggregating three years or more. I.R.C. § 121.

The South Carolina Equitable Apportionment of Marital Property Act requires the family court to take into consideration the tax consequences to each or either party as a result of any particular form of equitable apportionment. S.C. Code Ann. § 20-7-472(11) (Law. Co-op. Supp.).

4. REDEMPTIONS BY A CORPORATION

The ownership of a closely held corporation is not uncommon in the divorce context. In these situations the wife and husband hold shares in the company and, as a part of the division and distribution of the marital estate, the party getting the corporation wants the other spouse to transfer his or her shares to them. The temptation is for the corporation to purchase or redeem the shares. The issue of who pays the tax where a redemption is ordered by a family court or is provided for in a property division agreement is currently unsettled. The courts appear to favor taxing the spouse who benefits from the redemption, regardless of which spouse has formal title. However, the specific facts and circumstances could vary the result and each instance should be closely examined and tax advice should be obtained.

E. FILING STATUS

Filing status determines the rate at which income is taxed as well as the amount of the standard deduction. It is also important in determining whether the individual is entitled to claim certain other deductions and credits. Generally, the appropriate filing status is determined by the taxpayer's marital status on the last day of the taxable period (usually December 31).

1. SINGLE

The federal tax rules allow a person to file as single if the person is unmarried or "legally separated" from his or her spouse and does not qualify to file as head of household. It is not clear whether the single filing status for federal or state returns is available in South Carolina in any situation other than where a final judgment of divorce or annulment has been rendered. This is a significant issue, for the single filing status is a more favor able filing status than "married filing separately," unless the party qualifies as "head of household" (see below).

Some uncertainty arises because the meaning of "legally separated" is not clear and no reported court decision in South Carolina has yet addressed the issue. The rule obviously contemplates that some marital status in addition to "unmarried" will enable a person to file as "single." The rule would clearly encompass those people who had obtained a divorce *a mensa et thoro* (also known as a "legal separation"), but this cause of action is not recognized in South Carolina (see the chapter on separate support and maintenance).

It appears that "legally separated" would not include situations in which a divorce action is pending and a temporary order has been issued, such as a "*pendente lite* order," "temporary order," or "temporary order for separate maintenance and support." However, even this is not clear. In *Dunn v. Commissioner*, 70 T.C. 361 (1978), *aff'd*, 601 F.2d 599 (7th Cir. 1979), the tax court ruled that a person could not file as a single person where a temporary order of support and maintenance had been issued during the pendency of a divorce action. However, the *Dunn* court noted that the parties had the option under Wisconsin law to seek a divorce *a mensa et thoro*, which they had not done. This is not an option in South Carolina. The only cause of action through which parties can obtain family court acknowledgment of their separation in South Carolina is an action for separate support and maintenance. Thus, *Dunn* does not clearly resolve the issue in relation to South Carolina proceedings. It has also been brought to the authors' attention that I.R.S. agents have told some people operating under *pendente lite* orders in South Carolina that they could file under the single status.

Perhaps the most important unanswered question is whether parties who have obtained a final order in a separate support and maintenance action will be allowed to file using the single status. This is as close as a person can come to being "legally separated" in South Carolina. *Dunn* did not reach this question, although some of the language in *Dunn* suggests that the courts might require some actual change in the marital status of the parties before the single filing status can be used. An action for separate support and maintenance does not change one's marital status in South Carolina.

Although the questions are not yet fully resolved, most Certified Public Accountants appear to be advising South Carolina taxpayers that they cannot use the single filing status unless they have obtained a judgment of divorce.

If a taxpayer is divorced under a final decree by the last day of the taxable year, he or she is considered to have been single for the entire year.

2. MARRIED FILING JOINTLY

Taxpayer spouses are considered to have been married for the entire year and, therefore, they are entitled to file as married if, on the last day of the tax year, they are (1) married and living together as husband and wife; (2) living together as common law husband and wife in a state recognizing common law marriage; (3) married and living apart, but not "legally separated"; or (4) separated under an interlocutory (not final) decree of divorce. Option four cannot be used in South Carolina because interlocutory divorce decrees are not available under South Carolina law.

In general, if an individual has filed a separate return for a taxable year for which a taxable return could have been made by the taxpayer and the taxpayer's spouse, and the time for filing has expired, the taxpayer and spouse may file a joint return within three years.

A spouse can be liable for the tax owed on a joint return. The most important thing an individual can do to avoid tax liability for a joint return is to file a timely return stating the individual is "married filing separately." This will alert the IRS to a problem if a joint return is filed in the individual's name in the same year he has filed his own return.

3. MARRIED FILING SEPARATELY

This status may be selected by taxpayers who are not divorced as of the last day of their tax year. Generally in a domes tic action environment, this method may benefit one party where there exists a need to segregate responsibility for tax positions. Depending on the relative incomes of the parties, such filing status may result in a greater total tax than filing under married filing jointly status.

4. HEAD OF HOUSEHOLD

The head of household rates are more favorable than the single rates. A taxpayer is entitled to use the head of household status if he or she is unmarried or is "considered unmarried" on the last day of the year and pays more than one-half of the cost of maintaining a home for an unmarried child, grandchild, or adopted child, among other qualifying individuals. In order to qualify for this status, the child need not be a dependent. There are special rules for qualifying married children and relatives who live in the taxpayer's household. Unlike the single filing status, the taxpayer may be entitled to qualify under head of household for the earned income credit and the child care credit.

In qualifying for head of household status, the taxpayer is "considered unmarried" if all of the following tests are met:

1) The taxpayer must file a separate return;

2) The taxpayer must pay more than one-half the cost of maintaining his or her home for the year;

3) The taxpayer's spouse did not live in the home during the last six (6) months of the year; and

4) The taxpayer's home was the main home of his or her unmarried child, grandchild, or adopted child.

See I.R.C. § 7703.

If a qualified custodial spouse files as head of household before the marriage has been dissolved, it creates a hardship for the other spouse who is forced also to file under the married filing separately status, the least favorable filing status.

F. INNOCENT SPOUSE

Where there has been a substantial understatement of tax by one spouse, the other spouse can be relieved of liability for the error by establishing that he or she is an "innocent spouse." The following conditions must exist: (1) in signing the return the innocent spouse did not know, and had no reason to know, that there was such substantial understatement; and (2) taking into account all the facts and circumstances, it is inequitable to hold the other spouse liable for the deficiency in tax attributable to the substantial understatement. If these conditions are established, the innocent spouse will be relieved of liability for tax, interest, penalties and other amounts, for such taxable year to the extent such liability is attributable to such substantial understatement. I.R.C. § 6013(e).

G. ATTORNEYS' FEES AND LITIGATION EXPENSES

Generally, attorneys' fees paid for a divorce are personal expenses and are not deductible.[56] *U.S. v. Gilmore*, 372 U.S. 39, 83 S.Ct. 623, 4 L.Ed.2d 570 (1963).

---

[56] A client who is expecting to pay attorneys' fees or litigation costs may want to consider paying such amount as additional lump sum alimony. If properly worded in the agreement, and order if there is one, such payment would be deductible to the payor spouse and taxable to the payee spouse. To the extent that the payee spouse can legitimately deduct his or her own attorneys' fees, such

However, the Internal Revenue Code permits a deduction for all ordinary and necessary expenses paid or incurred for the production or collection of income, for the management, conservation, or maintenance of property held for the production of income, or in connection with the determination, collection or refund of any tax. I.R.C. § 212. This section is generally believed to permit the deduction of a portion of attorneys' fees and litigation expenses incurred in a divorce action in which the cited issues are involved.

A spouse can deduct attorney's fees actually paid or incurred for tax advice. I.R.C. § 202(c); Treas. Reg. § 1.212-1(l); *Carpenter v. U.S.*, 338 F.2d 366 (Ct. Cl. 1964); *Munn v. U.S.*, 455 F.2d 1028 (Ct. Cl. 1972).[57] *But see U.S. v. Davis*, 370 U.S. 65, 82 S. Ct. 1190, 8 L. Ed. 2d 335 (1962), which holds that attorneys' fees paid by a husband to his spouse's tax counsel in a divorce proceeding were not deductible because the expenses had been incurred in connection with advice about her tax problems, not his.

Revenue Ruling 72-545 requires documentation. The ruling gives the following examples of circumstances justifying fees as deductible:

a. The taxpayer at the time of his divorce engaged a law firm to advise him of the federal income tax consequences of a proposed property settlement agreement in which he transferred his interest in certain properties to his wife in exchange for the transfer to him of her interest in other properties and the release by her of marital rights in certain other properties owned by him. The law firm limited its practice to matters involving state and federal taxation.

---

deduction will offset the taxable alimony. In drafting such a provision, care must be taken to assure that the aggregate alimony paid does not violate the recapture rules.

[57] In the materials for a S.C. Bar Hot Tips CLE on May 6, 1994, Harvey Golden, Esq., questions whether it is wise for lawyers to charge for "tax advice." "Personally, I would advise the usual practitioner to stay away from billing for tax advice as it can be more trouble than it is worth. Of course, if you are Ray McKay or anyone who specializes in tax advice, then it is a different story."

b. The taxpayer, at the time of the divorce, engaged tax counsel to advise him of the federal income, gift and estate tax consequences of establishing a trust to make periodic payments to his wife during her life in discharge of his support obligation. The law firm also handled certain nontax aspects of the divorce, and the tax matters were handled by a department of the firm that specialized in taxation. The firm's bill allocated a portion of the fee to tax matters. The allocation was based primarily on the time required, the difficulty of the tax question involved, and the amount of taxes involved.

c. The taxpayer engaged a practitioner to represent him in a divorce. The legal services included tax counsel concerning his right to claim the children as dependents for federal income tax purposes in years after divorce. The practitioner's statement to the taxpayer allocated the fee between the tax advice and other nontax matters based on the amount of the attorney's time attributable to each, the fee customarily charged in the locality for such services and the results obtained in the divorce negotiations.

Legal fees can be deducted which are related to winning or collecting alimony. "Generally, attorney's fees and other costs paid in connection with a divorce, separation or decree for support are not deductible by either the husband or the wife. However, the part of an attorney's fee and the part of the other costs paid in connection with the divorce, legal separation, written separation agreement, or a decree for support, which are properly attributable to the production or collection of amounts includible in gross income under section 71 are deductible by the wife under section 212." Treas. Reg. § 1.262-1(b)(7). *See also Wild v. Commissioner*, 42 T.C. 706 (1964), and *Elliott v. Commissioner*, 40 T.C. 304 (1963) (both allowing expenses incurred in litigation about alimony to be deducted); *Marion R. Hesse*, 60 T.C. 685 (1973) (allowing legal expenses incurred in obtaining certain payments in lieu of alimony to be deducted).

Attorneys' fees can be deducted along with other miscellaneous itemized deductions not excluded by section 67(b) of the *Internal Revenue Code*, but only to the extent that the aggregate of these deductions exceeds 2% of the individual's adjusted gross income. I.R.C. § 67(a).

The costs incurred in defending or protecting title to property constitute a part of the cost of the property and are not deductible expenses. However, they can be added to the basis of the property. I.R.C. § 1016(a)(i); Treas. Reg. § 1.212-1(K).

The following is a proposed tax letter to be sent at the end of the case to the client (Source: Dennis L. Dabney, C.P.A.):

> In my opinion, based upon my review of your file and my first-hand knowledge of the case, I estimate that (percentage or amount) of my fees and costs for legal services are deductible under section 212 of the *Internal Revenue Code* as ordinary and necessary expenses paid in connection with our efforts to secure and produce taxable income (alimony) for you and in connection with the tax advice that I have given to you in this matter.
>
> Under section 67 of the *Internal Revenue Code*, all miscellaneous itemized deductions (which include section 212 expenses) would be aggregated and only the amount that exceeds 2% of your adjusted gross income could be deducted.
>
> You should consult with you tax preparer concerning the deductibility of these expenses, and he or she can further advise you concerning their deductibility.

MARITAL LITIGATION IN SOUTH CAROLINA
Substantive Law
TABLE OF CASES

MARITAL LITIGATION IN SOUTH CAROLINA
Substantive Law
TABLE OF STATUTES AND REGULATIONS

SOUTH CAROLINA CONSTITUTION

STATUTES
S.C. Code Ann.

S.C. CODE REGS.

FEDERAL STATUTES AND REGULATIONS

MARITAL LITIGATION IN SOUTH CAROLINA
Substantive Law
INDEX

ATTORNEYS' FEES

BANKRUPTCY

DIVORCE

SPOUSAL SUPPORT.

STANDARD OF LIVING

STANDING

SUBJECT MATTER JURISDICTION